Prolegomena to a History of Islamicate Manichaeism

Comparative Islamic Studies
Series Editor: Brannon Wheeler, US Naval Academy

This series, like its companion journal of the same title, publishes work that integrates Islamic studies into the contemporary study of religion, thus providing an opportunity for expert scholars of Islam to demonstrate the more general significance of their research both to comparativists and to specialists working in other areas. Attention to Islamic materials from outside the central Arabic lands is of special interest, as are comparisons which stress the diversity of Islam as it interacts with changing human conditions.

Notes from the Fortune-Telling Parrot:
Islam and the Struggle for Religious Pluralism in Pakistan
David Pinault

Earth, Empire and Sacred Text:
Muslims and Christians as Trustees of Creation
David L. Johnston

Ibn Arabi and the Contemporary West:
Beshara and the Ibn Arabi Society
Isobel Jeffery-Street

Orientalists, Islamists and the Global Public Sphere:
A Historical Genealogy of the Modern Image of Islam
Dietrich Jung

Prophecy and Power:
Muhammad and the Qur an in the Light of Comparison
Marilyn Robinson Waldman
Edited by Bruce B. Lawrence

The Qur'ān:
A New Annotated Translation
Edited by A. J. Droge

East by Mid-East:
Studies in Cultural, Historical and Strategic Connectivities
Edited by Brannon Wheeler and Anchi Hoh

Prolegomena to a History of Islamicate Manichaeism

John C. Reeves

SHEFFIELD UK BRISTOL CT

Published by Equinox Publishing Ltd.

UK: Kelham House, 3 Lancaster Street, Sheffield, S3 8AF
USA: ISD, 70 Enterprise Drive, Bristol, CT 06010

www.equinoxpub.com

Paperback edition published 2013.

British Library Cataloguing-in-Publication Data
A catalogue record for this book is available from the British Library.

Library of Congress Cataloging-in-Publication Data
Reeves, John C.
Prolegomena to a History of Islamicate Manichaeism / John C. Reeves.
p. cm. — (Comparative Islamic studies)
Includes bibliographical references and index.
ISBN 978-1-904768-52-4 (hb)
1. Manichaeism—History. 2. Manichaeism—Relations. I. Title. BT1410.R45 2010
297.8'3—dc22

2010008755

ISBN: 978 1 904768 52 4 (hardback)
ISBN: 978 1 78179 038 0 (paperback)

Typeset and edited by Queenston Publishing, Hamilton, Canada
Printed and bound in the UK by Lightning Source UK Ltd., Milton Keynes and Lightning Source Inc., La Vergne, TN

In Memoriam

Ben Zion Wacholder (ז״ל)
Exemplary scholar, teacher, and mentor

Contents

Preface

The present volume represents the fruition of approximately a decade of work on most of the important Islamicate sources pertaining to the Mesopotamian prophet Mani and the survival of his religion among early and medieval Muslim polities. My goal in preparing the work was to supply scholars with a roughly sorted mass of raw data for producing more nuanced histories and studies of Manichaeism in the Arabophonic cultural sphere; hence the title *Prolegomena to a History of Islamicate Manichaeism*, an admittedly overambitious label which deliberately mimics those chosen by Julius Wellhausen over a century ago for his justly celebrated pair of monographs devoted to the identification and elucidation of the signal primary texts which permit a plausible reconstruction of both biblical and early Muslim history. It is my hope that modern researchers more erudite than I can likewise exploit the materials contained in this book to re-conceive and expound the history of Manichaeism (as well as dualist religious thought more generally) under Islam.

I appreciate very much the continuing encouragement which I received from a host of interested colleagues and students over the lengthy period of this volume's gestation and preparation. As always, I remain profoundly grateful to the Blumenthal Foundation for its continuing financial support of my research efforts in Jewish and cognate studies at the University of North Carolina, Charlotte. For this volume, my work was also facilitated and accelerated by my residency as a Ruth Meltzer Distinguished Fellow at the Center for Advanced Judaic Studies at the University of Pennsylvania during the fall of 2007, a fantastic privilege whose collegial and scholastic rewards I am still reaping years after the fact. Finally, I want to append here a special note of thanks to Janet Joyce and Valerie Hall of Equinox Publishing for their extraordinary patience and kindness while awaiting the final delivery of this manuscript.

John C. Reeves
University of North Carolina, Charlotte

Abbreviations and Conventions

( ) mark the translator's additions in order to improve the English sense

[ ] mark textual lacunae and/or editorial restorations

< > mark emendation of the orthography of the text

PRIMARY SOURCES

Ant.	Josephus, *Jewish Antiquities*
Apoc. Adam	*Apocalypse of Adam*
Apoc. Paul	*Apocalypse of Paul*
b.	Babylonian Talmud (Bavli)
CMC	*Cologne Mani Codex*
Col	Colossians (Christian Bible)
1 Cor	1 Corinthians (Christian Bible)
Dan	Daniel (Bible)
1 En.	*1 Enoch* (Ethiopic Book of Enoch)
Gal	Galatians (Christian Bible)
Gen	Genesis (Bible)
Gos. Eg.	*Gospel of the Egyptians*
Gos. Thom.	*Gospel of Thomas*
Homil.	*Manichäische Homilien*. Edited by Hans Jakob Polotsky. Stuttgart, 1934.
Ḥul.	*Ḥullin*
Isa	Isaiah (Bible)
Jub.	*Book of Jubilees*
Judg	Judges (Bible)
Keph.	*Manichäische Handschriften der Staatlichen Museen, Berlin, Band I: Kephalaia, 1. Hälfte*. Edited by H. J. Polotsky and A. Böhlig. Stuttgart, 1934-40. *2. Hälfte (Lfg. 11/12)*. Stuttgart, 1966.
1 Kgs, 2 Kgs	1 Kings, 2 Kings (Bible)
Lk	Luke (Christian Bible)
M	Middle Iranian Manichaean texts and fragments

Matt	Matthew (Christian Bible)
Meg.	*Megillah*
Mk	Mark (Christian Bible)
Ms.	Manuscript
NHC	Nag Hammadi Codex
Num	Numbers (Bible)
1 Pet	1 Peter (Christian Bible)
PGM	*Papyri Graecae Magicae.* 2nd ed. 2 vols. Edited by Karl Preisendanz and Albert Henrichs. Stuttgart, 1973-74.
Prov	Proverbs (Bible)
Ps-Bk.	*Manichaean Manuscripts in the Chester Beatty Collection, vol. II: A Manichaean Psalm-Book, pt. II.* Edited by C. R. C. Allberry. Stuttgart, 1938.
Q	Qur'ān
Qidd.	*Qiddushin*
Rom	Romans (Christian Bible)
Sanh.	*Sanhedrin*
Šebu.	*Shevu'ot*
t.	*Tosefta*

SECONDARY SOURCES

ANF	*Ante-Nicene Fathers.* 10 vols. Edited by Alexander Roberts and James Donaldson. Buffalo, 1885–96.
AOS	American Oriental Series
APAW	*Abhandlungen der königlichen preussischen Akademie der Wissenschaften (Berlin)*
BSO(A)S	*Bulletin of the School of Oriental (and African) Studies*
BZAW	Beihefte zur Zeitschrift für die alttestamentliche Wissenschaft
CFM	Corpus Fontium Manichaeorum
CRINT	Compendia rerum iudaicarum ad Novum Testamentum
CSCO	Corpus scriptorum christianorum orientalium
CSHB	Corpus scriptorum historiae byzantinae
EI[1]	*The Encyclopaedia of Islam,* first edition. 9 vols. Leiden, 1913–38.
EI[2]	*The Encyclopaedia of Islam,* new edition. 12 vols. Leiden, 1954–2002.
EncIr	*Encyclopaedia Iranica.* 14 vols. to date. Edited by Ehsan Yarshater. London & New York, 1982– .
EncQur	*Encyclopaedia of the Qur'ān.* 6 vols. Edited by Jane Dammen McAuliffe. Leiden, 2001–2006.

ERE	*Encyclopaedia of Religion and Ethics*. 13 vols. Edited by James Hastings. New York, 1908–1927.
FRLANT	Forschungen zur Religion und Literatur des Alten und Neuen Testaments
GCS	Die griechische christliche Schriftsteller der ersten [drei] Jahrhunderte
JAOS	*Journal of the American Oriental Society*
JNES	*Journal of Near Eastern Studies*
JRAS	*Journal of the Royal Asiatic Society*
JSOTSup	Journal for the Study of the Old Testament Supplement Series
LCL	Loeb Classical Library
NHMS	Nag Hammadi and Manichaean Studies
NHS	Nag Hammadi Studies
NovTSup	Novum Testamentum Supplements
OIP	Oriental Institute Publications
OLA	Orientalia Lovaniensia Analecta
OrChrAn	Orientalia christiana analecta
PW	*Paulys Realencyclopädie der classischen Altertumswissenschaft*. New edition edited by Georg Wissowa. 49 vols. München, 1980.
RGRW	Religions in the Graeco-Roman World
RHR	*Revue de l'histoire des religions*
RSO	*Rivista degli studi orientali*
SBE	Sacred Books of the East
SBLEJL	Society of Biblical Literature Early Judaism and Its Literature
SBLTT	Society of Biblical Literature Texts and Translations
SPAW	*Sitzungsberichte der preussischen Akademie der Wissenschaften*
TSAJ	Texte und Studien zum antiken Judentum
TU	Texte und Untersuchungen
WUNT	Wissenschaftliche Untersuchungen zum Neuen Testament
ZDMG	*Zeitschrift der deutschen morgenländischen Gesellschaft*
ZNW	*Zeitschrift für die neutestamentliche Wissenschaft und die Kunde der älteren Kirche*

— 1 —

Introduction

Perhaps the most successful attempt at implementing an authoritative succession of revelatory prophetic instruction prior to the emergence of Islam is found in Manichaeism, a religion born in third-century Mesopotamia, but one which rapidly spread during the next few centuries to become the first serious claimant to distinctive recognition as a 'world religion.'[1] During its heyday, Manichaeism achieved a geographical spread which ranged from the coast of North Africa to the deserts of central Asia, and Manichaean evangelists succeeded in adapting the religion's teachings and ritual behaviors to the prevailing religions and linguistic registers of these different regions. Due to successive waves of persecution at the hands of Christians, Zoroastrians, and Muslims, Manichaeism was eventually eradicated as a formal religious affiliation within both the Byzantine and Islamicate[2] realms, although its ideology continued to attract followers and sympathizers even after the community's physical suppression well into the medieval eras of both cultural circles. Manichaean refugees furthermore were able to find a safe haven in the distant provinces of central Asia, Tibet, and China, and there is literary and archaeological evidence for the survival of Far Eastern Manichaean communities up to the sixteenth or seventeenth century.

---

1. See Birger A. Pearson, "Jewish Sources in Gnostic Literature," in *Jewish Writings of the Second Temple Period* (CRINT 2.2; ed. Michael E. Stone; Assen/Philadelphia: Van Gorcum/Fortress, 1984), 480; D. A. Scott, "Manichaean Responses to Zoroastrianism (Politico-Religious Controversies in Iran, Past to Present: 3)," *Religious Studies* 25 (1989): 435; Jonathan Z. Smith, "A Matter of Class: Taxonomies of Religion," *Harvard Theological Review* 89 (1996): 396; reprinted in his *Relating Religion: Essays in the Study of Religion* (Chicago, IL: University of Chicago Press, 2004), 169. My employment here of the criticized category 'world religion' is strictly geolinguistic as opposed to the more nefarious usages cataloged and analyzed by Tomoko Masuzawa, *The Invention of World Religions, Or, How European Universalism was Preserved in the Language of Pluralism* (Chicago, IL: University of Chicago Press, 2005).
2. I follow Marshall Hodgson's suggestion to use the adjective 'Islamicate' to refer 'not directly to the religion, Islam, itself, but to the social and cultural complex historically associated with Islam and the Muslims, both among Muslims themselves and even when found among non-Muslims.' See Marshall G. S. Hodgson, *The Venture of Islam: Conscience and History in a World Civilization* (3 vols.; Chicago, IL: University of Chicago Press, 1974), 1:57–60; the quotation is taken from p. 59.

1. Who was Mani?

Manichaeism takes its name from that of its founder, a Babylonian prophet by the name of Mani. Biographical information about his career comes from sources from both within and outside of the Manichaean tradition itself. Perhaps the most important of these accounts is the autobiographically couched *Cologne Mani Codex*, a Greek work from Egypt that first came to scholarly attention during the 1970s, and which has since revolutionized the study of Mani's religion.[3] This text consists of a series of excerpted testimonia regarding the early formative experiences of the sage that are attributed to prominent teachers and leaders of third-century Manichaeism. These testimonia represent Mani as speaking in the first person, and may preserve authentic reminiscences of his pedagogic style. The *Codex* also features a small number of quotations from purportedly literary sources, some of which allegedly were authored by Mani himself. Prior to the discovery and publication of the *Codex*, Carl Schmidt had identified a similar biographical composition among the early twentieth-century Medinet Madi find of Coptic Manichaean texts.[4] Unfortunately that text was never published, and it apparently perished during the devastation wrought in Germany by the Second World War. Apart from the Greek *Codex* and some fragmentary remains of hagiographical and/or biographical content that were recovered from central Asia by explorers during the early decades of the last century, the two most significant repositories of biographical information about Mani are contained in Islamicate heresiography. One was compiled in Syriac by the eighth-century Nestorian patriarch Theodore bar Konai.[5] The other was prepared in Arabic on the basis of earlier sources, which were also apparently transmitted in Arabic, by the tenth-century Muslim encyclopaedist Ibn al-Nadīm.[6] By utilizing the least tendentious

3. Ludwig Koenen and Cornelia Römer, *Der Kölner Mani-Kodex. Über das Werden seines Leben: Kritische Edition* (Papyrologica Coloniensia 14; Opladen: Westdeutscher Verlag, 1988), with references to the initial publications. A partial English translation (up to 99.9) was prepared by Ron Cameron and Arthur J. Dewey, *The Cologne Mani Codex (P. Colon. inv. nr. 4780): "Concerning the Origin of his Body"* (SBLTT 15; Missoula, MT: Scholars Press, 1979); for English translations of the remaining legible text, see Ellen Bradshaw Aitken, "The Cologne Mani Codex," in *Religions of Late Antiquity in Practice* (ed. Richard Valantasis; Princeton: Princeton University Press, 2000), 169–74; Iain Gardner and Samuel N. C. Lieu, eds., *Manichaean Texts From the Roman Empire* (Cambridge: Cambridge University Press, 2004), 65–73.

4. Carl Schmidt and H. J. Polotsky, *Ein Mani-Fund in Ägypten: Originalschriften des Mani und seiner Schüler* (Berlin: Akademie der Wissenschaften, 1933), 26–29.

5. Henri Pognon, "Extraits du «Livre des Scholies» de Théodore bar Khouni," in idem, *Inscriptions mandaïtes des coupes de Khouabir* (Paris, 1898; repr., Amsterdam: Philo Press, 1979), 125.11-126.31 (text); Theodore bar Konai, *Liber Scholiorum* (CSCO 55, 69; 2 vols.; ed. A. Scher; Paris: Carolus Poussielgue, 1910–12), 2:311.12–313.9 (text).

6. Gustav Flügel, *Mani: Seine Lehre und seine Schriften* (Leipzig, 1862; repr., Osnabrück: Biblio Verlag, 1969), 49.1–52.10; 69.5–15 (text). Regarding Ibn al-Nadīm and his *Fihrist*, see especially G[ustav] Flügel, "Ueber Muhammad bin Iṣhâq's Fihrist al-'ulûm," *ZDMG*

parts of these hostile sources in conjunction with the traditions related by the Greek *Codex*, we can reconstruct the following account of Mani's life.

Mani was born in 216 CE near the city of Ctesiphon, a Parthian foundation that was situated directly across the Euphrates River from the ancient city of Babylon. His father Pattikios is represented as a pious man who frequented the temples of that region: we are informed by Ibn al-Nadīm that during one of these visits, not long after Mani's birth, Pattikios heard a voice commanding him to abstain from meat, wine, and sex. The same voice moreover bade him to join a particular communitarian sect who resided in the marshes south of the city. Pattikios obeyed the mysterious oracle, abandoned his marriage and former secular pursuits, and took up residence with that sect, taking along with him the now four-year old Mani. Mani grew up among the sect and remained with them for some twenty years, during which time he occasionally experienced 'revelations' mediated through an angelic figure known as 'the Twin.' Due to his increasingly disruptive behavior as a result of these 'revelations,' Mani was forced to leave the sect (Theodore bar Konai claims that he was formally expelled; the *Codex* speaks of a trial after which Mani quietly withdrew from the community). Two erstwhile sectarian adherents accompanied him in exile to Ctesiphon, where his father Pattikios soon rejoined him.

Mani's break with the baptist sect[7] inaugurates a new phase within his life. Emboldened by the messages received from 'the Twin,' Mani began a series of missionary journeys throughout the Sasanian realm for the purpose of promulgating his 'new' religion, the religion which comes to be known to its detractors and modern historians as 'Manichaeism.' He soon managed to win the favor of the Sasanian ruler Shāpūr I, a crucial factor for the early success of his enterprise. Trusted disciples were dispatched by Mani to the West, particularly to Syria, Arabia, and Egypt, where additional converts were added to the rapidly expanding religion. It was undoubtedly during this period (the mid-third century) that most of the Manichaean scriptures first appeared in written form, all (save one) reportedly authored by Mani himself in his native Aramaic. Didactic and liturgical works were also produced after the master's death by the initial generations of Mani's disciples.[8] The early expansion of Manichaeism beyond the bounds of

13 (1859): 559-650; Reynold A. Nicholson, *A Literary History of the Arabs* (2nd ed.; Cambridge: The University Press, 1930), 362–64; Chase F. Robinson, *Islamic Historiography* (Cambridge: Cambridge University Press, 2003), 3–8.

7. They are identified within the *Codex* as Elchasaites, a Jewish-Christian sect founded by the late first century or early second-century Palestinian prophet Elchasai. Patristic testimonies about this group occur in Hippolytus, *Refutatio* 9.13.1–16.4; Origen *apud* Eusebius, *Historia ecclesiastica* 6.38; Epiphanius, *Panarion* 19.1.1–6.4; 53.1.1–9. These early sources have been conveniently collected in A. F. J. Klijn and G. J. Reinink, *Patristic Evidence for Jewish-Christian Sects* (NovTSup 36; Leiden: Brill, 1973). For further cross-cultural observations, see John C. Reeves, "The 'Elchasaite' Sanhedrin of the Cologne Mani Codex in Light of Second Temple Jewish Sectarian Sources," *Journal of Jewish Studies* 42 (1991): 68–91.

8. These include works like the Greek *Codex*, the Coptic *Kephalaia*, *Homilies*, and *Psalm-*

Mesopotamia necessitated an organized program of literary translation whereby the new religion's scriptures could be quickly rendered from Aramaic into Greek, Coptic, and other regional vernaculars. Presciently appreciative of the impact of visual media in public communication, Mani also prepared an illustrated synopsis of his revelatory teachings, the so-called *Ardahang*, a 'picture-book' regarding which the fourth-century witness Ephrem Syrus states:

> According to some of his disciples, Manī also illustrated (the) figures of the godless doctrine which he fabricated out of his own mind, using pigments on a scroll. He labeled the odious (figures) 'sons of Darkness' in order to declare to his disciples the hideousness of Darkness, so that they might loathe it; and he labeled the lovely (figures) 'sons of Light' in order to declare to them 'its beauty so that they might desire it.' He accordingly states: 'I have written them in books and illustrated them with colors. Let the one who hears about them verbally also see them in visual form, and the one who is unable to learn them (the teachings) from [words] learn them from picture(s).'[9]

By the end of the third century, the growth of Manichaeism and its hegemonic claims to spiritual primacy would attract the attention of both state and ecclesiastical authorities in the Roman Empire. The emperor Diocletian officially proscribed Manichaeism as a 'Persian' aberration, lumping Manichaeans together with other allegedly despicable deviants like 'astrologers' and 'sorcerers.'[10] During the same period or slightly thereafter an anonymous Christian disputant composed a fictional account of a moderated debate between the Persian Mani—who was lured to the contest on a pretext—and an 'orthodox' Christian bishop by the name of Archelaus. The resultant *Acta Archelai* would come to be regarded as 'historical' and exert an enormous influence upon the depiction of Mani and his religion in almost all subsequent Christian discussions.[11]

Book, and various other anthologies of hymns, confessions, and prayers fragmentarily extant in Coptic, Middle Iranian languages, Old Turkish, and Chinese. Extended excerpts from these and similar works are available in Gardner-Lieu, *Manichaean Texts*; Jes P. Asmussen, *Manichaean Literature: Representative Texts Chiefly from Middle Persian and Parthian Writings* (Delmar, N.Y.: Scholars' Facsimiles and Reprints, 1975); Jes P. Asmussen and Alexander Böhlig, *Die Gnosis III: Der Manichäismus* (Zürich: Artemis, 1980); Hans-Joachim Klimkeit, *Gnosis on the Silk Road: Gnostic Texts from Central Asia* (San Francisco, CA: HarperCollins, 1993); Willis Barnstone and Marvin Meyer, eds., *The Gnostic Bible* (Boston, MA: Shambhala, 2003), 569–654.

9. C. W. Mitchell, ed., *S. Ephraim's Prose Refutations of Mani, Marcion, and Bardaisan* (2 vols.; London: Williams and Norgate, 1912–21), 1:126.31–127.11; the translation is from John C. Reeves, "Manichaean Citations from the *Prose Refutations* of Ephrem," in *Emerging from Darkness: Studies in the Recovery of Manichaean Sources* (NHMS 43; ed. Paul Mirecki and Jason BeDuhn; Leiden: Brill, 1997), 263.

10. The Latin text of the edict is available in Alfred Adam, ed., *Texte zum Manichäismus* (2nd ed.; Berlin: W. de Gruyter, 1969), 82–83. For an English rendering, see Gardner-Lieu, *Manichaean Texts*, 117–18; also Beate Dignas and Engelbert Winter, *Rome and Persia in Late Antiquity: Neighbours and Rivals* (Cambridge: Cambridge University Press, 2007), 216–17.

11. Hegemonius, *Acta Archelai* (GCS 16; ed. Charles Henry Beeson; Leipzig: J. C. Hinrichs,

Meanwhile events had taken a sinister turn in the Mesopotamian homeland. The death of Shāpūr in 272 CE deprived Mani and his movement of their royal protector. Shāpūr's immediate successor was his son Hormizd, who unfortunately ruled for less than a year, and who was in turn replaced by the decidedly less tolerant Bahrām I. Mani rapidly lost favor under the new regime. Summoned to the royal court at Gundešāpūr, he was arrested, imprisoned, and eventually executed as an offender against Zoroastrian orthodoxy. Legend has it that Mani's corpse was flayed, its skin stuffed with straw, and then affixed and exposed to public ridicule at the principal gate of the city. Later generations of Manichaean tradents would portray Mani as a martyr to his cause, thereby encouraging a rhetorical assimilation of his tragic fate to that of Jesus in Roman Palestine. Since Mani and Jesus were (from the Manichaean perspective) at root actually one and the same entity, this deliberate interpretative response to the death of the founder is not unwarranted.

2. Manichaean Prophetology

Manichaeism, insofar as it is consciously founded on traditions grounded in a biblical sphere of discourse, exhibits a profound emphasis upon prophetic authority. One of the core principles of Manichaeism as a religion is a distinctive 'prophetology'; i.e., it has a particular conception of the manifestations and historical progress of divine revelation since the creation of humanity. According to Manichaeism, there exists a series of authentic emissaries from the divine world that extends back to the earliest generations of human existence. Although these prophets bear different names and exercise their office at different times and among different peoples, they are in actuality one divine figure—the Apostle of Light—proclaiming an identical message.

The human guises of these 'prophets' are articulated in a number of our sources. The succession of prophets is composed initially of certain biblical forefathers—Adam, Seth, Enosh, Enoch, and Shem. It is then augmented with Zoroaster, the Buddha, and Jesus, and culminates with the purportedly self-declared 'seal of the prophets,' Mani himself.[12] Their authority as legitimate conduits of heav-

---

1906). For a discussion of this work's importance and influence, see Samuel N. C. Lieu, "Fact and Fiction in the *Acta Archelai*," in *Manichaean Studies: Proceedings of the First International Conference on Manichaeism, August 5-9, 1987* (ed. Peter Bryder; Lund: Plus Ultra, 1988), 69–88; also available in idem, *Manichaeism in Mesopotamia and the Roman East* (RGRW 118; Leiden: Brill, 1994), 132–52. See now the various essays collected in Jason BeDuhn and Paul Mirecki, eds., *Frontiers of Faith: The Christian Encounter with Manichaeism in the Acts of Archelaus* (NHMS 61; Leiden: Brill, 2007).

12. Given the application of this same epithet to Muḥammad (see Q 33:40), the label 'seal of the prophets' is sometimes thought to have been appropriated by nascent Islam from Manichaeism. Note how 1 Cor 9:2 has been adapted and applied to Mani in *CMC* 72.4–7: οἱ δὲ μαθηταὶ αὐτοῦ ἐγίγνοντο σφραγὶς αὐτοῦ τῆς ἀποστολῆς 'his disciples became the seal of his apostleship.' See, e.g., Karl Ahrens, *Muhammad als Religionsstifter* (Leipzig: F. A. Brockhaus, 1935), 154; Alfred Louis de Prémare, "«Comme il est écrit»:

enly wisdom is explicitly grounded by Manichaean tradition in their 'writings,' which in turn rely upon an 'ascent experience' to the heavenly realm supposedly undergone by each authentic prophet.[13] The aforementioned *Cologne Mani Codex*, for example, supplies such an ascent experience for each of the biblical forefathers mentioned above, claiming that it has excerpted these testimonies from 'writings' (literally 'apocalypses') authored by Adam, Seth, Enosh, Shem, and Enoch. Although these alleged citations display a familiarity with the interpretive penumbra surrounding these figures in Jewish, Christian, and gnostic literature and traditions, they are not otherwise found in any extant Jewish or Christian works, and are most likely Manichaean forgeries composed to bolster the prophetic status of that religion's founder.[14] Mani also allegedly 'ascended to heaven,'[15] and he too is the author of a roster of books which purportedly relate heavenly secrets based upon revelatory wisdom. His career in broad outline can be made to mimic those of Adam, Seth, Jesus, and the other worthy predecessors who were revered in Manichaean circles. Moreover, a careful study of the narrative accounts associated with this chain of 'true prophets' can shed light upon the ultimate significance of Mani's mission, who as 'seal' brings both affirmation and closure to the list.

Given the cardinal importance of some early (and later) biblical characters to the formulation of its prophetology, we should not be surprised to learn that Manichaeism exhibits a distinctive reading of the written texts associated with

---

L'histoire d'un texte," *Studia Islamica* 70 (1989): 45; idem, "Les textes musulmans dans leur environment," *Arabica* 47 (2000): 407; Kathryn Babayan, *Mystics, Monarchs, and Messiahs: Cultural Landscapes of Early Modern Iran* (Cambridge, MA: Harvard University Press, 2002), xxxvii. Some cross-cultural resonances are provided by I[gnaz]. Goldziher, "Bemerkungen zur neuhebräischen Poesie," *Jewish Quarterly Review* o.s. 14 (1902): 724–26. The notion of 'seal' connotes 'endorsement' or 'confirmation' and not necessarily 'finality' as per the illuminating remarks of Josef van Ess, *The Flowering of Muslim Theology* (trans. Jane Marie Todd; Cambridge, MA: Harvard University Press, 2006), 23–24. There are however no clear pre-Islamic applications of this epithet to Mani himself; see especially Gedaliahu G. Stroumsa, "'Seal of the Prophets': The Nature of a Manichaean Metaphor," *Jerusalem Studies in Arabic and Islam* 7 (1986): 61–74. François de Blois has recently suggested that Manichaeism and Islam independently inherit this epithet from a shared 'Jewish-Christian' heritage; see his "Elchasai—Manes—Muḥammad: Manichäismus und Islam in religionshistorischem Vergleich," *Der Islam* 81 (2004): 31–48, esp. 44–46.

13. See John C. Reeves, *Heralds of That Good Realm: Syro-Mesopotamian Gnosis and Jewish Traditions* (NHMS 41; Leiden: Brill, 1996), 7–30.

14. Note especially David Frankfurter, "Apocalypses Real and Alleged in the Mani Codex," *Numen* 44 (1997): 60–73.

15. *CMC* 63.2–72.7 embeds Mani within its chain of 'true prophets' (63.13–14) on the basis of such experiences. Two further instances of 'ascent' are discussed by John C. Reeves, "Jewish Pseudepigrapha in Manichaean Literature: The Influence of the Enochic Library," in *Tracing the Threads: Studies in the Vitality of Jewish Pseudepigrapha* (SBLEJL 6; ed. John C. Reeves; Atlanta, GA: Scholars Press, 1994), 179–81.

the initial chapters of the biblical book of Genesis as well as early gospel and apostolic traditions, apparently transmitting some of its stories and exhortations in the form of what some scholars misleadingly term 'rewritten Bible.' This however is a problematic category for nascent Manichaeism: there must first *be* a 'Bible' before it can be 'rewritten,' and neither the Jewish nor the Christian versions of the works eventually codified under this title function as canonical entities (at least as they are defined by modern religious apologists or institutions) during the third century. Like other contemporaneous religious groups who anchored much of their discourse and practices onto biblically based characters, stories, and themes, Manichaeans utilized a rich variety of narrative lore which emanated from a diverse array of traditional sources and whose sole criterion of authority was a close association with a communally endorsed prophet. As is exemplified by the opaque transmission history of the *Book of Giants*,[16] it seems possible that Mani knew about or actually possessed 'alternative' versions of the 'biblical' compositions that were more expansive in scope or more primitive in form than those that would achieve widespread recognition in a later age as 'canonical' books. And if such indeed proves to be the case, there may thus be some currency to the recurrent charge of textual corruption or falsification leveled by Manichaeans against contemporary Christians, Zoroastrians, and Buddhists, or at least more than modern scholars are accustomed to granting to it.

3. The Manichaean Worldview

According to the religion of Mani, the universe once consisted of two perfectly balanced yet separate 'Realms': a Realm of Light or of Goodness, and a Realm of Darkness or of Evil, with each realm populated by immaterial entities who shared the essential nature of the respective realms, the so-called 'sons of Light' and 'sons of Darkness.'[17] The Realm of Light was a paradisal locale, filled with pleasant fragrances and abundant fruits, but the Realm of Darkness was foul and filthy and populated by an unruly horde of monstrous fiends. This initial state of separation and balance between the two primal domains is occasionally termed the 'First Time.'

Consumed with lust for violence and sensual gratification, the sons of Darkness initiate an attack upon the Realm of Light in an attempt to gain possession of it by conquest. The ruler of the Realm of Light, an entity named the Father of Greatness, responds to the assault by creating a figure termed Primal Man. Primal Man proceeds to the border to confront the invaders, but he is promptly defeated, taken within the Realm of Darkness to be held as prisoner, and stripped of his shining armament. This gleaming panoply—sometimes referred to as the 'five sons of Primal Man'—is ravenously devoured by the sons of Darkness. Primal

16. See Chapter 3, below.

17. Ephrem Syrus, one of our oldest witnesses to Manichaeism's Syriac iteration, occasionally uses this terminology. See, e.g., his observations about Mani's *Ardahang* quoted above.

Man's defeat and the consumption of his 'children' represent a catastrophic 'mixture' of the two previously unsullied Realms, a situation of contamination which characterizes the so-called 'Second Time,' and which necessitates the creation of the physical universe as a means of purifying the captive portions belonging to the Realm of Light and restoring them to their original home.

Primal Man is rescued from his plight by agents from the Realm of Light, but the recovery of the elements of Light that were consumed by the sons of Darkness will require a more complicated means of extraction and purification. A number of divine entities are called into service in order to supervise this lengthy process. During the liberation of Primal Man, a certain group of the sons of Darkness termed 'archons' or 'demons' were taken into custody by the forces of Light. Some of these archons are now killed, flayed, and dismembered: their detached skins are fashioned into what becomes the canopy of the heavens, and the rest of their carcasses are used for the fabrication of the physical surface of the earth.[18] Those elements of Light trapped within their bodies are now dispersed throughout what has become the material order of existence. In order to effect their extraction from matter, the sun, the moon, and the stars are placed in the heavens to shine upon the earth and thereby attract the earth-bound particles of Light in an upward direction toward their proper domicile within the Realm of Light. The remaining captive archons, two hundred in number, are incarcerated in the heavens in preparation for a further stage of recovery, an episode popularly labeled 'the seduction of the archons.'

The 'seduction' is performed by an androgynous entity known as the Third Evocation or Messenger. This emissary promenades nude before the bound captive archons, displaying its considerable female charms to the male archons and its handsome male form to the female archons. Uncontrollably excited by this sight, the male archons ejaculate semen wherein is concentrated the previously engulfed particles of Light. Their semen falls to the surface of the earth where it becomes the origin of vegetal life. Similarly the pregnant female archons suffer miscarriages, and their ejected fetuses fall to earth to become animal life, among which figure a group of monstrous beings termed 'abortions.' These 'abortions' feed upon the newly sprouted plants, engage in riotous and destructive behavior, and further disperse and mix the trapped elements of Light within the material order. They however also nostalgically recall the alluring forms of the Messenger beheld by their archon parents in the heavens, and they therefore resolve to create facsimiles of those same male and female images upon the earth. By a sordid process involving both cannibalism and sexual congress, the 'abortions' successfully spawn the first human couple—Adam and Eve.

18. There is a certain irony that Mani's physical fate at the hands of his Persian torturers roughly parallels the painful experience of this group of unfortunate archons. This coincidence was not lost on Ephrem: 'and they (Mani's executioners) fittingly skinned Mani the deceitful: he who said that Darkness was skinned, (an entity) which possesses neither skin nor shed skin!' (Ephrem Syrus, *Prose Refutations* [ed. Mitchell], 1:15.20–26; Reeves, "Citations from Ephrem," 262).

Alarmed by these new and apparently unforeseen developments upon earth, the Father of Greatness dispatches a heavenly messenger to the newly created Adam in order to educate him about the true nature of the created order. Adam receives instructions regarding the ways by which he can assist the supernal process of recovering and restoring the bound particles of Light: he must completely abstain from sexual activity, observe strict dietary regulations, and devote himself to the performance of a series of elaborate prayers and purificatory rituals—in sum, the core regimen characteristic of a Manichaean *electus* or *zaddīq*.[19] If correctly implemented, these prescriptions would halt the continuing dispersal of the elements of Light throughout the material world and eventually produce their liberation, thereby restoring the uncontaminated status of the Realm of Light, the so-called 'Third Time' wherein the original ontological stasis would be re-attained.

Despite its singular formulation, readers of the foregoing summary cannot fail to notice a number of instances where Manichaean discourse and behaviors echo and intersect with more familiar Near Eastern myths of creation, ethnic legendry, communal identity, and eschatology. A systematic exposition of these numerous intriguing correspondences, including a demonstration of their exegetical grounding within both biblical and parabiblical writings, lies however well beyond the purview of the present work.

4. Manichaeism and Islam

Students of Manichaeism during the initial years of the twenty-first century are enjoying the fruits of a rich harvest of scholarly resources recently assembled for the study of that religion. New archaeological discoveries at Kellis (Ismant el-Kharab in the Dakhleh Oasis in Upper Egypt) have augmented the literary and documentary corpus surviving from early Egyptian Manichaeism,[20] helping to

19. There were two main classes of Manichaean 'believers': (1) the so-called 'elect' (Latin pl. *electi*) who observed all of the precepts in order to assist the release of the trapped particles of Light in the world, and (2) the so-called 'hearers' (Latin pl. *auditores*); i.e., the laity whose occupational labors and alms supported the 'elect' in their redemptive work. Syriac and Arabic sources indicate that Mani's Aramaic term for the 'elect' was *zaddīqā*; i.e., 'righteous one, pious one,' and that the self-designation for the religion itself was *zaddīqātā* '(true) righteousness, piety.' See the discussion of the Arabic term *zandaqa* below.

20. General discussion and some initial publication of a portion of the recent manuscript finds at Kellis can be found in Iain Gardner, "A Manichaean Liturgical Codex Found at Kellis," *Orientalia* 62 (1993): 30–59; I. M. F. Gardner and Samuel N. C. Lieu, "From Narmouthis (Medinet Madi) to Kellis (Ismant el-Kharab): Manichaean Documents from Roman Egypt," *Journal of Roman Studies* 86 (1996): 146–69; Iain Gardner and K. A. Worp, "Leaves from a Manichaean Codex," *Zeitschrift für Papyrologie und Epigraphik* 117 (1997): 139–55; C. A. Hope, "The Archaeological Context of the Discovery of Leaves from a Manichaean Codex," ibid., 156–61; Iain Gardner, "The Manichaean Community at Kellis: A Progress Report," in *Emerging from Darkness* (see above), 161–75. Official publication of the textual remains is in the Dakhleh Oasis Project Monograph series, of which

clarify some of the thorny issues surrounding the translation of early Manichaean scriptures from their eastern Aramaic *Vorlagen* into Greek and Coptic.[21] The justly renowned identification and publication of the Greek *Cologne Mani Codex* has revolutionized our understanding of Mani's religious roots within third-century Mesopotamia,[22] and continues to pose intriguing questions regarding the catalytic influence of both biblical and parabiblical writings upon nascent Manichaeism. At the same time, scholars persistently probe and extend our awareness of the great manuscript finds from the early decades of this century: the gradual but continual publication, translation, and discussion of the Medinet Madi (Coptic), Turfan (Middle Iranian and Old Turkish), and Dunhuang (Old Turkish and Chinese) texts have vastly increased the primary sources available for the study of Manichaeism in its various regional forms.[23] Older monographic syntheses of data and analysis have been supplanted in many respects by the recent comprehensive presentations of Lieu and Tardieu;[24] however, the pace of discovery and

---

a number of volumes have appeared over the past decade: the initial bibliographic details for this series are available in Gardner-Worp, "Leaves," 139 n.2.

21. For example, it is now clear (despite the reservations of the modern volume editors) that the Coptic Manichaean writings were translated directly from Syriac into Coptic. Such a procedure was already suspected by H. H. Schaeder almost seventy years ago; see his "Rezension von Carl Schmidt und H. J. Polotsky, *Ein Mani-Fund in Ägypten*," *Gnomon* 9 (1933): 337–62, reprinted in Geo Widengren, ed., *Der Manichäismus* (Wege der Forschung 168; Darmstadt: Wissenschaftliche Buchgesellschaft, 1977), 70–97, on p. 74. The lexical lists and other pertinent data are available in Iain Gardner, ed., *Kellis Literary Texts: Volume 1* (Dakhleh Oasis Project Monograph No. 4; Oxford: Oxbow Books, 1996), 101–31. See also the remarks of Majella Franzmann, "The Syriac-Coptic Bilinguals from Ismant el-Kharab (Roman Kellis): Translation Process and Manichaean Missionary Practice," in *Il Manicheismo, nuove prospettive della richerca: Dipartimento di Studi Asiatici Università degli Studi di Napoli "L'Orientale," Napoli, 2-8 Settembre 2001* (ed. Aloïs van Tongerloo and Luigi Cirillo; Turnhout: Brepols, 2005), 115–22.

22. The best edition of this important source is Koenen-Römer, *Der Kölner Mani-Kodex* (see n.2 above). As to its significance, see Julien Ries, *Les études manichéennes: Des controverses de la Réforme aux découvertes du XXe siècle* (Louvain-la-Neuve: Centre d'histoire des religions, 1988), 229–39; moreover, the proceedings of the two international conferences devoted to its explication: Luigi Cirillo and Amneris Roselli, eds., *Codex Manichaicus Coloniensis: Atti del Simposio Internazionale (Rende-Amantea 3-7 settembre 1984)* (Cosenza: Marra Editore, 1986), and Luigi Cirillo, ed., *Codex Manichaicus Coloniensis: Atti del Secondo Simposio Internazionale (Cosenza 27-28 maggio 1988)* (Cosenza: Marra Editore, 1990).

23. Ries (*Études*, 210–18) adequately synopsizes the work done on these texts up to the mid-1980s; for information about subsequent developments, see Lieu, *Manichaeism in Mesopotamia*, 64–105; idem, *Manichaeism in Central Asia and China* (NHMS 45; Leiden: Brill, 1998), 1–58.

24. Samuel N. C. Lieu, *Manichaeism in the Later Roman Empire and Medieval China* (2nd ed.; Tübingen: J. C. B. Mohr, 1992); Michel Tardieu, *Le manichéisme* (Paris: Presses Universitaires de France, 1981; 2nd ed.; Paris: Presses Universitaires de France, 1997). See now Michel Tardieu, *Manichaeism* (trans. M. B. DeBevoise; Urbana: University of Illinois Press, 2008).

publication is such that each of these newer books is now in need of fresh revision.[25] An International Association of Manichaean Studies links scholars who are active in this discipline and organizes and coordinates periodic conferences for the public dissemination of the latest discoveries and analytical discussions; in the United States, the Manichaeism Group program unit has fulfilled a similar networking role under the auspices of the Society of Biblical Literature.[26] Finally, a monumental publishing effort—the *Corpus Fontium Manichaeorum*—promises to bring together and reissue the most important primary texts and testimonies pertaining to Manichaeism (many of which, thanks to the obscurity of their original publication, prove difficult for the individual student to assemble) in order to enhance scholarly access to these essential materials.[27]

In spite of these praiseworthy efforts, one area of Manichaean studies remains remarkably underdeveloped amidst the current renascence of scholarly activity. This largely neglected realm of inquiry involves the study of the history and influence of Manichaeism as a viable minority religion within the orbit of Islam. Serious students of Manichaeism recognize that the information supplied by Islamicate sources constitutes some of the most important data we have pertaining to the history of Near Eastern dualist and 'gnostic' movements. It is clear that a number of these writers were privy to Manichaean writings—either authored in or at some point translated into Arabic—that in most cases are no longer extant. Some of these works formed part of the original Manichaean scriptural canon whose titles are known to us from earlier sources, whereas other cited writings were apparently authored, presumably in Arabic, by subsequent generations of Manichaean teachers and evangelists. Several of these Islamicate writers—to judge from their comments—had occasion to observe or to interact with individual members of active Manichaean communities, or at least participated in dialogues with intellectuals who allegedly exhibited some sympathy with Man-

25. While not intended as a comprehensive survey of Manichaeism, a nevertheless pathbreaking contribution to its modern study is Jason David BeDuhn, *The Manichaean Body: In Discipline and Ritual* (Baltimore, MD: The Johns Hopkins University Press, 2000).

26. This program unit is unfortunately now defunct.

27. Published to date are the following volumes: Gregor Wurst, *Die Bema-Psalmen* (CFM Series Coptica 1; Liber Psalmorum, Pars II, Fasc. 1; Turnhout: Brepols, 1996); Siegfried G. Richter, *Die Herakleides-Psalmen* (CFM Series Coptica 1; Liber Psalmorum, Pars II, Fasc. 2; Turnhout: Brepols, 1998); Sarah Clackson, et al., eds., *Dictionary of Manichaean Texts Vol. I: Texts from the Roman Empire* (CFM Subsidia II; Turnhout: Brepols, 1998); Hendrik Gerhard Schipper and Johannes van Oort, *St. Leo the Great, Sermons and Letters Against the Manichaeans: Selected Fragments* (CFM Series Latina 1; Turnhout: Brepols, 2000); Desmond Durkin-Meisterernst, *Dictionary of Manichaean Texts Vol. III, Part 1: Dictionary of Manichaean Middle Persian and Parthian* (CFM Subsidia; Turnhout: Brepols, 2004); François de Blois and Nicholas Sims-Williams, eds., *Dictionary of Manichaean Texts Vol. II: Texts from Iraq and Iran* (CFM Subsidia; Turnhout: Brepols, 2006); Nils Arne Pedersen, *Manichaean Homilies* (CFM Series Coptica 2; Turnhout: Brepols, 2006); Gunner B. Mikkelsen, *Dictionary of Manichaean Texts Vol. III, Part 4: Dictionary of Manichaean Texts in Chinese* (CFM Subsidia; Turnhout: Brepols, 2006).

ichaean ideology, an allegiance or affiliation which was most often termed in Muslim sources the heresy of *zandaqa*. This label, allegedly deriving from an Iranian loanword originally applied to the Manichaeans during the Sasanian period by Zoroastrian critics,[28] was adopted and amplified by ʿAbbāsid jurists to denote a broad spectrum of dualist speculation and antinomian behavior.[29] Given the fundamental importance of the information preserved and transmitted by Muslim tradents, as well as the notices and testimonies contained in the contemporaneous Jewish, Christian, Zoroastrian, and gnostic sources produced within the Islamicate realm, it is disappointing that so little attention has been devoted to date to a close analysis and integration of this material into comprehensive synthetic treatments of the history of Manichaeism, or even, at the most basic level, to the preparation of a history of Islamicate Manichaeism.

This unfortunate policy of neglect can be primarily attributed to a single cause. Excepting the basic treatments of Manichaeism supplied by Ibn al-Nadīm, Bīrūnī, and Shahrastānī together with their largely nineteenth-century commentators, the vast bulk of the Islamicate testimony to Manichaeism and kindred sects remains largely unavailable to western, and particularly Anglophone, scholarship. The standard collections of translated sources simply omit much of the relevant Muslim evidence, and as a consequence, the more recent synthetic studies follow

28. This is the standard explanation for the origin of this term, and it has been strongly endorsed again recently by van Ess, *Flowering*, 27. Renewed consideration, however, should be given to the possibility that *zandaqa* and its reflexes derives directly from the Syriac designations (*zaddīqā, zaddīqātā*; note Arabic *ṣiddīqūn*) for Manichaeism and its adherents, where medial /*nd*/ may be due to the dissimilation of /*dd*/. See A. A. Bevan, "Manichaeism," *ERE* 8:398–99 n.5; Edward G. Browne, *A Literary History of Persia* (4 vols.; London and Cambridge, 1902–24; repr., Cambridge: The University Press, 1964), 1:159–60; Nicholson, *Literary History of the Arabs*, 375 n.2; W[ladimir]. Ivanow, *Ibn al-Qaddah (The Alleged Founder of Ismailism)* (2nd rev. ed.; Bombay: Ismaili Society, 1957), 79; Otakar Klíma, *Mazdak: Geschichte einer sozialen Bewegung im sassanidischen Persien* (Praha: Nakladatelství Československé Akademie Věd, 1957), 201–203; Chaim Rabin, *Qumran Studies* (Oxford: Oxford University Press, 1957), 127 n.2; Yoram Erder, "The Origin of the Name Idrīs in the Qur'ān: A Study of the Influence of Qumran Literature on Early Islam," *JNES* 49 (1990): 349 n.83; F[rançois]. C. de Blois, "Zindīḳ," *EI*[2] 11:511. The derivation from Syriac is simply presumed without argument by the influential seventeenth-century orientalist Barthélemy d'Herbelot in his *Bibliothèque orientale, ou Dictionaire universel* (Paris: Compagnie des Libraires, 1697), 548: 'Zendik, c.a. le Saduceen'; also ibid., 415: 'les Zendik ou Sadduceens ... Ces Sadduceens étoient les Manicheens.'

29. Francesco Gabrieli, "La «zandaqa» au Ier siècle abbasside," in *L'élaboration de l'Islam: Colloque de Strasbourg, 12-13-14 juin 1959* (Paris: Presses Universitaires de France, 1961), 23–38; Louis Massignon, *The Passion of al-Ḥallāj: Mystic and Martyr of Islam* (4 vols.; trans. Herbert Mason; Princeton: Princeton University Press, 1982), 1:381–85; Roberto Giorgi, *Pour une histoire de la zandaḳa* (Firenze: La Nuova Italia Editrice, 1989), 13–26; Josef van Ess, *Theologie und Gesellschaft im 2. und 3. Jahrhundert Hidschra: Eine Geschichte des religiösen Denkens im frühen Islam* (6 vols.; Berlin: W. de Gruyter, 1991–96), 1:416–26; idem, *Flowering*, 24-29; Melhem Chokr, *Zandaqa et zindiqs en Islam au second siècle de l'hégire* (Damas: Institut français de Damas, 1993), 9–14.

suit. This situation is due in part to linguistic factors, inasmuch as a substantial number of the Arabic and New Persian testimonia have never been rendered into English, but it is also explicable on the basis of the general obscurity and institutional rarity of the few published *western* editions, translations, and commentaries devoted to these writers. Little progress can be made in crafting a critical re-description of Islamicate Manichaeism without taking into account the fuller range of evidence that is in fact available for its delineation.

Approximately fifty years ago a convenient anthology gathering together several hundred Arabic and New Persian excerpts pertaining to Manichaeism was published in Tehran by S. H. Taqīzādeh and A. A. Šīrāzī.[30] Unfortunately their work has never been made available to scholars in a western language. Since the labors of these editors over a half century ago, some additional important Islamicate texts have surfaced, and the new information which these witnesses provide requires their integration and study among the previously known sources. A streamlined English edition of the more important texts contained in this valuable collection of primary materials can in fact serve as the nucleus for a more comprehensive compilation of testimonies about the history of Manichaeism within the Islamicate realm.

The present work is a modest attempt to address the problem of raw accessibility by providing Anglophone researchers with a critically annotated English translation of a series of important Islamicate sources for the study of Manichaeism. Translations and brief commentary are provided not only for a number of the Arabic and Persian materials previously isolated by Taqīzādeh-Šīrāzī, but also for several pertinent later publications of Muslim texts as well as some relevant Hebrew, Syriac, Mandaic, and Judaeo-Arabic testimonia produced by a variety of minority religious communities living under the rule of Islam. The compilation and publication of such a resource is intended as a first step toward embracing the larger and more complex problem of reconstructing the history and cultural influence of Islamicate Manichaeism.

A new reading of these testimonies regarding Manichaean teachings and practices preserved in the Islamicate sources is long overdue. Having convenient access to these materials should enhance scholarly awareness of and appreciation for these sources and presumably help shed new light on the textual and cultural affiliations of Arabic language Manichaica. We should gain through this effort a more nuanced understanding of the complex interrelationships among these testimonies, their presumed sources, and their literary affinities.[31] Once

30. S. H. Taqīzādeh and A. A. Šīrāzī, *Mānī va dīn-e-ū* (Teheran: Ānjuman-e Irānshināsī, 1335 AH/1956).

31. See especially Carsten Colpe, "Anpassung des Manichäismus an den Islam (Abū 'Īsā al-Warrāq)," *ZDMG* 109 (1959): 82–91; Michael H. Browder, "Al-Bîrûnî's Manichaean Sources," in *Manichaean Studies* (ed. Bryder), 19–28; David Thomas, "Abū 'Īsā al-Warrāq and the History of Religions," *Journal of Semitic Studies* 41 (1996): 275–90; François de Blois, "New Light on the Sources of the Manichaean Chapter in the *Fihrist*," in *Il Manicheismo, nuove prospettive della richerca: Dipartimento di Studi Asiatici Università degli Studi*

the contours of textual transmission are better understood, we are then better prepared to tackle the engrossing issues surrounding the possible attraction that Manichaean imagery, mythemes, and behavioral attitudes had for certain intellectual and/or religious movements within and on the margins of Islam.[32] The ultimate goal of the present study, however, is a much more modest one. It is to provide in an accessible form the analytical data—the raw material—one needs for the gestation and birth of the more sophisticated synthetic studies of religious esoteric movements in the Islamicate world.

---

di Napoli "L'Orientale," Napoli, 2-8 Settembre 2001 (ed. Aloïs van Tongerloo and Luigi Cirillo; Turnhout: Brepols, 2005), 37-45. I am grateful to Prof. de Blois for kindly sharing with me his unpublished manuscript reconstruction of Abū 'Īsā al-Warrāq's account of Manichaeism.

32. Note for example Dimitri Gutas, *Greek Thought, Arabic Culture: The Graeco-Arabic Translation Movement in Baghdad and Early 'Abbāsid Society* (London and New York: Routledge, 1998), 70-71: '... the fact remains that *zandaqa* ... influenced enormously the course and development of Islam as a religion and ideology during the early 'Abbāsid era. The question is, how, precisely. Van Ess [*Theologie und Gesellschaft*, 1:423-27] has most recently suggested that ... certain Muslim intellectuals found in Manichaeism and related dualistic systems certain things that the Islam of their time could not offer them. It was therefore a matter of intellectuals coming in contact not with religious sects but with an ambience of intellectualism.' The 'intellectualist' mystique of Manichaeism within the Muslim world has also been noted by Róbert Simon, "Mānī and Muḥammad," *Jerusalem Studies in Arabic and Islam* 21 (1997): 123 n.28.

Biographical Testimonia about Mani

One of the thorniest problems in Manichaean studies revolves around the establishment of a precise chronology and the recovery of an 'objective' biographical framework for the most significant events of the founder's life. Part of the blame for this murky situation falls upon a parallel uncertainty surrounding the proper dating of the regnal years for both the mid-third century Roman rulers[1] and the early Sasanian emperors:[2] historical sources invariably synchronize the dates of Mani's birth, missionary activities, or death with the names and reigns of these imperial figures. Since there are uncertainties surrounding the lengths of reign and sequential ordering of these rulers, any synchronizations based upon these rulers share and perpetuate these discrepancies. Another complicating factor is a frequent confusion and conflation among these sources between widely separate events in Mani's life; for example, between that of his birth and that of his initial appearance as a representative of the new religion at the court of Shāpūr I. Henri-Charles Puech, who was perhaps the most reliable twentieth-century scholar of Manichaeism, characterizes this latter confusion as one between Mani's 'spiritual birth' (*naissance spirituelle*) and his 'actual birth' (*naissance charnelle*).[3] Chronographic notices exhibiting such confusion effectively compress Mani's activities on behalf of his new religion to the final years of his life in the mid-

1. See E. J. Bickerman, *Chronology of the Ancient World* (2nd ed.; Ithaca, NY: Cornell University Press, 1980), 212 note.
2. Note S. H. Taqizadeh and W. B. Henning, "The Dates of Mani's Life," *Asia Major* 6 (1957): 106-21; Albert Henrichs and Ludwig Koenen, "Ein griechischer Mani-Codex," *Zeitschrift für Papyrologie und Epigraphik* 5 (1970): 116–32; Richard N. Frye, "The Political History of Iran under the Sasanians," in *The Cambridge History of Iran, Volume 3(1): The Seleucid, Parthian and Sasanian Periods* (ed. Ehsan Yarshater; Cambridge: Cambridge University Press, 1983), 118–19.
3. Henri-Charles Puech, *Le manichéisme: Son fondateur — sa doctrine* (Paris: Civilisations du Sud, 1949), 17, 20, 42–43. Some reasons for this confusion are offered by Werner Sundermann, "Mani's Revelations in the Cologne Mani Codex and in Other Sources," in *Codex Manichaicus Coloniensis: Atti del Simposio Internazionale (Rende-Amantea 3-7 settembre 1984)* (ed. Luigi Cirillo and Amneris Roselli; Cosenza: Marra Editore, 1986), 205–14.

270s CE. Finally, the literary presentation of what might at first glance appear to be an 'objective' biographical narrative has in fact been manipulatively shaped by both hagiographical and heresiological interests. Authentically Manichaean testimonia tend to read the life of Mani through the lens of his self-announced role as Apostle of Light: his *vita* was creatively conformed to echo and re-present legendary aspects of the terrestrial careers of the Apostle's earlier *avatars*; namely, some select antediluvian biblical forefathers (like Adam or Enoch), Zoroaster, Buddha, and especially Jesus. On the other hand, and probably in direct response to this sympathetic reading, hostile Christian witnesses paint an unflattering portrait of Mani as a conniving imposter and unscrupulous opportunist. Their most successful effort was the so-called *Acta Archelai*,[4] a lengthy work of fiction ascribed to an otherwise unknown Hegemonius which was produced sometime during the first half of the fourth century.[5] The *Acta Archelai* would exert a profound influence upon almost every subsequent Christian discussion of Mani and Manichaeism:[6] it was particularly popular in the East among Syriac and Christian Arabic writers and even came to the notice of a few Muslim witnesses.[7]

Our intention in this chapter is not to produce indubitable certitude by resolving these various issues, but is simply to present the relevant data that is contributed by Islamicate sources to the delineation of Mani's life and career in order that present and future researchers might enjoy an unimpeded recourse to the broadest range of relevant material. The chapter sub-divides into three sections: (1) a series of brief chronological and synchronic notices pertaining to Mani's *floruit* culled from Syriac and Arabic sources; (2) an assemblage of materials for the recovery of what possibly are authentic biographical trajectories, largely recognizable from the evidence contributed by newly discovered sources

4. Hegemonius, *Acta Archelai* (GCS 16; ed. Charles Henry Beeson; Leipzig: J. C. Hinrichs, 1906). English translations are available in *ANF* 6:179–233 (trans. S. D. F. Salmond); Hegemonius, *Acta Archelai: The Acts of Archelaus* (trans. Mark Vermes; Turnhout: Brepols, 2001). The contents of the 'Mani-vita' contained in the *Acta Archelai* are summarized by Puech, *Le manichéisme*, 22–24.

5. Apparently still unknown to Eusebius (note his *Historia ecclesiastica* 7.31.1–2), material reflective of the distinctive contents of the *Acta* initially surface within the catechetical homilies of Cyril of Jerusalem (ca. 350 CE).

6. See especially Puech, *Le manichéisme*, 17–18; 99–100 n.10.

7. A longstanding issue involves the original linguistic provenance of the *Acta*. It is extant in its entirety only in Latin; some portions linger in Greek in Cyril of Jerusalem and in the *Panarion* of Epiphanius. According to Jerome (*De vir. inl.* 72), the work was first composed in Syriac and then translated into Greek (*Archelaus episcopus Mesopotamiae librum disputationis suae, quam habuit adversum Manichaeum exeuntum de Perside Syro sermone composuit, qui translatus in Graecum habetur a multis*), but almost all modern scholars accept Greek as its original language of composition. In addition to Greek and Latin, recognizable versions of the *Acta* are extant in Coptic, Syriac, and Arabic. Given the *Acta*'s immense popularity in the East, the matter of its linguistic diffusion probably deserves a new study.

like the *Cologne Mani Codex*, but often blended with brief accounts or traditions which betray a dependence upon the hagiographic portrayals surviving in Coptic and Middle Iranian Manichaean works; and (3) a presentation of the polemical themes deriving from the *Acta Archelai* and its satellites. Following the seriatim presentation of these materials are some concluding pages of analysis and reflection on these sources' relative worth to a plausible reconstruction of the *vita* of the third-century Babylonian prophet.

1. Chronological and Synchronic Notices

Chronicon Edessenum (ed. Guidi):[8]

Year 551:[9] Mānī was born.[10]

Chronicon Maroniticum (ed. Brooks):[11]

Also in the fourth year of Aurelian,[12] which according to the Greek reckoning is year [5]83,[13] [M]anī the lunatic propagated (his) false doctrine. He was at this time

8. Ignatius Guidi, ed., *Chronica Minora I* (CSCO 1; Paris, 1903; repr., Louvain: Imprimerie Orientaliste, 1960), 3.27–28.

9. I.e., according to the Seleucid era (SE), whose point of departure in Babylonia was 311 BCE. 551 SE would thus be equivalent to 240 CE. Mani however was born in 216 CE, not 240; see the next note.

10. The same notice is repeated in *Chronicon Anonymum ad A.D. 819* (see J.-B. Chabot, ed., *Anonymi auctoris Chronicon ad annum Christi 1234 pertinens* [CSCO 81–82; 2 vols.; Paris: Reipublicae, 1916–20], 1:3.23) and in the *Opus chronologicum* of Elias of Nisibis (see E. W. Brooks, ed., *Eliae metropolitae Nisibeni Opus chronologicum* [CSCO 62-63a; 2 vols. in 4; Paris: Reipublicae, 1909–10], 1:92.15–17). The one indisputable date in the biographical tradition is the date of Mani's birth, regarding which both the Arabic and Chinese traditions (Ms. Stein 3969) confirm as 8 Nisannu (= 14 April) 216. See the testimony of Bīrūnī below, as well as G. Haloun and W. B. Henning, "The Compendium of the Doctrines and Styles of the Teaching of Mani, the Buddha of Light," *Asia Major* 3 (1953): 184-212. Hence Ludwig Hallier proposed emending this chronicle's 'was born' (ܐܬܝܠܕ) to 'became known' (ܐܬܝܕܥ) in his *Untersuchungen über die Edessenische Chronik* (TU 9.1; Leipzig: J. C. Hinrichs, 1892), 92.

11. E.-W. Brooks, ed., *Chronica Minora II* (CSCO 3; Louvain: Secrétariat du CorpusSCO, 1904), 58.21–24. For information about this chronicle, which should probably be dated to the mid-seventh century, see Andrew Palmer, *The Seventh Century in the West-Syrian Chronicles* (Liverpool: Liverpool University Press, 1993), 29. The remainder of this chronicle's presentation of 'biographical' information about Mani appears below.

12. 274 CE. This synchronization with Aurelian stems ultimately from the largely lost *Chronicle* of Eusebius; see Epiphanius, *Panarion* 66.1.2 and Rudolf Helm, ed., *Eusebius Werke VII Band: Die Chronik des Hieronymus* (3rd ed.; Berlin: Akademie-Verlag, 1984), 222–23. The same traditions found here are repeated almost verbatim by a number of derivative sources; see, for example, Michael Syrus below. Puech asserts (based on Epiphanius, *Panarion* 66.1.1) that the 'fourth year of Aurelian' originally marked the date of the arrival of the Manichaean mission in Palestine (*Le manichéisme*, 19 and 101 n.17).

13. The result is 272 CE if one completes this computation. A more glaring erroneous correla-

thirty-three years old,[14] for he was b[orn] in the year [55]1.

Chronicon miscellaneum ad ann. p. Chr. 724 pertinens **(ed. Brooks):**[15]

In the year 573: Mānī the seducer appeared.[16]

Zūqnīn Chronicle **(ed. Chabot):**[17]

Year 2273 *anno mundi*.[18] The holy Cyril was bishop of Antioch, and Eutychianus was (bishop) of Rome for eight months; after him Gaianus was (bishop) for fifteen years. The holy Theonas was (bishop) over Alexandria for nineteen years. At that time pernicious destroyers of humankind—the Manichaeans—came into the world. Now this Manī was a barbarian of Arab ethnicity.[19] He came and befouled the land of Egypt,[20] and his demonic heresy spread corruption by means of (its) foolish language. He was deranged and insane. He devoted himself to those who imitated him. He decided to model himself after the image of Our Lord: he an-

---

tion is made between the fourth year of Aurelian and 592 SE in Michael Syrus; see below.

14. Should probably be corrected to 24/25 years old in line with the authentic biographical traditions contained in the *Cologne Mani Codex* and Ibn al-Nadīm's *Fihrist*. On the other hand, having Mani begin his teaching activities at the age of thirty-three would cement a conceptual association with the figure of Jesus, who according to one popular eastern tradition 'was on earth for thirty-three years' (*Chronica Minora II* [ed. Brooks], 97.27–29). Thus the 'thirty-three' may stem from an authentic Manichaean source. Compare Coptic *Keph.* 14.3 which employs the rhetoric of a seamless transition between the respective 'apostolates' of Jesus and Mani; translations available in Carl Schmidt and H. J. Polotsky, *Ein Mani-Fund in Ägypten: Originalschriften des Mani und seiner Schüler* (Berlin: Verlag der Akademie der Wissenschaften, 1933), 54; Iain Gardner and Samuel N. C. Lieu, eds., *Manichaean Texts From the Roman Empire* (Cambridge: Cambridge University Press, 2004), 74.

15. *Chronica Minora II* (ed. Brooks), 149.14.

16. I.e., 262 CE. See Henri-Charles Puech, "Dates manichéennes dans les chroniques syriaques," in *Mélanges syriens offerts à Monsieur René Dussaud* (2 vols.; Paris: Librairie Orientaliste Paul Geuthner, 1939), 2:594, where he notes that this year corresponds with the ninth year of Valerian and Gallienus, a synchronization mentioned by Epiphanius for the dating of the legendary disputation with Archelaus; see also Palmer, *Seventh Century*, 20.

17. J.-B. Chabot, ed., *Incerti auctoris Chronicon Pseudo-Dionysianum vulgo dictum* (CSCO 91, 104; 2 vols.; Paris: Reipublicae, 1927–33), 1:145.24–146.8.

18. This corresponds to 259 CE.

19. Possibly an echo of the ethnic profile of Scythianus provided in the *Acta Archelai* (see below), but in light of the place and era during which this chronicle was compiled (775 CE), it is more likely a deliberate misrepresentation of Mani as 'Muḥammad' for the purpose of denigrating Islam.

20. Despite this claim and a similar statement found in the *Chronicon ad annum Christi 1234* (see below), there is no evidence that Mani himself ever undertook a journey to Egypt. Egypt was however an important site for early Manichaean missionary activity as evidenced by both primary Manichaean and secondary polemical sources.

nounced that he himself was the Spirit, the Paraclete. Carried away by his madness and mimicking Christ, he selected twelve disciples for himself.[21]

Chronicon anonymum ad ann. p. Chr. 846 pertinens (ed. Brooks):[22]

During those times Mānī the maniac flourished.[23]

Mas'ūdī, _Tanbīh_ (ed. de Goeje):[24]

Second: Sābūr b. Ardašīr ruled for thirty-one years and six months. It was during his reign that Mānī was active, and the Manichaeans,[25] adherents of dualism, are connected to him.

Third: Hurmuz b. Sābūr ruled for one year and ten months.

Fourth: Bahrām b. Hurmuz[26] ruled for three years and three months. He executed Mānī and attacked some of his followers. This took place in the city of Sābūr-Fārs.[27]

---

21. Compare Eusebius, *Historia ecclesiastica* 7.31.1, the likely source for some of this information. See also Witold Witakowski, "Sources of Pseudo-Dionysius of Tel-Mahre for the Christian Epoch of the First Part of His *Chronicle*," in *After Bardaisan: Studies on Continuity and Change in Syriac Christianity in Honour of Professor Han J. W. Drijvers* (Orientalia Lovaniensia Analecta 89; ed. G. J. Reinink and A. C. Klugkist; Leuven: Peeters, 1999), 353.

22. *Chronica Minora II* (ed. Brooks), 190.3–4.

23. The 'times' in question are during, or immediately prior to, the reign of Diocletian (284-305 CE). This notice, as pointed out by Puech ("Dates," 594–95), is dependent on Eusebius, *Historia ecclesiastica* 7.31.1–2, and also reproduces the Greek pun found there that spoofs Mani's name.

24. Mas'ūdī, *Kitâb at-Tanbîh wa'l-Ischrâf* (2nd ed.; Bibliotheca Geographorum Arabicorum 8; ed. M. J. de Goeje; Leiden: Brill, 1967), 100.12–16; also S. H. Taqīzādeh and A. A. Šīrāzī, *Mānī va dīn-e-ū* (Teheran: Ānjuman-e Irānshināsī, 1335 AH/1956), 133–34 (§22); Gustav Flügel, *Mani: Seine Lehre und seine Schriften* (Leipzig, 1862; repr., Osnabrück: Biblio Verlag, 1969), 357.

25. The usual Arabophone designations for the followers of Mani are the Mānawiyya (as here) or the Manāniyya; rarely, the Māniyya. See Guy Monnot, "Thanawiyya," *EI*[2] 10:439; C. E. Bosworth, "Mānī b. Fāttik," *EI*[2] 6:421; François de Blois, "Glossary of Technical Terms and Uncommon Expressions in Arabic (and in Muslim New Persian) Texts Relating to Manichaeism," in *Dictionary of Manichaean Texts, Vol. II: Texts from Iraq and Iran (Texts in Syriac, Arabic, Persian and Zoroastrian Middle Persian)* (ed. François de Blois and Nicholas Sims-Williams; Turnhout: Brepols, 2006), 75–76.

26. Bahrām I (273–276 CE) was the elder brother, not the son, of Hurmuz I (272–273 CE). This error is widespread throughout the Muslim chronographic tradition.

27. Perhaps a mistaken reference to Pērōz-Shāpūr, the new name of the city Anbār on the Euphrates where Shāpūr defeated the Roman emperor Gordian III in 244 CE? The location of Mani's imprisonment and execution is usually identified as Gundešāpūr (Syriac Bēth Lapaṭ; Arabic Jundaysābūr), a site about thirty kilometers east of Susa; see the testimonies below and W. B. Henning, "Mani's Last Journey," *BSOAS* 10 (1939–42): 941–53. A Parthian Manichaean text which discusses the death of Mani (M 5569) identifies the city as *byl'b'd*; i.e., Bēlāpāt or Bēth Lapaṭ; see F. C. Andreas and W. B. Henning, "Mitteliranische Manichaica aus Chinesisch-Turkestan III," *SPAW* (1934): 861. A copious list-

Mas'ūdī, *Tanbīh* (ed. de Goeje):[28]

Thirty-fourth: Claudius the second ruled for one year,[29] and it was during his reign that Mānī appeared. The Manichaeans among the dualist sects are connected to him. Mention of him has already been made previously in this book within the account of the second (group) of Persian kings, the Sasanians, during the reign of Sābūr b. Ardašīr, and (a notice was given of) how he had been put to death during the reign of Bahrām b. Hurmuz b. Sābūr.[30]

Ḥamza al-Iṣfahānī, *Ta'rīkh sinī mulūk al-arḍ wa'l-anbiyā'* (ed. Taqīzādeh-Šīrāzī):[31]

Mānī appeared in the time of Šābūr b. Ar[da]šir.

Ibn al-Nadīm, *Fihrist* (ed. Flügel):[32]

The Manichaeans have said: He came out on the day Sābūr b. Ardašīr became king and placed the crown on his head. It was a Sunday, the first day of (the month) Nīsān,[33] and the sun was in (the constellation) Aries. Accompanying him were two men who followed after his teaching: one of them was named Šam'ūn and the other Zakwā.[34] Also with him was his father, watching what would happen.[35]

---

ing of the sources treating of Mani's final days is supplied by Puech, *Le manichéisme*, 141 n.225; see also the texts assembled by Gardner-Lieu, *Manichaean Texts*, 79–108. Anbār corresponds to talmudic Neharde'ā; see Moshe Gil, *A History of Palestine, 634–1099* (trans. Ethel Broido; Cambridge: Cambridge University Press, 1992), 305. For another translation, see B. Carra de Vaux, *Maçoudi: Le livre de l'avertissement et de la revision* (Paris: L'Imprimerie Nationale, 1896), 144.

28. *Tanbīh* (ed. de Goeje), 135.5–9; Taqīzādeh-Šīrāzī, *Mānī va dīn-e-ū*, 134 (§22).

29. Bar Hebraeus mentions this Roman ruler in his notice below.

30. See the previous extract. For another translation, see Carra de Vaux, *Le livre de l'avertissement*, 187–88.

31. Taqīzādeh-Šīrāzī, *Mānī va dīn-e-ū*, 136 (§23).

32. Flügel, *Mani*, 51.4–13; Ibn al-Nadīm, *Kitāb al-Fihrist* (ed. Riḍa Tajaddud; [Teheran: Maktabat al-Assadī, 1971]), 392; Taqīzādeh-Šīrāzī, *Mānī va dīn-e-ū*, 150-51 (§27).

33. The first month of the year in the Babylonian calendar. This date for Shāpūr's coronation corresponds to April 12, 240 CE.

34. Compare *CMC* 106.15-19, where Mani's first two named disciples are [Συμεώ]ν and 'Αβιζαχίας. The latter figure may be identical with the early Manichaean missionary Abzakyā (ܐܒܙܟܝܐ) who is known from the Syriac narrative about the martyrs of Karkā de-Bēth Selōk; see Paul Bedjan, ed., *Acta martyrum et sanctorum syriace* (7 vols.; Paris, 1890–97; repr., Hildesheim: Georg Olms, 1968), 2:512.12-13; Puech, *Le manichéisme*, 49. A teacher named 'Zakū' or 'Mar Zaku' also figures among Mani's early followers; note, e.g., the end of the Parthian crucifixion hymn M 104 R ll.15–17 (Andreas-Henning, "Mitteliranische Manichaica ... III," 882). A different list of names for Mani's initial disciples is supplied by the *Acta Archelai* tradition; see below.

35. According to the *Cologne Mani Codex*, Pattikios (Mani's father) left the baptist sect soon after Mani's departure and joined his son near Ctesiphon.

Muḥammad b. Isḥaq[36] said: Mānī appeared in the second year of the rule of Gallus the Roman.[37] Marcion had appeared about a hundred years prior to him in the reign of Titus Antoninus, in the first year of his rule.[38] Ibn Dayṣān (i.e., Bardaiṣan) appeared about thirty years after Marcion; he was named Ibn Dayṣān because he was born by a river which was called Dayṣān.[39]

Bīrūnī, *Āthār al-bāqiya ʻan-il-qurūn al-khāliya* (ed. Sachau):[40]

He (Mānī) says in this book (the *Shābuhragān*)[41] in the chapter about the advent of the apostle that he was born in Babylon in the year 527 according to the astronomical chronology of Babylon, meaning the chronology of Alexander (i.e., Seleucid era),[42] and four years past the accession to rule of Ādharbān the king, whom I think is the final Ardavān (i.e., Artabanus IV or V, the last Arsacid monarch).[43] In this chapter he maintains that revelation came to him when he was thirteen years old,[44] and this was in the year 539 of the astronomical chronology of Babylon,[45]

36. I.e., Ibn al-Nadīm, the compiler of the *Fihrist*. Here he cites himself as the authority for what follows.
37. Presumably Trebonianus Gallus, who was proclaimed emperor in 251 CE and then killed in 253.
38. Antoninus Pius (138-61 CE)? The dates supplied for Marcion and Bardaiṣan are approximately correct.
39. This river flows through the city of Edessa. The same explanation for the name appears in the biography of Bardaiṣan contained in the twelfth-century *Chronicle* of Michael Syrus: 'While they were crossing over the river which (runs) by the city, (his mother) Nahshiram gave birth, and they called the name of the child "Bardaiṣan" after the name of the river.' Text translated from the extract published by F. Nau, "Bardesanes: Liber legum regionum," in *Patrologia Syriaca* (3 vols.; ed. R. Graffin; Paris: Firmin-Didot, 1894-1926), 2:522–23. See also Flügel, *Mani*, 84–85; Konrad Kessler, *Mani: Forschungen über die manichäische Religion* (Berlin: Georg Reimer, 1889), 385–86; Bayard Dodge, *The Fihrist of al-Nadīm: A Tenth-Century Survey of Muslim Culture* (2 vols.; New York: Columbia University Press, 1970), 2:775–76; Gardner-Lieu, *Manichaean Texts*, 75.
40. Bīrūnī, *Kitāb al-āthār al-bāqiya ʻani'l-qurūn al-khāliya: Chronologie orientalischer Völker von Albêrûnî* (ed. C. E. Sachau; Leipzig, 1878; repr., Leipzig: Otto Harrassowitz, 1923), 118.15–21; Taqīzādeh-Šīrāzī, *Mānī va dīn-e-ū*, 203 (§34).
41. Bīrūnī quotes the same information later in the *Āthār* with the title of Mani's work explicitly identified; see the next excerpt.
42. This dating for Mani's birth (year 527 of the Seleucid era) is independently confirmed by the so-called Chinese *Compendium*. See Haloun-Henning, "Compendium," 190, 196–97.
43. 213–224 CE.
44. Note the testimony of Ibn al-Nadīm below: 'When he completed the age of twelve years, a revelation came to him ....'
45. This date (539 SE = 228 CE) is confirmed by the Manichaean Parthian fragment (M 5910) published by Werner Sundermann, *Mitteliranische manichäische Texte kirchengeschichtlichen Inhalts* (Berliner Turfantexte 11; Berlin: Akademie-Verlag, 1981), 19.22–23. Note also Samuel N. C. Lieu, *Manichaeism in the Later Roman Empire and*

two years having passed of the years of Ardašīr, the King of Kings.

He stipulates by this that the space of time between Alexander and Ardašīr was 537 years, and that the space of time between Ardašīr and the accession to rule of Yazdgird[46] was 406 years. This is correct, taking as testimony (what) has been recorded in a bound volume with which a religion is governed.

Bīrūnī, *Āthār* (ed. Sachau):[47]

According to what he related in the book *Shābūraqān* (i.e., the *Shābuhragān*) in the chapter about the advent of the apostle, the birthplace of Mānī was in Babylon in a village called Mardīnū near the upper canal of Kūtha in the year 527 of the era of the Babylonian astronomers, meaning the chronology of Alexander (i.e., Seleucid era), four years having passed of the years of Ādharbān the king. Revelation came when he was thirteen years old in the year 539 of the era of the Babylonian astronomers and after two years had passed of the years of Ardašīr, the King of Kings.[48] We have already verified this portion in what preceded (the section about) the length of time the 'Ašakāniyyah[49] and petty kings ruled.[50]

Michael Syrus, *Chronicle* (ed. Chabot):[51]

In the fourth year of Aurelian, which correlates with year 592 according to the Greek reckoning,[52] Mānī flourished. At that time he was thirty-three years old.[53]

***Chronicon ad annum Christi 1234* (ed. Chabot):**[54]

A different Antoninus ruled for seven years. At that time the heretic Mānī became known when he came to Alexandria.[55]

Medieval China (2nd ed.; WUNT 63; Tübingen: J. C. B. Mohr, 1992), 44.

46. The final Sasanid ruler Yazdgird III (633–651 CE).

47. *Āthār* (ed. Sachau), 208.7–12; Taqīzādeh-Šīrāzī, *Mānī va dīn-e-ū*, 205 (§34).

48. See the remarks of Theodor Nöldeke, *Geschichte der Perser und Araber zur Zeit der Sasaniden aus der arabischen Chronik des Tabari* (Leiden, 1879; repr., Leiden: Brill, 1973), 409.

49. The Arabic name for the Arsacid royal dynasty or Parthian empire. See Nöldeke, *Geschichte der Perser und Araber*, 26 n.1. See also the testimony of Ibn al-Nadīm below regarding the family of Mani's mother.

50. For another translation, see Gotthard Strohmaier, *In den Gärten der Wissenschaft: Ausgewählte Texte aus den Werken des muslimischen Universalgelehrten* (2nd ed.; Leipzig: Reclam-Verlag, 1991), 141.

51. J.-B. Chabot, ed., *Chronique de Michel le Syrien, patriarche jacobite d'Antioche, 1166–1199* (4 vols.; repr., Bruxelles: Culture et Civilisation, 1963), 4:116.40–117.1.

52. On this erroneous correlation, see Puech, "Dates," 597.

53. Compare with the *Chronicon Maroniticum* above.

54. J.-B. Chabot, ed., *Anonymi auctoris Chronicon ad annum Christi 1234 pertinens* (CSCO 81–82; 2 vols.; Paris: Reipublicae, 1916–20), 1:136.3–5.

55. Apart from the *Zuqnīn Chronicle* (see above), there are no other traditions which speak of Mani journeying to Egypt. Probably the present text simply equates the advent of 'Mani' in Alexandria with the late third-century arrival of Manichaean missionaries in Egypt.

Bar Hebraeus, *Chronicon syriacum* (ed. Bedjan):[56]

After Maximinus Caesar, Gordian Caesar reigned for six years, who was killed within the boundaries of Persia. During his reign Mānī was born ....[57]

After Claudius Caesar (II),[58] Aurelian Caesar reigned six years. During his first year (of rule) he conquered the Palmyrenes and subdued the Gauls.[59] During his reign Mānī flourished.

Ibn Abī Uṣaybi'a, '*Uyūn* (ed. Taqīzādeh-Šīrāzī):[60]

I found in an epitome of Roman history that Asfāsiyānūs (Vespasian?) ruled for fifteen years, and it was during his time that Mānī appeared.

2. Authentic Biographical Trajectories

Theodore bar Konai, *Liber scholiorum* (ed. Scher):[61]

Many stories are related about this wicked one (i.e., Mani). Some have said that he was (originally) named Qūrqabyōs,[62] and that he first learned the heresy of the 'Pure Ones' because they purchased him (as a slave).[63] His hometown was named 'Abrūmya[64] and his father was Paṭīq.[65]

56. Paul Bedjan, ed., *Gregorii Barhebraei Chronicon Syriacum* (Paris: Maisonneuve, 1890), 56.9–10; 57.9–11.

57. Gordian III ruled Rome 238–244 CE. Hence Bar Hebraeus's information correlates with that of the *Chronicon Edessenum* above.

58. 268–270 CE.

59. These events took place during 273–274, when Aurelian destroyed Palmyra and recovered the allegiance of Gaul.

60. Taqīzādeh-Šīrāzī, *Mānī va dīn-e-ū*, 268 (§58).

61. Theodore bar Konai, *Liber Scholiorum* (CSCO 55, 69; 2 vols.; ed. A. Scher; Paris: Carolus Poussielgue, 1910–12), 2:311.12–19. See also Henri Pognon, *Inscriptions mandaïtes des coupes de Khouabir* (Paris, 1898; repr., Amsterdam: Philo Press, 1979), 125.11–17.

62. ܩܘܪܩܒܝܘܣ. This represents a slightly garbled transcription into Syriac characters of Greek Κούβρικος (cf. Latin *Corbicius*), a name derived from *Acta Archelai* 64.2–3 (ed. Beeson, 92–93).

63. An intriguing combination (Theodore's?) of authentic biographical data with two motifs (Mani's 'original' name and social status) drawn from the *Acta Archelai*. Both the *Cologne Mani Codex* and Ibn al-Nadīm's *Fihrist* know Mani's 'sectarian' background, the former terming them 'baptists' (βαπτισταί) and later identifying them as followers of Elchasai (*CMC* 94.10–12), a Jewish-Christian prophet active in the Transjordan during the last decade of the first century CE.

64. Compare the excerpt from Bīrūnī above, where Mani himself reportedly stated that his birthplace was a village named Mardīnū. Henning ("Mani's Last Journey," 948) suggests emending 'Mardīnū' to 'Barūmyā.' For a detailed attempt to sort out the discrepancies, see Puech, *Le manichéisme*, 34–35, 116–17 nn.111–17.

65. So in many Syriac and Arabic sources; the Greek form (known from the *Cologne Mani Codex* and Byzantine abjuration formulae) is Pattikios (Παττίκιος). This name for Mani's biological father is confirmed by a number of sources; see Puech, *Le man-*

But since the 'Pure Ones[66]'—those (also) called 'the (wearers of) White Garment(s)'[67]—were unable to endure him, they expelled him from among them,[68] terming him a 'vessel of evil' (*mānā de-bīštā*), and it is from this (expression) that he is named 'Mānī.'[69]

Jāḥiẓ, *Kitāb al-tarbīʿ wa'l-tadwīr* (ed. Pellat):[70]

Recount to me how prophetic pretenders and artful liars compare with those who are qualified to prophesy and who do not publicize their claim (to such credentials), or who have announced (it) and embarrassed themselves, or with those whose summons I might obey and it is in no way obligatory ... or those whose form and situation are in accord with what appears in previous prophe-

---

ichéisme, 35-36, 117–18 n.124.

66. ܕܟܝ̈ܐ. For a discussion of this name, see H. H. Schaeder, "Die Kantäer," *Die Welt des Orients* 1 (1947–52): 297–98. Note the final specific entry in Mārūtā of Maypherqaṭ's fifth-century list of heresies: 'The next heresy is that of the Cathari (ܩܬܪ̈ܐ; Greek καθάριοι) who are termed in Syriac "Pure Ones" (ܕܟܝ̈ܐ)'; text cited from Arthur Vööbus, ed., *The Canons Ascribed to Mārūtā of Maipherqaṭ and Related Sources* (CSCO 439, scrip. syri t. 191; Louvain: Peeters, 1982), 26.21-22. Werner Sundermann connects the Syriac term with the enigmatic *mktky* of the Kirdēr inscription(s); see his "Parthisch 'bšwdg'n 'die Täufer'," *Acta Antiqua Academiae Scientiarum Hungaricae* 25 (1977): 241; note also H. W. Bailey, "Note on the Religious Sects Mentioned by Kartīr (Kardēr)," in *The Cambridge History of Iran, Volume 3(2): The Seleucid, Parthian and Sasanian Periods* (ed. Ehsan Yarshater; Cambridge: Cambridge University Press, 1983), 907-908. For further references, see Shaul Shaked, *Dualism in Transformation: Varieties of Religion in Sasanian Iran* (London: School of Oriental and African Studies, 1994), 11–12 n.15.

67. Reading ܕܠܒܫܐ ܚܘܪܐ in place of the text's ܕܚܝܠܐ ܚܘܪܐ 'White Power.' The wearing of white garments as a distinctive garb was favored by a number of Mediterranean and Syro-Mesopotamian religious groups in late antiquity.

68. The *Cologne Mani Codex* also seems to envision a 'trial' followed by Mani's formal expulsion from the sect. See John C. Reeves, "The Elchasaite Sanhedrin of the Cologne Mani Codex in Light of Second Temple Jewish Sectarian Sources," *Journal of Jewish Studies* 42 (1991): 68–91. Several Muslim sources speak of an otherwise unattested 'expulsion' of Mani from the Sasanian Empire itself.

69. Puns on Mani's name (Mani the 'maniac, madman') are a favorite feature of the polemical traditions. For an echo of Theodore's Semitically based wordplay in the Greek tradition (τὸ σκεῦος τοῦ διαβόλου), see Sarah Stroumsa and Gedaliahu G. Stroumsa, "Aspects of Anti-Manichaean Polemics in Late Antiquity and under Early Islam," *Harvard Theological Review* 81 (1988): 38 n.5; Samuel N. C. Lieu, *Manichaeism in Mesopotamia and the Roman East* (RGRW 118; Leiden: Brill, 1994), 256–57. Additional translations are available in Pognon, *Inscriptions*, 181-82; Alfred Adam, ed., *Texte zum Manichäismus* (2nd ed.; Berlin: Walter de Gruyter, 1969), 75–76; Robert Hespel and René Draguet, *Théodore bar Koni, Livre des scolies (recension de Séert): II. Mimrè VI-XI* (CSCO 432, scrip. syri t. 188; Louvain: E. Peeters, 1982), 232. For the continuation of this passage, see below in section 3.

70. Charles Pellat, *Le Kitāb at-tarbīʿ wa-t-tadwīr de Ǧāḥiẓ* (Damas: Institut français de Damas, 1955), 75 (§133); also Taqīzādeh-Šīrāzī, *Mānī va dīn-e-ū*, 98 (§7).

cies and with what is found in genuine scriptures, or the other ones regarding whom there happens to be some doubt. Talk (for example) about Seth b. Adam,[71] and talk about Zarādusht (i.e., Zoroaster) and Mānī and Paul, and about what they claim with regard to Mark, Matthew, Luke, and John.[72]

Ya'qūbī, *Ta'rīkh* (ed. Houtsma):[73]

Mānī b. Ḥammād[74] the *zindīq* appeared during the time of Sābūr b. Ardašīr. He invited Sābūr (to convert) to his dualism, finding fault with his (the king's) religious belief. And Sābūr inclined to him ….[75]

So Sābūr agreed to this doctrine from him, and imposed it upon the people of his kingdom. This was distressful to them, and the wise men among the people of his kingdom joined together to resist him regarding this (choice), but he did not do (what they wanted) ….[76]

Sābūr persisted in this doctrine about ten years. Then the *mōbadh* (Zoroastrian priest)[77] came to him and said, 'This one (Mani) has corrupted your religion!

---

71. A number of Near Eastern religious communities accorded the figure of Seth prophetic credentials and assigned writings or even the establishment of a distinctive 'religion' (Arabic *dīn*) to him. For some examples, see A. F. J. Klijn, *Seth in Jewish, Christian and Gnostic Literature* (NovTSup 46; Leiden: Brill, 1977); John C. Reeves, *Heralds of That Good Realm: Syro-Mesopotamian Gnosis and Jewish Traditions* (NHMS 41; Leiden: Brill, 1996), 36–37, 111–40. Note the prophetic legend recounted by al-Kisā'ī about the so-called 'Ṣābians' of Ḥarrān who refuse to join Abraham in his migration to Canaan and who pledge their allegiance to 'the religion (*dīn*) of Seth, Enoch, and Noah'; see *Qiṣaṣ al-anbiyā': Vita Prophetarum auctore Muḥammed ben 'Abdallah al-Kisa'i* (2 vols.; ed. Isaac Eisenberg; Leiden: Brill, 1922–23), 1:71.15; D. Chwolsohn, *Die Ssabier und der Ssabismus* (2 vols.; St. Petersburg: Kaiserlichen Akademie der Wissenschaften, 1856), 2:503.

72. For other translations, see Maurice Adad, "Le *Kitāb al-Tarbī' wa-l-Tadwīr* d'al-Ğāḥiẓ: Traduction française, III," *Arabica* 14 (1967): 184; *Sobriety and Mirth: A Selection of the Shorter Writings of al-Jāhiz* (trans. Jim Colville; London and New York: Kegan Paul, 2002), 291.

73. M. T. Houtsma, ed., *Ibn Wadih qui dicitur al-Ja'qubi historiae …* (2 vols.; Leiden: Brill, 1883), 1:180–82; Taqīzādeh-Šīrāzī, *Mānī va dīn-e-ū*, 103-105 (§13).

74. Otherwise unattested as a name for Mani's father.

75. *Ta'rīkh* (ed. Houtsma), 1:180.4–5.

76. *Ta'rīkh* (ed. Houtsma), 1:181.1–3. According to the Coptic *Homil.* 48.2–9, Shāpūr and Mani enjoyed a close relationship and corresponded with one another.

77. For this religious office, see especially Michelangelo Guidi and Michael G. Morony, "Mōbadh," *EI*[2] 7:213–16. The anonymous priest of Ya'qūbī is presumably the Magian zealot Kirdēr, regarding whose career see Jacques Duchesne-Guillemin, "Zoroastrian Religion," in *Cambridge History of Iran 3(2)*, 878–85; Josef Wiesehöfer, *Ancient Persia: From 550 BC to 650 AD* (trans. Azizeh Azodi; London and New York: I. B. Tauris, 1996), 212–15. An important study is James R. Russel[l], "Kartīr and Mānī: A Shamanistic Model of Their Conflict," in *Iranica Varia: Papers in Honor of Professor Ehsan Yarshater* (Leiden: Brill, 1990), 180–93. Was the rivalry between Kirdēr and Mani—apparently historical—the stimulus for the generation of the *Acta Archelai* legendry?

Arrange a meeting between him and me so that I might dispute with him.' So he arranged a meeting between them, and the *mōbadh* prevailed over him in argument, and Sābūr reverted from dualism to Zoroastrianism. He planned to execute Mānī, but he escaped and went to the country of India,[78] where he remained until Sābūr died.

Hurmuz, son of Sābūr, became king after Sābūr. He was a brave man,[79] and he was the one who built the city of Rām-Hurmuz, but his days (as king) were not long. He reigned only one year.

Then Bahrām, son of Hurmuz, became king. He was infatuated with (his) slaves and amusing diversions. So Mānī's disciples wrote to him, saying: 'The king who now reigns is young in years (and) greatly preoccupied.' Hence he came to the land of Persia, his deeds became notorious, and his location became known. Then Bahrām summoned him and questioned him regarding his doctrine, and he recounted to him his situation. Then he arranged a meeting between him and the *mōbadh* who had disputed with him.[80] Then the *mōbadh* said to him, 'Let him melt lead for me and for you and pour (it) on my stomach and on your stomach, and whichever one of us is unhurt by this (ordeal), he will be correct.' But [Mānī] protested, 'This is a deed of Darkness!'[81] So Bahrām ordered him fettered[82] and said to him, 'When morning comes I will summon you and execute you (with) a

78. Most of the sources agree that Mani traveled to India, but disagree over why he made the journey. A competing biographical tradition (see, e.g., Bīrūnī below) asserts that Mani was exiled by the monarch to India. By contrast, Manichaean sources invariably characterize Mani's eastern wanderings as voluntary in nature.

79. This specific characterization reflects his standard epithet in Persian sources (*nēv* 'the brave'). See Henning, "Mani's Last Journey," 941 n.2; Sundermann, *Texte kirchengeschichtlichen Inhalts*, 127 n.1; and note Coptic *Homil.* 42.18. See also Ibn Qutayba, *Kitāb al-ma'ārif* (2nd ed.; ed. Tharwat 'Ukkāsha; Cairo: Dār al-Ma'ārif, 1969), 654.16; Maqdisī, *Kitāb al-bad' wa'l-ta'rīkh* (6 vols.; ed. Cl. Huart; Paris: Leroux, 1899-1919), 3:158.8.

80. See the Parthian Manichaean fragment M 6031 (published in Henning, "Mani's Last Journey," 948): 'then Kirdīr the priest (*mgbyd* = *mōbadh*) together with friends who attended the king plotted ....' Note also Coptic *Homil.* 45.15–16, where the name 'Kardel' (= Kirdēr) also occurs. The text of M 6031 is also available in Mary Boyce, *A Reader in Manichaean Middle Persian and Parthian* (Acta Iranica 9; Leiden: Brill, 1975), 43–44 §m. See the discussion of Sundermann, *Texte kirchengeschichtlichen Inhalts*, 71.

81. Note Edward G. Browne, *A Literary History of Persia* (4 vols.; London & Cambridge, 1902-24; repr., Cambridge: The University Press, 1964), 1:157 n.1 for some other references to this ordeal. Zoroaster allegedly vouchsafed the veracity of his own revelations by allowing molten copper to be poured on his chest: by suffering no harm, he was shown to be a true prophet. See Richard J. H. Gottheil, "References to Zoroaster in Syriac and Arabic Literature," in *Classical Studies in Honour of Henry Drisler* (New York: Macmillan and Company, 1894), 40–41; S. [H.] Taqizadeh, "A New Contribution to the Materials Concerning the Life of Zoroaster," *BSOS* 8 (1935–37): 947–54.

82. Cf. Coptic *Homil.* 48.19–22; 60.7–12; also Bīrūnī below, who seems to be dependent upon this source. See also Coptic *Ps-Bk.* 16.19–30 (Mani spent twenty-six days imprisoned in chains in Bēth Lapaṭ prior to his death); 18.30–19.7.

means of death like no one before you has been executed!'

While it was yet night Mānī was flayed, until his spirit disintegrated. And when it was morning, Bahrām summoned him, but they found him already dead. He ordered his head to be cut off[83] and his body to be stuffed with straw. Moreover, he persecuted his followers and executed many people from among them. And Bahrām the son of Hurmuz reigned for three years.[84]

Dīnawarī, *Akhbār al-ṭiwāl* (ed. Guirgass):[85]

It was during the time of Sābūr that Mānī the *zindīq*[86] appeared and led the people astray. Sābūr died before he could overcome him—Sābūr ruled for thirty-one years. His son, Hurmuz b. Sābūr, attained the throne after him. He arrested Mānī[87] and ordered that his skin be stripped off and then stuffed with straw, and he suspended him from a gate of the city of Jundaysābūr (i.e. Gundešāpūr). To this day it is still called the 'Mānī-gate.' He prosecuted his followers, and after subjecting them to interrogation he executed all of them. He ruled for thirty years.[88]

Ibn al-Faqīh, *Kitāb al-buldān* (ed. Taqīzādeh-Šīrāzī):[89]

Mānī, the leader of the *zanādiqa* (i.e., plural of *zindīq*), appeared during the reign of Sābūr b. Ardašīr, and he invited Sābūr to (convert to) his doctrine. He did not abandon it (i.e., his orthodox religion); instead, he delayed and postponed until he could make investigation as to what his thinking was. He discovered that he was an apostle

83. A similar tradition about the decapitation of Mani is recounted in Iṣṭakhrī and Bīrūnī below. Note also Coptic *Ps-Bk.* 19.29–31: 'lo, his body was brought forth in the city of these sinners, when they had cut off his head and hung it up amid the whole multitude' (Gardner-Lieu, *Manichaean Texts,* 101).

84. *Ta'rīkh* (ed. Houtsma), 1:181.12–182.11. For another translation, see Browne, *Literary History,* 1:155–57.

85. Abū Ḥanīfah Aḥmad ibn Dāwūd al-Dīnawarī, *Kitāb al-akhbār al-ṭiwāl* (ed. Vladimir Guirgass; Leiden: Brill, 1888), 49.4–9; see also Taqīzādeh-Šīrāzī, *Mānī va dīn-e-ū,* 103 (§12).

86. This term is the most common Arabic appellation for a dualist heretic and can be traced back into pre-Islamic Armenian and Iranian sources. Although many scholars today hold that the term is of Persian origin, it seems more likely that it represents an early transcription, with nasal dissimilation, of the original eastern Aramaic self-designation of a Manichaean *electus;* namely, a *zaddīq* or 'righteous one.' See A. A. Bevan, "Manichaeism," *ERE* 8:398–99 n.5; F. C. de Blois, "Zindīḳ" *EI*[2] 11:511.

87. Only Dīnawarī and Maqdisī credit Hurmuz with Mani's arrest and execution; his successor Bahrām is the usual culprit. By contrast, the Manichaean sources (listed by Puech, *Le manichéisme,* 135 n.198) stress that Mani and Hurmuz enjoyed good relations with one another.

88. The reign of Shāpūr I is usually calculated at thirty years. His son Hurmuz by contrast reigned for less than two years, and is usually portrayed as tolerant of Mani. Either Dīnawarī or his source has conflated traditions which belong separately to Shāpūr, Hurmuz, and Bahrām I.

89. Taqīzādeh-Šīrāzī, *Mānī va dīn-e-ū,* 344 (§95).

for Satan. He issued orders that his skin be stripped off, stuffed with straw, and suspended from the gate of the city of Jundaysābūr (i.e., Gundešāpūr). The gate is now called the 'Mānī-gate,' and *zanādiqa* make pilgrimage to it and glorify this spot.

Ṭabarī, *Ta'rīkh ar-rusul wa-l-mulūk* (ed. de Goeje):[90]

It was during the reign of Sābūr that Mānī the *zindīq* appeared ....

As mentioned, Mānī the *zindīq* invited him (Bahrām I) to embrace his religious teachings, but he put what he taught to a test and discovered him to be an apostle of Satan. He issued orders for his execution: he stripped off his skin, stuffed it with straw, and suspended him from one of the gates of the city of Jundaysābūr (i.e., Gundešāpūr), the one which is called the 'Mānī-gate.' He moreover executed some of his followers and those who had joined his religion.[91]

Iṣṭakhrī, *Kitāb al-masālik wa'l-mamālik* (ed. Taqīzādeh-Šīrāzī):[92]

While one says that Mānī was executed and gibbeted there (i.e., in Rām Hurmuz[93]), another says that he died a natural death in the prison of Bahrām, who then beheaded him and exposed his corpse.[94]

Ma'sūdī, *Murūj al-dhahab* (ed. Barbier de Meynard-de Courteille):[95]

Then Bahrām b. Hurmuz ruled after him for three years. He engaged in military campaigns against eastern dynasts. It is reported that Bahrām brought before him Mānī b. Yazīd,[96] the disciple of Qārdūn,[97] and he expounded his dualistic doctrine

90. Abū Ja'far Muḥammad b. Jarīr al-Ṭabarī, *Ta'rīkh ar-rusul wa-l-mulūk: Annales quos scripsit Abu Djafar Mohammed ibn Djarir at-Tabari* (15 vols.; ed. M. J. de Goeje; Leiden, 1879–1901; repr., Leiden: Brill, 1964–65), 1/2:830, 834; Taqīzādeh-Šīrāzī, *Mānī va dīn-e-ū*, 114 (§15).

91. For other translations featuring some useful annotations, see Nöldeke, *Geschichte der Perser und Araber*, 40, 47; C. E. Bosworth, *The History of al-Tabarī (Ta'rīkh al-rusul wa'l-mulūk), Volume V: The Sāsānids, the Byzantines, the Lakhmids, and Yemen* (Albany: State University of New York Press, 1999), 45.

92. Taqīzādeh-Šīrāzī, *Mānī va dīn-e-ū*, 355 (§102). The same tradition is quoted verbatim in Ibn Ḥawqal, *Kitāb ṣūrat al-arḍ*, 2:256; see Taqīzādeh-Šīrāzī, *Mānī va dīn-e-ū*, 364 (§106).

93. A city reportedly founded by Hurmuz b. Shāpūr; note the testimony of Ya'qūbī above. See Vladimir Minorsky and C. E. Bosworth, "Rām-Hurmuz," *EI*[2] 8:416–17.

94. A variant report about Mani's demise which is related to those found in the Coptic Manichaica and in Bīrūnī below. The notice about Mani's 'natural death,' as opposed to execution, is probably indebted to Ya'qūbī.

95. Abū al-Ḥasan 'Alī b. al-Ḥusayn b. 'Alī al-Mas'ūdī, *Murūj al-dhahab wa-ma'ādin al-jawhar: Les prairies d'or* (9 vols.; ed. C. Barbier de Meynard and Pavet de Courteille; Paris: Imprimerie impériale, 1861-77), 2:167; Taqīzādeh-Šīrāzī, *Mānī va dīn-e-ū*, 130 (§21).

96. *Sic.* Pellat and Monnot correct to 'Fātak' or 'Fāttak.'

97. I.e., Cerdo, a second-century gnostic teacher whom Irenaeus (*Adv. haer.* 1.27.1; 3.4.3) identifies as a follower of Simon Magus and an important intellectual influence upon Marcion. The association of Cerdo with Mani suggests either that a correct chronological sequencing of Marcion and Mani was mistakenly reversed, or that the

to him. He (Bahrām) deceptively agreed with him about it until he (Mānī) had recalled his missionaries who were dispersed among the various lands, they being his adherents who summoned the people to embrace his dualistic doctrines. Then he executed him and he also put to death the leaders among his followers.

Ḥamza al-Iṣfahānī, *Ta'rīkh sinī mulūk al-arḍ wa'l-anbiyā'* (ed. Taqīzādeh-Šīrāzī):[98]

During his reign Bahrām b. Hurmuz vanquished Mānī, the one who propagandized heresy,[99] (capturing him) after he had been a fugitive and had concealed himself for two years. He convoked against him an assembly of scholars. They engaged him in dispute and obliged the leader of the proceedings (i.e., Bahrām) to acknowledge the superiority of their arguments to his (i.e., Mani's). He (Bahrām) commanded regarding him that he be executed, his skin stripped off and stuffed with straw, and hung from one of the gates of the city of Jundayšābūr (i.e., Gundešāpūr).

Maqdisī, *Kitāb al-bad' wa'l-ta'rīkh* (ed. Huart):[100]

It was during his time (the reign of Shāpūr I) that Mānī the *zindīq* appeared. This was the first manifestation on earth of the phenomenon of *zandaqa*; however, there are different names for it. At the present time it (*zandaqa*) is termed 'esoteric knowledge' (*'ilm al-bāṭin*) and (flourishes among) the Bāṭiniyya ....[101]

Then Hurmuz 'the brave' became king after him (i.e., after Shāpūr I); he was also called Hurmuz 'the bold.'[102] Mānī came to Hurmuz and invited him to adopt *zandaqa*. But he replied: 'Toward what end do you invite me?' He answered: 'To effect the destruction of the present world and to leave behind the prosperity enjoyed in it for the next one!' Thereupon he (Hurmuz) said: 'Let me instead destroy your body!' He then ordered him put to death and his skin stuffed with straw. He was suspended on a gate at Jundaysābūr (i.e., Gundešāpūr), and up to this day it is still referred to as 'the Mānī-gate.' But it is (also) reported that it (i.e., Mani's body) was taken [and suspended] on a gate at Nīsābūr in Khurāsān.[103]

---

conceptually distinct Marcionite and Manichaean teachings have undergone some amalgamation at the hands of eastern heresiologists.

98. Taqīzādeh-Šīrāzī, *Mānī va dīn-e-ū*, 136–37 (§23); Flügel, *Mani*, 330.

99. Literally 'propagandist for the heretics (*zanādiqa*).'

100. Maqdisī, *K. al-bad' wa'l-ta'rīkh* (ed. Huart), 3:157.5–8; 158.8–13; see also Taqīzādeh-Šīrāzī, *Mānī va dīn-e-ū*, 145 (§25).

101. This is a polemical remark directed against the Shi'ite group known as the Ismā'īliyya who based their doctrines upon a self-described 'esoteric' exegesis of the Qur'ān. See Edgar Blochet, *Le messianisme dans l'hétérodoxie musulmane* (Paris: Librairie Orientale et Américaine, 1903), 50.

102. See the note on Hurmuz in the testimony of Ya'qūbī cited above.

103. This variant apparently conflates the fate of Mani with that of Bihāfrīd, a Zoroastrian pseudo-prophet captured and executed by the 'Abbāsid standard-bearer Abū Muslim in 748/49 CE. According to Shahrastānī, Bihāfrīd was put to death and suspended from the *bāb al-jāme'* in Nīsābūr. For some useful information about his movement, see M.

His reign lasted for one year and ten months.[104] Some say it was actually his son Bahrām b. Hurmuz who executed Mānī.[105]

Ibn al-Nadīm, *Fihrist* (ed. Flügel):[106]

Muḥammad b. Isḥaq said:[107] Mānī b. Fattiq Bābak b. Abū Barzām was related to the Ḥaskānīyah.[108] The name of his mother was Mays, but some say Utākhīm and some say Mar Maryam,[109] a descendant of the Arsacid royal line.[110] It is said that Mānī was bishop[111] ...[112] (and stemmed?) from the people of <Jawkhai>[113] and the districts of Bādarāyā and Bākusāyā.[114] He suffered from a distortion of the

---

Th. Houtsma, "Bih'afrid," *Wiener Zeitschrift für die Kunde des Morgenlandes* 3 (1889): 30–37; Gholam Hossein Sadighi, *Les mouvements religieux iraniens au IIe et au IIIe siècle de l'hégire* (Paris: Les Presses Modernes, 1938), 111–31; S. M. Stern, "Abū Ḥātim al-Rāzī on Persian Religion," in idem, *Studies in Early Ismāʿīlism* (Jerusalem: The Magnes Press, 1983), 40–45.

104. This correlates with the chronographic notice supplied by Masʿūdī above.

105. For another translation, see Cl. Huart, *Le livre de la création et de l'histoire de Motahhar ben Ṭâhir el-Maqdisî* (Paris: Ernest Leroux, 1903), 161–62.

106. Flügel, *Mani*, 49.1–51.4; 51.16–52.10; Ibn al-Nadīm, *K. al-Fihrist* (ed. Tajaddud), 391–92; Taqīzādeh-Šīrāzī, *Mānī va dīn-e-ū*, 149–51 (§27).

107. I.e., the compiler of the *Fihrist*.

108. Flügel (*Mani*, 117) cites the *Qāmūs* of Fīrūzābādī wherein it states that Ḥaskān was the name of an important family in Nīshāpūr, a city in Khurāsān. François de Blois plausibly suggests emending the reading (presumably upon the basis of manuscripts L and V in Flügel's apparatus) to 'Kamsaragān,' a prominent Parthian family whose name also figures in the biographical information supplied by the Chinese *Compendium*; see his "Glossary," 72.

109. I.e., 'St. (masculine!) Mary,' thereby effecting a typological association with the mother of Jesus.

110. On the possible royal descent of Mani's mother, see W. B. Henning, "The Book of the Giants," *BSOAS* 11 (1943-46): 52 n.4.

111. Read with manuscript V of Flügel's apparatus, and see the testimony of ʿAbd al-Jabbār below.

112. The text is hopelessly corrupt and should probably be restored at least in part on the basis of ʿAbd al-Jabbār, *Tathbīt* (ed. ʿUthmān), 1:169.11. Note the emendations suggested by de Blois, "Glossary," 28–29.

113. Or perhaps Jūkhā (Latin Cauchae; Syriac Gaukay), a region east of the Tigris adjoining Mesene. The obscure gnostic sectarian Battai, or at least his 'master' Papā, was from Gaukay (ܓܘܟܝ); note Theodore bar Konai, *Scholion* (ed. Scher), 2:343.12–15. See Erik Peterson, "Urchristentum und Mandäismus," *ZNW* 27 (1928): 56–57; Henning, "Mani's Last Journey," 945–48; Moshe Gil, "The Creed of Abū ʿĀmir," *Israel Oriental Studies* 12 (1992): 17 n.16.

114. Two of the administrative subdivisions of the district of Nahrawān, an area east of the Tigris along the lower Diyālā river which had an extensive canal system. See Nöldeke, *Geschichte der Perser und Araber*, 239–40; Henning, "Mani's Last Journey," 945; Bosworth, *History of al-Tabarī V*, 254.

foot.[115]

It is said that his father was originally from Hamadān. He moved to Babylon and took up residence in al-Madā'in in the place known as Ctesiphon.[116] An idol-temple was located there which Fattiq would frequent as the remainder of the people did. One day a voice called out to him from the sanctuary of the idol-temple, 'O Fattiq! Eat no meat! Drink no wine! Be married to no one!' This event recurred for him a number of times over a three day period. When Fattiq recognized this, he joined a group of people near Dast-(i)-Maysān[117] known as the Mughtasila.[118] Remnants of them are still in the districts of al-Batā'iḥ[119] in our own time. They were the sect which Fattiq was ordered to join while his wife was pregnant with Mānī.

When she gave birth to him, they claim that she experienced favorable dreams about him and that when she awoke, she watched while a certain entity took him and ascended with him into the air. Then he returned him, but possibly he remained (in the heavens) for one or two days before he reappeared.

Then his father sent for and brought him to the place in which he was dwelling, and he grew up with him and was instructed in accordance with his religion.[120] Even when young, Mānī would speak words of wisdom. When he completed the

---

115. A possible allusion to Mani as a 'crippled fiend' appears in the Zoroastrian *Dēnkard*; see A. V. Williams Jackson, *Researches in Manichaeism* (New York, 1932; repr., New York: AMS Press, 1965), 209; the same epithet is also cited by Manfred Hutter, "Manichaeism in Iran in the Fourth Century," in *Studia Manichaica: IV. Internationaler Kongress zum Manichäismus, Berlin, 14.-18. Juli 1997* (ed. Ronald E. Emmerick, Werner Sundermann, and Peter Zieme; Berlin: Akademie-Verlag, 2000), 310. Gil ("Creed," 17) suggests the crucial phrase should be translated: '(he was) the most *ḥanīf* of men'; i.e., Mani was viewed as an exemplary representative of a non-sectarian monotheism. Kessler, by contrast, presaged Gil's linguistic argument but reached an opposite conclusion based on the connotation of the cognate term *ḥanpā* in Syriac as 'pagan'; viz. '(he was) the vilest of men' (*Mani*, 332–33). See below for a possible solution to this problem.

116. Al-Madā'in ('the cities') refers to the Sasanian metropolis of Seleucia-Ctesiphon. See M. Streck and Michael G. Morony, "al-Madā'in," *EI*² 5:945–46.

117. See M. Streck and Michael G. Morony, "Maysān," *EI*² 6:918–23.

118. 'Mughtasila' are 'baptists' or 'those who wash themselves.' They are presumably identical with the 'baptists' (βαπτισταί) of the *Cologne Mani Codex* and the 'pure ones' (ܚܘܪ̈ܐ) mentioned in Theodore bar Konai's synopsis of the early life of Mani. According to a further report found in Ibn al-Nadīm, the Mughtasila were founded by a leader named Elchasai, presumably the same sectarian Jewish-Christian prophet mentioned by the church fathers Hippolytus, Origen, and Epiphanius, and the 'founder' of the *CMC* 'baptist' community among whom Mani was raised.

119. I have slightly emended the text here to accord with that in another section of the *Fihrist* which speaks of this same sect (reproduced by Flügel, *Mani*, 133). The locale 'al-Batā'iḥ' refers to the swamps south of Baṣra in southern Mesopotamia.

120. I have followed here the readings of Taqīzādeh-Šīrāzī, *Mānī va dīn-e-ū*, 150. Note the remarks of Flügel, *Mani*, 138–39.

age of twelve years, a revelation came to him[121] which he said was from the King of the Gardens of Light, who according to what he says is (the same as) God Most Exalted. The angel who brought him the revelation was named al-Tawm, which is Aramaic[122] and which means 'companion.'[123] He said to him, 'Depart from this religion, for you are no longer one of its members. You are to maintain purity and to forsake carnal desires. However, it is not time for you to manifest yourself due to your youthfulness.' When he had completed his twenty-fourth year, al-Tawm came to him (again)[124] and said, 'The time has come for you to emerge and proclaim your message.'

The words which al-Tawm spoke to him (on that occasion were): 'Greetings, O Mānī, from myself and from the Lord who sent me to you and who has chosen you for his mission. He commands you to issue the invitation for your teaching, to announce the glad tidings of truth which comes from him, and to persist in this (task) with all of your might ....'

... Mānī wandered through the land for about forty years prior to meeting with Sābūr.[125] Then he won over (to his teachings) Fīrūz,[126] the brother of Sābūr b. Ardašīr, and Fīrūz introduced him to his brother, Sābūr. The Manichaeans say that when he came to him, there were on his shoulders what seemed like two lamps shedding light.[127] When he (Sābūr) saw him, he extolled him and he (Mānī) enjoyed favor in his eyes. He had previously decided to assassinate or to execute him, but after he met him awe came over him, and he was pleased with him. He asked him for what reason he had come to him, and he promised him that he could return to him (whenever he chose?). Mānī presented him with numerous requests, a few of which were that he should support his followers in the lands and in the rest of the provinces of the empire, and that they might travel wherever they might

121. See the testimony of Bīrūnī above which similarly situates Mani's revelatory experience during his thirteenth year. As Sundermann has pointed out ("Mani's Revelations," 212–14), only Mani's *Shābuhragān* and those sources dependent upon its biographical traditions are familiar with a revelation during the prophet's thirteenth year.

122. Literally 'Nabataean,' but this label is commonly wielded in Arabic literature to refer more broadly to Aramaic-speaking peoples and cultures. See the remarks of Theodor Nöldeke, "Die Namen der aramäischen Nation und Sprache," *ZDMG* 25 (1871): 113–31.

123. Literally 'twin,' assuming that Aramaic תיומא and Syriac ܬܐܘܡܐ comprise this term's background. The same entity is termed ὁ σύζυγος in Greek, ⲥⲁϊϣ in Coptic, and *nrjmyg* in Middle Persian texts.

124. Compare *CMC* 18.1–17.

125. Almost surely a corruption for 'four years'; so Geo Widengren, "Manichaeism and its Iranian Background," in *Cambridge History of Iran 3(2)*, 969. According to Coptic *Keph.* 15.24–31, Mani traveled to India prior to his audience with Shāpūr.

126. At this time the governor of Khurāsān.

127. One might compare the Mandaean legend recounting the wondrous conception and birth of John the Baptist which refers to 'three lights' which hover above and accompany his father Abā Sabā Zakhrīa. See Mark Lidzbarski, *Das Johannesbuch der Mandäer* (2 vols.; Giessen: Alfred Töpelmann, 1905-15), 2:71.

wish throughout the provinces. Sābūr granted him all that he requested, so that Mānī propagated (his message) to India, China, and the peoples of Khurāsān. He appointed one of his followers (to take responsibility) for each region.[128]

Ibn al-Nadīm, *Fihrist* (ed. Flügel):[129]

Mānī was put to death during the reign of Bahrām b. Sābūr. After he executed him, he suspended him in two pieces, one half over a certain gate and the other half over a different gate of the city of Jundaysābūr (i.e., Gundešāpūr).[130] The(se) two places received the designations 'the upper part of the Lord' and 'the lower (part) of the Lord.'[131] It is said that he had been previously imprisoned by Sābūr, but after Sābūr died Bahrām freed him. It is also said that he died while in prison,[132] but there is no uncertainty regarding his 'crucifixion.'[133]

Some people relate that he had two misshapen feet whereas others said that it was his right foot (only).[134]

'Abd al-Jabbār, *Tathbīt* (ed. 'Uthmān):[135]

Similar to what Paul did with Rome by supporting them in their religion and abandoning the (actual) religion of Christ[136] was done by Mānī the priest,[137] who

128. Compare the translations of Flügel, *Mani*, 83–85; Kessler, *Mani*, 382–86; Adam, *Texte*², 23–25, 118; Dodge, *Fihrist*, 2:773-76; Gardner-Lieu, *Manichaean Texts*, 46–47, 75–76.

129. Flügel, *Mani*, 69.5–11; Ibn al-Nadīm, *K. al-Fihrist* (ed. Tajaddud), 398; Taqīzādeh-Šīrāzī, *Mānī va dīn-e-ū*, 159 (§27).

130. See Coptic *Homil.* 45.9–10: '... he (Mani) arrived in Belapat (= Bēth Lapaṭ or Jundaysābūr), the place of crucifi[xion] and the place where the [bitter?] cup would be mixed for him.'

131. Arabic مار 'lord,' a loan-word from Syriac and Mani's customary title in Manichaean devotional literature; e.g., Mār Mani or 'the Lord Mani.' Compare de Blois, "Glossary," 75.

132. According to Ya'qūbī (see above), he died while being tortured in prison.

133. The Arabic verb that is employed in this account of Mani's dismemberment and suspension is the one also used for 'crucifixion.' This is a clear lexical indicator of a hagiographic leveling of the *vitae* of Jesus and Mani.

134. Given its reiteration, this particular tradition may be indebted to a Jewish polemical motif which brands 'false prophets' (e.g., Balaam, Muḥammad) with lameness or orthopedic deformity. See *b. Soṭah* 10a; *Sanh.* 105a ('Balaam was crippled in one foot'); *Ba'al ha-Ṭūrim* to Num 23:3; and the remarks of Alexander Altmann, "'The Ladder of Ascension'," in *Studies in Mysticism and Religion presented to Gershom G. Scholem on his Seventieth Birthday by Pupils, Colleagues and Friends* (Jerusalem: Magnes Press, 1967), 9-11. See also Flügel, *Mani*, 99–100; Dodge, *Fihrist*, 2:794.

135. 'Abd al-Jabbār b. Aḥmad al-Hamadhānī, *Tathbīt dālā'il al-nubūwwah* (2 vols.; ed. 'Abd al-Karīm 'Uthmān; Beirut: Dār al-Arabiyah, 1966-67), 1:169.9–12; 170.9–12.

136. An example of anti-Pauline rhetoric similar to what is visible in the Pseudo-Clementines or other allegedly 'Jewish-Christian' sources. For further discussion, see Shlomo Pines, "Studies in Christianity and in Judaeo-Christianity Based on Arabic Sources," *Jerusalem Studies in Arabic and Islam* 6 (1985): 107–61.

137. Mani's alleged background as a renegade Christian 'priest' (القس) also figures in the

became the leader of the Manichaeans. He lived a long time after Paul and achieved a prominent office. After having been a priest, he became an archbishop over the Christians in Iraq, (a region) in the Persian empire ....[138]

... his fame grew among them (i.e., the general public). They followed him and claimed that he performed miracles and signs.[139] But one of the kings of the Persians arrested him in order to examine him, and he began an investigation about his activities. It turned out that he was a liar and a heretic,[140] an opportunist in quest of authority: he was currying favor with the Persians and the Zoroastrians with respect to what they loved so that he might disseminate among them that which does not (actually) belong to the Christian religion. The king executed

---

biographical sketches supplied by the *Chronicon Maroniticum*, the *Chronicon Seertensis*, the *Chronicle* of Michael Syrus, and Bar Hebraeus's *Historia compendiosa dynastiarum*, all of which are excerpted below in the section devoted to the reception history of the *Acta Archelai* polemical traditions. The *Acta* itself never admits such a pedigree, but does concede that his disciples deceptively advertised him as a *magistro Christianorum* or 'Christian teacher' (*Acta Archelai* 4.4 [ed. Beeson, 5]). For discussion of the Arabic term, see Henri-Charles Puech, "Liturgie et pratiques rituelles dans le manichéisme (Collège de France, 1952–1972)," in idem, *Sur le manichéisme et autres essais* (Paris: Flammarion, 1979), 383–84; F. C. de Blois, "[Review of *Atti del terzo congresso internazionale di studi "Manicheismo e Oriente Cristiano Antico"*]," *JRAS* series 3,9,3 (1999): 441–42; and note also the careful discussion of Manfred Hutter, "Mani und das persische Christentum," in *Manichaica Selecta: Studies Presented to Professor Julien Ries on the Occasion of his Seventieth Birthday* (ed. Alois van Tongerloo and Søren Giversen; Louvain: International Association of Manichaean Studies, 1991), 129–31.

138. Ibn al-Nadīm (see above) also makes Mani a 'bishop.' Some scholars have questioned this attribution, arguing that an onomastic confusion between Mani and Mari, a Christian missionary in Persia and founder of a monastery in Qoni, is the likely culprit; see for example W. B. Henning, "Zwei Fehler in der arabisch-manichäischen Überlieferung," *Orientalia* 5 (1936): 84–86; Gardner-Lieu, *Manichaean Texts*, 46 n.4. On the other hand, the possession of an ecclesiastical office, or the failure to attain such, is a standard trope in Christian heresiography. Both Marcion and Bardaiṣan are associated with bishoprics, and it is hence not surprising to see an equivalent status extended to Mani in this genre of literature.

139. Mani indeed enjoyed fame as a thaumaturge and healer. *CMC* 121.11-123.13 and 130.1–135.6 depict two early miracles performed by Mani, and M 47 attaches the conversion of Mihrshāh to Mani's ability to ascend at will to the Paradise of Light. During his final fateful interrogation by Bahrām I (see M 3 *apud* Henning, "Mani's Last Journey," 951–52; Boyce, *Reader*, 44–45 §n), Mani protests that he has performed numerous successful healings and demon-expulsions. Bīrūnī (see below) confirms that one faction of Manichaeans attached a special importance to Mani's miracles and wonder-working. Even the Nestorian bishop Theodore bar Konai grudgingly concedes that Mani was 'familiar with the art of healing.'

140. Or with a slight emendation 'swindler.' See Gabriel Said Reynolds, *A Muslim Theologian in the Sectarian Milieu: 'Abd al-Jabbār and the Critique of Christian Origins* (Leiden: Brill, 2004), 113 n.132.

him, just as that (Roman) king did to Paul.[141]

Miskawayh, *Tajārib al-umum* (ed. Taqīzādeh-Šīrāzī):[142]

And the reign of Sābūr lasted for thirty glorious years, and it was during his reign that Mānī the *zindīq* first appeared, and likewise (he was active) during the reign of Hurmuz his son ... Then too the reign of his son Bahrām b. Hurmuz came to an end: he executed Mānī and had him skinned.

Tha'ālibī, *Ghurar akhbār mulūk al-Furs wa-siyarihim* (ed. Taqīzādeh-Šīrāzī):[143]

Account of Mānī the *zindīq*, a pseudo-prophet (may he be cursed by God!):

This damnable one appeared during the days of Sābūr, but he did not reveal his message until the time of Bahrām, for he supposed due to his inexperience he could be deceived by his embellished doctrine and his false religion. Maqdisī has mentioned in his book entitled *Kitāb al-bad' wa'l-ta'rīkh* that he was the first manifestation on earth of the phenomenon of *zandaqa*; however, there are different names for it. At the present time it is termed Bāṭiniyya.[144]

When Mānī arrived with his deception(s),[145] Bahrām ordered an assembly of *mōbadhs*[146] to engage him in a disputation in his presence. The chief *mōbadh* said to him: 'What is the message which you are proclaiming to us?' He said: 'Rejection of the world so as to effect its dissolution; renunciation of sexual relations with women in order to cease procreation and to make this corrupt material world disappear. (These must happen) because spirits of the Pure Divinity have become mixed with filthy Ahrimanic (*sic*) bodies, and the deity[147] suffers harm in this mixture. He will have relief when a separation is effected between them so as to bring into existence a final created order and to establish the world as He intended.' The *mōbadh* said to him: 'Which is better, destruction or construction?' He replied: 'The destruction of bodies results in prosperity for spirits!' He said: 'Tell us—should someone kill you, would it be (considered) constructive or

141. Other translations are available in Shlomo Pines, "Two Passages Concerning Mani," in his *The Jewish Christians of the Early Centuries of Christianity According to a New Source* (Proceedings of the Israel Academy of Sciences and Humanities 2.13; Jerusalem: The Israel Academy of Sciences and Humanities, 1966), 66–68; Guy Monnot, *Penseurs musulmans et religions iraniennes: 'Abd al-Jabbār et ses devanciers* (Paris: J. Vrin, 1974), 277–79; Reynolds, *Muslim Theologian*, 113, 169.

142. Taqīzādeh-Šīrāzī, *Mānī va dīn-e-ū*, 181 (§29).

143. Taqīzādeh-Šīrāzī, *Mānī va dīn-e-ū*, 182–83 (§30). See also H. Zotenberg, *Histoire des rois des Perses: Texte arabe publié et traduit* (Paris: Imprimerie nationale, 1890), 501–503.

144. Or 'esotericism.' See the testimony of Maqdisī above.

145. Effecting a rare pun in the Arabic language on the name 'Mānī.'

146. I.e., Zoroastrian clergy.

147. Persian *yazdān*. It would appear that Tha'ālibī is familiar with the attested Manichaean proclivity to couch the wording of their distinctive message in the vernacular of the 'local' religion. It may also signal that he considered Mani to be a Zoroastrian (as opposed to a Christian) 'heretic.'

destructive?' He replied: 'This would destroy (only) the body.' He said: 'Then it is incumbent that we put you to death in order to bring about the destruction of your body and the prosperity of your spirit!' (This illustrates the scriptural passage): 'And the one who was an infidel was confounded' (Q 2:258).[148]

Bahrām said: 'We will start with the destruction of your body and deal with you in accordance with what you teach!' He then commanded that his skin be stripped off, stuffed with straw, and suspended over one of the gates of Jundaysābūr (i.e., Gundešāpūr); this gate is referred to even now as the 'Mānī-gate' (*bāb-Mānī*). He also put to death twelve thousand followers of Mānī and was tenacious in sniffing out anyone who had 'the smell of *zandaqa*' about him. The populace esteemed him and praised him for this action.[149]

Bīrūnī, *Āthār* (ed. Sachau):[150]

According to what the Christian Yaḥyā b. al-Nu'mān has related about him in his book on the Magians, Mānī was named by the Christians Qūrbīqūs b. Fatak.[151] When he appeared, many people accepted him and became his followers ....

His power did not diminish but grew under Ardašīr, his son Sābūr, and Hurmuz his son until the reign of Bahrām b. Hurmuz. He (Bahrām) searched for him until he found him, and then he said: 'This person has come forth summoning people to destroy the world. Therefore we must begin by destroying him, before the thing which he desires comes to pass.' It is widely known in any case that he put Mānī to death, stripped off his skin, stuffed it with straw, and suspended it at the gate of the city of Jundaysābūr (i.e., Gundešāpūr), the one which is known in our own time as the 'Mānī-gate.' He also killed a number of the people who had answered his (Mani's) summons.[152]

Jibrā'īl b. Nūḥ the Christian[153] has related in his response to the refutation of the Christians authored by Yazdānbakht[154] that a certain disciple of Mānī had a book

148. The qur'ānic passage features an exchange between Abraham and Nimrod which parallels in several respects the present dialogue.

149. Another translation is available in Zotenberg, *Histoire*, 501–503.

150. *Āthār* (ed. Sachau), 208.12–13, 15–22; 209.7–10; Taqīzādeh-Šīrāzī, *Mānī va dīn-e-ū*, 205–206 (§34).

151. As in Theodore bar Konai's testimony above, we have a combination of authentic biographical information (the name of Mani's father) with a polemical motif drawn from the *Acta Archelai* trajectory. It is possible that Theodore and Bīrūnī have drawn from a common source.

152. Note Ya'qūbī, Dīnawarī, Ṭabarī, and Mas'ūdī above as well as Coptic *Homil.* 45.9–10. It is possible that Bahrām I has been conflated with Bahrām II (276–93 CE), the latter of whom perpetrates an extensive persecution of Manichaean leaders and sympathizers.

153. Presumably the ninth-century Nestorian theologian Gabriel b. Nūḥ al-Anbārī, regarding whom see Hans Daiber, "Nestorians of Ninth Century Iraq as a Source of Greek, Syriac and Arabic: A Survey of Some Unexploited Sources," *Aram* 3 (1991): 45–46.

154. A prominent ninth-century Manichaean leader who resided in Baghdad.

which informed about his fate.[155] (It said) that he was imprisoned because of a relative of the king who was convinced that he was possessed by a demon. He (Mānī) promised to cure him, but when he could not do it,[156] both his feet and hands were placed in chains until he died in prison. His head was set up at the entrance of the pavilion, and his corpse was flung into the street in order for it to be a warning and lesson ....[157]

I heard the *isbahbadh* (i.e., ruler)[158] Marzubān b. Rustam say that Sābūr banished him from his kingdom, adhering to the way prescribed to them by Zarādusht; (namely, that) one should expel those posing as prophets from the land. He imposed upon him the condition that he was to never return. Hence he journeyed to India, China, and Tibet, and announced his message there. Then he returned, and at that time Bahrām arrested him and put him to death for having violated the condition, for it was now permissible to take his life.[159]

Bīrūnī, *Taḥqīq mā lil-Hind* (ed. Sachau):[160]

When Mānī was expelled from Iran,[161] he went to India ....

Ibn Ḥazm, *Kitāb al-faṣl fī al-milal wa'l-ahwā' wa'l-niḥal* (ed. Taqīzādeh-Šīrāzī):[162]

Mānī was a monk in Ḥarrān and invented this religion. He was the one whom

155. The mention of an 'internal book' about Mani's death is apparently a reference to the Manichaean 'Passion Narrative,' a large portion of which survives fragmentarily in Coptic translation in Hans Jakob Polotsky, ed., *Manichäische Homilien* (Stuttgart: W. Kohlhammer, 1934); an edition now superseded by Nils Arne Pedersen, *Manichaean Homilies* (CFM Series Coptica 2; Turnhout: Brepols, 2006). See Coptic *Homil.* 42.9–85.34 for the relevant section. Note also Henning, "Mani's Last Journey," 941; Werner Sundermann, "Studien zur kirchengeschichtlichen Literatur der iranischen Manichäer II," *Altorientalische Forschungen* 13 (1986): 260–61.

156. This episode about Mani's failure to heal a member of the king's family stems ultimately from the *Acta Archelai*, where it is the king's son who perishes despite Mani's therapy. The same episode is also mentioned by Michael Syrus and Bar Hebraeus below.

157. Note that the motifs of the fettering of Mani, his (natural?) death in prison, his decapitation, and the exposure of his headless corpse cohere with the variant tradition about Mani's demise that stems ultimately from authentic Manichaean sources.

158. Derived from the Middle Persian for 'general' and which comes to signify a 'ruler' in central Asia.

159. According to Ya'qūbī (see above), Mani fled to India in order to escape arrest by Shāpūr. After the eventual accession of Bahrām, Mani returned to Persia but was finally caught and executed by that monarch.
For another translation, see Strohmaier, *In den Gärten*², 141–43.

160. Edward Sachau, ed., *Kitāb fī taḥqīq mā l'il-Hind: Alberuni's India: An Account of the Religion, Philosophy, Literature, Chronology, Astronomy, Customs, Laws and Astrology of India about A.D. 1030* (London: Trübner, 1887), 27.8; Taqīzādeh-Šīrāzī, *Mānī va dīn-e-ū*, 212 (§37).

161. This presupposes a biographical tradition whereby Mani suffered an involuntary deportation from Persia by the Sasanian monarch.

162. Taqīzādeh-Šīrāzī, *Mānī va dīn-e-ū*, 227 (§41).

the king Bahrām b. Bahrām put to death when he conducted in his presence his disputation with the chief *mōbadh* Ādhurbadh-Mahrspand(ān),[163] undergoing interrogation about the prohibition of sexual relations and the rapidly approaching end of the world. The *mōbadh* said to him: 'You are the one who pronounces a ban on marriage in order to hasten the destruction of the world and the return of every created thing to its maker. Is this truly necessary?' Mānī replied to him: 'It is necessary for one to assist the Light in freeing itself from what it is in by prohibiting sexual relations.' Ādhurbadh said to him: '(It follows) then from this necessary truth that one can hasten this liberation for you—the one you are proclaiming for it—and you can thereby assist the dissolution of this loathsome mixture!' Mānī being unable to reply, Bahrām ordered that Mānī be executed. He and a group of his followers were put to death.

Marwazī, *Kitāb ṭabāʾiʿ al-ḥayawān* (ed. Kruk):[164]

One whose case was similar[165] was the pseudo-prophet Mānī. He was important and had many followers. His birthplace was in Babylon in a village called Nardīnū (*sic*)[166] near the upper canal of Kūthā. He resorted to a knowledge of his own making; no person was his equal in the practice of piety. He attained such skill in making figures and pictures that he used to spread open a piece of Chinese silk whose length was more than twenty cubits, then take the *khāma*—this is an instrument used by illuminators—and draw with it a line on the piece from the beginning to the end, and the line would never go beyond a single silken thread of the warp of the piece. He would draw a circle freehand, and when the compass was put on it, it would exactly match it ....[167]

Then King Shābūr banished him from his kingdom, adhering to the way prescribed by Zarādusht; (namely, that) one should expel those posing as prophets from the land. He imposed upon him the condition that he was to never return.

---

163. A blatant anachronism. Ādhurbadh-ī-Mahrspandān was chief *mōbadh* during the reign of Shāpūr II (309-379 CE) and renowned in Zoroastrian tradition for supervising a textual redaction of the Avesta. He reportedly bore witness to the accuracy of his labors by voluntarily submitting himself to the ordeal of having molten metal poured on his stomach; for the details, see the passage from the *Ardā Wirāz Nāmag* cited by H. W. Bailey, *Zoroastrian Problems in the Ninth-Century Books* (Oxford: Clarendon Press, 1971), 152; note also Arthur Christensen, *L'Iran sous les Sassanides* (2nd ed.; Copenhagen: Ejnar Munksgaard, 1944), 142; Hutter, "Manichaeism in Iran in the Fourth Century," 310–11.

164. Ms. UCLA Ar. 52 fol. 5a.20–5b.6; 6a.2–12; 6b.1–10, as published by Remke Kruk, "Sharaf az-Zamân Ṭâhir Marwazî (fl. ca. 1100 A.D.) on Zoroaster, Mânî, Mazdak, and Other Pseudo-Prophets," *Persica* 17 (2001): 65–66.

165. Marwazī had been discussing the career of Zoroaster.

166. Read Mardīnū as in Bīrūnī.

167. Mani was renowned in later Muslim tradition for his artistic talents. Almost all of those testimonia are associated with his infamous 'Picture-Book' or *Ardahang*; see Chapter Three below.

So he journeyed to India and announced his message there, and a large throng responded to him. From there he extended (his journey) to Tibet and summoned the people to his teachings. They responded to him and accepted him, and he prescribed laws for them, and he enjoined illustration, ornamentation, and the use of images for the worship and supplication of God Most High ....

... The peoples of China, Tibet, and a part of India adopted his religion, and having accomplished what he sought in those realms, his soul longed for his birthplace. So he moved on to Babylon, thinking he might accomplish there what had taken place in China and India for his power had increased (beyond what it was) in the days of Ardašīr and the days of his son Shābūr and the days of Hurmuz. But when Bahrām b. Hurmuz became king after Mānī had returned from China, he searched for him and said: 'This one commands the destruction of the world; would it not be better that he suffer destruction?' Then he gave the order to put him to death.

It is said that the reason he was killed was because he had broken the agreement and violated the condition when he returned to Babylon, for when he had been banished, a condition was put upon him that he would never return.[168] Hence he was killed, his skin stripped off and filled with straw, and it was suspended by the gate of the city Jadda-Shābūr (*sic*),[169] and to this day that gate is still known as the 'Mānī-gate.'[170]

Shahrastānī, *Kitāb al-milal wa'l-niḥal* (ed. Badrān):[171]

The Manichaeans (are) followers of Mānī b. Fātak, the sage who appeared in the time of Sābūr b. Ardašīr, and whom Bahrām b. Hurmuz b. Sābūr put to death. This was after (the time of) Jesus b. Maryam, peace be upon him!

Sam'ānī, *Kitāb al-ānsāb* (ed. Taqīzādeh-Šīrāzī):[172]

When Bahrām the king heard his message, he commanded that his skin be stripped from him while he was still alive. (This took place) in the city of Jundaysābūr. He <stuffed (it) with straw>[173] and suspended (it).

Fakhr al-Dīn al-Rāzī, *I'tiqād firaq al-muslimīn w'al-mushrikīn* (ed. Taqīzādeh-Šīrāzī):[174]

The first group (of dualists) are the Manichaeans, the followers of Mānī, a man

168. See Bīrūnī above.
169. A scribal error for Jundaysābūr.
170. Another translation is provided by Kruk, "Marwazî," 55–56.
171. Muḥammad b. Fatḥ Allāh Badrān, ed., *Kitāb al-milal wa'l-niḥal l'il-Shahrastānī* (2 vols.; [Cairo]: Matba'at al-Azhar, [1951–55]), 1:619.2–5; note also William Cureton, ed., *Kitāb al-milal wa al-niḥal: Book of Religious and Philosophical Sects by Muhammad al-Shahrastáni* (London, 1846; repr., Leipzig: Otto Harrassowitz, 1923), 188.11–12; Taqīzādeh-Šīrāzī, *Mānī va dīn-e-ū*, 240–41 (§45); Flügel, *Mani*, 331.
172. Taqīzādeh-Šīrāzī, *Mānī va dīn-e-ū*, 246 (§46).
173. Read with the textual apparatus supplied in Taqīzādeh-Šīrāzī, *Mānī va dīn-e-ū*, 246.
174. Taqīzādeh-Šīrāzī, *Mānī va dīn-e-ū*, 258 (§51).

who was a nimble-fingered artist.[175] He appeared at the time of Sābūr b. Azdašīr[176] b. Bābak and claimed to be a prophet. He said the universe had two principles (lit. 'roots'), Light and Darkness, both of which were eternal. Sābūr accepted his doctrine, but after he died (and) it became the turn of Bahrām to rule, he arrested Mānī, skinned him, stuffed his skin with straw, and suspended it. He also executed his companions, except for those who fled and reached China. They proclaimed there the religion of Mānī, and the people of China accepted it from them. To this very day the people of China belong to the religion of Mānī.

Ibn al-Āthīr, *Kāmil fī al-tārīkh* (ed. Taqīzādeh-Šīrāzī):[177]

It was during the reign of Sābūr when Mānī the *zindīq* appeared and pretended to be a prophet. Numerous people followed him. They are the ones who are called Manichaeans.

Ibn al-Āthīr, *Kāmil fī al-tārīkh* (ed. Taqīzādeh-Šīrāzī):[178]

And he (Bahrām) killed Mānī the *zindīq*, skinned him, stuffed his skin with straw, and suspended (it) from one of the gates of Jundaysābūr: it is named the 'Mānī-gate.'

Ibn al-Āthīr, *Lulāb fī tahdhīb al-ānsāb* (ed. Taqīzādeh-Šīrāzī):[179]

The king commanded that his skin be stripped from him while he was still alive. He stuffed (it) with straw and suspended it over a gate of the city of Jundaysābūr.

Nuwayrī, *Nihāyat al-arab fī funūn al-adab* (ed. Taqīzādeh-Šīrāzī):[180]

It was during his reign (i.e., that of Shāpūr I) when Mānī the *zindīq*, the disciple of Qārdūn,[181] appeared and propounded dualism. Sābūr examined the doctrine of Mānī and the teaching about Light and about purification from Darkness, but then he returned to the religion of Zoroastrianism and gave up being a Manichaean, which was the name for those belonging to the religion of dualism ....

Then Hurmuz b. Sābūr became king after his father ... then Bahrām b. Hurmuz became king after his father. He declared (that) since he was (now) king, Mānī the *zindīq* should come before him and expound to him the teachings of dualism. He (Mānī) responded to his deceptive trick: he brought with him his missionaries who had been dispersed throughout the various lands where they were inviting people to embrace the teachings of dualism. When they arrived before him (Bahrām), he killed them. He also executed Mānī and stripped off his skin.

175. For Mani's artistic prowess, see the testimony of Mīrkhwānd below and the discussion of the *Ardahang* in Chapter Three.

176. An orthographic error. Read instead 'Ardašīr.'

177. Taqīzādeh-Šīrāzī, *Mānī va dīn-e-ū*, 263 (§55).

178. Taqīzādeh-Šīrāzī, *Mānī va dīn-e-ū*, 263 (§55).

179. Taqīzādeh-Šīrāzī, *Mānī va dīn-e-ū*, 265 (§56).

180. Taqīzādeh-Šīrāzī, *Mānī va dīn-e-ū*, 275 (§63).

181. This detail indicates that Mas'ūdī was Nuwayrī's ultimate primary source for information about Mani.

... Bahrām put this Mānī to death, suspending him from one of the gates of one of the cities of Iraq. This gate was sometimes referred to as the 'gate of Mānī.'

Ibn al-Murtaḍā, *K. al-munya* (ed. Taqīzādeh-Šīrāzī):[182]

There are nine sects of dualists. That of the Manichaeans gets its name from a man whose name was Mānī b. Wānī (*sic*),[183] a Syrian sage who arose during the time of Sābūr b. A<r>dašīr[184] and claimed to be a prophet. The Magians opposed him and advised Sābūr to put him to death. Bahrām b. Hurmuz b. Sābūr executed him; (this event took place) after the time of Jesus, upon whom be peace! His doctrine continues to have adherents.[185]

Ibn al-Shiḥnah, *Rawḍ al-manāẓir fī akhbār al-awā'il wa'al-awākhir* (ed. Taqīzādeh-Šīrāzī):[186]

Mānī the *zindīq* appeared during his (i.e., Shāpūr's) reign. He laid claim to a prophetic revelation, and many people became his followers. They are called Manichaeans. With the exception of Diqyānūs (Decius? Diocletian?), the rulers of the Greeks gave him assistance.[187] He wrote about philosophy and relocated it (i.e., philosophy) among the Persians. He invented the musical instrument called the lute (*'ūd*).[188]

Mīrkhwānd, *Rawḍat al-ṣafā* (ed. Taqīzādeh-Šīrāzī):[189]

Mas'ūdī has said that Shāpūr initially entered into his religion; afterwards, he publicly renounced his doctrine and began to issue rebukes against Mānī.[190] He made his escape, going from Kashmīr to the land of India, and from that place he turned toward Turkestān and northern China. Mānī was a painter without equal. They say for example he would draw a circle whose diameter was five cubits with his finger, and when they would examine it with a compass, none of its constituent parts

182. Taqīzādeh-Šīrāzī, *Mānī va dīn-e-ū*, 299 (§74); Kessler, *Mani*, 346 (text).

183. Kessler (*Mani*, 349 n.3) urges an emendation from وانى to فاتق 'Fātak,' a suggestion that is orthographically reasonable.

184. Read اردشير in place of ازدشير.

185. See also Kessler, *Mani*, 349–50.

186. Taqīzādeh-Šīrāzī, *Mānī va dīn-e-ū*, 296 (§72); cf. Kessler, *Mani*, 369.

187. If the reference is to the Roman emperor Diocletian, this otherwise cryptic notice preserves a factual reminiscence of Diocletian's 297 CE decree against Manichaeism.

188. Kessler (*Mani*, 212; 369–70) provides a text and translation. For some suggestive connections between Mani and music, see Flügel, *Mani*, 380–81; Kessler, *Mani*, 237–38; Peterson, "Urchristentum," 73; and especially Geneviève Gobillot, *Le livre de la profondeur des choses* (Villeneuve d'Ascq: Presses Universitaires du Septentrion, 1996), 148–49. According to Mas'ūdī, the lute was invented by the biblical forefather Lamech, but the same historian in other places attributes its manufacture to the Greeks.

189. Taqīzādeh-Šīrāzī, *Mānī va dīn-e-ū*, 525–26 (§190); cf. the slightly variant text in Kessler, *Mani*, 377–79.

190. A number of tradents report Shāpūr's initial infatuation with and even conversion by Mani, but Mas'ūdī does not relate this story.

ever fell outside the circumference of that circle. He was generally in great demand in the lands of India and northern China, and he could effect a consummate ornamentation because of the extraordinary pictures which he could produce. He traveled to and fro without interruption within certain districts of the Orient.[191]

Mānī turned towards the kingdom of Persia, imagining that he could also deceive the people of those regions. When he arrived in the land of Iran, he arranged a meeting with Bahrām, inviting him to (accept) his religion. The devious emperor at first consented to listen to his words in order to put his mind at ease (and allow) followers to be assembled. Then he summoned the imperial theologians (*ʿulamā*), and they came to the place to dispute with and oppose Mānī. Mānī failed to answer them; he suffered condemnation. When his impiety (*kufr*) and error had been completely exposed, they called on him to recant. Mānī refused to submit. Bahrām gave the order to remove the skin from his body and to suspend it on the city gate so that it could be an example for people to see. Immediately thereafter they rounded up his adherents and followers.[192]

3. The *Acta Archelai* and its Satellites

***Chronicon Maroniticum* (ed. Brooks):**[193]

... there was a ma[n from the city of Lapat (i.e., Bēth Lapaṭ) whose na]me was Paṭ[īq[194] who had a] son b[y] Ṭa[qsh]īt [his wi]fe. [His parents] named him Qūrūbīqōs.[195] When he wa[s] seven years old, [the wi]fe of a certain Arab [whose nam]e was Sqūtīna[196] (i.e., Scythianus) purchased him. Sh[e] was from the Upper The[baid][197] (and her husband) [for her sake] spent much time in Egypt. While (there) Scythianus became learned in the teac[hings] of the Egyptians, (and) he introduced the here[sy](s) of Pōdqlīs[198] (Empedocles) and Pyth[agoras] against-

191. For the continuation of this passage, see Chapter Three under the entry for *Ardahang*.

192. See also Flügel, *Mani*, 331–32; Kessler, *Mani*, 379–81.

193. *Chronica Minora II* (ed. Brooks), 58.24–60.9. This account, which probably dates from the seventh century, is closely related to and reconstructed where necessary from the one preserved in the twelfth-century *Chronicle* of Michael Syrus. See below.

194. Spelled ܦܐܬܝܩ in Michael Syrus. This is obviously the same name as Pattikios in Greek and Fatak/Fātak/Fatik in Arabic sources. This name is either suppressed by or unknown to the author of the *Acta Archelai*. The *Chronicon Maroniticum* has thus combined both authentic and spurious elements within its Mani *vita*, inaugurating a narrative trend which will be slavishly followed by subsequent tradents.

195. ܩܘܪܘܒܝܩܘܣ; spelled ܩܘܪܒܝܩܘܣ in Michael Syrus.

196. ܣܩܘܛܝܢܐ; spelled ܣܩܛܝܢܐ and ܣܩܘܛܝܢܐ in Michael Syrus. His Arab ethnicity stems from the *Acta Archelai*.

197. This source and *Acta Archelai* remain silent about her occupation. Epiphanius says that she was a prostitute.

198. ܦܘܕܩܠܝܣ; spelled ܦܐܕܘܩܠܝܣ in Michael Syrus. There Chabot emends to ܐܡܦܕܘܩܠܝܣ 'Empedocles' on the basis of Socrates, *Hist. eccl.* 1.22. *Acta Archelai* 62.3 provides only the name of Pythagoras.

the Christia[ns].[199] He had [a certain] disciple [whose name] was Būdōs (Buddha?) who was form[erly called] Ṭ[erebī]nt[ō]s[200] (i.e., Terebinthus). When Scythianus [died], this one (Būdōs/Terebinthus) came with [the wif]e of Scythianus to Babylon[ia] and clai[med] about himself that he was born [of a virgi]n and that he was raised among [the mountains].[201] He prepared f[our] books: one whose title was [*Mysteries*], another called *G*[*ospe*]*l*, the third [*Treasuries*], and the fourth *Kephal*[*a*]*ia*.[202] [While pretend]ing to expound some v[isions, he was beaten] by a spirit [and died].[203] When [the woman] who was living with him perceived this, she to[ok the gold] which he had amassed and purch[ased] the boy whom we m[entioned (earlier) who]se name was Qūrūbīqōs. After [she had instructed him] in the teaching of those fo[ur] books, that woman [also] died. She [left] him [those] books of Terebinthus wherein he had set down the teaching which he had received [from] S[cy]thianus, and all of their w[ealth]. Qūrūbīqōs t[ook] all of the books [and the gold and went] to the land [of the Persian]s.[204] He came to the house of his par[ents], and there he named [himself] Manī.[205]

And (acting) [as if] these books [had been com]posed by himself, he [transmitted] them under the label of '[Christia]n' to those whom he [led astray] with them. When they saw that he o[ccupied himself] with the t[eaching] of the Nazarenes, they made him then and there a [pr]iest.[206] He became an expos[itor] of the Scrip-

199. The 'heresy(s)' supposedly introduced by Scythianus into Christianity are dualism and recourse to the occult sciences. See the note to the corresponding section in the testimony of Theodore bar Konai below; note also *Acta Archelai* 68.6 (ed. Beeson, 99).

200. Spelled ܛܪܒܝܢܬܘܣ in Michael Syrus.

201. Compare *Acta Archelai* 63.2 (ed. Beeson, 91): *ex quadam autem virgine natum se esse simulavit et ab angelo in montibus enutritum* 'he (i.e., Terebinthus) pretended that he had been born from a virgin, and nurtured by an angel on the mountains'; also Socrates, *Historia ecclesiastica* 1.22: φάσκων ἐκ παρθένου γεγενῆσθαι καὶ ἐν ὄρεσιν ἀνατετράφθαι '(Terebinthus) was claiming that he was born of a virgin and brought up among the mountains.' Translation of the *Acta* is quoted from Vermes, *Acta Archelai*, 142.

202. ܕܪ̈ܫܐ in Michael Syrus; Chabot counsels to read there as here ܪ̈ܫܐ 'Heads,' i.e., Greek *Kephalaia*.

203. According to *Acta Archelai* 63.6 (ed. Beeson, 92), while Terebinthus was engaged in a magical ritual on the housetop, *sub terras eum detrudi per spiritum iubet et continuo de summo deiectus exanime corpus deorsum praecipitatum est* 'he (i.e., God) decreed that he be knocked down to the ground by a spirit, and at once he was hurled from the height (and) a lifeless body was cast down.' Interestingly *PGM* IV.2507-9 warns a magician against conjuring without the protection of an amulet (φυλακτήριον); should a magician foolishly ignore this precaution, the deity 'casts them from aloft onto the ground' (ἀπὸ τοῦ ὕψους ἐπὶ τὴν γῆν ῥῖψαι).

204. Mani takes up residence in the city of [Bēth] Lapaṭ in Michael Syrus; Susa in Agapius and the *Chronicon Seertensis*.

205. Spelled ܡܐܢܝ 'Mānī' in Michael Syrus.

206. Michael Syrus reads here as follows: 'He led astray many by means of those books. He ascribed them as Christian. When they beheld that he occupied himself with the Christian

tures and [disputed] against both [Jews] and pagans.[207] He acquired [thr]ee disciples: [Addā], whom he sent forth [to instruct] Bēth [A]ramāyē;[208] [Thoma]s, who we[n]t to India ;[209] [and another wh]ose name was [Hermeias.[210] But when] they returned [and reported to him that no] one [had accepted them] (i.e., as authentic exponents of Christianity), he became angr[y] and abandoned Christian doctrines. He however did not understand it (i.e., Christianity) correctly from the start, for he called himself 'Christ' and 'the Holy Spirit.' In imitation of what the 'authentic Christ' did, he thereupon chose for himself twelve disciples and infused them with a spirit.[211]

---

teaching, they made him a priest.' See the note to the Michael Syrus excerpt below.

207. For Mani's reputation as a disputant and public debater, see Lieu, *Manichaeism in Mesopotamia*, 148–49.

208. I.e., lower Mesopotamia. Addā (variants Addas; Addai) was a prominent Manichaean missionary active during the second half of the third century in the eastern Roman Empire. See F. C. Andreas and W. B. Henning, "Mitteliranische Manichaica aus Chinesisch-Turkestan, II," *SPAW* (1933): 301 nn.2–3; H. J. W. Drijvers, "Addai und Mani: Christentum und Manichäismus im dritten Jahrhundert in Syrien," in *IIIe Symposium Syriacum, 1980: Les contacts du monde syriaque avec les autres cultures, Goslar 7–11 septembre 1980* (OrChrAn 221; ed. René Lavenant; Rome: Pontificium Institutum Studiorium Orientalium, 1983), 171–85; idem, "Early Syriac Christianity: Some Recent Publications," *Vigiliae Christianae* 50 (1996): 164–65, 171–72; Giulia Sfameni Gasparro, "Addas-Adimantus unus ex discipulis Manichaei: For the History of Manichaeism in the West," in *Studia Manichaica: IV. Internationaler Kongress* (ed. Emmerick, Sundermann, and Zieme), 546–59.

209. The mission of an apostle Thomas to India is based upon the third-century *Acts of Thomas*, a parascriptural romance of Syrian provenance which exhibits a number of intriguing connections with Manichaeism. Mani's own association with proselytization in India may have had a hand in shaping this legend. For the possible Manichaean affinities of the *Acts of Thomas*, see Wilhelm Bousset, "Manichäisches in den Thomasakten," *ZNW* 18 (1917–18): 1–39; Günther Bornkamm, *Mythos und Legende in den apokryphen Thomas-Akten: Beiträge zur Geschichte der Gnosis und zur Vorgeschichte des Manichäismus* (FRLANT 31; Göttingen: Vandenhoeck and Ruprecht, 1933); Jean-Daniel Kaestli, "L'utilisation des actes apocryphes des apôtres dans le manichéisme," in *Gnosis and Gnosticism: Papers read at the Seventh International Conference on Patristic Studies (Oxford, September 8th–13th 1975)* (NHS 8; ed. Martin Krause; Leiden: Brill, 1977), 113–14. According to Sam Lieu, 'the *Acts of Thomas* ... played a significant part in the formation of Mani's views on soteriology' (*Manichaeism*[2], 87).

210. Michael Syrus only names Addā and Thomas. According to *Acta Archelai* 13.4 (ed. Beeson, 22), Addas (*sic*) went east; Thomas operated in the 'Syrian territories' (τὴν Σύρων γῆν), and Hermeias (Ἑρμείας) went to Egypt. But in *Acta Archelai* 64.6 (ed. Beeson, 93), Addas goes to Scythia, Thomas to Egypt, and the third disciple Hermas (*sic*) remains behind with Mani in Persia.

211. Michael Syrus: 'and blew into them a so-called "spirit."' Compare Ephrem Syrus, *Hymnus contra haereses* 22.14.2–4: 'He infused his prophets (ܢܒܝ̈ܘܗܝ) with a deceptive spirit (ܪܘܚ ܛܘܥܝܐ), broke his body for his disciples, and divided the earth among his heralds (ܟܪ̈ܘܙܘܗܝ).' The same hymn also refers to Mani appropriating to himself the titles 'Christ' (22.14.1, 5) and 'Paraclete' (22.14.9). Text of Ephrem cited from Edmund Beck, ed., *Des Heiligen Ephraem des Syrers Hymnen contra Haereses* (CSCO 169;

They then went forth and led astray the world.[212]

Theodore bar Konai, *Scholion* (ed. Scher):[213]

There are others[214] who say that he was manumitted (from the aforementioned sect) by the wife of (a certain) Budōs.[215] Now this Budōs was the pupil of a man whose name was Sqūntyōs (Scythianus). He was one who accepted the teachings of the Egyptian philosophers, for he had gone thither (i.e., Egypt) in order to study with the sages who were in Egypt at that time. He became learned in Egyptian and Greek lore, and in the works of Pythagoras and <Empedocles>.[216] He ventured to introduce the teachings of paganism into Christianity, and he furthermore taught that there are two principles, one Good and the other Evil, as also did <Empedocles> who gave to Evil the designation 'conquest' and to Good the designations 'desire' and 'love.'[217]

Scythianus had a student, Budōs, whom we mentioned above. This one (Budōs) was originally named Ṭerōbintōs (Terebinthus). Using the doctrines which he received from Scythianus, he authored four books: the first he called *[Book of] Mysteries*, the next *Gospel*, the third *[Book of] Treasures*, and the fourth *[Book of] Kephalaia*. After he composed these books, he went down to Babylon and led many astray. While celebrating certain secret magical rites, he was severely beaten by a spirit and (so) died. And that woman who lived with him <buried him>,[218] for it was she that inherited everything that Budōs left. She acquired (from the aforementioned sect) a servant-boy who was about seven years old whose name was Qūrqabyōs, and after she freed him, she taught him letters, and he became learned in the books of Budōs. After his mistress died and he had come of age,

---

Louvain: Imprimerie orientaliste L. Durbecq, 1957), 82–83.

212. For another translation, see Wassilios Klein, "War Mani Priester der Perserkirche?" in *Atti del terzo congresso internazionale di studi "Manicheismo e Oriente Cristiano Antico": Arcavacata di Rende-Amantea 31 agosto – 5 settembre 1993* (Manichaean Studies 3; ed. Luigi Cirillo and Alois van Tongerloo; Turnhout: Brepols, 1997), 203–204.

213. Theodore bar Konai, *Scholion* (ed. Scher), 2:311.19–313.9; Pognon, *Inscriptions*, 125.17–126.31.

214. For what preceded this passage, see section 2 above.

215. This character is of course the same as Būdōs, or Terebīntōs, of the *Chronicon Maroniticum* above.

216. The text has 'Proclus' (ܦܪܘܩܠܘܣ) which is undoubtedly a corruption of 'Empedocles'; compare the testimony of the *Chronicon Maroniticum* and Michael Syrus.

217. Based on Socrates, *Historia ecclesiastica* 1.22: ὡς καὶ 'Εμπεδοκλῆς νεῖκος ὀνομάζων τὴν πονηρὰν, φιλίαν δὲ τὴν ἀγαθήν. See Joel L. Kraemer, *Humanism in the Renaissance of Islam: The Cultural Revival during the Buyid Age* (2nd rev. ed.; Leiden: Brill, 1992), 141–43; Majid Fakhry, *A History of Islamic Philosophy* (3rd ed.; New York: Columbia University Press, 2004), 19.

218. The text as it stands is incomprehensible. Pognon (*Inscriptions*, 183 n.2) suggests emending the verb ܘܣܒܪܬܗ to ܘܩܒܪܬܗ, a change that also brings Theodore's narrative in line with that of the *Acta Archelai* at this point.

he departed those places where Budōs had taught, changed his name, and called himself Mānī.

He declared that the four books of Budōs were his own (compositions), and claimed the teaching(s) (of Budōs) for himself. He was familiar with the art of healing, as well as that of magic, and although he reasoned about everything from a pagan point of view, he also sought to use the name of Christ (in his system), with the result that he was able to lead many astray. He taught that one should worship evil spirits as gods and adore the sun, moon, and stars, for he also cast destinies and horoscopes.[219] He denied the Law of Moses and the Prophets and the God who was the giver of the Law.[220] With regard to our Savior he said that it was only opinion that he (Jesus) was born and suffered, for in truth he was not a human being as he appeared to be.[221] He said that human bodies derive from (the) Evil (principle), and he denied the resurrection. He taught about the world that part of it was from God and another part was from Matter,[222] and he forbade the eating of that which was animate. All of the members of his group are wicked: they sacrifice human beings and impudently fornicate during (their) demonic mysteries.[223] They are devoid of compassion and completely hopeless.

Shabūr the King flayed Mānī, stuffed his skin with straw, and fastened him before the gate of Bēth Lapaṭ, a city of the Elamites.[224]

---

219. Earlier eastern writers like Aphrahat and Mārūtā accuse Manichaeans of practicing 'Chaldeanism,' a popular late antique label for the art of astrology. For the place of astrology in Manichaeism, see Lieu, *Manichaeism*^{2}, 177–79; F. Stanley Jones, "The Astrological Trajectory in Ancient Syriac-Speaking Christianity," in *Atti del terzo congresso* (ed. Cirillo and van Tongerloo), esp. 194–99.

220. Note 'Abd al-Jabbār, Ibn al-Nadīm, and Shahrastānī for similar accusations. See also Ephrem Syrus, *Hymnus contra haereses* (ed. Beck) 51.14.1–4, who charges that Mani 'rabidly abused Moses and the prophets.'

221. Mani taught a docetic Christology: as an authentic Apostle of Light, Jesus only seemed to have a mortal body. The Jews mistakenly crucified a look-alike double instead of Jesus. See the discussion and references given by Jes P. Asmussen, *Manichaean Literature: Representative Texts Chiefly from Middle Persian and Parthian Writings* (Delmar, NY: Scholars' Facsimiles and Reprints, 1975), 103–09; and compare Q 4:157–59. For more on docetism as a heresiological trope, see especially Israel Friedlaender, "Jewish-Arabic Studies," *Jewish Quarterly Review* n.s. 2 (1912): 507–16; also Kurt Rudolph, *Gnosis: The Nature and History of Gnosticism* (trans. Robert McLachlan Wilson; San Francisco: Harper & Row, 1983), 157–71.

222. ܗܘܠܐ, i.e., Greek ὕλη or 'matter,' another common designation for the Realm of Darkness.

223. These lurid accusations are of course based on popular rumors. See especially the section below in Chapter Five on the Manichaean blood-libel.

224. Note that Shāpūr I is identified as the executioner in this tradition, as opposed to Bahrām I. Additional translations are available in Pognon, *Inscriptions*, 182–84; Adam, *Texte*^{2}, 76–78; Hespel-Draguet, *Théodore*, 232–33.

Sāwīrūs b. al-Muqaffaʿ, *Taʾrīkh al-baṭārikah* (ed. Seybold):[225]

At the time of this ruler[226] there appeared an abominable man whose name was Mānī, and this one also proclaimed and performed abominable things. He uttered blasphemies against the Lord the Protector of all and against the Only Son and against the Holy Spirit which proceeds from the Father, and he insolently claimed he was the Paraclete. But this Mānī was (originally) Qurwīqōs, a slave owned by a widowed woman. She acquired great wealth after a powerful magician from Palestine who was lodging with her fell from the top of the roof and died. That woman then purchased the wicked slave and taught him the scribal arts. When he reached puberty, she gave to him those books owned by the magician, and after he read and learned magical knowledge from them, he went away to Persia and took up residence at a place wherein sorcerers, fortune-tellers, and astrologers were resident. When he had achieved proficiency in criminal lore, Satan appeared to him, emboldened him, and took pleasure in him. He hated the Church and caused a large number of people to go astray on account of his magic. (Duped Christians) would convey their riches to him, and young boys and young girls would gratify his depraved lusts. He enslaved them with his magic and seduced a group of the populace. He would tell them that he was the Paraclete, the one whom the Lord Christ had promised to send in the Gospel of John.[227]

Now there was a rich Christian man named Marcellus who was the mayor of a city in the province of Syria. The city had a bishop whose name was Āršlāūs (i.e., Archelaus). This mayor was endowed with the spirit and generosity of Abraham, Isaac, and Jacob, and he was a disciple of the Church and attended to it morning and evening like a destitute man who possessed nothing. He would listen to the sermons of the bishop as was his duty, and with his wealth he accomplished good things for the people of his city. His door—like that of the blessed Job—was open for all to enter, whether they were fellow citizens, persons unjustly treated by banishment, or any others.

It was shortly after this time that Persia captured the people of a small town belonging to it (i.e., that province). They devastated the region and killed many people. The prisoners came to him and asked whether he could exercise mercy on their behalf, and he replied to their question affectionately: he made an appeal to the Persian official and obtained from him the number of the captives, and when he came to him, he produced money for him and the group with him. He said to them: 'Take whatever you wish for these prisoners!' When they beheld his charitable deed, they refused this (request). They said to him: 'We cannot do this, but pay us whatever you wish for these men whom we have.' They settled between them upon a price of three *dīnārs* for each person, and he thus rescued all of them from being with them (i.e., the Persians). He furnished them with money

225. Chr. Fred. Seybold, ed., *Severus ben el Moqaffaʿ Historia patriarcharum alexandrinorum* (CSCO script. arabici 8-9; 2 vols.; Paris: Carolus Poussielgue, 1904–10), 1:46.15–50.2.

226. The emperor Aurelian (270–75 CE).

227. See John 14:16–17, 26; 15:26; 16:7.

and showed them every sort of courtesy. Finally, apart from the payment and the restoration of those who had been captured from among them, he looked after them for seven days and occupied himself with their sick ones as if they were his own children. He came to their region and buried those whom the Persians had killed. Afterwards he rebuilt for the survivors their locales which they (i.e., the Persians) had destroyed, and he restored stability for those who were left in the region. He rebuilt all their churches and resettled them within their region.[228]

When the sinful Mānikhāūs (*sic*)[229] heard about what this man had accomplished, he reflected (on it) and said: 'If I were to gain power and mastery over this man, then the whole of Syria would be subject to my authority!' Therefore he wrote a letter to him. It said in it: 'The Paraclete Mānī writes to Marcellus. I have heard about the munificence of your deeds, and so I will teach you to become my elect disciple in order to apprise you about the correct path regarding which Christ has transmitted to me to instruct the people. Now your previous teachers have led you astray when they say that the speech of the Great God descended[230] into the womb of a woman, or that the prophets spoke a true message about Christ. For the Old (Testament) God is wicked: he is not willing for anything to be obtained from him; whereas the New (Testament) God is the One Who is virtuous.'[231] He did not say whether they obtained (anything) from Him. He expressed in it (i.e., the letter) many blasphemous doctrines which is improper to mention here; even Satan never spoke the way he did.

He gave the letter to a certain person like himself and sent him to Marcellus. When the messenger came to Syria, none of the people on his way welcomed him to lodge with them or offered him sustenance. In great distress due to hunger, he sustained himself on herbs until he reached Marcellus.[232] After Marcellus had received the letter and read it, he sent it to the bishop Āršlāūs. He prepared a place for the messenger to stay, and attended to his needs for the present. When the bishop had read the letter, he tore (some) hair from his head and exclaimed, 'Would that I might have died and not read such a blasphemous letter!' He sent to Marcellus and had the messenger brought to him. He questioned him about the behavior of this Mānī, and how he fared. The messenger informed him about these things, and he made petition to remain with them after he had listened to their conversations and had seen their beneficence and their liberality. Marcel-

228. This description of the pious deeds in which Marcellus engaged on behalf of the war captives is based very loosely on *Acta Archelai* 1.4–3.6 (ed. Beeson, 1–4).

229. Note that this spelling of Mani's name reflects at least one of its creative permutations as developed by Manichaean scribes and described by Augustine, *de Haeresibus* 46.1 (cf. Adam, *Texte*[2], 65; Gardner-Lieu, *Manichaean Texts*, 187). See also *CMC* 66.4; Coptic *Homil.* 7.3–5; Lieu, *Manichaeism*[2], 136.

230. Read with Seybold's apparatus.

231. Falsely ascribing a Marcionite view to Mani.

232. Clearly modeled upon the lack of hospitality extended to Mani's emissary Turbo as described in *Acta Archelai* 4.5 (ed. Beeson, 4).

lus suggested that he could take back an answer to the letter and even offered him three *dīnārs*, but he said to him: 'Forgive me, my lord! I cannot go back to him!' Then they rejoiced at the deliverance of his soul from the deadly snare.

Marcellus thereupon wrote Mānī a response to his letter, dispatching it to him with one of his servants. The (holy) father Āršlāūs told that servant not to accept anything from him (i.e., from Mani), and not to eat or to drink (anything) with him. Then he sent him out. After seven days Mānī came to Āršlāūs. He was wearing a fine *āskīm*[233] around his torso and a thin *istikhārat*[234] beneath it, and he was wrapped in a striped garment coming down over his feet which was adorned with figures on its front and its back.[235] Accompanying him were thirty-two young men and women who were his followers.[236] When he entered the residence of Marcellus, he proceeded to the chair which was at the center of the residence and sat upon it, assuming that they had invited him in order to learn from him. Marcellus then sent for the bishop Āršlāūs.

When he (i.e., Āršlāūs) beheld him sitting in the chair, he was astonished by his impudence. The bishop questioned him and said to him: 'What is your name?' He answered him: 'Paraclete is my name!' Āršlāūs said to him: 'Are you the Paraclete whom the Lord Christ said He would send to us?' He responded: 'Yes, I am the one.' The bishop asked him: 'How old are you?' He answered: 'I am thirty-five years old.'[237] The bishop Āršlāūs said to him: 'Christ the Savior told his disciples that they should remain in Jerusalem and not depart or engage in missionary activity until they were armored by a power from above.[238] This was the Paraclete: the Holy Spirit. And ten days after His ascension to heaven, just as He said, the Paraclete descended upon the apostles on the Day of Pentecost, and this was completed fifty days after Easter. And are the disciples now waiting for you in Jerusalem? You should remember this thing—that for a duration of about three hundred years[239] they have been evangelizing: their voices have gone forth to the entire world, and their message has reached the farthest regions of the inhabited world. But had the thing transpired as you claim, they would not have evange-

---

233. A loan from Greek σχῆμα, defined as a 'bonnet des prêtres grecs' or 'l'habit angélique' by R. Dozy, *Supplément aux dictionnaires arabes* (2 vols.; Leiden: E. J. Brill, 1881), 1:23. Note also W. E. Crum, *A Coptic Dictionary* (Oxford: Clarendon Press, 1939), 777.

234. Presumably a reflex of Greek στιχάριον, defined as a 'thin tunic or shirt' by G. W. H. Lampe, *A Patristic Greek Lexicon* (Oxford: Clarendon Press, 1961), 1260.

235. Very little of the elaborate description of Mani's appearance supplied in *Acta Archelai* 14.3 survives in this rendition.

236. According to *Acta Archelai* 14.2 (ed. Beeson, 22), Mani's entourage consisted of 'twenty-two elect young men and women.'

237. In *Acta Archelai* 64.4 (ed. Beeson, 93), Mani is said to be sixty years old prior to embarking upon the public part of his prophetic vocation.

238. This story is based on Acts 1:2-11.

239. The three hundred-year duration between the eras of Jesus and Mani is mentioned in passing in *Acta Archelai* 31.4; also 31.7.

lized nor would they even still be alive in Jerusalem at the present time. In what place did you see the Lord Christ?[240] You are only thirty-five years old! He once said that a person should not seat themselves in the most prominent position when they attend a gathering,[241] and lo, you have assumed a seat in the most honored spot of the house!'

Mānī said to him: 'Does the Gospel not say "I will send the Paraclete to you?"' Āršlāūs answered him: 'Do you accept the Gospel? For it also says with respect to the Blessed Virgin Mary that "the Holy Spirit will settle upon you and a supernal power will overshadow you, and the One whom you will give birth to will be holy and will be called the Son of God (Lk 1:35)."' Then he produced for him his letter which he had sent to Marcellus wherein he had rejected the physical birth of Christ from a woman, argued about His death, and denied there was a resurrection from the dead. Then Mānī began to expound his worthless teachings; namely, that there are two deities, one of whom is Light and the other Darkness, and other things similar to this from (his) blasphemy. But the bishop Āršlāūs said to him: 'Even if I condemn you in proportion to your dishonesty, you will still resist me for the sake of your teachings. Let me however send for (and) bring to you some people who do not know God; i.e., the God of heaven, in order (to show) that they will condemn you for your statements.' So he sent for (and) brought to him some men, each of whom were knowledgeable, and another who was a scribe, and he said to them: 'Listen to what this man says. Are there in your books statements which you accept and (other) statements which you reject?' They responded: 'No, we accept everything that is in our writings and we do not reject any part of them. And when we make distinctions between one thing and another, the readings which are unacceptable are not kept.'

The bishop answered and said to them: 'This man announces and says that he is Christ, yet he despises the instructions of Christ!' They replied to him: 'We neither accept him nor do we engage ourselves with his instructions.' When he (i.e., Mani) spoke and the crowd heard his words which were full of blasphemy, they rushed toward him to kill him, but the bishop prevented them from (harming) him. He said to them: 'He will suffer death at the hands of someone else, not us.'[242] Then he expelled him from the city and said to him: 'Take care that you do not die, (for such will be the result) should you be discovered in our district!'

When he left, he came to a small village wherein the priest showed beneficence to the stranger and offered him lodging.[243] He remained with him for a month,

240. Compare Archelaus admonishing Mani in *Acta Archelai* 40.5: 'Who of those who live in Jerusalem have ever seen you?' Translation is that of Vermes, *Acta Archelai*, 105.

241. An allusion to Matt 23:6; Mk 12:38-39; Lk 11:43; 14:7–11; 20:46. Cf. Prov 25:6–7.

242. Compare *Acta Archelai* 43.1–2 which provides a different justification for why Mani escaped mob violence.

243. Both the village and the priest bear the name 'Diodorus' in *Acta Archelai* 44.4. This final paragraph represents a drastic abbreviation and reworking of *Acta Archelai* 44.4–66.3.

and he (i.e., the priest) did not know who he was. Then he told the priest some of his teachings. The priest said to him: 'I have never heard these teachings. However, let me send for Āršlāūs to come and hear from you what you are teaching. If he finds no fault with it, then I will accept it.' When Mānī heard the name 'Āršlāūs,' he grew agitated on account of the acuity, courage, and divine wisdom which the latter possessed, and so he returned at that time to the land of Persia. As was his habit, he continued to promote his blasphemies. The real Paraclete then pronounced judgment on him. The king of Persia took him into custody, stripped off his skin, threw him down to the animals, and they ate him.[244]

Agapius of Mabbug, *Kitāb al-Unvān* (ed. Vasiliev):[245]

The story of the accursed Mānī. The father of Mānī was a man from Susa who was called Fatīq,[246] and his family was from Ahwāz. He had a wife whose name was Yūsīt, and she bore him a son whom he named Qūrbīqōs. After he grew and became seven years old, he was taken captive[247] and brought down into Egypt.[248] A woman from the Maghrib (North Africa) who was called Šūsannah bought him. Her husband was called Sqūsy,[249] and he had Egyptian teachers. This one believed the idea(s) of Pythagoras and <Empe>docles. He had a disciple who was called Bardōrōs (i.e., Budos) who was (also) known by the name of Terebinsōs (i.e., Terebinthus). After the woman's husband Sqūsy died, his disciple—the one we said was named Bardōrōs—married her and assumed the burden of (supporting) the woman and the boy whom she had purchased. He engaged in deceptions until he came to Babylon. (There) he told the Persians that he had been born of a virgin

244. Compare Cyril of Jerusalem, *Catecheses ad illuminandos* 6.30: καὶ τὸ μὲν λοιπὸν σῶμα θηρίων παρεδόθη βορᾷ 'and the rest of the corpse (i.e., Mani's) was given as food to the animals.' A Coptic version of the last part of this account was rendered in English by W. E. Crum, "Eusebius and Coptic Church Histories," *Proceedings of the Society of Biblical Archaeology* 24 (1902): 76–77; note also the references supplied by D. W. Johnson, "Coptic Reactions to Gnosticism and Manichaeism," *Le Muséon* 100 (1987): 207. For another translation (including an edition of the Arabic text), see B. Evetts, "History of the Patriarchs of the Coptic Church of Alexandria," *Patrologia Orientalis* 1 (1907): 195–202.

245. Alexandre Vasiliev, "*Kitāb al-Unvān*: Histoire universelle écrite par Agapius (Mahboub) de Menbidj," *Patrologia Orientalis* 7 (1911): 531–35; Taqīzādeh-Šīrāzī, *Mānī va dīn-e-ū*, 350–52; 353 (§100).

246. The text reads فتبق, but this is an error for فتيق.

247. A new motif that is unknown to the earlier sources.

248. In the Latin *Acta Archelai*, Cyril of Jerusalem, Socrates, the *Chronicon Maroniticum*, and Theodore bar Konai, the slave boy is not acquired until after Terebinthus relocates to Babylonia. Yet this discrepancy may explain why the *Zūqnīn Chronicle* and the *Chronicon ad annum 1234* claim that Mani visited Egypt; viz., he arrived there in his youthful capacity as a household slave.

249. A corruption for Scythianus.

mother and that he had been raised among the mountains.[250] He wrote four books: he named the first one the *Book of Mysteries*, he named the next one the *Gospel*, the third the *Book of Treasure*, and the fourth the *Book of Disputation*.[251] He did not cease swindling the people with his sorcery, insolence, and trickery until he had amassed a large amount of wealth. Then he suffered an unfortunate demise.

After Sūsannah (*sic*) his wife had buried him, she devoted herself to the boy. Placing herself in his hands, as well as a small portion of the fortune accumulated by her former husband and the books which her second husband had authored, she took him in marriage—that is, the boy Qūrbīqōs—as her third husband.[252] The boy copied passages from those books and diligently studied the knowledge (contained therein) for a time. Then that woman died and the boy inherited the fortune and the books. He took the money and the books and came to Susa, his original homeland and birthplace. He renamed himself Mānī and claimed that he was the author of those books. He pretended to be a Christian, the bishop of Ahwāz made him a priest, and he began teaching and interpreting the scriptures there. He engaged in disputations with pagans, Jews, Zoroastrians, or any one who was opposed to Christianity.

Some of the people believed his innovations, and he acquired disciples: the name of one of them was Addai, the name of another Thomas, and the name of a third was Marādai.[253] In order to summon people to his doctrine, he sent his disciple Addai to Yemen and Thomas to India, while Marādai remained behind with him in Susa. His disciples returned and informed him that no one followed their instructions or received them. He became angry at this and renounced the Christianity which he was feigning and fabricated some new fables.

He called himself the Paraclete, the one whom the Lord Christ (to Him be the glory!) had promised to send to his disciples.[254] He appointed twelve disciples and 'breathed the spirit' into them, just as the Lord Christ (to Him be the glory!) had done with his disciples. He and they (thereupon) went out and led the world astray ....[255]

Sābūr the son of Ardašīr, king of Persia, killed him (Mānī), flayed his skin, stuffed it with straw, and hung it up (lit. 'crucified it').[256]

250. See the *Chronicon Maroniticum* above and the discussion below.

251. Arabic كتاب الجدال. This spurious title results from a misreading of the Syriac characters ܪ̈ܫܐ '[Book] of Heads (i.e., *Kephalaia*) as ܕܪܫܐ 'controversy, disputation.'

252. Another creative expansion of the *Acta Archelai* tradition.

253. مرادى. This disciple's name is usually given as 'Hermas'; it has undoubtedly undergone some corruption.

254. See the *Zūqnīn Chronicle* above, and especially Ibn al-Nadīm in Chapter Four below.

255. The doctrinal portion of the testimony of Agapius is omitted here. See Chapter Four below.

256. An almost identical ending to that of Theodore bar Konai. For another translation, see Vasiliev, "Kitāb al-Unvān," 531-35.

***Chronicon Seertensis* (ed. Scher):**[257]

An account of Mānī with an exposition of his teaching:

To begin with, his father's name was Fasiq[258] and his mother's name was Nūšīt. When he was born, they named him Qūrbīqōs. After seven years passed, he was taken captive, and an Arab woman who called herself Sūsbah bought him. Now her husband was educated in the lore of the Egyptians and believed the idea(s) of Pythagoras. He had a disciple who was called Yūdhūrōs.[259]

The husband of the woman died, and she married his disciple. He assumed the burden of (supporting) her and the boy whom she had purchased. He engaged in deceptions until he came to Babylon. He told the Persians that he had been born of a virgin mother and that he had seen (visions?)[260] while in the mountains. He wrote four books, designating them with (distinctive) titles: the first was the *Full of Mysteries*, the second the *True Gospel*, the third the *Source of Treasures*, and the fourth the *Principle(s) of Disputation and Strife.*[261] Yet he did not cease terrorizing[262] the people with his sorcery. This took place during the reign of Philip emperor of Rome (i.e., Philip the Arab)[263] and King Sābūr son of Ardašīr (i.e., Shāpūr I, Sasanian ruler of Persia). He taught the people the doctrine of two creating and constantly generating deities, (who were) Good and Evil. Good is virtuous and luminous, whereas Evil is wicked and dark. He (the disciple) amassed great wealth, but (eventually) departed to the flames of Hell.

His wife Sūsbah took possession of the books, his wealth, and the property of her first husband. She fell in love with Mānī,[264] for he was handsome in appearance. She furnished him with a portion of that hoard and some of the books and took him to herself as a third husband. In this way he became educated and learned (in) the books. Her former husband had inoculated him with his blasphemy, and she supported him (with) the great wealth until she had rendered

257. Addai Scher, "Histoire Nestorienne inédite (Chronique de Séert)," *Patrologia Orientalis* 4 (1908): 225–28; reprinted in Taqīzādeh-Šīrāzī, *Mānī va dīn-e-ū*, 380–83 (§118). Note also Felix Haase, *Altchristliche Kirchengeschichte nach orientalischen Quellen* (Leipzig: Verlag Otto Harrassowitz, 1925), 33. Most authorities date this chronicle to the eleventh century; for an argument that it must date prior to 1019, see Pierre Nautin, "L'auteur de la «Chronique de Séert»: Išōʿdenaḥ de Baṣra," *RHR* 186 (1974): 113–26. Compare however the remarks of J.-M. Fiey, "Īšōʿdnāḥ et la Chronique de Séert," *Parole de l'Orient* 6–7 (1975–76): 447–59; Louis R. M. Sako, "Les sources de la Chronique de Séert," *Parole de l'Orient* 14 (1987): 155–66.

258. A corruption of Fatīq; see Agapius above.

259. Apparently a further corruption of the name 'Bardōrōs' occurring in Agapius.

260. Agapius (see *supra*) has the correct reading here: 'he was raised (ربّى) among the mountains.' Note also Scher, "Histoire," 225 n.5.

261. Perpetuating the wrong reading first found in Agapius; see above.

262. Compare Agapius above.

263. 244–249 CE.

264. The chronicler has not yet effected the equation between the slave boy and Mani!

him proficient and diligent in the quest for knowledge. But Sūsbah died before she could obtain what she wanted from him.[265]

He thereupon took the wealth and the books and proceeded to Susa, the land which was his birthplace. He renamed himself Mānī and claimed (that) he was the author of those books. He pretended that he was a Christian. The bishop of Ahwāz made him a priest, and he began teaching and interpreting the scriptures there. He engaged in disputations with pagans, Jews, Zoroastrians, or any one who was opposed to Christianity.

Then this hypocrite claimed that he was the Paraclete. He promoted the filth of the occult sciences. Mimicking the model set by the disciples of Christ, he took to himself twelve disciples. He denied the validity of (the doctrine of) corporeal rebirth and resurrection. He maintained that fire, water, and trees possess a spiritual component, and that one who uproots a tree or extinguishes a fire or spills water is guilty of murder. (He claimed) that the sun and moon were two ships which ferry souls to the Realm of the Good. He (also) invented things and divulged secrets too disgusting to mention.

Among his disciples were (those) named Thomas and Addai. In order to seduce the populace with his fables, he sent Addai to Yemen and the one named Thomas to India. One of his disciples named Mārī remained with him there,[266] and abode with him in Susa.[267] Meanwhile, the two who had gone to Yemen and India returned and informed him that no one had been deceived by their message or had accepted their interpretation(s). He became angry at this and was seized by rage: he renounced the Christianity which he hypocritically had exhibited and devised (further) abominable novelties.[268] At that time he announced that he was the Paraclete whom Christ had promised his disciples that he would send to them. He together with his disciples then set out and began to wander throughout the various lands and he taught that (doctrine) which he had formerly spoken about ....

When he won adherents (among) the people and his doctrine and heresy spread, Sābūr killed him and hung (lit. 'crucified') him on one of the gates of Susa. Hence the cursed one of God got what he deserved![269]

265. We are not told what sinister plan she envisioned. Is it possible that the attention which this later Nestorian chronicle devotes to the character of a 'wealthy widow' financially supporting a despised religious innovator is meant to evoke in the mind of the reader the analogous courtship and marital relationship between Khadīja and Muḥammad?

266. Compare *Acta Archelai* 64.6 (ed. Beeson, 93): the disciple named Hermias remains with Mani while Addai and Thomas embark on their respective missionary journeys, whereas Agapius (see above) relates that a certain 'Marādai' remains with Mani.

267. Interestingly all three of these names—Thomas, Addai, and Mārī—are associated with the orthodox Christianization of Mesopotamia and its environs. For the last named, see now Amir Harrak, *The Acts of Mār Mārī the Apostle* (Atlanta: Society of Biblical Literature, 2005).

268. For a translation of some of these passages, see also Klein, "War Mani Priester?" 205.

269. For another translation, see Scher, "Histoire," 225–28.

Michael Syrus, *Chronicle* (ed. Chabot):[270]

A certain man from (Bēth) Lapaṭ whose name was Pātīq had a son by Taqšīt and they named him Qūrbīqōs. When he was seven years old, the wife of an Arab man whose name was Sūtīna (*sic*; read Scythianus) purchased him. Becoming versed in the teaching of the Egyptians, he introduced the heresy of Pādōmīs (read: Empedocles) and Pythagoras among the Christians. He had a student whose name was Būdūs, formerly named Tabrīntōs (i.e., Terebinthus). This one came to Babylonia with the wife of Sqūtya (*sic*; i.e., Scythianus) and claimed about himself that he was born of a virgin.[271] He composed four books: one whose title was *Mysteries*, another (called) *Gospel*, the third *Treasuries*, and the fourth *Expositions* (read *Kephalaia*). While he was expounding the forms of some visitations and visions, he was beaten by a spirit and died. After burying him, the woman who lived with him took the gold which he had amassed and purchased the boy whom we spoke of (above), the one who was called Qūrbīqōs, and after she had instructed him in those writings, (then) she died. He then took the wealth and the writings, (and) came to (Bēth) Lapaṭ, and there he renamed himself Mānī.

He led astray many by means of those books, for he transmitted them under the name of 'Christian.' When they saw that he occupied himself with the Christian teaching, they made him a priest.[272] He became an expositor of the Scriptures and disputed against both Jews and pagans. He dispatched from among those whom were with him Addā in order to instruct Bēth Aramāyē and Thomas to India. But when they returned and reported to him that no one had accepted them (as authentic exponents of Christianity), he abandoned Christian doctrines and declared himself to be 'Christ' and 'the Holy Spirit.' He assembled twelve disciples and blew into them a so-called 'spirit.' Going forth, they led astray the world ....[273]

Mānī, having promised the king of Persia that he would heal his son but then proving unable to do so, fled to Mesopotamia.[274] However the king of Persia found him, flayed him, stuffed his skin with straw, and hung it up upon a wall. This was the end of the impious Mānī.

270. *Chronique de Michel le Syrien* (ed. Chabot), 4:117.3-118.7; 119.3-8. This account is closely related to that of the *Chronicon Maroniticum*.

271. A truncated version of *Acta Archelai* 63.2 and the *Chronicon Maroniticum*.

272. Note also the passages cited herein from 'Abd al-Jabbār, *Chronicon Maroniticum*, *Chronicon Seertensis*, and Bar Hebraeus.

273. For another translation up to this point, see Klein, "War Mani Priester?" 204. Note also Haase, *Altchristliche Kirchengeschichte*, 360-61.

274. Clearly dependent upon *Acta Archelai* 64.7-66.3.

Bar Hebraeus, *Historia compendiosa dynastiarum* (ed. Pococke):[275]

And at this time[276] Mānī the dualist became known. At first, this one appeared to be Christian, and he became a priest in Ahwāz. He taught and interpreted the Scriptures, and engaged Jews, Zoroastrians, and pagans in disputations. Then he renounced the true faith and termed himself 'Christ.' He took twelve disciples and sent them out to all the countries of the East, even to India and to China ....[277]

It is said that Sābūr, the king of Persia, executed Mānī, stripped off his skin, stuffed it with straw, and attached it upon the wall of the city. (This transpired) because he feigned a grandiose claim, but he proved incapable of curing his son of the illness present in him.[278]

***Kitāb al-sinkisār*; i.e., the Copto-Arabic Synaxarion (ed. Taqīzādeh-Šīrāzī):**[279]

[14 Baramouda[280]]: And it was during the time of this saint[281] that a man appeared from the East whose name was Mānī. He spoke about himself (saying) that he was the Paraclete, the Holy Spirit. He came to Syria and engaged in disputation with a holy bishop named Āršlāūs (i.e., Archelaus), and after he defeated him and exposed his errors, he expelled him from his country, and so he returned to Persia and announced (his) prophetic message (*sic*!). Bahrām, the king of Persia,[282] arrested him and cut him into two halves. He seized two hundred persons who followed him and buried them in the ground up to their waists upside down until they died.[283]

275. Edward Pococke, ed., *Historia compendiosa Dynastiarum authore Gregorio Abul-Pharagio* ... (2 vols.; Oxoniae: Excudebat H. Hall ... impensis Ric. Davis, 1663), 1:129–31; Kessler, *Mani*, 401-402; Taqīzādeh-Šīrāzī, *Mānī va dīn-e-ū*, 271 (§60). For the final paragraph, see Flügel, *Mani*, 332.

276. The accession-year of Hurmuz.

277. Another translation of this passage is in Klein, "War Mani Priester?" 204.

278. The same tradition (deriving from *Acta Archelai*) is also in Bīrūnī and in Michael Syrus. For another translation and brief discussion, see Carsten Colpe, "Bar Hebräus über die Manichäer," in *Pietas: Festschrift für Bernhard Kötting* (ed. Ernst Dassmann and K. Suso Frank; Münster [Westfalen]: Aschendorffsche Verlagsbuchhandlung, 1980), 237–42.

279. Taqīzādeh-Šīrāzī, *Mānī va dīn-e-ū*, 454 (§159).

280. The Coptic month corresponding to April 9–May 9.

281. Dionysius, bishop of Alexandria during the middle of the third century CE (d. 264) and whose epistles are extensively quoted by Eusebius in books 6 and 7 of his *Historia ecclesiastica*. The synchronization of Mani and Dionysius is likewise indebted to Eusebius.

282. Eutychius (see Taqīzādeh-Šīrāzī, *Mānī va dīn-e-ū*, 123 [§19]) identifies this king as Bahrām II who ruled after Bahrām I; it is the latter monarch who is typically named as the one responsible for the execution of Mani.

283. According to some sources, a remarkably similar form of execution is carried out by the Sasanian ruler Khusrau Anōshirvān (531–79 CE) against the followers of Mazdak, an early sixth-century social agitator. Mani, Mazdak, and their respective followers become increasingly intertwined in Islamicate sources. See Chapter Five below.

He then remarked: 'I have planted a garden of people!'[284]

4. Imagining Mani

As was indicated earlier in this chapter, the extant biographical representations of Mani oscillate between the binary poles of saint and scoundrel. His admirers and followers devotedly rhapsodized him as an inspired agent of the celestial realm, a gifted wonder-worker and charismatic teacher who repeatedly and brilliantly confirmed his claim to be an authentic messenger sent from beyond this world and who thereby deservedly won respect and recognition from a succession of temporal authorities. His detractors on the other hand pointedly mocked and derided his reputed sagacity, insinuated that he was simply a crass opportunist and deceitful huckster, and cleverly punned on his name by branding him as 'demented' (Μανής – μανείς) or as a 'vessel of the Devil' (τὸ σκεῦος τοῦ διαβόλου).[285] The undisputed source for many of these derogatory motifs, as we have seen, was a Christian composition whose actual author and original provenance remain shrouded in mystery, the so-called *Acta Archelai*. Given the demonstrable importance of this latter work for the subsequent eastern representations of the life and missionary career of Mani, a closer examination of its major structural components and distinctive themes seems justified at this point.[286]

The *Acta Archelai* is a fictional narrative discourse cast in the form of a staged disputation between Mani and an otherwise unknown Christian bishop named Archelaus.[287] The physical confrontation between the bishop and the heresiarch

284. This account is closely related to that supplied by the tenth-century Christian chronicler Saʿīd b. al-Biṭrīq (Eutychius) which also conflates the execution of Mani with the fall of Mazdak. See Chapter Five below.

285. Lieu, *Manichaeism*^{2}, 136; idem, *Manichaeism in Mesopotamia*, 234, 256–57; and see Theodore bar Konai above. Syriac *mānā* can be parsed as 'vessel; garment.' Note also *Acta Archelai* 40.2 (ed. Beeson, 59): *Vas es Antichristi et neque bonum vas, sed sordidum et indignum* 'You are the vessel of the Antichrist; and not a good vessel, but a filthy and worthless one.' Translation is that of Vermes, *Acta Archelai*, 104. It is very likely that the fourth-century Christian writer Aphrahat's dismissive references to the 'doctrines of the vessels of evil' (*Demonstrationes* 6.18; 8.24; cf. 1.19) signify Manichaean teachings and exploit the same word-play.

286. Important studies of the *Acta Archelai* include Samuel N. C. Lieu, "Fact and Fiction in the *Acta Archelai*," in *Manichaean Studies: Proceedings of the First International Conference on Manichaeism ...* (ed. Peter Bryder; Lund: Plus Ultra, 1988), 69–88; Madeleine Scopello, "Vérités et contre-vérités: La vie de Mani selon les *Acta Archelai*," *Apocrypha* 6 (1995): 203–34; idem, "Hégémonius, les *Acta Archelai* et l'histoire de la controverse anti-manichéenne," in *Studia Manichaica: IV. Internationaler Kongress* (ed. Emmerick, Sundermann, and Zieme), 528-45. See also the essays collected in Jason BeDuhn and Paul Mirecki, eds., *Frontiers of Faith: The Christian Encounter with Manichaeism in the Acts of Archelaus* (NHMS 61; Leiden: Brill, 2007)

287. The attribution of the work to 'Hegemonius' is dependent upon the testimony of a certain Heracleon, bishop of Chalcedon, who is so quoted in the ninth-century *Bib-*

reputedly took place *in Carcharis civitate Mesopotamiae* 'in Carchar, a city of Mesopotamia' (1.1), a difficult toponym whose obscurity engendered several variant renderings in dependent sources (Κασχάρων, Καλχάρων, Καρχάρων)[288] and whose intended urban referent continues to generate dispute among modern scholars:[289] the text of the *Acta* alleges it to be a journey of five days from Mani's pre-disputation domicile in Persia (4.3). Introductory and concluding narrative sketches surround the disputation proper, which is itself largely concerned with arguments about doctrinal issues, and it is these framing accounts which supply much of the biographical 'data' that will be copied and perpetuated by the later critics of Mani and his religion.

Attracted by the philanthropic munificence exhibited by a certain Marcellus, a wealthy resident of the city of Carchar, and intending to effect a conversion for the financial benefit of his own religious cause, Mani is represented as first engaging in correspondence with and then journeying westward to solicit the favor of this prospective patron. Unknown however to the heresiarch is that waiting anxiously for him at the house of Marcellus is Archelaus, a local bishop who is understandably resistant to the prospect of losing a rich parishioner and who has taken upon himself the cause of exposing Mani 'the Christian teacher' (4.4) as a fraud and a charlatan. Once the two have been brought together, Marcellus persuades them to argue their respective cases before a panel of learned judges which he selects from among the most prominent citizens of the town, a group of four men whom the author curiously labels *religione gentiles* 'belonging to the national religion' (14.5), an expression presumably signifying they were disinterested non-Christian indigenes or 'pagans.' This intriguing detail is undoubtedly designed to underscore the larger rhetorical point that the inherent absurdity and irrationality of Mani's teachings can be easily demonstrated even to those reasonably intelligent citizens of the empire who did not align themselves with any variety of fourth-century biblically inspired cultic groups.[290] Moreover, at the same time, the author can subtly introduce and artistically situate on stage a prominent target audience for whom Manichaean teachings and behavioral precepts historically were to prove especially appealing; namely, dissident elitist intellectuals and

---

liotheca of Photius. See Lieu, *Manichaeism in Mesopotamia*, 108–109; Scopello, "Vie de Mani," 204; idem, "Hégémonius," 532–33.

288. These different forms occur in the testimonia to the Greek version(s) of the *Acta* that are found in Cyril of Jerusalem, Epiphanius, Socrates, and Photius.

289. See Flügel, *Mani*, 19-25; M.-L. Chaumont, *La christianisation de l'empire iranien: Des origines aux grandes persécutions du IVᵉ siècle* (CSCO 499; Louvain: E. Peeters, 1988), 92–96; Lieu, *Manichaeism*², 131 n.61; Lieu, "Introduction," *apud* Vermes, *Acta Archelai*, 16–23.

290. One might compare the similar use of 'Zoroastrian referees' during the christological disputations staged by Simeon of Bēth Arsham, the notorious 'Persian debater,' against the Nestorians he encountered in the Sasanian realm. See E. W. Brooks, ed., *John of Ephesus, Lives of the Eastern Saints, I* (Patrologia Orientalis 17; Paris: Firmin-Didot, 1923), 144; also Joel Thomas Walker, *The Legend of Mar Qardagh: Narrative and Christian Heroism in Late Antique Iraq* (Berkeley: University of California Press, 2006), 176–77.

other members of the educated classes who exhibited varying degrees of disaffection with the prevailing structures and mechanisms of social power. Personalities like an Augustine (in Roman Africa) or an Ibn al-Muqaffaʿ (in ʿAbbāsid Baghdad) are representative of the type of individual who was often attracted to the Manichaean message and symbol system and for whom it seemed to serve as a plausible metaphysic and way of life. When the *Acta* positions such local figures as 'judges' for the disputation, it effectively juxtaposes a potentially gullible intelligentsia who might succumb to the seductive lure of Manichaeism with what the author portrays as a battery of philosophically sound counter-arguments and reasoned objections. It is these latter refutations which Archelaus strategically articulates, and hence the outcome of the disputation is in fact foreordained: Archelaus will prevail, while the perfidy of Mani will be devastatingly demonstrated.

The 'biographical' framework of the *Acta* seeks to justify its representation of Mani's philosophical naiveté and rhetorical ineptness by exposing the fraudulent nature of the claims which he and his adherents made about himself and his work. An enumeration of the most important characteristic motifs from the *Acta* rendition of Mani's life follows.

1. Pseudo-philosophers and/or magicians bearing exotic proper names like Scythianus, Terebinthus, and Buddos (or their orthographic variants) are the actual sources for Mani's purported prophetic revelations. Due to their endemic foolishness or wickedness, they suffer untimely demises.

Very little if any historical veracity resides in the popular charge against Mani of 'unoriginality.'[291] Apart from the *Acta* and its dependencies, the names of these alleged intellectual progenitors do not figure in any other work which treats of Mani and his doctrines. 'Scythianus'[292] (Greek Σκυθιανός)[293] is described as a desert Arab (*ex genere Saracenorum*) who was persuaded by his newlywed wife to take up residence in her native land of Egypt.[294] The name is symbolic, probably chosen to evoke the aura of a primitive barbarism insofar as one influential piece of early Christian rhetoric (Col 3:11) twins the gentilic 'Scythian' with Greek 'barbarian' to connote various uncivilized peoples who inhabit the remote corners of the inhabited world: the roughly contemporaneous heresiological compendium

291. According to Ephrem Syrus, *Hymnus contra haereses* (ed. Beck) 41.8.1–3, Mani 'stole' his doctrines from like-minded predecessors.

292. Variant spellings of the name 'Scythianus' signaled by Beeson (p. 90) include 'scitianus,' 'ex scythia scutianus,' 'excytiamus,' 'stutianus,' and 'excutianus.'

293. For the Greek spelling, see the so-called 'short Greek abjuration-formula' in Adam, *Texte*[2], 94.34.

294. *Acta Archelai* 62.4 (ed. Beeson, 90); Vermes, *Acta Archelai*, 141. According to Epiphanius (*Panarion* 66.2.3–4), he was an itinerant merchant who purchased a beautiful prostitute in 'the city called Hypsele in the Thebaid' in Upper Egypt and made her his wife. Scopello suggests that the portrait of Scythianus constructed by the *Acta* and its epigones is modeled upon that of the Christian arch-heretic Simon Magus; see her "Vie de Mani," 216–17.

of Epiphanius begins its exposition of deviant religious movements with successive chapters devoted to 'barbarism' and 'Scythianism' (*Panarion* 1.1–2.13). Scythianus is thus the quintessential 'pagan.' He is depicted as a seeker after wisdom and a devotee of Pythagoras, and he predictably develops an interest in the magical and ritual lore notoriously associated with Egyptian shrines and priests. Cyril of Jerusalem situates him in Alexandria and claims he adopted an 'Aristotelian lifestyle,' motifs which picturesquely abet his alleged 'philosophical' pretensions.[295] A disciple, one 'Terebinthus'[296] (Greek Τέρβινθος),[297] 'wrote' (copied?) four books for him bearing distinctive titles that will later designate important works included among authentic Manichaean literature. Making his way to Babylonia after the untimely demise of his teacher (which the *Acta* author attributes to his planned tour of Judaea),[298] 'Terebinthus' engaged in extravagant postures and made extraordinary claims about himself to the inhabitants of that region: '[saying] that he was brimming with all the wisdom of the Egyptians, and that he was no longer to be called Terebinthus but Buddha,[299] as this was the name given him.[300] He pretended that he had been born from a virgin, and nurtured by an angel on the mountains.'[301] Alleged credentials like those of miraculous birth and supernatural pedagogy are well attested *topoi* associated with authoritative teachers/saviors in the Near East of late antiquity.[302] Despite his best efforts, he was successful in acquiring only one follower, an elderly widow with whom he resided. While engaged in an otherwise nondescript conjuration on the roof of a house, something goes awry and he is fatally injured as a result of his fall from this height.

295. *Catecheses ad illuminandos* 6.22.

296. For variant spellings, see the apparatus of Beeson (p. 91).

297. So Epiphanius. Other sources preserving a Greek rendering (Cyril of Jerusalem, Socrates, the so-called 'long Greek abjuration-formula') have Τερέβινθος.

298. *Acta Archelai* 62.7 (ed. Beeson, 91); Vermes, *Acta Archelai*, 142.

299. *Acta Archelai* 63.2 (ed. Beeson, 91): *sed Buddam nomine sibique hoc nomen inpositum.* According to Epiphanius (*Panarion* 66.1.7), the name 'Buddha' (Βουδδά) was an 'Assyrianism' (κατὰ τὴν τῶν Ἀσσυρίων γλῶτταν). It is unclear what background Epiphanius meant to convey by his linguistic gloss.

300. Given to him by whom? Scopello suggests the name was granted him during the course of a theophany ("Vie de Mani," 219).

301. *Acta Archelai* 63.2 (ed. Beeson, 91); translation quoted from Vermes, *Acta Archelai*, 142.

302. For a suggestive roster featuring a series of 'miraculous births' and 'angelic nurturings,' see the Coptic *Apoc. Adam* (NHC V, 5) 77.18–83.4. Dio Chrysostom (*Borysthenitica Or.* 36.40) states that Zoroaster sequestered himself 'on a mountain' prior to promulgating his religious message; a similar tradition is found in the thirteenth-century Muslim geographer Qazwīnī: see A. V. Williams Jackson, *Zoroaster: The Prophet of Ancient Iran* (New York, 1899; repr., New York: AMS Press, 1965), 236; also Gottheil, "References to Zoroaster," 40–42. Some Mandaean sources also attribute intriguingly analogous 'birth' and 'mountain' traditions to John the Baptist; see Lidzbarski, *Johannesbuch*, 2:115–18; E. S. Drower, *The Haran Gawaita and The Baptism of Hibil-Ziwa* (Città del Vaticano: Biblioteca Apostolica Vaticana, 1953), 5–6.

Why was Terebinthus on the roof? His demise squares with a pattern of mortality that is sometimes applied to disreputable practitioners of the occult arts in the biblically based literatures of late antiquity. Several scholars have rightly called attention to the obvious overlaps with the fate of the arch-heretic Simon Magus as it has been depicted in Christian legendry. There is also a talmudic tale set in Babylonia, the same locale where Terebinthus enacts his performance, which constructs or imports an identical type of demise for its 'heretic' (*mīn*) protagonist.[303] But perhaps the most intriguing possibility for interpreting the actions attributed to Terebinthus surfaces in later accounts describing a ruse successfully perpetrated by the mid-eighth-century Zoroastrian dissident Bihāfrīd. Bīrūnī has the following account:

> He (i.e., Bihāfrīd) acquired his authority by first disappearing to China for seven years. Then he returned bearing with him some choice items, among which was a large green shirt so fine and soft it could be folded up in a person's fist. He climbed up to the *nāwūs*[304] during the night and then came down from it early the next morning, and a man who was ploughing his field noticed him as he was approaching the ground. He told him that during his absence from them he had been in heaven, and that Paradise and the Fire had been shown to him. God had spoken to him, had clothed him in this shirt, and had lowered him down to earth at that very moment. The ploughman believed him, and he informed people that he had witnessed him descending from heaven. As a result, from the very beginning a large group of Zoroastrians became followers of what he was prophesying and proclaiming.[305]

Although the Simonian associations of 'a fall from a rooftop' are admittedly powerful, it also seems possible to wonder whether the author was positioning Terebinthus for some type of Bihāfrīd-like performance whereby he might mislead people into thinking that he had just descended from the sky.

While the name 'Terebinthus' resists a facile resolution,[306] the application of the title 'Buddha' signals the *Acta* author's recognition that the historical Mani

---

303. See *b. Ḥul.* 87a.

304. Arabic ناووس probably from Greek νάος. In Arabic literature, the word usually refers to a burial chamber or sarcophagus, and is there especially applied to Christian cemeteries (Dozy, *Supplément*, 2:737). Lane points out that it is also used in Egypt of the pyramids. Its unusual presence in this text is due to a conflation of two originally distinct stories about the mysterious disappearance of Bihāfrīd. According to one tale, he hid in a mausoleum; according to another, he traveled to China.

305. Bīrūnī, *Āthār* (ed. Sachau), 210.11-16. It has been noticed that Bihāfrīd here essentially reproduces a 'stunt' associated with the hagiographic vita of Zoroaster. See Marijan Molé, "Le problème des sectes zoroastriennes dans les livres pehlevis," *Oriens* 13 (1960–61): 23.

306. The Bible frequently associates the sacred tree often rendered as 'terebinth' (Hebrew אלון, אלה) with idolatrous; i.e., 'pagan' shrines or rites. In light of the eventual fate of Terebinthus ('cast down' from a roof-top), one might also compare the language of the Greek versions of Isa 1:30; 6:13.

actually utilized linguistic markers and perhaps even teachings that were associated with the earlier Indian sage.[307] Mani expressly included 'Buddha' among his approved prophetic forebears, situating him within a sequential line of true 'apostles of Light' beginning with the biblical Adam and continuing through '... Bu]ddha to the east, and Aurentes (**ⲁⲩⲣⲉⲛⲧⲏⲥ**), and the other ... who were sent to the orient; from the advent of Buddha (**ⲃⲟⲩⲇⲇⲁⲥ**) and Aurentes up to the advent of Zarathustra to Persia ....'[308] This prophetological chain, familiar to us from a number of authentic and hostile sources, continued chronologically with references to Jesus, Paul, possibly a pair of 'righteous ones,'[309] and then Mani himself as the final terrestrial manifestation of the Living Paraclete. Other lists sometimes reverse the sequential ordering of the Buddha and Zoroaster, but it is unlikely that this represents a revision or 'correction' of what was perceived to be an earlier erroneous listing.[310] It seems obvious from this list of predecessors that Mani possessed more than a superficial appreciation for the important role played by the Buddha and the subsequent spread of Buddhism in the East. Such knowledge should not be deemed surprising: a sporadic but constant flow of diplomats, adventurers, and merchants had moved between India and the Mediterranean

---

307. Bevan, "Manichaeism," *ERE* 8:396: 'The assertion that Terebinthus took the name of Budda seems to be a confused reminiscence of the fact that Mānī represented the Indian Buddha as one of a series of prophets who had preceded him.' For recent discussions of possible Buddhist influences upon Mani and nascent Manichaeism, see David A. Scott, "Manichaean Views of Buddhism," *History of Religions* 25 (1985): 99–115; Lieu, *Manichaeism*², 72–75.

308. Coptic *Keph.* 12.15–18; translation quoted from Gardner-Lieu, *Manichaean Texts*, 263. This section of the *Kephalaia* (subtitled 'about his coming to the world' [9.15]) is almost certainly based on information contained in Mani's *Shābuhragān* which according to Bīrūnī featured an identically named 'chapter' (see Chapter Three below). The reference to 'Aurentes' remains somewhat enigmatic; most scholars view it as a transcription of Sanskrit *arha(n)t*, a term which designates a Buddhist 'saint.' See the references supplied by Werner Sundermann, "Manichaean Traditions on the Date of the Historical Buddha," in *The Dating of the Historical Buddha/Die Datierung des historischen Buddha* (ed. Heinz Bechert; 3 vols.; Göttingen: Vandenhoeck and Ruprecht, 1991), 1:430 n.28; Prods Oktor Skjærvø, "Venus and the Buddha, or How Many Steps to Nirvana? Some Buddhist Elements in Manichaean Literature," in *Iranian and Indo-European Studies: Memorial Volume of Otakar Klíma* (ed. Petr Vavroušek; Praha: Enigma Corporation, 1994), 248; Nicholas Sims-Williams, "*Aurentēs*," in *Studia Manichaica: IV. Internationaler Kongress* (ed. Emmerick, Sundermann, and Zieme), 560–63. For a variant rendering of this same passage in the Dublin codex of the Coptic *Kephalaia*, see David Scott, "Manichaeism in Bactria: Political Patterns and East-West Paradigms," *Journal of Asian History* 41 (2007): 113.

309. Coptic *Keph.* 13.30–35, where it is clear more than one figure is envisioned. If they are two in number, Marcion and Bardaiṣan are possible candidates: see Schmidt-Polotsky, *Ein Mani-Fund*, 61.

310. As argued by Sundermann, "Manichaean Traditions," 431–35.

world since the time of Alexander.[311] During Mani's childhood an embassy from India to the emperor Elagabalus (217–222 CE) was met by the Aramaean philosopher Bardaiṣan in probably either Edessa or Ḥarrān: this alleged 'teacher of Mani' wrote a book about his encounter which unfortunately no longer survives, but it was referenced by Porphyry and Jerome and briefly excerpted by Stobaeus, and it is evident from the fragment which the latter anthologist quotes that Bardaiṣan devoted some space to a discussion of the different brands of religiosity represented among the foreign visitors.[312] It is highly likely that Mani was conversant with Bardaiṣan's treatise, and should 'the passage to India' motif featured in the various representations of his *vita* be trustworthy, Mani would have further augmented his derivative knowledge of Buddhist teachings and fabulation during his initial evangelistic travels through and beyond the eastern boundaries of the Sasanian realm. Hence the *Acta* provides important evidence for an early western association of the 'heresy' of Mani with the exotic doctrines of the Orient, thereby opening it to polemical condemnation as a 'deviant' form of 'Christianity.'

2. The proper name 'Mani' is actually a later self-designation; his original name was Cubricius (or an orthographic variant thereof).

Only those accounts which repeat the *Acta Archelai* legend are familiar with the charge that "Mani' was not the Babylonian prophet's original cognomen. This motif obviously mimics the pattern set by his predecessor Terebinthus when the latter undertook his fraudulent campaign to market himself as a purveyor of celestial mysteries, and thus it serves to reinforce the theme of 'unoriginality' that was emphasized above. A change of identity also can be represented as a deceptive attempt to conceal the base social origin of the heretic: 'he called himself Mani (Μάνην) instead of Cubricus (Κουβρίκου) to negate the shame of slavery's name.'[313] 'Cubricius' (or its variant spellings) exhibits no obvious symbolic etymologies or unflattering connotations and its rhetorical import, apart from exposing Mani's servile origin, remains unclear.[314] Its occurrence in later reports about the life and teachings of Mani is an incontrovertible sign of dependence upon the *Acta* or one of its derivatives.

3. He is originally a slave who was purchased as a young boy by the widowed heiress of Scythianus, et al. She oversees his primary education, but soon dies herself.

311. For a useful summary of these contacts coupled with further references, see Garth Fowden, *Empire to Commonwealth: Consequences of Monotheism in Late Antiquity* (Princeton: Princeton University Press, 1993), 82–85. See also David A. Scott, "Christian Responses to Buddhism in Pre-Medieval Times," *Numen* 32 (1985): 88–91; Grant Parker, *The Making of Roman India* (Cambridge: Cambridge University Press, 2008).

312. For the quotations from these sources, see H. J. W. Drijvers, *Bardaiṣan of Edessa* (Assen: Van Gorcum, 1966), 173–76.

313. Cyril of Jerusalem, *Catecheses ad illuminandos* 6.24.

314. Note especially the remarks of Puech, *Le manichéisme*, 25; 108–109 n.73.

The notion that Mani grew up as a slave is a transparent polemical assault against the Manichaean claim that its founder could boast of a royal lineage.[315] According to the genealogical data preserved in the section devoted to Manichaeism in the *Fihrist* of the tenth-century encyclopaedist Ibn al-Nadīm, Mani's father stemmed from a prominent Parthian family, and his mother was related to the Arsacid family who ruled Persia prior to the advent of the Sasanian state.[316] The so-called Chinese *Compendium*, a synopsis of Manichaean teachings prepared for the purpose of persuading Chinese authorities to extend religious toleration to Manichaeans living under their rule in the early eighth century, similarly depicts 'Mani the Buddha of Light' as having been born 'in the country of Su-lin (i.e., Babylonia) at the royal palace of Pa-ti (i.e., Pattikios) by his wife Man-yen (i.e., Maryam) of the house Chin-sa-chien (i.e., Kamsar[a]gān, a branch of the Arsacid family).'[317] The Chinese *Compendium* in fact makes it clear that eastern advocates for the spread of the Manichaean message consciously sought to model the course of Mani's earthly career after that of illustrious oriental predecessors like Zoroaster, Lao-tzu,[318] and the Buddha. Accordingly Mani's *vita* was invested with certain details that were familiar to them from the extant legendary narratives about the birth and upbringing of the Buddha. Mani, for example, becomes the product of a virginal conception and his mother gives birth to him through her chest,[319] singular attributes which were almost certainly borrowed from the Buddha birth-narratives popularized by parascriptural works like the *Buddhacarita* and the *Lalitavistara*. Since the *Acta*'s Terebinthus/Buddos already mouths an analogous parthenogenetic claim,[320] it is possible that the legend of the Buddha's miraculous conception and unusual birth was already familiar to fourth-century western writers,[321] perhaps due in part to an early and deliberate Manichaean exploitation of this motif in tandem with certain gospel accounts of the conception and birth of Jesus.[322] While it is widely accepted by modern scholars

315. Puech, *Le manichéisme*, 36; Scopello, "Vie de Mani," 223; idem, "Hégémonius," 541.

316. Ibn al-Nadīm, *Fihrist* (*apud* Flügel, *Mani*, 49.1–3); note also Flügel, *Mani*, 119–20.

317. Haloun-Henning, "Compendium," 190–91; cf. also Henning, "Book of the Giants," 52 n.4.

318. For this identification, see the references supplied in Samuel N. C. Lieu, *Manichaeism in Central Asia and China* (NHMS 45; Leiden: Brill, 1998), 102–103, 111–15, 133, 165–67, 183, 194–95.

319. Haloun-Henning, "Compendium," 191.

320. *Acta Archelai* 63.2 (ed. Beeson, 91).

321. E.g., the slightly later Jerome, *Contra Jovianus* 1.42 knows the legend about Buddha being born 'through the side of a virgin.' See Scott, "Christian Responses," 90.

322. The *Buddhacarita* ('Acts of the Buddha') is a Sanskrit *vita* attributed to the second-century poet Aśvaghoṣa. Fragments of a later Manichaean translation of this work in Old Turkish (rendered in turn from Sogdian) have been recovered from central Asia; for an English translation, see Hans-Joachim Klimkeit, *Gnosis on the Silk Road: Gnostic Texts from Central Asia* (San Francisco: HarperSanFrancisco, 1993), 313–14; also Aloïs van Tongerloo, "The Buddha's First Encounter in a Manichaean Old Turkic Text," in *Il Manicheismo: Nuove prospettive della richerca: Dipartimento di studi asiatici Università*

that Manichaeans dwelling in Sogdiana are the most likely culprits in the literary adaptation and the eventual western diffusion of the traditional legends surrounding the birth and early life of the Buddha Śākyamuni in the guise of the tale of *Barlaam and Joasaph*,[323] it is less well known that it was scribes of Parthian and Sogdian ethnicity who were responsible for the initial translations of Buddhist scriptures into Chinese during the first two centuries of the Common Era.[324] One of the earliest of these translators, An Shih-kao, was allegedly a Parthian prince who surrendered his claim to the Arsacid throne in order to become a Buddhist monk,[325] a world-renouncing action which imitates the paradigmatic abandonment of his royal privileges by the historical Buddha and which curiously echoes the 'royal' genealogy that is awarded to Mani by Ibn al-Nadīm and the Chinese *Compendium*.

It therefore seems possible that the recurrent claims made about Mani's supposedly royal lineage might be rooted in hagiographic 'soil,' a fertile layer that encouraged and nourished the growth of a homologous blue-blooded profile for its prophetological heroes. By the same token, polemical attacks launched from outside the community against representations of this sort strive to blacken the reputations of these purported 'princes' by stressing their supposedly ignoble or base social origins, a verbal strategy of denigration that simply responds to the public 'portrait' cultivated by advocates and supporters, but which does not necessarily reflect actual biographical circumstances. One detects, for example, an analogous dialectical process of hagiographic enhancement and class-rooted disparagement in the lush growth of messianic legendry surrounding the cruel fate of the mid-eighth-century spearhead of the 'Abbāsid revolt against the Umayyad caliphate, the Khurāsānian general Abū Muslim.[326] It was thanks in large part to

---

degli studi di Napoli "L'Orientale" Napoli, 2–8 settembre 2001 (Manichaean Studies 5; ed. Aloïs van Tongerloo and Luigi Cirillo; Turnhout: Brepols, 2005), 385–96. Wassilios Klein has recently made a similar point about western knowledge of Buddhist legends; see his "The Epic *Buddhacarita* by Aśvaghoṣa and its Significance for the 'Life of Mani'," in *Il Manicheismo* (ed. van Tongerloo and Cirillo), 223–32.

323. See Prosper Alfaric, "La vie chrétienne du Bouddha," *Journal asiatique* 10, 11th ser. (1917): 269–88; also Werner Sundermann, "Bodhisattva," *EncIr* 2:318, who supplies the latest references.

324. For detailed descriptions of this enterprise, see especially Kōgen Mizuno, *Buddhist Sutras: Origin, Development, Transmission* (Tokyo: Kōsei Publishing Co., 1982), 41–76; Richard C. Foltz, *Religions of the Silk Road: Overland Trade and Cultural Exchange from Antiquity to the Fifteenth Century* (New York: St. Martin's Press, 1999), 37–59. Note also the important observations of Jan Nattier, "Church Language and Vernacular Language in Central Asian Buddhism," *Numen* 37 (1990): 202–204; Ronald E. Emmerick, "Buddhism among Iranian Peoples I: In Pre-Islamic Times," *EncIr* 2:492–96.

325. Mizuno, *Buddhist Sutras*, 45; Foltz, *Religions*, 50; Lieu, *Manichaeism*², 225.

326. For summary discussions of this figure, see Sabatino Moscati, "Abū Muslim," *EI*² 1:141; Ğ. Ḥ. Yūsofī, "Abu Moslem Ḵorāsānī," *EncIr* 1:341–44. A more detailed examination is provided by Bertold Spuler, *Iran in früh-islamischer Zeit: Politik, Kultur, Verwaltung und öffentliches Leben zwischen der arabischen und der seldschukischen Eroberung, 633 bis*

the latter's effective military and administrative skills that the ʿAbbāsid cause was able to achieve victory and stabilize its gains in the formation of a new imperial government, but tragically it was jealousy of the potentially disruptive effect of these same talents that fueled the suspicions of his erstwhile collaborators and sealed his fate. Summoned by the second ʿAbbāsid caliph al-Manṣūr to an audience in Kūfa early in the year 755, the unwitting Abū Muslim was set upon by assassins and treacherously murdered. For approximately a century following his sudden demise, a number of Persianate resistance movements arose which denied his death, asserted his occlusion, proclaimed his status as prophet and *imām*, or anticipated his return as a type of 'messiah' at a future date.[327] Grandiose conflicting claims were advanced about his genealogy and class origins: some authorities viewed him as akin to the ʿAbbāsid family, while others made him a descendant of ʿAlī, and still others linked him with prominent officials in the displaced Sasanian court. On the other hand, some less flattering traditions regarding his social position were also in circulation, such as the charge that he was 'a slave of Persian origin.'[328] We thus witness a recurring literary pattern, one that is probably folkloric in origin,[329] in the competing narrative depictions of the kinship ties and social background of popular religious heroes like a Mani or an Abū Muslim. This ultimately rhetorical feature possesses obvious implications for sifting out historical data from the posited claims about Mani's 'family' background.

1055 (Wiesbaden: Franz Steiner Verlag, 1952), 39–49; Jacob Lassner, "Abū Muslim al-Khurāsānī: The Emergence of a Secret Agent from Kurāsān, Irāq, or Was It Iṣfahān?," *JAOS* 104 (1984): 165–75; idem, *Islamic Revolution and Historical Memory: An Inquiry into the Art of ʿAbbāsid Apologetics* (AOS 66; New Haven, Conn.: American Oriental Society, 1986), 99–133.

327. See, for example, the discussion and references in W. Barthold and C. E. Bosworth, "Mā Warāʾ al-Nahr," *EI*[2] 5:855; Blochet, *Le messianisme*, 42–47; Browne, *Literary History*, 1:246–47; Elton L. Daniel, *The Political and Social History of Khurasan under Abbasid Rule, 747–820* (Minneapolis and Chicago: Bibliotheca Islamica, 1979), 125–47. William F. Tucker declares that the messianic status of Abū Muslim was 'the cardinal tenet' of the Khurramiyya, a collective name for these militant groups; see his *Mahdis and Millenarians: Shīʿite Extremists in Early Muslim Iraq* (Cambridge: Cambridge University Press, 2008), 111.

328. Cited by Moscati, "Abū Muslim," *EI*[2] 1:141. Another disparaging slur casts Abū Muslim as a 'saddle-maker'; see Israel Friedlaender, "Jewish-Arabic Studies," *Jewish Quarterly Review* n.s. 3 (1912): 282, ʿAbd al-Ḥusain Zarrīnkūb, "The Arab Conquest of Iran and its Aftermath," in *The Cambridge History of Iran, Volume 4: The Period from the Arab Invasion to the Saljuqs* (ed. R. N. Frye; Cambridge: Cambridge University Press, 1975), 54. Abū Muslim and his memory also come under attack in medieval Zoroastrian sources; see Touraj Daryaee, "Apocalypse Now: Zoroastrian Reflections on the Early Islamic Centuries," *Medieval Encounters* 4 (1998): 192–95.

329. Note the equivalent oscillation between the ranks of 'prince' and 'slave' or 'bastard' which surfaces during a synoptic reading of the hagiographic and polemical representations of the *vitae* of a Moses or of a Jesus.

4. After the death of the widow, 'Mani' comes into possession of her estate, which includes a small collection of unorthodox books authored by her ill-fated husband(s). Following a move to the Persian capital city (Ctesiphon?) and a long period of study, during which he supplements the books with 'old wives' tales'[330] and attempts to pass them off as his own compositions, he manages to win three disciples named Thomas, Addas, and Hermas.

A feature of Manichaeism which no informed critic in antiquity disputed was its emphatic scriptural fixation.[331] In addition to a strident appeal to the extant written records of what it termed the 'ancestral religions,'[332] a label which encoded a reference to social groups who preserved and transmitted earlier revelatory writings by authentic prophets like Seth, Enoch, Zoroaster, and Jesus, the Manichaean community also treasured and disseminated a small library of written works supposedly authored by Mani himself which encapsulated his distinctive teachings and doctrines.[333] The author of the *Acta* shows that he is familiar with the book culture fostered by Manichaeism and with the insider claim that its founder was likewise the recipient of divine revelations which he disseminated among the public in a written format. What is more, he shows that he knows the titular designations for at least a 'tetrateuch' of Manichaean writings.[334] The names he provides for these works—*Mysteriorum*, *Capitulorum*, *Euangelium*, and *Thesaurum*[335]—coincide with the titles of four books whose Manichaean provenance is well attested by other sources. Most of the lists which heresiologists supply of the literature produced and circulated among Manichaean communities mention three distinct works which Mani himself authored bearing the names 'Gospel' (=*Euangelium*), 'Mysteries' (=*Mysteriorum*), and 'Treasury' (=*Thesaurum*).[336] Moreover, Latin *Capitulorum* 'Chapters' (lit. 'Heads') clearly alludes to the important early Manichaean didactic collection of dialogues known as the *Kephalaia*, a lengthy work surviving in a two volume Coptic translation recovered in 1929 from Medinet Madi in the Egyptian Fayum.[337]

---

330. The phrase is *anilibus fabulis*. See *Acta Archelai* 64.5 (ed. Beeson, 93); Vermes, *Acta Archelai*, 144.

331. Note Puech, *Le manichéisme*, 66, where he terms Manichaeism 'une religion du Livre'; Jürgen Tubach, "Mani, der bibliophile Religionsstifter," in *Studia Manichaica: IV. Internationaler Kongress* (ed. Emmerick, Sundermann, and Zieme), 622–38.

332. Middle Persian *dyn 'y pyšyng'n*. See especially M 5794 I in Boyce, *Reader*, 29–30 §a; Gardner-Lieu, *Manichaean Texts*, 109, and 265–68 for the parallel in Coptic *Keph.* 370.16–375.15.

333. See Chapter Three below.

334. Scopello, "Hégémonius," 532.

335. *Acta Archelai* 62.6 (ed. Beeson, 91).

336. For further details, see Chapter Three below.

337. These two 'volumes' or codices are customarily referred to as the Berlin codex and the Dublin codex based upon their respective archival locations. The former bears the running title *The Kephalaia of the Teacher*, whereas the latter is labeled *The Kepha-*

It remains unclear when the category of 'written scripture' emerges as an essential vehicle of Mani's claim to religious authority. The surviving leaves of the *Cologne Mani Codex* are silent about authorial activity on Mani's part during the years immediately following his removal from the baptist sect, and it does not record their production prior to this rupture. Yet tradition holds that Mani presented Shāpūr I with a dedicatory copy of the work known as the *Shābuhragān* at the time of their initial encounter shortly after the ruler's sole accession to the throne in the spring of 242 CE.[338] There are moreover numerous references to books and scribes in the surviving accounts about the initial dissemination of the new religion within and beyond the borders of the Sasanian realm during Mani's lifetime. Extant fragments from an early narrative history of Mani's teaching activities (M 216c + M 1750) provocatively associate 'books of Light' (*nbyg'n rwšn*) with the mission of '[Pattikios] the teacher, Addā the bishop, [and M]ani the scribe to Rome.'[339] The same text states that they commenced their journey from Weh-Ardashīr (i.e., Ctesiphon), but there is unfortunately no way to determine at what point in Mani's career this mission was supposed to have taken place. Another text which may describe the same mission (M 2 I) portrays Mani dispatching to Addā in Rome a copy of his *Gospel* along with 'two other books' (*'ny dw nbyg*) and 'three scribes' (*s<u>h</u> dbyr*). Therein Addā is encouraged by Mani to prolong his mission and to act 'like a merchant who collects treasure';[340] as a result of this exhortation, Addā made copies of the scriptures which Mani sent him and used them to confront the other 'religions' which he encountered during his journey through the eastern Roman empire.[341] A Sogdian version of the same account names the *Treasure/y of Life* (*sm'ttyx'*) as one of the 'books' which 'Pattī the teacher ..., Addā the bishop, and Mani the abbott' take with them on this western trip.[342] Mani's initial missionary ventures to the eastern

laia of the Wisdom of My Lord Mani. In spite of this discrepancy, it is likely that the Dublin codex represents a continuation of the Berlin volume. See Wolf-Peter Funk, "The Reconstruction of the Manichaean *Kephalaia*," in *Emerging From Darkness: Studies in the Recovery of Manichaean Sources* (NHMS 43; ed. Paul Mirecki and Jason BeDuhn; Leiden: Brill, 1997), 143–59; Gardner-Lieu, *Manichaean Texts*, 38 n.58. Iain Gardner and Jason BeDuhn are now engaged in the preparation of an edition and translation of the Dublin codex.

338. For this dating, see Wiesehöfer, *Ancient Persia*, 288.

339. Andreas-Henning, "Mitteliranische Manichaica ... II," 301 n.2; Sundermann, *Texte kirchengeschichtlichen Inhalts*, 26; Asmussen, *Manichaean Literature*, 21; Klimkeit, *Gnosis*, 203.

340. This trope has received an exemplary study in Christelle Jullien and Florence Jullien, *Apôtres des confins: Processus missionnaires chrétiens dans l'empire iranien* (Res Orientales 15; Bures-sur-Yvette: Groupe pour l'Étude de la Civilisation du Moyen-Orient, 2002), 215–22.

341. Andreas-Henning, "Mitteliranische Manichaica ... II," 301–302; Boyce, *Reader*, 39–40 (§h); Asmussen, *Manichaean Literature*, 21; Klimkeit, *Gnosis*, 202. According to this text, the terminus of his mission was Alexandria.

342. Sundermann, *Texte kirchengeschichtlichen Inhalts*, 35-36; Klimkeit, *Gnosis*, 203.

parts of the Sasanian empire similarly feature the employment of scribal technologies and scriptural resources. One of the remarkable talents of ʻMār Ammō the teacher' is his prowess with Parthian script and language, and his judicious use of a passage from the *Treasure/y of Life* wins him and his entourage admittance to the eastern province of Kushān.[343] He is represented as being accompanied on his travels by a team of calligraphers and an illustrator. A later epistle to the same missionary (M 5815 II) by an unnamed correspondent speaks of sending him copies of Mani's *Book of Giants* and the *Ardahang*.[344] Archaeological evidence from the recent excavations of a late Roman era village at Kellis in Egypt also bears witness to the importance of translation and publication activities in the distribution of Manichaean scriptures among the populace.[345] It is thus apparent that a burgeoning Manichaean book culture must have played a crucial role in the public announcement and promulgation of the new teaching.

The notion that Mani had only altered and supplemented a system of dualist teachings which originally belonged to his teacher finds an intriguing parallel in the writings of the tenth-century Ismāʻīlī teacher Abū Ḥātim al-Rāzī. According to Abū Ḥātim, the prophetic revelation vouchsafed to the Iranian prophet Zoroaster underwent a profound corruption at the hands of his later disciples: as an authentic conduit for the mediation of divine truths, he should not be blamed for the later aberrations of his Magian adherents. These pernicious modifications were allegedly introduced by an individual named <Z>āraṭos ʻwho arose among the Magians after Zoroaster' and who was influenced by a disciple of Pythagoras who had immigrated to Persia.[346] Presumably the name ʻZāraṭos' reflects that of Zarādusht b. Khurrakān of Fasā, the enigmatic religious innovator sometimes associated with the notorious Zoroastrian reformer Mazdak.[347] A tangled web of assertions and claims, most of which are overstated, persistently amalgamate the purported aspirations, doctrines, and fates of Mani and Mazdak, and the

343. Andreas-Henning, "Mitteliranische Manichaica ... II," 302–306; Boyce, *Reader*, 40–41; Asmussen, *Manichaean Literature*, 21-22; Klimkeit, *Gnosis*, 203-204. Cf. also Sundermann, *Texte kirchengeschichtlichen Inhalts*, 27; 39–41.

344. Andreas-Henning, "Mitteliranische Manichaica ... III," 857–58; Boyce, *Reader*, 48–49 (§q); Asmussen, *Manichaean Literature*, 23; Klimkeit, *Gnosis*, 260.

345. See Gardner-Lieu, *Manichaean Texts*, 44–45.

346. Abū Ḥātim al-Rāzī, *Aʻlām al-nubuwwah (The Peaks of Prophecy)* (ed. Salah al-Sawy; Teheran: Imperial Iranian Academy of Philosophy, 1977), 146.1–5, with an emendation of وارطوس to زارطوس. See Henry Corbin, "From the Gnosis of Antiquity to Ismaili Gnosis," in idem, *Cyclical Time and Ismaili Gnosis* (London: Kegan Paul International, 1983), 190-91; Farhad Daftary, *The Ismāʻīlīs: Their History and Doctrines* (2nd ed.; Cambridge: Cambridge University Press, 2007), 227.

347. Ibn al-Nadīm terms him ʻthe elder Mazdak' to distinguish him from his sixth-century heir. See also Bedjan, *Acta martyrum*, 2:517.1–3; Yaʻqūbī, *Ta'rīkh* (ed. Houtsma), 1:185–86; Ṭabarī, *Ta'rīkh* (ed. de Goeje), 1/2:893–94; Molé, "Le problème," 19–21; Patricia Crone, "Kavād's Heresy and Mazdak's Revolt," *Iran* 29 (1991): 24. Further sources and discussion are provided in Chapter Five below.

present homology fits comfortably within that same pattern of heresiographic assimilation. The story recounted by Abū Ḥātim signals its indebtedness to the *Acta Archelai* complex of biographical themes by its combination of the motifs of Pythagorean heresy, intellectual dishonesty, and relocation to Persia.

The tradition that Mani began the public phase of his religious mission with the assistance of three named disciples is one that is also attested outside the tendentious orbit of the *Acta Archelai* invectives.[348] According to the *Cologne Mani Codex*, when Mani departed the baptist sect within which he was raised, he was accompanied by 'two youths from the baptists, [Simeo]n and Abzakyā, who had been my neighbors (πλη[σιόχω]ροι)'; soon, the young renegade and his two 'helpers' (συνερ[γοί]) were joined by his father Pattikios.[349] The identical tradition reappears in the *Fihrist* of Ibn al-Nadīm.[350] The names 'Pattikios' and 'Abzakyā' (or obvious permutations of these same consonant clusters) recur in a number of sources which pertain to the early missionary journeys of Mani's disciples,[351] whereas the name 'Simeon' or its analogues is otherwise unattested.[352] The *Acta Archelai* trajectory however identifies the three named disciples as Adda(s), Thomas, and Herm(ei)as: the subsequent witnesses to this stream of tradition in Syriac and Christian Arabic continue to retain recognizable forms of these three cognomens.[353]

It has been noticed that several of the names of Mani's earliest missionaries or closest disciples are congruent with those that are borne by some of the initial 'orthodox' Christian evangelists of the East.[354] Henning has proposed that

348. *Contra* F. Forrester Church and Gedaliahu G. Stroumsa, "Mani's Disciple Thomas and the Psalms of Thomas," *Vigiliae Christianae* 34 (1980): 48.

349. *CMC* 106.16-19; 111.5–8.

350. Flügel, *Mani*, 51.7–8 (see above). It is on the basis of the *Fihrist* report that the name 'Simeon' has been restored in the *CMC* lacuna.

351. For Pattikios, see the Middle Iranian texts cited above. Abzakyā (and Addai) were exposed as early Manichaean agents in the northern city of Kirkūk (Bedjan, *Acta martyrum*, 2:512.11–14). He also may appear in the company of Sethel in a missionary journey to the so-called 'Tower of Abiran' in the Roman province of Arabia; see Nils Arne Pedersen, "A Manichaean Historical Text," *Zeitschrift für Papyrologie und Epigraphik* 119 (1997): 193–201.

352. The name 'Simeon' or 'Simon' may betray a typological brush: both Jesus and Elchasai have a prominent successor who bears this name.

353. *Acta Archelai* 13.4 = Epiphanius, *Panarion* 66.31 (ed. Beeson, 22); *Acta Archelai* 64.6 (ed. Beeson, 93). See also Epiphanius, *Panarion* 66.5; 66.12; Cyril of Jerusalem, *Catecheses ad illuminandos* 6.31; Theodoret, *Haereticarum fabularum compendium* 1.26; *Chronicon Maroniticum* (ed. Brooks), 59.29–60.2, and cf. Michael Syrus, *Chronicle* (ed. Chabot), 4:117.41-118.1; Agapius of Mabbug, *Kitāb al-Unvān* (ed. Vasiliev), 533; *Chronicon Seertensis* (ed. Scher), 227. See especially Church-Stroumsa, "Mani's Disciple Thomas," 47–49.

354. Han J. W. Drijvers, "Jews and Christians at Edessa," *Journal of Jewish Studies* 36 (1985): 91; idem, "Early Syriac Christianity," 164–65, 171–72; de Blois, "[Review of *Atti*]," 441-42; Jullien-Jullien, *Apôtres des confins*, 77–78.

the curious tradition that Mani originally held a prominent office in the Christian ecclesiastical hierarchy before 'defecting' from the Church reflects an early confusion of the name of the heresiarch with that of the shadowy Mār Mārī, a likely legendary saint whom the Church of the East (i.e., Nestorian Christians) promoted as the apostle responsible for the christianization of Mesopotamia and the establishment of the seat of its catholicus at Seleucia/Ctesiphon.[355] Complicating that proposal, however, is the absence of Mārī's name among the rosters of Mani's collaborators in those west Syrian texts which arguably should have endorsed such a slur (*Chronicon Maroniticum*, Agapius, Michael Syrus) coupled with its puzzling presence within the type of source that should have rejected such a slur; namely, in the Nestorian *Chronicon Seertensis*! Prominent associates in Mār Mārī's labors include Addai, Thomas, and Pāpā, each of whom is connected with a particular geographical region or sphere of operation wherein he founds churches and makes converts. According to the Mār Mārī legend, Addai is identical with the figure bearing the same name in the infamous *Doctrina Addai*,[356] the Christian missionary who was reportedly dispatched by Judas Thomas from Jerusalem to Edessa after the crucifixion of Jesus and who successfully introduced into Mesopotamia a brand of Christianity associated with the closest disciples of Jesus many generations prior to the birth of corrupting heresiarchs like Marcion, Bardaiṣan, and Mani. The apologetic interests of such a tale are patently obvious. Mārī is associated with Addai in his evangelistic work in Edessa, and is eventually sent out by the latter as an authorized bearer of the 'authentic' apostolic gospel to Babylonia and southern Mesopotamia. Pāpā becomes the successor of Mārī and builds upon his predecessor's legacy upon the latter's demise.

It is indeed intriguing that there are so many overlaps in nomenclature among the famous 'Christian' teachers of the east, regardless of their alleged doctrinal sympathies and affiliations. According to the fourth-century exposition of Manichaeism authored by the philosopher Alexander of Lycopolis, emissaries named 'Papos' and 'Thomas' were the first representatives of Mani to reach Egypt.[357] As we have already seen above, a figure known as 'Addā the bishop' is active in the spreading of the Manichaean message within the Roman empire. He is elsewhere the companion of Mani himself when the latter is represented as having to flee the Persian court due to his ineffective ministrations as a royal physician.[358] The

355. Henning, "Zwei Fehler," 84–86. Henning viewed the confusion as orthographic in origin, whereas later scholars see a vicious polemic at work. For the probable fictionality of Mār Mārī, see Rubens Duval, *La littérature syriaque* (3rd ed.; Paris: Librairie Victor Lecoffre, 1907), 108–11; also Christelle Jullien and Florence Jullien, "Les *Actes de Mār Mārī*: Une figure apocryphe au service de l'unité communautaire," *Apocrypha* 10 (1999): 177–94. His historicity has recently been defended by Harrak, *Acts of Mār Mārī*, esp. xxxii-xxxvi.

356. George Howard, *The Teaching of Addai* (Chico, Calif.: Scholars Press, 1981).

357. Augustus Brinkmann, ed., *Alexandri Lycopolitani contra Manichaei opinions disputatio* (Lipsiae: B. G. Teubner, 1895), 4.16–19.

358. Bedjan, *Acta martyrum*, 3:463.4–5: 'Then Mānī fled to the West along with his disciple Addai.'

figure of 'Thomas,' aspects of the legendry growing up around that name, and the writings attributed to or linked to his name have a number of analogues in Manichaean myth and history:[359] it is even possible that the popular biographical motif of Mani's 'passage to India'[360] is ultimately modeled on the missionary journey traditionally ascribed to Jesus's disciple and hagiographically narrated in the apocryphal *Acts of Thomas*. As for Herm[ei]as, there is nothing either within or outside of Manichaean literature that permits us to say anything further about this purported disciple.[361]

5. He dispatches these disciples abroad in the hope of gaining further adherents for his cause, but this scheme fails miserably. He then feigns an adoption of Christianity and begins to attract notice. He claims to be the Paraclete who was predicted by Jesus in the Gospel of John and deceptively models his image and message upon those of Jesus.

According to the *Acta*, Mani is initially unsuccessful in the wider marketing of his plagiarized teachings, and his fortunes do not turn until he is informed by his disciples of the success stories they witnessed among Christian missionaries. Mani therefore disguises himself as a Christian teacher, cloaking his absurdities within a veil of deceit and mystery. The notion that he deliberately mimicked the example of Jesus by gathering twelve disciples around himself goes back to the pre-*Acta* portrait of Mani's activities that is supplied by Eusebius during the first half of the fourth century in his *Historia ecclesiastica*. We read therein: '[Mani] attempted to pose as Christ: at one time giving out that he was the Paraclete ... at another time choosing, as Christ did, twelve disciples as associates in his newfangled system.'[362] This alternate depiction of the number of Mani's apostolic associates (i.e., an inner circle of twelve) is one that recurs even among those

359. See the note on Thomas appended to the translation of the *Chronicon Maroniticum* supplied above. Add to that roster the important observations of Paul-Hubert Poirier, "Les *Actes de Thomas* et le manichéisme," *Apocrypha* 9 (1998): 263–90; Jullien-Jullien, *Apôtres des confins*, 95–97. It should be noted that the apocryphal *Gospel of Thomas* is sometimes assigned to Mani's disciple Thomas; see Cyril of Jerusalem, *Catecheses ad illuminandos* 6.31; a Byzantine scholion on *Codex Iustinianus* 1.5.21 (quoted and translated by Lieu, *Manichaeism in Central Asia*, 126); the so-called 'long' Greek abjuration formula (*apud* Adam, *Texte*^{2}, 101 lines 154–55).

360. The 'passage to India' motif: (1) authentic Manichaean sources locate this journey prior to Mani's initial audience with Shāpūr and characterize it as voluntary; (2) Ibn al-Nadīm says that Shāpūr granted Mani permission to go there during their initial audience; (3) *Acta Archelai* and its epigones say that Mani sent others (namely, Thomas) to India; (4) Ya'qūbī says that Mani 'escaped' from Shāpūr and fled to India, while Bīrūnī and Marwazī hold that Mani was banished by Shāpūr from Persia, and hence he made his way to India.

361. Note Church-Stroumsa, "Mani's Disciple Thomas," 50.

362. Eusebius, *Historia ecclesiastica* 7.31.1. See Eusebius, *The Ecclesiastical History* (LCL; 2 vols.; trans. Kirsopp Lake and J. E. L. Oulton; repr., Cambridge, Mass.: Harvard University Press, 1994), 2:226–27

heresiologists who reproduce the scheme featuring three named disciples that was popularized by the *Acta Archelai*.[363]

An interesting difference emerges between the way the *Acta* reconstructs Mani's career and the way most of its imitators represent his vita. For the *Acta Archelai*, Mani is essentially a 'pagan' teacher who passes himself off as 'Christian' only after his initial efforts to win widespread recognition as a religious leader have failed: jealousy and opportunism fuel his worldly ambitions.[364] However, for many of the heirs of the *Acta*, Mani begins his public life as a Christian and often attains a church office such as that of priest or even bishop. His failure to garner wider recognition or prestige within the Church then pushes him toward a self-declared identification with Christ and/or the Paraclete and prompts his delusional parody of what the sources hold to be 'orthodox' teachings.[365] Both of these distinct heresiological trajectories overlap in different ways with Manichaean writings, where Mani is invariably portrayed as a Christian emissary intent on restoring the authentic gospel teachings which the early generations of disciples had corrupted.

A key component of Mani's supposedly revamped message invokes his widely decried claim to be the fulfillment of a scriptural prophecy envisioning the future advent of an authoritative figure who will explain the teachings and complete the mission of an earlier prophet or teacher. His own suitability as a candidate for this sort of status is already presaged in the *Cologne Mani Codex*, wherein his fellow baptist sectarians argue with him and debate among themselves about his possible 'messianic' significance (85.13–88.15). Some of them apply to Mani an oracle 'which our teac[hers prop]hesied, saying: "a certain young man will a[rise] from our midst, come forw[ard] as a new [teach]er, and overturn our entire doctrine ..."' (*CMC* 86.17–87.2).[366] Others on the basis of his insights were willing to accord him recognition 'as a prophet and a teacher ... a Living Word (ζῶν λόγος) is proclaimed through him;[367] let us make him a teacher of our doctrine' (*CMC* 86.1–9). The apparently historical furor surrounding Mani's appropriation of the title 'Paraclete' underscores the importance of the issue for recovering his self-understanding of his mission and reconstituting the way that he wished to be perceived by his followers.

363. Theodoret, *Haereticarum fabularum compendium* 1.26; Augustine, *de Haeresibus* 46.16 (for this source, see Adam, *Texte*², 69–70; Gardner-Lieu, *Manichaean Texts*, 190); *Chronicon Maroniticum* (ed. Brooks), 60.7; Agapius of Mabbug, *Kitāb al-Unvān* (ed. Vasiliev), 533–34; *Chronicon Seertensis* (ed. Scher), 226; Michael Syrus, *Chronicle* (ed. Chabot), 4:118.5–6.

364. A similar reading of Mani's religious identity is found in Theodore bar Konai's *Scholion*.

365. This latter model coheres with a popular heresiological formula that traces a heresiarch's deviance from orthodoxy to frustrated ambition.

366. This oracle has been characterized as a citation from 'eine alchasaitische Apokalypse'; see Ludwig Koenen and Cornelia Römer, eds., *Der Kölner Mani-Kodex: Über das Werden seines Leibes: Kritische Edition* (Opladen: Westdeutscher Verlag, 1988), 61 n.2.

367. Cf. Acts 7:38; 1 Pet 1:23.

In the farewell discourse to his disciples that is presented in the canonical Gospel of John, Jesus promises the future advent on earth of the Paraclete (ὁ παράκλητος), an enigmatic entity who would 'remind you of all the things I have said to you' (14:26) and continue his mission of condemning wrongdoing and exhorting 'righteousness' (15:26; 16:7–11). Although the texts of the biblical passages already define this entity as equivalent to 'the spirit of truth' (14:17; 15:26; 16:13) or even 'the holy spirit' (14:26), it is clear that these identifications are *ex post facto* scribal glosses which seek to circumvent claims that Jesus envisioned the advent of another prophetic figure who would continue or perhaps even complete his earthly mission. Mani famously saw himself as the fulfillment of this particular oracle,[368] and he was not the only post-Johannine biblically inspired community leader who would exploit its interpretative possibilities.

Werner Sundermann has shown that the Manichaean concept of the Paraclete as it is exhibited in western sources such as the Coptic *Kephalaia* and the *Cologne Mani Codex* is also visible in Middle Iranian Manichaean texts emanating from central Asia, thus confirming the likely centrality of this notion for the earliest strata of tradition.[369] Interestingly, the appropriation of the Christian title 'Paraclete' is mirrored in some eastern Manichaean sources by Mani's assumption of the designation 'Maitreya,' a name employed by Buddhists for the final manifestation of the Buddha in the present age.[370] It however remains unclear whether Mani or his adherents adopt the analogous Zoroastrian idea of the future savior figure of the 'Saoshyant' and view his third-century advent as a fulfillment of that role.[371] The so-called *Prophecy of Zardūsht* provides some suggestive testimony that this concept may have also played a role in Manichaean prophetology.[372]

6. Boastful too about his wonder-working abilities, he nevertheless fails to cure Shāpūr's son of a fatal illness. The king imprisons him, attempts to round up his followers, and forms plans to execute him. But before they can be actualized, Mani bribes his guards and effects an escape. It is during this time while Mani is a fugitive from justice that he has his fateful encounter with Archelaus. However, royal officers eventually catch up with him, recapture him, and bring him back to the king who then executes him.

368. See Coptic *Keph.* 14.4-10; 16.23–31; Eusebius, *Historia ecclesiastica* 7.31.1; as well as the numerous texts cited above.

369. Werner Sundermann, "Der Paraklet in der ostmanichäischen Überlieferung," in *Manichaean Studies* (ed. Bryder), 201–12.

370. M 42 and M 801 contain unambiguous declarations of this identity, including the notion that Mani fulfills a saying of the historical Buddha to that effect. For a recent discussion of these texts, see Scott, "Manichaeism in Bactria," 114–18.

371. This was negatively appraised by D. A. Scott, "Manichaean Responses to Zoroastrianism (Politico-Religious Controversies in Iran, Past to Present: 3)," *Religious Studies* 25 (1989): 456 n.1.

372. John C. Reeves, "Reconsidering the 'Prophecy of Zardūšt'," in *A Multiform Heritage: Studies on Early Judaism and Early Christianity in Honor of Robert A. Kraft*, ed. Benjamin G. Wright (Atlanta: Scholars Press, 1999), 167–82.

Both Manichaean and hostile witnesses represent Mani as a healer. When pressed by an anonymous king to identify himself, Mani supposedly replied: 'I am a physician (*bzyšk*) from the land of Bab[ylon] ....' and then on the reverse side of this same textual fragment gives a demonstration of his abilities by restoring the health of a maiden.[373] During his final fateful encounter with the Sasanian ruler Bahrām I,[374] Mani defends himself against his detractors by invoking his numerous successful healings and demon-expulsions. Even the Nestorian bishop Theodore bar Konai grudgingly concedes that Mani was 'familiar with the art of healing,' even if he immediately qualifies that remarkable admission with the charge that Mani accomplished his cures via sorcery.[375] The *Acta* and its literary epigones are more harshly critical of his purported medical talents, portraying them as thoroughly fraudulent and linked to a sense of false bravado: in other words, they provide another instance of his habitual deceit and opportunism. According to some of these sources, Mani exploits the severe illness of a royal family member in order to gain the favor of the Persian monarch. His failure to bring about a cure lands him instead in the royal dungeon.[376] A Christian source cited by Bīrūnī knows a version of this tradition,[377] although it assumes that Mani then perished in prison and does not speak (like the *Acta* and its satellites) of Mani's temporary escape from incarceration to Roman ruled lands.

Comparable farcical anecdotes about Mani's medical incompetence occur in Syriac martyrological accounts. These interestingly emplot their protagonist as an 'anti-Mani': their authors creatively reinscribe the settings and narrative movements which were undoubtedly familiar from the *Acta Archelai* legend and from authentic Manichaean hagiography in order to denigrate the heresiarch and celebrate the triumph of a self-defined Christian 'orthodoxy' in the Persian empire. The scene wherein the main narrative action transpires remains that of the Sasanian court of Shāpūr. Mani's audience with the king matches the profile that was promulgated by the *Acta*: he promises a miraculous healing, but in fact produces a more serious medical crisis. Mani is thoroughly discredited and eventually is executed by the enraged monarch. But then a new element is introduced by these martyrologies into the storyline: a Christian saint now comes to the rescue and repairs the damage effected by the heresiarch. Thanks to this timely

373. M 566 I in Sundermann, *Texte kirchengeschichtlichen Inhalts*, 23–24; see also Klimkeit, *Gnosis*, 208.

374. M 3 in Boyce, *Reader*, 44–45 §n; cf. Henning, "Mani's Last Journey," 951–52. Note also Vermes, *Acta Archelai*, 145–46 n.325.

375. Theodore bar Konai, *Scholion* (ed. Scher), 2:312.20–21.

376. *Acta Archelai* 64.7–65.7 (ed. Beeson, 93–94); Cyril of Jerusalem, *Catecheses ad illuminandos* 6.25–26; Socrates, *Historia ecclesiastica* 1.22; Theodoret, *Haereticarum fabularum compendium* 1.26; Michael Syrus, *Chronicle* (ed. Chabot), 4:119.3–8; Bar Hebraeus, *Historia compendiosa dynastiarum* (excerpted in Flügel, *Mani*, 332).

377. Bīrūnī, *Āthār* (ed. Sachau), 208.19–22. The Christian tradent is there identified as Jibrā'īl b. Nūḥ.

intervention, the Persian king gratefully endorses the saint's request for permission to propagate the gospel and expand Christian institutions within his realm. The ideological utility of this kind of legend for the regional legitimacy of the Church of the East is transparent. It must however not be overlooked that this reward was precisely the sort of boon that the 'hagiographic Mani' (i.e., the one promoted by his own followers) supposedly received during his initial audience with Shāpūr I!

In a curious narrative which bears the introductory rubric *Account of Mār Awgīn*,[378] we find for example the following story:

> Now two of King Shabūr's sons had fallen ill. One would cry out due to a demon, and as for the other, all of his limbs shriveled. The insane Mānī[379] thought that he could heal his two sons. When he initially approached the older (of the two)—the one whose limbs were shriveled—he treated him with incantations for two days, but the boy rapidly died. Then Mānī fled to the West along with his disciple Addai.[380]
>
> King Shabūr heard about this, and he sent for (and) apprehended him and sent him down to the city of Bēth Lapaṭ and incarcerated him in prison. Now that sorcerer concocted a plan with his disciples to throw himself from the wall (of the city) and escape. They promised the heretic and said to him: 'We will lay down garments for you at such-and such a place so that they will be beneath you.'
>
> When he arrived (at the spot) in the evening, he hastily glanced to see whether his disciples had done as they had told him, and lo, due to divine action a pack of dogs had assembled there, and his sight was hindered by the power of God so that he could not discern whether dogs or garments were present there. (This happened) so that he might be made an object of scorn just as his teacher Simon (Magus) was made an object of scorn in order to fulfill the word of the holy Mār Awgīn.[381] For Mānī thought to himself—'These are garments!'—and casting himself from the wall he fell down upon them. Highly disturbed, and because it was their custom (i.e., the Zoroastrians') to throw down corpses to them, the dogs attacked him and mauled his entire body. At daybreak they came and discovered him prostrate and torn apart by the dogs. Shabūr commanded them to strip off his skin, stuff it with straw, and hang it from the wall. He even became an object of derision and a laughing-stock among all of his disciples.[382]

---

378. See Puech, *Le manichéisme*, 109 n.75. Mār Awgīn is the alleged founder of Christian monasticism in the Sasanian realm. See J[érôme]. Labourt, *Le christianisme dans l'empire perse sous la dynastie sassanide (224–632)* (Paris: Librairie Victor Lecoffre, 1904), 302–15.

379. A calque reproducing the popular Greek pun.

380. Thus setting in motion the train of events which leads to his debate with Archelaus, the hero of the *Acta Archelai*. Mani's disciple Addai was indeed involved in the Manichaean mission to the West.

381. He had earlier predicted that God would deal with Mani the same way that he had dealt with Simon Magus; namely, to cast him down from a great height.

382. Bedjan, *Acta martyrum*, 3:462.17–464.3.

The denouement of this episode occurs in the related *Account of Mār Daniel the Physician:*[383]

> King Shabūr heard about the holy man Mār Awgīn who was dwelling among the mountains of 'Izla which were above Nisibis, for they said of him that he was a powerful man who could work miracles and produce signs. So he sent for him in order that he might come and heal two of his sons who were possessed by demons. Mānī the heretic—the 'vessel'[384] of Satan—had introduced these devils into them, and because of this (error) they stripped him of his skin, stuffed him with straw, and hung his corpse upon the (city) wall. Afterwards his carcass was (given) to the dogs in the same manner as that of the adulterous Jezebel.[385]
>
> When the holy saint Mār Awgīn came to Shabūr at Nisibis, the king told him about the affliction of his sons. Then that holy man, having put his trust in God, answered the king: 'My God can heal them!' After he stood and prayed over them, he expelled from them the demons which Mānī had introduced into them. When Shabūr saw that the boys had been freed from the power of Satan, he said to the holy saint Mār Awgīn: 'Ask of me and receive for yourself anything which you might seek!' The holy saint said to him: 'I ask for neither gold nor silver from you. Instead, grant my followers permission to travel throughout the land which you rule and to build (there) monasteries and convents.'[386]

Mār Awgīn thus undoes the mischief that Mani had wrought through his earlier inept treatment of the sons of Shāpūr. The grateful monarch in turn grants the saint's request to travel throughout the realm and found 'monasteries and convents,' centers which would serve as bases of support for later efforts to christianize the empire. Mār Awgīn's alleged success in fact mimes the favorable reception that was given to Mani by the Sasanian ruler in the extant Manichaean descriptions of their initial encounter.[387]

But perhaps the most fascinating example of this motif occurs in the the Syriac narrative about the Christian martyrs of Karkā de-Bēth Selōk; i.e., the modern

---

383. Bedjan, *Acta martyrum*, 3:493.14–494.12.

384. The familiar wordplay.

385. Cf. 1 Kgs 21:23; 2 Kgs 9:10, 33–37. But according to the *Account of Mār Awgīn* (see above), Mani's body had been mutilated by dogs prior to its flaying, stuffing, and exposure on the wall.

386. Another somewhat confused reference to this healing story is in E. A. Wallis Budge, *The Book of Governors: The Historia Monastica of Thomas Bishop of Margâ A.D. 840* (2 vols.; London: Kegan Paul, Trench, Trübner, 1893), 1:cxxix-cxxx. Given the present account's conscious framing as a 'counter-narrative' to Manichaean claims about the medical prowess of Mani, compare the healing miracle and ensuing dialogue between Mani and the governor of Ganazak presented in *CMC* 121.6–123.13. 'Ask from me anything you want,' the grateful governor offers, to which Mani replies: 'I have no need for any of your goods—neither gold nor silver. I ask only for a daily allowance of provisions for the brethren of the (Manichaean) community.' See also Scopello, "Vie de Mani," 229 n.101.

387. Compare the language of Ibn al-Nadīm, *Fihrist* (ed. Flügel), 51.16-52.10 (see above); Coptic *Keph.* 15.28–33.

city of Kirkūk in Iraqi Kurdistan. There we encounter the following notice about the public excitement attending the miracles performed by the Christian ascetic 'Aqablahā:

> News of his exploits spread and eventually reached Bahrām b. Shabūr, the king of Persia. Now he (the king) had a daughter who was being tormented by a foul demon. After he summoned the holy 'Aqablahā there, he laid (his) hand upon the girl and she was cured. He then petitioned the king not to destroy the (Christian) churches and to allow those already destroyed to be rebuilt. The king hearkened to him and permitted him to act as he wished.[388]

The Persian ruler in this account is not Shāpūr but his son Bahrām, the king historically responsible for the imprisonment and death of Mani. This nomenclatural departure from the traditional cast of characters popularized by the invective of the *Acta Archelai* does not appear to be accidental. According to that latter source, it was Mani's failure to cure the royal prince that eventually leads to his demise. The Christian saint's success in exorcising the royal princess—one who is the daughter of Mani's imperial nemesis—effectively juxtaposes the figures of Mani and 'Aqablahā as narrative symbols competing for the elusive prize of Christian hegemony in the Sasanian realm.[389]

388. Bedjan, *Acta martyrum*, 2:516.15–517.1. For another translation, see Georg Hoffmann, *Auszüge aus syrischen Akten persischer Märtyrer* (Leipzig, 1880; repr., Nendeln, Liechtenstein: Kraus Reprint Ltd., 1966), 49.

389. One may in fact view this literary juxtaposition as another instance of what Peter Brown has labeled 'the antithesis of saint and sorcerer,' a narrative articulation where 'saints positively needed sorcerers.' See his *The Making of Late Antiquity* (Cambridge, MA: Harvard University Press, 1978), 21–23, 60–62.

— 3 —

Fragments of Manichaean Scripture: A Classified Collection of Islamicate Testimonia

Manichaeism may well be the earliest example of what Islam will later term a 'people of the Book'; i.e., a scripturally based religious community. Both internal and external sources bear witness to the signal role played by a distinctive canon of authoritative writings in the rapid and widespread promulgation of Mani's teachings, and the modern archaeological investigation of recognizably Manichaean settlements or missionary outposts has uncovered abundant material evidence which points to book production and distribution as an important activity pursued therein. Given the slippery notion of just what constitutes 'scripture' among the various biblically grounded groups of the third century, it does not seem far-fetched to view Mani's authorial efforts as catalytic in the eventual determination of the physical content and conceptual boundaries of Jewish, Christian, and even Zoroastrian scripture.[1]

Diocletian's condemnation of the Manichaean infiltration of Egypt—the earliest western notice of this religion—is insightfully cognizant of the insidious part played by a written literature in the diffusion of their 'poison' among his provincial subjects: he orders that the Manichaean books be confiscated and publicly burnt.[2] The spurious biography of Mani embedded within the polemical

1. Note Roy Mottahedeh, *The Mantle of the Prophet: Religion and Politics in Iran* (new ed.; Oxford: Oneworld Publications, 2000), 159. For the possible role of Manichaeism in the textualization of the Avesta, see the sources cited by Jonathan P. Berkey, *The Formation of Islam: Religion and Society in the Near East, 600–1800* (Cambridge: Cambridge University Press, 2003), 28 n.60. See also the remarks of Manfred Hutter, "Manichaeism in Iran in the Fourth Century," in *Studia Manichaica: IV. Internationaler Kongress zum Manichäismus, Berlin, 14.–18. Juli 1997* (ed. Ronald E. Emmerick, Werner Sundermann, and Peter Zieme; Berlin: Akademie-Verlag, 2000), 313–15; Josef Wiesehöfer, *Ancient Persia from 550 BC to 650 AD* (trans. Azizeh Azodi; London and New York: I. B. Tauris, 2001), 200; Yaakov Elman, "Middle Persian Culture and Babylonian Sages: Accommodation and Resistance in the Shaping of Rabbinic Legal Tradition," in *The Cambridge Companion to the Talmud and Rabbinic Literature* (ed. Charlotte Elisheva Fonrobert and Martin S. Jaffee; Cambridge: Cambridge University Press, 2007), 167.

2. There is some debate regarding whether the edict should be dated to either 297 or

Acta Archelai associates its antagonist with four named writings (*Gospel*, *Secrets*, *Treasure/y*, and *Kephalaia*) whose titles actually correlate with those of genuine Manichaean works.[3] Brief citations from or allusions to the first three of these titles can be found in a variety of sources (see below), and a large portion of a Manichaean work in Coptic bearing the title *Kephalaia* was fortuitously recovered in the early twentieth century from the site of Medinet Madi in Egypt.[4] In spite of this subtle gesture by the Christian heresiographer toward historical verisimilitude, the *Acta* actually impugn Mani's authorial integrity by confiding that the books which Mani disseminated as his own had their origin in the blasphemous teachings of an itinerant Arab magician who fancied himself a devotee of the dualist systems ascribed to the Hellenic philosophers Pythagoras and Empedocles. In a war of dueling scriptures, Mani's are thereby derided as utterly fraudulent.

Despite having only a limited knowledge of the accusations leveled against Mani by works like the *Acta Archelai*, Muslim writers largely shared that Christian treatise's suspicion of his motives and integrity. His books, moreover, were like lethal weapons which undermined societal mores and norms. According to Bīrūnī, the infamous Muslim 'freethinker' Abū Bakr al-Rāzī explicitly 'endorsed the books of Mānī and his followers for circumventing religions, even Islam.'[5] And, in accord with what was first recommended by the emperor Diocletian, we sometimes read about a deliberate state-sanctioned destruction of Manichaean writings.

Catalogs of Manichaean scriptures are extant in a number of linguistic traditions, and despite the regional diversification of Manichaeism over the passage of many centuries, their rosters of titles are remarkably consistent.[6] Most of these lists specify a core collection of about a half a dozen or so works which Mani himself authored, supplemented with a more variable group of titles that appear to emanate from Manichaean teachers who belong among the early generations of

302 CE. For the Latin text, see Alfred Adam, ed., *Texte zum Manichäismus* (2nd ed.; Berlin: Walter de Gruyter, 1969), 82–83; an English translation and brief discussion are provided by Beate Dignas and Engelbert Winter, *Rome and Persia in Late Antiquity: Neighbours and Rivals* (Cambridge: Cambridge University Press, 2007), 216–19. Note also the remarks of Samuel N. C. Lieu, *Manichaeism in the Later Roman Empire and Medieval China* (2nd ed.; WUNT 63; Tübingen: J. C. B. Mohr, 1992), 121–25.

3. *Acta Archelai* 62.6 (ed. Beeson, 91). See the Syriac and Christian Arabic versions of this legend provided in Chapter 2 above.

4. Carl Schmidt and H. J. Polotsky, *Ein Mani-Fund in Ägypten: Originalschriften des Mani und seiner Schüler* (Berlin: Verlag der Akademie der Wissenschaften, 1933).

5. Bīrūnī, *Risālah lil-Bīrūnī fī fihrist kutub Muḥammad ibn Zakarīyyā al-Rāzī*, as published in S. H. Taqīzādeh and A. A. Šīrāzī, *Mānī va dīn-e-ū* (Teheran: Ānjuman-e Irānshināsī, 1335 AH/1956), 208 (§36). See also Sarah Stroumsa, *Freethinkers of Medieval Islam: Ibn al-Rāwandī, Abū Bakr al-Rāzī, and Their Impact on Islamic Thought* (Leiden: Brill, 1999), 105–106.

6. For a representative presentation and discussion, see John C. Reeves, *Jewish Lore in Manichaean Cosmogony: Studies in the Book of Giants Traditions* (Cincinnati, OH: Hebrew Union College Press, 1992), 9–19.

Mani's successors. There are also indications that an expanding library of doctrinal and liturgical tractates continued to be produced by community leaders well into the Islamicate period (see below). Converging testimonia from Christian and Muslim writers inform us that Mani wrote his scriptures in Aramaic,[7] the common language of the native, gnostic, Jewish, and Christian populaces of Mesopotamia during the centuries preceding the Islamic conquest—the only exception was the work known as the *Shābuhragān*, a treatise which according to tradition (and its title) was specially prepared in Persian for the edification of the Sasanian ruler Shāpūr I. This promotional strategy seems to have achieved its intended effect: as a result of his audience with Shāpūr, Mani secured imperial permission to propagate his teachings throughout Shāpūr's realm, and an important aspect of this missionary enterprise would be the dispatch of teams of scribes and translators both east and west to produce and distribute attractive editions of Mani's scriptures in the various languages and dialects of the Sasanian and ultimately Roman worlds.

The translation of Mani's writings into various regional and national vernaculars marks an important practical step in the popular promotion of scriptural religions in Near Eastern late antiquity, one that finds a logistical parallel in the gradual and ultimately irreversible transformation of the Indian Buddhist canon of scriptures from an oral Māghadī (an eastern Prakrit likely spoken by Buddha Śākyamuni) to the Pali, Gāndhārī, hybrid Sanskrit, Khotanese, Chinese, and Tibetan linguistic registers.[8] By contrast, Iranian Zoroastrianism places strict limitations upon the public dissemination of its scriptures,[9] and it is well known that Islam deems the Qur'ān to be inimitable apart from its original language of

7. *Acta Archelai* 40.5 (ed. Beeson, 59); Titus of Bostra, *Adversus Manichaeos* 1.14; Epiphanius, *Panarion* 66.13.3; Ibn al-Nadīm, *Fihrist* (in Gustav Flügel, *Mani: Seine Lehre und seine Schriften* (Leipzig, 1862; repr., Osnabrück: Biblio Verlag, 1969), 72.10–11): 'Mānī authored seven books, one of them in Persian, and six in Syriac (i.e., Aramaic), the language of Syria.' With regard to the dialect of Aramaic used by Mani, see especially Mark Lidzbarski, "Warum schrieb Mānī aramäisch?" *Orientalistische Literaturzeitung* 30 (1927): 913–17; Franz Rosenthal, *Die aramaistische Forschung seit Th. Nöldeke's Veröffentlichungen* (Leiden, 1939; repr., Leiden: Brill, 1964), 207–11, 222; Riccardo Contini, "Hypothèses sur l'araméen manichéen," *Annali di Ca' Foscari: Rivista della Facoltà di lingue e letterature straniere di Ca' Foscari dell'Università di Venezia* 34 (1995): 65–107.

8. On this process, see Kōgen Mizuno, *Buddhist Sutras: Origin, Development, Transmission* (Tokyo: Kōsei Publishing, 1982), 26–39; Jan Nattier, "Church Language and Vernacular Language in Central Asian Buddhism," *Numen* 37 (1990): 195–219. Note too that the early fifth-century Chinese pilgrim Faxian (Fa-hsien) encountered considerable difficulties during his quest in India for early Buddhist manuscripts. The tale of his journey is recounted in *The Travels of Fa-hsien (399–414 A.D.), or Record of the Buddhistic Kingdoms* (trans. H. A. Giles; Cambridge, 1923; repr., Westport, CT: Greenwood Press, 1981).

9. See the brief discussion with references in Shaul Shaked, *Dualism in Transformation: Varieties of Religion in Sasanian Iran* (London: School of Oriental and African Studies, 1994), 76–80.

expression.[10] Classical Judaism, unlike Christianity, exhibits a deep suspicion of the Greek and Aramaic translations of the Bible.[11] Should the tradition be historically accurate, it already shows that Mani himself authorized the manufacture of a translation—the *Shābuhragān*—in order to win the assent of the political establishment for his cause. Some of Mani's surviving epistles, provided they are genuine, also confirm the founder's concern that apostolic missions be furnished with copies of the scriptures and competent teams of scribes and translators. And as in Buddhism, where few if any indigenous language versions of the Buddha's teachings seem to have survived, so too the Manichaean impetus toward translation ironically insured the almost total loss of the Aramaic base texts from which the early scribes would have originally worked.[12] Contiguous pieces of Manichaean literature, some of which are quite extensive, are extant in Greek, Latin, Coptic, Middle Iranian, Old Turkish, and Chinese; only isolated words and phrases, some fragmentary lexical lists, and a limited number of possible citations or paraphrases in certain Syrian church fathers bear witness to the Aramaic substrate of the Manichaean scriptures.[13]

It is therefore of signal importance to note that a number of Muslim writers refer to the existence of or display some knowledge of the contents of Manichaean

---

10. The most recent treatment is that of Richard C. Martin, "Inimitability," *EncQur* 2:526–36.

11. Note *t. Meg.* 3.41; *b. Qidd.* 49a: 'R. Yehudah has said: One who translates a passage literally is a liar, and one who adds to its content is a blasphemer.' With regard to the ambivalent attitudes toward translation that are evidenced in rabbinic literature, see Moshe Simon-Shoshan, "The Tasks of the Translators: The Rabbis, the Septuagint, and the Cultural Politics of Translation," *Prooftexts* 27 (2007): 1–39. Note also the extensive collection of testimonia assembled by Abraham Wasserstein and David J. Wasserstein, *The Legend of the Septuagint: From Classical Antiquity to Today* (Cambridge: Cambridge University Press, 2006).

12. It remains unclear how long Mani's works survived in their original Aramaic dress. For a suggestive indication that they were still extant in that form at the end of the fifth century, see Lucas Van Rompay, "Bardaisan and Mani in Philoxenus of Mabbog's *Mēmrē Against Habib*," in *Syriac Polemics: Studies in Honour of Gerrit Jan Reinink* (OLA 170; ed. Wout Jac. Van Bekkum, Jan Willem Drijvers, and Alex C. Klugkist; Leuven: Peeters, 2007), 77–90.

13. For Manichaean Syriac fragments recovered from Egypt, see D. S. Margoliouth, "Notes on Syriac Papyrus Fragments from Oxyrhynchus," *Journal of Egyptian Archaeology* 2 (1915): 214–16, (Ms. Oxford Bodl. Syr. d 13, 14); W. E. Crum, "A 'Manichaean' Fragment from Egypt," *JRAS* (1919): 207–208, (Ms. Brit. Lib. Or. 6201 c); the foregoing were collected together and published by F. C. Burkitt, *The Religion of the Manichees* (Cambridge: The University Press, 1925), 111–19; note also Samuel N. C. Lieu, *Manichaeism in Mesopotamia and the Roman East* (RGRW 118; Leiden: Brill, 1994), 62–64. The excavations at Kellis have yielded some more samples; see Iain Gardner, ed., *Kellis Literary Texts: Volume 1* (Dakhleh Oasis Project Monograph No. 4; Oxford: Oxbow Books, 1996), 101–31, with an index of Syriac words on pp. 173–77; idem, *Kellis Literary Texts: Volume 2* (Dakhleh Oasis Project Monograph 15; Oxford: Oxbow Books, 2007), 136–37.

writings in the Islamicate world. Since almost none of these writers were conversant with Syriac or the languages of the daughter versions in which Manichaean texts circulated on the periphery of the Muslim Near East, it is virtually certain that they were reliant upon sources available to them in the Arabic language. It however remains unclear from precisely whom these translations originate or even at what stage in the growth and spread of the religion they were produced. There are some intriguing traditions that point to an initial exposition of Manichaean teachings to certain Arab rulers and tribes beginning in the second half of the third century at urban centers in Roman Arabia like Palmyra, Bostra, and al-Ḥīra; that is, at precisely the same time the first Manichaean missionaries were infiltrating Syria and Egypt. Moreover, the ethnic dimension of the *Acta Archelai*'s association of Mani's perfidy with an itinerant *Arab* merchant Scythianus should not fail to be noted.[14] If the usual evangelistic patterns pursued by Manichaean envoys were also followed in these cases, one might reasonably expect that direct translations of Manichaean books from Aramaic into Arabic were extant prior to the birth of Islam.[15]

On the other hand, reliable Muslim sources (Mas'ūdī, Bīrūnī) inform us that a few dissident intellectuals engaged in the promotion of heretical dualist (including Manichaean) writings among elite literate circles in Baghdad during the eighth and ninth centuries. Perhaps the most prominent of these alleged propagandists was the learned 'Abd Allāh Ibn al-Muqaffa',[16] a gifted translator and court official involved in the rendition of choice Pahlavi literary classics into Arabic, and probably the key person responsible for insuring the continued westward migration and acculturation of the popular Indian collection of animal fables known as the *Pañcatantra*. Another figure who may also have been involved in the textual commodification of Manichaean ideas and literature was the enigmatic Abū 'Īsā al-Warrāq,[17] an assiduous compiler of data about non-Muslim religions and philosophical schools who becomes the most frequently cited authority about Manichaeism by Muslim traditionists and heresiographers. A close reading of the testimonia preserved in Arabic does not conclusively resolve the source issue: while there are hints that some of the material may have come from Middle Persian, there are also places where an intimate connection with

14. For a thorough discussion of these traditions, see my essay, "Assessing the Evidence: Manichaeism in Roman Arabia," in my *Shades of Light and Darkness: Studies in Chaldean Dualism and Gnosis* (forthcoming).

15. Titus of Bostra, a fourth-century Christian bishop whose refutation of Manichaeism survives partially in Greek and more fully in Syriac, exhibits an extensive knowledge of Manichaean doctrine and literature, and indeed quotes from the latter in several instances. Although Titus is aware that Mani wrote his scriptures in Aramaic (τῇ Σύρων φωνῇ χρώμενος), should we assume that the Manichaean scriptures available to him in Bostra were also in this language?

16. See Chapter Five below, as well as Carl Brockelmann, "Kalīla wa-Dimna," *EI*[2] 4:503–506.

17. S. M. Stern, "Abū 'Īsā Muḥammad b. Hārūn al-Warrāḳ," *EI*[2] 1:130; Carsten Colpe, "Anpassung des Manichäismus an den Islam (Abū 'Īsā al-Warrāq)," *ZDMG* 109 (1959): 82–91.

Syriac texts can be posited. Yet there are some curious instances where distinctive terminology (e.g., the proper names of divine beings or mythological characters) is simply unparalleled in other sources. One must reckon too with the well documented Manichaean proclivity to adapt both the names of the entities in their pantheon and the vocabulary of their teachings to the familiar usages of the dominant religious discourse in a particular region. Despite a series of increasingly savage persecutions, Manichaeism remained a living presence in its Mesopotamian homeland even at the end of the tenth century, and would continue to hang on in the eastern provinces of the ʿAbbāsid realm for another couple of centuries. An indigenous Arabophonic Manichaeism may have sponsored 'new' translations of the older scriptures; it would most certainly have produced new texts and devotional literature designed for contemporary religious life. Unfortunately the ultimate source for most of the extant Arabic Manichaica remains frustratingly opaque.

The present chapter initially gives the most important Islamicate catalogs of Manichaean titles, followed by a seriatim assemblage of citations from and testimonia about certain named Manichaean books. Those entries in the catalogs that provide some indication of the contents of named works are reprised under their appropriate rubric.

1. Generic Remarks on Manichaean Script and Scriptures

Yaʿqūbī, *Ta'rīkh* (ed. Houtsma):[18]

And Mānī authored books wherein he affirmed the two entities;[19] and among those (books) which he (Mani) composed was his book which he named *Treasure of Life*, (in which) he describes what exists in the soul (deriving) from the redemptive activity of Light and the corruptive activity of Darkness, and attributes evil deeds to Darkness; and a book which he named *Shāburaqān*, in which he describes the redeemed soul and the mixture with satans and imperfections; and (wherein) he makes the celestial sphere a flat surface, and he says that the world is upon a sloping mountain around which the uppermost celestial sphere revolves; and a book which he named *Book of Guidance and Organization*; and twelve <read twenty-two> *Gospel*(s), naming each gospel by a letter of the alphabet, (in which) he spoke of prayer, and what one must necessarily do for the redemption of the soul; and a *Book of Mysteries*, in which he discredits the signs of the prophets; and a *Book of Giants*; and he has numerous other books and epistles.[20]

---

18. M. T. Houtsma, ed., *Ibn Wadih qui dicitur al-Jaʿqubi historiae* ... (2 vols.; Leiden: Brill, 1883), 1:181.3–12; also Taqīzādeh-Šīrāzī, *Mānī va dīn-e-ū*, 104 (§13).

19. I.e., the ontological priority of Light and Darkness.

20. For other translations, see Konrad Kessler, *Mani: Forschungen über die manichäische Religion* (Berlin: Georg Reimer, 1889), 328–29; Edward G. Browne, *A Literary History of Persia* (4 vols.; London and Cambridge, 1902–24; repr., Cambridge: The University Press, 1964), 1:156.

Mas'ūdī, *Tanbīh* (ed. de Goeje):[21]

A summary containing what I previously wrote (in) a more detailed description: The doctrine of the Manichaean sect holds him (Mani) to be the Paraclete, the one whom Christ promised (would come). Mānī speaks of this in his *Gospel*,[22] in his book which was translated as *Shāburaqān*,[23] and in the *Book of Books* (*sic*),[24] as well as the rest of his writings. (I also discussed) the dispute(s) among the various dualist sects, such as the Manichaeans, Dayṣāniyya,[25] Marcionites, and the rest of them, pertaining to (their) philosophy(s) of ontological principles, etc., and how often Mānī mentioned the Marcionites and Dayṣāniyya in his books.[26]

Ibn al-Nadīm, *Fihrist* (ed. Tajaddud):[27]

A discussion about Manichaean script:
Just as the doctrine was put together from Zoroastrianism and Christianity, the Manichaean mode of writing characters was taken from Persian and Syriac, (and) Mānī produced it.[28] It has more letters than the Arabic letters. They write their gospels and their prescriptive books with this script. The people of Sogdia (lit. 'what is beyond the river,' i.e., the Oxus) and Samarkand write religious books using this script, and therefore it is named 'the script of religion.'

The Marcionite sect also has a script which is peculiar to it. A trustworthy source informed me that he had seen it. He said: 'It resembles Manichaean (script), but it is different.'[29] This is the Manichaean (form of writing) letters:

---

21. Mas'ūdī, *Kitâb at-Tanbîh wa'l-Ischrâf* (2nd ed.; Bibliotheca Geographorum Arabicorum 8; ed. M. J. de Goeje; repr., Leiden: Brill, 1967), 135.9–15. See also Flügel, *Mani*, 356–57; Taqīzādeh-Šīrāzī, *Mānī va dīn-e-ū*, 134 (§22).

22. Emending the text from الجبلة to انجيله.

23. That is, the *Shābuhragān*. See the discussion below.

24. A common corruption of the title *Book of Mysteries*.

25. Adherents of the second-century Syrian philosopher Bardaiṣan, whose teachings were gnosticized by later followers. Ephrem Syrus terms Bardaiṣan the 'teacher' of Mani.

26. See also B. Carra de Vaux, *Maçoudi: Le livre de l'avertissement et de la revision* (Paris: L'Imprimerie Nationale, 1896), 188.

27. Ibn al-Nadīm, *Kitāb al-Fihrist* (ed. Riḍa Tajaddud; [Teheran: Maktabat al-Assadī, 1971]), 19. See also Flügel, *Mani*, 166–67; Taqīzādeh-Šīrāzī, *Mānī va dīn-e-ū*, 165 (§27).

28. Compare Ibn al-Nadīm, *Fihrist* (ed. Flügel, *Mani*), 51.13–16 rendered in Chapter Four below. Mani's alleged invention of Manichaean script and its relationship to Syriac ductus are briefly discussed by A. A. Bevan, "Manichaeism," *ERE* 8:397; P. Oktor Skjærvø, "Aramaic Scripts for Iranian Languages," in *The World's Writing Systems* (ed. Peter T. Daniels and William Bright; New York and Oxford: Oxford University Press, 1996), 530–31; James R. Russell, "Alphabets," in *Late Antiquity: A Guide to the Postclassical World* (ed. G. W. Bowersock, Peter Brown, and Oleg Grabar; Cambridge, MA: Harvard University Press, 1999), 289; for a recent lengthier treatment, see Desmond Durkin-Meisterernst, "Erfand Mani die manichäische Schrift?" in *Studia Manichaica: IV. Internationaler Kongress* (ed. Emmerick, Sundermann, and Zieme), 161–78.

29. See the remarks of Wilferd Madelung, "Abū 'Īsā al-Warrāq über die Bardesaniten,

[a 'greatly corrupted and disfigured'[30] sample alphabet is inserted here]. They (i.e., the Marcionite letters) have the shape but the lettering differs. They write some of them as follows: the *ṣād* as [ ], the *mīm* as [ ], the *ḥā* as [ ], the *kāf* as [ ], the *qāf* as [ ] or [ ], and the *hā* as [ ] or [ ].[31]

Bīrūnī, *Risālah lil-Bīrūnī fī fihrist kutub Muḥammad ibn Zakarīyyā al-Rāzī* (ed. Sachau):[32]

... and this I read (in) his *Book on Divine Knowledge*,[33] and he begins with arguments against the books of Mānī, especially his book called *Book of Mysteries*. The title enticed me in the same way that another is enticed by (the colors) white and yellow in (the practice of) alchemy. The novelty, or rather, the inaccessibility of the truth stimulated me to search for these *Mysteries* among my acquaintances in (various) countries and regions, but I remained in a state of longing (for this work) some forty years until there came to me in Khwārizm a soldier from Hamadān bearing books which Faḍl b. Sahlān had come across, and he informed me that they (these books) were very dear to him. Among them was a volume filled with the writings of the Manichaeans, containing the *Pragmateia*, the *Book of Giants*, the *Treasure of Life*, the *Dawn of Truth and Foundation*, the *Gospel*, the *Shābūraqān*, and a number of epistles of Mani; and the goal of my search, the *Book of Mysteries*. Happiness over this discovery overwhelmed me, as those who are thirsty are overwhelmed at the sight of a drink, but also sadness in the end, as when one is stricken with gas from contaminated (water?), and I experienced the truth of the word of God Most High: "He to whom God does not grant light has no light" (Q 24:40).[34]

Marcioniten und Kantäer," in *Studien zur Geschichte und Kultur des Vorderen Orients: Festschrift für Bertold Spuler zum siebzigsten Geburtstag* (ed. Hans R. Roemer and Albrecht Noth; Leiden: Brill, 1981), 220.

30. The adjectives are quoted from Browne, *Literary History*, 1:165.

31. For other translations, see Flügel, *Mani*, 167-68; Bayard Dodge, *The Fihrist of al-Nadīm* (2 vols.; New York: Columbia University Press, 1970), 1:32–33.

32. C. E. Sachau, ed., *Kitāb al-āthār al-bāqiya 'ani'l-qurūn al-khāliya: Chronologie orientalischer Völker von Albêrûnî* (Leipzig, 1878; repr., Leipzig: Otto Harrassowitz, 1923), XXXIX.10–19; Taqīzādeh-Šīrāzī, *Mānī va dīn-e-ū*, 209–10 (§36).

33. A work by the ninth-century physician and skeptic Abū Bakr Muḥammad b. Zakariyyā al-Rāzī. For more on this important intellectual figure, see especially Stroumsa, *Freethinkers of Medieval Islam*.

34. Translation adapted from that of Reeves, *Jewish Lore*, 40. See also Kessler, *Mani*, 178–79; Julius Ruska, "Al-Birūni als Quelle für das Leben und die Schriften al-Rāzi's," *Isis* 5 (1923): 31–32; Gotthard Strohmaier, *In den Gärten der Wissenschaft: Ausgewählte Texte aus den Werken des muslimischen Universalgelehrten* (2nd ed.; Leipzig: Reclam-Verlag, 1991), 147; idem, "Al-Bīrūnī (973–1048) über Mani und Manichäer," in *Studia Manichaica: IV. Internationaler Kongress* (ed. Emmerick, Sundermann, and Zieme), 594–95.

Bīrūnī, *Āthār al-bāqiya 'an-il-qurūn al-khāliya* (ed. Sachau):[35]

He composed many books such as his *Gospel*, the *Shārbūqān* (*sic*), the *Treasure of Life*, the *Book of the Giants*, the *Book of Books* (*sic*),[36] and numerous (other) treatises. He said in it (his *Gospel*?) that he had amplified what Christ had only hinted at.[37]

Marwazī, *Kitāb ṭabā'i' al-ḥayawān* (ed. Kruk):[38]

He composed the book *al-Shābūraqān*, the *Treasury of Stories*,[39] the *Book of Confusion*,[40] the *Vessels of Secrets*,[41] and many other epistles and treatises. He said in it (?) that he had amplified what Christ had only hinted at.[42]

Shams-i Qays, *al-Mu'jam fī ma'āyīr ash'ār al-'ajam* (ed. Mudarris Raḍavī):[43]

Moreover I have read in some of the books of the Persians that the religious sages during the age of Bahrām (i.e., Bahrām Gūr, 420–438 CE) saw nothing to condemn in his morals and circumstances except for the composition of poetry. When therefore he first attained the kingdom and dominion, the learned Adhurbād b. Zarādustān came before him and firmly reproached him. The advice which he voiced on that occasion was: 'O king! Know that composing poetry is one of the worst vices for rulers and is contemptible conduct for kings. For that (process; i.e., composing poetry) is based on deceit and falsehood, and that (activity) is founded on excessive distortions and extravagant exaggerations. Therefore the great philosophers of religion have been averse to that (activity) and consider it to be despicable. They reckon the satirizing of the poets to be among the causes of the destruction of bygone kingdoms and past peoples, and they identify it as one of the preludes to the loss of wealth and the ruin of countries. *Zanādiqa* and those who denied prophecy have fallen into wild fantasies: they revile the revealed scriptures and the divinely sent prophets only by means of composing

35. *Āthār* (ed. Sachau), 208.13–15; Taqīzādeh-Šīrāzī, *Mānī va dīn-e-ū*, 205 (§34).

36. A common corruption for the *Book of Mysteries*.

37. For another translation, see Strohmaier, *In den Gärten*², 141.

38. Ms. UCLA Ar. 52 fol. 5b.21–6a.2, as published by Remke Kruk, "Sharaf az-Zamân Ṭâhir Marwazî (fl. ca. 1100 A.D.) on Zoroaster, Mânî, Mazdak, and Other Pseudo-Prophets," *Persica* 17 (2001): 65.

39. Arabic كنز الاخبار. Compare Bīrūnī, *Āthār* (ed. Sachau), 208.14: كنز الاحياء 'Treasury/e of Life.'

40. Arabic سفر الحائرة. Compare Bīrūnī, *Āthār* (ed. Sachau), 208.14: سفر الجبابرة 'Book of the Giants.' One is tempted to see in Marwazī's حائر a corrupt reflex of Aramaic עירין 'Watcher(s),' hence 'Book of Watchers' or the title of the Jewish Enochic source underlying Mani's *Book of Giants*.

41. Arabic سفن الاسرار. Compare Bīrūnī, *Āthār* (ed. Sachau), 208.14: سفر الاسفار 'Book of Books,' which is an alternative name for the *Book of Mysteries*.

42. The final sentence is a verbatim reproduction of Bīrūnī, *Āthār* (ed. Sachau), 208.14-15. For another translation, see Kruk, "Marwazî," 55.

43. Shams-i Qays, *al-Mu'jam fī ma'āyīr ash'ār al-'ajam* (ed. Muḥammad Qazvīnī; rev. Muḥammad Taqī Mudarris Raḍavī; Teheran: Dānishgāh-i Tihrān, 1959), 199–200.

(their) words as poetry. Their contrary thoughts are expressed exclusively by means of cultivating the habit of rhythm and rhyme. ... the first created being who composed poetry about asceticism, self-improvement, and the praise and sanctification of God was one of the cherubim angels,[44] yet it is agreed that the first creature who glorified himself using poetry and who bragged about himself over others was Iblīs (i.e., Satan), may a curse be upon him!' Bahrām Gūr repented of that behavior and after that never spoke poetry.[45]

2. *Gospel*[46]

The work which bears the title *Gospel*, occasionally glossed as the *Living Gospel* or *Gospel of the Living*, was likely Mani's most important scriptural expression. Its conscious mimicry of a rubric exclusively associated with Christian textual productions would have guaranteed it at least an initial hearing among that religion's various sects in light of the widespread proliferation of so-called 'apocryphal gospels' during the pre-canonical age.[47] The *Gospel* figures prominently, usually as the first entry, in almost every catalog of Manichaean scriptures prepared by both western and eastern heresiologists. According to several of our surviving sources, the book featured twenty-two separate sections or chapters which were arranged sequentially according to the order and number of the letters of the Aramaic alphabet; if it bore an acrostic structure, each chapter's initial statement or paragraph would have started with its corresponding letter.[48] This editorial arrangement has been confirmed by the archaeological recovery of some Middle Iranian fragments (S 1) of an index to a liturgical collection which displays two entries stating 'the Gospel *alaph* is taught' and 'the Gospel *taw* is taught';[49] there

44. Cf. Q 4:172, where according to Bayḍāwī the angels there termed *al-muqarrabūn* 'the closest ones (to God)' are identified as *karūbiyyūn* 'cherubim.' See Thomas Patrick Hughes, *A Dictionary of Islam* (London, 1885; repr., Chicago, IL: Kazi Publications, 1994), 50.

45. See also Alessandro Bausani, *Religion in Iran: From Zoroaster to Baha'ullah* (trans. J. M. Marchesi; New York: Bibliotheca Persica Press, 2000), 250; Mottahedeh, *Mantle of the Prophet*, 161.

46. For an excellent discussion of Mani's *Gospel*, see Henri-Charles Puech, "Gnostic Gospels and Related Documents," in Edgar Hennecke, *New Testament Apocrypha* (2 vols.; ed. Wilhelm Schneemelcher; Philadelphia: The Westminster Press, 1963–65), 1:355–61.

47. Responsible scholars of the history of the New Testament are reluctant to speak about the existence of a 'canon' of Christian scriptures prior to the latter half of the fourth century CE.

48. Note Coptic *Homil.* 94.18–19: 'my *Great Go[spel* from] *alpha* to *omega*.'

49. Carl Salemann, "Ein Bruchstük (*sic*!) manichäischen Schrifttums im Asiatischen Museum," in *Mémoires de l'Academié Impériale des Sciences de Saint-Pétersbourg*, 8ème série, VI.6 (1904): 2–7; Mary Boyce, *A Reader in Manichaean Middle Persian and Parthian* (Acta Iranica 9; Leiden: Brill, 1975), 186; Hans-Joachim Klimkeit, *Hymnen und Gebete der Religion des Lichts: Iranische und türkische liturgische Texte der Manichäer Zentralasiens* (Opladen: Westdeutscher Verlag, 1989), 183; Puech, "Gnostic Gospels," in *New*

is another textual fragment (M 17), presumably from the *Gospel* itself, which has the superscription 'the Gospel *arb* (i.e., *alaph*) is taught.'[50]

Three early quotations from Mani's *Gospel* are also available in Greek in the *Cologne Mani Codex* (65.23-70.9).[51] It has recently been argued by Byard Bennett that some of the anonymous citations from an unknown Manichaean work contained in a sixth-century homily of Severus of Antioch may stem from the *Living Gospel*.[52]

Ya'qūbī, *Ta'rīkh* (ed. Houtsma):[53]

And Mānī authored ... twelve <read twenty-two> *Gospel*(s), naming each gospel by a letter of the alphabet, (in which) he spoke of prayer, and what one must necessarily do for the redemption of the soul.[54]

'Abd al-Jabbār, *Tathbīt* (ed. 'Uthmān):[55]

But you surely know that Mānī the priest[56] claims precision about Christ, that he (claims to be) among his followers, that no one follows his (Christ's) religious laws and injunctions except for he (Mani) and his followers,[57] and that the *Gospel* which he has is his (Christ's) gospel.

Testament Apocrypha (Hennecke-Schneemelcher), 1:357.

50. Boyce, *Reader*, 32; Klimkeit, *Hymnen und Gebete*, 184-85; D. N. MacKenzie, "I, Mani ...," in *Gnosisforschung und Religionsgeschichte: Festschrift für Kurt Rudolph zum 65. Geburtstag* (ed. Holger Preissler and Hubert Seiwert; Marburg: Diagonal-Verlag, 1994), 183–98; Iain Gardner and Samuel N. C. Lieu, *Manichaean Texts From the Roman Empire* (Cambridge: Cambridge University Press, 2004), 157.
51. For a translation, see Gardner-Lieu, *Manichaean Texts*, 156–59.
52. Byard Bennett, "*Iuxta unum latus erat terra tenebrarum*: The Division of Primordial Space in Anti-Manichaean Writers' Descriptions of the Manichaean Cosmogony," in *The Light and the Darkness: Studies in Manichaeism and its World* (NHMS 50; ed. Paul Mirecki and Jason BeDuhn; Leiden: Brill, 2001), 68–78.
53. Ya'qūbī, *Ta'rīkh* (ed. Houtsma), 1:181; Taqīzādeh-Šīrāzī, *Mānī va dīn-e-ū*, 104 (§13); cf. Kessler, *Mani*, 206.
54. For other translations, see Kessler, *Mani*, 206; Browne, *Literary History*, 1:156; Adam, *Texte*², 1; Michael H. Browder, "Al-Bîrûnî's Manichaean Sources," in *Manichaean Studies: Proceedings of the First International Conference on Manichaeism, August 5–9, 1987* (ed. Peter Bryder; Lund: Plus Ultra, 1988), 25.
55. 'Abd al-Jabbār b. Aḥmad al-Hamadhānī, *Tathbīt dālā'il al-nubūwwah* (2 vols.; ed. 'Abd al-Karīm 'Uthmān; Beirut: Dār al-Arabiyah, 1966–67), 1:114.13–15.
56. See the note on this appellation in Chapter Two above.
57. Compare Augustine, *Contra Faustum* 5.1, where the Manichaean teacher Faustus is represented as voicing an analogous claim. See Elizabeth A. Clark, *Reading Renunciation: Asceticism and Scripture in Early Christianity* (Princeton: Princeton University Press, 1999), 42 n.144.

'Abd al-Jabbār, *Tathbīt* (ed. 'Uthmān):[58]

But nevertheless they (the Manichaeans) claim that they are followers of Christ and of the religion of Christ, and that the *Gospel* which they possess is the authentic one. The one which you (the Christians) possess is inferior.[59]

Bīrūnī, *Āthār* (ed. Sachau):[60]

Each one of the sects of Marcion and of Bardaiṣan possesses a gospel whose parts disagree with parts of those (other) gospels. The adherents of Mānī have a separate *Gospel*, filled from beginning to end with differences from the Christian (version), but they adhere to these faithfully and say that it is correct and that it is in conformity with the one by Christ and the one which He brought. Any other one is false and those who would follow such are mistaken about Christ.[61]

There is a copy of it[62] called *The Gospel of the Seventy* which is attributed to Balāmis.[63] It begins by saying that <Salām b.>[64] 'Abdallāh b. Salām wrote it down at the dictation of Salmān al-Fārisī.[65] Whoever examines it will easily see that it is a forgery; neither the Christians nor anyone else acknowledges it. Thus one finds there are no gospels informed by the writings of the prophets upon whom one might rely.[66]

---

58. 'Abd al-Jabbār, *Tathbīt* (ed. 'Uthmān), 1:184.13–14.

59. See also Guy Monnot, *Penseurs musulmans et religions iraniennes: 'Abd al-Jabbār et ses devanciers* (Paris: J. Vrin, 1974), 281.

60. *Āthār* (ed. Sachau), 23.9–15; Taqīzādeh-Šīrāzī, *Mānī va dīn-e-ū*, 200-201 (§34); cf. Kessler, *Mani*, 206–207.

61. See also Adam, *Texte*[2], 1. The Manichaean claim to be in possession of the 'true' gospel was repeatedly emphasized by 'Abd al-Jabbār. Note also the verbal lobbying of a religious seeker by a band of Manichaeans imagined by Theodore Abū Qurra in Chapter Four below.

62. It is doubtful whether Bīrūnī is still speaking of Mani's *Gospel*, but some scholars think that this is the case. For a sober assessment of this particular testimony, see Puech, "Gnostic Gospels," in *New Testament Apocrypha* (Hennecke-Schneemelcher), 1:269–71.

63. As Kessler and Puech suggest, presumably a corruption of the name Iklāmīs; i.e., Clement.

64. Delete these two words.

65. These two figures are prominent Companions of the Prophet Muḥammad, the former representative of Jewish and the latter Iranian converts to the new faith. It is unclear how either name would be relevant to the production of Christian gospels. Note however the intriguing observations of Steven M. Wasserstrom, *Between Muslim and Jew: The Problem of Symbiosis Under Early Islam* (Princeton, NJ: Princeton University Press, 1995), 176.

66. Other translations of this entire passage are in Kessler, *Mani*, 206–207; Strohmaier, *In den Gärten*[2], 133–34.

Bīrūnī, *Āthār* (ed. Sachau):[67]

He says in his *Gospel*—which he compiled following each letter of the twenty-two letters of the *abjad* alphabet—that he is the Paraclete announced by Christ and that he is the seal of the prophets.[68]

Marwazī, *Kitāb ṭabā'i' al-ḥayawān* (ed. Kruk):[69]

He composed many books like his *Gospel*, which he compiled following each letter of the twenty-two letters of the *abjad* alphabet, and he maintained that he was the Paraclete announced by Christ and that he was the seal of the prophets.[70]

Shahrastānī, *Kitāb al-milal wa'l-niḥal* (ed. Badrān):[71]

The sage Mānī in the first chapter of his *Jibilla*[72] and in the beginning of the *Shāburaqān* says that the Ruler of the World of Light is in all of His land: nothing is devoid of Him, and that He is both visible and concealed, and that He has no end apart from where His land ends at the land of His foe.[73] He says also that the Ruler of the World of Light (is situated) in the center of His land. He mentions that the ancient mixing was a mixing of heat, cold, moisture, and dryness; but the recent mixing is one of Good and Evil.[74]

Ibn al-Murtaḍā, *Kitāb al-munya* (ed. Taqīzādeh-Šīrāzī):[75]

Among his books are the *Gospel* and *Shāburaqān* (...).

Mani maintained in the *Gospel* and in the *Shāburaqān* that the Ruler of the World of Light was in the center of His land, but he states in the first chapter[76] of his *Gospel* and at the beginning of the *Shāburaqān* that He (i.e., the Ruler) is in all of

67. *Āthār* (ed. Sachau), 207.18–19; Taqīzādeh-Šīrāzī, *Mānī va dīn-e-ū*, 204 (§34).
68. The identical epithet is applied to Muḥammad by Q 33:40. For other translations, see Kessler, *Mani*, 206; Adam, *Texte*[2], 1; Strohmaier, *In den Gärten*[2], 140.
69. Ms. UCLA Ar. 52 fol. 5b.19–21, as published by Kruk, "Marwazî," 65.
70. Although he does not claim to be quoting Mani's *Gospel*, it is clear from Bīrūnī that this is the source. For another translation, see Kruk, "Marwazî," 55.
71. Muḥammad b. Fatḥ Allāh Badrān, ed., *Kitāb al-milal wa'l-niḥal* (2 vols.; [Cairo]: Matba'at al-Azhar, [1951–55]), 1:628.11–629.2. See also William Cureton, ed., *Kitāb al-milal wa-l-niḥal: Book of Religious and Philosophical Sects, by Muhammad al-Shahrastáni* (London, 1846; repr., Leipzig: O. Harrassowitz, 1923), 192.1–6, reprinted by Taqīzādeh-Šīrāzī, *Mānī va dīn-e-ū*, 244 (§45).
72. Prosper Alfaric, *Les écritures manichéennes* (2 vols.; Paris: E. Nourry, 1918–19), 1:126 identifies this as the *Book of Giants*; see also 1:81. Kessler, *Mani*, 342 states that 'ohne Zweifel' the *Book of Giants* is to be read here. The correct reading however is 'his *Gospel*.'
73. For other translations of this passage, see Kessler, *Mani*, 191; Adam, *Texte*[2], 6; Browder, "Al-Bîrûnî's Manichaean Sources," 25.
74. Compare Ibn al-Murtaḍā and 'Abd al-Jabbār below.
75. Taqīzādeh-Šīrāzī, *Mānī va dīn-e-ū*, 299, 301 (§74); Kessler, *Mani*, 346, 349.
76. Literally 'the *aleph*-chapter.' Most testimonia about Mani's *Gospel* remark its sequential arrangement in accordance with the order of the Aramaic alphabet.

his land, and that He is both visible (and) hidden, and that He has no end apart from where His land ends at the land of His foe.[77]

Mīrkhwānd, *Rauḍat al-ṣafā* (ed. Taqīzādeh-Šīrāzī):[78]

He (i.e., Mani) would show a book—the *Gospel*—and would say: 'This book has come down from heaven.'[79]

3. *Shābuhragān*

The title of the *Shābuhragān* signals its identity as the special tractate supposedly prepared by Mani for Shāpūr I. If it was indeed presented to the emperor during their initial audience of 241/2, as tradition holds, it would rank as one of Mani's earliest written compositions. It was supposedly written in Persian, unlike the rest of Mani's writings which were composed in Aramaic. While some scholars have labeled it a digest of Manichaean doctrine, the true scope of its contents remains unclear. The evidence preserved by Bīrūnī suggests that the work featured a first-person promotional announcement by Mani advertising his religious credentials: twice Bīrūnī refers to a discrete section of the book which he labeled 'the chapter about the advent of the apostle.'[80] The same writer also indicates that the *Shābuhragān* contained precepts or rules of conduct for the organization of communal life.[81] Some historical, biographical, and doctrinal background was included, particularly with regard to how Mani's teachings could be fit among those of earlier socially recognized eastern prophets like Zoroaster or the Buddha. Other traditionists seem to confuse the *Shābuhragān* with the *Gospel*, attributing the same information to both works.[82] Most of the Middle Iranian fragments of this work recovered to date exhibit not a hagiographical but eschatological tone;[83] perhaps the genre of apocalypse was deemed a more

77. See also Kessler, *Mani*, 350, 354; Schmidt-Polotsky, *Ein Mani-Fund*, 36. Note Shahrastānī above; also 'Abd al-Jabbār below.

78. Taqīzādeh-Šīrāzī, *Mānī va dīn-e-ū*, 525 (§190); Persian text reproduced by Kessler, *Mani*, 377.

79. Similar claims are associated with the prophetic missions of Elchasai and Muḥammad. For the former, see Eusebius, *Historia ecclesiastica* 6.38; Theodoret, *Haereticarum fabularum compendium* 2.7; for the latter, John of Damascus, *De haeresibus* 100.14–15, as published in Bonifatius Kotter, ed., *Die Schriften des Johannes von Damaskos, IV: Liber de haeresibus; Opera polemica* (Berlin and New York: Walter de Gruyter, 1981), 60–61.

80. Bīrūnī, *Āthār* (ed. Sachau), 118.15; 208.8.

81. Bīrūnī, *Āthār* (ed. Sachau), 118.21. Note Jason David BeDuhn, *The Manichaean Body: In Discipline and Ritual* (Baltimore and London: The Johns Hopkins University Press, 2000), 282 n.39.

82. Of course some information could have actually been repeated in these works.

83. See Mary Boyce, *A Catalogue of the Iranian Manuscripts in Manichaean Script in the German Turfan Collection* (Berlin: Akademie-Verlag, 1960), 31–32; idem, *Reader*, 76–81; D. N. MacKenzie, "Mani's *Šābuhragān*," *BSOAS* 42 (1979): 500–534; 43 (1980): 288–310; Werner Sundermann, *Mitteliranische manichäische Texte kirchengeschichtlichen Inhalts* (Berlin:

suitable literary vehicle for a suppliant who sought royal recognition of his prophetic vocation. Apparently the *Shābuhragān* circulated only in the east since no western writers display explicit cognizance of it.[84]

Ya'qūbī, *Ta'rīkh* (ed. Houtsma):[85]

And Mānī authored ... a book which he named *Shāburaqān*, in which he describes the redeemed soul and the mixture with satans and imperfections; and (wherein) he makes the celestial sphere a flat surface, and he says that the world is upon a sloping mountain around which the uppermost celestial sphere revolves.[86]

Abū Ḥātim al-Rāzī, *Kitāb a'lām al-nubuwwa* (ed. Ṣāwī):[87]

He (i.e., Abū Bakr al-Rāzī) mentioned what the Zoroastrians claim on the authority of Zoroaster with regard to Ahriman and Ohr[mazd], and what Mānī asserted about it; (namely), that the Word became separated from the Father and it dispersed the devils[88] and killed (them); that the heavens originate from the skins of the (slain) devils;[89] that thunder is (caused by) the cries of demons and that earthquakes are (caused by) the commotion of devils beneath the earth;[90] that Mānī elevated Sābūr, the one for whom he prepared the *Shāburaqān*, into the air and concealed him there for a time;[91] that Mānī would suddenly be carried away by his Spirit from their presence (and) it would situate him opposite the sun: he would tarry as long

Akademie-Verlag, 1981), 92–98; Manfred Hutter, *Manis kosmogonische Šābuhragān-Texte: Edition, Kommentar und literaturgeschichtliche Einordung der manichäisch-mittelpersischen Handschriften M 98/99 I und M 7980–7984* (Wiesbaden: Otto Harrassowitz, 1992).

84. Note however Coptic *Keph.* 14.3–16.2 and Coptic *Homil.* 7.8–42.8, both of whose contents may ultimately rely on the *Shābuhragān*.
85. Ya'qūbī, *Ta'rīkh* (ed. Houtsma), 1:181; Taqīzādeh-Šīrāzī, *Mānī va dīn-e-ū*, 104 (§13).
86. For other translations, see Kessler, *Mani*, 190-91; Browne, *Literary History*, 1:156; Adam, *Texte*², 6.
87. Abū Ḥātim al-Rāzī, *A'lām al-nubuwwah (The Peaks of Prophecy)* (ed. Salah al-Sawy; Teheran: Imperial Iranian Academy of Philosophy, 1977), 70.10–71.4; see also Taqīzādeh-Šīrāzī, *Mānī va dīn-e-ū*, 120 (§17).
88. Literally 'satans,' and so throughout this paragraph.
89. An authentic mytheme of Manichaean cosmogony, which holds that eleven heavens were fashioned from the skins of the slain archons of Darkness. Their flayed bodies formed the substance of eight earths. See the fuller discussion and references in Chapter Four below, as well as Henri-Charles Puech, *Le manichéisme: Son fondateur – sa doctrine* (Paris: Civilisations du Sud, 1949), 170–71 nn.319–20.
90. Compare *Acta Archelai* 8.2 (ed. Beeson, 11–12), where however an agent of the Realm of Light is to blame for the occurrence of earthquakes. See also *Acta Archelai* 9.5 (ed. Beeson, 15).
91. Compare Bīrūnī, *Āthār* (ed. Sachau), 209.5–6: 'the king Sābūr came to believe in him the time when he (Mani) raised him with himself to heaven and they both stood in the air between heaven and earth. He displayed marvels to him during this (feat).'

as for an hour, but sometimes he tarried for days.[92] He (Abū Bakr al-Rāzī) quoted novel absurdities like these which had been invented by the Zoroastrians and the Manichaeans, and he combined them with what was in the revealed scriptures and the stories about the prophets, thereby attributing these (absurdities) to the holy messengers of God who are blameless in all this. He maintained that this was in their writings and that this (shows) incongruity and contradiction in their arguments. He adduced this in order to argue against (the idea of) prophecy.[93]

Abū Yaʿqūb al-Sijistānī, *Kitāb al-yanābīʿ* (ed. Corbin):[94]

... in the gospel which says:[95] 'Truly the Lord will assemble the righteous and the unrighteous in one place. Then He will say to the righteous, "You have done and acted well in light of My situation![96] I was hungry and you fed Me. I was thirsty and you gave Me drink. I was naked and you covered Me. I was imprisoned and you released Me." They shall answer Him by saying, "Our Lord! When were You ever hungry, thirsty, naked, and imprisoned so that we fed You, gave You drink, covered You, and released You?" Then God will say to them, "You are correct; however, all that you have done for your own selves you have actually done for Me!"[97] Then He will say to the unrighteous, "You have acted wickedly in light of My situation! I was hungry, but you did not feed Me, etc." They shall say, "Our Lord! When were You ever like this?" And He will reply, "Yes, you are correct; however, all that you did not do for your own selves[98] was as if you did not do

---

92. Compare ʿAbd al-Jabbār, *Tathbīt* (ed. ʿUthmān), 1:184.10–12: 'Angels would come to him and carry him off so that he would ascend to the sun, and it would happen to him while his companions were present with him'; Bīrūnī, *Āthār* (ed. Sachau), 209.6–7: 'They say that he would ascend from among his companions to heaven, remain there a few days, and then descend to them.' Note also *CMC* 126.4–12.

93. For another translation, see Stroumsa, *Freethinkers of Medieval Islam*, 101–102.

94. Henry Corbin, *Trilogie ismaelienne: Textes édités avec traduction française et commentaires* (Bibliothèque iranienne 9; Teheran: Departement d'iranologie de l'Institut franco-iranien, 1961), 88–89 (text).

95. What follows is ostensibly a quotation of Matt 25:31–46, a passage which however was also used and reinterpreted by Mani in his *Shābuhragān*. See MacKenzie, "Mani's *Šābuhragān*," 506–509; cf. also Coptic *Homil.* 35.12–38.27.

96. I.e., dispersed throughout material existence and suffering pain during His imprisonment by Darkness.

97. Corbin notes the singularity of this variant reading and realizes its import for a gnostic anthropogony, but he does not identify the quotation as possibly coming from the *Shābuhragān*. See Corbin, *Trilogie*, 114–16; idem, "From the Gnosis of Antiquity to Ismaili Gnosis," in idem, *Cyclical Time and Ismaili Gnosis* (London: Kegan Paul International, 1983), 162–65.

98. Compare M 537a I lines 47–48 (*apud* MacKenzie, "Mani's *Šābuhragān*, II," 296): 'and he [followed?] the false teaching of Ahriman ... and he [did not perform?] pious deeds (*kyrdg'n*) for his own soul.'

anything for Me!"'[99]

Ibn al-Nadīm, *Fihrist* (ed. Flügel):[100]

The book *Shāburaqān*, and it contains a chapter on the 'release'[101] of the *auditores*; a chapter on the 'release' of the *electi* (?);[102] (and) a chapter on the 'release' of the wrongdoers (i.e., non-Manichaeans).[103]

'Abd al-Jabbār, *Mughnī* (ed. Ḥusayn):[104]

They have differing opinions about the Ruler of the World of Light, for some of them say He is its major occupant and its spiritual essence, and whatever is adjacent to it and its substance occupies the same position as a human body. Part of it (i.e., a body) is a mind which exercises cognition and perception, and part of it lacks this (component). Other members of the group say that the Ruler of the World of Light totally fills His world (and that) nothing is devoid of Him, and others say that He is in the middle of His world.

And Mānī says in the first part of the *Sāburaqān*: 'The Ruler of the World of Light is in all of His land: nothing is devoid of Him, and He is both visible and concealed. He has no end apart from where His land ends at the land of His foe.'[105]

---

99. See also Corbin, *Trilogie*, 112 (translation); Paul E. Walker, *The Wellsprings of Wisdom: A Study of Abū Ya'qūb al-Sijistānī's Kitāb al-Yanābī'* (Salt Lake City: University of Utah Press, 1994), 105.

100. Flügel, *Mani*, 73.7–9; Ibn al-Nadīm, *K. al-Fihrist* (ed. Tajaddud), 399; Taqīzādeh-Šīrāzī, *Mānī va dīn-e-ū*, 161 (§27).

101. Literally 'freeing' or 'unbinding.' Given the eschatological tone of the Middle Iranian fragments of the *Shābuhragān*, this term may signal the final dissolution of the bound constituents of their material bodies. In those fragments, however, humanity is divided into two (rather than three) groups: the 'religious' and the 'wrongdoers.'

102. There is a wide range of textual variants for this term. See the list compiled by Taqīzādeh-Šīrāzī, *Mānī va dīn-e-ū*, 176; note also Kessler, *Mani*, 181 n.1.

103. Compare Ibn al-Nadīm, *Fihrist* (ed. Flügel, *Mani*, 71.9–12): 'Mānī said: "These are three paths apportioned for the souls of humans. One of them leads to Paradise (lit. 'the Gardens'), and they (who travel on it) are the Elect. The second leads (back) to the world and (its) terrors, and they (who travel on it) observe the religion and provide assistance to the Elect. The third leads to Jahannam (i.e., Hell), and they (who travel on it) are the wicked people."'
Other translations are in Kessler, *Mani*, 180–81; Dodge, *Fihrist*, 2:798; Gardner-Lieu, *Manichaean Texts*, 155.

104. 'Abd al-Jabbār b. Aḥmad al-Hamadhānī, *Al-Mughnī fī abwāb al-tawḥīd wa'l-'adl* (14 vols.; ed. Ṭāhā Ḥusayn, et al.; Cairo: Al-Shirkah al-'Arabīyah lil-Tibā'ah wa'l-Nashr, 1958–66), 5:14.14–15.3.

105. The same quotation is found in Shahrastānī and Ibn al-Murtaḍā, where both the *Shābuhragān* and the *Gospel* are given as the source. For other translations, see Georges Vajda, "Note annexe: L'aperçu sur les sectes dualistes dans *al-Muġnī fī abwāb al-tawḥīd wa-l-'adl* du cadi 'Abd al-Ğabbār," *Arabica* 13 (1966): 120–21; Monnot, *Penseurs*, 162.

'Abd al-Jabbār, *Mughnī* (ed. Ḥusayn):[106]

[According to the *Shābuhragān*],[107] the first whom God Most Exalted sent with knowledge (*'ilm*) was Adam, then Seth, and then Noah. Then he sent Zarādusht (i.e., Zoroaster) to Persia, the Buddha to India, Jesus the Christ to the countries of the West, and then, Mānī, 'seal of the prophets' (Q 33:40).[108]

Bīrūnī, *Āthār* (ed. Sachau):[109]

Now we will leave it altogether and we will accept a correction of it from the book of Mānī that is known as the *Shābūraqān*, because among Persian books[110] it is reliable for what transpires after the advent of Ardašīr. Mānī is one who obeys a prohibition against the telling of lies, and he has no need to falsify history.

... He (Mānī) says in this book in the chapter about the advent of the apostle that he was born in Babylon in the year 527 according to the astronomical chronology of Babylon, meaning the chronology of Alexander (i.e., Seleucid era) ... In this (same) chapter he maintains that revelation came to him when he was thirteen years old, and this was in the year 539 of the astronomical chronology of Babylon, two years having passed of the years of Ardašīr, the King of Kings.

He stipulates by this that the space of time between Alexander and Ardašīr was 537 years, and that the space of time between Ardašīr and the accession to rule of Yazdgird[111] was 406 years. This is correct, taking as testimony (what) has been recorded in a bound volume with which a religion is governed.[112]

Bīrūnī, *Āthār* (ed. Sachau):[113]

He states at the beginning of his book which is called *al-Shābūraqān* (i.e., the *Shābuhragān*), which is the one he composed for Shābūr b. Ardašīr: 'Apostles of God have constantly brought wisdom and deeds in successive times.[114] In one era

106. 'Abd al-Jabbār, *Mughnī* (ed. Ḥusayn), 5:15.13–15.

107. Although the title of a book is not cited here, it is clear from the parallel testimony of Bīrūnī that the *Shābuhragān* is the textual source for this statement. Shahrastānī transmits a slightly variant form of this same statement below. See Monnot, *Penseurs*, 125.

108. See also Monnot, *Penseurs*, 163.

109. *Āthār* (ed. Sachau), 118.12–21; Taqīzādeh-Šīrāzī, *Mānī va dīn-e-ū*, 203 (§34); cf. Kessler, *Mani*, 189 n.6.

110. Does 'Persian' refer here to language or cultural orbit? Did Bīrūnī know a Persian version of this work?

111. The final Sasanid ruler Yazdgird III (633–651 CE).

112. For another translation, see C. Edward Sachau, *The Chronology of Ancient Nations: An English Version of the Arabic Text of the Athâr-ul-bâkiya of Albîrûnî* (London: William H. Allen and Co., 1879), 121; Kessler, *Mani*, 190.

113. *Āthār* (ed. Sachau), 207.14–18; Taqīzādeh-Šīrāzī, *Mānī va dīn-e-ū*, 204 (§34); cf. Kessler, *Mani*, 187.

114. Compare a surviving passage from a Middle Iranian version of the *Shābuhragān*: 'Then Xradeshahr ... *from time to time and from [age] to age sent wisdom and knowledge*

they were brought by the apostle al-Bud (i.e., the Buddha) to the land of India, in another (era) by Zardāsht (i.e., Zoroaster) to Persia, and in another (era) by Jesus to the West. Now this revelation has descended and this prophecy is promulgated during this final era by me, Mānī, the apostle of the God of truth to Babylonia.'[115]

Bīrūnī, *Āthār* (ed. Sachau):[116]

According to what he related in the book *Shābūraqān* (i.e., the *Shābuhragān*) in the chapter about the advent of the apostle, the birthplace of Mānī was in Babylon in a village called Mardīnū near the upper canal of Kūtha in the year 527 of the era of the Babylonian astronomers, meaning the chronology of Alexander (i.e., Seleucid era), four years having passed of the years of Ādharbān the king. Revelation came when he was thirteen years old in the year 539 of the era of the Babylonian astronomers and after two years had passed of the years of Ardashīr, the King of Kings.[117]

Marwazī, *Kitāb ṭabā'i' al-ḥayawān* (ed. Kruk):[118]

In the time of Shābūr b. Ardašīr he came forth and announced himself to be a prophet. He said: 'Apostles of God have constantly brought wisdom and pious deeds in successive times. In one era they were brought by the apostle al-Budū (i.e., the Buddha) to the land of India and in another by Jesus to the land of the Arabs (*sic*). In this era prophecy has come to me and is promulgated by me, for I, Mānī, am the apostle of the God of truth to Babylonia.'[119]

Shahrastānī, *Kitāb al-milal wa'l-niḥal* (ed. Badrān):[120]

(See the entry for this source under *Gospel*).

---

to mankind.' As is visible in this passage, it is likely that 'wisdom and knowledge' is a better reading than Bīrūnī's 'wisdom and deeds'; see the parallel passages in 'Abd al-Jabbār and Shahrastānī as well as John C. Reeves, *Heralds of That Good Realm: Syro-Mesopotamian Gnosis and Jewish Traditions* (NHMS 41; Leiden: Brill, 1996), 23 n.40. The passage from the *Shābuhragān* is quoted from MacKenzie, "Mani's *Šābuhragān*," 505. One might also compare the language used in the final sentence of the Coptic Nag Hammadi tractate *On the Origin of the World* (NHC II, 5): 'For each one *by his deeds and his knowledge* will reveal his nature' (127.16–17).

115. For other translations, see Kessler, *Mani*, 187–88; Adam, *Texte*², 5–6; Strohmaier, *In den Gärten*², 140.

116. *Āthār* (ed. Sachau), 208.7–11; Taqīzādeh-Šīrāzī, *Mānī va dīn-e-ū*, 205 (§34).

117. Twice Bīrūnī juxtaposes a birth notice of Mani with a reference to the timing of his first revelation during his thirteenth year. The *Shābuhragān* may have had this same structure.

118. Ms. UCLA Ar. 52 fol. 5b.7–11, as published in Kruk, "Marwazî," 65.

119. The attribution of this quotation to the *Shābuhragān* is found in Bīrūnī. For another translation, see Kruk, "Marwazî," 55.

120. *Kitāb al-milal wa'l-niḥal* (ed. Badrān), 1:628.11–629.2.

Shahrastānī, *Kitāb al-milal wa'l-niḥal* (ed. Badrān):[121]

His doctrine regarding the Law and the Prophets was that the first whom God Most Exalted commissioned with knowledge and wisdom was Adam, the ancestor of humanity; then [He commissioned] Seth after him; then Noah after him; then Abraham after him,[122] upon them be blessings and peace! Then he sent the Buddha to India, Zoroaster to Persia, the (Christian) Messiah—the Word of God and His Spirit[123]—to Rome and the West, and Paul after the Messiah to those (same regions). Finally the Seal of the Prophets came to the land of the Arabs.[124]

Sam'ānī, *Kitāb al-ānsāb* (ed. Taqīzādeh-Šīrāzī):[125]

The first one to be designated by this term (i.e., *zindīq*) was Mānī b. Fābiq Māmān (*sic*) whose floruit was during the reign of Bahrām b. Hormuz b. Sābūr. He perused the ancestral scriptures. He was a Zoroastrian. He wished that fame and renown might be his, and so he founded his religious order and put together a book whose title was *Sāburqān* and said: 'This *zand* was for <the scripture of>[126] Zoroaster'; (using) the *zand* will enable you to attain the interpretation,' by which he meant (the interpretation of) the scripture of Zoroaster.[127] But his followers call the writing the *Book of Mānī*.[128] He adorned it with pictures and colors and set out in it Light and Darkness.

Shahrazūrī, *Šarḥ ḥikmat al-ishrāq* (ed. Corbin):[129]

He (i.e., Mānī) said [in his *Shābuhragān*]:[130] 'The Ruler of the World of Light is in all

121. *Kitāb al-milal wa'l-niḥal* (ed. Badrān), 1:629.10–630.5.

122. For another instance where the name of Abraham figures among Manichaean prophets, see Augustine, *Contra Faustum* 19.3.

123. An allusion to Q 4:171, where Jesus is characterized as 'His (i.e., God's) Word communicated to Mary and a Spirit from Him.'

124. Clearly an Islamicizing reference to the mission of Muḥammad. Missing from this prophetological roster is any reference to Mani himself, who is typically styled in Islamicate sources as the 'seal of the prophets.' Some think that the 'seal' here is actually Mani: see Julien Ries, *Les études manichéennes: Des controversies de la Réforme aux découvertes de XXe siècle* (Louvain-la-Neuve: Centre d'Histoire des Religions, 1988), 74. Compare 'Abd al-Jabbār, *Mughnī* (ed. Ḥusayn), 5:15.13–15: 'He sent Zoroaster to Persia, the Buddha to India, Jesus the Christ to the countries of the west, and last, Mānī, seal of the prophets.' Note Vajda, "Note annexe," 122 n.2. For another translation of this passage, see Kessler, *Mani*, 188–89.

125. Taqīzādeh-Šīrāzī, *Mānī va dīn-e-ū*, 246 (§46).

126. Reading with the textual apparatus supplied in Taqīzādeh-Šīrāzī, *Mānī va dīn-e-ū*, 246.

127. Note the remarks of F. C. de Blois, "Zindīḳ" *EI*^{2} 11:510–11.

128. Arabic مصحف ماني.

129. Henry Corbin, *Œuvres philosophiques et mystiques de Shihabaddin Yahya Sohrawardi I (Opera metaphysica et mystica II)* (Bibliothèque iranienne 2; Teheran/Paris: Institut franco-iranien/Adrien-Maisonneuve, 1952), 234 (text); Taqīzādeh-Šīrāzī, *Mānī va dīn-e-ū*, 254 (§48).

130. It seems clear from the numerous parallel testimonia that this quotation stems from the *Shābuhragān*.

of His land: nothing is devoid of Him; and that He is both visible and concealed, and that He has no end apart from where His land ends at the land of His foe. He says also that the Ruler of the World of Light (is situated) in the center of His land.'[131] If he intends by this (statement) an allusion to what we have related about him (i.e., this entity) or to what approximates him, then he is correct; but if not, then he errs.[132]

4. *Book of Mysteries*

The *Book of Mysteries*, sometimes referred to as the *Book of Books*, is already associated with Mani in the fourth-century *Acta Archelai*. If the relatively complete synopsis of its contents that is provided by Ibn al-Nadīm (see below) is accurate, it apparently featured a number of topical discourses which served to align the distinctive teachings of Mani with those that were supposedly propounded by Jesus the Messiah and his true predecessors in their guise as Manichaean heralds. The book also devoted several chapters to differentiating and refuting the doctrines of the followers of Bardaiṣan, a rival dualist sect whose advocates competed with those of Mani and other Christian proponents in Syria and Mesopotamia from the third through the fifth centuries CE. Interestingly, Bardaiṣan is also explicitly credited with authoring a *Book of Mysteries*;[133] it is possible that in mimicking this title, Mani was deliberately attempting to attract and convert the adherents of Bardaiṣan to his new faith. The Dayṣāniyya nevertheless continued to lead a shadowy existence on the fringes of religious orthodoxy well into the 'Abbāsid period, by which time they appear to have merged and conflated a number of their doctrinal and behavioral precepts with those of the Manichaeans.

Ya'qūbī, *Ta'rīkh* (ed. Houtsma):[134]

And Mānī authored ... a *Book of Mysteries*, in which he discredits the signs of the prophets.[135]

Abū Ḥātim al-Rāzī, *Kitāb a'lām al-nubuwwa* (ed. Ṣāwī):[136]

He (i.e., Abū Bakr al-Rāzī) maintained that they (certain biblical passages) were

131. Compare Shahrastānī, *Kitāb al-milal wa'l-niḥal* (ed. Badrān), 1:628.11–629.3.

132. For this final sentence, see also Corbin, *Œuvres*, 52. This paragraph is also translated in Christian Jambet, *The Act of Being: The Philosophy of Revelation in Mullā Sadrā* (trans. Jeff Fort; New York: Zone Books, 2006), 326.

133. Ephrem Syrus, *Hymnus contra haereses* 56.9.4: 'nor Bardaiṣan's *Book of* Foul *Mysteries*'; cf. also 1.14.2, both cited from the edition of Edmund Beck, ed., *Des Heiligen Ephraem des Syrers Hymnen contra Haereses* (CSCO 169; Louvain: Imprimerie orientaliste L. Durbecq, 1957). See also H. J. W. Drijvers, *Bardaiṣan of Edessa* (Assen: Van Gorcum, 1966), 163.

134. Ya'qūbī, *Ta'rīkh* (ed. Houtsma), 1:181; Taqīzādeh-Šīrāzī, *Mānī va dīn-e-ū*, 104 (§13); cf. Kessler, *Mani*, 192 n.3.

135. For other translations, see Kessler, *Mani*, 192; Browne, *Literary History*, 1:156; Adam, *Texte*[2], 9.

136. Abū Ḥātim al-Rāzī, *A'lām al-nubuwwah* (ed. Sawy), 122.1–4.

fictive and their use (in arguments) was something to be scoffed at and ridiculed. He cited the claim of the Manichaeans that Moses was among the apostles of the satans, and he said: 'Let anyone who is concerned about this read the *Book of Books* of the Manichaeans. Then he will become acquainted with the admirable things in their statements about Judaism from the time of Abraham until the time of Jesus.'[137]

Mas'ūdī, *Tanbīh* (ed. de Goeje):[138]

... a chapter in his book (entitled) *Book of Mysteries*[139] (treats) the Dayṣānīyya.[140]

Ibn al-Nadīm, *Fihrist* (ed. Flügel):[141]

... a book (known as) the *Book of Mysteries*,[142] and it contains (these) chapters: (1) a chapter discussing the Dayṣāniyya;[143] (2) a chapter (devoted to) the testimony of Yistāsaf (*sic*) about the Beloved;[144] (3) a chapter (on) the testimony about Himself to Ya'qūb;[145] (4) a chapter (on) the son of the widow, who according to Mānī was the crucified Christ; i.e., the one whom the Jews crucified;[146] (5) a chapter (on) the

137. For another translation and some illuminating discussion, see Wasserstrom, *Between Muslim and Jew*, 149.

138. *Tanbīh* (ed. de Goeje), 135.16. See also Flügel, *Mani*, 357; Taqīzādeh-Šīrāzī, *Mānī va dīn-e-ū*, 134 (§22).

139. Emending the text from سفر الاسفار 'Book of Books' to سفر الاسرار.

140. For other translations, see Kessler, *Mani*, 204; Carra de Vaux, *Le livre de l'avertissement*, 188.

141. Flügel, *Mani*, 72.11–73.5; Ibn al-Nadīm, *K. al-Fihrist* (ed. Tajaddud), 399; Taqīzādeh-Šīrāzī, *Mānī va dīn-e-ū*, 161 (§27).

142. A manuscript variant reads *Book of Books*.

143. I.e., the followers of Bardaiṣan. Note Mas'ūdī above.

144. Yistāsaf is the ancient Persian king Vištaspa (Greek Hystaspes), the legendary royal patron of the Iranian prophet Zoroaster. See especially Adam, *Texte*², 115. For an explication of this particular passage, see John C. Reeves, "An Enochic Citation in *Barnabas* 4:3 and the *Oracles of Hystaspes*," in *Pursuing the Text: Studies in Honor of Ben Zion Wacholder on the Occasion of his Seventieth Birthday* (JSOTSup 184; ed. John C. Reeves and John Kampen; Sheffield: Sheffield Academic Press, 1994), 269–72.

145. Or perhaps 'by Ya'qūb'? A James apocalypse? Several are known from Nag Hammadi. *Pace* Flügel, this Ya'qūb is almost certainly James, the brother of Jesus. The reflexive referent ('Himself') can be either Christ or Mani.

146. The 'son of the widow' who is referenced here is presumably the resurrected son of the widow at Nain (Lk 7:11–17), a story also included in the *Diatessaron*. Some docetic narratives of the crucifixion relate that another person (e.g., Simon of Cyrene) was crucified in the place of Jesus. This passage would seem to indicate that Mani applied a similar argument to the 'son of the widow.' See the remarks of Tor Andrae, *Mohammed: The Man and His Faith* (trans. Theophil Menzel; New York: Harper and Brothers, 1960), 112–13. Note also Ibn al-Nadīm, *Fihrist* (ed. Flügel, *Mani*, 69.13–15) and the testimony of Evodius alleging that Mani claimed Satan was tricked into taking the place of Jesus on the cross; Monnot, *Penseurs*, 84.

testimony of Jesus about Himself while in Judaea; (6) a chapter (on) the beginning of the testimony of the 'right hand' after its victory;[147] (7) a chapter (on) the seven spirits; (8) a chapter (on) the teachings about the four wondrous spirits; (9) a chapter (on) laughter; (10) a chapter (on) the testimony of Adam about Jesus;[148] (11) a chapter (on) lapsing from the (Manichaean) religion; (12) a chapter (on) the teachings of the Dayṣāniyya about the soul and the body; (13) a chapter (containing) a refutation of the Dayṣāniyya on the Living Soul;[149] (14) a chapter (on) the three ditches; (15) a chapter (on) protecting the world; (16) a chapter (on) the three days; (17) a chapter (on) the prophets;[150] (18) a chapter (on) resurrection. This is what the *Book of Mysteries* contains in it.[151]

Ibn Sīnā, *Risālah* (ed. Taqīzādeh-Šīrāzī):[152]

And as for books by prophets, like the book *al-Āstā* (i.e., the Avesta) and the *Zand* and *Bāzand* of Zaradusht ... and like the book *Anklyōn* (Gospel?) and the *Book of Books* of Mānī the deceitful dualist.

Bīrūnī, *Taḥqīq mā lil-Hind* (ed. Sachau):[153]

He (Mani)[154] says in the *Book of Mysteries*: 'Since the disciples knew that souls are

147. The expression 'right hand' serves as a *terminus technicus* in Manichaean myth and ritual. See *Acta Archelai* 7.4–5 (ed. Beeson, 10–11): καὶ διὰ τοῦτο Μανιχαῖοι ἐὰν συναντήσωσιν ἀλλήλοις δεξιὰς διδόασιν ἑαυτοῖς σημείου χάριν, ὡς ἀπὸ σκότους σωθέντες 'on account of this (the Living Spirit's rescue of Primal Man), the Manichaeans when they meet one another extend to each other the right hand as a sign of greeting as (an indication) they have been saved from Darkness.' For further references in Manichaean literature, see Reeves, *Heralds*, 123–24; 180 n.39. Puech has called attention to the Mandaean ritual gesture termed *kušṭā*, regarding which see especially Kurt Rudolph, *Die Mandäer* (2 vols.; Göttingen: Vandenhoeck and Ruprecht, 1960–61), 2:140–49.

148. A composition presumably akin to the Christian pseudepigraphon known as the *Testament of Adam*.

149. The Living Soul or Self is the Manichaean term for the portions of Light which are trapped within material existence. See also the excerpt from Bīrūnī's *Taḥqīq mā lil-Hind* below.

150. To judge from some of the other testimonia, this chapter evaluated the claims of various figures such as Moses to prophethood.

151. For other translations, see Flügel, *Mani*, 102-103; Kessler, *Mani*, 192; Dodge, *Fihrist*, 2:797–98; Adam, *Texte*², 8–9; Browder, "Al-Bîrûnî's Manichaean Sources," 20; Gardner-Lieu, *Manichaean Texts*, 155.

152. Taqīzādeh-Šīrāzī, *Mānī va dīn-e-ū*, 373 (§112).

153. Edward Sachau, ed., *Kitāb fī taḥqīq mā l'il-Hind: Alberuni's India: An Account of the Religion, Philosophy, Literature, Chronology, Astronomy, Customs, Laws and Astrology of India about A.D. 1030* (London: Trübner, 1887), 27.8–15; Taqīzādeh-Šīrāzī, *Mānī va dīn-e-ū*, 212 (§37).

154. The preceding sentence states that Mani had learned about the transmigration of souls during a forced exile to India. See Chapter Two above.

immortal and that they repeatedly undergo transformation into the likeness of any form which it can wear, shaped as an animal or like any form cast from a hollow mold, they asked Christ about the fate of those souls who did not accept the truth or learn about the reason for their existence. He said, "Every infirm soul which does not obey its summons from Truth will perish (and) have no repose."'[155] He means by its 'perishing' its 'punishment,' not its annihilation. For he says also: 'The Dayṣāniyya are of the opinion that the ascension and purification of the Living Soul takes place in the human body. They do not know that the body is the enemy of the soul and that it (the body) forbids it (the soul) to make ascent, for it (the body) is a prison and an instrument of torture for it (the soul).[156] If this human form was associated with Truth, its creator would not let it wear out or experience harm, and he would not need it to propagate sexually by means of semen in wombs.'[157]

Ibn Ḥazm, *Kitāb al-faṣl fī al-milal wa'l-ahwā' wa'l-niḥal* (ed. Taqīzādeh-Šīrāzī):[158]

The *mutakallimūn* say that Dayṣān (i.e., Bardaiṣan) was the disciple of Mānī, but this is wrong. Instead he preceded Mānī, for Mānī mentions him in his books and argues against him. They are in agreement about everything we have stated except for Darkness, which Mānī holds to be alive, but Dayṣān says is inanimate (lit. 'dead').

Ms. Or. Brit. Mus. 8613 fol. 16b-17a (ed. Taqīzādeh-Šīrāzī):[159]

And also Mānī says a similar thing in his scriptural *Book of Mysteries*: in it he impugned the miracles performed by Moses (upon whom be peace!).[160]

5. *Treasure/y of Life*

The *Treasure* or *Treasury of Life*, or alternatively, the *Living Treasure*, was another work authored by Mani which receives prominent mention in the surviving lists and catalogs of Manichaean scriptures. According to a tradition preserved in the

155. See Puech, "Gnostic Gospels" in *New Testament Apocrypha* (Hennecke-Schneemelcher), 1:268–69.

156. Note Georges Vajda, "Le témoignage d'al-Māturidī sur la doctrine des manichéens, des dayṣānites et des marcionites," *Arabica* 13 (1966): 28 n.5.

157. For other translations, see Edward Sachau, *Alberuni's India: An Account of the Religion, Philosophy, Literature, Geography, Chronology, Astronomy, Customs, Laws and Astrology of India about A.D. 1030* (2 vols.; London: K. Paul, Trench, Trübner, 1888), 1:54–55; Adam, *Texte*², 9–10; Browder, "Al-Bîrûnî's Manichaean Sources," 20–21. The second quotation is also translated in Drijvers, *Bardaiṣan of Edessa*, 204.

158. Taqīzādeh-Šīrāzī, *Mānī va dīn-e-ū*, 227 (§41).

159. Taqīzādeh-Šīrāzī, *Mānī va dīn-e-ū*, 376–77 (§115).

160. Franz Rosenthal, *Aḥmad b. aṭ-Ṭayyib as-Saraḫsî* (New Haven: American Oriental Society, 1943), 37 n.116: 'According to a hasty note of mine, which I mention here in the hope that someone might verify it, this ms. "quotes Mani from the *sifr al-srâr* about the miracles of Moses."'

Coptic *Kephalaia*, this book manifested itself as a 'gift' from the supernal Column of Glory.[161] The *Acta Archelai* already identify a book named *Treasure/y* (*Thesaurum*) as one of the four scandalous writings which the youthful Mani allegedly inherited after the deaths of Scythianus and Terebinthus. The Latin church father Augustine presented excerpts from what he termed the second and the seventh 'books' of the *Treasure*,[162] but it remains unclear whether he was familiar with the entire work. Unfortunately very little is known about its contents: the extant manuscripts of Ibn al-Nadīm are lacunose where we would expect to find a synopsis of its chapters,[163] and quotations from or references to it are rare in the later literature. One chapter or section apparently bore the rubric 'The Closing of the Gates' (Middle Persian *hrwbyšn 'y dr'n*), where the term 'gates' signified the five bodily senses which the Manichaean *electus* must learn to control.[164] Judging from these limited testimonia, the book must have included a narrative presentation of the fundamental Manichaean cosmogonic myths, an exposition which was perhaps conducted in dialogue with the teachings of rival systems such as that of Marcion. Such a compendium would certainly prove useful for catechesis: a Sogdian historical text refers to an unnamed Manichaean 'apostle' (Mani himself?) distributing the 'Treasure of Life (*sm'ttyx'* = ܣܝܡܬ ܚܝܐ) along with other scriptures.'[165]

Ya'qūbī, *Ta'rīkh* (ed. Houtsma):[166]

And Mānī authored ... his book which he named *Treasure of Life*, (in which) he describes what exists in the soul (deriving) from the redemptive activity of Light

161. Coptic *Keph.* 355.9–10, first published in Schmidt-Polotsky, *Ein Mani-Fund*, 85 as *kephalaion* 148, with translation ibid., 34–35. See now Gardner-Lieu, *Manichaean Texts*, 154. For more on the Column of Glory or Radiance, see below.

162. Schmidt-Polotsky, *Ein Mani-Fund*, 37. The Latin texts are quoted in Adam, *Texte*², 2–4; translated in Gardner-Lieu, *Manichaean Texts*, 159–60; cf. also Lieu, *Manichaeism*², 19.

163. Ibn al-Nadīm, *Fihrist* (ed. Flügel, *Mani*, 73.9): 'a book (known as) the *Book of the Living*; and it contains [...].' The attribute 'Life/Living' frequently modifies two distinct works of Mani, the *Gospel* and the *Treasure/y*. It is notable that the former title is curiously missing from this catalog, and given its centrality to the dissemination of the Manichaean message, it is quite possible that *Gospel* is actually the intended referent.

164. M 2 R II 34-36 and V I 14-16; see F. C. Andreas and W. B. Henning, "Mitteliranische Manichaica aus Chinesisch-Turkestan, II," *SPAW* (1933): 304; Boyce, *Reader*, 41; G. Haloun and W. B. Henning, "The Compendium of the Doctrines and Styles of the Teaching of Mani, the Buddha of Light," *Asia Major* 3 (1953): 205; Sundermann, *Mitteliranische manichäische Texte*, 17; Jes P. Asmussen, *Manichaean Literature: Representative Texts Chiefly from Middle Persian and Parthian Writings* (Delmar, N.Y.: Scholars' Facsimiles and Reprints, 1975), 22; Hans-Joachim Klimkeit, *Gnosis on the Silk Road: Gnostic Texts from Central Asia* (San Francisco: HarperCollins, 1993), 217 n.25; BeDuhn, *The Manichaean Body*, 287–88 n.155.

165. Sundermann, *Mitteliranische manichäische Texte*, 35; Klimkeit, *Gnosis*, 203.

166. Ya'qūbī, *Ta'rīkh* (ed. Houtsma), 1:181; Taqīzādeh-Šīrāzī, *Mānī va dīn-e-ū*, 104 (§13); cf. Kessler, *Mani*, 204.

and the corruptive activity of Darkness, and attributes evil deeds to Darkness.[167]

Mas'ūdī, *Tanbīh* (ed. de Goeje):[168]

A chapter in his book translated[169] as *The Treasure* singles out the Marcionites.[170]

Bīrūnī, *Taḥqīq mā lil-Hind* (ed. Sachau):[171]

Among the scriptural religions[172] and their adherents, the Manichaeans resemble the Christians.[173] Mānī uses this rhetoric in a book (entitled) *The Treasure of Life*: 'The shining warriors are termed "maidens," "virgins," "fathers,"[174] "mothers," "sons," "brothers," and "sisters" because this is the style followed in the books of the prophets. (Nevertheless) in the region of delight[175] there is neither male nor female: sexual organs are lacking. All of them bear living bodies. As divine bodies, they do not differ from one other with regard to frailty or vigor, or to length or shortness, or to form or appearance: (they are) like identical lamps lit from a single prized lamp; it alone supplies them. However, the reason for this terminology (is due to) the contention of the Two Realms. When the lower regions of Darkness rose up from its depth(s) and were perceived by the upper luminous realm to be pairs of male and female forms, the latter (provided) the same external forms to its members[176] who departed to do battle, so that each kind stood opposed to its kind.'[177]

---

167. For other translations, see Kessler, *Mani*, 204; Browne, *Literary History*, 1:156; Adam, *Texte*², 4.

168. *Tanbīh* (ed. de Goeje), 135.15–16. See also Flügel, *Mani*, 357; Taqīzādeh-Šīrāzī, *Mānī va dīn-e-ū*, 134 (§22).

169. This verb suggests that the book was available to Mas'ūdī in Arabic.

170. For other translations, see Kessler, *Mani*, 204; Carra de Vaux, *Le livre de l'avertissement*, 188; Adam, *Texte*², 4. Note also Flügel, *Mani*, 369.

171. *Kitāb fī taḥqīq mā l'il-Hind* (ed. Sachau), 19.2–9; also available in Taqīzādeh-Šīrāzī, *Mānī va dīn-e-ū*, 211 (§37).

172. Literally 'people of the Book' (*ahl al-kitāb*), the qur'ānic locution for licit scriptural religions, primarily Judaism and Christianity. For the most recent exposition of this phrase, see Moshe Sharon, "People of the Book," *EncQur* 4:36–43.

173. The subject being discussed is the use of gendered language with regard to heavenly entities; e.g., speaking of God as 'father' or Jesus as 'son of God,' etc.

174. Note, e.g., Theodore bar Konai, *Scholion* (ed. Scher, 2:315.1–2): 'How do the Fathers, the sons of light, fare in their city?'; also ibid., 2:317.24: 'and he (Jesus) showed him the Fathers on high.' According to Shahrastānī, the Ṣābian community of Ḥarrān designate the spiritual beings who guide the seven planets 'fathers'; see Yves Marquet, "Sabéens et Iḫwān al-Ṣafā'," *Studia Islamica* 24 (1966): 65.

175. I.e., the Realm of Light.

176. Literally 'its children.'

177. For other translations, see Sachau, *Alberuni's India*, 1:39; Adam, *Texte*², 4–5.

6. *Book of Giants*

Perhaps the most exotic text found in the Manichaean canon is the work known as the *Book of Giants*. The 'giants' of which it speaks are the infamous *ha-gibborim* of Gen 6:4, a fierce race of savage beings whom older forms of Jewish story view as the miscegenate offspring of a small group of rebellious divine beings and human women prior to the onset of the universal Flood. While the salient details of this ancient myth were deliberately obscured in the present editions of the biblical narrative, more primitive versions of the story remain available in Second Temple Jewish parascriptural sources like *1 Enoch* and the *Book of Jubilees*. Further narrative motifs ultimately deriving from these pre-canonical traditions resurface in fascinating ways within much later Jewish, Christian, and Muslim compositions. Finally, Martin Schwartz has recently shown that some magical conjurations from a medieval Arabic collection of incantations and apotropaic spells are most likely dependent upon an Arabic version of the Manichaean *Book of Giants*.[178]

Substantial fragments emanating from Mani's *Book of Giants* were identified by W. B. Henning among the multilingual Manichaean texts recovered from central Asia during the initial decades of the twentieth century, and the same scholar compellingly demonstrated that Mani consciously exploited and adapted the Jewish Enochic literature in order to produce the Manichaean version of the *Book of Giants*.[179] Several decades later an actual literary archetype for the *Book of Giants* was discovered among the non-biblical Qumran or so-called Dead Sea scrolls, an intriguing Aramaic composition which exhibited a number of verbal and thematic parallels with the extant Manichaean renditions from approximately a millennium later.[180] We are thus afforded a rare glimpse into the creative appropriation of an earlier scriptural resource by Mani and his editorial successors.[181]

---

178. Martin Schwartz, "Qumran, Turfan, Arabic Magic, and Noah's Name," in *Charmes et sortilèges, magie et magiciens* (Res Orientales 14; ed. Rika Gyselen; Bures-sur-Yvette: Groupe pour l'Étude de la Civilisation du Moyen-Orient, 2002), 231–38.

179. W. B. Henning, "Ein manichäisches Henochbuch," *SPAW* (1934): 27–35; idem, "Neue Materialen zur Geschichte des Manichäismus," *ZDMG* 90 (1936): 1–18; idem, "The Book of the Giants," *BSOAS* 11 (1943–46): 52–74. Further fragments of the *Book of Giants* continue to be identified and published. See Werner Sundermann, *Mittelpersische und parthische kosmogonische und Parabeltexte der Manichäer* (Berliner Turfantexte 4; Berlin: Akademie-Verlag, 1973), 76–78; idem, "Ein weiteres Fragment aus Manis Gigantenbuch," in *Orientalia J. Duchesne-Guillemin emerito oblata* (Leiden: Brill, 1984): 491–505; Jens Wilkens, "Neue Fragmente aus Manis Gigantenbuch," *ZDMG* 150 (2000): 133–76.

180. Credit for this discovery must go to J. T. Milik, "Problèmes de la littérature hénochique à la lumière des fragments araméennes de Qumran," *Harvard Theological Review* 64 (1971): 333–78; idem, "Turfân et Qumran: Livre des Géants juif et manichéen," in *Tradition und Glaube: Das frühe Christentum in seiner Umwelt* (ed. Gert Jeremias, Heinz-Wolfgang Kuhn, and Hartmut Stegemann; Göttingen: Vandenhoeck and Ruprecht, 1971), 117–27; idem, *The Books of Enoch: Aramaic Fragments of Qumrân Cave 4* (Oxford: Clarendon Press, 1976), 298–339.

181. See Reeves, *Jewish Lore*, passim; Werner Sundermann, "Mani's 'Book of the Giants'

This stupendous discovery serves to confirm a recurrent claim found in Manichaean sources that Mani simply expropriated and restored the 'ancient scriptures' to their 'true' form for the use of his religion.

Jacob of Edessa, *Scholion* to Gen 6:1–4:[182]

From the tenth *scholion*, when he (i.e., Jacob) comments about those giants regarding whom it is written that they were born before the Flood to the daughters of Cain:

Some tales about them are recorded and recounted which are ancient and which are fuller than those belonging to the Hebrews.[183] (These relate) that since God wished to destroy them and their wickedness even prior to that total wrath (expressed) by means of the Flood, He allowed them to perish through the evil machinations of their (own) minds: they fell upon each other as if waging war, exercising neither reason nor sense.[184] Moreover, according to the narrative of the tale, (this took place) so that during all the subsequent eras of the world human beings would not experience combat, destruction, and ruin of a magnitude comparable to this one.

Thus the destruction of those arrogant and insolent giants—the evil offspring of those who violated their covenant, being those who were illicitly born from the daughters of Cain—(transpired) in such a manner that many *stadia* of the earth were rendered putrid by their blood and by the foul discharge from their (rotting) carcasses. Large and mighty heaps of their bones were compiled from the corpses. These things are in accordance with what the tale has said. It happened that the visible sign of their destruction remained evident until the Flood.[185]

---

and the Jewish Books of Enoch," in *Irano-Judaica III: Studies Relating to Jewish Contacts with Persian Culture Throughout the Ages* (ed. Shaul Shaked and Amnon Netzer; Jerusalem: Yad Izhak Ben-Zvi, 1994), 40–48; Prods Oktor Skjaervø, "Iranian Epic and the Manichean *Book of Giants*: Irano-Manichaica III," *Acta Orientalia Academiae Scientiarum Hungaricae* 48 (1995): 187–223.

182. Ms. Brit. Libr. Add. 17.193 fol. 61v–62r. I am grateful to Dirk Kruisheer for kindly providing me with a copy of this as yet unpublished text.

183. A clear reference to apocryphal written accounts, as pointed out by Dirk Kruisheer, "Reconstructing Jacob of Edessa's *Scholia*," in *The Book of Genesis in Jewish and Oriental Christian Interpretation: A Collection of Essays* (ed. Judith Frishman and Lucas Van Rompay; Louvain: Peeters, 1997), 195. For the Jewish 'Book of Giants' recovered from Qumran, see Loren T. Stuckenbruck, *The Book of Giants from Qumran: Texts, Translation, and Commentary* (TSAJ 63; Tübingen: Mohr Siebeck, 1997). Note also J. T. Milik, *Books of Enoch*, 298–339; Reeves, *Jewish Lore*.

184. Cf. *1 En.* 7:2–5; 10:9, 12; 86:4–87:1; 88:2; *Jub.* 5:7, 9–10; 7:21–25. One might also compare M 101 frag. j line 26: 'thereupon the giants began to kill each other and [....' (Henning, "Book of the Giants," 60); M 5900 *apud* Sundermann, *Kosmogonische und Parabeltexte*, 77–78, which contains references to the slaying of both giants and angelic Watchers; and U 217 frag. 3 verso, which provides a description of the death of the giants and a possible notice of them 'killing each other' (Wilkens, "Neue Fragmente," 163).

185. For the pollution of the biosphere and the visible survival of the giants' skeletal

The entirety of this (destruction?) was so great and marvelous that heretical and erring persons of a pagan orientation even composed poetical fables about them which were full of foolishness and error.[186] They say that the earth was compacted from their excrement and that the heavens had been stretched out using their skins.[187]

Abū Isḥāq Ibrāhīm b. Muḥammad al-Tibrīzī (al-Ghaḍanfar) (ed. Sachau):[188]

The *Book of Giants* of Mānī the Babylonian is full of stories about these giants,[189] among whom are numbered Sām and Narīmān, names which he took from the Avesta of Zoroaster.[190]

7. *Pragmateia*

This commonly listed yet nominally un-referenced title, an Arabic transcription of a Greek term which was probably mediated through Syriac, is usually thought to bear the significance of 'treatise' or 'tractate.' No explicit citations from this

---

remains, see Pseudo-Clementine *Homilies* 8.17.1–2 (ed. Rehm and Strecker, 128); Pseudo-Clementine *Recognitions* 1.29.3 (ed. Rehm and Strecker, 25). The stichometry of these sources is that employed in Bernhard Rehm and Georg Strecker, eds., *Die Pseudoklementinen, [Bd.] I: Homilien* (GCS; 3d ed.; Berlin: Akademie Verlag, 1992); idem, eds., *Die Pseudoklementinen, [Bd.] II: Rekognitionen in Rufins Übersetzung* (GCS; 2nd ed.; Berlin: Akademie Verlag, 1994).

186. A reference to the Manichaean appropriation of the Jewish Enochic literary corpus, of which Mani's adaptation of the *Book of Giants* is perhaps the most blatant example. It seems possible that Jacob relies more on the 'Manichaean' than the 'Jewish' versions of the Enoch legend.

187. See the testimony of Abū Ḥātim al-Rāzī above. Jacob's cosmogonic 'citation' here erroneously conflates the 'giants' with their angelic forebears; for some authentic references to these concepts, see John C. Reeves, "Manichaean Citations from the *Prose Refutations* of Ephrem," in *Emerging from Darkness: Studies in the Recovery of Manichaean Sources* (NHMS 43; ed. Paul Mirecki and Jason BeDuhn; Leiden: Brill, 1997), 281–82, as well as Chapter Four below.
Another translation was published by Kruisheer, "Reconstructing Jacob of Edessa's *Scholia*," 194–95.

188. *Āthār* (ed. Sachau), XIV, reproduced in Kessler, *Mani*, 199-200, and Reeves, *Jewish Lore*, 43 n.87. Little is known about this author. Besides Sachau, see Franz Rosenthal, "Some Pythagorean Documents Transmitted in Arabic," *Orientalia* 10 (1941): 104 n.1; Fuat Sezgin, *Geschichte des arabischen Schriftums* (9 vols.; Leiden: Brill, 1967-1995), 3:251.

189. The author had been speaking of widespread traditions about the association of 'giants' with the antediluvian period and with the construction of the Tower of Babel (cf. Gen 11:1–9).

190. Translation adapted from that of Reeves, *Jewish Lore*, 22. See also Kessler, *Mani*, 199; Schmidt-Polotsky, *Ein Mani-Fund*, 39; E[mile] Benveniste, "Le témoignage de Théodore bar Kōnay sur le zoroastrisme," *Le Monde Oriental* 26 (1932): 213–14; Henning, "Book of the Giants," 72; Adam, *Texte*[2], 10–11.

work survive in any language.[191] Michel Tardieu has argued at length that the title should be interpreted in the sense of 'legends,' proposing that this work may have served as the principal source for Theodore bar Konai in his extensive narrative recountal of the details of Manichaean cosmogony, but few have been convinced by his arguments.[192] In the most recent attempt to resolve this problem, Werner Sundermann has suggested that the *Pragmateia* is in fact identical with the work known from Arabic and Persian sources as the *Ardahang* or 'Picture-Book.'[193]

A simpler solution involves a re-examination of the semantic dimensions of the lexeme in question. One primary meaning of koine Greek πραγματεία and its borrowed forms in eastern Aramaic dialects is 'business, trade; merchandise.'[194] Given the historical connection between the seasonal movement of trading caravans and voyages among the urban centers of the Roman and Sasanian East and the wide dissemination of the Manichaean message, a title like '(Costly) Merchandise' or '(Precious) Cargo' would be a singularly fitting label for one of the valuable wares being distributed to customers by the merchants. Such a rubric would also cohere with the popular homiletic trope likening the Manichaean missionary effort to merchants marketing their goods.[195]

8. *Epistles*

The canonical Christian Acts of the Apostles devotes more than two-thirds of its narrative account to the missionary wanderings of the apostle Paul. Almost half of what becomes the Christian New Testament consists of topical epistles which this same Paul purportedly dispatched to the different communities of believers which he left in his wake. Manichaean accounts of the apostolic career of Mani similarly focus on their own protagonist's peregrinations throughout the far-flung regions of the Sasanian realm for the purpose of spreading his revela-

191. Brief discussions of this obscure work are provided by Kessler, *Mani*, 205; Schmidt-Polotsky, *Ein Mani-Fund*, 38.

192. Michel Tardieu, *Le manichéisme* (Paris: Presses Universitaires de France, 1981), 55–57; repeated in his *Manichaeism* (trans. M. B. DeBevoise; Urbana: University of Illinois Press, 2008), 41–43.

193. Werner Sundermann, "Was the *Ārdhang* Mani's Picture-Book?" in *Il Manicheismo, nuove prospettive della richerca: Dipartimento di Studi Asiatici Università degli Studi di Napoli "L'Orientale," Napoli, 2–8 Settembre 2001* (ed. Aloïs van Tongerloo and Luigi Cirillo; Turnhout: Brepols, 2005), 373–84.

194. Walter Bauer, *A Greek-English Lexicon of the New Testament and Other Early Christian Literature* (2nd ed.; rev. and trans. William F. Arndt and F. Wilbur Gingrich; Chicago: University of Chicago Press, 1979), 697; Michael Sokoloff, *A Dictionary of Jewish Babylonian Aramaic of the Talmudic and Geonic Periods* (Ramat-Gan: Bar Ilan University Press, 2002), 939; R. Payne Smith, ed., *Thesaurus Syriacus* (2 vols.; Oxford: Clarendon, 1879–1901), 2:3235–36.

195. Victoria Arnold-Döben, *Die Bildersprache des Manichäismus* (Köln: E. J. Brill, 1978), 62–63.

tory message. The Pauline model of epistolary exchange was probably deliberately cultivated as a favored means for maintaining contact with and imparting instruction to the newly established groups of converts: the tenth-century jurist ʿAbd al-Jabbār perceptively remarked on this specific simulacrum,[196] and there are indications within early Manichaean literature that the figure of Paul loomed large for Mani's own understanding of his prophetic role.

It is uncertain whether the *Epistles* of Mani, soon coupled with missives attributed to the various figures who succeeded him as leader of his church, ever existed as an integral collection of letters with a fixed table of contents. The rubric *Epistles* occurs as a separate book-title in a number of the extant catalogs of Manichaean scriptures, but only Ibn al-Nadīm provides a synopsis of its contents, and it is unclear whether the copy he (or his source) used was normative in any sense. A Coptic papyrus codex containing some of Mani's *Epistles* was among a group of early Manichaean books recovered from the Medinet Madi site in the Egyptian Fayyūm and then removed to Berlin during the early decades of the twentieth century,[197] but it unfortunately perished during the Second World War before its full contents could be divulged. Recently it has been announced that approximately one hundred papyrus fragments from what was presumably an anthology of Mani's *Epistles* have been identified among the hoard of Coptic Manichaean literature recovered from Kellis.[198] Further fragments of individual epistles attributed to Mani also survive in Greek,[199] Latin,[200] and Middle Iranian.[201]

Ibn al-Nadīm, *Fihrist* (ed. Flügel):[202]

The Titles of Mānī's *Epistles* and (those) of the community leaders after him:

(1) an epistle on the Two Principles; (2) an epistle on the Esteemed Ones;[203] (3) the long epistle to India;[204] (4) an epistle on the Condition of Piety; (5) an epistle

196. ʿAbd al-Jabbār, *Tathbīt* (ed. ʿUthmān), 1:170.3–4: 'And he would write: "From Mānī, the servant of Jesus," just like Paul used to write. He imitated him (i.e., Paul) and followed his example.'

197. Schmidt-Polotsky, *Ein Mani-Fund*, 23–26.

198. Gardner-Lieu, *Manichaean Texts*, 166–68. These have now been published in *Kellis Literary Texts: Volume 2* (ed. Gardner), 11–93.

199. *CMC* 64.8–65.22 (epistle to Edessa); Adam, *Texte*², 33–34 (epistles to Odas, Kondaros, Zebinas).

200. Adam, *Texte*², 27–30 (so-called *Epistuli fundamenti*); 30 (epistle to Pattikios); 31–33 (epistle to Menoch). The severely damaged Tebessa Codex may also have been epistolary.

201. Boyce, *Reader*, 184–85.

202. Flügel, *Mani*, 73.11–76.6; Ibn al-Nadīm, *K. al-Fihrist* (ed. Tajaddud), 400; Taqīzādeh-Šīrāzī, *Mānī va dīn-e-ū*, 161-62 (§27).

203. Flügel suggests this epistle may have discussed ancestral saints and holy personages.

204. Note David A. Scott, "Manichaean Views of Buddhism," *History of Religions* 25 (1985): 101; Lieu, *Manichaeism*², 75.

on the Judicial Discharge of Justice;[205] (6) an epistle to Kaskar;[206] (7) the long epistle to Fatiq;[207] (8) the epistle to Armenia;[208] (9) the epistle to Amūlyā the unbeliever; (10) the 'one-leaf'[209] epistle to Ctesiphon; (11) an epistle on the Ten Words;[210] (12) an epistle of the Teacher on Social Relations;[211] (13) the epistle of Vaḥman[212] on the Seal of the Mouth;[213] (14) the epistle of/to Khabarhāt on Patience; (15) the epistle of/to Khabarhāt on [...];[214] (16) an epistle of/to Umm Husam of Ctesiphon; (17) the epistle of/to Yaḥyā on Perfume; (18) the epistle of/to Khabarhāt on [...];[215] (19) the Ctesiphon epistle to the Hearers;[216] (20) an epistle of/to Fāfī;[217] (21) the short

205. With regard to this epistle and the one immediately preceding it, see *Kellis Literary Texts: Volume 2* (ed. Gardner), 63; 82–83.

206. Perhaps Kashkar, a southern Mesopotamian city which legend holds underwent Christianization during the early second century. This city name also appears as a variant reading in the manuscript traditions underlying the fourth-century *Acta Archelai* as the geographic site for the fictive debate between the bishop Archelaus and Mani. See Flügel, *Mani*, 19-26; Lieu, *Manichaeism*², 10 n.64; idem, *Manichaeism in Mesopotamia*, 140–41.

207. I.e., Pattikios, the biological father of Mani and an important early disciple.

208. This epistle is apparently referenced in M 915 (Sogdian) ll.12–13. See Haloun-Henning, "Compendium," 206.

209. Literally 'on a sheet of paper.'

210. Presumably addressing the Ten Ordinances or Commandments laid upon the Manichaean laity. See Ibn al-Nadīm, *Fihrist* (ed. Flügel, *Mani*, 64.4, 11–14), translated in Chapter Four below, and especially BeDuhn, *The Manichaean Body*, 53–56. Note too the phrase 'I have written to you *these ten sayings*' in the new epistle fragment from Kellis published in Gardner-Lieu, *Manichaean Texts*, 167; *Kellis Literary Texts: Volume 2* (ed. Gardner), 56–57; 82.

211. The epithet 'Teacher' is sometimes applied to Mani; e.g., 'the *Kephalaia* of the Teacher.' The 'social relations' addressed in this epistle may pertain to interactions with non-Manichaeans; see the lexical remarks of Georges Vajda, "Les zindîqs en pays d'Islam au début de la période abbaside," *RSO* 17 (1937-38): 177 n.2.

212. Vaḥman is the usual Middle Persian designation for the heavenly entity known as 'the great Nous,' essentially a personified form of the Manichaean church. See Andreas-Henning, "Mitteliranische Manichaica ... II," 328 n.2. A variant manuscript spelling yields the Aramaic name Raḥmay. In either case, this is the name of an otherwise unattested early Manichaean leader.

213. The Seal of the Mouth signifies the Manichaean dietary regimen. For further discussion, see Chapter Four below.

214. The topic of this epistle is lacking in all witnesses.

215. The topic of this epistle is lacking in all witnesses.

216. I.e., the *auditores* or Manichaean laity. See Flügel, *Mani*, 286–89.

217. Presumably Papos (Πάπος), whom according to Alexander of Lycopolis was the first Manichaean missionary to Egypt. See Flügel, *Mani*, 374; Schmidt-Polotsky, *Ein Mani-Fund*, 14–15. The testimony of Alexander, an early fourth-century Egyptian Neoplatonist, is found in his *Contra Manichaei opiniones disputatio* (ed. Augustus Brinkmann;

epistle on Conduct; (22) the epistle of Sīs[218] which has two meanings;[219] (23) the great epistle to Babylon;[220] (24) the epistle of Sīs and Fatiq on Illustrations;[221] (25) an epistle on Paradise; (26) the epistle of Sīs on Time; (27) the epistle of/to Sa'yūs on The Tithe;[222] (28) the epistle of Sīs on Pledges; (29) an epistle on Organization; (30) the epistle of Abā to a pupil;[223] (31) the epistle of Mānī[224] to Edessa;[225] (32) the epistle of Abā on Love; (33) the epistle to Maysān (i.e., Mesene) on The Day;[226] (34) an epistle of Abā on [...];[227] (35) the epistle of Baḥrānā on The Terrible; (36) the epistle of Abā on Commemorating the Good; (37) the epistle of 'Abd Yasū' on Associations; (38) the epistle of Baḥrānā on Social Relations;[228] (39) the epistle of Shāyil and Saknay; (40) the epistle of Abā on Almsgiving; (41) the epistle of Ḥadānā on The Dove;[229] (42) the epistle of Afqūryā on Time; (43) the epistle of Zakū on Time;[230] (44) the epistle of Suhrāb on The Tithe;[231] (45) the epistle of Karkh and 'Urāb; (46)

Leipzig: B. G. Teubner, 1895), 4.17–19; see also Adam, *Texte*², 54.

218. Sisinnios (Σισίννιος), who succeeded Mani as the church leader after the latter's demise. See Flügel, *Mani*, 316-17, and the note on this figure in the testimony of Ibn Abī Uṣaybi'a in Chapter Five below.

219. Literally 'two faces,' which in exegetical contexts often signifies multiple layers of meaning. Perhaps Sisinnios encoded an esoteric message in an otherwise seemingly innocuous message?

220. A possible Sogdian reference to this epistle is signaled by Haloun-Henning, "Compendium," 212.

221. Perhaps relevant to the *Ardahang*? This epistle is also referenced in M 915 (Sogdian) ll.20–22; see Haloun-Henning, "Compendium," 206.

222. See Shahrastānī, *Kitāb al-milal wa'l-niḥal* (ed. Badrān), 1:629.6: 'Mānī imposed upon his followers a tithe upon all their property.'

223. Reading with Flügel's manuscript C.

224. Reading with Flügel's manuscripts L and V.

225. A portion of this epistle is quoted in Greek in *CMC* 64.3–65.22 (ed. Koenen-Römer, 44-45). See also Lieu, *Manichaeism in Mesopotamia*, 38–39.

226. A quotation from a 'Mesene-epistle' (*prwrdg myšwn*) survives in the Middle Persian fragment M 731; the topic however differs from what is stated here. See Boyce, *Reader*, 185; Klimkeit, *Gnosis*, 258; BeDuhn, *The Manichaean Body*, 135.

227. The subject of this epistle is lacking in all manuscripts.

228. See the note on epistle #12 above.

229. One wonders whether this oddity is the result of an oral confusion between 'dove' (الحمامة) and 'Hummāma' (الهمامة), the term sometimes used in Arabic literature for the 'ruler' or 'spirit' of the Realm of Darkness.

230. Zakū may be the same figure as the Zakwā mentioned earlier by Ibn al-Nadīm (*Fihrist* [ed. Flügel, *Mani*, 51.8]) and the Mār Zaku whose *parinirvana* is commemorated in the Parthian hymn M 6. See F. C. Andreas and W. B. Henning, "Mitteliranische Manichaica aus Chinesisch-Turkestan, III," *SPAW* (1934): 865 n.3; Boyce, *Reader*, 139.

231. See the note on epistle #27 above.

the epistle of Suhrāb to Persia; (47) an epistle of/to Abrāḥyā;[232] (48) an epistle of/ to Abū Yasām the architect; (49) an epistle to Abrāḥyā the unbeliever;[233] (50) an epistle on Baptismal Ablutions; (51) the epistle of Yaḥyā on Money; (52) the epistle of Afʿand on The Four Tithes.

And moreover there are: (53) the epistle of Afʿand on the First Good Fortune;[234] (54) the epistle of [?][235] which mentions Pillows;[236] (55) the epistle of Yuḥannā about the administration of Alms; (56) an epistle to the Hearers on Fasting and Vows; (57) the epistle to the Hearers on the Great Fire;[237] (58) the epistle to Ahwāz which mentions the Angel; (59) the epistle to the Hearers containing the declaration of Yazdānbakht;[238] (60) the first epistle to Maynaq the Persian;[239] (61) the second epistle to Maynaq; (62) an epistle on Tithing and Alms; (63) the epistle to Ardašīr and Maynaq; (64) the epistle of/to Salam and ʿAnṣirā; (65) the epistle of/ to Ḥaṭā;[240] (66) the epistle of Khabarhāt on the Angel; (67) the epistle to Abrāḥyā on the Healthy and the Sick; (68) the epistle of Ardad on Animals; (69) the epistle of Ajā on Boots; (70) the epistle on the Two Luminous Burdens;[241] (71) the epistle of Mānī[242] about the Crucifixion (of Jesus?);[243] (72) the epistle to Mihr the Hearer;

232. Perhaps read here (and in #49 and #67) Abzakyā, the name of one of Mani's earliest disciples; see F. W. K. Müller, "Eine Hermas-Stelle in manichäischer Version,"*SPAW* (1905): 1083.

233. Presumably different from epistle #47.

234. A manuscript variant reads 'the First People.'

235. ىسو. Flügel suggests Yannū, possibly a rendering of the name of the early Manichaean leader Innaios (Ἰνναῖος). See also Schmidt-Polotsky, *Ein Mani-Fund*, 28.

236. Manuscript variant reads 'Epistles.'

237. The 'Great Fire' (Middle Iranian *'dwr wzrg*) is the world conflagration, which according to Manichaean eschatology will consume the material order once the elements of Light have been successfully recovered. See Boyce, *Reader*, 80–83; *Acta Archelai* 13.1 (ed. Beeson, 21): τὸ μέγα πῦρ; Ibn al-Nadīm, *Fihrist* (ed. Flügel, *Mani*, 58.1–10).

238. Head of the Manichaean community during the early decades of the ninth century.

239. There exists a Latin epistle of Mani to a Persian woman named Menoch (the so-called 'Epistle to Menoch') whose authenticity many scholars dispute. For further particulars, see Adam, *Texte*[2], 31–33; Gardner-Lieu, *Manichaean Texts*, 172–74.

240. I.e., northern China. According to Mīrkhwānd, Mani himself journeyed to 'India and Ḥaṭā.' But according to Johann Fück, the proper noun refers instead to 'al-Khaṭṭ in Baḥrain'; see his "The Rôle of Manicheism under the Early Abbasids," in idem, *Arabische Kultur und Islam im Mittelalter: Ausgewählte Schriften* (Weimar: H. Böhlaus, 1981), 258 n.2. This same epistle appears to be cited in M 733 (*apud* Boyce, *Reader*, 184): *prwrdg 'y ht'* 'Epistle pertaining to Hatā.' See Klimkeit, *Gnosis*, 258.

241. Presumably referring to the sun and moon in their capacities as vessels bearing cargoes of Light to their original domicile.

242. Reading with Flügel's manuscripts L and V.

243. Note the so-called 'Epistle to Kondaros' preserved in Greek. See Adam, *Texte*[2], 33; Lieu, *Manichaeism in Mesopotamia*, 111; Gardner-Lieu, *Manichaean Texts*, 175.

(73) the epistle of/to Fīrūz and Rāsīn;[244] (74) the epistle of 'Abd Yāl about the *Book of Mysteries*; (75) the epistle of/to Šam'ūn and Zamīn;[245] (76) the epistle of 'Abd Yāl on Garments.[246]

'Abd al-Jabbār, *Tathbīt* (ed. 'Uthmān):[247]

The sect of Mānī remained after him: they promulgated his prophetic status and established (the texts of?) his *Epistles* and his *Gospel*. His *Epistles* are probably more numerous than (those of) the apostles or the epistles of Paul.

9. *Ardahang*[248]

One of the more unusual textual productions associated with Mani was the so-called *Ardahang* (Persian *Ertheng/k*), which reportedly was a book filled with pictures presenting the teachings of Manichaeism in a vivid visual form. In fact Mani's reputation as an illustrator and painter is perhaps the most enduring facet of his religious legacy among medieval and modern Arab and Persian writers.[249]

The *Ardahang* appears to have played an important role in Manichaean missionary work from an early stage in the history of the religion. An intriguing epistle perhaps sent by Sisinnios, Mani's immediate successor in Mesopotamia as leader of the nascent movement, indicates that copies of the book were already being successfully produced and distributed during the last decades of the third century.[250] In the late third or early fourth century Coptic *Kephalaia*, an early lay adherent upbraids Mani for failing to include an illustration of the afterlife fate of the Auditors in a so-called 'Picture-Book' (Εἰκών),[251] an otherwise unknown

244. Henning suggests correcting the latter name to 'Rāštēn' and identifies him with the Manichaean 'brother' named Raschtin (*r'štyn*) mentioned in M 5815 II R I 137–42; see Andreas-Henning, "Mitteliranische Manichaica ... III," 858 n.5; Boyce, *Reader*, 49.

245. This 'Šam'ūn' is probably the same as the 'Šam'ūn' who was identified as one of Mani's first followers. See Ibn al-Nadīm, *Fihrist* (ed. Flügel, *Mani*, 51.6–7). The same name also belongs to an important Elchasaite; see Flügel, *Mani*, 133–34.

246. For other translations, see Flügel, *Mani*, 103-105; Dodge, *Fihrist*, 2:799–801; Gardner-Lieu, *Manichaean Texts*, 165–66. See especially Flügel, *Mani*, 369–85; Kessler, *Mani*, 213–39 for exhaustive discussions of Ibn al-Nadīm's list.

247. 'Abd al-Jabbār, *Tathbīt* (ed. 'Uthmān), 1:170.12–14.

248. See Kessler, *Mani*, 205–13, although together with a number of early scholars (e.g., Thomas Hyde [cf. Flügel, *Mani*, 383]) he confounds *Gospel* and *Ardahang*; Schmidt-Polotsky, *Ein Mani-Fund*, 44 n.3.

249. See especially Asmussen, *Manichaean Literature*, 25; the references to Mani in *Calligraphers and Painters: A Treatise by Qāḍī Aḥmad, son of Mīr-Munshī (circa A.H. 1015/A.D. 1606)* (trans. V. Minorsky; Freer Gallery of Art Occasional Papers vol. 3, no. 2; Washington, D.C.: Smithsonian Institution, 1959); Kathryn Babayan, *Mystics, Monarchs, and Messiahs: Cultural Landscapes of Early Modern Iran* (Cambridge, MA: Harvard University Press, 2002), 47–56.

250. M 5815 II R I 134-36 (Andreas-Henning, "Mitteliranische Manichaica ... III," 858); also Boyce, *Reader*, 49. See also Lieu, *Manichaeism*[2], 175.

251. Coptic *Keph.* 234.25-236.6.

title which most scholars equate with the *Ardahang*. The same work finds mention elsewhere in the Coptic Manichaean corpus,[252] and Ephrem Syrus seems familiar with its contents: 'He (i.e., Mani) accordingly states, "I have written them in books and illustrated them with colors. Let the one who hears about them verbally also see them in visual form, and the one who is unable to learn them (the teachings) from [words] learn them from picture(s)."'[253] Ephrem's statement supplies the motivation behind presenting religious teachings in this format: it embodied the Manichaean outreach to that substantial proportion of the provincial populations who were non-literate and thereby unresponsive to subtle philological arguments and intricate verbal proofs expressed in written form. To judge from the remarks made in passing by its opponents in both its eastern and western spheres of dissemination, Manichaeism always enjoyed a certain cachet among the elite philosophical and intellectual strata of late antique and early medieval social circles: in a conscious effort to broaden its appeal, the *Ardahang* was presumably conceived as the most effective medium for reaching the unlettered masses.

Later testimonia which narrate its alleged origin and miraculous reception from heaven consciously exploit the widespread prestige and religious authority granted to the 'heavenly book' and its human recipient in Near Eastern religions of late antiquity. An intriguingly parallel account to Mani's reputed charade for procuring his *Ardahang* from 'heaven' (see below) is associated with the eighth-century Zoroastrian agitator Bihāfrīd. It relates that this self-declared prophet pretended to die and be interred within his tomb, only to return miraculously after the passage of a year showing a piece of green cloth which he alleged that God had given him as a 'heavenly garment' and as a sign of his divinely favored mission.[254] Suggestive in this latter regard is the British Museum manuscript 'portrait' of Mani recently published by Robert Irwin which depicts the dualist prophet clothed in a mint-green tunic.[255] It nevertheless remains unclear whether some Muslim tradents consciously shape their literary (or artistic) representation of Mani to accord with the heretical profile manifested by Bihāfrīd, or whether Bihāfrīd was in fact exploiting Manichaean teachings for the formulation of his own distinctive syncretic program of religious resistance against Islamic hegemony.

252. Note Coptic *Homil.* 18.5–6; 25.5.

253. Reeves, "Citations from Ephrem," 263. See Chapter One above for a fuller quotation of this source.

254. Bausani, *Religion in Iran*, 122, with reference to a story recounted by Tha'ālibī (for which see M. Th. Houtsma, "Bih'afrid," *Wiener Zeitschrift für die Kunde des Morgenlandes* 3 [1889]: 30–37, at 34–35). Other accounts speak of his 'seven year absence' in China. The most important sources for Bihāfrīd's 'occultation' are analyzed in Gholam Hossein Sadighi, *Les mouvements religieux iraniens au IIe et au IIIe siècle de l'hégire* (Paris: Les Presses Modernes, 1938), 118–20.

255. Robert Irwin, *Islamic Art in Context: Art, Architecture, and the Literary World* (New York: Harry N. Abrams, 1997), fig. 1.

This book apparently circulated in tandem with a verbal commentary.[256] Copies of the work were apparently still extant in southern China during the twelfth century.[257]

Bīrūnī, *Taḥqīq mā lil-Hind* (ed. Sachau):[258]

Many from among religious communities have turned to the depiction of images in (their) scriptures and temples, such as the Jews, Christians, and especially the Manichaeans.[259]

'Asadī, *Kitāb lughat-i Furs* (ed. Taqīzādeh-Šīrāzī):[260]

Ertheng: It was (the title) of a book of figures by Mānī. And I have seen the same word in the Darī language,[261] from which it derives.

Abu'l-Ma'ālī, *Bayān al-adyān* (ed. Taqīzādeh-Šīrāzī):[262]

The doctrine of Mānī. This was a man who excelled in the art of painting. He manifested himself among the Magians at the time of Shāpūr b. Ardašīr and pretended to be a prophet. His proof (for this claim) was artistry with the pen and painting. They say that on a piece of white silk he could draw a line in such a manner that when they extracted a single silk thread that line disappeared. He composed a book having many kinds of pictures which they call the '*Erzheng* of Mānī,' and it is in the treasury at Ghazna.[263] His system was the same as that of Zaradusht, and he professed a dualist doctrine, an example of which we next make mention.[264]

---

256. See Boyce, *Reader*, 83; Haloun-Henning, "Compendium," 210.

257. Entitled *T'u ching*, or 'the sacred illustrated scripture.' See Antonino Forte, "Deux études sur le manichéisme chinois," *T'oung Pao* 59 (1973): 240–41.

258. *Kitāb fī taḥqīq mā l'il-Hind* (ed. Sachau), 53.13–14; also available in Taqīzādeh-Šīrāzī, *Mānī va dīn-e-ū*, 212 (§37).

259. See also Sachau, *Alberuni's India*, 1:111; Strohmaier, *In den Gärten*², 167.

260. Taqīzādeh-Šīrāzī, *Mānī va dīn-e-ū*, 488 (§175).

261. The term applied by some later authors to the spoken and written language of the Sasanian royal court.

262. Taqīzādeh-Šīrāzī, *Mānī va dīn-e-ū*, 491 (§177). See also Ch[arles] Schefer, *Chrestomathie persane à l'usage des élèves de l'École spéciale des langues orientales vivantes* (2 vols.; Paris: Ernest Leroux, 1883–85), 1:145.8–14; Kessler, *Mani*, 370–71.

263. Schefer thinks that Abu'l-Ma'ālī has actually seen this book (*Chrestomathie*, 1:133). Further references are provided by Kruk, "Marwazî," 57; Thomas W. Arnold, *Painting in Islam: A Study of the Place of Pictorial Art in Muslim Culture* (Oxford, 1928; repr., New York: Dover Publications, 1965), 62; Haloun-Henning, "Compendium," 210; Geo Widengren, *Mani and Manichaeism* (trans. Charles Kessler; New York: Holt, Rinehart and Winston, 1965), 110; Babayan, *Mystics*, 49. The early thirteenth-century anecdotist 'Awfī states that Mani's *Ardahang* could still be viewed among the treasures hoarded by the Chinese emperors; see Taqīzādeh-Šīrāzī, *Mānī va dīn-e-ū*, 511 (§184); Sadighi, *Mouvements*, 102 n.3.

264. The following section of Abu'l-Ma'ālī's treatise is entitled 'dualist doctrine.'

Marwazī, *Kitāb ṭabā'i' al-ḥayawān* (ed. Kruk):[265]

He (Mani) often traveled through the wilder regions of China and its mountains, and one day he paused by a fissure in the mountain leading to a remote cave. He sent someone into it to ascertain its suitability as an abode, and he reported back to him that at its bottom was a large bright spacious area and fresh water. He endeavored to collect there enough food and clothing to last him for a year, and he also gathered there a large quantity of things for producing decorations. Then he said to his followers: 'God Most Exalted has summoned me, and it is necessary to go to Him and remain in His presence.' He fixed a time for them regarding his return and said: 'This fissure in the mountain will be my path to Him: I will go down it, and I will not need food or drink until I return.' He charged his followers to bring his riding animal every day to the opening of that fissure.

Then he descended it, remained alone, and collected his ideas. He had taken a scroll that resembled paper, but which was very fine and completely white. He painted it with remarkable images, and he drew pictures of every (kind of) demon and crime, such as robbery, fornication, and so on, and beside the crimes the required punishments, and he drew underneath the illustration of each demon a picture of what it produces. He completed this during the time period which he had fixed.

Then he came forth from the cave with the illustrated scroll in his hand. He said: 'I have been alone with my Lord, and He has commanded me to establish His ordinances. This is a book that comes from God Most Exalted!' They looked at it and saw that a human being would be incapable of producing its like or its equal, and so they believed him. He named this (scroll) *Arthank*,[266] and it still exists today in the libraries of their rulers under the name of '*Arthank* of Mānī.' Its antiquity is confirmed.[267]

Shams-i Munshī, *Ṣiḥāḥ al-Furs* (ed. Taqīzādeh-Šīrāzī):[268]

Arthang: it has several meanings. First, it is a collection of pictures which Mānī the painter made. Second, it is an idol temple.... Third, it is the name for Mānī's book of figures, and this meaning is the most sound one. The learned 'Asadī Ṭūsī has said: 'I have noticed the same name for this book in the Darī language, because the letter *sā'i* (ث) is not (used) in the Darī language except in (the name) *Arthang*.'

Mīrkhwānd, *Rawḍat al-ṣafā* (ed. Taqīzādeh-Šīrāzī):[269]

Mānī was a painter without equal. They say for example he would draw a circle whose diameter was five cubits with his finger, and when they would examine it with a compass, none of its constituent parts ever fell outside the circumfer-

265. Ms. UCLA Ar. 52 fol. 6a.7–6b.1, as published in Kruk, "Marwazî," 66.

266. Arabic ارثنك.

267. For another translation, see Kruk, "Marwazî," 56.

268. Taqīzādeh-Šīrāzī, *Mānī va dīn-e-ū*, 520 (§187).

269. Taqīzādeh-Šīrāzī, *Mānī va dīn-e-ū*, 525–26 (§190). A variant text is published in Kessler, *Mani*, 377–79.

ence of that circle. He was generally in great demand in the lands of India and northern China, and he could effect a consummate ornamentation because of the extraordinary pictures which he could produce. He traveled to and fro without interruption within certain districts of the Orient.

It is said that while traveling he arrived at a mountain which had a spacious cave containing fresh air and a fountain of water. This cave did not have more than one way (to enter). He clandestinely brought in a year's supply of food to that cave, and he said to those who followed him: 'I am going to heaven, and my stay in heaven will last for one year. After one year, I will come from heaven to earth and I will give you information from God.' Actually ignorant of what comes from God, he said to that group of people: 'At the beginning of the second year, be for me at a certain place' which was close to the way out of that same cave. Following this instruction, he disappeared from human sight, entered the aforementioned cave, (and) occupied himself for one year with painting. He produced marvelous pictures on a tablet, and he termed this tablet the *Erzheng of Mānī*.

After the passage of a year, he reappeared before the people near the place of that cave. He held the previously mentioned tablet in his hand, painted with marvelous pictures (and) decorated with diverse illustrations. Everyone who saw it said: 'The world has brought forth a thousand figures, but there is not one comparable to what is painted here.' While the people were expressing (their) astonishment about this tablet, Mānī asserted: 'I myself brought this from heaven to be my prophetic miracle.' (Then) the people accepted his religion.[270]

Ḥājjī Khalīfah, *Kašf al-ẓunūn* (ed. Taqīzādeh-Šīrāzī):[271]

Artang is the title of a book by Mānī the artist. It is said that it is an original work (*dastūr*) of Mānī; bizarre pictures and odd figures are contained in it.[272]

10. Unattributed, 'Noncanonical,' or Post-Mani Literary Citations

It remains difficult to gauge the actual extent and contents of the Manichaean 'canon' insofar as a significant number of citations or quotations occur without any formal attribution to a named work. Moreover, in addition to the standard titles ascribed to Mani that are found within most lists of the Manichaean 'canon,' Manichaean missionaries appear to have authored and circulated a substan-

270. See also Flügel, *Mani*, 383–84; Kessler, *Mani*, 380; Geo Widengren, *Muhammad, The Apostle of God, and His Ascension* (Uppsala: A.-B. Lundequistska Bokhandeln, 1955), 83–84; idem, *Mani and Manichaeism*, 109–10; Zsuzsanna Gulácsi, "Mani's 'Picture-Box'? A Study of a Chagatai Textual Reference and its Supposed Pictorial Analogy from the British Library (Or. 8212–1691)," in *Il Manicheismo, nuove prospettive della richerca* (ed. van Tongerloo and Cirillo), 150 n.5.

271. Arabic text available in Taqīzādeh-Šīrāzī, *Mānī va dīn-e-ū*, 317 (§79). Regarding this historian, see O. Ş. Gökyay, "Kātib Čelebi," *EI*[2] 4:760–62.

272. See also Flügel, *Mani*, 384; Barthélemy d'Herbelot, *Bibliothèque orientale, ou Dictionaire universel* (Paris: Compagnie des Libraires, 1697), 293 and esp. 317.

tial number of parascriptural works during the centuries following the death of the founder. Such a procedure might be expected from a religion which placed strong emphasis upon the preservation and transmission of its scriptural truths in a formal written register, whose publication were in turn frequently enhanced by decorative ornamentation and interspersed authoritative commentary. According to the initial chapters of the Coptic *Kephalaia*, it was Mani himself who encouraged the creation and dissemination of such 'apocryphal' works by his successors and disciples: 'Every writer, if he reveals these three great lessons: that one is the writer of truth. Also, every teacher, if he gives instruction and proclaims these three lessons, is the teacher of truth' (5.29–32).[273]

To judge from the titles of the *Epistles* preserved by Ibn al-Nadīm (see above), Mani's successors were actively engaged in the production of exhortatory and instructional literature. This impression is confirmed by testimonial evidence emanating from literary sources. The Byzantine bibliographer Photius informs us that a tractate entitled *Modios* was authored by Addai, a prominent emissary and teacher among the first generation of Mani's disciples; some early polemicists, such as Titus of Bostra and Diodorus of Tarsus, mistakenly thought the book was by Mani himself and quote from it as such.[274] Several Manichaean texts themselves hint that Addai composed as well as distributed religious writings.[275] Bīrūnī's catalog of writings authored by the notorious Muslim dissident Abū Bakr al-Rāzī lists among them a work bearing the title *Refutation of Sīsan the Dualist*,[276] 'a book which alternates (statements) between he (i.e., al-Rāzī) and Sīsan the Manichaean,'[277] the latter presumably taken from one or more treatises written by Mani's immediate successor Sisinnios.[278] If this early literary activity serves as any indication, undoubtedly a number of commentaries and parascriptural expositions were produced by the first few generations of Manichaean sages, almost all of which though have perished due to Christian, Zoroastrian, and Mus-

273. Gardner-Lieu, *Manichaean Texts*, 153–54.

274. The Greek text and an English translation are provided by Lieu, *Manichaeism in Mesopotamia*, 108. See also the discussion in Lieu, *Manichaeism*², 91–92.

275. Note M 1750 + M 216c in Sundermann, *Mitteliranische manichäische Texte*, 26; M 18220 in ibid., 38. See also the brief discussion and further references supplied by Michel Tardieu, "Principes de l'exégèse manichéenne du Nouveau Testament," in *Les règles de l'interpretation* (ed. Michel Tardieu; Paris: Éditions du Cerf, 1987), 133–34.

276. See Taqīzādeh-Šīrāzī, *Mānī va dīn-e-ū*, 210 (§36).

277. Ibn Abī Uṣaybiʿa, *ʿUyūn* 1:315; see Taqīzādeh-Šīrāzī, *Mānī va dīn-e-ū*, 269 (§58). Note also Julius Lippert, *Ibn al-Qifti's Tar'īḫ al-Ḥukamā'* (Leipzig: Dieterich'sche Verlagsbuchhandlung, 1903), 273.15.

278. Interestingly, *Acta Archelai* 61.3-4 (ed. Beeson, 89) imagines Sisinnios as renouncing his Manichaean past and converting to 'orthodox' Christianity. The fictional quality of this claim is thoroughly undermined by the primary evidence summarized by Schmidt-Polotsky, *Ein Mani-Fund*, 23-25. See also the perceptive remarks of Madeleine Scopello, "Vérités et contre-vérités: La vie de Mani selon les *Acta Archelai*," *Apocrypha* 6 (1995): 211.

lim suppression. Nevertheless devotion to the written word and its dissemination remained a vital mode of religious expression, for even as late as the ninth century the Baghdadi Manichaean leader Yazdānbakht was still associated with the publication of Manichaean literature.

'Abd al-Jabbār, *Mughnī* (ed. Ḥusayn):[279]

Mānī has indeed said: 'Our Father of Greatness[280] dispatched His angels to do battle; what He sought was battle against Hummāma[281] and its demons. He gave them orders to quarantine what had become a mixture of Light and Darkness, for they would construct the world from it.'

He said in another passage: 'Light will effect a separation between the Spirit of Darkness and its members so that it is incapable of repeating the mixture (of Light and Darkness).'

And he said in another passage: 'He will effect a deed against it; He will not permit it to repeat the mixture, and its state will be the state of a stallion when emasculated: it cannot reproduce.'[282]

Miskawayh, *Tajārib al-umam* (ed. Taqīzādeh-Šīrāzī):[283]

And Abraham the prophet (may God bless him!) was a contemporary of Daḥḥāk,[284] and therefore people maintain that he (Daḥḥāk) is identical with Namrūd (i.e., biblical Nimrod), or at least that Namrūd was an official in his administration.[285] But a thing of this sort is not communicated by reports about him (may he have peace!), which (is) our reason for citing it in this book. It is nothing but a tale of Mānī and far removed from truth; therefore one should not quote it or dare to mention it.[286]

---

279. *Mughnī* (ed. Ḥusayn), 5:14.8–13; Vajda, "Note annexe," 120 n.5.

280. Or: 'for the sake of His greatness, our Father ....' The moniker 'Father of Greatness' (*abū al-'aẓama*) for the Manichaean Ruler of the World of Light is well known from a variety of sources. See, e.g., 'Abd al-Jabbār, *Mughnī* (ed. Ḥusayn), 5:19.10: 'and the Father of Greatness is the ruler of the principle of Light and its world.'

281. Many sources record this as the proper name of the Ruler of the Realm of Darkness. For a fuller discussion, see Chapter Four below.

282. For other translations, see Vajda, "Note annexe," 120; Monnot, *Penseurs*, 161–62.

283. Taqīzādeh-Šīrāzī, *Mānī va dīn-e-ū*, 181 (§29).

284. Regarding the sinister figure of Daḥḥāk in pre-Islamic Iranian epic, see Ehsan Yarshater, "Iranian National History," in *The Cambridge History of Iran, 3(1): The Seleucid, Parthian and Sasanian Periods* (ed. Ehsan Yarshater; Cambridge: Cambridge University Press, 1983), 426–27.

285. See Ṭabarī, *Ta'rīkh* (ed. de Goeje), 1/1:252–53. The assimilation of these two characters is effected by their common association with the city of Babylon.

286. A different reason is given by Ṭabarī for questioning this Irano-Semitic equation. See his *Ta'rīkh* (ed. de Goeje), 1/1:323–24.

Baghdādī, *al-Farq bayn al-firaq* (ed. Taqīzādeh-Šīrāzī):[287]

The Manichaeans also have embraced the doctrine of metempsychosis. This is because Mānī says in one of his books: 'Souls which depart their bodies are two sorts: the souls of the righteous (i.e., the Elect), and the souls of those who are lost. When the souls of the righteous depart their bodies, they rise in the Column of Radiance[288] to the Light which is above the celestial sphere and remain in that world in eternal bliss. But (as for) the souls of those who are lost, when they depart their bodies and seek to join the supernal Light, they are sent back to the lower world to transmigrate into the bodies of animals until they are purified of the pollutions effected by Darkness. Then they join the supernal Light.'[289]

Bīrūnī, *Āthār* (ed. Sachau):[290]

However, I discovered (that) the author of the *Book on Sexual Relations*, who is one of their group (i.e., a Manichaean) and a missionary for them, upbraids the adherents of the three (Abrahamic) religions for turning toward one direction (in prayer) in lieu of another. He quarrels with them about other things, and he indicates that one praying to God may dispense with turning toward a *qibla*.[291]

Bīrūnī, *Taḥqīq mā lil-Hind* (ed. Sachau):[292]

On this[293] Mānī has constructed his declaration: 'The apostles asked Jesus (upon whom be peace!) about the life of inanimate things, and he said to them, "(As for the) dead thing, when the life that is mixed with it departs and separates itself, it returns to an inanimate state (and) no longer lives; but the life which departed from it never dies."'[294]

---

287. Taqīzādeh-Šīrāzī, *Mānī va dīn-e-ū*, 190 (§32).

288. See also Shahrastānī, *Kitāb al-milal wa'l-niḥal* (ed. Badrān), 1:627.8. It is termed by Jāḥiẓ, *Kitāb al-ḥayawān* (ed. Taqīzādeh-Šīrāzī, *Mānī va dīn-e-ū*, 85, 87) and Ibn al-Nadīm, *Fihrist* (ed. Flügel, *Mani*, 57.11) a 'Column of Praise'; cf. ܐܣܛܘܢ ܫܘܒܚܐ 'Column of Glory, Praise' in Ephrem Syrus (*apud* Reeves, "Citations from Ephrem," 264). For some thoughts on this differing terminology, see Henry Corbin, *Spiritual Body and Celestial Earth: From Mazdean Iran to Shī'ite Iran* (trans. Nancy Pearson; Bollingen Series 91:2; Princeton, NJ: Princeton University Press, 1977), 305 n.4.

289. See also Abū Manṣūr 'Abd al-Qāhir b. Tāhir al-Baghdādī, *Moslem Schisms and Sects (Al-Fark Bain al-Firak) Part II* (ed. Abraham S. Halkin; Tel Aviv, 1935; repr., Philadelphia, PA: Porcupine Press, 1978), 91–92.

290. *Āthār* (ed. Sachau), 331.20–22; Taqīzādeh-Šīrāzī, *Mānī va dīn-e-ū*, 206 (§34); note also Kessler, *Mani*, 242 n.2.

291. I.e., a fixed point for directing prayer, such as Mecca for Muslims or Jerusalem for Jews.

292. *Kitāb fī taḥqīq mā l'il-Hind* (ed. Sachau), 23.20–24.1; Taqīzādeh-Šīrāzī, *Mānī va dīn-e-ū*, 212 (§37).

293. The theory that matter acts due to an innate disposition.

294. See also Sachau, *Alberuni's India*, 1:48; Adam, *Texte*², 26; Browder, "Al-Bîrûnî's Manichaean Sources," 21–22; Puech, "Gnostic Gospels," in *New Testament Apocrypha*

Bīrūnī, *Taḥqīq mā lil-Hind* (ed. Sachau):[295]

And this (idea)[296] was taken up by Mānī, for he says: 'Know that the affairs of the world have changed and altered, and similarly the ability to make predictions has been corrupted, for the heavenly *'sfyr't* (spheres?);[297] i.e., the celestial spheres, have changed, and the prognosticators can no longer obtain knowledge of the stars in their movement(s) similar to what their ancestors could obtain. All of them lead (people) astray by practicing deception, and whereas something may conform with what they say, often it does not happen.'[298]

Bīrūnī, *Taḥqīq mā lil-Hind* (ed. Sachau):[299]

Furthermore Mānī holds this to be so[300] in his statement that 'adherents of (other) religions reproach us because we worship the sun and the moon and set them up as images, yet they have no knowledge of their true significance. They (the sun and moon) are our road and the gate through which we depart to the world where we originated, in accordance with what Jesus testified.' They say he maintained so.[301]

Ibn al-Murtaḍā, *Kitāb al-munya* (ed. Taqīzādeh-Šīrāzī):[302]

Yazdānbakht[303] asserted in his book that Adam was the first prophet, then Seth, (and) then Noah. Then He (i.e., God) sent the Buddha to India, Zarādusht to Persia, Jesus to the West, and then Mānī the Paraclete, 'seal of the prophets' (Q 33:40) and guide of the attested prophets. Thus also has Mānī related in his book.[304]

(Hennecke-Schneemelcher), 1:268. Therein Browder and Puech (following H. H. Schaeder?) ascribe this quotation to Mani's *Book of Mysteries*.

295. *Kitāb fī taḥqīq mā l'il-Hind* (ed. Sachau), 191.13–15; also available in Taqīzādeh-Šīrāzī, *Mānī va dīn-e-ū*, 214–15 (§37).

296. The increase of evil and voiding of astrological rules at the *kaliyuga*.

297. A loan-word from Greek σφαῖραι or Persian; compare Hebrew ספירות.

298. See also Sachau, *Alberuni's India*, 1:381; Adam, *Texte*², 26; Mansour Shaki, "The Cosmogonical and Cosmological Teachings of Mazdak," in *Papers in Honour of Professor Mary Boyce* (Acta Iranica 24–25; 2 vols.; ed. Jacques Duchesne-Guillemin and Pierre Lecoq; Leiden: E. J. Brill, 1985), 2:540.

299. *Kitāb fī taḥqīq mā l'il-Hind* (ed. Sachau), 283.21–284.2; also available in Taqīzādeh-Šīrāzī, *Mānī va dīn-e-ū*, 215 (§37), and see also Vajda, "Les zindîqs," 216 n.2.

300. Namely, that the rays of the sun serve as a pathway to the heavens for the soul.

301. See also Sachau, *Alberuni's India*, 2:169; Adam, *Texte*², 26.

302. Taqīzādeh-Šīrāzī, *Mānī va dīn-e-ū*, 301 (§74); Kessler, *Mani*, 349.

303. A prominent ninth-century Manichaean teacher mentioned also by Ibn al-Nadīm and Bīrūnī and who participated in court-sponsored inter-religious disputations under the protection of Ma'mūn. See Chapter Five below.

304. Namely in the *Shābuhragān*, as above. See also Kessler, *Mani*, 354–55; Sadighi, *Mouvements*, 87 n.4. It is possible that Yazdānbakht was responsible for the Arabic language rendition of Mani's *Shābuhragān*; see Josef van Ess, *Theologie und Gesellschaft*

Berlin Ms. Or. 4198 fol. 532b-533b (ed. Taqīzādeh-Šīrāzī):[305]

This is the book of Mānī (*kitāb Mānī*) the apostle of God. He was one who was empowered by the holy spirit of God, Jesus (may the grace of God and His peace be upon him!).[306] He says: 'This is the writing (*sifr*) wherein I expound, explain, summarize, and make expert pronouncements to those who seek understanding about that secret pertaining to 'the divine craft' (i.e., alchemy). [These are ...][307] unknown by the ignorant, (but) commonly known by the sages; valued as lofty by the one who knows it, (but) rated as despicable by the one who fails to recognize it. It is the stone wherein are four natures,[308] mixed in equal proportions, and it is the best thing in this world and of what exists in it.'

He says: '[...] the greatest gnosis is divided into four parts: the first involves knowledge of the thing and how it came to be; the second is its putrefaction and what relates to it; the third is cultivation of *hw'w'h* and its procedures; and the fourth is its mixture. He was an authoritative angel, and he was in possession of the greatest secret ....'

Take the aforementioned noble stone and allow a flame[309] to damage it in a container until you see that it no longer exudes drops. Then strike it and return it to the flame ....

[...][310]

Comment about incenses for the seven planets:

Zuḥal (Saturn): its incense is storax, pitch, opoponax gum, scales of *al-knrb*, eggshells. Al-Mushtarī (Jupiter): its incense is ladanum[311] .... The moon: (its) incense is white and red sandalwood, ostrich egg, fern, *qṭry*.

The book is finished with the aid of God, the gracious King.

---

im 2. und 3. Jahrhundert Hidschra: Eine Geschichte des religiösen Denkens im frühen Islam (6 vols.; Berlin and New York: Walter de Gruyter, 1991–97), 1:420.

305. Taqīzādeh-Šīrāzī, *Mānī va dīn-e-ū*, 302–303 (§75). See Alfred Siggel, *Katalog der arabischen alchemistischen Handschriften Deutschlands* (3 vols.; Berlin: Akademie-Verlag, 1949-56), 1:113; George Sarton, "[Review of Siggel, *Katalog*, vol. 1]," *Journal of Near Eastern Studies* 10 (1951): 285; Guy Monnot, "Les écrits musulmans sur les religions non-bibliques," in idem, *Islam et religions* (Paris: Éditions Maisonneuve et Larose, 1986), 75.

306. Cf. Q 4:171; 21:91.

307. I have omitted some obscure expressions.

308. I.e., the qualities hot, cold, moist, and dry. See Syed Nomanul Haq, *Names, Natures and Things: The Alchemist Jābir ibn Ḥayyān and his* Kitāb al-Aḥjār *(Book of Stones)* (Dordrecht/Boston/London: Kluwer Academic Publishers, 1994), 57–62.

309. Read with the critical apparatus.

310. I have omitted more obscure material.

311. See Alfred Siggel, *Arabisch-deutsches Wörterbuch der Stoffe aus den drei Naturreichen, die in arabischen alchemistischen Handschriften vorkommen* (Deutsche Akademie der Wissenschaften zu Berlin, Institut für Orientforschung Veröffentlichung Nr. 1; Berlin: Akademie-Verlag, 1950), 65.

11. On Manichaean Scripturalism: Some Concluding Reflections

The earliest literary portrait we have of Mani, one that is found in the mid-fourth century *Acta Archelai*,[312] depicts Mani in outlandishly garish Persian garb, brandishing an ebony staff in his right hand and carrying a 'Babylonian book' (*Babylonium ... librum*) under his left arm. One might compare to this gaudy image of an exotic Chaldean mage the more modest rendering preserved by Bīrūnī relating the marvelous advent of the prophet Zoroaster at the royal court of the ancient Iranian ruler Vishtaspa: '[Zarādusht] was in a garment split at both sides on the right and the left (that was) bound with a belt (*zunnār*) of palm fiber, (and) a woolen cloth (*fadām*) covering his mouth.[313] He had with him some writing(s) in a piecemeal state, carried in his hand next to his chest.'[314] While the disparity of costuming might be attributed to the differing rhetorical agendas of their depictors, it is surely no accident that both of these oriental prophets are represented as bearers of inscribed objects. Zoroaster was to achieve signal renown in the Greco-Roman world as a privileged source of revelatory knowledge and a teacher of the occult arts, especially divination and astrology, much of which came to be registered in books and writings tied to either his name or to those of some of his closest disciples. As we have seen, Mani too enjoyed fame as a producer and distributor of written texts whose authority rested upon the claim that their author was privy to authentic knowledge about the creation and mechanical workings of the physical universe. Unlike his Magian predecessor, however, whose scriptural productions had only a limited circulation among indigenous ritual specialists or within occidental circles of intellectual or esoteric enthusiasts, Mani and his followers oversaw a deliberate diffusion of his own writings and teachings throughout the literate world of late antiquity, translating and subtly adapting his distinctive teachings into the languages and iconographies of the various communities and polities where Manichaeism spread over the course of its one-and-a-half millennia of missionary activity. The result was a remarkably rich and diverse collection of religious writings whose vocabulary and figural motifs mirrored those utilized by the dominant religious discourses of their host societies—Christian, Muslim, Buddhist, Daoist, and so on—but whose syntactic structure of discursive relationships and themes remained faithful to

312. *Acta Archelai* 14.3 (ed. Beeson, 22–23).

313. A reference to the veil (*padām/n*) worn over his mouth by a Zoroastrian priest to prevent his breath from polluting the altar fire. See Martin Haug, *Essays on the Sacred Language, Writings, and Religion of the Parsis* (3rd ed.; ed. E. W. West; London: Kegan Paul, Trench, Trübner, 1884), 243 n.1.

314. This important text is missing from Sachau's edition of Bīrūnī's *Āthār*. See S. H. Taqizadeh, "A New Contribution to the Materials Concerning the Life of Zoroaster," *BSOS* 8 (1935-37): 947–54, which is corrected in turn by the Arabic text published by Johann Fück, "Sechs Ergänzungen zu Sachaus Ausgabe von al-Bīrūnīs „Chronologie Orientalischer Völker"," in *Documenta Islamica Inedita* (ed. Johann Fück; Berlin: Akademie-Verlag, 1952), 75.8–9.

the core teachings of the founder.[315] It is thanks to the discoveries and recovery efforts of modern archaeologists and philologists that we are able to view (relatively) extensive samples of the Manichaean scriptural corpus embedded within its regional habitats.

Given this external veneer of what many have erroneously described as a 'conscious syncretism,'[316] it seems important to stress that Mani does not seem to view himself as a doctrinal innovator or *bricoleur*. According to our earliest and most reliable testimonies, Mani considers himself an apostle for Christianity, and what is more, a Christianity which he deemed to be more closely aligned with the ideas and practices of its initial proponents than those forms of it propounded by other third-century clergy, teachers, and missionaries. The 'ancestral' or 'former religions' (*pyšyng'n dyn*)—i.e., those expositions of what he endorsed as true religiosity which had preceded his own advent among humanity—exhibited a number of crippling corruptions and distortions due to their geographic restriction, their parochial forms of expression, and the appalling ignorance and incompetence of the generations of disciples and followers who supervised their promulgation after the removal of their founding teachers. Mani thus counted himself as the ultimate restorer and perfecting agent of a more pristine revelation, one which required a careful restatement and vigorous reinforcement in a world which had repeatedly altered or forgotten it. Conceived in these terms, his mission was remarkably akin to that of a later Near Eastern prophet who similarly viewed a core motive of his own work as a timely summons to his local community to return to the older 'religion of Abraham' (*millat Ibrāhīm*).[317]

To be 'Christian' in third-century Mesopotamia (or for that matter, in the west also) was to wrap oneself within a rather permeable cloak of religious identity that had little doctrinal, ritual, or institutional uniformity apart from its professed allegiance to the eponymous figure of Jesus Christ and its adherence to a set of allied scriptural teachings that purportedly bore witness to Jesus and to the God about whom he taught. Terming this latter collection of scriptures 'the Bible' can be somewhat problematic, since that particular label misleadingly connotes a structural and editorial rigidity which the Christian scriptures had yet to achieve among the regionally diverse communities which used them. A brief glance at the physical contents of early Christian (and Jewish) 'Bibles' demonstrates that a wide variety of named works functioned as 'scriptures' for Christian (and Jewish) groups inhabiting Palestine, Egypt, Anatolia, North Africa, Gaul, Armenia, Syro-Mesopotamia, and Ethiopia. Moreover, these formally marked rosters of titles are bolstered by the innumerable citations of and allusions to clearly authori-

---

315. Termed by Guy Stroumsa 'cultural' as opposed to 'linguistic' translations; note the astute remarks in his *The End of Sacrifice: Religious Transformations in Late Antiquity* (trans. Susan Emanuel; Chicago, IL: University of Chicago Press, 2009), 36–41.

316. Lidzbarski, "Warum schrieb Mani," 913, a judgment that has been repeatedly parroted in subsequent scholarly literature.

317. See Q 2:135; 3:95; 4:125; 6:161; 16:123.

tative interpretive lore which undoubtedly circulated in both written and oral form and which found tangible expression in a vast library of apologies, polemical treatises, homilies, martyrologies, commentaries, liturgies, doctrinal expositions, and figural remains. Manichaeism unsurprisingly relies upon and usually cites from this same corpus of Christian textual remains when it is challenged by its opponents to defend its conceptual underpinnings, and it is even possible that Mani and his community were privy to what might be deemed 'earlier' or 'more primitive' forms of some of the literary works which circulated under the label of 'scripture' during the initial centuries of the Common Era.[318] Even though Manichaeism would eventually sport a distinctive canon composed of Mani's own works and a series of didactic works which expound that corpus, it cannot be overemphasized that it is the Christian Bible and its interpretive penumbra that are the generative foundation for Mani's self-image, rhetoric, and mission.

318. Illustrated, for example, by their interest in and possession of textual traditions tied to the antediluvian forefathers of the biblical Book of Genesis and its affiliated literatures. This point is argued at greater length in my essay "Manichaeans as *Ahl al-Kitāb*: Studies in Scriptures and Scripturalism," a portion of my monograph-in-progress entitled *Shades of Light and Darkness: Studies in Chaldean Dualism and Gnosis*.

Testimonia about Manichaean Teachings

Islamicate sources cluster the particular teachings associated with Manichaeism around a relatively fixed set of doctrines and behaviors. It is unlikely that this general congruence in description derives from direct experience with bona fide adherents of the movement, even though such encounters might be construed as historically plausible at certain times and locales in the Muslim world. Much of the information about Manichaean beliefs and practices in these sources stems from literature that is patently 'heresiological,' and it would be a huge mistake to read a religion's heresiology—its internal catalog of perceived errors and deviations from a putative norm—as a disinterested report about historical or social realia.[1] While some texts undoubtedly reflect the conscious incorporation of or contemporary interaction with authentically Manichaean sources and informants, it is also clear that a number of tradents are excerpting and thus artificially perpetuating a fairly stable sequence of expository prose which they encountered among the generically similar scholastic products of their predecessors. The likely originary fount for this recurrent textual complex is the alleged crypto-Manichaean Abū 'Īsā al-Warrāq.[2]

The present chapter subdivides the most important Islamicate testimonia into groupings bearing the religious labels Jewish, Mandaean, Christian, Zoroastrian, and Muslim, wherein the entries under each heading exhibit a roughly chronological arrangement. Given the quantity of information that is contained in the Muslim sources, a further subdivision into general topical categories has been introduced into that section and will be briefly outlined at that juncture.

1. See the perceptive caveats of Averil Cameron, "How to Read Heresiology," *Journal of Medieval and Early Modern Studies* 33 (2003): 471–92.

2. His (now largely lost) *Kitāb al-maqālāt* 'must be regarded as the main source on dualist teachings for later Muslim heresiographers'; quoted from David Thomas, "Abū 'Īsā al-Warrāq and the History of Religions," *Journal of Semitic Studies* 41 (1996): 279. For a convenient summary of what little is known about the 'historical' figure, see David Thomas, ed., *Early Muslim Polemic Against Christianity: Abū 'Īsā al-Warrāq's "Against the Incarnation"* (Cambridge: Cambridge University Press, 2002), 21–36.

1. Jewish Discussions

R. Sa'adya ben Joseph, *Refutation of Ḥiwī al-Balkhī* (ed. Davidson):[3]

You know every wicked thing which your mind knows,[4] for your Lord is eaten, drunk, burnt, and commingled (throughout the created order).[5]

R. Sa'adya ben Joseph, *Kitāb al-amānāt wa'l-i'tiqādāt* (ed. Landauer):[6]

The fifth way is the doctrine of the one who asserts there are two eternal creators. May God guide you well! Those who hold this view are more ignorant than all those who were previously mentioned. They deny that there could be two (opposing) acts performed by a single agent,[7] and claim they have never seen anything like this (occurring in real time).[8]

The gist of what they agree on is as follows. They state: 'We see that everything contains both good and evil, impairment and benefit. It follows then that the good that is in them derives from a principle[9] that is wholly good, and the evil that is in them derives from a principle that is entirely evil.' This impels them to think that the source of Good is infinite in extent in five directions, they being upwards, the east, the west, the south, and the north, but that it has a boundary below where it comes into contact with the source of Evil. Similarly the source

3. Israel Davidson, *Saadia's Polemic Against Ḥiwi al-Balkhi: A Fragment Edited from a Genizah MS* (New York: The Jewish Theological Seminary of America, 1915), 68–69.
4. Cf. 1 Kgs 2:44.
5. Davidson assumes this is a reference to the Christian eucharist, but Shlomo Pines correctly recognized it as a description which fits the dispersed elements of the Manichaean 'Living Soul.' See his article "Jewish Philosophy," in *The Encyclopedia of Philosophy* (8 vols.; ed. Paul Edwards; New York: Macmillan, 1967), 4:261–77; reprinted in Shlomo Pines, *The Collected Works of Shlomo Pines, Volume V: Studies in the History of Jewish Thought* (ed. Warren Zev Harvey and Moshe Idel; Jerusalem: Magnes Press, 1997), 4. See also Julius Guttmann, "The Sources of Hiwi al-Balkhi," in *Alexander Marx Jubilee Volume: On the Occasion of his Seventieth Birthday* (2 vols.; New York: The Jewish Theological Seminary, 1950), 95–102 (Hebrew); Salo W. Baron, *A Social and Religious History of the Jews* (2nd ed.; 18 vols.; Philadelphia and New York: Jewish Publication Society and Columbia University Press, 1952-83), 6:299–306. Paul Kraus opined that the infamous Jewish skeptic Ḥiwī al-Balkhī was clearly influenced by Manichaeism; note his "Beiträge zur islamischen Ketzergeschichte: Das *Kitâb az-Zumurrud* des Ibn-ar-Râwandî," *Rivista degli Studi Orientali* 14 (1933–34): 365 n.3; reprinted in Paul Kraus, *Alchemie, Ketzerei, Apokryphen im frühen Islam: Gesammelte Aufsätze* (ed. Rémi Brague; Hildesheim: Georg Olms Verlag, 1994), 176 n.3.
6. S. Landauer, ed., *Kitâb al-Amânât wa'l-I'tiqâdât von Sa'adja b. Jûsuf al-Fajjûmî* (Leiden: Brill, 1880), 48.12–49.8.
7. Note the examples adduced by Ya'qūbī below.
8. See the poem of Abū Nuwās quoted in Chapter Five; also Sarah Stroumsa and Gedaliahu G. Stroumsa, "Aspects of Anti-Manichaean Polemics in Late Antiquity and under Early Islam," *Harvard Theological Review* 81 (1988): 46.
9. Literally 'root.'

of Evil is infinite in extent in five directions, they being downwards, the east, the west, the south, and the north, but that it has a boundary above where it comes into contact with the source of Good.

They also claim that these two principles had always been separate from one another. Then they mixed, and as a result of their mixture, bodies were produced. But they disagree about the cause of the mixture. Some of them maintain that Good was its cause, seeking to calm the border where Evil was meeting it. Some maintain that Evil was the cause: it craved Good so that it could enjoy what was delectable in it. But they agree that this mixture will continue for only a limited time, and when it is reversed, Good will be triumphant, whereas Evil will be tamed and its activity curtailed.[10]

Abū Yūsuf Ya'qūb al-Qirqisānī, *Tafsīr Bereshit* (*sic*) (British Library Ms. Or. 2557):[11]

And we will talk about the issues raised by obscure passages and the passages which are allegedly contradictory that have been remarked by disputants and heretics such as the Manichaeans and others.[12]

Qirqisānī, *Kitāb al-anwār wa'l-maqārib* (ed. Nemoy):[13]

However, the Manichaeans are among those who reject final punishments com-

---

10. For other translations, see M[oise] Ventura, *La philosophie de Saadia Gaon* (Paris: J. Vrin, 1934), 127; Alexander Altmann, *Saadya Gaon: The Book of Doctrines and Beliefs: Abridged Edition* (Oxford: East and West Library, 1946), 69–70; Samuel Rosenblatt, *Saadia Gaon: The Book of Beliefs and Opinions* (Yale Judaica Series 1; New Haven, CT: Yale University Press, 1948), 58–59; Georges Vajda, "Le témoignage d'al-Māturidī sur la doctrine des Manichéens, des Dayṣānites et des Marcionites," *Arabica* 13 (1966): 8–9. An important discussion remains that of J[acob] Guttmann, *Die Religionsphilosophie des Saadia dargestellt und erläutert* (Göttingen: Vandenhoeck and Ruprecht, 1882), 53–58.

11. Hartwig Hirschfeld, *Qirqisāni Studies* (Jews' College Publication 6; London: Oxford University Press, 1918), 39.11–12. It is now known that the text published by Hirschfeld is actually Qirqisānī's introduction to his much lengthier commentary on the narrative sections of the Pentateuch. His briefer commentary (called by Chiesa an 'epitome') on Genesis (*Tafsīr Bereshit*) is extant as British Library Ms. Or. 2492. See Bruno Chiesa, "A New Fragment of al-Qirqisānī's *Kitāb al-Riyāḍ*," *Jewish Quarterly Review* 78 (1987–88): 175–85. Further important remarks on this manuscript are in Haggai Ben-Shammai, *The Doctrines of Religious Thought of Abū Yūsuf Ya'qūb al-Qirqisānī and Yefet ben 'Elī* (2 vols.; Ph.D. dissertation, Hebrew University, Jerusalem, 1977); idem, "Jewish Thought in Iraq in the 10th Century," in *Judaeo-Arabic Studies: Proceedings of the Founding Conference of the Society for Judaeo-Arabic Studies* (ed. Norman Golb; Amsterdam: Harwood Academic Publishers, 1997), 15–32, esp. 18–19.

12. For other translations, see Leon Nemoy, *Karaite Anthology: Excerpts from the Early Literature* (Yale Judaica Series 7; New Haven, CT: Yale University Press, 1952), 53; Georges Vajda, "Du prologue de Qirqisānī à son commentaire sur la Genèse," in *In Memoriam Paul Kahle* (BZAW 103; ed. Matthew Black and Georg Fohrer; Berlin: A. Töpelmann, 1968), 223.

13. Qirqisānī, *Kitāb al-anwār wa'l-maqārib* (5 vols.; ed. Leon Nemoy; New York: Alexander Kohut Memorial Foundation, 1939–43), 2:251.13–17.

pletely. They claim that the one meting out punishment who does not put something right by his punishment of the one being punished, or who does not change it, or who does not (at least) vent his anger or anything else is a tyrant,[14] because he has imposed punishment where it has no proper place. Consequently they say since God (may He be honored and esteemed!) would not be rehabilitating the people being punished, nor would they be changed because of His punishment, nor would He punish them to vent His anger, there is no punishment when facing judgment in the hereafter.[15]

Yūsuf al-Baṣīr, *Kitāb al-muḥtawī* (ed. Vajda-Blumenthal):[16]

I think I can dispense here from formulating a detailed argument against the Manichaeans, the Dayṣānites,[17] the Zoroastrians, and the Christians, since our earlier treatments have sufficiently refuted their positions ....[18]

The Manichaean and Dayṣānite argument, according to which Light and Darkness are eternal, affects in no way the issue which we are presently discussing; namely, the refutation of a second eternal being who possesses the same attributes as God. As far as we know, no such doctrine can be supported. The Manichaean position is self-contradictory, because according to them Light is wise while Darkness is stupid; the former naturally produces what is good, and the latter what is evil. It is a well known fact that we perceive both Light and Darkness. Light consists of white particles which serve as the substrate of whiteness, whereas Darkness consists of dark particles which serve as the substrate of blackness. Their teaching finds its refutation in what we have already demonstrated with regard to the making of a material entity and its properties. The *mutakallimūn* compelled them to defend absurdities when they showed that their arguments implied such follies as the immoral nature of authority and of prohibition, the abolition of praise and of blame, (and) the immoral nature of repentance. That which we have said should suffice.[19]

---

14. Reading *jā'ir* in place of the text's *jā'iz*.
15. For another translation, see Nemoy, *Karaite Anthology*, 336.
16. Georges Vajda, *Al-Kitāb al-Muḥtawī de Yūsuf al-Baṣīr: Texte, traduction et commentaire* (ed. David R. Blumenthal; Leiden: Brill, 1985), 44b (685.20–21); 47a-b (687.21–688.2).
17. Adherents of the teachings ascribed to the second-century Syrian philosopher Bardaiṣan. It remains unclear just how long this sect survived as an integral community. Islamicate texts often conflate the Dayṣāniyya with Manichaeans and other 'dualist' brands.
18. Compare Georges Vajda, "La démonstration de l'unité divine d'après Yūsuf al-Baṣīr," in *Studies in Mysticism and Religion presented to Gershom G. Scholem on his Seventieth Birthday* (Jerusalem: Magnes Press, 1967), 299; Vajda-Blumenthal, *Yūsuf al-Baṣīr*, 134. Vajda (ibid.) reports that the Hebrew translator inserts the following glosses: 'Manichaeans are those who say that Darkness causes evil and Light what is good; Dayṣānites and Zoroastrians are those who say that it is Satan who made what is evil, and God what is good; Christians are those uncircumcised ones who profess the Trinity.'
19. Compare Vajda, "La démonstration," 304; Vajda-Blumenthal, *Yūsuf al-Baṣīr*, 139.

Yūsuf al-Baṣīr, *Kitāb al-muḥtawī* (ed. Vajda-Blumenthal):[20]

As for the problem of physical suffering, opinions are divided. According to the dualists, it can only be evil, and this position leads them to affirm (the existence of an entity) Darkness which inflicts it. The Zoroastrians are also of this opinion, attributing physical suffering to Satan.[21]

Abraham bar Ḥiyya, *Sefer megillat ha-megalleh* (ed. Poznanski):[22]

I have found in the historical books of the gentile nations that it was during the time of this conjunction[23] that the wicked Mānī formed a conspiracy in the region of Mesopotamia. He was the one who spoke of two deities—one ruling over that which is Good, and the other ruling over that which is Evil—and the rest of the foolish things which he had devised to seduce (people) into his heresy by which means he led the world astray.

This Mānī was one of the prominent members of his family,[24] and his fame spread throughout the land of the Chaldeans and Persians and the whole region of Mesopotamia, and he seduced many people with his words and his foolishness. A very large and mighty force gathered about him, and it came into his mind to go up to Babylon and lay siege to it: this happened during the time of Shabūr the king, who was called Bahram son of Bahram,[25] and he was the seventh of the rulers who were called Shabūr.[26] Now when Shabūr the king heard this report about

---

For further information on this author, see Moshe Gil, *A History of Palestine, 634–1099* (trans. Ethel Broido; Cambridge: Cambridge University Press, 1992), 814–15.

20. Vajda-Blumenthal, *Yūsuf al-Baṣīr*, 87b (719.10–13).
21. Vajda-Blumenthal, *Yūsuf al-Baṣīr*, 335–36.
22. Adolf Poznanski and Julius Guttmann, eds., *Sefer Megillat ha-Megalle von Abraham bar Chija* (Berlin: H. Itzkowski, 1924), 138.6–139.18; note also 145.15-16: '... at that time there appeared the wicked Mānī, whose words were not believed and whose days were not prolonged.' The Hebrew text was partially reproduced by Jacob Guttmann, "Ueber Abraham bar Chijja's ‚Buch der Enthüllung'," *Monatsschrift für Geschichte und Wissenschaft des Judentums* 47 (1903): 564–65 n.1.
23. 'The great conjunction (of Jupiter and Saturn) from the air trigon initiating in the constellation Libra.'
24. This characterization appears to echo the well attested claim that Mani's family belonged among the Parthian aristocracy. Note also the polemical theme broached below where in contrast to the 'noble' or even 'royal' patrimonies ascribed by their advocates to Jesus and Mani, Muḥammad reportedly issued from much humbler stock.
25. Only the Egyptian Christian chronicler Sa'īd ibn al-Biṭrīq (Eutychius) and the Andalusian Muslim jurist Ibn Ḥazm use this locution to identify the executioner of Mani as Bahrām II.
26. There were no more than three Sasanian rulers who bore the name 'Shāpūr.' It seems likely that the Hebrew name 'Shabūr' serves here as a generic designation for 'the Persian king' just as Hebrew קיסר 'Caesar' is used in Jewish literature for any Roman emperor. Note *b. Šebu.* 6b for a possible instance of this usage. The seventh Sasanian king however was not Bahrām II (276–293), but Narseh (293–302).

him and about the large multitude of people who had gathered around him, he grew fearful of him and was afraid to fight with him. He instead formulated in his mind a clever and crafty plan. He dispatched messengers to him from among the noblest of his officials and servants to inform him that he believed his words and accepted his prophetic status and wished to enroll himself in his heresy. He persuaded him to come to him in Babylon in order that he might learn from him the regulations of his religion and so that he might strengthen his hand and assist him until all nations had entered into his heresy.

When Mānī heard the words of the messengers sent by Shabūr, they pleased him and he believed them, and thus he was duped by his words. He and all the prominent citizens of the province who believed in him came with those messengers to Babylon: his patrons amounted to about four hundred persons. The king of Babylon came out to meet him, received him cordially, and seated him upon the imperial throne in the presence of the people. He commanded that all those who had come with him be conducted to his royal palace to dine first. However when they had entered his palace compound, all of them were slain upon a stone, and he gave orders to suspend them on the trees in the park which was within the compound.

Then he said to Mānī: 'Arise, and let us proceed to the palace, and I will show you there the truth of your prophecy and the correctness of your words!' He then brought him into that park where his companions had been suspended, and he said to him: 'You have said there are two deities. That one which rules over that which is evil ordered me to kill all these (people) and to hang them up in order to teach all the world's inhabitants that his power is greater than that of the second deity who rules over that which is good. I think that a great argument has broken out between them, where one sanctioned your mission and the other did not sanction (it). The proper course of action for a man in your position is to have himself suspended along with his people who professed belief in him, inasmuch as the controversy between the two deities arose on his account!' He thereupon issued orders to kill him and hang him with them. Thus that wicked one died, and all his people, and their memory has perished from the world in accordance with what the courses of the heavenly bodies indicate in this constellation.

It seems to me that Daniel spoke about this wicked Mānī (in the verse which reads) 'there will arise in his place one who removes an oppressor, an ornament of rule; but in a few days he will be destroyed, although not by opposition or in battle' (Dan 11:20). For in an earlier verse he had revealed to us the rebellious acts of the wicked Constantine with respect to his idols and his turning to the wicked heresy of the crucified Jesus, as scripture states: 'a ruler will put an end to his own shame; nevertheless, he will return his shame to him' (Dan 11:18). Now this criminal did exchange one shame for another one; he put an end to one disgraceful thing but acquired another disgraceful thing. And after him the practice of the wicked Mānī is revealed to us, for he acted like he (i.e., Constantine) did and attempted to erect one shame in place of another, as scripture affirms: 'and there will arise in his place' (Dan 11:20); that is to say, he presented himself and behaved in accordance with his practice 'removing an oppressor, an ornament of rule' (ibid.), for he planned to remove the kingdom of Babylon and subdue its majesty. 'But in a few days he will be destroyed, although not by opposition or in battle' (ibid.): for he only endured in a position of influence for a short time, but then was destroyed and suddenly cut down without rancor or military action. Therefore the entire (scriptural) context fits the case of the wicked Mānī.

The passage interprets all these matters so as to inform us about the nature of all the religions which would be invented in the world during this period of (our) exile, and that there would come into being three religions. The one which was in the middle (temporally speaking) was violently suppressed, and it perished.[27] But the first and third of them have enjoyed a prolonged existence, a circumstance which accords with what is said after this in this (same) prophecy: 'and two of them kings, their minds set on doing evil' (Dan 11:27). These are the two wrong religions which were invented in the world, and they continue to inflict misfortune upon Israel. And after that verse which contained a hint within it about the heresy of the wicked Mānī and his demise and the brevity of his life, there is one which contains another hint about the heresy of the 'madman' (i.e., Muḥammad).[28] It states: 'and there will arise in his place a despicable man, one upon whom they did not confer royal majesty' (Dan 11:21); that is to say, he will act in the same way as those (previous) two deceivers (i.e., Jesus and Mani) and lead the world astray. 'A despicable man' (ibid.) who lacks 'royal majesty' (ibid.): this indicates that even though his predecessors (i.e., Jesus and Mani) were totally wicked, they stemmed from royal or noble lineages, whereas this criminal (Muḥammad) will be (of) 'despicable' and contemptible (lineage) even among his own people.[29]

27. Namely Manichaeism, which is juxtaposed temporally between Christianity and Islam. An analogous tripartite historical progression of pseudo-prophetic religions occurs in the *Iggeret Teman* of Maimonides, but he does not disclose the name of the founder of the second religion (Judaeo-Arabic *dīn*), for which few details are provided (see Abraham S. Halkin, ed., *Moses Maimonides' Epistle to Yemen: The Arabic Original and the Three Hebrew Versions* [New York: American Academy for Jewish Research, 1952], 14-15). Some have sought to see in this cryptic passage a reference to Mani and the Manichaeans; e.g., Salo W. Baron, "The Historical Outlook of Maimonides," *Proceedings of the American Academy for Jewish Research* 6 (1934-35): 9-10 n.6; 72 n.141.

28. Hebrew משוגע, a term commonly used in medieval Jewish literature to designate Muḥammad. See Moritz Steinschneider, *Polemische und apologetische Literatur in arabischer Sprache zwischen Muslimen, Christen und Juden, nebst Anhängen verwandten Inhalts* (Leipzig, 1877; repr., Hildesheim: Georg Olms, 1966), 302-303; Halkin, *Moses Maimonides' Epistle to Yemen*, 14-15 n.16.

29. For a broader discussion of this work, see Guttmann, "Abraham bar Chijja's Buch," 446-68; 545-69, esp. 563-65 for the Mani narrative.

Judah Halevi, *Kuzari* 5.14 (ed. Baneth):[30]

When you find a group of people that agrees on a particular view, this is not because (independent) examination and the inferences produced informs their view. Instead, they blindly follow after the spokesman for a single party like the party of Pythagoras, Empedocles, <Hippocrates>,[31] Aristotle, Plato, and the others; or (of) the party of Darkness <and Light>;[32] or (of) those who are from the party of Aristotle.[33]

Judah b. Elijah Hadassi, *Sefer Eshkol ha-kofer:*[34]

The Manichaeans (אלמנ״יאה)[35] shout and open their 'mouth infinitely wide' (Isa 5:14) when they say that Light is the creator and that it is wise and makes what is good; and so too Darkness is a creator and that it is insolent and wicked and makes everything that is bad, damaged, ugly, and loathsome in the world, both thereby expressing their essential nature. But their words are wrong, for 'a hook

---

30. Judah ha-Levi, *Kitāb al-radd wa-'l-dalīl fī 'l-dīn al-dhalīl (al-Kitāb al-Khazarī)* (ed. David H. Baneth; Jerusalem: The Magnes Press, 1977), 212.8–11. See also Hartwig Hirschfeld, ed., *Das Buch al-Chazarî des Abû-l-Ḥasan Jehuda Hallewi* (Leipzig: Otto Schulze, 1887), 328.21–26.

31. So the early Hebrew translation of Ibn Tibbon.

32. Literally the Judaeo-Arabic text of the Oxford manuscript reads 'the party of shade and brightness,' a phrase rendered in the twelfth-century Hebrew translation of Judah Ibn Tibbon as בעלי החשך והאור (*Das Buch al-Chazarî* [ed. Hirschfeld], 329.15). In accordance with a suggestion first made by Ignaz Goldziher (see his review of Hirschfeld's edition in *ZDMG* 41 [1887]: 705), modern scholars emend Judaeo-Arabic *w'lmyḍ'n* to *w'lmš''yn* 'walkers,' i.e., Peripatetics, and this emendation is actually incorporated into Baneth's text. Yet in light of the author's preceding specification of the followers of Pythagoras and Empedocles, a reference to a prominent dualist sect is hardly out of line here.

33. For another translation, see *Le Kuzari: Apologie de la religion méprisée* (trans. Charles Touati; Louvain and Paris: Peeters, 1994), 216–17.

34. Judah ben Elijah Hadassi, *Sefer Eshkol ha-kofer* (Eupatoria, 1836; repr., [Farnborough]: Gregg, 1971), §95, 40b.

35. This form is a clear indication of its Arabic language origin. Compare the testimony of the fourteenth-century Karaite Aaron b. Elijah of Nicomedia, *Etz Ḥayyim* (ed. Delitzsch): 'The second opinion is the opinion of the Manichaean (אלמניאה) sect. They are the ones who say Light makes what is good and Darkness makes what is bad.' Translated from the Hebrew text edited by Franz Delitzsch, *Etz Ḥayyim: Ahron ben Elia's aus Nikomedien des Karäers System der Religionsphilosophie* (Leipzig: Verlag von Johann Ambrosius Barth, 1841), 118.23–24. Since Aaron b. Elijah worked within the Byzantine (rather than Islamicate) cultural sphere, his work will not be considered further here. For his report about Manichaeism, see especially S. Dörfler, "Ahron ben Elia über die Manichäer," *Le Muséon* 38 (1925): 57–65; Harry Blumberg, "Theories of Evil in Medieval Jewish Philosophy," *Hebrew Union College Annual* 43 (1972): 155; Daniel Frank, *The Religious Philosophy of the Karaite Aaron ben Elijah: The Problem of Divine Justice* (Ph.D. diss., Harvard University, 1991), 85–90.

has come into the hand of a drunkard' (Prov 26:9) when they expound them.[36] For thus is it written: 'Fashioner of light and creator of darkness, maker of weal and creator of woe: I—the Lord—do all these things' (Isa 45:7) in your world!

Abraham Ibn Daud, *Sefer ha-qabbalah* (ed. Neubauer):[37]

It was during his reign (i.e., Shāpūr's) that Mānī[38] appeared. He maintained that there are two deities in the universe. One of them is a generator of life and brings about all the good things which exist in the universe, and the other is a destroyer and brings about all the bad things which exist in the universe. He invented for the Zoroastrians[39] a Torah from his own heart, and (his teachings) brought into being a mighty nation. However, using his cleverness Shabūr the king put him to death.[40]

R. Simeon b. Ṣemaḥ Duran, *Sefer Magen Avot:*[41]

They say there was a man named Maynay[42] who chose to believe in two deities, one of whom made the good things and one of whom made the bad. They (*sic*) became a great nation: they were the Zoroastrians,[43] the ones termed in Arabic *al-Majūs* (i.e., Magians). Shabūr the king of Persia became afraid that they might cause him to lose his kingdom. So he sent him (*sic*) a letter stating that he was sympathetic to their religion; however, he desired that he might come to him alone and instruct him in the evidences for this (belief). When the man had come to him, he spoke to him in private and said to him: 'You should know that the two deities have come to me in a dream. One of them ordered me to show you favor, but the other commanded me to put you to death. So I would like to test which of them is the more powerful (entity).' Thereupon he executed him and then abolished this religion. For this reason those who believe in two deities are called

36. The reader is expected to remember the second half of the biblical verse: 'a clever saying in the mouth of fools.'

37. Adolf Neubauer, ed., *Mediaeval Jewish Chronicles and Chronological Notes: Edited from Printed Books and Manuscripts* (2 vols.; Oxford, 1887–95; repr., Amsterdam: Philo Press, 1970), 1:60-61. See also Gerson D. Cohen, *A Critical Edition with a Translation and Notes of the Book of Tradition (Sefer ha-Qabbalah) by Abraham ibn Daud* (Philadelphia: The Jewish Publication Society of America, 1967), 30–31 (text); Micha Joseph Bin Gorion, *Mimekor Yisrael: Classic Jewish Folktales* (3 vols.; ed. Emanuel Bin Gorion; Bloomington and London: Indiana University Press, 1976), 3:1475–76.

38. Hebrew מאני.

39. Hebrew אמגושים.

40. For another translation, see Cohen, *Book of Tradition*, 41 (translation). Note also Baron, *History*, 6:208.

41. R. Simeon b. Ṣemaḥ Duran, *Sefer Magen Avot* (Livorno: Abraham Isaac Qastillo, 1784/5), 4b.

42. Spelled מינאי, a corruption of מאני. But the 'misspelling' serves an ulterior purpose in the faux-etymology offered at the end of his narrative.

43. Hebrew האמגושים.

minim (מינים)[44] after the name of Maynay (מינאי).[45]

Isaac b. Moses Arama, *'Aqedat Yiṣḥaq*:[46]

And let him not mentally entertain the fraudulent statement which says there are two or more originaries responsible for the different classes of things which have emanated from above. For it is recounted in the gentile chronicles that during the time of the Caesar Constantine there arose a foolish man[47] from the land of Shinar whose name was Mānī (מא״ני). He led the world astray by saying to them that there were two deities, one of whom ruled over Good and the other of whom ruled over Evil. He gathered around him a very large force, and it came into his mind to go up and lay siege to Babylon: this took place during the reign of the seventh king Shabūr. When Shabūr the king heard this report about him, he concocted a scheme to deal with him.

He first dispatched to him messengers from among the noblest of his officials to inquire after his welfare and to contract an agreement with him. (They were) to inform him that he (i.e., Shabūr) was a member of his (i.e., Mani's) faith, and to beg him to come to him in Babylon along with his principal sages so that they might physically appear together with him and ground him perfectly in that faith so that he might in turn aggressively force the nations into turning to it (i.e., Mani's religion). The simpleton actually believed his words and trusted him! He came to him with four hundred of the greatest philosophical supporters of his religion, and the king of Babylon came out to meet him. They (*sic*) conducted him to his palace and he seated him on his throne. He (Shabūr) ordered that all those who accompanied him (Mani) were to enter and eat a meal in his palace. Bringing them inside the palace, he conducted them in pairs while walking through the garden, and they slaughtered them and hung them from the trees.

After their private banquet, the king said to Mānī: 'Arise and let us go in the palace, for your people await us there, and there the truth of your prophetic message and the correctness of your word(s) will become manifest!' When they reached the middle of the garden where those who had accompanied him were hanging from the cypress trees, he said to him: 'You have said that there are two deities. The one of them who rules over Evil commanded me to try all of these and to hang them in order to indicate to all the world's inhabitants that his power is greater than that of the second god, the one who rules over Good. It seems to me that a mighty dispute has broken out between them, for this one approves your mission but the other one does not approve! The proper course of action for

44. The rabbinic Hebrew designation for religious heretics. Its scope and etymology are much disputed.

45. This report is referenced in Guttmann, "Abraham bar Chijja's Buch," 564–65 n.1. For another instance of this spurious etymology, see the talmudic lexicon entry for Hebrew מין prepared by Elijah Levita below.

46. Isaac ben Moses Arama, *Sefer 'Aqedat Yiṣḥaq* (5 vols.; Pressburg: Verlag von Victor Kittseer, 1849), 5:26a–b.

47. Hebrew איש סכל.

a man in your position is to have himself suspended along with his people who professed belief in him, since controversy has arisen between the two deities!' He issued the command, they slaughtered him, and they hung him up with them. 'So will perish all Your enemies, O Lord!' (Judg 5:31).[48]

Elijah Levita, *Sefer ha-Tishbi*:[49]

The Sages of blessed memory term a religious skeptic (lit. 'one who has no religion') a *min* (מין) ... I wonder whether it is derived from the books of the Greeks wherein there is a man whose name was Mānī (מאני) who was not religiously observant, and hence all those who were drawn after him came to be named *minin* (מינין) in the same way that the Epicureans take their name from Epicurus.[50]

2. Mandaean Discussions

***Right Ginzā* 9.1.228 (ed. Shapira):**[51]

My followers, I further declare to you[52] that there is still another gate (to perdition) which resulted from (the mission) of the Christ. They are the ones called *zandiqia* and *mardmania*.[53] They sow seed in secret and assign to Darkness its portion.

48. This report is referenced in Guttmann, "Abraham bar Chijja's Buch," 564–65 n.1.

49. Elijah Levita, *Sefer ha-Tishbi: le-Eliyahu ha-Tishbi shoroshav ke-minyan Tishbi* (Isny: [Paul Fagius], 1540/41), s.v. מין.

50. Note Natan b. Yeḥiel, *'Arukh ha-shalem* (9 vols.; ed. Alexander Kohut; repr., New York: Pardes, 1955), 5:168; also David Cassel, ed., *Sefer ha-Kuzari: Das Buch Kuzari des Jehuda ha-Levi, nach dem hebräischen Texte des Jehuda Ibn-Tibbon* (Leipzig: A. M. Colditz, 1853), 2 n.2 and 309 n.3, where reference is made to this same fanciful etymology. It is undoubtedly sources like these that undergird the more modern arguments for the same correlation; see, e.g., Alan F. Segal, *Two Powers in Heaven: Early Rabbinic Reports about Christianity and Gnosticism* (Leiden, 1977; repr., Leiden: Brill, 2002), 11.

51. A Hebrew character transcription of this text is provided by Dan D. Y. Shapira, "Manichaeans (Marmanaiia), Zoroastrians (Iazuqaiia), Jews, Christians and Other Heretics: A Study in the Redaction of Mandaic Texts," *Le Muséon* 117 (2004): 273. It presumably is based upon the *editio princeps* of H. Petermann, *Thesaurus s. Liber Magnus vulgo "Liber Adami" appellatus opus Mandaeorum summi ponderis* (2 vols.; Lipsiae: P. O. Weigel, 1867).

52. The speaker is the heavenly entity known as Mandā de-Ḥayyē, the principal divinity in Mandaeism.

53. *Zandiqia* is clearly a reflex of *zanādiqa*, the common Arabic term for Manichaeans. *Mardmania* is more difficult; perhaps a corrupt rendering of Persian *mard* 'man, men' fused to the proper name 'Mani'? Alternatively, since 'the lord Mani' (*marmania*) is referenced later in this passage, perhaps the *-d-* is a mistake. An emendation to **marmania* here could then be rendered 'those who follow the lord Mani.' See Shapira, "Manichaeans," 245 for an assessment of the possibilities; note also Mark Lidzbarski, ed., *Ginzā: Der Schatz oder das grosse Buch der Mandäer* (Göttingen: Vandenhoeck and Ruprecht, 1925), 229 n.6; E. S. Drower and R. Macuch, *A Mandaic Dictionary* (Oxford: Clarendon Press, 1963), 253.

Women and men lie with one another, (then) take the 'seed,' put it into wine, give it to the people (lit. 'souls') to drink, and say: 'It is pure.' They invoke wind, fire, and water, and sing hymns of praise to the sun and the moon. Once their soul(s) die, they are like flies which sit on the top of a chamber-pot. The fumes rise up and reach them; they lose their wings, are stricken, and fall inside. They are termed the elect ones whom Mār Mānī has chosen.[54] Any Mandaean who eats of their food[55] will descend into the Great Sea of Reeds (i.e., the infernal waters).[56]

Canonical Prayerbook Hymn 357 (ed. Drower):[57]

Who ate *zidqa*?[58] ... the *zandiqia*, who are sitting on the Column of the Lie,[59] sitting on the Column of the Lie, who cut off their seed from the world, ate it.[60]

3. Christian Discussions

Mārūtā of Maypherqaṭ, *On Heresies* (ed. Vööbus):[61]

The heresy of the school of Mānī: these proclaim two beings—Good and Evil—and reject the (doctrine of) corporeal resurrection. They worship the sun and the moon,[62] abhor marriage, and pronounce foods unclean. They declare that

54. The expression 'Mār Mānī' (Mandaic *marmania*); i.e., 'Lord Mani,' is authentically Manichaean.

55. An idiom for 'who ascribes to their doctrines.' Compare the analogous usages in the *Cologne Mani Codex* of gustatory phraseology (e.g., 'he wants to eat Greek bread') in order to accuse Mani of doctrinal heterodoxy.

56. Other translations are available in *Right Ginzā* (ed. Lidzbarski), 229.17–27; Edmondo Lupieri, *The Mandaeans: The Last Gnostics* (trans. Charles Hindley; Grand Rapids, Mich.: William B. Eerdmans, 2002), 209–10; Shapira, "Manichaeans," 244, also 273–74. Some initial comparative observations on this passage were made long ago by Erik Peterson, "Urchristentum und Mandäismus," *ZNW* 27 (1928): 74–75.

57. E. S. Drower, *The Canonical Prayerbook of the Mandaeans* (Leiden: Brill, 1959), 379–80 (text); see also Shapira, "Manichaeans," 254.

58. The term *zidqa* refers to an offering or a ritual meal. See Drower and Macuch, *Mandaic Dictionary*, 165.

59. A derogatory reference to the Manichaean Column of Radiance/Praise. Mandaic *'ṣṭunia d-kadba* puns on Syriac ܐܣܛܘܢ ܫܘܒܚܐ, or as Shapira suggests (p. 247 n.18), perhaps an unattested ܐܣܛܘܢ ܕܒܗܪܘܬܐ. Another reference to this same image occurs in *Right Ginzā* (ed. Lidzbarski), 374.27–30.

60. 'Eating' again seems to serve here as a metaphor for the imbibing of heretical teachings. For other translations, see Drower, *Canonical Prayerbook*, 251; idem, "Mandaean Polemic," *BSOAS* 25 (1962): 445–46; Shapira, "Manichaeans," 255.

61. Arthur Vööbus, ed., *The Canons Ascribed to Mārūtā of Maipherqaṭ and Related Sources* (CSCO 439, scrip. syri t. 191; Louvain: Peeters, 1982), 24.9–16.

62. Cf. Alexander of Lycopolis, *Contra Manichaei opiniones disputatio* (ed. Augustus Brinkmann; Leipzig: B. G. Teubner, 1895), 7.27–8.1: τιμῶσι δὲ μάλιστα ἥλιον καὶ σελήνην οὐχ ὡς θεούς, ἀλλ´ ὡς ὁδὸν δι´ ἧς ἔστιν πρὸς θεὸν ἀφικέσθαι 'and they show

everything in the world possesses a soul. They possess much deviousness[63] in their doctrines, and utter blasphemy and confusion against God. They proclaim the seven and the twelve.[64] They speak of the existence of fates, destinies, and zodiacal signs, and they practice the Chaldean sciences and are accomplished in divination.[65]

Synodicon Orientale (ed. Chabot):[66]

In the land of the Persians from the time of the apostles until the present (612 CE) not a single heretic appeared who introduced dissensions and divisions into this faith (i.e., Christianity). But in the land of the Romans from the time of the apostles until the present there were many different heresies, and many (people) were corrupted. And when they were chased out from there, afterwards their 'darknesses' found asylum here, such as (that of) the Manichaeans,[67] the Marcionites, and also those Severans—the 'God-sufferers'[68]—with their destructive doctrine.[69]

Chronicon Maroniticum (ed. Brooks):[70]

Manī says in his teaching that there were two original beings (ܐܝܬܝ̈ܐ): God and Hyle (ܗܘܠܐ). One was Good and possessed the east, north, west, and upper re-

---

special honor to the sun and the moon, not as gods, but as the way by which one comes to the realm of divinity.'

63. Read ܘܥܩܡܘܬܐ in place of ܘܥܩܡܡܘܬܐ in Vööbus's printed text. This was presumably a misprint.
64. I.e., the astral powers associated with the seven planets and the twelve signs of the zodiac.
65. For other translations, see Adolf Harnack, *Der Ketzer-Katalog des Bischofs Maruta von Maipherkat* (Texte und Untersuchungen zur Geschichte der altchristlichen Literatur, neue Folge 4.1b; Leipzig: J. C. Hinrichs, 1899), 9; Felix Haase, *Altchristliche Kirchengeschichte nach orientalischen Quellen* (Leipzig: Otto Harrassowitz, 1925), 362; Arthur Vööbus, ed., *Canons Ascribed to Mārūtā of Maipherqaṭ and Related Sources* (CSCO 440, scrip. syri t. 192; Louvain: Peeters, 1982), 19.
66. J. B. Chabot, ed., *Synodicon orientale ou Recueil de synods nestoriens* (Paris: Imprimerie nationale, 1902), 567.18–24.
67. Ironically just as the West disparaged Manichaeism as a 'poison' spread from Persia (e.g., the edict of Diocletian), here the Church of the East officially brands Manichaeism as a pernicious import from Rome.
68. I.e., Monophysites or Jacobites.
69. See also Alfred Adam, ed., *Texte zum Manichäismus* (2nd ed.; Berlin: W. de Gruyter, 1969), 83–84; Samuel N. C. Lieu, *Manichaeism in the Later Roman Empire and Medieval China* (2nd ed.; WUNT 63; Tübingen: J. C. B. Mohr, 1992), 125; Joel Thomas Walker, *The Legend of Mar Qardagh: Narrative and Christian Heroism in Late Antique Iraq* (Berkeley: University of California Press, 2006), 94 n.28.
70. E.-W. Brooks, ed., *Chronica Minora II* (CSCO 3, scrip. syri, t.3; Louvain: Secrétariat du CorpusSCO, 1904), 60.9–22.

gions; and the other being that he called Hyle which was Evil possessed the southern regions.[71] This so-called Hyle was in a perpetual state of uproar.[72] Its members[73] — demons, fire, water, and idols — confronted one another and were chasing and putting each other to flight. When they arrived at hea[v]en, the Region of Light, they sought to mix their Darkness with the Good and the Light. But when God beheld them, he imprisoned them [th]ere, and taking a small portion of Light he threw it down to Hyle in the likeness of a hook,[74] and when Hyle swallowed it, he was cau[gh]t by it. For this reason Go[d] was compelled, so to speak, to create [the universe ...].[75]

Theodore bar Konai, *Scholion* (ed. Scher):[76]

Regarding his abominable teaching:

It is however proper that we record in this book a little of the absurd blasphemy of the wicked Mānī in order to confound the Manichaeans. He (Mani) says

71. Compare Michael Syrus: 'He said there was a god in the Light and he possessed the eastern, western, northern, and upper regions; and another which was Hyle whose name was evil and he possessed the southern and lower regions.' The sacral topography outlined here corresponds with that propounded in Mandaeism; to wit, that South is the locality of evil spirits, and that North, East, and West are associated with benevolent ones. The opposite situation prevails in Zoroastrianism, where North is associated with evil, and South, East, and West with good. Note also Bīrūnī, *Āthār* (ed. Sachau), 331 reproduced below: the idolators of Ḥarrān turned in prayer (*qibla*) toward the south, whereas the Ṣābians (Mandaeans?) turn toward the north. Bīrūnī thinks that Manichaeans also turn in prayer toward the north, although a later Manichaean author denies any such *qibla*. For some discussion, see Kurt Rudolph, *Die Mandäer* (2 vols.; Göttingen: Vandenhoeck and Ruprecht, 1960–61), 1:179 n.2; also I. Scheftelowitz, *Die Entstehung der manichäischen Religion und des Erlösungsmysteriums* (Giessen: A. Töpelmann, 1922), 16.

72. Well attested across a broad spectrum of both western and eastern sources, 'uncoordinated movement is a major characteristic of these negative forces.' The quotation comes from Aloïs van Tongerloo, "The Father of Greatness," in *Gnosisforschung und Religionsgeschichte: Festschrift für Kurt Rudolph zum 65. Geburtstag* (ed. Holger Preissler and Hubert Seiwert; Marburg: diagonal-Verlag, 1994), 331. Compare Severus of Antioch, *Homily 123*: 'the cause that led them to ascend from here up to the Worlds of Light was their turbulence (ܫܓܘܫܝܐ).' This passage is cited from the edition of Maurice Brière, "Les Homiliae Cathedrales de Sévère d'Antioche, traduction syriaque de Jacques d'Édesse CXX à CXXV," *Patrologia Orientalis* 29 (1960): 164.11–12; note also 'Abd al-Jabbār, *Mughnī* (ed. Ḥusayn), 5:19.13–14 (see below).

73. Literally 'its progeny' (ܒܢܝ̈ܗ).

74. The 'form' of the Light not mentioned in Michael Syrus.

75. The remainder of the *Chronicon Maroniticum* notice on Mani is missing from here on, but Michael Syrus preserves what is lacking. See below.
See also Adam, *Texte*[2], 75.

76. Theodore bar Konai, *Liber Scholiorum* (CSCO 55, 69; 2 vols.; ed. A. Scher; Paris: Carolus Poussielgue, 1910-12), 2:313.10–318.4. See also Henri Pognon, *Inscriptions mandaïtes des coupes de Khouabir* (Paris, 1898; repr., Amsterdam: Philo Press, 1979), 127.1-131.7.

that before heaven and earth and all that they contain came into being, there existed two entities (ܟܝ̈ܢܝܢ): one Good and the other Evil. The Good entity dwelt in the Region of Light, and he terms him the Father of Greatness, and he says that there were dwelling (there) in addition to him (the Father) his five 'shekinahs':[77] mind, knowledge, intellect, thought, (and) reflection. The Evil entity he terms the <King>[78] of Darkness, and he says that he dwelt in the Land of Darkness with his five 'aeons' (ܥܠ̈ܡܐ): the aeon of smoke, the aeon of fire, the aeon of wind, the aeon of water, and the aeon of darkness. He says that when the <King> of Darkness contemplated ascending to the Region of Light, those five shekinahs (there) became agitated, and he says that at that time the Father of Greatness took thought and said: 'I will not send from my worlds any of these five shekinahs to do battle because they were created by me for tranquility and peace. Instead, I myself will go[79] and do battle.'

He says that the Father of Greatness evoked the Mother of Life, and the Mother of Life evoked the Primal Man, and Primal Man evoked his five sons, like a man who puts on armor for battle. He says that an angel whose name was *Nḥšbṭ*[80] went out in front of him, holding in his hand a crown of victory,[81] and he says that he spread (or shed) light before Primal Man. When the <King> of Darkness saw him, he (the King) took thought and said, 'The thing that I desired which was distant, I have discovered nearby!' Then Primal Man gave himself and his five sons as food to the five sons of Darkness, just as a man who has an enemy mixes deadly poison in a cake (and) gives (it) to him.

And he says that when they had eaten them, the reasoning power of the five luminous deities was removed, and they became like a man bitten by a rabid dog or a serpent due to the venom of the sons of Darkness. He says that Primal Man regained his rationality and prayed seven times to the Father of Greatness, and

77. These five 'shekinahs' are equivalent to the five 'limbs' of the King of the Light-Paradises mentioned by Ibn al-Nadīm, *Fihrist* (*apud* Flügel, *Mani*), 52.15–16; see below. On the plurality of 'shekinahs,' and also this word's employment as a Mandaean *technicus terminus*, see the important remarks of Gershom Scholem, *On the Mystical Shape of the Godhead: Basic Concepts in the Kabbalah* (trans. Joachim Neugroschel; New York: Schocken, 1991), 150–51; also Pierre Jean de Menasce, *Une apologétique mazdéenne du IXᵉ siècle: Škand-Gumānīk Vičār* (Fribourg: Librairie de l'Université, 1945), 261. Mandaic *škynt'* signifies a heavenly residence or domicile; see Mark Lidzbarski, *Das Johannesbuch der Mandäer* (2 vols.; Giessen: Alfred Töpelmann, 1905–15), 2:5 n.2.

78. Read ܡܠܟ in place of ܡܠܐܟ. The same emendation is required several more times below.

79. Theodore bar Konai, *Scholion*, 2:313.26: ܐܠܐ ܒܢܦܫܝ ܐܙܠ 'Instead, I *myself* will go ....' Compare Ibn al-Nadīm, *Fihrist* (*apud* Flügel, *Mani*, 54.4): 'He (i.e., Mānī) said: "Those who were his (i.e., the King's) armies had the power to subdue him; however, he wanted to take on this (opponent) *himself* (بنفسه).'"

80. Vocalization and etymology unknown.

81. Presumably the same entity referred to in the longer Byzantine abjuration as Στεφανηφόρον or 'crown-bearer.' See Adam, *Texte*², 97–98.

he (the Father) evoked the Second Evocation,[82] the Beloved of the Lights.[83] The Beloved of the Lights evoked the Great *Ban*, and the Great *Ban* evoked the Living Spirit. The Living Spirit evoked his five sons: the Ornament of Splendor[84] from his mind, the Great King of Honor from his knowledge, the Adamos of Light from his intellect, the King of Glory from his thought, and the Porter from his reflection. They came to the Land of Darkness and found Primal Man and his five sons engulfed by Darkness. Then the Living Spirit cried out with his voice, and the voice of the Living Spirit was like a sharp sword,[85] and it uncovered the form of Primal Man, and he said to him: 'Greetings to you, O Excellent One among evil entities, O Luminous One in the midst of Darkness, O Divine One dwelling among wrathful beasts who have no knowledge of <his> glory!'[86] Then Primal Man answered him and said: 'Come in peace, O bringer of the merchandise of tranquility and peace!' And he said: 'How do our Fathers,[87] the sons of Light, fare in their city?' The Caller answered him: 'They are faring well!' The Caller and the Respondent joined together and ascended to the Mother of Life and the Living Spirit. The Living Spirit clothed himself with the Caller, and the Mother of Life clothed herself with the Respondent, her beloved son, and they descended to the Land of Darkness where Primal Man and his sons were.

Then the Living Spirit commanded three of his sons, that each should kill and should skin the archons, the sons of Darkness, and bring (them) to the Mother of Life. The Mother of Life stretched out the heavens from their skins,[88] and she

82. ܘܩܪܐ ܩܪܝܬܐ ܕܬܪܬܝܢ ܠܚܒܝܒ ܢܗܝܪܐ. Since Manichaean theogony employs the verb ܩܪܐ as its primary verb of action, the word ܩܪܝܬܐ might legitimately be translated as 'creation.' See Pognon, *Inscriptions*, 185 n.1, 187 n.3; Theodor Nöldeke, "[Review of Pognon, *Inscriptions*]," *Wiener Zeitschrift für die Kunde des Morgenlandes* 12 (1898): 358.

83. This same character figures in a parallel account supplied by Ibn al-Nadīm (see below). There he is solely credited with the rescue of Primal Man from his plight.

84. See the remarks of Pognon, *Inscriptions*, 187 n.3; also Riccardo Contini, "Hypothèses sur l'araméen manichéen," *Annali di Ca' Foscari: Rivista della Facoltà di lingue e letterature straniere di Ca' Foscari dell'Università di Venezia* 34 (1995): 74.

85. Cf. Ibn al-Nadīm, *Fihrist* (*apud* Flügel, *Mani*, 55.6-7): فدعا روح الحياة الانسان القديم بصوت عالى كالبرق فى سرعة 'and the Living Spirit called out to Primal Man in a loud voice (which was) like lightning in its rapidity.'

86. Compare the Middle Iranian rhetorical parallels found in Werner Sundermann, *Mittelpersische und parthische kosmogonische und Parabeltexte der Manichäer* (Berlin Turfantexte 4; Berlin: Akademie-Verlag, 1973), 17–18.14–19; 43–44.797–801; 53.

87. See the instruction of Adam by Jesus below, and Yves Marquet, "Sabéens et Iḫwān al-Ṣafā'," *Studia Islamica* 24 (1966): 65.

88. On constructing the 'heavens' from 'skins,' see the references to Ephrem Syrus, Epiphanius, John of Damascus, and the Zoroastrian *Škand-Gumānīk-Vičār* cited in John C. Reeves, "Manichaean Citations from the *Prose Refutations* of Ephrem," in *Emerging From Darkness: Studies in the Recovery of Manichaean Sources* (NHMS 43; ed. Paul Mirecki and Jason BeDuhn; Leiden: Brill, 1997), 281–82 n.79. Note also the testimony of Abū Ḥātim al-Rāzī cited in Chapter Three above.

made eleven heavens (*sic*!).[89] They threw down their bodies to the Land of Darkness, and they made eight earths.[90] And the five sons of the Living Spirit each completed their task—the Ornament of Splendor is the one who holds the five luminous deities by their loins, and below their loins the heavens were spread out, and the Porter is the one who bends upon one of his knees and supports the earths. After the heavens and earths were made, the Great King of Honor took a seat in the midst of the heavens and kept watch over the whole.

Then the Living Spirit revealed his forms (*sic*) to the sons of Darkness, and he strained out (some) light from the light that these had consumed from those five luminous deities,[91] and made (from it) the sun and the moon, and from the light which remained (after making these) vessel(s) he made 'wheels' of wind, water, and fire.[92] He descended (and) forged them near the Porter. The King of Glory evoked and raised over them a covering so that they (the sun and moon?) can ascend over those archons who are subjugated in the earths, so that they may

---

89. Usually 'ten' heavens, although if the zodiacal sphere is counted, 'eleven' is the proper sum. See Coptic *Keph.* 88.6-7; F. C. Andreas and W. B. Henning, "Mitteliranische Manichaica aus Chinesisch-Turkestan, I," *SPAW* (1932): 177 n.7; 183 n.2; W. B. Henning, "A Sogdian Fragment of the Manichaean Cosmogony," *BSOAS* 12 (1947–48): 306-18; Sundermann, *Kosmogonische und Parabeltexte*, 56.1054; Franz Cumont and M.-A. Kugener, *Recherches sur le manichéisme* (Bruxelles: H. Lamertin, 1908–12), 28 n.2; A. V. Williams Jackson, *Researches in Manichaeism* (New York, 1932; repr., New York: AMS Press, 1965), 314–20. The motif of 'ten heavens' also plays a role among the Ophites, Valentinians, Mazdakites, Pythagoreans, and in the so-called 'long' version of *2 Enoch*. Note also *Apoc. Paul* (NHC V, 2) 24.5–7, and the remarks of David Frankfurter, "The Legacy of Jewish Apocalypses in Early Christianity: Regional Trajectories," in *The Jewish Apocalyptic Heritage in Early Christianity* (CRINT III.4; ed. James C. VanderKam and William Adler; Minneapolis: Fortress, 1996), 159.

90. See Sundermann, *Kosmogonische und Parabeltexte*, 45–46.846–47; Jackson, *Researches*, 314–20.

91. Foreshadowing the 'seduction of the archons' motif normally associated with the behavior of the Messenger below. See Werner Sundermann, "Der Lebendige Geist als Verführer der Dämonen," in *Manichaica Selecta: Studies Presented to Professor Julien Ries on the Occasion of his Seventieth Birthday* (ed. Aloïs van Tongerloo and Søren Giversen; Louvain: International Association of Manichaean Studies, 1991), 339–42.

92. Cumont-Kugener, *Recherches*, 31 n.2. See *Keph.* 171.4–5, 23–24: 'The fourth watch, over which the King of Glory has governance, contains the three "wheels" ... the motion and the ascent of the three wheels of wind, water, and fire was hindered.' According to *Keph.* 91.27-29; 113.31-32; 172.16, it is the King of Glory who is responsible for 'turning' the wheels. Note also *Ps-Bk.* 2.15–17; 37.4–5; 138.46–48; 144.32–145.2; Augustine, *Contra Faustum* 15.6; 20.10; M 292 I V? I line 3 (Sundermann, *Kosmogonische und Parabeltexte*, 48.885). These 'wheels' are often termed 'garments'; see *Keph.* 107.20–26; M 98 I V lines 1–5 (*apud* Manfred Hutter, *Manis kosmogonische Šābuhragān-Texte: Edition, Kommentar und literaturgeschichtliche Einordung der manichäisch-mittelpersischen Handschriften M 98/99 I und M 7980–7984* [Wiesbaden: Otto Harrassowitz, 1992],12); Sundermann, *Kosmogonische und Parabeltexte*, 46.847–48 (and n.16); 56.1055; 61.1161–62; Jackson, *Researches*, 61 n.85.

serve the five luminous deities and not be harmed by the venom of the archons.

He says then the Mother of Life and Primal Man and the Living Spirit rose in prayer and beseeched the Father of Greatness. The Father of Greatness hearkened to them and evoked the Third Evocation, the Messenger. The Messenger evoked twelve virgins with their garments, crowns, and attributes—the first is majesty, the second wisdom, the third victory, the fourth persuasion, the fifth chastity, the sixth truth, the seventh faith, the eighth patience, the ninth uprightness, the tenth grace, the eleventh justice, and the twelfth light.[93] When the Messenger came to those vessels (i.e., sun and moon), he appointed three servants to make the vessels move. He commanded the Great *Ban* to construct a new earth and three wheels for their (the vessels') ascending. When the vessels moved and reached the midst of heaven, the Messenger then revealed his male and female forms and became visible to all the archons, the sons of Darkness, both male and female. At the appearance of the Messenger, who was attractive in his forms, all of the archons became excited with desire, the males for the female image and the females for the male image. Due to their lust, they began to eject the light which they had consumed from the five luminous deities. Then the sin that was in them devised a plan. It mixed itself with <the light>[94] that came forth from the archons like a portion (of yeast) in bread-dough,[95] and sought to enter within (the emitted light). Then the Messenger concealed his forms, and separated the light of the five luminous deities from the sin that was with them, and it (the sin) fell back upon the archons from whom it had issued, but they did not receive it back, just like a man who feels loathing for his own vomit. It (the sin) thereupon fell upon the earth, half of it upon moist ground and half of it upon dry. (The half which fell upon moist ground) became an odious beast in the likeness of the King of Darkness, and the Adamos of Light was sent against her (*sic*!) and he did battle with her and defeated her, and turned her over upon her back, and struck her <with a spear>[96] in her heart, and thrust his shield over her mouth, and set one of his feet upon her thighs and the other upon her breast.[97] That (half) which fell upon dry ground sprouted up into five trees.

He says that these daughters of Darkness were previously pregnant of their

93. For further references to this group of powers in a wide variety of Manichaean texts, see especially Jason David BeDuhn, *The Manichaean Body: In Discipline and Ritual* (Baltimore: The Johns Hopkins University Press, 2000), 313-14 n.173.

94. Following Chabot's suggested emendation of ܢܘܗܪܐ for ܣܘܗܪܐ.

95. See Samuel N. C. Lieu, "[Review of Reeves, *Jewish Lore in Manichaean Cosmogony*]," *Journal of Semitic Studies* 40 (1995): 162.

96. Following Cumont's suggested emendation of ܒܕܘܪܡܚܐ for ܒܐܘܪܡܚܐ.

97. Compare Sundermann, *Kosmogonische und Parabeltexte*, 48–49.907–13. On the motif of the Adamos of Light as a 'Marduk-like warrior,' see Carl H. Kraeling, *Anthropos and Son of Man: A Study in the Religious Syncretism of the Hellenistic Orient* (New York: Columbia University Press, 1927), 97–102. This conceptual affinity is somehow unnoticed by Mehmet-Ali Ataç, "Manichaeism and Ancient Mesopotamian 'Gnosticism'," *Journal of Ancient Near Eastern Religions* 5 (2005): 1–39.

own nature, and when they beheld the attractive forms of the Messenger, their embryos aborted and fell to the earth. These ate the buds of the trees. Then the abortions took counsel together and recalled the form(s) of the Messenger that they had seen and said: 'Where is the form(s) that we saw?' And Ašaqlūn, son of the King of Darkness, said to the abortions: 'Give me your sons and daughters, and I will make for you a form like the one you saw.' They brought (them) and gave (them) to him. He ate the males, and the females he gave to <Namrāēl>[98] his wife. Namrāēl and Ašaqlūn then united together, and she became pregnant from him and gave birth to a son, naming him Adam. She (again) became pregnant and bore a daughter, naming her Eve.

He (then) says that Jesus the Splendor approached the unsuspecting Adam and roused him from the sleep of death so that he might be delivered from the 'Great Spirit.'[99] As (when) one who is righteous comes across a man possessed by a strong demon and calms him by his skill, so likewise it was with Adam when the Beloved One[100] found him prostrate in deep sleep. He roused him, shook him, and woke[101] him up. He chased the deceptive demon away from him, and bound the great (female) archon apart from him. Then Adam examined himself and recognized who he was, and (Jesus) showed him the Fathers on high, and (revealed to him) regarding his own self (i.e., Jesus's) all that into which he (i.e., Jesus) had been cast—into the teeth of leopard(s) and the teeth of elephant(s), swallowed by voracious ones and absorbed by gulping ones, consumed by dogs, mixed and imprisoned in all that exists, and bound in the stench of Darkness. He (Mani) says that he (Jesus) raised him (Adam) up and made him taste of the Tree of Life.

---

98. In place of the text's ܢܡܟܐܝܠ. This same entity is named ܢܒܪܘܐܝܠ 'Nebrūēl' by Michael Syrus; note also Theodoret, *Haereticarum fabularum compendium* 1.26 (Νεβρώδ) and the same name in the shorter Byzantine abjuration *apud* Adam, *Texte*[2], 95. See Wilhelm Bousset, *Hauptprobleme der Gnosis* (Göttingen, 1907; repr., Göttingen: Vandenhoeck and Ruprecht, 1973), 47–50. Sakla 'the great angel' and 'Nebruel the great demon' figure also in *Gos. Eg.* (NHC III, 2) 57.5–58.21; cf. now *Gospel of Judas* 51.12–23 for the names Saklas and Nebro. Translations of both Coptic texts are available in Marvin Meyer, ed., *The Nag Hammadi Scriptures: The International Edition* (New York: HarperOne, 2007).

99. One is tempted to translate simply as the 'Great Rūhā,' inasmuch as Rūhā is the evil Mandaean entity associated with the World of Darkness and in some myths shares responsibility for the material fabrication of Adam's body. She is also known as Namrus, a designation which might be related to that of Namrāēl. See Bousset, *Hauptprobleme der Gnosis*, 28-37; Henri-Charles Puech, *Le manichéisme: Son fondateur – sa doctrine* (Paris: Civilisations du Sud, 1949), 125 n.150; Rudolph, *Die Mandäer*, 1:184 n.5.

100. For this *terminus technicus*, see John C. Reeves, "An Enochic Citation in *Barnabas* 4.3 and the *Oracles of Hystaspes*," in *Pursuing the Text: Studies in Honor of Ben Zion Wacholder on the Occasion of his Seventieth Birthday* (JSOTSup 184; ed. John C. Reeves and John Kampen; Sheffield: Sheffield Academic Press, 1994), 269–72.

101. Following Mandaic usage. See Pognon, *Inscriptions*, 187 n.3, 192 n.3; Nöldeke, "[Review of Pognon]," 358.

Then Adam saw[102] and wept, and raised his voice loudly like a lion that roars and tears (prey). He cast (himself down), beat (his breast),[103] and said: 'Woe, woe to the one who formed my body, and to the one who bound my soul, and to the rebels who have enslaved me.'[104]

Theodore Abū Qurra, *On the Existence of the Creator and the True Religion* (ed. Dick):[105]

Then I left these (i.e., proponents of Christianity), and people from the Manichaeans met me. They are the ones who are called *zanādiqa*, and they said: 'Be wary of following the Christians or giving credence to the word of their gospel! The true Gospel is in our possession: it is the one which the twelve apostles have written.[106] There is no Church[107] except for the one which we have, and no one is (truly) Christian except for us. No one discerns the (proper) interpretation of the

---

102. Reading ܘܚܙܝܢ ܫܘ in place of ܘܚܝ ܕܝܢ ܠܢܐ in accordance with Scher's note (2:318 n.1). Correct the earlier translations in John C. Reeves, *Jewish Lore in Manichaean Cosmogony: Studies in the Book of Giants Traditions* (Cincinnati: Hebrew Union College Press, 1992), 193; idem, *Heralds of That Good Realm: Syro-Mesopotamian Gnosis and Jewish Traditions* (NHMS 41; Leiden: Brill, 1996), 79 accordingly.

103. Following Mandaic usage. See Pognon, *Inscriptions*, 187 n.3; Nöldeke, "[Review of Pognon]," 358.

104. Other translations are available in Pognon, *Inscriptions*, 184–93; R. Reitzenstein and H. H. Schaeder, *Studien zum antiken Synkretismus aus Iran und Griechenland* (Leipzig: B. G. Teubner, 1926), 342–47; Adam, *Texte*², 15–23; Robert Hespel and René Draguet, *Théodore bar Koni, Livre des scolies (recension de Séert): II. Mimrè VI-XI* (CSCO 432, scrip. syri t. 188; Louvain: E. Peeters, 1982), 234–37. Note also the commentaries provided in Reeves, *Jewish Lore*, 185–206; idem, *Heralds*, 67–109.

105. Ignace Dick, ed., *Théodore Abuqurra: Traité de l'existence du Créateur et de la vraie religion* (Patrimoine arabe chrétien 3; Rome: Pontificio Istituto Orientale, 1982), 205.14–208.11.

106. For some ancient testimonies about a 'gospel' ascribed to the 'twelve apostles,' see J. Rendel Harris, *The Gospel of the Twelve Apostles Together With the Apocalypses of Each One of Them* (Cambridge: The University Press, 1900), 11–17; Philip Vielhauer, "Jewish-Christian Gospels," in Edgar Hennecke, *New Testament Apocrypha* (2 vols.; ed. Wilhelm Schneemelcher; Philadelphia: The Westminster Press, 1963–65), 1:153–54; Henri-Charles Puech, "Gnostic Gospels and Related Documents," in ibid., 1:263–71. It has been suggested that the apostolic 'book' referenced in Coptic *Keph.* 7.26 is this same 'Gospel of the Twelve Apostles'; see Michel Tardieu, "Principes de l'exégèse manichéenne du Nouveau Testament," in *Les règles de l'interprétation* (ed. Michel Tardieu; Paris: Les Éditions du Cerf, 1987), 129 n.25.

107. Literally دين 'religion,' but in view of the context the term is used here apologetically to promote Manichaeism as the only legitimate form of Christianity. Note François de Blois, "Glossary of Technical Terms and Uncommon Expressions in Arabic (and in Muslim New Persian) Texts Relating to Manichaeism," in *Dictionary of Manichaean Texts, Vol. II: Texts from Iraq and Iran (Texts in Syriac, Arabic, Persian and Zoroastrian Middle Persian)* (ed. François de Blois and Nicholas Sims-Williams; Turnhout: Brepols, 2006), 46.

Gospel apart from Mānī, our founder.[108]

Thus has he taught us: Before this world was created, there were two gods whose substances were each different. One of them was Light, Good—it is the good deity—and the other was Evil, Darkness; namely, Satan. In the beginning, each one of them occupied its own territory. Then Darkness noticed the Radiant One and its beauty and its excellence. Filled with desire for it, it pounced upon it and fought with it, wishing to capture it. The Radiant One strove to combat it, but Darkness was on the verge of gaining victory over it. As the Radiant One was in mortal fear, it lopped off a piece of itself and flung it to it, and Darkness swallowed it. Heaven and earth and everything between them[109] were created from the nature of Darkness and from the nature of the piece that the Radiant One threw to him: they came into being by means of (their) combination.'[110]

For example, humans are created having an internal soul and an external body. They claim that the soul derives from the nature of the Radiant One and the body derives from the nature of Satan, the Dark One. So too for the condition of all things: whatever in them that is good and pleasant is from the nature of the Radiant One, and whatever is not good and harmful is from the nature of the Dark One. For example, water drowns the one who is submerged in it but invigorates and pleases the one who drinks it. The part (of water) that invigorates is from the Radiant One, while that which drowns and ruins is from Darkness. As for serpents, scorpions, lions, leopards, crawling creatures, and their sort, all these are from Darkness.[111] This is the foundation of the religion and the distinguishing attribute(s) of their gods.

As for the permitted and the forbidden, they give free rein to the worldly desires of those who wish to experience pleasure by doing whatever they wish. They are not commanded to marry; instead, whoever desires a woman embraces her, and the same is true for women with regard to men. This same interpretation they apply to the Gospel: they claim that when Christ said, 'Give it to the one asking you' (Matt 5:42), this does not mean that when the poor beg for alms, you should give alms to them. Since it was God who caused the poor to experience misfortune in this world, no one is permitted to give them anything or give them alms.[112]

---

108. For this paragraph, see also Puech, "Gnostic Gospels," 1:268.

109. This phraseology closely mimics a frequent qur'ānic locution; see Q 5:17–18; 15:85; 19:65; 20:6 plus fourteen more occurrences.

110. It would appear that Theodore's framing of the narrative in the first person ends here.

111. Compare the testimony of 'Abd al-Jabbār below regarding the 'five kinds of animals' generated by the 'Queen of Darkness,' as well as Augustine, *de Haeresibus* 46.8 (cited below).

112. Theodore here distorts Manichaean warnings about distributing food and drink indiscriminately due to their harboring of elements from the realm of Light whose release would thereby be frustrated. See the passages from Augustine cited by Iain Gardner and Samuel N. C. Lieu, *Manichaean Texts From the Roman Empire* (Cambridge: Cambridge University Press, 2004), 245–46. Jason BeDuhn has concisely phrased it: "Alms within the Manichaean community are literally *korban*, set aside for the altar of sacrifice and forbidden to profane consumption." Quoted from his *The Manichaean Body*, 171.

Otherwise we impugn God, the one who if He so desires makes them miserable, and if He so desires makes them live in comfort. If God had desired to give them a comfortable life, He would have given them corresponding wealth and would not have impoverished them. But the meaning of the words of Christ—'Give it to the one asking you'—(actually) refers to men and women. He is saying to the woman: 'Do not refuse any man who asks you for yourself,' and similarly to the man: 'Give yourself to a woman who asks you for [yourself].' This along with similar things do they teach about the permitted and the forbidden and about divine power.[113]

Theodore Abū Qurra, *On Free Will* (ed. Samir):[114]

Now, if that which overpowered freedom was not something created [by God], then it was most certainly His adversary, for it attacked what He created and perverted it without His permission. The one who follows this line of thought has arrived at something similar to the teaching of Mānī, the fool who introduced two entities, a Good One and an Evil One, and he claimed that the soul was free of the Evil Entity. He said: 'The body subdued the soul and overpowered it because Satan, who is the prince of Evil, captured souls from God, who is in charge of Good, and he imprisoned them in bodies.'[115]

... How remarkable is your ignorance, O Mānī! You find evidence for the confirmation of the Two Entities—those which were invented by your perverse mind—in what our holy Gospel says: 'A good tree is not capable of producing bad fruit, nor is a bad tree capable of producing good fruit' (Matt 7:18).[116] Then you say: 'Souls are from the Good substance, but they act 'Evil' when conjoined with bodies.'[117] ... At any rate, your commandments and proscriptions cannot be reconciled with how you interpret the words of the Gospel.

... We have no wish to linger over the teaching of Mānī and thus depart from our course. Were we to proceed to occupy ourselves with his book,[118] then we would need to compose many volumes in order to expose its most disgusting and foolish things. By my life, one who is adrift in his dream is not as deluded about

113. See also Guy Monnot, "Abū Qurra et la pluralité des religions," *RHR* 208 (1991): 58–60; *Theodore Abū Qurrah* (Library of the Christian East 1; trans. John C. Lamoreaux; Provo: Brigham Young University Press, 2005), 4–5.

114. Samir Khalil Samir, ed., *Teodoro Abū Qurra: La libertà* (Patrimonio culturale arabo cristiano 6; trans. Paola Pizzi; Torino: Silvio Zamorani, 2001), 162.16–164.13; 168.14–170.7; 174.1–2; 194.12–196.3.

115. This appears to be a quotation from one of Mani's writings. For similar materials, see the citations collected in Reeves, "Citations from Ephrem," 250–56.

116. See also Lk 6:43; *Gos. Thom.* 43 and 45. This was a popular text in Manichaean apologetic; see *Acta Archelai* 5.4 (ed. Beeson, 7); Coptic *Keph.* 16.33–23.13; John of Damascus, *Contra Manichaeos* §2 (ed. Kotter, 352); and note Reeves, "Citations from Ephrem," 252.

117. Another likely quotation from a Manichaean work; compare Reeves, "Citations from Ephrem," 250–56.

118. It is unclear which 'book' of Mani's that Theodore is using.

what he sees in his dreams as is Mānī with what his mind has imagined![119]

Agapius of Mabbug, *Kitāb al-unvān* (ed. Vasiliev):[120]

He (Mani) said: 'Were I to say that the One God makes Himself known through Three Persons, I could not be taken seriously.' Rather, this is what he steadfastly wrote and never abandoned; namely, that there are Two eternal beings. One of them is God, who produces Good and is the source of Light and Righteousness, and the other is Hyle, principle of Evil and the source of Ignorance, Darkness, and Corruption. God extends upward without limit, but they both impinge upon one another from the center outwards, and they are both corporeal (entities). The principle of Evil was once in a state of tumult and its progeny were recklessly rushing against each other. These (progeny) were satans, demons, fire, and water. Their combat with one another did not cease until they arrived at the Region (controlled by the principle) of Good. They overshadowed its Light, and (then) went and said to one another: 'Let us pounce, and that (Light) will be food for our consumption or a beverage for our drinking!' They thereupon resolved to pounce upon it. But when God—who is the principle of Righteousness—beheld this (scheme), He forfeited a portion of Himself and threw it to them, and so the principle of Evil absorbed a portion of God.[121] It imprisoned it and mingled itself with it and became mixed up with it. It is on account of its (Light's) mixture within it (Hyle) that the world came into being. God Most High appointed His two beloved ones (to be) at the boundary of the Evil Realm,[122] and God will reclaim the portion which He surrendered to Evil, and God will gradually reunite it to Himself. He will secure Himself against Evil to the point that the latter could not prevail against Him in a second attack.[123]

119. See also Lamoreaux, 198-203. A cogent exposition of Theodore's exploitation of Manichaeism in this work is provided by Sidney H. Griffith, "Free Will in Christian Kalām: The Doctrine of Theodore Abū Qurrah," *Parole de l'Orient* 14 (1987): 94–96, 99–102.

120. Alexandre Vasiliev, "*Kitāb al-Unvān*: Histoire universelle écrite par Agapius (Mahboub) de Menbidj," *Patrologia Orientalis* 7 (1911): 534–35; Taqīzādeh-Šīrāzī, *Mānī va dīn-e-ū*, 352–53 (§100).

121. Regarding this depiction of the initial encounter between Darkness and Light, compare the *Chronicon Maroniticum* above as well as the testimony of al-Misma'ī related in 'Abd al-Jabbār, *Mughnī* (ed. Ḥusayn), 5:19.8–20.1 below. This material is related to the unknown Manichaean source which is cited in Severus of Antioch, *Homily 123* (ed. Brière, 164.10–166.15), a report made available in English translation by Reeves, *Jewish Lore*, 169–70; see also Gardner-Lieu, *Manichaean Texts*, 162–63. For further analysis of this source and an intriguing suggestion as to its identity, see Byard Bennett, "*Iuxta unum latus erat terra tenebrarum*: The Division of Primordial Space in Anti-Manichaean Writers' Descriptions of the Manichaean Cosmogony," in *The Light and the Darkness: Studies in Manichaeism and its World* (NHMS 50; ed. Paul Mirecki and Jason BeDuhn; Leiden: Brill, 2001), 68–78.

122. It is unclear which two entities are meant. Vasiliev suggests they are the sun and the moon.

123. See Vajda, "Le témoignage d'al-Māturidī," 9.

He (Mānī) denied the resurrection of the dead. He said that the Lord Christ was the son of God, possessing His (i.e., God's) nature and substance, and that He had sent him to those portions (of Light) which came from His realm into (that of) Evil in order to announce to them that they would be delivered from that which belongs to Evil and eventually return to Him, together with those portions (of Light) now dispersed throughout Evil and who do not realize it. (Mani said) that he (Christ) was not related to anything (terrestrial); rather, he resembled an apparition. He moreover said that he (Christ) was not really crucified or made to suffer death, and that his crucifixion and death were only apparent; that is to say, the principle of Evil stirred up its demons against him and they were under the impression that they killed him and crucified him, but actually this was not so. He (actually) escaped from them and rejoined the *pleroma* of God. He (also) said that souls transmigrate (from one body to another). He said that he himself was a messenger of Christ and that he himself derived from the pure substance of God and that the body which was visible (to his followers) was (actually) an apparition.[124]

***Chronicon Seertensis* (ed. Scher):**[125]

God is known as Three Persons and the one who preaches this should not cease from doing so, but (Mani said) there are two entities: one of them—God—who produces Good and who is the source of Light, Righteousness, and Piety, and the other (of them) Hyle, creator of Evil and the source of Ignorance, Darkness, and Depravity. God extends upward without limit, and Evil extends downward without limit, but they both impinge upon one another from the center outwards. They are both corporeal entities. The creator of Evil was once in a state of tumult and its progeny were recklessly rushing against each other—these being satans, demons, fire, and water. Their contention with one another did not cease until they arrived at the region (controlled by the principle) of Righteousness. They beheld its Light and became envious of it. They said, '(Let us)[126] violate it, and that (Light) will be food for our consumption, or a beverage for our quaffing!' They thereupon resolved upon that (course of action). But when God—who is the Righteous One—beheld this (scheme), he detached a portion of Himself and threw it to them. The principle of Evil discovered this piece of God.[127] It mingled itself with it and became mixed (with it), and due to its mixture with it this world came into being. Parts of God are imprisoned among parts of the Evil Realm. But God will reclaim the portion which he surrendered to Evil, and gradually He will reunite it to His 'being' and regain control[128] from Evil to the extent that the lat-

124. See also the translation of Vasiliev, "Kitāb al-Unvān," 534–35.

125. Addai Scher, "Histoire Nestorienne inédite (Chronique de Séert)," *Patrologia Orientalis* 4 (1908): 227–28; Taqīzādeh-Šīrāzī, *Mānī va dīn-e-ū*, 382 (§118).

126. See Taqīzādeh-Šīrāzī, *Mānī va dīn-e-ū*, 382 n.2.

127. Note the parallel sections in *Chronicon Maroniticum* and Agapius above, as well as Michael Syrus and 'Abd al-Jabbār below.

128. Taqīzādeh-Šīrāzī (following Scher, "Histoire," 228 n.1) suggest emending the text to

ter will not be in a position to repeat its hostile actions.

This devil-possessed heretic—may God's curse be upon him because of his lies—repudiated the resurrection. He said that Christ was the son of that God of Righteousness, and that he (i.e., Christ) was His messenger to those portions (of God) which came from His Realm into (that of) Evil, so as to proclaim liberation from the imprisonment of Evil and to lead (them) back to Him (i.e., God). He maintained that souls transmigrate (from one body to another), and he announced that he was a messenger of Christ and possessed the same nature (as Christ).[129]

Michael Syrus, *Chronicon* (ed. Chabot):[130]

He said there was a deity in the Light[131] and he possessed the eastern, western, northern, and upper regions; and another which he named Hyle (ܗܘܠܐ) who was evil (and) who possessed the southern and lower regions. This so-called Hyle was in a perpetual state of uproar. Its members — demons, fire, water, and idols — confronted one another and were chasing and putting each other to flight. When they arrived at heaven, the Region of Light, they sought to mix their Darkness with the Light and the Good. But when God beheld them, he imprisoned them there, and taking a small portion of Light he sent it to (the Region of) Hyle, and when Hyle swallowed it, he was caught by it. For this reason God was compelled, so to speak, to create the universe.

They say that Adam and Eve derive from Saqla (ܣܩܠܐ) the ruler of Hyle and from Nabrōēl (ܢܒܪܘܐܝܠ). They say that the sun and the moon are ships which receive human souls and every (portion) of the Good that is mixed with Hyle. They ascend (with this cargo) to the Region of Light until all of the Light is set free from (its) mixture with Evil. Then God will deliver over Hyle to fire along with those souls who do not believe in Mānī ... [three words unintelligible]. They say that marriage stems from Evil, and they deny the resurrection, (holding instead) that souls migrate from body to body; that everything has a soul, even earth and water; and that our Lord did not receive a (mortal) body or soul, but rather he became visible and suffered only in appearance. And they say there are twenty-five gods who have twelve wives, along with the rest of their disgraceful mysteries.

Bar Hebraeus, *Historia compendiosa dynastiarum* (ed. Pococke):[132]

They promulgated the doctrine of dualism: the world had two deities, one of them

---

يتورع or يتولى (382 n.3); I have accordingly followed the latter form here.

129. See also Scher, "Histoire," 227–28.

130. J.-B. Chabot, ed., *Chronique de Michel le Syrien, patriarche jacobite d'Antioche, 1166–1199* (4 vols.; repr., Bruxelles: Culture et Civilisation, 1963), 4:118.7–119.3. The initial paragraph is based upon the last surviving paragraph of *Chronicon Maroniticum*.

131. Read ܒܗܘܪܐ for ܒܗܘܠܐ.

132. Edward Pococke, ed., *Historia compendiosa Dynastiarum authore Gregorio Abul-Pharagio ...* (2 vols.; Oxoniae: Excudebat H. Hall ... impensis Ric. Davis, 1663), 1:129–31. This specific passage is reprinted in Taqīzādeh-Šīrāzī, *Mānī va dīn-e-ū*, 271 (§60); also Konrad Kessler, *Mani: Forschungen über die manichäische Religion* (Berlin: Georg Reimer, 1889), 401-402.

being Good and the source of Light, whereas the other was Evil and the source of Darkness. Both of them were mixed with one another, and the Good was elevated above the Evil. Evil proceeded to the southern region to make a world there in order to rule over it.[133] But when it began by making the 'Bear-constellations' near the south pole like those near the north pole, angels (intervened and) made peace between them, for some of the Good had dropped down on to Hyle, and hence there was a world liable to generation[134] and corruption over which Evil could rule. Because Good acted only out of its reluctance, it was obliged to create in the heavens two great ships, the sun and the moon. It began to collect within them human souls and to reclaim that portion of it which Evil held captive so as to gradually empty Hyle of the vestiges of the Good and to nullify the sovereignty of Evil.

He (Mani) spoke of the transmigration of souls and of how there was a soul interwoven within all things. He was extravagant with regard to the glorification of fire and the exaltation of its nature, and he acclaimed its consecration and praiseworthiness, all on account of its luminescence and its splendor, and he situated it in the middle (of the universe) in the locale between the sphere and the elements. The earth he held in contempt since its 'nature' derived from Darkness: its interior cannot be illumined either actually or potentially. This teaching was already an ancient one in Persia; Mānī did not innovate it, nor did he support it with persuasive arguments.[135] Correct is the response from the venerable master Abū 'Alī Ibn Sīnā (i.e., Avicenna) when he said: 'How can it be possible for the concept of 'fire' to be exclusively located (only) in the Realm of Good, and for the concept of 'earth' to be exclusively located (only) in the Realm of Evil? For the earth is (also) the region (which provides) for the maintenance and sustenance of animals and plants,[136] whereas fire (also) has a voracious nature, causing damage by disrupting the component parts of a compounded entity and (effecting) its disintegration.'[137]

Abu'l-Barakāt Ibn Kabar, *Miṣbāḥ al-ẓulmah fī īḍāḥ al-khidmah* (ed. Taqīzādeh-Širāzī):[138]

Regarding the religious community called Manichaeans:

They are the followers of Mānī, the one nicknamed the 'madman.'[139] They are the ones who believe in two gods, a good one and a bad one. They maintain that the good one creates Light and Goodness, and the bad one creates Darkness and

133. Compare Bīrūnī, *'Ifrād al-maqāl fī 'amr al-ẓilāl* (ed. Taqīzādeh-Šīrāzī), 207 (§35): '... for there are some Manichaeans who believe that the north is the locale of sublime things and the south is the locale of decadent and corrupt things.'

134. Literally 'being, existence.'

135. A translation of this and the preceding two sentences was provided in Haase, *Altchristliche Kirchengeschichte*, 362.

136. Surely a 'good' activity?

137. In certain circumstances a disastrous event.

138. Taqīzādeh-Šīrāzī, *Mānī va dīn-e-ū*, 456–57 (§160).

139. A reflex of the popular Greek pun on the name 'Mani.'

Evil. They say there is no resurrection, resuscitation, or (final) reckoning for humans. They worship the sun, moon, and the seven planets, and they compute horoscopes using the twelve zodiacal signs of the astronomers and constantly speak about the power of the stars. They totally prohibit marriage and constantly speak of fasting and they pronounce foodstuffs unclean. They declare that everything in the world is infused with a soul, whether they are kinds of herbs, seeds, fruits, or the like. They fabricate lies about the Mighty and Powerful God and believe in fates and the reckoning of nativities, and they practice magic and incantations and astral calculations.[140]

That which has been related about the story of Mānī—his departure to the land of Persia, his escape from prison, and his execution by a certain king—is recorded in the *Qāqsīs*; that is, a volume of the deeds which are attributed to Saint Cyrus.[141] It is a book of disputations which includes (the following synopsis): they proclaim two deities, a good one and a wicked one. They worship the sun and the moon and the remainder of the seven planets, and they extol the twelve signs of the zodiac and the (celestial) luminaries. They are of the opinion that the substances of water, fire, and plants possess a spiritual component, so that whoever pours out water effects destruction, or whoever extinguishes the flame of a fire or uproots a plant has in fact slain an 'innocent person.'[142] They prohibit the acquisition of women whether for wives or for maidservants, and they declare slaughtered animals to be unclean.

4. Zoroastrian Discussions

Škand-Gumānīk Vičār §10.58-60 (ed. de Menasce):[143]

I have completely escaped the doubts, errors, delusions, and seductions of the heterodox sects, especially those of the featherbrained Mānī, the greatest imposter and the worst teacher, whose doctrine is sorcery and (whose) religion is deceit and (whose) teaching is wicked and (whose) custom is secretiveness.[144]

140. This particular report is very closely related to the early Syriac one supplied by Mārūtā; see above.

141. The Melkite patriarch of Alexandria at the time of the Muslim conquest of Egypt in the seventh century. The title *Qāqsīs* is apparently a corruption of the enigmatic epithet 'Muqawqis' that is often applied to Cyrus by Arab historians. See especially Alfred J. Butler, *The Arab Conquest of Egypt and the Last Thirty Years of the Roman Dominion* (Oxford: Clarendon Press, 1902), 508–26; also Paul Casanova, *Mohammed et la fin du monde: Étude critique sur l'Islam primitif* (2 vols.; Paris: Librairie Paul Geuthner, 1911–24), 1:25–27; 230–34.

142. Literally 'a pure soul.' For the above translation, see Q 18:74.

143. de Menasce, *Une apologétique mazdéenne*, 116. Note especially Dieter Tailleu, "Glossary to the Zoroastrian Middle Persian Polemics Against Manichaeism," in *Dictionary of Manichaean Texts, Vol. II* (ed. de Blois and Sims-Williams), 121–45.

144. For other translations, see de Menasce, *Une apologétique mazdéenne*, 117; Jackson, *Researches*, 182; R. C. Zaehner, *The Teachings of the Magi: A Compendium of Zoroastrian*

Škand-Gumānīk Vičār §16.1–52 (ed. de Menasce):[145]

Now with regard to the error of Mānī, there is written (here) only one (thing) out of the thousand and ten thousand (that could be written), for I am incapable of writing a complete description of the foolishness, twaddle, and deception of Mānī and the Manichaeans: this would require much trouble and hard daily work on my part.

You should know, O Mazdaean adherents of Zoroaster, that the statement(s) of Mānī pertain initially to the existence of infinite Principles, next to (their) mixture, and finally to the separation of Light from Darkness, which is more like a lack of separation.

Furthermore, (he states) this: the material world is a corporeal formation of Ahriman; all corporeal formation is a creation of Ahriman. To say it another way: the sky was created from the skin, the earth from the flesh, the mountains from the bones, and the vegetation from the hair of the demon Kunī (Kundag).[146] Rain is the semen of the Māzandarān[147] who are attached to the celestial sphere. Humanity is a demon with two legs, and animals are quadripedal demons. Kunī is the army commander of Ahriman who, in the first battle, swallowed the Light emanating from the god Ohrmazd.[148] Then, in the second battle, the demon Kunī and many other demons were captured. Some of them were fettered to the celestial sphere, whereas Kunī was slain. The macrocosm was taken and made from him.

The sun and the moon were situated beyond the highest heaven. By a purifying and extracting process carried out by the sun and the moon, they gradually purify and draw up that Light which the demons swallowed. However, Ahriman presciently realized that the Light would be quickly purified and separated through the purifying and extracting process of the sun and the moon. So that the Light

Beliefs (repr., New York: Oxford University Press, 1976), 53.

145. de Menasce, *Une apologétique mazdéenne*, 252-54. See also Jackson, *Researches*, 176–180; Tailleu, "Glossary," 121–45.

146. For this demon, see also the passage from the third book of the *Dēnkard* that is cited and briefly discussed in de Menasce, *Une apologétique mazdéenne*, 231–32. See also E[mile] Benveniste, "Le témoignage de Théodore bar Kōnay sur le zoroastrianisme," *Le Monde Oriental* 26 (1932): 170–215, esp. 203–204; W. B. Henning, "[Review of Jackson, *Researches in Manichaeism*]," *Orientalistische Literaturzeitung* 37 (1934): 754–55; M 731 lines 75–76 in F. C. Andreas and W. Henning, "Mitteliranische Manichaica aus Chinesisch-Turkestan, III," *SPAW* (1934): 856; Hans-Joachim Klimkeit, *Gnosis on the Silk Road: Gnostic Texts from Central Asia* (San Francisco, CA: HarperCollins, 1993), 259; Philippe Gignoux, *Man and Cosmos in Ancient Iran* (Roma: Istituto italiano per l'Africa e l'Oriente, 2001), 71–72. Note especially the insightful remarks of Alessandro Bausani, *Religion in Iran: From Zoroaster to Baha'ullah* (trans. J. M. Marchesi; New York: Bibliotheca Persica Press, 2000), 151–52.

147. I.e., the 'monstrous ones.' See W. B. Henning, "The Book of the Giants," *BSOAS* 11 (1943–46): 53–54.

148. The name 'Ohrmazd' thus encodes the Manichaean entity otherwise known as Primal Man.

would not be separated quickly from the Darkness, he fashioned this microcosm after the pattern and model of the macrocosm, (fashioning) humanity, cattle, and other animals, as well as other material creations. He bound and imprisoned (vital) soul and Light in the body so that the Light which is drawn up by the sun and moon is nevertheless hindered by the sexual reproduction and birthing of living creatures, thus slowing down their separation.

Rain is the semen of the Māzandarān. This is why: when the Māzandarān who had swallowed the Light were attached to the celestial sphere, a novel means, stratagem, and procedure was devised by Zurwān[149] to extract the Light from them. Twelve glorious daughters of Zurwān expose themselves before the male Māzandarān so that sight of them excites the lust of those Māzandarān and they ejaculate their semen. The Light which is contained in the semen pours down upon the earth. Trees, plants, and grains grow from it, and (thus) the Light which was inside the Māzandarān is extracted from them via the semen. That (Light) which is contained within the earth is extracted from the earth by means of vegetation.

He states moreover with regard to the different natures of the (vital) soul and the body that the (vital) soul is bound and imprisoned within the body. And since Ahriman is the creator and maintainer of the bodies of all material entities, it follows that one should not procreate or establish a familial posterity because one then co-operates with Ahriman in the perpetuation of people and cattle and in causing the retention of the (vital) soul and Light within their bodies. Nor should one cultivate plants and grains.

Moreover, they contradict themselves when they say that this same Ahriman is the destroyer of creation; and therefore, one is not permitted to kill any creature because it is an act engaged in by Ahriman.

They say moreover that whereas the world is maintained by Ahriman, God will finally prevail in separating the (vital) souls from the bodies. He will eventually destroy the world of living beings so that it cannot be re-established. There will be no resurrection or 'future body.'[150]

They say moreover that those Two Principles will always remain and exist side by side like sunshine and shade, with no void or space being between them.[151]

---

149. The name employed in Iranian and Old Turkic Manichaean texts for the deity most often termed in other linguistic traditions 'the King of the Light-Paradises' or 'Father of Greatness.' See D. N. MacKenzie, "Mani's *Šābuhragān*," *BSOAS* 42 (1979): 506 (B verso line 76: *zrw'n* 'Zurwān'); Prods Oktor Skjærvø, "Iranian Elements in Manicheism, A Comparative Contrastive Approach: Irano-Manichaica I," in *Au carrefour des religions: Mélanges offerts à Philippe Gignoux* (Res Orientales 7; ed. Rika Gyselen; Bures-sur-Yvette: Group pour l'étude de la civilisation du Moyen-Orient, 1995), 269–72; van Tongerloo, "Father of Greatness," 329–42, esp. 333–39. As Skjærvø points out, Manichaean adoption of the name 'Zurwān' does not imply an endorsement of the mythology or theology associated with so-called 'Zurvanism.'

150. See the remarks of Bausani, *Religion in Iran*, 20–21.

151. For other translations, see E. W. West, *Pahlavi Texts: Part III* (SBE 24; Oxford, 1855; repr., Delhi: Motilal Banarsidass, 1970), 243–46; Jackson, *Researches*, 177–81; de Me-

5. Muslim Discussions

For ease of reference and in order to facilitate comparative readings, the following extracts have been subdivided into four topical groupings. 'Doctrinal' assembles the various statements expressing how Mani represented his prophetic vocation and revelatory teachings in relation to older and rival religious groupings and concerns. This section also includes a series of largely second-order Muslim distillations of the way Manichaeism purportedly structured empirical reality and explained its natural processes. The label 'mythological' brings together accounts which articulate the distinctive Manichaean myth regarding the origin of the material world and its inhabitants: it features colorful episodes and *dramatis personae* familiar from much earlier testimonia like those provided by the Coptic Manichaica, Ephrem Syrus, and Augustine. 'Ritual and behavioral' collects information about the lifestyles embraced by the two classes of believers, the so-called 'Elect' and the catechumens (*Auditores* or 'Hearers'). Finally, the rubric of 'eschatological' presents Manichaean teachings about the fate of individual souls, the afterlife, and the cosmic events associated with the eschaton.

a. Doctrinal

Jāḥiẓ, *Kitāb al-ḥayawān* (ed. Taqīzādeh-Šīrāzī):[152]

This is what the Manichaeans maintain: the universe with its contents derives from ten kinds (of things). Five of them are Good and Light, and five of them are Evil and Darkness, and each of them is sentient and passionate.

Humans are composed of all these 'kinds,' but in variant proportions: in each person some of the 'good' kinds outweigh the 'bad' kinds, and some of the 'bad' kinds outweigh the 'good' kinds. Humans possess five senses, and there is present in each sense the main parts of the five kinds and their opposites. Whenever a person beholds a merciful sight, this sight derives from what is Light and Good, but when they behold a threatening sight, this sight derives from Darkness. The same holds true for all the senses.

The sense of hearing is a separate 'kind.' That which is in the sense of sight that derives from Good and Light does not assist that which derives from Good in the sense of hearing, but it nevertheless does not oppose it. Nor does it corrupt it or obstruct it: it does not assist it to a different situation or 'kind,' nor does it help it, although it is not an opponent.

The 'kinds' belonging to Evil differ from one another and oppose the 'kinds' which belong to Good. The 'kinds' belonging to Good differ from one another, but do not oppose (their Evil counterparts). Cooperation and accomplishment does not occur among that which differs from it or is opposed to it, but only occurs among that which agrees with it.[153]

---

nasce, *Une apologétique mazdéenne*, 253–55.

152. Taqīzādeh-Šīrāzī, *Mānī va dīn-e-ū*, 88-89 (§4).

153. For other translations, see Charles Pellat, "Le témoignage d'al-Jāḥīẓ sur les Mani-

Jāḥiẓ, *Kitāb al-tarbīʿ wa'l-tadwīr* (ed. Pellat):[154]

Why do you not bite into Mānī and give him pain?[155]

Jāḥiẓ, *Kitāb ḥujaj al-nubuwwa* (ed. Taqīzādeh-Šīrāzī):[156]

Jews, Christians, Zoroastrians, *zanādiqa*, materialists, and the worshippers of Buddha images reject the Prophet (may God bless and protect him!).[157]

Yaʿqūbī, *Ta'rīkh* (ed. Houtsma):[158]

Mani said that the ruler of the world is binary, and (that) they are two eternal entities, Light and Darkness, both creators, for one creates Good and the other Evil. Darkness and Light each name for themselves five concepts: color, taste, smell, palpability, and sound; and both of them hear, see, and think. That which is good and beneficial is from the Light, and that which is harmful and distressful is from the Darkness. They were (originally) unmixed with each other; then they mixed. The evidence of this (is) that there were (at first) no tangible things; then it (materiality) happened. Darkness initiated the mixing with the Light, for they impinge upon each other after the manner of a shadow and the sun. The evidence for this is the impossibility of the coming-into-being of a thing from that which does not exist. Darkness initiated the mixing with the Light, because the mixture of the Darkness with the Light is harmful to it (Light). It would be impossible for the Light to have initiated (such an action), for the Light is essentially Good. And the evidence that these two, Good and Evil, are eternal is that if a single entity exists, two contrary actions cannot come about from it. For example, a hot burning fire cannot produce something cold, while that which chills cannot produce heat from itself; and that from which good results cannot produce evil, while good cannot be produced from that which produces evil. And the evidence that they are two living and active entities is that good persists by its action, and

---

chéens," in *Essays in Honor of Bernard Lewis: The Islamic World, From Classical to Modern Times* (ed. C. E. Bosworth, et al.; Princeton, NJ: Darwin Press, 1989), 272; Josef van Ess, *Theologie und Gesellschaft im 2. und 3. Jahrhundert Hidschra: Eine Geschichte des religiösen Denkens im frühen Islam* (6 vols.; Berlin: Walter de Gruyter, 1991–97), 6:116–17.

154. Charles Pellat, *Le Kitāb at-tarbīʿ wa-t-tadwīr de Ǧāḥiẓ* (Damas: Institut français de Damas, 1955), 79 (§145); also Taqīzādeh-Šīrāzī, *Mānī va dīn-e-ū*, 98 (§7).

155. Perhaps this is an allusion to the well known Manichaean doctrine which embeds the so-called 'Living Soul' in the material world. Although it is unusual for Mani himself to be equated with this entity, it is not unparalleled: see *CMC* 23.7–11; Coptic *Ps-Bk.* 86.27-30. For other translations of the passage from Jāḥiẓ, see Maurice Adad, "Le *Kitāb al-Tarbīʿ wa-l-Tadwīr* d'al-Ǧāḥiẓ: Traduction française, III," *Arabica* 14 (1967): 188; *Sobriety and Mirth: A Selection of the Shorter Writings of al-Jāhiz* (trans. Jim Colville; London: Kegan Paul, 2002), 293.

156. Taqīzādeh-Šīrāzī, *Mānī va dīn-e-ū*, 97 (§6).

157. See also *Sobriety and Mirth* (trans. Colville), 115.

158. M. T. Houtsma, ed., *Ibn Wadih qui dicitur al-Jaʿqubi historiae ...* (2 vols.; Leiden: Brill, 1883), 1:180.5–181.1. See also Taqīzādeh-Šīrāzī, *Mānī va dīn-e-ū*, 104–105 (§13).

evil persists by its action ....[159]

Ḥasan b. Mūsā al-Nawbakhtī *apud* Ibn al-Jawzī, *Talbīs Īblīs* (ed. Taqīzādeh-Šīrāzī):[160]

Account of the deception perpetrated by the dualists:

These are the people who say the creator of the world is two (entities). The one producing good is Light, and the one producing evil is Darkness. They are both eternal, they both never cease being and will never cease being, (and) they are powerful, sentient, hearing, (and) seeing (entities).[161] They differ from one another with regard to essence and form and are opposites with regard to (their) activity and organization. The substance of Light is beautiful, excellent, shining, pure, unmixed, pleasant of odor, (and) beautiful in appearance, and its essence is one that is good, noble, wise, producing benefits: from it comes what is good, delightful, joyous, and pious, and there is nothing in it that is harmful or evil. The substance of Darkness is the opposite of this: turbid, imperfect, rotten in odor, and ugly in appearance, and its essence is one that is wicked, greedy, stupid, stinking, (and) ignorant: from it comes what is wicked and corrupt.

Such does al-Nawbakhtī report about them.[162] He (also) says: Some of them maintain that Light was always located above Darkness, but some of them say that each one of them is located next to the other. Most of them say that Light has always been elevated toward the north and Darkness sunken toward the south, and that each one of them had always been separate from the other.

Nawbakhtī says: They claim that each of them has five parts, of which four are corporeal and the fifth spiritual. The four corporeal parts of Light are fire, wind, earth, and water; and its spiritual component is *šabaḥ* (?),[163] and it is always in motion in these bodies. The four corporeal parts of Darkness are fire, darkness, (hot) wind, and fog; and its spiritual component is smoke. They term the parts of Light 'angels,' and they term the parts of Darkness 'satans' and 'demons.'[164]

159. For another translation, see Edward G. Browne, *A Literary History of Persia* (4 vols.; London and Cambridge, 1902–24; repr., Cambridge: The University Press, 1964), 1:155–56.

160. Taqīzādeh-Šīrāzī, *Mānī va dīn-e-ū*, 255–56 (§49).

161. The latter two attributes echo the relatively frequent (ten times) qur'ānic designation of God as the 'all-hearing, all-seeing One'; see, e.g., Q 17:1.

162. Nawbakhtī was a primary channel through which one stream of traditions about dualist religions—those originally compiled by Abū 'Īsā al-Warrāq—were transmitted to later theologians and heresiologists. See J[oel]. L. Kraemer, "al-Nawbakhtī, al-Ḥasan b. Mūsā," *EI*^{2} 7:1044; Wilferd Madelung, "Abū 'Īsā al-Warrāq über die Bardesaniten, Marcioniten und Kantäer," in *Studien zur Geschichte und Kultur des Vorderen Orients: Festschrift für Bertold Spuler* (ed. Hans R. Roemer and Albrecht Noth; Leiden: Brill, 1981), 210-11.

163. Arabic الشبح, almost certainly an orthographic corruption of النسيم 'air.' See also de Blois, "Glossary," 80.

164. See also Ibn al-Murtaḍā, *Kitāb al-munya* (in Taqīzādeh-Šīrāzī, *Mānī va dīn-e-ū*, 300

Some of them say Darkness engenders satans and Light engenders angels, and that Light is incapable of evil and does not sanction it, while Darkness is incapable of good and does not sanction it.

He has mentioned their various teachings as they pertain to Light and Darkness—silly teachings! For example, it is prescribed for them that they should gather only enough food for a single day. Some of them say that a person should fast a seventh part of his life, should renounce deceit, greed, magic, idolatry, fornication, and robbery, and should not harm anything which has a 'spirit.' They concocted novel doctrines using their stupid tales.[165]

Yaḥyā b. Bishr al-Nihāwandī[166] has mentioned that some of them who are called Dayṣāniyya maintain that the constitution of the world was a coarse material and that it was for a time an imitation of the body of the creator, the one who is Light. He became irritated with it, and after he tired of it, he resolved to remove it from him. But he became mired within it and mixed up with it, and so this world came to be composed of Light and Darkness. Whatever there is that seems good is from Light, and whatever there is that seems corrupt is from Darkness. They murder people and strangle them, claiming that they are rescuing Light from Darkness. What silly teachings![167]

Abū Ḥātim al-Rāzī, *Kitāb a'lām al-nubuwwa* (ed. Ṣāwī):[168]

He (i.e., Abū Bakr al-Rāzī) said: 'Jesus claimed that he was the son of God, while Moses claimed that He had no son, and Muḥammad claimed that he (i.e., Jesus) was created, like the rest of humanity. But Mānī and Zoroaster both differed with Moses, Jesus, and Muḥammad in regard to ancient times, the existence of the world, and the reason for good and evil. Moreover Mānī differed with Zoroaster about the two entities and their (respective) worlds.'[169]

[§74]); Kessler, *Mani*, 347.

165. A translation up to this point is available in Guy Monnot, *Penseurs musulmans et religions iraniennes: 'Abd al-Jabbār et ses devanciers* (Paris: J. Vrin, 1974), 301–302.

166. For this authority, see the remarks of Guy Monnot, "Les écrits musulmans sur les religions non-bibliques," in idem, *Islam et religions* (Paris: Éditions Maisonneuve et Larose, 1986), 78–79; also Charles Genequand, "Philosophical Schools as Viewed by Some Medieval Muslim Authors," in *Muslim Perceptions of Other Religions: A Historical Survey* (ed. Jacques Waardenburg; Oxford: Oxford University Press, 1999), 201 n.21.

167. See also D. S. Margoliouth, "'The Devil's Delusion' of Ibn al-Jauzi," *Islamic Culture* 9 (1935): 1–21, at 14–15; Vajda, "Le témoignage d'al-Māturidī," 13, 30–31; Roberto Giorgi, *Pour une histoire de la zandaka* (Firenze: La Nuova Italia Editrice, 1989), 132.

168. Abū Ḥātim al-Rāzī, *A'lām al-nubuwwah (The Peaks of Prophecy)* (ed. Salah al-Sawy; Tehran: Imperial Iranian Academy of Philosophy, 1977), 69.4–8; Taqīzādeh-Šīrāzī, *Mānī va dīn-e-ū*, 119–20 (§17).

169. Reading with Ms. B in al-Sawy's textual apparatus; the base text reads 'and their (respective) causes.' See also Sarah Stroumsa, *Freethinkers of Medieval Islam: Ibn al-Rāwandī, Abū Bakr al-Rāzī, and Their Impact on Islamic Thought* (Leiden: Brill, 1999), 99–100.

Abū Ḥātim al-Rāzī, *Kitāb al-iṣlāḥ* (ed. Mīnūchehr):[170]

... and he (Bihāfarīd) is regarded alongside Zardusht, Mazdak, and Mānī, for it is said that they (dualists) designate four as (their) prophets: Zardusht, Mazdak, Mānī, and Bihāfarīd.[171]

Māturīdī, *Kitāb al-tawḥīd* (ed. Kholeif):[172]

The master (may God have mercy on him!) said: The Manichaeans claim that things as they are derive from a mixture of Light and Darkness. The two were (originally) separate: the Light above, (extending) infinitely to the four cardinal directions (of) north, south, east, and west; and the Darkness below, (extending) likewise; (but) both of them ending at the side where they adjoin. Darkness lusted after Light and they mixed with one another, and in proportion to the mixture the world came into being due to their mixture.

Each one of them (viz., Light and Darkness) possesses five species: redness, whiteness, yellowness, blackness, and greenness. For each species, everything which comes from the substance of Light is Good, and that which comes from the substance of Darkness is evil. Similarly, each one of them (Light and Darkness) possesses five senses: audition, vision, taste, the sense of smell, and touch. That which the substance of Light perceives with one of these (senses) is Good, and that which the substance of Darkness perceives is Evil.[173]

Māturīdī, *Kitāb al-tawḥīd* (ed. Kholeif):[174]

Ibn Shabīb[175] maintains (that) the doctrine of the Ṣābians is the same as that of the Manichaeans,[176] except for a minor distinction between them which he does

170. Abū Ḥātim Aḥmad b. Ḥamdān al-Rāzī, *Kitâb al-Iṣlâḥ* (Wisdom of Persia 42; ed. Hasan Mīnūchehr; Teheran: Institute of Islamic Studies, 1998), 162.1–2.

171. See W[ladimir]. Ivanow, *Ibn al-Qaddah (The Alleged Founder of Ismailism)* (2nd rev. ed.; Bombay: Ismaili Society, 1957), 78.

172. Abū Manṣūr Muḥammad b. Muḥammad b. Maḥmūd al-Māturīdī al-Samarqandī, *Kitāb al-tawḥīd* (ed. Fathalla Kholeif; Beyrouth: Dar el-Machreq Éditeurs, 1970), 157.3–10.

173. For other translations, see Vajda, "Le témoignage d'al-Māturidī," 4-5; Guy Monnot, "Māturīdī et le manichéisme," in idem, *Islam et religions*, 147; Monnot, *Penseurs*, 303–304. The second paragraph is also translated into English in Māturīdī, *Kitāb al-tawḥīd* (ed. Kholeif), xli.

174. Māturīdī, *Kitāb al-tawḥīd* (ed. Kholeif), 171.7–8.

175. I.e., Muḥammad Ibn Shabīb, a Baṣran Mu'tazilī thinker. See J. Meric Pessagno, "The Reconstruction of the Thought of Muḥammad Ibn Shabīb," *JAOS* 104 (1984): 445–53; Ulrich Rudolph, *Al-Māturīdī und die sunnitische Theologie in Samarkand* (Leiden: E. J. Brill, 1997), 178–79.

176. This is a claim repeatedly made but which is extraordinarily problematic insofar as the designation 'Ṣābian' refers to several distinct non-Muslim communities in Islamicate discourse and these references are thoroughly intertwined: (1) the unknown scriptural group mentioned in Q 2:62; 5:69; and 22:17; (2) the residual 'pagan' adherents dwelling in and around the northern Mesopotamian city of Ḥarrān; and (3) the so-called 'true Ṣābians' or 'Ṣābians of the marshes,' a report-

not specify.[177]

Ma'sūdī, *Murūj al-dhahab* (ed. Barbier de Meynard-de Courteille):[178]

It was at the time of this Mānī that the term *zanādiqa* began to be used for those persons attached to *zandaqa*. According to what I previously set forth in the earlier genealogy,[179] at the time when Zarādusht b. Isbī[ta]mān brought to the Persians the book in the ancient language of the Persians among their writings known as the Avesta, he prepared a commentary for it, which is the *Zand*,[180] and he made for this commentary an exposition of it called the *Pāzand*.[181] This information accords with what I previously set forth.[182] (Hence) the *Zand* is an elucidation for the interpretation of a prior revealed scripture. And it is the case that whenever someone introduces into their (i.e., Zoroastrian) religious law something that deviates from the revealed scripture—that is the Avesta—and turns toward the interpretation—that is the *Zand*—they call such a person a *zandī*, ascribing to him (the title) of the interpretation. He has deviated from the literal meaning of the revealed scripture to an interpretation which is at variance with what was revealed. When the Arabs arrived, they borrowed this term from the Persians and arabicized its pronunciation as *zindīq*. And (so) the dualists are the *zanādiqa*, but it (the term) is also attached to all those who believe in an infinite pre-existence and those who deny the creation of the world.[183]

Maqdisī, *Kitāb al-bad' wa'l-ta'rīkh* (ed. Huart):[184]

The dualists have different opinions. Mānī and Ibn Abī al-'Awjā'[185] maintain that

---

edly Irano-Jewish syncretist group inhabiting the swamps of lower Mesopotamia and presumably identical with the Mandaeans. It is probably this last group whom Ibn Shabīb has in mind when he claims there is a doctrinal affinity between the 'Ṣābians' and the 'Manichaeans.'

177. See also Rudolph, *Al-Māturīdī*, 165 n.37.

178. Abū al-Ḥasan 'Alī b. al-Ḥusayn b. 'Alī al-Mas'ūdī, *Murūj al-dhahab wa-ma'ādin al-jawhar: Les prairies d'or* (9 vols.; ed. C. Barbier de Meynard and Pavet de Courteille; Paris: Imprimerie impériale, 1861–77), 2:167–68; Taqīzādeh-Šīrāzī, *Mānī va dīn-e-ū*, 130 (§21).

179. See Mas'ūdī, *Murūj* (ed. Barbier de Meynard-de Courteille), 2:123–24.

180. The *Zand* is actually a glossed Pahlavi translation of the Avesta.

181. The *Pazand* is a Pahlavi or New Persian text transcribed into Avestan characters.

182. See Mas'ūdī, *Murūj* (ed. Barbier de Meynard-de Courteille), 2:126.

183. For other translations, see Barbier de Meynard-de Courteille, 2:167–68; Charles Pellat, *Les prairies d'or* (5 vols.; Paris: Société asiatique, 1962–97), 1:222 (§594); Shaul Shaked, "Esoteric Trends in Zoroastrianism," *Proceedings of the Israel Academy of Sciences and Humanities* 3 (1969): 188; Monnot, *Penseurs*, 309-10; Giorgi, *Pour une histoire*, 130-31; note also F. C. de Blois, "Zindīḳ" *EI*² 11:510. Some of the same information is repeated in the testimony of Nuwayrī below.

184. Maqdisī, *Kitāb al-bad' wa'l-ta'rīkh* (6 vols.; ed. Cl. Huart; Paris: Leroux, 1899–1919), 1:90.12–91.2; see also Taqīzādeh-Šīrāzī, *Mānī va dīn-e-ū*, 144 (§25).

185. A leading proponent of Manichaeism during the early 'Abbāsid period.

Light is the creator of Good and Darkness is the creator of Evil. They are both eternal, animate, and sentient. Their actions in the world result from their meeting and mixture after they had not been mixed, and this world came into existence as a result of that same mixing. They thus acknowledge the bringing into being of a new thing by a pre-existent one, although without it having a necessary reason or intention to do so. They are like the Zoroastrians when they say that Good brought Evil into being unintentionally and without it willing to do so. [Bar] Dayṣān claims that Light is animate and that Darkness is inanimate.[186]

Maqdisī, *K. al-bad' wa'l-ta'rīkh* (ed. Huart):[187]

An account of the statements of the Manichaeans and the Ḥarrānians:

In general, the foundation of their belief is that in the beginning there were two entities, Light and Darkness. Light was high above and Darkness was down below. Both Light and Darkness were unsullied, except for where they intersected after the fashion of the shade and the sun. Then they mixed with each other, and it is from their mixing that this world with its contents came into being. These are the basic beliefs on which there is consensus.

They however diverge in their opinions after this. Ibn Dayṣān maintained that Light created Good and Darkness created Evil, (claiming this) after having said that Light was animate and sentient and that Darkness was inanimate (lit. 'dead'). How can something that is dead be an agent? When he (Ibn Dayṣān) perceived the inconsistencies and distortions (voiced) among the different sects of Manichaeans and Dayṣānites, he invented a new teaching: he claimed that the two entities—the Luminous and the Dark—existed eternally, and with them was a third eternal being who never ceases opposing them and who is outside of their exteriors. This being was the one who caused the two entities to intertwine and mix. Without this one to balance them, their substance(s) would remain separate and resistant ....

Zurqān[188] claims that they (i.e., the Ḥarrānians) teach a doctrine similar to that of the Manichaeans ....

As for the Zoroastrians, there are many kinds. They are raving mad and have fanciful tales whose measure and extent can hardly be perceived. Some of them profess the dualist doctrine, whereas others of them follow the teaching of the Ḥarrānians. The Khurramiyya can be classed among them;[189] they conceal themselves within Islam. They say that Light forms the basis for the world, but that some of it was supplanted and changed into Darkness.

186. For another translation, see Cl. Huart, *Le livre de la création et de l'histoire de Motahhar ben Ṭâhir el-Maqdisî* (Paris: Ernest Leroux, 1899), 82.

187. Maqdisī, *K. al-bad' wa'l-ta'rīkh* (ed. Huart), 1:142.8–143.16; Taqīzādeh-Šīrāzī, *Mānī va dīn-e-ū*, 144–45 (§25).

188. Aḥmad b. al-Ḥasan al-Misma'ī. See the testimony of 'Abd al-Jabbār below; also van Ess, *Theologie und Gesellschaft*, 4:119–21.

189. For this group, see Chapter 5.

As for the people of China, they are generally dualists, for many of them are adjacent to the Turks.[190]

Maqdisī, *K. al-bad' wa'l-ta'rīkh* (ed. Huart):[191]

All of the dualists and Manichaeans believe in Jesus. They assert that he is the Spirit of God, meaning that he is part of God. According to them, Light is a living sentient realm.[192]

Abū Ya'qūb al-Sijistānī, *Ithbāt al-nubū'āt* (ed. Tāmir):[193]

Zarādusht (i.e., Zoroaster), Bihāfrīdh, and Mazdak each connected what is in his religious teachings (*sharī'a*) to that of Abraham. Likewise Mānī, [Bar]-Dayṣān, and Marcion each connected what is in his religious teachings to Christ (upon whom be peace!). All of them maintain that they came to renew the religion of Abraham and of Christ because it had been extinguished.[194]

Ibn al-Nadīm, *Fihrist* (ed. Flügel):[195]

Mānī claimed that he was the Paraclete, the one whom Jesus, upon whom be peace, had predicted.[196] Mānī derived his doctrine from the Zoroastrians and the Christians. Likewise, the script with which he wrote books on religion was produced from Syriac and Persian.[197]

---

190. For another translation, see Huart, *Le livre de la création* (1899), 131–33.

191. Maqdisī, *K. al-bad' wa'l-ta'rīkh* (ed. Huart), 3:122.8–10; Taqīzādeh-Šīrāzī, *Mānī va dīn-e-ū*, 145 (§25).

192. For another translation, see Huart, *Le livre de la création* (1903), 126.

193. Abū Ya'qūb al-Sijistānī, *Kitāb ithbāt al-nubū'āt* (ed. 'Ārif Tāmir; Beirut: al-Maṭba'ah al-Kāthūlīkīyah, 1966), 83.12–15.

194. See also Ivanow, *Ibn al-Qaddah*, 78–79; S. M. Stern, "Abū Ḥātim al-Rāzī on Persian Religion," in idem, *Studies in Early Ismā'īlism* (Jerusalem: The Magnes Press, 1983), 35–36; Henry Corbin, "From the Gnosis of Antiquity to Ismaili Gnosis," in idem, *Cyclical Time and Ismaili Gnosis* (London: Kegan Paul International, 1983), 192.

195. Gustav Flügel, *Mani: Seine Lehre und seine Schriften* (Leipzig, 1862; repr., Osnabrück: Biblio Verlag, 1969), 51.13–16; Ibn al-Nadīm, *Kitāb al-Fihrist* (ed. Riḍa Tajaddud; [Tehran: Maktabat al-Assadī, 1971]), 392; Taqīzādeh-Šīrāzī, *Mānī va dīn-e-ū*, 151 (§27).

196. See John 14:16–17, 26; 15:26; 16:7; Coptic *Keph.* 14.3–16.31. In Islam, the same prophecy of Jesus is applied to Muḥammad. See Q 61:6; Ibn Isḥāq, *Sīra* (note Alfred Guillaume, *The Life of Muhammad: A Translation of Isḥāq's Sīrat Rasūl Allāh* [Oxford, 1955; repr., Karachi: Oxford University Press, 1967], 104 n.1); and the discussions of Alfred Louis de Prémare, "«Comme il est écrit»: L'histoire d'un texte," *Studia Islamica* 70 (1989): 44-47; Uri Rubin, *The Eye of the Beholder: The Life of Muḥammad as Viewed by the Early Muslims* (Princeton, NJ: The Darwin Press, 1995), 22–23.

197. See also Flügel, *Mani*, 85; Kessler, *Mani*, 386; Adam, *Texte*², 118; Bayard Dodge, *The Fihrist of al-Nadīm* (2 vols.; New York: Columbia University Press, 1970), 2:776.

Ibn al-Nadīm, *Fihrist* (ed. Flügel):[198]

Mānī said: 'When the Primal Iblīs[199] became embroiled in battle with Primal Man, five ingredients of Light were mixed with five ingredients of Darkness. The smoke (from the Realm of Darkness) mixed with the air (from the Realm of Light), and from them resulted this blended air. Whatever there is in it that is delightful and that gives refreshment for souls and life to animals derived from the air, and whatever there is in it that is destructive and harmful derived from the smoke. The fire (from the Realm of Darkness) mixed with the fire (from the Realm of Light), and whatever there is in it that burns, destroys, and corrupts derived from the (Evil) fire, and whatever there is in it that shines and illumines derived from the (Good) fire. The light mixed with the darkness, and whatever there is in it of dense substances like gold, silver, and things similar to them and also whatever there is in it that is pure, beautiful, clean, and beneficial derived from the light. Whatever there is in it that is dirty, turbid, coarse, and harsh derived from the darkness. The (hot) wind (from the Realm of Darkness) mixed with the wind (from the Realm of Light), and whatever there is in it that is beneficial and delightful derived from the wind, and whatever there is in it that is distressful, injurious, and harmful derived from the (hot) wind. The fog mixed with the water, and whatever there is in it that is pure, sweet, and suitable for vitality derived from the water, and whatever there is in it that drowns, strangles, destroys, burdens, and corrupts derived from the fog.'

Mānī said: 'After the five 'kinds' of Darkness had contaminated the (five) 'kinds'[200] of Light, Primal Man descended to the bottom of the depth(s) and severed the roots of the 'kinds' of Darkness in order that it not expand. Then he returned, making ascent to his station on the battlefield.'

He (i.e., Mānī) said: 'He[201] then commanded some angels to drag this mixture to (a locale) remote from the Land of Darkness, bordering (?) the Land of Light. They suspended them (i.e., the mixed ingredients) in the heights. Then he commissioned another angel and gave to him those mixed ingredients.'

Mānī said: 'The King of the World of Light ordered one of his angels to create this world and to construct it using those mixed ingredients in order to free those ingredients of Light from the ingredients of Darkness. As a result he constructed ten heavens and eight earths.[202] He appointed one angel to bear the heavens and another (angel) to lift up the earths. He made twelve gates for each heaven

198. Flügel, Mani, 55.8–57.17; Ibn al-Nadīm, *K. al-Fihrist* (ed. Tajaddud), 393–94; Taqīzādeh-Šīrāzī, *Mānī va dīn-e-ū*, 152–53 (§27).

199. A mythic personification of the Realm of Darkness equivalent to the 'King of Darkness' in the account supplied by Theodore bar Konai above.

200. Arabic الاجناس. This term alternates with 'elements' (عناصر) or 'ingredients' (اجزاء).

201. Presumably the King of the Light-Paradises. But perhaps Primal Man is intended.

202. Compare the variant cosmogonic account given by Theodore bar Konai above, where the Mother of Life is credited with the fabrication of the heavens and a group of divine entities seem to share demiurgic responsibilities.

with large, wide antechambers. Each gate was situated opposite the other, and in front of each of the antechambers was two doors. He made six thresholds in those antechambers within each one of the openings, and for each of the thresholds (he made) thirty paths and for each of the paths twelve rows. He made the thresholds, paths, and rows especially high, corresponding to the elevation of the heavens.'

He (i.e., Mānī) said: 'The atmosphere of the lowest earth was joined to the heavens, and around this world he constructed a ditch wherein to cast the Darkness which was cleared from the Light. He fashioned a wall at the rear of that ditch so that none of the Darkness which had been separated from the Light could escape.'

Mānī said: 'Then he created the sun and the moon in order to extract the (portions of) Light which are (mixed) in the world. The sun extracts the Light which was mixed with the satans of heat, and the moon extracts the Light which was mixed with the satans of cold. This (i.e., what is extracted) ascends in a Column of Praise together with what is removed by (the chanting of hymns of) glorification, (invocations of) sanctification, proper speech, and pious deeds.'[203]

He (i.e., Mānī) said: 'This (i.e., what is extracted) reaches the sun, and the sun propels it onward to the Light that is above it in the 'World of Praises' (*sic*), and it circulates in this world (until it reconnects) to the uppermost, pure Light.'[204]

Ibn al-Nadīm, *Fihrist* (ed. Flügel):[205]

An account of the Land of Light and the Atmosphere of Light, which two are eternally coexistent with the God of Light:

Mānī said: 'The Land of Light has five limbs,[206] (which are) air, wind, light, water, and fire; and the Atmosphere of Light has five limbs, (which are) intellect, knowledge, intelligence, what is invisible, and sagacity.'

---

203. For the instrumental role of liturgical recitation and certain sanctioned behaviors (e.g., fasting) in the liberation of Light from the material order, see especially the evidence supplied by Ephrem Syrus, *Prose Refutations* (ed. Mitchell), 2:204 (*apud* Reeves, "Citations from Ephrem," 243–44): 'Let us state further against Manī—(who said) that it was possible to restore the one cast like a thing from its domain into "sin" by means of *zaddīqūtā* (i.e., the Manichaean ethos) and the observance of commandment(s), and (that) although the *ziwane* (i.e., the particles of Light) were mixed with "sin" in Darkness, they could be refined through fasting and prayer ....'; also note BeDuhn, *The Manichaean Body*, 144–45; 258, to which this Arabic language evidence should be added.

204. See also Flügel, *Mani*, 88-90; Kessler, *Mani*, 390–92; Adam, *Texte*², 121–23; Dodge, *Fihrist*, 2:780–82.

205. Flügel, *Mani*, 61.14–62.13; Ibn al-Nadīm, *K. al-Fihrist* (ed. Tajaddud), 395-96; Taqīzādeh-Šīrāzī, *Mānī va dīn-e-ū*, 156 (§27).

206. As in component 'bodily parts; members.' See Flügel, *Mani*, 178–80; Vajda, "Le témoignage d'al-Māturidī," 14–18. English 'limbs' also preserves a possible association with the older arboreal symbolism of the Tree of Life and the Tree of Death for the realms of Light and Darkness respectively.

He (i.e., Mānī) said: 'The <Father of>[207] Greatness is all these ten limbs which belong to the Atmosphere and the Land.'

He (i.e., Mānī) said: 'This luminous Land possesses a corporeality which is brilliant and beautiful, shining and radiant. There shines upon it the clarity of its purity and the beauty of its form, (consisting of) various shapes, lovelinesses, brightnesses, transparencies, beauties, lights, rays of light, sights, goodnesses, pleasant things, gates, towers, dwellings, domiciles, gardens, trees (with) branches loaded down with limbs and fruits having a beautiful appearance and a radiant luminosity (and) exhibiting different colors, some of them more excellent and brilliant than the others; as well as clouds and shady spots. That luminous god who is in this Land is an eternal deity.'

He (i.e., Mānī) said: 'The deity of this Land has twelve great beings who are termed "virgins."[208] Their form is similar to his form. Each of them is knowledgeable and intelligent.'

He (i.e., Mānī) said: 'And great beings who are termed "vigorously laboring inhabitants"[209] (are also there).'

He (i.e., Mānī) said: 'Air is the life of the world.'[210]

Ibn al-Nadīm, *Fihrist* (ed. Flügel):[211]

An account of the Land of Darkness and its heat:

Mānī said: 'Its Land contains pits, caves, tracts, layers, barriers, tangled growths, and swamps: a disordered, divided Land filled with discord, and smoke pours from it[212] through each area and every barrier. Fire pours from it through each area, and darkness also pours across each area. Some of this (Land) is higher than the rest, and some is lower. The smoke which pours from it is a deadly poison.[213] It flows from a source, the deepest part of whose foundations is entirely (comprised?) of earth and tangled growths of fire, intensely darkened wind, and brackish water.[214] Darkness is adjacent to that luminous Land (which is) above (it), and that one (i.e., Darkness) is below. There is no boundary for the one on its

207. Restore with de Blois, "Glossary," 64, and note Flügel, *Mani*, 272.

208. See Theodore bar Konai, *Scholion* (ed. Scher), 2:316.1–8, where each of the so-called 'twelve virgins' (ܬܪ̈ܬܥܣܪܐ ܒ̈ܬܘܠܬܐ) is identified by name.

209. Perhaps a reference to the five 'sons' of the Living Spirit? According to Theodore bar Konai (*Scholion* [ed. Scher], 2:316.9), three of them are 'workers, servitors' (ܦܠܚ̈ܐ).

210. See also Flügel, *Mani*, 93–94; Kessler, *Mani*, 396–97; Dodge, *Fihrist*, 2:786–87.

211. Flügel, *Mani*, 62.14–63.7; Ibn al-Nadīm, *K. al-Fihrist* (ed. Tajaddud), 396; Taqīzādeh-Šīrāzī, *Mānī va dīn-e-ū*, 156 (§27).

212. Read with the emendation suggested by Flügel, *Mani*, 62 n.14.

213. Literally 'the poison (or fever) of death.' This is presumably a corrupted reference to the 'Hummāma of Death,' an entity mentioned by al-Misma'ī *apud* 'Abd al-Jabbār, *Mughnī* (ed. Ḥusayn), 5:19.8–20.1 (see below).

214. The text of this sentence is extremely difficult, and the translation reflects many of the variants recorded in the textual apparatus supplied by Flügel, *Mani*, 63.

upper side, or for Darkness on its lower side.'[215]

Ibn al-Nadīm, *Fihrist* (ed. Flügel):[216]

Mānī disparaged the rest of the prophets in his writings. He found fault with them and charged them with lies, and maintained that devils[217] had taken possession of them and had spoken using their tongues. He even says in certain passages of his books that they themselves (i.e., certain biblical prophets) were devils, and he maintained that Jesus, a renowned figure among us and the Christians, was Satan.[218]

'Abd al-Jabbār, *Tathbīt* (ed. 'Uthmān):[219]

Similarly he (i.e., Aristotle) has said about fire: 'You can observe that it hardens things, like an egg or something similarly (soft), but it melts things like copper, lead, gold, and silver or something similarly (solid). It whitens these things, but blackens those things. Thus you learn from this that all things are alive, capable of speech, audition, sight, and action.'

This was the teaching of Mānī insofar as he taught (the same thing) about every material body found in the world and every constituent part of it, even saying this about iron, stones, and wood. Manichaeans speak about the noises which can be heard when sesame and eggplant are roasted, or the sounds associated with

215. See also Flügel, *Mani*, 94; Kessler, *Mani*, 397–98; Dodge, *Fihrist*, 2:787–88.

216. Flügel, *Mani*, 69.11–15; Ibn al-Nadīm, *K. al-Fihrist* (ed. Tajaddud), 398; Taqīzādeh-Šīrāzī, *Mānī va dīn-e-ū*, 159 (§27).

217. Literally 'satans' (الشياطين). Testimony to Mani's disparagement of most of the biblical prophets is supplied by the fourth-century tradents Titus of Bostra and Ephrem Syrus, and is also visible in Theodore bar Konai and 'Abd al-Jabbār above. For the Syriac sources, see John C. Reeves, "Jewish Pseudepigrapha in Manichaean Literature: The Influence of the Enochic Library," in *Tracing the Threads: Studies in the Vitality of Jewish Pseudepigrapha* (SBLEJL 6; ed. John C. Reeves; Atlanta: Scholars Press, 1994), 191 n.1.

218. Or simply 'a devil.' Presumably the non-docetic crucified figure propounded by classical Christianity is meant, since Jesus the Messiah was accepted as an authentic prophet by Mani (and Muḥammad); otherwise, it is a baseless calumny simply lifted from Christian polemic. Note also de Blois, "Zindīḳ" *EI*[2] 11:512. A curious passage found in Evodius (*De fide contra Manichaeos* 28, 964.7–10) which supposedly relies upon the *Epistula fundamenti* of Mani states *inimicus quippe qui eundem saluatorem iustorum patrem crucifixisse se speravit ipse est crucifixus, quo tempore aliud actum est atque aliud ostensum* 'the enemy, who hoped to have crucified that same saviour, the father of the righteous, was himself crucified: for at that time, appearance and real event were distinct.' Translation of the Latin text of Evodius cited from Gardner-Lieu, *Manichaean Texts*, 171; for discussion, see especially Flügel, *Mani*, 255–56; Monnot, *Penseurs*, 84–85; Lieu, *Manichaeism*[2], 163; idem, *Manichaeism in Mesopotamia and the Roman East* (EPRO 118; Leiden: Brill, 1994), 286–87.
For other translations of this passage, see Flügel, *Mani*, 100; Dodge, *Fihrist*, 2:794.

219. 'Abd al-Jabbār b. Aḥmad al-Hamadhānī, *Tathbīt dālā'il al-nubūwwah* (2 vols.; ed. 'Abd al-Karīm 'Uthmān; Beirut: Dār al-Arabiyah, 1966–67), 1:80.4–14.

pots boiling, or the sounds accompanying the splitting of firewood. Each of these (sounds) is its cry or its scream which has been induced by these sufferings.[220]

The Manichaeans maintain that the philosophers adopted these doctrines from their (own system). But I have only mentioned this in this context to acquaint you with the measure of intelligence exhibited by the *zanādiqa* and the heretics. Had not certain leaders, writers, and ministers been led astray by them, we would not have mentioned them.[221]

'Abd al-Jabbār, *Tathbīt* (ed. 'Uthmān):[222]

But you surely know that Mānī the priest[223] claims precision about Christ, that he (claims to be) among his followers, that no one follows his (Christ's) religious laws and injunctions except for he (Mani) and his followers, and that the *Gospel* which he has is his (Christ's) gospel.[224]

'Abd al-Jabbār, *Tathbīt* (ed. 'Uthmān):[225]

He (i.e., Mani) was on intimate terms with the Persians: he lauded Light and condemned Darkness in accordance with what the Zoroastrians believe. Moreover he praised Zarādusht (i.e., Zoroaster), the Zoroastrian prophet,[226] and said (that) Light had chosen him and sent him to the East, whereas it had sent Christ to the West. He however disparaged Abraham, Ishmael, and those prophets whom Christ regarded as authentic. The Persians used to disavow them (as well), and Mānī supported them, so that he was (doctrinally) close to them in disparaging these (prophets). He said: 'Satan sent them.'[227] And he would write: 'From Mānī, the servant of Jesus,'[228] just like Paul used to write. He imitated him (i.e., Paul) and followed his example.[229]

220. A reference to the Manichaean doctrine of the Living Soul or Living Self, the divine 'substance' which is dispersed throughout the created order on account of the initial mixture of Darkness with Light. For an illustration of the 'pain' suffered by the cutting of wood or the harvesting of vegetables, see *CMC* 6.8–10.16. The definitive discussion of this Manichaean doctrine is now that of BeDuhn, *The Manichaean Body*, 72–88.

221. For another translation, see Monnot, *Penseurs*, 279–80.

222. 'Abd al-Jabbār, *Tathbīt* (ed. 'Uthmān), 1:114.13–15.

223. See the note on this appellation in Chapter 2 above.

224. See also Shlomo Pines, "Two Passages Concerning Mani," in his *The Jewish Christians of the Early Centuries of Christianity According to a New Source* (Proceedings of the Israel Academy of Sciences and Humanities 2.13; Jerusalem: The Israel Academy of Sciences and Humanities, 1966), 66.

225. 'Abd al-Jabbār, *Tathbīt* (ed. 'Uthmān), 1:169.12–170.9; 170.12–16.

226. The name of Zoroaster frequently figures in authentic Manichaean rosters of recognized prophets.

227. A similar charge is found in Ibn al-Nadīm below.

228. Arabic: من مانى عبد اليسوع. Compare Rom 1:1; Gal 1:10.

229. H. D. Betz echoes this important observation: 'The quotations from Mani's own writings (CMC 64.8–68.5) confirm previous knowledge: Paul's apostleship served as the

He adopted the Avesta, which was the book of Zarādusht, the prophet of the Zoroastrians. It is a book which is not in the language of the Persians or in any language at all. No one understands what it is. It sounds like murmuring. They recite its words (i.e., of the Avesta), but they truly do not know what it means. However, Mānī the priest maintained that he could understand it and knew what it meant.

Mānī claimed that he was the Messenger of Light.[230] He invented foolish things for them and said: 'This is the interpretation of the Avesta!' The general public was fascinated and his fame grew among them. They followed him and claimed that he performed miracles and signs ....[231] The sect of Mānī remained after him: they promulgated his prophetic status and established (the texts?) of his *Epistles* and his *Gospel*. His *Epistles* are probably more numerous than (those of) the apostles or the epistles of Paul.[232]

Many among (the adherents of) these three (Christian) sects[233] believe in his teaching, but they hardly reveal this due to fear of the Christians and of the Muslims for those of them dwelling in an Islamic land, because the Manichaeans are not recognized by Muslims as having a protected status.[234]

'Abd al-Jabbār, *Tathbīt* (ed. 'Uthmān):[235]

The sect of the Manichaeans has prevailed throughout the east not by military conquest or by the distribution of wealth. They claim that their religion is the strictest and most difficult of religions, for they do not eat meat or harm any kind of animal. They eat only what has been harvested from the soil. Their religious devotion is expressed through numerous lengthy prayers and arduous fasts. They do not despise riches. They claim that prophetic miracles compel them to profess this religion, and they say that the most perceptive of your (Christian) monks and your leaders were actually some of them (Manichaeans). They term

model for Mani's understanding of his own vocation and mission.' Quoted from his "Paul in the Mani Biography (Codex Manichaicus Coloniensis)," in *Codex Manichaicus Coloniensis* (ed. Cirillo and Roselli), 215–34, at 217. For another translation of this paragraph, see Gabriel Said Reynolds, *A Muslim Theologian in the Sectarian Milieu: 'Abd al-Jabbār and the* Critique of Christian Origins (Leiden: Brill, 2004), 169–70.

230. رسول النور.

231. Mani indeed enjoyed fame as a thaumaturge and healer. *CMC* 121.11–123.13 and 130.1-135.6 depict two early miracles performed by Mani, and M 47 attaches the conversion of Mihrshāh to Mani's ability to ascend at will to the Paradise of Light. During his final fateful interrogation by Bahrām I (see M 3 *apud* Henning, "Mani's Last Journey," 951–52), Mani protests that he has performed numerous successful healings and demon-expulsions. Bīrūnī (see below) attests that one faction of Manichaeans gave special importance to Mani's miracles and wonder-working. Even Theodore bar Konai grudgingly concedes that Mani was 'familiar with the art of healing.'

232. For a catalogue of Mani's *Epistles*, see Ibn al-Nadīm in Chapter 3.

233. Namely the Chalcedonian, Monophysite, and Nestorian branches of eastern Christianity.

234. See also Pines, "Two Passages," 66–68; Monnot, *Penseurs*, 277–79.

235. 'Abd al-Jabbār, *Tathbīt* (ed. 'Uthmān), 1:184.2–17.

themselves 'Magian sages.'[236]

They say: 'However, unlike the Jews, Christians, or Zoroastrians, we are not accorded *dhimma* status by the Muslims.[237] Whenever we profess our religion to them, they kill us.' They say: 'The rulers of Rome do the same to us.'

Among the signs and miracles of Mānī, they recount that he was totally encompassed by pure light and that he cast no shadow when he was in sunlight. Angels would come to him and carry him off so that he would ascend to the sun, and it would happen to him while his companions were present with him, and they continue to transmit this (tradition) from group to group and congregation to congregation. They claim that his followers (also) performed miracles.

But nevertheless they (the Manichaeans) claim that they are followers of Christ and of the religion of Christ, and that the *Gospel* which they possess is the authentic one. The one which you (the Christians) possess is inferior. It is appropriate that they should establish (their religion) analogously to yours, and the (basis) then for them are the signs and miracles, similar to what you have claimed for yourselves. They possess books which record his signs and miracles, and they (the signs and miracles) are perhaps more numerous than those of your own apostles and (more numerous) than the signs which you ascribe to any missionary for Christianity.[238]

'Abd al-Jabbār, *Mughnī* (ed. Ḥusayn):[239]

An account of the doctrine of the Manichaeans.

According to the report of al-Ḥasan b. Mūsā [al-Nawbakhtī], the Manichaeans—they being the followers of Mānī the dualist—say that the world is composed of two things: Light and Darkness. They are primal entities which have always existed and which will never cease to exist. They deny the existence of any created or composed thing in the absence of a prior primal (generative) principle. We perceive, they would say, only two (entities who are) endowed with sensation, power, understanding, hearing, and vision who nevertheless differ from each other in identity[240] and form and who oppose one another in (their) activities and plans.[241] The substance of Light is excellent, pleasing, distinguished by clarity,

236. هرابذة المجوس.

237. I.e., Manichaeism was not a legally protected religion under Islamic law. For the complications which this created, see especially Yohanan Friedmann, *Tolerance and Coercion in Islam: Interfaith Relations in the Muslim Tradition* (Cambridge: Cambridge University Press, 2003), 139–43.

238. For another translation, see Monnot, *Penseurs*, 281–82.

239. 'Abd al-Jabbār b. Aḥmad al-Hamadhānī, *Al-Mughnī fī abwāb al-tawḥīd wa'l-'adl* (vols.; ed. Ṭāhā Ḥusayn, et al.; Cairo: Al-Shirkah al-'Arabīyah lil-Tibā'ah wa'l-Nashr, 1958–66), 5:10.2-12.5.

240. Literally 'soul; essence; nature' (*nafs*).

241. Compare the account attributed to Abū 'Īsā al-Warrāq below by Shahrastānī, *Kitāb al-milal wa'l-niḥal* (2 vols.; ed. Muḥammad b. Fatḥ Allāh Badrān; [Cairo]: Matba'at al-Azhar, [1951-55]), 1:620.1–5.

purity, a pleasant odor, and a beautiful appearance. Its essence is good, noble, (and) beneficial, and from its action comes everything that is good, proper, and delightful. There is nothing within it that is evil or harmful. The substance of Darkness contrasts with this (profile): it is imperfect, turbid, rotten in odor, and of ugly appearance. Its essence is evil, ignorant, stupid, rotten, (and) harmful, and from it derives everything that is evil, harmful, sorrowful, and corrupt.[242]

They maintain that the two were always separate but after a time became mixed with each other. They also maintain that their two Worlds extend infinitely in each direction except for the side where they meet. But then they differ, for some of them say that Light is always above Darkness, which latter matches it below.

But Abū ʿĪsā al-Warrāq relates that the majority of them (holds) that Light is always high toward the north, and Darkness is low toward the south. Some of them say that they lie adjacent to each other. According to some, the place where they contact is governed by where (Darkness?) is raised up vertically, for Darkness is (usually) in a horizontal position.[243] They differ about their intersection: some of them—and this is the majority opinion—say they touch each other without anything separating them similar to the way the sun and a shadow 'touch' one another. But others among them say that their point of contact is one of adjacency and that there is a gap between them.[244]

They claim that each of them (i.e., Light and Darkness) has five 'parts,'[245] four of which are corporeal. Those which belong to Light are fire, light, wind, and water; the fifth, which is spiritual, is air, and the air is in motion in this body. The corporeal component of Darkness consists of fire, darkness, hot wind, and mist, and its spiritual component is smoke, which they term Hummāma.[246] They maintain with regard to the corporeal (elements) of Light that some parts differ from other parts, but share with one another an existence in Light. The spiritual (element) of Light always helps its bodily (parts), and its bodily (parts) help it; but the spirit of Darkness harms its bodily (parts), and its bodily (parts) in turn are injurious to it. It is said with regard to them that the five parts are black, white, red, yellow, and green. That which is white which is in the World of Light is good, and that which is of that color in the World of Darkness is evil. They (Light and Darkness) have five senses: what is in Light is good, and what is in Darkness is evil. The

242. Compare the first three entries in the synoptic chart contrasting the characteristics of the two Realms provided by Shahrastānī, *Kitāb al-milal wa'l-niḥal* (ed. Badrān), 1:621.1–9 (see below).

243. A very problematic statement; compare the renderings and notes of Vajda, "Le témoignage d'al-Māturidī: Note annexe," 116; Monnot, *Penseurs*, 154.

244. For a parallel to this minority opinion within the testimony of Augustine, see Bennett, "Primordial Space," 75–78.

245. Also referred to as 'elements,' 'principles,' 'limbs,' or even 'deities.' See especially Reeves, "Citations from Ephrem," 269–70 n.9, which supplies a select number of lists of these elements from Greek, Coptic, Syriac, and Middle Iranian Manichaean sources.

246. Compare Shahrastānī, *Kitāb al-milal wa'l-niḥal* (ed. Badrān), 1:622.1–7.

majority of them claims that the parts[247] and the spiritual entities are completely alive (and) endowed with senses. Some of them say that it is the Two Spirits that are alive, and (that) the corporeal (elements) of Light live a pure life save that it is not a life of perception or discernment; and (that) the corporeal (elements) of Darkness and its parts are lifeless (and) putrid.

He (i.e., al-Nawbakhtī) reports that Abū ʿĪsā al-Warrāq said that the actions of each of them (i.e., of Light and Darkness) are voluntary; however, their ability to choose does not go against their essential nature. Yet they say things differ with respect to being good or bad, or being pleasant or foul, or being knowledgeable or ignorant: (the explanation is that) a part of this one is present quantitatively to a greater degree than a part of the other, by which are meant parts of Light and Darkness. And he says with regard to the mixture that it took place in the World of Darkness below the World of Light.

The *mutakallimūn* have reported that they reject accidents.

But al-Warrāq, who was a dualist, said in his book (that) they divide into three groups. One group rejects accidents, another affirms them as being adjuncts to substances, and the third claims that they are qualities and that it cannot be said that they are substances or something else.[248]

They disagree regarding the purification of Light from Darkness after the mixture occurred. Some of them say that all (the particles of) Light will be purified of Darkness, but others among them say that some of it (i.e., Light) will remain (mixed) in Darkness, for at the time Light purifies itself it will make a barrier between the two (Realms) out of Darkness and the parts of Light which are still bound within it to prevent it (i.e., Darkness) from returning to it (i.e., Light) and harming it. They also disagree when some of them say that at the time Darkness overpowered Light and the period (of its subjection) became prolonged, it (i.e., Light) performed its (i.e., Darkness's) actions. However, the rest of them deny this. The same disagreement pertains to the (future) time when Light overpowers Darkness.[249]

ʿAbd al-Jabbār, *Mughnī* (ed. Ḥusayn):[250]

Some of them say that the mixture of the Two Principles comprises only a portion of their corporeal components (and) excludes their spiritual components. In the (created) world are many pure things which are not part of the mixture, like the sun, moon, and the daytime: each one of these consists of unmixed Light, just as night[251] consists of unmixed Darkness.

---

247. Monnot suggests that a copyist mistakenly wrote 'parts' for 'corporeal entities'; see his *Penseurs*, 155 n.1.

248. See Thomas, "Abū ʿĪsā al-Warrāq," 280.

249. For other translations, see Georges Vajda, "Le témoignage d'al-Māturidī sur la doctrine des Manichéens, des Dayṣānites et des Marcionites: Note annexe," *Arabica* 13 (1966): 115–17; Monnot, *Penseurs*, 152–56.

250. ʿAbd al-Jabbār, *Mughnī* (ed. Ḥusayn), 5:15.4–8.

251. See the critical note in Vajda, "Le témoignage d'al-Māturidī: Note annexe," 121 n.3;

He (i.e., Mani) alleges that heat, cold, dampness, and dryness were always present in the World of Darkness and are always present in a mixed state in a pre-existent mixture.[252] The 'new mixture' is a mixture of Good and Evil.[253]

'Abd al-Jabbār, *Mughnī* (ed. Ḥusayn):[254]

[According to the *Shābuhragān*], the first whom God Most Exalted sent with knowledge (*'ilm*) was Adam, then Seth, and then Noah. Then he sent Zarādusht (i.e., Zoroaster) to Persia, the Buddha to India, Jesus the Christ to the countries of the West, and then, Mānī, seal of the prophets.[255]

Baghdādī, *al-Farq bayn al-firaq* (ed. Taqīzādeh-Šīrāzī):[256]

Among the astonishing things about al-Naẓẓām[257] in this matter is that he composed a book about dualism, and he showed surprise in it with regard to the teaching of the Manichaeans which praises Light as a form perfectly suited for producing what is Good. It is incapable of Evil, and it is incorrect that it could produce any kind of injury.[258] He showed surprise that the dualists blame Darkness for producing Evil when they teach at the same time that Darkness is unable to produce what is Good, but can only produce what is Evil.[259]

Baghdādī, *al-Farq bayn al-firaq* (ed. Taqīzādeh-Šīrāzī):[260]

The sixth of his (i.e., al-Naẓẓām's) mistakes: his declaration that it is the nature of fire to ascend above every thing .... And he said with regard to the soul that when it parts from the body, it rises .... This is the same as the teaching of the dualists that when those portions of Light which were mixed with portions of Darkness become separated from it, they rise to the World of Light, and when Light achieves stability beyond the heavens, the souls join it. Thus he is a dualist.[261]

Monnot, *Penseurs*, 162 n.9.

252. I.e., within the World of Darkness only.

253. For other translations, see Vajda, "Le témoignage d'al-Māturidī: Note annexe," 121; Monnot, *Penseurs*, 162–63.

254. 'Abd al-Jabbār, *Mughnī* (ed. Ḥusayn), 5:15.13–15.

255. See also Vajda, "Le témoignage d'al-Māturidī: Note annexe," 122; Monnot, *Penseurs*, 163.

256. Taqīzādeh-Šīrāzī, *Mānī va dīn-e-ū*, 186–87 (§32).

257. Abū Isḥāq Ibrāhīm al-Naẓẓām (d. 845), a radical Mu'tazilite theologian. See Josef van Ess, "al-Naẓẓām," *EI*[2] 7:1057–58.

258. A similar view as to God's incapability of doing evil was espoused by al-Naẓẓām. See van Ess, "al-Naẓẓām," 7:1058.

259. See also Abū Manṣūr 'Abd-al-Ḳāhir b. Ṭāhir al-Baghdādī, *Moslem Schisms and Sects: Being the History of the Various Philosophic Systems Developed in Islam* (trans. Kate Chambers Seelye; Columbia University Oriental Studies 15; New York, 1920; repr., New York: AMS Press, 1966), 139.

260. Taqīzādeh-Šīrāzī, *Mānī va dīn-e-ū*, 188 (§32).

261. See also Seelye, *Moslem Schisms*, 142–43.

Baghdādī, *al-Farq bayn al-firaq* (ed. Taqīzādeh-Šīrāzī):[262]

Another surprising thing is that he finds fault with the Manichaean teaching that al-Hummāma,[263] the one who in their opinion is the Spirit of Darkness, traversed its native regions and arrived at their uppermost side with the result that it beheld Light. He (i.e., al-Naẓẓām) said to them: 'If its native regions do not have a termination point on their lowest side, then how can al-Hummāma traverse them? It is absurd to cross over that which is limitless.' ... Even more astonishing than this, he accepted (the teaching of) the dualists that Light and Darkness are bounded on each side of the six directions.[264] (He accepted) their teaching for this reason: each one of them terminates on the side where the one meets the other.[265]

Baghdādī, *al-Farq bayn al-firaq* (ed. Taqīzādeh-Šīrāzī):[266]

They (i.e., representatives of 'normative' Islam) say there is a difference between (the status of) 'messenger' (*rasūl*) and 'prophet' (*nabī*). Anyone who has received a revelation from God Most Exalted by means of information mediated by an angel and who can perform various sorts of miracles which contravene the ordinary course of events is a 'prophet.' Whoever accomplishes this (prodigious activity) over a long period of time and moreover confers a new law or annuls some of the precepts of that law which had been previously received is a 'messenger.'

They say that while there have been many prophets, there have been (only) three hundred and thirteen messengers. The first messenger was the father of all humanity; namely, Adam (upon whom be peace!), and the last of them was Muḥammad (may God bless him and grant him salvation!). In opposition to this is the doctrine of the Zoroastrians, for they claim that the father of all humankind is Kayūmart (i.e., Gayōmart) who is called *gilshāh* (i.e., 'clay-king'),[267] and their

262. Taqīzādeh-Šīrāzī, *Mānī va dīn-e-ū*, 188 (§32).

263. Read with the critical apparatus provided by Taqīzādeh-Šīrāzī.

264. I.e., the four cardinal points plus above and below.

265. I.e., where Light is adjacent to Darkness. For another translation, see Seelye, *Moslem Schisms*, 145.

266. Taqīzādeh-Šīrāzī, *Mānī va dīn-e-ū*, 191 (§32).

267. An epithet found, e.g., in the *Dēnkard*. Note Ibn al-Nadīm, *K. al-Fihrist* (ed. Tajaddud), 15.1: 'It is said that the first one who spoke Persian was Jayōmart, and the Persians call him *al-kilshāh*, which means "king of clay."' See also Sven S. Hartman, "Les identifications de Gayōmart à l'époque islamique," in *Syncretism* (ed. Sven S. Hartman; Stockholm: Almqvist and Wiksell, 1969), 266; Shaul Shaked, "Some Islamic Reports Concerning Zoroastrianism," *Jerusalem Studies in Arabic and Islam* 17 (1994): 54 n.15. Based on the evidence of other Pahlavi texts, it has been suggested that *gilshāh* may be an error for *garshāh* 'mountain-king'; see Mansour Shaki, "Gayōmart," *EncIr* 10:345–47, at 346; but note the important observation regarding the orthographic ambiguity of Pahlavi script in Shaul Shaked, "First Man, First King: Notes on Semitic-Iranian Syncretism and Iranian Mythological Transformations," in *Gilgul: Essays on Transformation, Revolution and Permanence in the History of Religions* (ed. S[haul] Shaked, D[avid] Shulman, and G[uy] G. Stroumsa; Leiden: E. J. Brill, 1987), 247.

teaching regarding the final messenger is also different: (it is) Zarādusht (i.e., Zoroaster). A different doctrine is maintained by some of the Khurramiyya: they think that there is no finality for messengers.

They[268] teach that the prophecy of Moses applied only to its own time. A different teaching is that of the Barāhima who disavow it (i.e., the existence of prophecy),[269] and there are also Manichaeans who deny it,[270] as well as Manichaeans who acknowledge (the prophetic rank of) Jesus (upon whom be peace!) ....

They teach the heretical status of all those who posed as prophets, whether (they did so) before Islam like Zoroaster, Būdāsaf,[271] Mānī, [Bar] Dayṣān, Marcion, and Mazdak; or after it like Musaylima,[272] Sajāḥ,[273] al-Aswad b. Zayd al-'Ansī,[274] and the rest of those persons subsequent to them who called themselves 'prophets.'[275]

Baghdādī, *al-Farq bayn al-firaq* (ed. Taqīzādeh-Šīrāzī):[276]

The legal experts of Islam agree about allowing (the consumption of) animals slaughtered by Jews, Samaritans, and Christians; about the legality of contracting marriage with their women; and about the legality of accepting the *jizya* from them. However they disagree regarding the amount of the *jizya* ....[277]

---

268. Representatives of normative Islam? Or the Khurramiyya? Either antecedent will work.

269. For a convincing exposition of this problematic group, see especially Stroumsa, *Freethinkers*, 145–62.

270. Perhaps a reference to Abū 'Īsā al-Warrāq? Note the assumption of Māturīdī as reported by Stroumsa, *Freethinkers*, 70.

271. Emending the text's يوراسف to بوداسف.

272. An enigmatic religious leader roughly contemporary with Muḥammad who claimed to be a prophet. See W. Montgomery Watt, "Musaylima," *EI*² 7:664–65; idem, *Muhammad at Medina* (Oxford: Clarendon Press, 1956), 134–36; Charles Pellat, *The Life and Works of Jāḥiẓ* (trans. D. M. Hawke; Berkeley: University of California Press, 1969), 162–64; Jaakko Hämeen-Anttila, "Arabian Prophecy," in *Prophecy in its Ancient Near Eastern Context: Mesopotamian, Biblical, and Arabian Perspectives* (Atlanta: Society of Biblical Literature, 2000), 135–39; M. J. Kister, "The Struggle Against Musaylima and the Conquest of Yamāma," *Jerusalem Studies in Arabic and Islam* 27 (2002): 1–56.

273. An Arab prophetess who emerged after the death of Muḥammad. See V. Vacca, "Sadjāḥ," *EI*² 8:738–39; Watt, *Muhammad at Medina*, 139-41; Hämeen-Anttila, "Arabian Prophecy," 138; Robert G. Hoyland, *Arabia and the Arabs: From the Bronze Age to the Coming of Islam* (London and New York: Routledge, 2001), 157.

274. Yet another religious opponent of Muḥammad during his final years. See Watt, *Muhammad at Medina*, 128–29; idem, "al-Aswad b. Ka'b al-'Ansī," *EI*² 1:728; Hämeen-Anttila, "Arabian Prophecy," 139.

275. For another translation, see Abū Manṣūr 'Abd al-Qāhir b. Tāhir al-Baghdādī, *Moslem Schisms and Sects (Al-Fark Bain al-Firak) Part II* (ed. Abraham S. Halkin; Tel Aviv, 1935; repr., Philadelphia, PA: Porcupine Press, 1978), 199–200.

276. Taqīzādeh-Šīrāzī, *Mānī va dīn-e-ū*, 191–92 (§32).

277. The tax paid by non-Muslim subjects to the government.

They (i.e., the two legal schools of Shāfiʿī and Abū Ḥanīfa) disagree about the dualists such as the Manichaeans, the Dayṣāniyya, and the Marcionites: those who habitually speak of the pre-existence of Light and Darkness and who maintain that the world is composed of these two (entities). (They claim) that what is good and beneficial originates from Light, and that what is evil and harmful originates from Darkness. Some of the legal experts assert that their situation is like that of the Zoroastrians and allow the receipt of *jizya* from them, although they proscribe (consumption of) their slaughtered animals and (marrying) their women. But the correct opinion among us is that their situation with regard to contracting marriage (with Muslims), (our consuming their) slaughtered animals, and the *jizya* is equivalent to the situation of the worshippers of idols and images,[278] and we have already expounded that (case) prior to this one.[279]

Bīrūnī, *Āthār al-bāqiya ʿan-il-qurūn al-khāliya* (ed. Sachau):[280]

Then after them (i.e., Bardaiṣan and Marcion) came Mānī the disciple of Fādrūn (*sic*).[281] Being versed in the teaching of the Zoroastrians, Christians, and dualists, he proclaimed himself a prophet ....[282]

He said in it (one of his books) that he had amplified what Christ had only hinted at ....

(With regard to the thaumaturgical prowess of their prophet Mānī), they (the Manichaeans) are of two opinions: one group says that no miracle can be ascribed to Mānī and relates that he (only) informed about the advent of the signs denoting the coming of the Christ and his companions; whereas the other group maintains that he did work signs and miracles,[283] and that the king Sābūr came to believe in him the time when he (Mani) raised him with himself to heaven and they both stood in the air between heaven and earth. He displayed marvels to him during this (feat). They say that he would ascend from among his companions to heaven, remain there a few days, and then descend to them.[284]

278. I.e., all of these modes of social interaction are strictly forbidden.

279. See also Baghdādī, *Moslem Schisms* (ed. Halkin), 222–23.

280. Abu'l-Rayḥān Muḥammad b. Aḥmad al-Bīrūnī, *al-Āthār al-bāqiya ʿan-il-qurūn al-khāliya (Chronologie orientalischer Völker von Albêrûnî)* (ed. C. Eduard Sachau; Leipzig, 1878; repr., Leipzig: O. Harrassowitz, 1923), 207.13; 208.14–15; 209.3–7; Taqīzādeh-Šīrāzī, *Mānī va dīn-e-ū*, 204–206 (§34).

281. A corruption of the name Qārdūn (i.e., Cerdo). See above Masʿūdī, *Murūj*, 2:167; also Marwazī below.

282. Mani is frequently grouped with Marcion and Bardaiṣan in eastern polemical sources, a trajectory which stems ultimately from Ephrem Syrus. Later Muslim testimonia tend to 'manichaeize' the information which they transmit about Marcionites and the Dayṣanīyya, but it is unclear whether this reflects actual historical developments or a rhetorical shorthand. Note Guy Monnot, "T̲hanawiyya," *EI*² 10:439.

283. See the discussion about Mani's miracles above under the extract from ʿAbd al-Jabbār.

284. For ascent-traditions and Mani, see Reeves, "Jewish Pseudepigrapha," 179–81.

Bīrūnī, *Āthār* (ed. Sachau):[285]

The majority of philosophers and scholars acknowledge the existence of *jinn* and satans, like Aristotle when he depicts them as air-like and fiery entities and labels them 'human.' Similarly John Philoponus[286] like others acknowledges it when he depicts them (i.e., demons) as the corrupt parts of wavering souls after they were separated from their bodies. They are blocked from reaching their place of origin because they lack knowledge of the truth and behaved confusedly and stupidly. Mānī suggests something similar to this in his books, although his statements are cast in indistinct words.

Bīrūnī, *Taḥqīq mā lil-Hind* (ed. Sachau):[287]

When Mānī was expelled from Iran, he went to India and arrogated the idea of the transmigration of souls (*tanāsukh*) from their religion to his own.[288]

Bīrūnī, *Taḥqīq mā lil-Hind* (ed. Sachau):[289]

Mānī formed a similar belief about it[290] after he had heard from them (i.e., sages in India) that there was a demon (*'ifrīt*) in the sea: the rise and fall (of the waters) are from the drawing in and expulsion of its breath.[291]

Abu'l-Ma'ālī, *Bayān al-adyān* (ed. Taqīzādeh-Šīrāzī):[292]

Dualist doctrine. They say the same things that Zardusht said; namely, that there

285. Bīrūnī, *Āthār* (ed. Sachau), 237.7–12; Taqīzādeh-Šīrāzī, *Mānī va dīn-e-ū*, 206 (§34).

286. The sixth-century Alexandrian philosopher and commentator on Aristotle. See R. Wisnovsky, "Yaḥyā al-Naḥwī," *EI*[2] 11:251–53.

287. Edward Sachau, ed., *Kitāb fī taḥqīq mā l'il-Hind: Alberuni's India: An Account of the Religion, Philosophy, Literature, Chronology, Astronomy, Customs, Laws and Astrology of India about A.D. 1030* (London: Trübner, 1887), 27.8; Taqīzādeh-Šīrāzī, *Mānī va dīn-e-ū*, 212 (§37).

288. India is renowned in Muslim ethnographic literature as the source of this doctrine; see especially the discussion of Daniel Gimaret, "Tanāsu<u>kh</u>," *EI*[2] 10:181–83. Ephrem Syrus had previously accused Mani of importing religious ideas from India: 'Moreover, deceit originating from India gained control over Manī; the one who introduced two powers warring with one another' (*Hymnus contra haereses* [ed. Beck] 3.7.3–4). See the remarks of Sidney H. Griffith, "The Thorn Among the Tares: Mani and Manichaeism in the Works of St. Ephraem the Syrian," *Studia Patristica* 35 (2001): 411; also Lieu, *Manichaeism*[2], 73–74.

289. *Kitāb fī taḥqīq mā l'il-Hind* (ed. Sachau), 253.10–11; Taqīzādeh-Šīrāzī, *Mānī va dīn-e-ū*, 215 (§37).

290. The cause of the tides.

291. See also Sachau, *Alberuni's India*, 2:105. This same creature is referenced in Coptic *Keph*. 113, where it is termed 'the sea-giant,' and in Middle Persian M 99 V 22–23 'the sea monster' (*apud* Mary Boyce, *A Reader in Manichaean Middle Persian and Parthian* [Acta Iranica 9; Leiden: Brill, 1975], 62). See also Henning, "The Book of the Giants," 54, where his reference to 'Beruni, *India*, 203' should be corrected to '253.'

292. Taqīzādeh-Šīrāzī, *Mānī va dīn-e-ū*, 491–92 (§177). See also Ch[arles] Schefer, *Chrestomathie persane à l'usage des élèves de l'École spéciale des langues orientales vivantes* (2 vols.; Paris: Ernest Leroux, 1883-85), 1:145.14–18, 20-23; Kessler, *Mani*, 371.

are two creators. One is Light, who is the creator of what is good, and the other one is Darkness, who is the creator of what is evil. Whatever there is in the world that is pleasant, luminous, obedient, and good was endowed by the good creator, and whatever is evil, malignant, diseased, and dark is ascribed to the wicked creator. They say both creators exist eternally.

... They believe in the prophetic status of Adam (upon whom be peace!) and in the prophetic status of Seth, then [in the prophetic status of Noah (upon whom be peace!), then][293] in the prophetic status of a man from India who was named Buddha, and in the prophetic status of Zardusht from Persia and of Mānī whom they term 'the seal of the prophets.'[294] They maintain that Buddha was a great prodigy. The Ṣābians have the same doctrine.[295]

Marwazī, *Kitāb ṭabā'i' al-ḥayawān* (ed. Kruk):[296]

He was a disciple of the sage Qādrūn[297] and was versed in the teachings of the Christians, the Zoroastrians, and the dualists ....

He (i.e., Mani) invoked the realm of the Worlds of Light and he said that Light and Darkness were without beginning and uncreated.[298]

Many accepted him and followed him ....

Ibn al-Malāḥimī, *Kitāb al-mu'tamad fī uṣūl al-dīn* (ed. McDermott and Madelung):[299]

Among them (i.e., the dualist sects) are the Mānawiyya, who are sometimes called Manāniyya: they are the adherents of Mānī. Abū 'Īsa al-Warrāq has related about them that they maintain that the world was produced by two entities, one of them being Light and the other Darkness, and that both of them are primal entities. They claim that they are both eternally living sentient beings endowed with hearing and sight, but that they differ from one another with regard to their form and identity (and) oppose one another with regard to (their) activities. The essence of Light is goodness, excellence, nobility, wisdom, (and) produces benefits; nothing harmful comes from it, especially anything wicked. The essence of Darkness contrasts with this (profile) and is its opposite. It is comprised of

293. The bracketed passage is missing from the text published by Taqīzādeh-Šīrāzī.

294. Note the close relationship of this prophetic chain to the list supplied by Shahrastānī below.

295. See also Kessler, *Mani*, 372.

296. Ms. UCLA Ar. 52 fol. 5b.6–7, 11–12, 19 as published by Remke Kruk, "Sharaf az-Zamân Ṭâhir Marwazî (fl. ca. 1100 A.D.) on Zoroaster, Mânî, Mazdak, and Other Pseudo-Prophets," *Persica* 17 (2001): 65.

297. See Mas'ūdī and Bīrūnī above. Both Bīrūnī and Marwazī have garbled the name of this second-century gnostic teacher.

298. A demythologized version of what Bīrūnī states below.

299. Rukn al-Dīn Maḥmūd b. Muḥammad al-Malāḥimī al-Khuwārazmī, *Kitāb al-mu'tamad fī uṣūl al-dīn* (ed. Martin McDermott and Wilferd Madelung; London: Al-Hoda, 1991), 561.19–563.2.

wickedness, viciousness, vileness, putrescence, and insolence—blindly (and) senselessly killing, the origin of sins. They maintain that these characteristics (in the created order) derive from them. Light extends infinitely in five directions: upwards, right, left, before, and behind, and it is situated adjacent to Darkness. It terminates at the point where it encounters Darkness, and this is the direction (termed) 'below.' Similarly Darkness extends infinitely in five directions except for the direction where it encounters Light, where it is situated adjacent to Light. They name them (the) 'Two Entities' (*kīyānān*): Light is the higher entity, and the second entity is Darkness. They disagree about the manner in which they abut one another. Some of them say they touch each other the same way that a sunbeam and shadow do, whereas others among them assert that there is a gap situated between them, but that the gap does not thereby constitute a third entity. They claim that each one of them has five 'varieties,' one of them being spiritual and the other four corporeal. The spiritual component of Light is air, and the four corporeal (varieties) are fire, light, wind, and water. The spiritual component of Light never ceases moving among these corporeal parts. Darkness likewise has five varieties, (they being) smoke, fire, darkness, hot wind, and mist, and the spiritual component of Darkness is smoke, it being called by them Hummāma, and the four corporeal parts (are called) 'calamities.' They believe that the corporeal parts of Light each differ from one another, although all of them derive from Light. They term the varieties of Light 'angels.' They speak similarly about the different corporeal parts of Darkness, terming them 'satans.' The corporeal parts of Darkness are injurious to its Spirit, and the Spirit (of Darkness) never ceases harming its corporeal parts.

They say moreover about the five varieties (genera) that each one of them is black, white, yellow, red, or green. Whatever is white in the World of Light is good, whereas that which is white in the World of Darkness is evil. The same holds for the rest of the colors. They maintain that the two (Worlds) were eternally separate, with no third (realm) existing together with them. Then some of their parts mixed with one another, and this world came into being from their mixed parts.

Shahrastānī, *Kitāb al-milal wa'l-niḥal* (ed. Badrān):[300]

He (i.e., Mani) innovated a religion (which drew) some (elements) from Zoroastrianism and some from Christianity: he used to advocate the prophetic status of the Christ, peace be upon him, but did not propound the prophetic status of Moses, peace be upon him!

Muḥammad b. Hārūn, who is known as Abū 'Īsā al-Warrāq and who was originally a Zoroastrian acquainted with the doctrine of the sect, reported that the

300. *Kitāb al-milal wa'l-niḥal* (ed. Badrān), 1:619.6–624.14. See also William Cureton, ed., *Kitāb al-milal wa-l-niḥal: Book of Religious and Philosophical Sects, by Muhammad al-Shahrastáni* (London, 1846; repr., Leipzig: O. Harrassowitz, 1923), 188.12–190.15, which is reprinted by Taqīzādeh-Šīrāzī, *Mānī va dīn-e-ū*, 241–43 (§45); M. S. Kaylānī, ed., *Kitāb al-milal wa'l-niḥal* (2 vols.; Beirut: Dār al-Ma'rifah, n.d.), 1:244–46.

sage Mānī maintained that the world is made of a mixture of two pre-existent sources, one of them being Light, and the other Darkness, and that they both are eternal, neither one ceasing to be, and he denied the existence of any thing not from a pre-existent source. He maintained that both of them were incessantly powerful, in possession of sensory perceptions, discernment, (and the faculties of) hearing (and) seeing. Nevertheless, as to essence and form, and as to activity and organization, they are opposed to one another. As to realm, they parallel one another (like) a person and (their) shadow. Their substances and effects will be clarified by the chart opposite.

Sam'ānī, *Kitāb al-ānsāb* (ed. Taqīzādeh-Šīrāzī):[301]

He spoke of two deities: one of them created Light and the other created Darkness. Mention of them is made among the Manichaeans. He said that Good was from Light and Evil was from Darkness .... He publicly maintained that he was continuing the mission of Jesus (upon whom be peace!), but he was really a *zindīq*. He <harmonized>[302] Christianity and Zoroastrianism to form a sect distinct from both of them.

Shahrazūrī, *Šarḥ ḥikmat al-ishrāq* (ed. Corbin):[303]

Mānī the Babylonian was the one who adapted Zoroastrianism to the Christian religion. The dualists who bear his name advocate two deities. One of them is the good god and (his) created realm and is Light, and the other is the wicked god and (his) created realm and is Darkness.

Ibn al-Āthīr, *Lulāb fī tahdhīb al-ānsāb* (ed. Taqīzādeh-Šīrāzī):[304]

The term *zandī* refers ... to a book which Mānī the Zoroastrian wrote whose title was the *Zand* ... the floruit of Mānī was during the time of Bahrām b. Hormuz b. Sābūr. He was Zoroastrian, but he also propounded following after Christ (upon him be peace!). He sought fame for himself and so wrote this *Zand*; the term *zand* in their language signifies 'commentary.' Hence it means 'this is a commentary to the book of Zarādusht (i.e., Zoroaster).' In it is found his firm belief in two deities, Light and Darkness. Light created what is good, and Darkness created what is evil.

---

301. Taqīzādeh-Šīrāzī, *Mānī va dīn-e-ū*, 246 (§46).

302. Read with the textual apparatus supplied in Taqīzādeh-Šīrāzī, *Mānī va dīn-e-ū*, 246 n.14.

303. Henry Corbin, *Œuvres philosophiques et mystiques de Shihabaddin Yahya Sohrawardi I (Opera metaphysica et mystica II)* (Bibliothèque iranienne 2; Teheran/Paris: Institut franco-iranien/Adrien-Maisonneuve, 1952), 302.8–10 (text); Taqīzādeh-Šīrāzī, *Mānī va dīn-e-ū*, 253 (§48).

304. Taqīzādeh-Šīrāzī, *Mānī va dīn-e-ū*, 265 (§56).

	the Light	**the Darkness**
substance	Its substance is beautiful, excellent, noble, pure, unmixed, pleasant of odor, beautiful in appearance.	Its substance is ugly, imperfect, ignoble, turbid, evil, rotten in odor, ugly in appearance.
essence	Its essence is good, noble, wise, producing benefits, knowledgeable.	Its essence is wicked, base, stupid, producing harm, ignorant.
effect	Its effect is (what is) good and pious and beneficial and joyous and orderly and congruous and superior.	Its effect is (what is) wicked and corrupt and harmful and sorrowful and confused and broken and controversial.
realm	Its direction is the area above. Most of them regard it as elevated toward the north, but some of them maintain that it lies next to the Darkness.	Its direction is the area below. Most of them regard it as sunken toward the south, but some of them maintain that it lies next to the Light.
(its) parts	Its parts are five: four of them are corporeal and the fifth is spiritual. The corporeal entities are fire, light, wind, and water; and the spiritual (is) air,[305] and it is in motion within this body.	Its parts are five: four of them are corporeal and the fifth is spiritual. The corporeal entities are fire, darkness, hot wind, and mist; and the spiritual (is) smoke, and this is called Hummāma, and it is in motion within this body.[306]
qualities	Vital, beneficent, pure, and flawless. Some of them maintain (that) the World of Light is comparable in every respect to this world: it has a land and an atmosphere. The land of Light is of unceasing fineness, (constructed) not according to the form of this world, but rather according to the form of the body of the sun. Its rays are like the rays of the sun, and its aroma is the most excellent of aromas, and its colors are the colors of the rainbow. Some of them say there is nothing (there) that is not corporeal and that the substances are of three types: (those of) the land of Light, which are five (in number); another substance finer than this, which is the atmosphere and which is the 'soul' of the Light; and another substance finer than this (one), the air, which is the spirit of the Light. They say that [the Light] continually engenders angels, gods, and holy entities, not as married couples do, but rather as wisdom is produced from a sage, or elegant speech from an articulate speaker. [They say] that the Ruler of this world is its spirit, and his world unites what is good, praiseworthy, and light.	Lifeless, wicked, impure, and polluted. Some of them maintain (that) the World of Darkness is comparable in every respect to this world: it has a land and an atmosphere. The land of Darkness is of unceasing coarseness, (constructed) not according to the form of this world, but rather according to the form of that which is most dense and rigid. Its smell is disgusting, the most putrid of smells, and its colors are shades of black. Some of them say there is nothing (there) that is not corporeal and (that) the substances are of three types: (those of) the land of Darkness; another substance darker than this one, which is the atmosphere; and another substance darker than this one, which is the hot wind. They say that the Darkness continually engenders satans, archons, and demons, not as married couples do, but rather as vermin are produced from decay and filth. They say that the Ruler of this world is its spirit, and his world unites what is evil, blameworthy, and dark.

305. See Reeves, "Citations from Ephrem," 269–70 n.9. Note especially Ibn al-Nadīm, *Fihrist* (*apud* Flügel, *Mani*, 54.7-8) where these same 'parts' are glossed as 'deities': 'Primal Man armored himself with the five "parts," and they are the five deities air, wind, light, water, and fire.' Does 'air' correspond to Greek *pneuma*? So Richard Reitzenstein, *Hellenistic Mystery-Religions: Their Basic Ideas and Significance* (trans. John E. Steely; Pittsburgh, PA: Pickwick Press, 1978), 289 n.6.

306. Cf. Vajda, "Le témoignage d'al-Māturidī," 17.

Nuwayrī, *Nihāyat al-arab fī funūn al-adab* (ed. Taqīzādeh-Šīrāzī):[307]

It was during the time of this Mānī that the term *zanādiqa* was coined and used for those attached to *zandaqa*. This is a Persian word, for they have a book which they call Avesta,[308] and it has a commentary named the *Zand*. When one of them produces an amplification of what is in their book, they call it *zandī*. After the Arabs arrived, they borrowed this expression from Persian, arabicized it, and pronounced it *zindīq*. The *zanādiqa* are the dualists, but this term is also attached to all those who believe in an infinite pre-existence, those who deny the creation of the world, and those who reject (a doctrine of) resurrection.

The one who provided this book to the Persians was Zarādusht (who lived) during the time of the ancient Persians ... He was allegedly a prophet among the Magi, and he produced the book which we previously mentioned (i.e., the Avesta). He claimed that it was revealed to him from heaven. The language in which it is set down uses around seventy characters.[309] Since no one was able to perform a recitation of it, he abbreviated them and called the abridgment the *Zand*.

When Mānī emerged with his religion of dualism, the Zoroastrians named it *zanadīn* and named his adherents *zanādiqa*, for he had expanded their law which Zarādusht had laid down for them.[310]

Ibn al-Murtaḍā, *K. al-munya* (ed. Taqīzādeh-Šīrāzī):[311]

This group (i.e., the Manichaeans) teaches about the divinities Light and Darkness that they are both alive and powerful and that the universe is the result of their mixture. Their form and their nature are totally opposite. The substance of Light is beautiful, pure, pleasant of odor, (and) beautiful in appearance; and its essence is good, noble, vitalistic, beneficial, (and) it contains nothing wicked within it. The nature of Darkness is the opposite of these things.

They say these two were initially separate. Then they mixed unceasingly on every side except for the side where they intersected. They (i.e., the Manichaeans) disagree about their location. It is said by some that Light is located above Darkness. It is said by some that each is adjacent to the other. It is also said that Light is elevated to the northern side whereas Darkness is sunken to the south-

307. Taqīzādeh-Šīrāzī, *Mānī va dīn-e-ū*, 275 (§63).

308. The text (السا) is corrupt here, but Mas'ūdī has the correct reading.

309. A slightly garbled version of Mas'ūdī, *Murūj*, 2:124: 'The language of the book revealed by Zoroaster contains no less than sixty letters; no other known alphabet has a greater number of characters.' Both figures are somewhat exaggerated. For a cogent discussion and table of the Avestan alphabet, see Prods Oktor Skjærvø, "Aramaic Scripts for Iranian Languages," in *The World's Writing Systems* (ed. Peter T. Daniels and William Bright; Oxford: Oxford University Press, 1996), 527–28.

310. Compare the testimony of Mas'ūdī above.

311. Taqīzādeh-Šīrāzī, *Mānī va dīn-e-ū*, 299–300 (§74); Kessler, *Mani*, 346–47. For information on this author, see H. J. W. Drijvers, *Bardaiṣan of Edessa* (Assen: Van Gorcum, 1966), 123 n.1; Guy Monnot, "Les écrits musulmans sur les religions non-bibliques,"in idem, *Islam et religions*, 74–75.

ern side. They also disagree as to how it is they are in contact. Some say of their connection that it is analogous to that of the juncture of shade and sunlight, but it is said by others that there is a gap between them.[312] They maintain that each of them possesses five 'kinds,' four of which are corporeal and the fifth of which is immaterial (lit. 'spiritual'). The corporeal kinds (associated with Light) are fire, light, wind, and water,[313] and the immaterial kind (associated with Light) is air, and this latter is always in motion among these four (corporeal kinds). The corporeal kinds associated with Darkness are fire, blackness, (hot) wind, and fog, and its immaterial kind is smoke which is called by them al-Hummāma. They (furthermore) designate the physical entities associated with Light 'angels' and the physical entities associated with Darkness 'devils' and 'satans.'

They allege that the immaterial kind associated with Light is continually making good use of its corporeal complements, and it also receives benefit from them, so that each of its parts benefits the others. The immaterial kind associated with Darkness behaves in the opposite way from this. Some of them say that the (Two) Spirits and their 'kinds' are sentient living entities, whereas others say that it is only the Two Spirits (who can be described this way): the material kinds associated with Light sustain an intangible and imperceptible living phenomenon, but the material kinds associated with Darkness are dead (and) putrid. They say that everything that is good derives from Light and everything that is bad derives from Darkness. Some say this is natural, but others say it is due to choice; however, their choice cannot go against their essential nature. This means then, they say, that Light has chosen what is good due to (its) goodness and Darkness has chosen what is bad due to (its) wickedness. They say that all things vary with respect to attractiveness or ugliness in dependence upon the amount of the components of Light and Darkness (they contain), and there is no extant entity which is not composed out of them. They disagree over (their) non-essential attributes as to whether they are fixed or variable, but they agree that the composition of things is due to the mixture (of Light and Darkness).

Mīrkhwānd, *Rawḍat al-ṣafā* (ed. Taqīzādeh-Šīrāzī):[314]

Account of Mānī the painter. He is depicted in some books as having acquired the reputation of a *zindīq*. For Jesus (upon whom be peace!) enjoined: 'After me it will come to pass that the Paraclete will be sent. You should command your children that they become his followers.' Mānī pretended that the term 'Paraclete' referred to himself. The fact is that this word is among the special names of the blessed Prophet (may God bless and reward him!). Consequently he falsely imagined that he could lay claim to prophetic status. He would show a book—the *Gospel*—and would say: 'This book has come down from heaven.'

312. A partial translation to this point is provided by Vajda, "Le témoignage d'al-Māturidī," 14.

313. Replacing the problematic والهوى with والنور. Note Vajda, "Le témoignage d'al-Māturidī," 18.

314. Taqīzādeh-Šīrāzī, *Mānī va dīn-e-ū*, 525 (§190); cf. the slightly variant text in Kessler, *Mani*, 377–79.

b. Mythological

Qāsim b. Ibrāhīm, *K. al-radd ʿalā al-zindīq al-laʿīn Ibn al-Muqaffaʿ* (ed. Taqīzādeh-Šīrāzī):[315]

Their stories are nonsensical, they amuse themselves with fairy tales: (they are) joke(s) which cannot be taken seriously and which feature nothing which one feels obligated to refute. Woe to those for whom their hands write, and woe to those from whom they earn profit! What kind of drivel do they—may God slay them—produce? Have you not seen the titles which they name and with what care they extol them? Some used among them are the Father of Greatness, the fragrant[316] Mother of Life, the Beloved of the Lights, the Supervisors of the Trenches and the Walls, the Messenger, the Radiant One,[317] Primal Man, and what they say about the archons whom have been cursed by God, and what they say about a Column of Praise ....

Jāḥiẓ, *Kitāb al-ḥayawān* (ed. Taqīzādeh-Šīrāzī):[318]

And this proves what I (previously) said: in their (Manichaean) books there is no current proverb or singular story or artistically crafted narrative or marvelous wisdom or philosophy or dialectic inquiry or professional instruction. Nor is there (information) regarding the making of tool(s) or instruction about farming or advice regarding warfare or an apology for (their) religion or a defense of (their) sect. Instead, most of what is in them speaks about the Light and the Darkness, and (about) the marriages of the satans and copulations of the demons. Mention is made of al-Ṣindīd[319] and the intimidating Column of Praise, and (there are) stories about Šaqlūn[320]

---

315. Taqīzādeh-Šīrāzī, *Mānī va dīn-e-ū*, 82–83 (§3). See also Michelangelo Guidi, *La lotta tra l'Islam e il Manicheismo: Un libro di Ibn al-Muqaffaʿ contro il Corano confutato da al-Qāsim b. Ibrāhīm* (Roma: R. Accademia Nazionale dei Lincei, 1927), 52.20–53.2.

316. Or according to a textual variant: 'breezy.' See de Blois, "Glossary," 30.

317. Perhaps the supernal entity known from western sources as the Splenditenens or Custodian of Splendor, one of the five sons of the Living Spirit. See Guidi, *La lotta tra l'Islam*, 123 n.1; de Blois, "Glossary," 82.

318. Taqīzādeh-Šīrāzī, *Mānī va dīn-e-ū*, 85–86 (§4); also Alfred von Kremer, *Culturgeschichtliche Streifzüge auf dem Gebiete des Islams* (Leipzig: F. A. Brockhaus, 1873), 72. Part of the Arabic text is available in Kessler, *Mani*, 368–69; also in Charles Pellat, "Index des noms propres," *apud* his *Le Kitāb at-tarbīʿ wa-t-tadwīr*, 37. See also the citation from Jāḥiẓ in part one of Chapter 5 below.

319. This name is otherwise attested only in the Manichaean version of Genesis 2-4 preserved by Ibn al-Nadīm. See below.

320. Undoubtedly the same entity as Ašaqlūn, offspring of the Ruler of Darkness in Theodore bar Konai's account above. Both names (Ašaqlūn and Šaqlūn) are recognizable forms of the name 'Sakla(s),' a common designation for the demiurgic archon of classical gnostic literature. See also the testimony of Michael Syrus.

and about 'the head'[321] and Hummāma.[322] It is entirely nonsensical, inarticulate, fabulous, ridiculous, and delusive. One discerns within them no good lessons or pleasing tales or measures for planning one's lifestyle or for governing the masses or for organizing the upper classes.[323]

Jāḥiẓ, *Kitāb al-ḥayawān* (ed. Taqīzādeh-Šīrāzī):[324]

Every coiner of verbal expressions wins recognition from them. Similarly, all those on earth who are eloquent and masters of prosody and every poet [on the earth] and master of rhythmic speech will inevitably have expressions which they are fond of and accustomed to using, taking pains to use them over and over again in their discourse even if they possess extensive knowledge, have many ideas, and wield a large vocabulary. The *zanādiqa* (i.e., the Manichaeans) happen to have some terms which anticipate their spirit and which correspond to their nature and draw upon their expressions. (Terms like) *tanākuḥ* 'sexual relations'; *natā'ij* 'offspring'; *mizāj* 'mixture'; *nūr wa'l-ẓulma* 'light and darkness'; *daffā'* 'defense'; *mannā'* 'opposition'; *sātir* 'concealer'; *ghāmir* 'inundator'; *munḥall* 'dissolved'; *buṭlān* 'futility'; *wijdān* 'emotion'; *āthir* 'ether'; *ṣiddīq* 'righteous one; a Manichaean';[325] *'amūd al-subḥ* 'Column of Praise'; and *iškālā* 'obscurity, turbidity' are from this type of discourse. And it turns out that if it (such language) is strange, deemed nonsensical, or rejected by the adherents of our religion and our faith, or likewise, by our people or the general populace, it will only be used by palm-weavers[326] and theologians.[327]

Jāḥiẓ, *Kitāb al-tarbī' wa'l-tadwīr* (ed. Pellat):[328]

Speak to me about Šaqlūn and Ahriman and Kāweh and Kayūmarth[329] and Ayadadhash and Afradadhash and Abrushārash and Abrubārash and Khawanirath

321. This expression apparently alludes to the popular 'blood-libel' accusation which was leveled against Manichaeans in Islamicate society. For further discussion with sources, see Chapter Five below.

322. See also the testimonies of Māturīdī, Ibn al-Nadīm, 'Abd al-Jabbār, and Khwārazmī. For discussion of this entity, see Reeves, *Jewish Lore*, 124–26; Shaul Shaked, "Manichaean Incantation Bowls in Syriac," *Jerusalem Studies in Arabic and Islam* 24 (2000): 67–68 n.44; and now the lengthy entry of de Blois, "Glossary," 83–86.

323. For other translations, see Kessler, *Mani*, 368–69; von Kremer, *Streifzüge*, 38; Jâhiz, *Le cadi et la mouche: Anthologie du Livre des Animaux* (ed. Lakhdar Souami; Paris: Sindbad, 1988), 142–43; Pellat, "Le témoignage," 274. See also the discussion of Melhem Chokr, *Zandaqa et zindiqs en Islam au second siècle de l'Hégire* (Damas: Institut français de Damas, 1993), 66–68.

324. Taqīzādeh-Šīrāzī, *Mānī va dīn-e-ū*, 86–87 (§4).

325. Chokr, *Zandaqa et zindiqs*, 45 n.28.

326. Alternatively 'men of rank, nobles.'

327. See also Pellat, "Le témoignage," 273.

328. Pellat, *Le Kitāb at-tarbī' wa-t-tadwīr*, 43 (§77).

329. I.e., Gayōmart.

Bāmiya.[330]

Māturīdī, *Kitāb al-tawḥīd* (ed. Kholeif):[331]

[Ibn] al-Rāwandī says: 'I marvel at [Abū ʿĪsā] al-Warrāq who denies the accounts about the prophets with their clear evidence and advocates instead the acceptance of the doctrine of the Manichaeans and the necessary soundness of their foolish statements—such as the stretching out of the heavens from the skins of the satans,[332] and the corruption of the earth when it was teeming with serpents and scorpions—and the acceptance of their reports about the doings of Light and Darkness.'[333]

Ibn al-Nadīm, *Fihrist* (ed. Flügel):[334]

A report about what Mānī set forth and his doctrine about the attributes of the Primal Blessed and Exalted One, the creation of the world, and the struggles which took place between Light and Darkness:

Mānī said: 'Two entities form the basis for the world: one of them is Light, and the other is Darkness. Each of them was (originally) separate from the other. Light is the premier incomparably great One: it cannot be measured, and it is the deity, the King of the Light-Paradises. He has five limbs, (which are) intellect,[335] knowledge, intelligence, what is invisible, and sagacity,[336] and five other spiritual (limbs?) which are love, faith, fidelity, friendship,[337] and wisdom.' He also maintained that this (entity), along with its attributes, was eternal; and with it were two (other) eternal things, one of them being the atmosphere (of the land of Light) and the other the land (which Light inhabits).[338]

Mānī said: 'The atmosphere (of the land of Light) has five limbs, (which are) intellect, knowledge, intelligence, what is invisible, and sagacity; and the land (of Light) has limbs consisting of air, wind, light, water, and fire. The other

330. See also Maurice Adad, "Le *Kitāb al-Tarbīʿ wa-l-Tadwīr* d'al-Ǧāḥiẓ: Traduction française, II," *Arabica* 14 (1967): 51–52; *Sobriety and Mirth* (trans. Colville), 275.

331. Māturīdī, *Kitāb al-tawḥīd* (ed. Kholeif), 199.17–20.

332. See the report of Theodore bar Konai above and the other references cited there.

333. Ibn al-Rāwandī was a student of Abū ʿĪsā and achieved notoriety in his own right as a pernicious heretic. For discussion of this accusation, see Rudolph, *Al-Māturīdī*, 176–78; *Early Muslim Polemic* (ed. Thomas), 26–27. See also van Ess, *Theologie und Gesellschaft*, 6:478; for a partial translation of the present passage, see Stroumsa, *Freethinkers*, 42.

334. Flügel, *Mani*, 52.11–55.7; Ibn al-Nadīm, *K. al-Fihrist* (ed. Tajaddud), 392–93; Taqīzādeh-Šīrāzī, *Mānī va dīn-e-ū*, 151–52 (§27).

335. Or 'mind.' See Q 52:32.

336. These are undoubtedly the 'five shekinahs' which dwell alongside the Father of Greatness according to the testimony of Theodore bar Konai above. They are also referred to as 'aeons' (Arabic عالم) below.

337. Read with mss. C and H in Flügel's apparatus.

338. For a detailed description of these two, see above Flügel, *Mani*, 61.14–62.13.

entity, which is Darkness, (also) has its five limbs, (which are) fog, fire, (hot) wind, venom, and darkness.'

Mānī said: 'The Luminous entity was adjacent to the entity of Darkness; there was no fence between them. Light met Darkness on its surface. Light has no upward boundary, nor (is it bounded) on its right or left sides; and Darkness has no lower boundary, and it is (likewise not bounded) on its right or left sides.'

Mānī said: 'Satan came into being out of that Dark land. He himself is not eternal, but instead the substances of his constituent elements are eternal. These substances of his elements combined themselves and Satan came into being. His head was like the head of a lion, his torso was like the torso of a dragon, his wing was like the wing of a flying creature, his tail was like the tail of a large fish, and his four feet were like the feet of an animal.[339] When this Satan—who is termed the Primal Iblīs—had come into being from Darkness, he swallowed, gulped down, and befouled (his surroundings). He proceeded to the right and to the left, and he went down to the lowest part (of his world), befouling all this (area) and spoiling whatever he subdued.[340] Then he became enamored with the upper regions, for he saw the glistening of (the land of) Light but was unacquainted with it. Moreover he beheld its ascendancy, and he was thrown into commotion. Some of their portions commingled and he clung to its (i.e., Light's) elements. While he thus kept close to the upper regions, the Land of Light came to know about the conduct of Satan and what he (Satan) intended for it; namely, (its) slaughter and corruption. So after it had learned about him, it informed the Aeon of sagacity about him, then the Aeon of knowledge, then the Aeon of what is invisible, then the Aeon of intelligence, (and) then the Aeon of intellect.'

He (i.e., Mānī) said: 'Then the King of the Light-Paradises became cognizant of him, and he made plans for his subjection.'

He (i.e., Mānī) said: 'Those who were his (i.e., the King's) armies had the power to subdue him; however, he wanted to take on this (opponent) himself. Therefore he produced a child with the spirit of his right hand,[341] his five Aeons, and his twelve elements; namely, Primal Man, and he sent him to engage Darkness in battle.'

He (i.e., Mānī) said: 'Primal Man armored himself with the five 'kinds,' and these are the five deities air, wind, light, water, and fire.[342] He prepared them as

339. Note the analogous description found in Coptic *Keph.* 30.33–31.2. Compare also the sixth-century testimony of the Neoplatonist philosopher Simplicius: 'They (i.e., Manichaeans) describe Evil as a combination of five forms: those of a lion, a fish, an eagle, and of other animals which I cannot describe, and they fear an impending attack from it.' Translation cited from Lieu, *Manichaeism in Mesopotamia*, 127.

340. Read with Ms. L in the critical apparatus of Flügel, *Mani*, 53 n.17.

341. This is a problematic phrase. Presumably the Mother of Life is intended; compare the cosmogonic narrative in Theodore bar Konai above. See also Bousset, *Hauptprobleme der Gnosis*, 177; de Blois, "Glossary," 49. But note the suggestion of Jackson, *Researches*, 326–27.

342. Note that Theodore bar Konai also references this same pentad as 'deities' (*Scholion* [ed. Scher], 2:314.11).

weapons for himself. First he put on the air, and he put on over the mighty air diffused light, and he wrapped over the light the water which rises (?),[343] and he covered himself with the blowing wind. Then he took the fire in his hand like a shield and spear, and he swiftly descended from the (Light)-Paradises until he came as far as the border, near the one seeking conflict. Primal Iblīs attended to his five 'kinds,' they being smoke, fire, darkness, (hot) wind, and fog,[344] and he armored himself and made them a panoply for himself. He then met Primal Man, and they engaged in combat for a lengthy period of time. Eventually Primal Iblīs prevailed over Primal Man: he swallowed some of his light, and he engulfed him with his 'kinds' and elements. But the King of the Light-Paradises dispatched another deity after him, and he rescued him and prevailed over Darkness. This one, the one whom he sent after (Primal) Man, was called the Beloved of the Lights.[345] He descended and freed Primal Man from the hells and from the spirits of Darkness by whom he had been seized and hidden.'

He (i.e., Mānī) said: 'Then al-Bahijah[346] and the Living Spirit traveled to the border, and they gazed into the bottom of that lowest hell, and they discerned Primal Man and (his) angels surrounded by Iblīs and the ferocious shouting ones (?) and the dark beast(s).'

He (i.e., Mānī) said: 'The Living Spirit called out to Primal Man in a loud voice (which was) like lightning in its rapidity,[347] and it (i.e., the call)[348] became another deity.'[349]

Ibn al-Nadīm, *Fihrist* (ed. Flügel):[350]

The beginning of sexual reproduction according to the teaching of Mānī:

He (i.e., Mani) said: 'Then one of those archons, the stars, urgent force, desire, lust, and sin had sexual intercourse, and the result of their intercourse was the first man, who was Adam. That which produced this was (the union of) two

343. Text is obscure.

344. Note that this list of 'kinds' varies slightly from the rosters supplied by Flügel, *Mani*, 53.3-4 and ibid., 62.14-63.7; it is identical with that of 'Abd al-Jabbār, *Mughnī* (ed. Ḥusayn), 5:11.3-4.

345. This same entity also appears in the cosmogonic narrative supplied by Theodore bar Konai, *Scholion* (ed. Scher), 2:314.15-17.

346. The peculiar designation employed by Ibn al-Nadīm (or his source) for the divine entity who is more commonly termed the Mother of Life.

347. Compare Theodore bar Konai, *Scholion* (ed. Scher), 2:314.23-24. Therein the voice of the Living Spirit is likened to a 'sharp sword' which slices through the gloom to expose the supine 'form' of Primal Man.

348. Compare Theodore bar Konai, *Scholion* (ed. Scher), 2:314.22-315.7, where the voice of the Living Spirit is likewise personified.

349. For other translations, see Flügel, *Mani*, 86-88; Kessler, *Mani*, 386-90; Adam, *Texte*², 118-21; Dodge, *Fihrist*, 2:777-80.

350. Flügel, *Mani*, 58.11-61.13; Ibn al-Nadīm, *K. al-Fihrist* (ed. Tajaddud), 394-95; Taqīzādeh-Šīrāzī, *Mānī va dīn-e-ū*, 154-55 (§27).

archons, male and female. Then intercourse took place once more, and its result was the beautiful woman, who was Eve.'

He (i.e., Mani) said: 'When the five angels[351] saw the divine Light and Goodness which Desire[352] had plundered and bound as captive within those two who had been born, they asked al-Bashīr (= the Messenger), the Mother of Life, Primal Man, and the Living Spirit to send to this first-born creature someone to release and deliver him, to teach him knowledge and piety, and to deliver him from the satans.'

He (i.e., Mani) said: 'They thus sent Jesus, along with (another) deity.[353] They approached the two archons, confined them, and rescued the two who had been born.'

He (i.e., Mani) said: 'Then Jesus came and spoke to the one who had been born, who was Adam, and explained to him (about) the (Light)-Paradises, the deities, Jahannam, the satans, earth, heaven, sun, and moon. He also made him fear Eve, showing him how to suppress (desire) for her, and he forbade him to approach her, and made him fear to be near her, so that he did (what Jesus commanded). Then that (male) archon came back to his daughter, who was Eve, and lustfully had intercourse with her. He engendered with her a son, deformed in shape and possessing a red complexion, and his name was Cain, the Red Man. Then that son had intercourse with his mother, and engendered with her a son of white complexion, whose name was Abel, the White Man. Then Cain again had intercourse with his mother, and engendered with her two girls, one of whom was named Ḥakimat al-Dahr[354] and the other Ibnat al-Ḥirṣ.[355] Then Cain took Ibnat al-Ḥirṣ as his wife and presented Ḥakimat al-Dahr to Abel, and he took her as his wife.'

He (i.e., Mani) said: 'In Ḥakimat al-Dahr there was a residue of the Light of God and His Wisdom,[356] but there was none of this (present) in Ibnat al-Ḥirṣ. Then one of the angels came to Ḥakimat al-Dahr and said to her, "Watch yourself, for you will give birth to two girls who will fulfill the pleasure of God." He had sexual intercourse with her and she gave birth because of him to two girls, and she named one of them (Rau)-Faryād and the other Bar-Faryād.[357] When Abel learned of this,

351. Either the five 'limbs' or the five 'deities' of the Realm of Light referred to in the previous section; see Flügel, *Mani*, 249.

352. Personified as the demoness Āz in Middle Iranian versions of this anthropogenic myth.

353. Note that Jesus comes alone in Theodore bar Konai's account above.

354. Literally 'Wise (One) of the Age.' Flügel suggests that she corresponds to the figure of Sophia in classical gnostic sources (*Mani*, 260).

355. Literally 'Daughter of Greed.'

356. Note the recurrence of this phrase below in Seth's recommendation to his father regarding where they should dwell.

357. Literally 'Go for help' and 'Bring help' respectively. These are Persian names, suggesting that the source utilized by Ibn al-Nadīm stems from Iranian traditions. See Flügel, *Mani*, 261–62; Gedaliahu A. G. Stroumsa, *Another Seed: Studies in Gnostic Mythology* (NHS 24; Leiden: Brill, 1984), 151.

rage filled (him) and grief overcame him. He said to her, "From whom did you produce these two children? I think they are from Cain; it was he who consorted with you!" Although she described to him the form of the angel, he left her and came to his mother, Eve, and complained to her about what Cain had done. He said to her, "Have you heard what he did to my sister and wife?" When Cain learned this, he went to Abel and struck him with a rock, killing him. Then he took Ḥakimat al-Dahr for a wife.'

Mānī said: 'Then those archons and this al-Ṣindīd[358] and Eve were troubled at (the behavior) they saw (exhibited) by Cain. Al-Ṣindīd then taught Eve magical syllables in order that she might infatuate Adam.[359] She proceeded to act (by) presenting him with a garland from a flowering tree,[360] and when Adam saw her, he lustfully united with her, and she became pregnant and gave birth to a handsome male child of radiant appearance. When al-Ṣindīd learned about this, he was distressed and fell ill, and said to Eve, "This infant is not one of us; he is a stranger." Then she wished to kill him, but Adam seized him and said to Eve, "I will feed him cow's milk and the fruit of trees!"[361] Thus taking him he departed. But al-Ṣindīd sent the archons to carry off the trees and cattle, moving them away from Adam. When Adam saw this, he took the infant and encircled him within three rings. He pronounced over the first (ring) the name of the King of the (Light)-Paradises, over the second the name of Primal Man, and over the third the name of the Living Spirit. He spoke to and implored God, may His name be glorified, saying, "Even though I have sinned before you, what offense has this infant committed?" Then one of the three (invoked deities) hurried (to Adam bearing) a crown of

358. Jāḥiẓ (see above) also bears witness to this distinctive name or designation for the chief archon of the Realm of Darkness. The word seems to mean 'powerful one' or 'mighty one.' See the remarks of Flügel, *Mani*, 262–63. Stroumsa is undoubtedly correct in viewing him as equivalent to the figure of Sakla(s) or Ašaqlūn in earlier gnostic accounts of the creation of Adam (*Another Seed*, 149–50).

359. Note that the archetypal Genesis narrative (Genesis 2-4) displays an inverted form in its Manichaean analogue: the temptation and corruption of Adam now transpires *after* the story of Cain and Abel. Al-Ṣindīd thus performs the role of the serpent in the Genesis version of the myth.

360. The Tree of Knowledge in the Genesis myth.

361. This is a puzzling response to Eve's murderous intention. However, M 528 Fragment II produces the suspicion that Ibn al-Nadīm's narrative is truncated at this point: '(R) ... he appeared before Šaqlōn, and addressed him thusly: "Command that she give him milk immediately!" Then Šaqlōn sought to make Adam an apostate from the (correct) religion (V) ... (lacuna of approximately 20 lines) ... he saw the demons. He then quickly laid the child on the ground, and drew (around him) seven times a very wide circle, and prayed to the gods ....' We learn from this fragment that Eve had apparently decided to kill the child by starving it. Adam thereupon appeals to Šaqlōn to force Eve to nurse the infant, unaware that the archon desires the child's demise as well. When Adam finally realizes this, he takes the child in order to feed him himself. The text of M 528 Fragment II is cited from W. B. Henning, "Ein manichäisches Bet- und Beichtbuch," *APAW* 10 (Berlin, 1936): 48.

radiance, extending it in his hand to Adam. When al-Ṣindīd and the archons saw this, they departed (and went) away.'[362]

He (i.e., Mani) said: 'Then there appeared to Adam a tree called the lotus, and milk flowed from it, and he fed the boy with it. He named him (the boy) after its name, but sometime later he renamed him Shāthil (i.e., Seth).[363] Then that al-Ṣindīd declared enmity against Adam and those who were born, and said to Eve, "Reveal (yourself) to Adam; perhaps you may restore him to us." Then she made haste and seduced Adam, who lustfully united with her. When Shāthil saw him, he admonished and rebuked him (Adam), and said to him, "Arise, let us go to the East, to the Light and Wisdom of God."[364] So he left with him and resided there until he died and came to the (Light)-Paradises. Then Shāthil with Rau-Faryād and Bar-Faryād and Ḥakimat al-Dahr, their mother, practiced *ṣiddīqūt*,[365] following one way and one path until the time of their deaths, but Eve, Cain, and Ibnat al-Ḥiriṣ went to Jahannam.'"[366]

---

362. This same legend of Adam's resorting to magical praxis in order to protect the young Seth from demonic attack also appears in the Middle Iranian fragments (M 5566 + M 4501) published by Werner Sundermann. There however Adam inscribes seven circles, as opposed to the three mentioned here. This legend must also lie behind the curious invocation preserved on a sixth or seventh century incantation bowl recovered from the site of ancient Nippur in southern Iraq and published by James A. Montgomery, *Aramaic Incantation Texts from Nippur* (Philadelphia, PA: The University Museum, 1913), #10 lines 3-4 (later emended in accordance with J. N. Epstein, "Gloses babylo-araméennes," *Revue des études juives* 73 [1921]: 40): 'with that seal with which Adam the protoplast sealed his son Seth, and he (i.e., Seth) was delivered from d[emons], devils, tormentors, and satans.' For further discussion of these correlations, see John C. Reeves, "Manichaica Aramaica: Adam, Seth, and Magical Praxis," *JAOS* 119 (1999): 432–39.

363. This episode provides an aetiological explanation for the designation 'Sethel,' the usual name for this son of Adam within Syro-Mesopotamian gnostic circles. According to this tradition, the name 'Sethel' derives from a midrashic transposition and manipulation of the consonantal phonemes of the child's original name, '*Lothis*.'

364. A reflex of Gen 3:24, wherein Adam and Eve are involuntarily expelled from the Garden. Here, by contrast, Adam and Seth voluntarily separate themselves from further temptation. 'East' as the locale of divinely sanctioned 'Light' and 'Wisdom' is a recurring mytheme in Syro-Mesopotamian and Iranian gnosis. Note the apocryphal *Acts of Thomas* 108–113; the parable of the journey to India recounted in Judah Halevi, *Kuzari* 1.109; the valence of 'East' (the so-called *ḥikmat al-ishrāq*) in the writings of Avicenna and Suhrawardī (see Annemarie Schimmel, *Mystical Dimensions of Islam* [Chapel Hill, NC: University of North Carolina Press, 1975], 262; Bausani, *Religion in Iran*, 190); and especially the perspicacious remarks of Stroumsa, *Freethinkers*, 43.

365. I.e., the Manichaean precepts for the Elect. See the discussions of Flügel, *Mani*, 271; H. H. Schaeder, *Iranische Beiträge I* (Halle, 1930; repr., Darmstadt: Wissenschaftliche Buchgesellschaft, 1972), 282–85; Henri-Charles Puech, *Le manichéisme: Son fondateur - sa doctrine* (Paris: Civilisations du Sud, 1949), 143–44 n.238.

366. See also Reeves, *Heralds*, 79–81, 100–104; idem, "Manichaica Aramaica," 433 for 60.7-

Khwārazmī, *Kitāb mafātīḥ al-ʿulūm* (ed. Taqīzādeh-Šīrāzī):[367]

Hummāma is the Spirit of Darkness among the Manichaeans, and it manifests as smoke for them.

ʿAbd al-Jabbār, *Mughnī* (ed. Ḥusayn):[368]

Some of them say that the way mixture transpired was as follows: the World of Darkness was in a state of continual dissension until it reached the boundary of (the World of) Light at the moment when mixture transpired. But others say Darkness never ceased from wandering about its World until it chanced to come upon Light accidentally (and) not by design. The majority of them maintain of the cause of this (mixture) was that the corporeal parts of Darkness maliciously distracted their Spirit; once distracted, the Spirit then beheld and saw Light, and it was afterwards always cognizant that some entity foreign to it was nearby. Then it dispatched the corporeal parts to mix with Light, and they hurriedly obeyed due to (their) depravity. Darkness transferred a hideous shape into each of its five parts. When the Ruler of the World of Light saw this, he sent against it one of his angels with five parts from his (own) five varieties. He (i.e., the angel) overcame each of its (i.e., Darkness's) five forces and took them captive. Then the five luminous elements became mingled with the five elements of Darkness. The smoke mingled with the air: vitality and spirit derives from the air, but destruction derives from the smoke. The fire mingled with the fire: destruction and flame derive from the fire (of Darkness), but illumination and usefulness derive from the fire (of Light). Light and darkness mingled, and from them resulted dense visible substances like gold, silver, stone, dirt, and similar stuff. That which has beauty, clarity, and utility stems from Light, and that which has the contrary stems from Darkness. The hot wind mingled with the wind, and the fog with the water: those things which are beneficial come from Light, and those things which are harmful come from Darkness.[369]

Then Primal Man descended to the bottom of the lowest abyss and cut the roots of those captive troops of Darkness. Afterwards, turning around, he ascended to his place in the southern (*sic*!) region.[370] Then one of the angels dragged off those captive troops which had within them (portions of Light) to a portion of the Land of Darkness. He installed a powerful angel from the Land of Light in the space[371] between the World of Light and the mixed portions so that they could expel those portions to him.

61.13. Both of these treatments should be consulted for much fuller annotation and discussion. Other translations are available in Flügel, *Mani*, 90–93; Kessler, *Mani*, 393-96; Dodge, *Fihrist*, 2:783–86.

367. Taqīzādeh-Šīrāzī, *Mānī va dīn-e-ū*, 180 (§28).

368. ʿAbd al-Jabbār, *Mughnī* (ed. Ḥusayn), 5:12.6–13.19.

369. Compare Shahrastānī, *Kitāb al-milal wa'l-niḥal* (ed. Badrān), 1:625.3–626.8.

370. The World of Light is situated to the north.

371. Literally 'air.'

The Ruler of the World of Light commanded one of his angels to create this world and fashion it from those mixed portions. So he created it and fashioned it (as) ten heavens and eight earths beneath the resultant sphere for those mixed portions. He swept some of the demons of Darkness underneath the earths, and he approached the principal satans and cast them toward the heavens. He created a revolving heaven—the zodiacal sphere—and he attached the demons to it, making them close to (the World of) Light. He appointed one of his angels to administer the revolution so that he could direct those demons and guard against them and stop them from rising to the supernal Light and from further damaging the mixed (portions of) Light and to effect the purification of what was (mixed) therein by this means.

He appointed an angel to bear the heavens, another (angel) to hold up the earths, and he united the atmosphere at the lowest part of the earths to the highest part of the heavens. Around this world he made a ditch for containing Darkness after the (portions of) Light had been removed from it, (a place) where Darkness would remain segregated.

Then he set in motion the sun and the moon in order to extract (?)[372] the (portions of) Light which are (mixed) in the world. The sun extracts (?) the Light which was mixed with the satans of heat, and the moon extracts (?) the Light which was mixed with the satans of cold. The air which is on the earths does not cease transmitting the Light-powers which it contains and what it takes up from the earth and from vegetation ....[373]

'Abd al-Jabbār, *Mughnī* (ed. Ḥusayn):[374]

All of this Mānī has narrated. We could extend (discussion of) his tales, but this should suffice for the purposes of argument and the exposure of their fables to the one who reads them.[375]

'Abd al-Jabbār, *Mughnī* (ed. Ḥusayn):[376]

Now al-Misma'ī[377] has mentioned with regard to the Manichaeans[378] that the Light

372. The text literally has 'examine,' a variant wording which is likely corrupt. See the inconclusive remarks of de Blois, "Glossary," 57–58, 70.

373. This passage is continued in the subdivision devoted to eschatological teachings below. For other translations, see Vajda, "Le témoignage d'al-Māturidī: Note annexe," 117-20; Monnot, *Penseurs*, 156–60.

374. 'Abd al-Jabbār, *Mughnī* (ed. Ḥusayn), 5:15.16–17.

375. For other translations, see Vajda, "Le témoignage d'al-Māturidī: Note annexe," 122; Monnot, *Penseurs*, 164.

376. 'Abd al-Jabbār, *Mughnī* (ed. Ḥusayn), 5:19.8–20.1.

377. Identified more fully elsewhere by the same author as Aḥmad b. al-Ḥasan al-Misma'ī. For the problems involved in identifying this source, see Vajda, "Le témoignage d'al-Māturidī: Note annexe," 114 n.6 ; Monnot, *Penseurs*, 56-60. This same figure is sometimes referred to as 'Zurqān'; see Thomas, "Abū 'Īsā al-Warrāq," 284; Gotthard Strohmaier, *In den Gärten der Wissenschaft: Ausgewählte Texte aus den Werken des muslimischen Universalgelehrten* (2nd ed.; Leipzig: Reclam-Verlag, 1991), 280 n.374.

378. *Pace* de Blois ("Zindīḳ," *EI*[2] 11:511), there is no reason to assume that this report provides information about the doctrines associated with the eighth-century Man-

always was aware of the existence of the Darkness, for it knows everything,[379] whereas the Darkness was always in a state of ignorance. Eternally present in each of those two Principles was a powerful figure who was the ruler of that Principle and the one who governed it: al-Hummāma is the 'queen' of the Principle of Darkness and its world, and the Father of Greatness is the 'king' of the Principle of Light and its world. They maintain that there is eternally present in the middle of the World of Light a mountain which as it rises tapers from its lowest point to its highest and which has no limit for its elevation; moreover, eternally present in the World of Darkness is a deep pit which is named 'Womb of Darkness': as it descends through the World of Darkness it narrows and diminishes endlessly. Moreover, the 'Hummāma of Death' was in a state of commotion in the World of Darkness. (Its component parts?) were engaged in killing each other until it arrived at that pit. Then it entered it and came to the far border of Darkness which lay next to the Principle of Light. It gazed at its (i.e., Light's) World and beheld a beautiful sight. It attempted to embrace it, but found itself rejected,[380] and so it returned to its own World in order to collect itself (for further efforts).[381] It then entered the pit and brought into existence the trees and five (types of) animals—birds, reptiles, fish, those having legs, and vermin.[382] Then, oblivious to the consequences, it approached to do battle with the Light, and it effected a mixture with itself.[383] But the Father of Greatness, cognizant of the consequences, effected the mixture with (only) a portion of His realm and a group of His spirits.[384] Then he (i.e., al-Misma'ī) goes on to recount the entirety of the struggle. Afterwards, he mentions how the purification occurs and how the (physical) world and the

ichaean 'sect' led by Mihr (see Chapter Five below). Fifth and sixth-century testimonia supplied by Augustine, Theodoret (*Haer. fab. comp.* 1.26), and Severus of Antioch (in Latin, Greek, and Syriac respectively) corroborate the general accuracy of the report transmitted by al-Misma'ī.

379. Reading with the emendation suggested by Monnot, *Penseurs*, 171 n.1.

380. Note Monnot, *Penseurs*, 171 n.8.

381. See Vajda, "Le témoignage d'al-Māturidī: Note annexe," 126 n.3.

382. Compare Augustine, *de Haeresibus* 46.8: *In fumo nata animalia bipedia ...; in tenebris, serpentia; in igne, quadrupedia; in aquis, natatilia; in vento, volatilia* 'Two-footed animals were generated in smoke ...; serpents were generated in darkness; quadrupeds in fire; swimming creatures in the waters; flying creatures in the wind.' Text cited from Adam, *Texte*[2], 66; translation from Gardner-Lieu, *Manichaean Texts*, 188.

383. Or 'by itself,' in that it personally led the assault against the World of Light. The following sentence however suggests that an instrumental sense is intended.

384. This report is closely allied to those supplied by the *Chronicon Maroniticum* and Agapius above, which are in turn dependent upon the unknown *written* Manichaean source (ܟܬܝܒ ܠܗܘܢ ܕܝܢ) cited by the sixth-century Severus of Antioch in his *Homily 123* (ed. Brière, 164.10) and apparently also used by Theodoret (451–458 CE) in his *Haereticarum fabularum compendium* 1.26. For a detailed discussion of the Severus citation, see especially Reeves, *Jewish Lore*, 165–83.

heavenly spheres came into existence.[385]

Bīrūnī, *Āthār* (ed. Sachau):[386]

The stories about the coming into existence and condition of the world are inconsistent with what results from empirical evidence and proofs. He (i.e., Mani) invoked the realm of the Worlds of Light, Primal Man, and the Living Spirit. He said (that) Light and Darkness were without beginning and uncreated.[387]

Ibn al-Malāḥimī, *K. al-mu'tamad* (ed. McDermott and Madelung):[388]

They maintain that the mixture began because the corporeal parts of Darkness maliciously distracted its Spirit; once distracted, the Spirit immediately beheld and saw the Light, and it was afterwards always cognizant that some entity foreign to it was nearby. Similarly the corporeal parts of Darkness perceived that some entity foreign to it (i.e., the World of Darkness) was nearby. Then the Spirit dispatched those corporeal parts to mingle with the Light, and due to their depravity and their desire for it they complied. At that time the Spirit of Darkness contrived by means of those corporeal parts a great plot by (assuming) a hideous ugly shape. Then it approached the vicinity of the Light and arranged itself as five portions, each of them being a variety of the five varieties (genera) of Darkness. It set about mixing itself with the Light. When that [Ruler] of the World of Light saw (what was happening), he sent Primal Man—one of his angels—(armored) with five portions of his genera (of Light), mighty angels (as well). As soon as Primal Man became visible to Darkness, he looked down from the five Light-portions upon each army of its hosts, five portions, and he captured it using them, and he mingled the five Light-portions with the five (portions) of Darkness. The smoke (and) the air mingled together and from them resulted this blended air. Whatever there is in it that is delightful and that gives refreshment for souls and life to animals derived from the air, and whatever there is in it that is destructive, harmful, diseased, and disgusting derived from the smoke. The fire (from the Realm of Darkness) mixed with the fire (from the Realm of Light), and whatever there is in it that shines derived from the (Good) fire, and whatever there is in it that burns and destroys came from the (Evil) fire. The light mixed with the darkness, and within that (mixture) those bright dense substances like gold, silver, and things similar to them and also whatever there is in it that is pure, beautiful, clean, and beneficial derived from the light. Whatever there is in it that is turbid, gross, ugly, dirty, sour, broken, and painful derived from the darkness. The (hot) wind (from the Realm of Darkness) mixed with the wind (from the Realm of Light), and whatever there is in it that is beneficial derived from the wind,

385. For other translations, see Vajda, "Le témoignage d'al-Māturidī: Note annexe," 125–27; Monnot, *Penseurs*, 170–72.

386. *Āthār* (ed. Sachau), 207.20–21. See also Taqīzādeh-Šīrāzī, *Mānī va dīn-e-ū*, 204 (§34).

387. For another translation, see Strohmaier, *In den Gärten*², 140.

388. *Kitāb al-mu'tamad fī uṣūl al-dīn* (ed. McDermott and Madelung), 563.2–565.10; 565.20–566.3.

and whatever there is in it that is distressful and harmful derived from the (hot) wind. The fog mixed with the water, and whatever there is in it that is pure and sweet derived from the water, and whatever there is in it that drowns, strangles, and corrupts derived from the fog.

Then they maintain that since these Dark-portions remained bound with the Light-portions, Primal Man descended to the bottom of the depth and severed the roots of those five Dark forces from it. Afterward he returned upwards to his place. Then one of those angels dragged off the forces which had Light bound within them to a section of the Land of Darkness which was adjacent to the Land of Light, and they lifted them up and attached them to the heights. Then they installed a powerful angel beneath the Land of Light in the space (lit. 'air') which belonged to the World of Light. The Ruler of the World of Light commanded one of his angels, and he created this world from those mixed portions in order to purify those parts of Light which had become mingled with those of Darkness. He built from it (i.e., the mixture) ten heavens and eight earths, putting them under the authority of that angel who bears the mixed portions. He imprisoned some of the demons of Darkness beneath the earths, and he approached the principal satans and fastened them to the heavens. He made the encircling heaven a sphere for the stars and zodiacal signs, and he attached demons to the lowest heaven. He put them <next>[389] to the Light, and he appointed two of his angels to turn them in order to set in motion the demons that were on it and prevent them from ascending to the upper Light and from (further) damaging the Light mixed within them and so as to strain (it) by this means from them. He appointed an angel to bear the heavens and another to lift up the earths. Air formed a connection between the lowest of the earths and the uppermost heavens. He placed a ditch around this world to cast into it the Darkness after its Light had been filtered from it so that Darkness would remain separate, and he made a wall <beyond?>[390] that ditch so that none of this sequestered Darkness could escape from (the control of Light to recombine) with the Light which was in the world. Thus it (Darkness) could not harm it (Light) or mix with it. Then he set in motion the sun and the moon to filter out those portions of Light which were (mixed) in the world. The sun filters out the Light which is mixed with the satans of heat, and the moon filters out what is mixed with the satans of cold.

They maintain that the (Light-portion termed) 'air' which is (held) in the earths continually ascends, and that it causes the Light-powers which are in them and that which extricates itself from the ground, plants, and light (*sic!*) to ascend. Moreover it will continue rising in accordance with its lofty nature until it attains its former place and rids itself of Darkness, going (back) into its substance together with what has ascended due to (the mechanisms of) praise, sanctification, proper speech, and pious deeds which sustain the created order. All of this rises and flows through the Column of Praise to the sphere of the moon: the

389. Read مصاقبا in place of مصافا. See de Blois, "Glossary," 57.

390. Cf. the parallel accounts.

Column of Praise is that (instrument) through which the particles of Light ascend to the sphere of the moon. The moon constantly receives this (Light) from the first of the month until the full moon appears. Then—since it is full—it conveys it to the sun. The waxing of the moon is due to its reception over the course of the first day to the fourteenth night of the month of what is released and has ascended from the particles of Light (that were bound) in the earth, vegetation, water, and other things, as well as the pure portions of the Light of the world and the praises. Its waning from the time of the appearance of the full moon to the end of the month and to the time when the new moon appears is due to its propulsion of that (Light) to the sun. And the sun propels it to the Light which is above it in the World of Praise, and it travels through that World up to the pure supernal Light. By means of their activity this (purification) will not cease until there remains from the Light only a compressed thing which the sun and the moon are unable to render pure.

... Do they then differ over whether any portion from Light remains in Darkness after the process of purification? For some of them teach that a part of it remains in it, and others of them teach that none remains. They maintain that al-Hummāma, the Spirit of Darkness, is the entity that forms animals in the wombs of mothers and in the other places which are not wombs through which animals reproduce. She also causes plants to germinate in the ground. She does this in order to perpetuate the mixing and to leave progeny; in this way, Evil becomes more established and Good is diminished, for she is the one who is Desire and Lust.

Shahrastānī, *Kitāb al-milal wa'l-niḥal* (ed. Badrān):[391]

Moreover, the Manichaeans differ over the mixture and its cause, as well as over the 'refining' and its means. Some of them say that the Light and the Darkness became mixed haphazardly and by accident, not by design or by choice.[392] The majority says that the cause of the mixture was that the bodies of Darkness distracted[393] their spirit; once distracted, the spirit then beheld and saw the Light. It thereupon dispatched the bodies to mix with the Light, and they hurriedly obeyed him due to (their) evil (nature). When the Ruler of Light saw this, he sent against it one of his angels with five parts from his five parts, and the five light-elements became mixed with the five darkness-elements. The smoke mingled with the air, and truly that which is alive or spiritual in this world derives from the air, but destruction and failure (derives) from the smoke. Fire and fire, light

391. Shahrastānī, *Kitāb al-milal wa'l-niḥal* (ed. Badrān), 1:625.1–628.2; Taqīzādeh-Šīrāzī, *Mānī va dīn-e-ū*, 243 (§45).

392. This sentence expresses a view of the causes of 'mixture' (and 'redemption') that is characteristic of the sixth-century Zoroastrian sect of Mazdak, a group that is frequently confused in Arabic language sources with the Manichaeans. Compare Shahrastānī's report on the Mazdakites in Chapter 5 below.

393. Note the system of Bardaiṣan where the intermediary *itye* 'awaken' or 'rouse' the Darkness, thus initiating the mixture in his system.

and darkness, hot wind and wind, and mist and water mingled together. Whatever is in the world that is beneficial, good, and blessed stems from the parts of Light, and whatever is in it that is harmful, evil, and corrupt stems from the parts of Darkness.

When the Ruler of Light saw this mixture, he commanded one of his angels to create this world according to this form (so as) to rescue the parts of Light from the parts of Darkness. The sun, the moon, and the other celestial bodies and stars were set in motion in order to filter out the parts of Light from the parts of Darkness. The sun filters out the Light which was mixed with the satans of heat, and the moon filters out the Light which was mixed with the satans of cold.[394] The air which is in the land does not cease rising, for it is its nature to rise toward its world.[395] Similarly all the particles of Light will continually rise and ascend and the particles of Darkness will continually descend and sink until every particle will have been separated from the other. Then the mixture will be neutralized, the composition will unravel, and everything will regain its integrity and its world. This is the resurrection and the life to come.

He (i.e., Mānī) says that what aids the purification and the separation and the ascension of the particles of Light are (the chanting of hymns of) glorification, (invocations of) sanctification, proper speech, and pious deeds, and that by this (behavior) the particles of Light are lifted in a Column of Radiance[396] to the orbit of the moon. The moon constantly receives this (i.e., the flow of particles) from the first of the month to the middle (of the month); then it is full and becomes the full moon.[397] Then (the moon) conveys (it) to the sun until the end of the month,[398] and the sun propels it onward to the Light that is above it, and it circulates in this world until it rejoins the uppermost, pure Light.[399]

Ibn al-Murtaḍā, *K. al-munya* (ed. Taqīzādeh-Šīrāzī):[400]

But then they (i.e., different Manichaean groups) disagree where the mixture transpired. It is said by some that the World of Darkness was beneath the World

394. Cf. Dodge, *Fihrist*, 2:782.

395. See the superior version of this text that is supplied by ʻAbd al-Jabbār, *Mughnī* (ed. Ḥusayn), 5:13.16–19.

396. Cf. Ephrem Syrus, *Prose Refutations* (ed. Mitchell), 2:208.37-38 (*apud* Reeves, "Citations from Ephrem," 264); Jāḥiẓ, *Kitāb al-ḥayawān* (ed. Taqīzādeh-Šīrāzī, *Mānī va dīn-e-ū*, 85, 87 [§4]); Ibn al-Nadīm, *Fihrist* (ed. Flügel, *Mani*, 57.11); Baghdādī, *al-Farq bayn al-firaq*, 162 (*apud* Taqīzādeh-Šīrāzī, *Mānī va dīn-e-ū*, 190 [§32]).

397. Cf. Ephrem Syrus, *Prose Refutations* (ed. Mitchell), 1:15.27–34.

398. Cf. Ephrem Syrus, *Prose Refutations* (ed. Mitchell), 1:20.37–40.

399. Puech (*Le manichéisme*, 176-77 n.349) points out that the itinerary of the redeemed Light differs in the Arabic language sources from that specified in *Acta Archelai* and its dependent traditions. The former lists a sequential progression of 'Column of Glory-moon-sun-uppermost Light,' whereas the latter has 'twelve bowls-moon-sun-Column of Glory.'

400. Taqīzādeh-Šīrāzī, *Mānī va dīn-e-ū*, 300–301 (§74); Kessler, *Mani*, 347–48.

of Light, but others say there was a distance between them. They also disagree over the cause of the mixture. It is said (by some) that the World of Darkness extended infinitely and experienced no interruption until it reached the border with Light at the time of (their) mixture. It is said that Darkness was constantly engrossed with its own World and it happened upon (the World of) Light accidentally (and) unintentionally and the Two mixed together. Most of them say instead about the cause that the material kinds associated with Darkness were distracting one another and causing harm to its immaterial 'kind': the immaterial 'kind' then caught sight of and discerned the Light, and it summoned its material kinds to mix themselves with it. They were quick to respond due to (their) wickedness, and each of the five parts of the repulsive form of Darkness suddenly revealed itself (in order to effect the mixture). As soon as the Ruler of the World of Light saw that, he sent against it one of his angels from his five 'kinds' and supervised the results. It (i.e., Darkness?) captured him, and the luminous portions were combined with the parts of Darkness. Smoke combined with air, and so whatever is animate and endowed with spirit (in the physical universe) derives from the air, whereas whatever is destructive derives from the smoke. Fire combined with fire: that which is useful comes from the fire (associated with Light), and that which is detrimental comes from the fire (associated with Darkness). Light combined with Darkness, and the components of dense substances like gold, silver, and so forth stem from both of them. Whatever among them that is beneficial or attractive comes from the Light, whereas the opposite characteristics come from Darkness. The fog combined with water, and the hot wind with the wind.

The Ruler of the World of Light commanded that this universe and its botanical organisms be created from those mixed parts in order to rescue those parts (originating in Light) from Darkness. He created the heavens and the earth along with what is contained in them, and he appointed an angel to bear the earth and another (angel) to bear the heavens. He created the heavenly spheres and appointed an angel to set them in motion, and the sun and the moon move to seek out[401] what there is in this universe that derives from Light ....[402]

c. Ritual and Behavioral

Jāḥiẓ, *Kitāb al-ḥayawān* (ed. Taqīzādeh-Šīrāzī):[403]

Some Sufis[404] and Christians resemble *zanādiqa* in the way they reject animal

---

401. See de Blois, "Glossary," 57–58, 70.

402. For another translation, see Kessler, *Mani*, 352–53.

403. Taqīzādeh-Šīrāzī, *Mānī va dīn-e-ū*, 87 (§4).

404. A multi-faceted ascetic and mystical movement within Islam, the bibliography pertaining to which is enormous. For some initial guidance, see Ignaz Goldziher, *Introduction to Islamic Theology and Law* (trans. Andras and Ruth Hamori; Princeton, NJ: Princeton University Press, 1981), 116–66.

slaughter, hate the spilling of blood, and renounce the consumption of meat.[405]

Jāḥiẓ, *Kitāb al-ḥayawān* (ed. Taqīzādeh-Šīrāzī):[406]

He (Jāḥiẓ's informant) said: '*Zindīq* monks are itinerants. They engage in itinerancy instead of the Nestorian fondness for (inhabiting) subterranean caverns, or that of the Melkite for residing in hermitages or of the Nestorian for residing in caverns.'

He said: 'They (i.e., *zindīq* monks) always wander in pairs. Whenever you observe one of them, then look around, and you will (soon) see his companion. In their opinion, itinerancy means that none of them should lodge in the same spot for two nights.' He said: 'They wander about accompanied by four qualities—holiness, purity, truthfulness, and poverty. Regarding poverty, they eat from what has been begged and from what the people themselves are pleased to make over to them so that they eat nothing except what they have obtained (by those means). The one who desires more than that commits a sin. As for purity, they renounce sexual relations. With regard to truthfulness, they excel in not behaving deceitfully. And as for holiness, they excel in restraining their (urge to) sin and the desire for committing it.'

He said: 'Once two of their members came to Ahwāz.[407] One of them proceeded ahead in the direction of the tombs in order to use the toilet. The other sat down near a jeweler close to some wineshops. A woman emerged from one of the palaces bearing a small chest which contained within it some precious gems. When she was going up the road to the jeweler's shop, she slipped and the chest fell out of her hand. Now there was an ostrich which frequented some of those residential districts, and when the chest dropped, the lid fell off, and some of the stones which were in it scattered, and that ostrich swallowed the largest and most valuable stone which it contained. This (all) took place while the wanderer was watching. Meanwhile the jeweler and his slaves jumped up and gathered up those stones, and so too the people and their companions, but none of them had been nearby, and they failed to find that stone. The woman cried out, and the group looked more carefully but then gave up searching, for they could not find the stone. Then one of them said: "By God, was not the closest one of us (to the accident) this sitting monk? Should we not seek to see whether he has it?" They asked him about the stone. He realized that were he to inform them that it was in the belly of the ostrich, then he would be responsible for shedding the blood of a living being. So he said: "I have taken nothing." Then they searched him and spread out everything which he had and heaped blows upon him. His companion came forward and said: "May God grant (us His) protection!" But they seized him and said: "You must hand over to her what you have hidden!" He responded: "What thing should I hand over to her?" Then they brutally beat them both to the point of death, but while they were suffering this, a man who was passing by

405. For another translation, see Pellat, "Le témoignage," 272–73.

406. Taqīzādeh-Šīrāzī, *Mānī va dīn-e-ū*, 95–96 (§4).

407. A prominent city in Khūzistān in southwestern Iran.

realized (what had occurred) after soliciting the story from them and seeing the ostrich moving about (nearby). He said to them: "Was this ostrich frequenting the street when the chest fell?" They answered: "Yes." He said: "Who among you is the owner?" After they compensated the owners of the ostrich, they slaughtered it, split open its gizzard, and discovered the stone. It was already diminished in its size by half during the time it had remained in there.'[408]

Jāḥiẓ, *Kitāb al-ḥayawān* (ed. Taqīzādeh-Šīrāzī):[409]

I had always heard it said that the size of a man's ear served as a sign for the length of his life. They even maintain that there was a certain itinerant *zindīq*—may they be cursed by God Most High—whom they brought forth to suffer decapitation. One who had been fortunate to be his slave passed by him and said: 'Did you not always claim, O my master, that the one whose ear was long would be long-lived?' He answered: 'Certainly.' He said: 'But they are now executing you!!!' He responded: 'On the contrary; I maintain they will abandon the effort!'

Jāḥiẓ, *Kitāb al-radd 'alā al-naṣārā* (ed. Taqīzādeh-Šīrāzī):[410]

And when you give attention to their (i.e., Christians') language about mercy and forgiveness, and their reputation for wanderings, and their disparagement of anyone who eats meat, and their appetite for eating cereals and avoiding (the eating of) animals, and their abstinence from marriage and their rejection of the wish for offspring, and their praise of the catholicoi, metropolitans, bishops, and monks for renouncing marriage and rejecting procreation, and their glorification of (their) superiors, you become aware that there is a kinship between their religion (i.e., Christianity) and *zandaqa*, and that they exhibit an attachment to this ideology.[411]

Abū Bakr al-Rāzī, *Kitāb al-sīrat al-falsafīya* (ed. Taqīzādeh-Šīrāzī):[412]

Since it is the verdict of reason and justice that no person should cause another to suffer, it follows from this that no one should inflict suffering upon themselves as well. Indeed many things which the verdict of reason rejects come under this sentence; for example, the Indian method of seeking favor from God by scorching their bodies or flinging them down upon sharpened spikes; and, for example, those things Manichaeans impose upon themselves when they desire sexual

---

408. See Goldziher, *Introduction*, 142. Note also Jāḥiẓ's remarks in his *Kitāb al-radd 'alā al-naṣārā* which is excerpted below. For the possible Manichaean identity of these '*zindīq* monks,' see Louis Massignon, *Essay on the Origins of the Technical Language of Islamic Mysticism* (trans. Benjamin Clark; Notre Dame: University of Notre Dame Press, 1997), 57 n.182, 158.

409. Taqīzādeh-Šīrāzī, *Mānī va dīn-e-ū*, 96 (§4).

410. Taqīzādeh-Šīrāzī, *Mānī va dīn-e-ū*, 100 (§8).

411. See also Joshua Finkel, "A Risāla of al-Jāḥiẓ," *JAOS* 47 (1927): 331–32; *Sobriety and Mirth* (trans. Colville), 79.

412. Taqīzādeh-Šīrāzī, *Mānī va dīn-e-ū*, 118 (§16).

intercourse, their emaciation due to hunger and thirst, and their rendering themselves filthy by performing ablutions using urine instead of water.[413]

Maʿsūdī, *Murūj al-dhahab* (ed. Barbier de Meynard-de Courteille):[414]

As I have mentioned, the Christians took some of these (ecclesiastical) offices from the Ṣābians;[415] the Manichaeans did (likewise) with that of 'priest,' 'deacon,' and the rest, although not those of the 'electi,' 'auditores,' etc. Now Mānī came onto the scene after the *floruit* of Christ, as did Bardaiṣan and Marcion. The Manichaeans are the partisans of Mānī, the Marcionites those of Marcion, and the Dayṣāniyya those of Bardaiṣan. Subsequently ranks like 'electi' and the like developed among those who pursued the path of the dualist sects.[416]

Ibn al-Nadīm, *Fihrist* (ed. Flügel):[417]

What is required for a person to join the religion (*dīn*):

He (i.e., Mānī) said: 'One who wants to join the religion is required to test themselves. If one thinks they have the strength to suppress desire and greed; to give up eating meat, drinking wine, and marriage; and to avoid injury to water, fire, trees,[418] and soil,[419] then they may join the religion. But if one does not have the strength (to overcome) all of these things, then they may not join the religion.

If, however, one loves the religion but does not have the strength to suppress

413. Compare a passage found in the ninth-century so-called 'long' Greek abjuration: 'I anathematize those who pollute themselves with their own urine, and do not suffer their filth to be cleansed in water lest, they say, the water be defiled.' For the Greek text, see Adam, *Texte*², 100.113-15; the translation is that of BeDuhn, *The Manichaean Body*, 49. Note also Lieu, *Manichaeism in Mesopotamia*, 293–94. A twelfth-century Confucianist official levels the same charge: 'They (Manichaeans) consider urine as holy water and use it for their ablutions.' See Samuel N. C. Lieu, *Manichaeism in Central Asia and China* (NHMS 45; Leiden: Brill, 1998), 156.
Another rendering of the citation from Abū Bakr al-Rāzī can be found in A. J. Arberry, *Razi's Traditional Psychology* (Damascus: Islamic Book Service, n.d.), 13.

414. Masʿūdī, *Murūj* (ed. Barbier de Meynard-de Courteille), 1:200; Taqīzādeh-Šīrāzī, *Mānī va dīn-e-ū*, 128–29 (§21).

415. See the lengthy note above. It is unclear which of the various groups to whom medieval Islamicate writers applied the label 'Ṣābian' Masʿūdī has in view here.

416. For a different understanding of this passage, see the cautionary remarks of François de Blois, "*Naṣrānī* (Ναζωραῖος) and *ḥanīf* (ἐθνικός): Studies on the Religious Vocabulary of Christianity and of Islam," *BSOAS* 65 (2002): 7 n.32.

417. Flügel, *Mani*, 63.8-64.2; Ibn al-Nadīm, *K. al-Fihrist* (ed. Tajaddud), 396; Taqīzādeh-Šīrāzī, *Mānī va dīn-e-ū*, 156-57 (§27).

418. Reading والشجر in place of والسحر. See Flügel's critical apparatus and Nicholas Sims-Williams, "The Manichaean Commandments: A Survey of the Sources," in *Papers in Honour of Professor Mary Boyce* (Acta Iranica 24-25; 2 vols.; ed. Jacques Duchesne-Guillemin and Pierre Lecoq; Leiden: Brill, 1985), 2:577 n. 32.

419. Read with Flügel's manuscript V and compare Marwazī below; also Sims-Williams, "Manichaean Commandments," 2:577 n. 33.

desire and greed, then they should take the opportunity to support the religion and the Elect, and to effect an assuagement in view of their repugnant deeds (by the) periods of time during which they devote themselves to work, piety, nocturnal prayers, petitions, and supplications. That will protect them during life in this world and at their time of death, and their mode (of recompense) will be the second mode in the world to come.'[420] We will speak of it (i.e., this mode of recompense) in what follows, should God Most Exalted be willing.[421]

Ibn al-Nadīm, *Fihrist* (ed. Flügel):[422]

The religious law which Mānī produced and the precepts which he established:

With regard to his adherents, Mānī imposed ten precepts upon the Auditors, to which he attaches 'Three Seals'[423] and a seven-day fast in every month. The precepts involve (lit. 'are') belief in the four majestic ones:[424] God, His Light, His Power, and His Wisdom.[425] God (may His name be magnified!) is King of the Light-Paradises. The sun and the moon constitute His Light. His Power consists of five angels, and they are air, wind, light, water, and fire. His Wisdom is the Holy Church,[426] and it has five expressions: the teachers, (who are) the offspring of intellect; the deacons, (who are) the offspring of knowledge; the priests, (who

420. This 'mode' (literally 'form') is explained below in Ibn al-Nadīm's presentation of Mani's views on the afterlife.

421. See also Flügel, *Mani*, 94–95; Kessler, *Mani*, 398; Adam, *Texte*², 125; Dodge, *Fihrist*, 2:788.

422. Flügel, *Mani*, 64.3–66.7; Ibn al-Nadīm, *K. al-Fihrist* (ed. Tajaddud), 396–97; Taqīzādeh-Šīrāzī, *Mānī va dīn-e-ū*, 157–58 (§27).

423. Also attested as the *tria signacula* by Augustine in his *De moribus manichaeorum*; see Adam, *Texte*², 61-62; Gardner-Lieu, *Manichaean Texts*, 236–37. The phrase 'Three Seals' refers to the rigid discipline extended over one's mouth, hands, and breast, which respectively signify and govern dietary intake, acquisition of foodstuffs, and chastity. For a comprehensive discussion, see BeDuhn, *The Manichaean Body*, 33–45. As BeDuhn points out, the 'Three Seals' tend to overlap with the 'Five Commandments' which eastern Manichaean sources hold to be normative for the Elect.

424. Paralleling the common reference in Greek and Coptic sources to the quadruple or 'four-faced' Father of Greatness. For references, see Lieu, *Manichaeism*², 11.

425. For this same tetrad in an arrestingly similar context, see M 801, a bilingual (Middle Persian and Parthian) hymn to the deity known as the Messenger first published by Henning, "Ein manichäisches Bet- und Beichtbuch," 25.230–33 (Middle Persian *yzd* 'god,' *rwšn* 'light,' *zwr* 'power,' *whyh* 'wisdom'), 26.283–85 ('*who believe in* God, Light, Power, and Wisdom'); cf. also 31.450–53. The same text is also available in Boyce, *Reader*, 156–57 §§25 and 29. Note too M 36 V 20–21, published by F. C. Andreas and W. B. Henning, "Mitteliranische Manichaica aus Chinesisch-Turkestan, II," *SPAW* (1933): 326; cf. 324–25 n.7; 329 n.1. See also Bousset, *Hauptprobleme der Gnosis*, 236–37, and the important remarks of Gedaliahu G. Stroumsa, "'Seal of the Prophets': The Nature of a Manichaean Metaphor," *Jerusalem Studies in Arabic and Islam* 7 (1986): 68–69.

426. I.e., the Manichaean religion. See de Blois, "Glossary," 46.

are) the offspring of intelligence; the Elect, (who are) the offspring of what is invisible; and the catechumens, (who are) the offspring of sagacity.

The ten precepts[427] (imposed upon the Auditors are) ceasing the worship of idols; ceasing deceitful practices; forsaking greed; rejecting the taking of life; ceasing fornication; abandoning theft; not providing defective information (i.e., bearing false witness); ceasing magical practices; not supporting confusion; i.e., doubts about the religion; and not being slack or negligent in practice.

The precept governing the four or seven ritual prayers:[428]

While standing, the person washes with running water or something else.[429] Then still standing they turn to face the greatest luminary[430] (and) next prostrate themselves and say while prostrating: 'Blessed be our true guide, the Paraclete, the Apostle of Light! Blessed be His ministering angels and praised be His luminous hosts!' They say this while prostrate. Then they stand and do not remain prostrate, but assume an upright posture.

Afterwards, they say while prostrating a second time: 'Praised be you, O shining one, Mānī, our true guide, source (lit. 'root') of Light and branch of Life,[431] a great tree the whole of which gives healing!'[432]

They say while prostrating a third time: 'With a pure heart and a sincere tongue, I bow down and offer praise to the mighty deity, the Father of the Lights[433] and their elements! Praised and blessed are You, and all of Your greatness and the blessed Aeons[434] whom You called forth![435] The exalted one(s) among Your hosts extol You, along with Your beneficence, Your discourse, Your greatness, and Your good will, because You are the deity who is completely (representative of) Truth, Life, and Goodness!'

Then they say while (prostrating) a fourth time: 'I praise and bow down to all of the divinities and to all of the luminous angels and to all of the lights and to all of the hosts who owe their existence to the mighty deity!'

Then they say while (prostrating) a fifth time: 'I bow down and give praise

427. See Sims-Williams, "Manichaean Commandments," 2:577–82; BeDuhn, *The Manichaean Body*, 53–56.

428. The Auditors pray four times and the Elect seven times daily. See the testimony of Bīrūnī below.

429. In Islam, if suitable water is unavailable for ritual washing, another substance such as clean sand may be used. Perhaps a similar practice is envisioned here.

430. Depending upon the time of the prayer, either the sun or the moon.

431. Read with Flügel's Ms. H.

432. This arboreal symbolism is ultimately intertwined with Manichaean readings of the biblical legend of Genesis 2–3.

433. Middle Persian *pydr rwšn* as in M 2 lines 120–21, published by Andreas-Henning, "Mitteliranische Manichaica III," 853.

434. Read with Flügel's Mss. C and H.

435. An allusion to the asexual verbal process by which the Manichaean pantheon of lesser deities was produced. See, e.g., the cosmogonic description provided by Theodore bar Konai above.

to the noble hosts and to the shining deities who in their wisdom attacked and expelled Darkness, and suppressed it!'

Afterwards, they say while (prostrating) a sixth time: 'I bow down to and extol the mighty luminous Father of Greatness,[436] He Who endures forever!'[437] (They continue praying) in this manner until the twelfth prostration. When they finish ten prayers, another prayer is commenced in which they repeatedly glorify God. It is unnecessary for us to record it.

Now the first prayer takes place around noon, and the second prayer is between noon and sunset. Afterwards there is the evening prayer after sunset, and then the prayer for the first third of the night, taking place three hours after sundown. They perform for each prayer and prostration the same actions done during the first prayer, which is (known as) the prayer of al-Bashīr (i.e., the Messenger).

As for fasting, they fast for two days without a break between them when the sun is in the zodiacal sign of Sagittarius and the moon is full. When a new moon occurs, they also fast two days without a break between them. Besides these they fast when a luminary appears for two days in the zodiacal sign of Capricorn. Also whenever a new moon occurs and the sun is in the zodiacal sign of Aquarius, after eight days of the month have past, they begin fasting that day for thirty days, breaking the fast each day at sundown.

The first day of the week (i.e., Sunday) is venerated by the Manichaean laity, but their elite venerate the second day (i.e., Monday). Thus has Mānī made binding upon them.[438]

'Abd al-Jabbār, *Tathbīt* (ed. 'Uthmān):[439]

He (i.e., Mani) says about him (i.e., Jesus) that he laid down proscriptions upon himself and upon all their people (i.e., Christians) against (having sexual relations with) women, slaughtering animals, and eating meat; and (he asserts) that this had never been lawful nor would it become lawful (behavior). He cursed anyone who declared it to be lawful. He disowned any connection with Abraham, Moses, Aaron, Joshua, David,[440] and anyone who deemed it proper to kill animals, to cause them pain, to eat meat, and the like. He (Mani) cited as proof for this some passages from your own gospels! Yet according to you, he has lied and forged traditions about Christ, and is wrong in his interpretations. (You say) that it is clear that Christ pronounced those prophets to be righteous; this cannot be subverted by his inter-

---

436. The usual designation for the Manichaean supreme deity in Semitic language sources. See Theodore bar Konai above.

437. Arabic من العلمين is simply a transcription of Syriac ܡܢ ܥܠܡܝܢ 'forever.' See Andreas-Henning, "Mitteliranische Manichaica III," 853 n.2.

438. See also Flügel, *Mani*, 95–97; Adam, *Texte*², 126–28; Dodge, *Fihrist*, 2:789–91. The contents of the six prayers were also translated by A. A. Bevan, "Manichaeism," *ERE* 8:399.

439. 'Abd al-Jabbār, *Tathbīt* (ed. 'Uthmān), 1:114.15–115.2.

440. This assertion is akin to the Marcionite denial of a Jewish cultural lineage for Jesus.

pretations.[441]

'Abd al-Jabbār, *Tathbīt* (ed. 'Uthmān):[442]

The religion of the Manichaeans is more strict than the religion of the Christians, for they forbid the eating of any animal, the riding of one, or causing injury to one for any reason. They even forbid the killing of lions, serpents, and scorpions, instead tolerating the harm they may inflict. They forbid the hoarding of wealth, and they enjoin more fasts and prayers than do the Christians. They forbid any kind of sexual contact and all appetitive pleasures.[443]

'Abd al-Jabbār, *Mughnī* (ed. Ḥusayn):[444]

He (i.e., Mani) has imposed obligatory rules upon their followers and their leaders, such as to possess only clothing for a year and food for each day, (and) they practice many other rituals pertaining to prayer, almsgiving, and supplicating the True (God); and to abstain from taking life, deceit, greed, fornication, and theft; and not to do to a living being that which you would hate were it done to your own self.[445]

Bīrūnī, *Āthār* (ed. Sachau):[446]

He prohibited killing animals or causing (them) pain, and (he forbade) causing damage especially to fire, water, and vegetation. He prescribed ordinances which are obligatory for the Elect,[447] they being the Manichaean pietists and ascetics: to choose poverty over their own desires, to restrain greed and lust, to abandon the temporal world, to be ascetic while in it, to fast uninterruptedly, and to give alms insofar as one is able.[448] He forbade the acquisition of anything, except food for one day and clothing for one year. He (i.e., an Elect) must give up sexual relations and continually journey throughout the present world, engaging in missionary work and guiding people onto the right path.

He enjoined other regulations upon the Auditors, meaning their followers and attendants who are involved in worldly affairs: to give alms by tithing property, to fast a seventh part of one's life-time, to restrict oneself to a single wife, to support the Elect, and to drive away whatever distracts them.

It has been related that he permitted sexual gratification using young men,

441. See also Pines, "Two Passages," 66.

442. 'Abd al-Jabbār, *Tathbīt* (ed. 'Uthmān), 1:187.2–6.

443. See also Monnot, *Penseurs*, 279; Reynolds, *Muslim Theologian*, 82–83 n.32.

444. 'Abd al-Jabbār, *Mughnī* (ed. Ḥusayn), 5:15.9–12. Note also Shahrastānī, *Kitāb al-milal wa'l-niḥal* (ed. Badrān), 1:629.6–9. According to Vajda, they are here reliant upon a common source.

445. See also Vajda, "Le témoignage d'al-Māturidī: Note annexe," 121; Monnot, *Penseurs*, 163.

446. *Āthār* (ed. Sachau), 207.21–208.7. See also Taqīzādeh-Šīrāzī, *Mānī va dīn-e-ū*, 204–205 (§34).

447. Literally 'the truthful ones,' or 'the righteous ones.' On this terminology, see Flügel, *Mani*, 271, 283–85; BeDuhn, *The Manichaean Body*, 26.

448. The Elect were normally the *recipients* of the alms contributed by the *Auditores*. Note also BeDuhn, *The Manichaean Body*, 46.

should a man become inflamed by lust. It is cited as evidence for the truth of this that every Manichaean was attended by a beardless, hairless, young male servant.[449] However, I have not come across in what I have read from his books a single word which resembled this (report).[450] Rather, his way of life displays the opposite of what has been related.[451]

Bīrūnī, *Āthār* (ed. Sachau):[452]

And as for the inhabitants of Ḥarrān, they face the south pole (when praying), whereas the Ṣābians face towards the north pole.[453] I think that the Manichaeans also face this same pole (i.e., north), because according to them, it is the center of the dome of heaven and its highest place.[454] However, I discovered (that) the author of the *Book on Sexual Relations*, who is one of their group (i.e., a Manichaean) and a missionary for them, upbraids the adherents of the three (Abrahamic) religions for turning toward one direction (in prayer) in lieu of another. He quarrels with them about other things, and he indicates that one praying to God may dispense with turning toward a *qibla*.[455]

Bīrūnī, *'Ifrād al-maqāl fī 'amr al-ẓilāl* (ed. Taqīzādeh-Šīrāzī):[456]

The <Manichaean>[457] Elect have seven prayers. The first one is the prayer of the Column (of Radiance) at noon, (with) thirty-seven *raka'āt* (i.e., bowings of the head and body), and on Mondays two *raka'āt* are subtracted. Then (they pray at) the middle of the afternoon, (with) twenty-one *raka'āt*. Then (they pray) af-

449. According to Maqdisī (*K. al-bad' wa'l-ta'rīkh* [ed. Huart], 6:54–55), the disciples of late Umayyad heretic Ja'd b. Dirham were 'beardless men,' and he is branded by Ibn al-Nadīm as a *zindīq*. Note the suggestive remarks of Georges Vajda, "Les zindîqs en pays d'Islam au debut de la période abbaside," *RSO* 17 (1937–38): 181 n.*e*; also J. L. Kraemer, "Heresy Versus the State in Medieval Islam," in *Studies in Judaica, Karaitica and Islamica Presented to Leon Nemoy on his Eightieth Birthday* (ed. Sheldon R. Brunswick; Ramat-Gan: Bar-Ilan University Press, 1982), 172.

450. Note however Sam'ānī below.

451. For another translation, see Strohmaier, *In den Gärten*², 140–41.

452. *Āthār* (ed. Sachau), 331.18–22; Taqīzādeh-Šīrāzī, *Mānī va dīn-e-ū*, 206 (§34).

453. These two groups are often equated in Muslim literature. However, Bīrūnī distinguishes the pagan population of the northern Mesopotamian city of Ḥarrān from another community whom he terms the 'true Ṣābians' (*Āthār* [ed. Sachau], 204.17-206.19) whom he characterizes as an Irano-Jewish baptist sect, perhaps the forerunners of the Mandaeans.

454. Confirmation of Bīrūnī's supposition that the Manichaeans turn toward the north when praying is found in a Chinese language description of their ritual behaviors. See Kao Yu-Kung, "Source Materials on the Fang La Rebellion," *Harvard Journal of Asiatic Studies* 26 (1966): 217.

455. I.e., a fixed point for directing prayer, such as Mecca for Muslims or Jerusalem for Jews.

456. Taqīzādeh-Šīrāzī, *Mānī va dīn-e-ū*, 207 (§35).

457. Read with Taqīzādeh-Šīrāzī, *Mānī va dīn-e-ū*, 207 n.2.

ter sundown, (with) twenty-five *raka'āt*. Next (they pray) a half an hour into the night, (with) the same (number of *raka'āt*). Next (they pray at) midnight, (with) thirty *raka'āt*. Then (they pray at) daybreak, (with) fifty *raka'āt*. Finally (the prayer of) al-Bashīr (the Messenger) at the last part of the night and the initial part of day, (with) twenty-six *raka'āt*.[458] Their Auditors, the ones who occupy themselves with worldly affairs, perform four prayers at noon, nightfall, daybreak, and the time when the sun appears.[459]

Abu'l-Ma'ālī, *Bayān al-adyān* (ed. Taqīzādeh-Šīrāzī):[460]

They are obligated to provide a tithe of their property. They possess a single garment for each year, and they are forbidden to keep more food than is sufficient for them for one day. A seventh of their life is spent in fasting,[461] and they have four obligatory prayers.

Marwazī, *Kitāb ṭabā'i' al-ḥayawān* (ed. Kruk):[462]

He prohibited killing animals or causing (them) pain, and (he forbade) causing damage especially to fire, air, water, and soil.[463] He prescribed ordinances which are obligatory for the Manichaean ascetics: to choose poverty over their own desires, to restrain greed and lust, to abandon the temporal world, and to be abstemious while in it. He forbade the accumulation of anything except food for one day and dress for one year, and to restrict oneself to a single wife, and other similar ordinances; for example, to give alms by tithing property, to fast a seventh part of one's life-time, and continually journey throughout the present world, engaging in missionary work and guiding people onto the right path, and to support the Elect and to drive away whatever distracts them.[464]

Shahrastānī, *Kitāb al-milal wa'l-niḥal* (ed. Badrān):[465]

... Mānī imposed upon his followers a tithe upon all their property, four prayers (to be recited) daily and nightly, supplication(s) to God, abstention from deceit, killing,

458. Compare the summary of prayers provided by Ibn al-Nadīm in Flügel, *Mani*, 64.14–65.19.

459. See also de Blois, "Glossary," 58; idem, "The Manichaean Daily Prayers," in *Studia Manichaica: IV. Internationaler Kongress zum Manichäismus, Berlin, 14.–18. Juli 1997* (ed. Ronald E. Emmerick, Werner Sundermann, and Peter Zieme; Berlin: Akademie-Verlag, 2000), 50; BeDuhn, *The Manichaean Body*, 145.

460. Taqīzādeh-Šīrāzī, *Mānī va dīn-e-ū*, 491–92 (§177). See also Schefer, *Chrestomathie*, 1:145.18–20; Kessler, *Mani*, 371.

461. Note the same roster of behavioral prescriptions in Bīrūnī above.

462. Ms. UCLA Ar. 52 fol. 5b.12–19, as published by Remke Kruk, "Sharaf az-Zamân Ṭâhir Marwazî (fl. ca. 1100 A.D.) on Zoroaster, Mânî, Mazdak, and Other Pseudo-Prophets," *Persica* 17 (2001): 65.

463. Note the testimony of Ibn al-Nadīm above.

464. Essentially a compressed synopsis of the differentiated regimen presented in Bīrūnī's *Āthār* above.

465. Shahrastānī, *Kitāb al-milal wa'l-niḥal* (ed. Badrān), 1:629.6-9; Taqīzādeh-Šīrāzī, *Mānī va dīn-e-ū*, 244 (§45).

stealing, fornication, greed, sorcery, and worship of idols, and (the precept) not to do to a living being that which he would hate were it done to his own self.[466]

Sam'ānī, *Kitāb al-ānsāb* (ed. Taqīzādeh-Šīrāzī):[467]

He prohibited sexual relations with women because the origin of <carnal desire>[468] was from Satan. Consequently the child whom one engendered due to <carnal desire>[469] was nothing but a filthy jinn. He however permitted pederasty in order to put a stop to procreation. He forbade the slaughter of living creatures, but when one died of natural causes, he allowed it to be eaten.[470]

Ibn al-Āthīr, *Lulāb fī tahdhīb al-ānsāb* (ed. Taqīzādeh-Šīrāzī):[471]

He prohibited sexual relations with women because the origin of carnal desire was from Satan. The only thing engendered from carnal desire was filth. He permitted pederasty in order to put a stop to procreation. He forbade the slaughter of living creatures, but when one died of natural causes, he allowed it to be eaten.

Ibn al-Murtaḍā, *K. al-munya* (ed. Taqīzādeh-Šīrāzī):[472]

Mānī prescribed poverty for them. They should not accumulate things except dress for one year and food for each day. He imposed a tithe on their property and (commanded) it to be put at the disposition of its (the community's?) managers. He forbade them to enter idol-temples, and he prohibited fornication, theft, and causing pain to animals of any sort. He also prohibited marriage and agriculture.[473]

d. Eschatological[474]

Māturīdī, *Kitāb al-tawḥīd* (ed. Kholeif):[475]

Both Light and Darkness have a spirit. The spirit of Darkness is named Hummāma:[476]

---

466. Compare with the formulation found in 'Abd al-Jabbār above.

467. Taqīzādeh-Šīrāzī, *Mānī va dīn-e-ū*, 246 (§46).

468. Read with the textual apparatus supplied in Taqīzādeh-Šīrāzī, *Mānī va dīn-e-ū*, 246 n.12.

469. Read with the textual apparatus supplied in Taqīzādeh-Šīrāzī, *Mānī va dīn-e-ū*, 246 n.13.

470. Compare Middle Persian M 5794 II R 1–14 (*apud* Andreas-Henning, "Mitteliranische Manichaica II," 296–97; Boyce, *Reader*, 56): '... But dead flesh of any animals, wherever they find it, be it (naturally) dead or slaughtered, they [i.e., Manichaean auditors] may eat; and whenever they find it, either through trading or as a livelihood or as a present, they may eat.' Translation is that of BeDuhn, *The Manichaean Body*, 55.

471. Taqīzādeh-Šīrāzī, *Mānī va dīn-e-ū*, 265 (§56).

472. Taqīzādeh-Šīrāzī, *Mānī va dīn-e-ū*, 301 (§74); Kessler, *Mani*, 349.

473. See also Kessler, *Mani*, 354.

474. Excellent general overviews of Manichaean eschatology are Puech, *Le manichéisme*, 177 n.351; Guy G. Stroumsa, "Aspects de l'eschatologie manichéenne," *RHR* 198 (1981): 163-81; Skjærvø, "Iranian Elements," 275–81; Werner Sundermann, "Manichaean Eschatology," *EncIr* 8:569–75.

475. Māturīdī, *Kitāb al-tawḥīd* (ed. Kholeif), 157.11-16.

476. This name is first attested in Jāḥiẓ above.

it is alive (and) made the world for the purpose of imprisoning Light within it. Light experiences no sensations: whatever derives from it comes into being naturally and is completely Good. Hummāma experiences sensations.

Each one of them will eventually return to their (proper) realm. Then it will transpire that the upper things will be purer and the lower things more polluted; due to their distinct natures (one will be) light and (the other) heavy, and since their properties will be so different, that which is light will rise up and that which is heavy will sink down.

Time will pass until, just as they were once mixed, the two will finally be extracted from one another.[477]

Ibn al-Nadīm, *Fihrist* (ed. Flügel):[478]

[Mani said:] '... this activity (i.e., the refining of Light from material existence) will not cease until only a small amount of congealed Light is left (which) the sun and moon are unable to purify. At that time the angel who bears the earths will lift up, and the other angel will stop stretching the heavens, and that which is uppermost will mix with that which is lowest. A fire will heat up and burn these things, and it will not cease burning until what Light remains in them is set free.'

Mānī said: 'This burning will last for 1,468 years.'

He (i.e., Mani) said: 'When this administration passes away and al-Hummāma, the Spirit of Darkness, perceives the redemption of the Light and the exaltation of the angels, the hosts, and the guardians (of Light), then she will surrender. She will perceive the strife restraining her and the hosts who surround her, and she will retreat into a tomb previously made ready for her. Then it (i.e., Light) will close this tomb with a rock the same size as this world, and seal her in it, and Light will be relieved at that time from Darkness and its molestation.'

The Māsīyah, who are a Manichaean sect,[479] maintain that a certain amount of Light will still remain in Darkness.[480]

Ibn al-Nadīm, *Fihrist* (ed. Flügel):[481]

The Manichaean teaching about the hereafter:

Mānī said: 'When an Elect is visited by death, Primal Man sends to him a luminous deity in the form of the Wise Guide.[482] Accompanying him are three deities

477. See Vajda, "Le témoignage d'al-Māturidī," 4–23; Monnot, *Penseurs*, 304; idem, "Māturīdī et le manichéisme," 147–48; Giorgi, *Pour une histoire*, 131–32.

478. Flügel, *Mani*, 57.15–58.10; Ibn al-Nadīm, *K. al-Fihrist* (ed. Tajaddud), 394; Taqīzādeh-Šīrāzī, *Mānī va dīn-e-ū*, 153–54 (§27).

479. This name does not occur anywhere else in expositions of Manichaean sectarianism (regarding which see Chapter 5 below). 'Māsīyah' is most likely a corruption of 'Miqlāṣiyah'; see de Blois, "Glossary," 74, 77.

480. See also Flügel, *Mani*, 90; Adam, *Texte*², 123–25; Dodge, *Fihrist*, 2:782–83.

481. Flügel, *Mani*, 69.16–72.8; Ibn al-Nadīm, *K. al-Fihrist* (ed. Tajaddud), 398–99; Taqīzādeh-Šīrāzī, *Mānī va dīn-e-ū*, 160–61 (§27).

482. Cf. Coptic *Ps-Bk.* 84.16; also Coptic *Homil.* 6.19–21 (a luminous 'Great Splendor'

who bring a cup, a garment, turban, crown, and garland of light. A youth[483] comes with them who is similar to the soul of that Elect.[484] A devil symbolizing desire and lust will appear before them, along with other satans. When the Elect sees them, he will appeal to the divinity in the form of the Wise (Guide) and to the three deities for help, and they will draw near to him. When the satans behold them, they will turn around (and) flee. They (the deities) will then will take hold of the Elect and dress him in the crown, the garland, and the garment. They will put the cup in his hand and ascend with him in the Column of Praise to the lunar sphere and (then) to Primal Man and <al-Bahijah>,[485] the Mother of Life,[486] to where he was in the beginning in the Light-Paradises. That discarded body remains behind, and the sun, the moon, and the luminous deities strain out from it those species which are water, fire, and air. (The product of this filtration) ascends to the sun and becomes divine. The rest of the body, which is all Darkness, is cast down to Jahannam.'

'As for the person who is a soldier (struggling on behalf of Light) who accepted the religion (of Manichaeism) and (its) piety, providing service for these and the Elect[487]—when such a one is visited by death, those deities whom I mentioned arrive, and the satans are also present. He will appeal (to the former) for help, reminding (them) about how he labored for the sake of righteousness and served the religion and the Elect. Then they will rescue him from the satans, but he will

---

escorted by 'three angels').

483. The word employed (بكر) can be used of either a male or a female who has no sexual experience. Some scholars have called attention to the seemingly parallel Zoroastrian notion of meeting the *daēnā* or one's 'immaterial self' after death in the form of a beautiful maiden; see Flügel, *Mani*, 339–41; A. V. Williams Jackson, "A Sketch of the Manichaean Doctrine Concerning the Future Life," *JAOS* 50 (1930): 178; Werner Sundermann, "Zoroastrian Motifs in Non-Zoroastrian Traditions," *JRAS* series 3, 18, 2 (2008): 160–62. A Sogdian Manichaean fragment (see W. B. Henning, "Sogdian Tales," *BSOAS* 11 [1943–46]: 476–77) would seem to indicate that the 'virginal youth' is female, but this may reflect a subsequent stage of conceptual assimilation to Iranian traditions.

484. Compare the recently published Coptic prayer from Kellis which refers to the post-mortem advent of 'the image of my counterpart ... with her three angels' and gifts of 'the garment and the crown and the palm and the victory' (*T. Kell. Copt.* 2, Text A5; see Iain Gardner, ed., *Kellis Literary Texts: Volume 1* [Dakhleh Oasis Project Monograph No. 4; Oxford: Oxbow Books, 1996], 15, 25–30; Gardner-Lieu, *Manichaean Texts*, 257–58); also Skjærvø, "Iranian Elements," 276.

485. Such a restoration would seem certain based on a slight emendation of Flügel's Ms. L. This would seem preferable to the labored efforts to extract sense from a nonsensical 'Nahnahah,' as in Jackson, *Researches*, 328–31.

486. These deities are located in the solar sphere. The stages of the itinerary thus match those of the journey undertaken by the elements of Light reclaimed by the Elect during their dietary regimen while on earth.

487. I.e., an auditor.

not cease being part of the world: (he will be) like a person who sees terrible things while they sleep, and he will remain immersed in the mire and clay. He will not cease being like this until his light and spirit are rescued and he obtains membership among the Elect. He will wear their garment after a lengthy period of births and deaths (lit. 'comings and goings').'[488]

'As for[489] the sinful person who is possessed by desire and lust—when death visits, the satans come to him, seize him, beat him, and show him frightening things. Those (other) deities are present with that garment, and the sinful person will think that they have come to rescue him. However, they are present to condemn him, to remind him of his deeds, and to secure the evidence that he rejected giving assistance to the Elect. Therefore he will not cease birth and death in torment in the world until the time of retribution, and he will be thrown into Jahannam.'

Mānī said: 'These are three paths apportioned for the souls of humans. One of them leads to the Light-Paradises, and they (who travel on it) are the Elect.[490] The second leads (back) to the world and (its) terrors, and they (who travel on it) observe the religion and provide assistance to the Elect. The third leads to Jahannam (i.e., Hell), and they (who travel on it) are the wicked people.'[491]

What the condition of the hereafter will be after the passing away of the world, (and) the condition of Paradise and Hellfire:

He (i.e., Mānī) said: 'Then Primal Man will come from the world of Capricorn, al-Bashīr (will come) from the east, the Great Builder[492] (will come) from the south, and the Living Spirit (will come) from the world of the west. They will observe the large structure which is the new Paradise, (and) circumambulating that Hellfire, they will look within it. Then the Elect will come from the (Light)-Paradises

---

488. A reference to the transmigration of souls. The Auditor will eventually win rebirth as an Elect and then, after death, release from material existence. For the crucial role of metempsychosis in Manichaean thought, see Puech, *Le manichéisme*, 86, 179 n.360.

489. Read with Flügel's Mss. L and V.

490. Compare the language used in *CMC* 67.7–11 (ed. Koenen-Römer, 46), which is a Greek quotation from Mani's *Gospel*: 'I have chosen the Elect and I have shown a path (ἀτραπόν) to the height to those who ascend according to this truth.' Translation cited from BeDuhn, *The Manichaean Body*, 26.

491. A tripartite division of retribution for Elect, Auditors, and 'sinners' is also signaled by Coptic *Keph.* 15.15–19. Translations of and extensive religio-historical parallels to Ibn al-Nadīm's report up to this point are offered by R[ichard]. Reitzenstein, *Das iranische Erlösungsmysterium: Religionsgeschichtliche Untersuchungen* (Bonn a. Rh.: A. Marcus and E. Weber's Verlag, 1921), 28–42; Carsten Colpe, *Die religionsgeschichtliche Schule: Darstellung und Kritik ihres Bildes vom gnostischen Erlösermythus* (FRLANT 78, n.f. 60; Göttingen: Vandenhoeck and Ruprecht, 1961), 100–17.

492. A deity corresponding to the 'Great Ban' (ܒܢ ܪܒܐ) of Theodore bar Konai, *Scholion* (ed. Scher), 2:314.16; 316.10. See Reeves, "Citations from Ephrem," 286 n.116. Ephrem Syrus (d. 373) refers to this same deity as 'Ban the Builder' (ܒܢ ܒܢܝܐ).

to this Light (i.e., the new Paradise), and they will sit within it; afterwards, they will hasten to the assembled deities and stand around that Hellfire. Then they will watch the sinful evildoers turn over, shift back and forth, and sink deeper into that Hellfire.[493] That Hellfire cannot injure the Elect, and if those sinners catch sight of the Elect, they will implore them and petition them (for relief). But they will not respond to them in any way: nothing would be of use to them from (the Elect's) censure.[494] So the remorse, distress, and sorrow of the sinners will be compounded, and this will be their mode (lit. 'form') for eternity.'[495]

'Abd al-Jabbār, *Mughnī* (ed. Ḥusayn):[496]

... similarly this activity (i.e., the refining of Light from material existence) will not cease until only a small amount of congealed Light is left (which) the sun and moon are unable to purify. At that time the angel will lift up the earths, and the other angel will stop stretching the heavens, and that which is uppermost will be lowered onto that which is lowest. A fire will heat up and burn these things until what Light remains in them is set free.[497] This burning will last for 1,468 years.[498]

When the Spirit of Darkness[499] perceives the redemption of the Light, she will be furious and will strive to fight back. But those hosts who surround her will restrain her, and in fright she will retreat into a tomb previously made ready for her.[500] Then it (i.e., Light) will close the opening of this tomb with a rock the same

493. Compare M 470, a passage from Mani's *Shābuhragān* (see MacKenzie, "Mani's *Šābuhragān*," 517) as well as a Middle Persian fragment published by Henning, "Book of the Giants," 68.

494. By contrast, the *Shābuhragān* does feature a verbal rebuke of the imploring sinners by the Elect. See MacKenzie, "Mani's *Šābuhragān*," 519.

495. See also Flügel, *Mani*, 100-102; Kessler, *Mani*, 398–401; Dodge, *Fihrist*, 2:795–97.

496. 'Abd al-Jabbār, *Mughnī* (ed. Ḥusayn), 5:13.19–14.7.

497. Compare *Acta Archelai* 13.1 (ed. Beeson, 21): τότε ὁ Ὠμοφόρος ἀφίησιν ἔξω τὴν γῆν καὶ οὕτως ἀπολύεται τὸ μέγα πῦρ καὶ ὅλον ἀναλίσκει τὸν κόσμον 'then the Omophoros (i.e., Atlas, the bearer of the earth) will release the earth, and then the Great Fire is released and consumes the entire cosmos.'

498. See Coptic *Keph.* 75.20–23; Mani's *Shābuhragān* (in MacKenzie, "Mani's *Šābuhragān*," 516-17; also Boyce, *Reader*, 80); and the other testimonia cited in this section. Further references are supplied by H. J. Polotsky, "Manichäismus," *PW* 6:261–62. The number 1468 has been plausibly explained as one complete Sothis period (1461 years) plus an extra 'week' of years. See C. J. Ogden, "The 1468 Years of the World-Conflagration in Manichaeism," in *Dr. Modi Memorial Volume: Papers on Indo-Iranian and Other Subjects* (Bombay: Fort Printing Press, 1930), 102–105; Stroumsa, "Aspects de l'eschatologie manichéenne," 167 n.20; Ludwig Koenen, "Manichaean Apocalypticism at the Crossroads of Iranian, Egyptian, Jewish and Christian Thought," in *Codex Manichaicus Coloniensis: Atti del Simposio Internazionale (Rende-Amantea 3–7 settembre 1984)* (ed. Luigi Cirillo and Amneris Roselli; Cosenza: Marra Editore, 1986), 321.

499. Sometimes given the proper name Hummāma.

500. This 'tomb' or 'grave' was constructed by a deity variously referred to as 'Ban,' the

size as this world, and those numerous hosts will fill up the place of the present world until it is made equivalent to the Land of the World of Light.[501] Light will be relieved at that time from Darkness.[502]

Ibn al-Malāḥimī, *K. al-mu'tamad* (ed. McDermott and Madelung):[503]

Then the angel who is bearing the earths will lift up and the other angel will stop stretching the heavens, and that which is highest will sink down onto that which is lowest. A fire will flare up (and) burn these things, and it will continue burning until what remains in them from the Light is set free. This conflagration will last for 1,468 years. According to what is reported about them, some (of them) teach (the duration of the conflagration) is 1,460 years.

After the Light is set free and when Hummāma, the Spirit of Darkness—Death—sees (this) and those (redeeming) angels and forces, she will become enraged and bristle and ready herself for battle. But those forces who surround her will restrain her, and in fright she will fearfully retreat into a tomb previously made ready for her. Then this tomb will be plugged with a rock which is the same size as this world, and those luminous forces will remain outside the place of this world until it is made equivalent to the Land of the World of Light, and Light at that time will be relieved from Darkness. This according to them is the Resurrection.

Shahrastānī, *Kitāb al-milal wa'l-niḥal* (ed. Badrān):[504]

It will not cease (from) doing this until there is not left any portion of the particles of Light in this world (i.e., the created world) except for (what remains in) a small amount of congealed matter that the sun and moon are unable to purify. At that time, the angel who bears the earth will lift up, and the angel who spreads out the heavens will stop doing so, and that which is uppermost will collapse upon that which is lowest. Then a fire will burn until the uppermost and the lowest are set ablaze, and it will remain burning until that which is in it (the congealed matter) from the Light is set free.

The duration of the burning will be 1,468 years.

... Abū Sa'īd the Manichaean,[505] one of their leaders, maintained that (the time) which had elapsed from the period of mixture up to his own lifetime—which

'Great Ban,' or 'Ban the Builder.'

501. For the 'tomb' and the 'filling up' of earth, see Coptic *Homil.* 41.5–15; M 2 lines 120–48, as published by Andreas-Henning, "Mitteliranische Manichaica III," 853. The latter text is rendered into English by Jes P. Asmussen, *Manichaean Literature: Representative Texts Chiefly from Middle Persian and Parthian Writings* (Delmar, NY: Scholars' Facsimiles & Reprints, 1975), 136–37.

502. See also Vajda, "Le témoignage d'al-Māturidī: Note annexe," 120; Monnot, *Penseurs*, 160–61.

503. *Kitāb al-mu'tamad fī uṣūl al-dīn* (ed. McDermott and Madelung), 565.10–19.

504. Shahrastānī, *Kitāb al-milal wa'l-niḥal* (ed. Badrān), 1:628.3–9; 630.6–13; Taqīzādeh-Šīrāzī, *Mānī va dīn-e-ū*, 243–44 (§45).

505. Flügel, *Mani*, 408 n.429; Vajda, "Les zindîqs," 191.

was year AH 271[506]—was 11,700 years, and that (the time) which remained until the period of purification was 300 years. According to his teaching, the period of mixture would last 12,000 years.[507] There continues to remain of this period in our own time—which is 521 AH[508]—50 years. Hence we (should perceive) the end of the mixture and the beginning of the (final) purification, for in fifty years the complete liberation and the dissolution of the components (of the universe takes place).

Shahrazūrī, *Šarḥ ḥikmat al-ishrāq* (ed. Corbin):[509]

The sage (*sic*!) Mānī[510] has indicated something similar to this when he said: 'When the Ruler of Light beheld the mixing of the Light, he commanded some of his angels to create this world in order to separate that which belongs to Light from that which belongs to Darkness. Hence the sun and moon and stars move in order to purify the portions of Light of those of Darkness: the sun cleanses the Light which was mixed with the satans of heat, and the moon (cleanses) what was mixed with the satans of cold. Initially all of the portions of Light were located above and the portions of Darkness were located below. Engaging in praise, sanctification, proper speech, and pious deeds were required (of Manichaeans) for the purification and ascension of the portions of Light. By this (activity) the luminous portions rise up in a Column of Radiance to the lunar sphere, which receives this Light from the first of the month until its midpoint when it forms a full moon. Then it is conveyed to the sun until the end of the month. The sun propels <it> to the Light that is above it, and it circulates in this world until it rejoins the uppermost, pure Light. It will not cease (from) doing this until there is not left any portion of the particles of Light in this world (i.e., the created world) except for (what remains in) a small amount of congealed matter that the sun and moon are unable to purify. At that time, the angel who bears the earth will lift up, and the angel who bears the heavens (will cease doing so), and that which is uppermost will collapse upon that which is below. Then a fire will burn, and the uppermost will be set ablaze upon the lowest, and it will set free what remains from the Light in it. The duration of the burning will be 1,468 years.'[511]

506. I.e., 884/5 CE.

507. Eastern Manichaeans, influenced by Indian chronology, seem to have added an extra century to each millennium in order to 'postpone' the eschaton. See G. Haloun and W. B. Henning, "The Compendium of the Doctrines and Styles of the Teaching of Mani, the Buddha of Light," *Asia Major* 3 (1953): 201–204.

508. I.e., 1127 CE.

509. Corbin, *Œuvres*, 233 (text); Taqīzādeh-Šīrāzī, *Mānī va dīn-e-ū*, 253–54 (§48). See also Corbin, *Œuvres*, 52, 64–71; idem, *Spiritual Body and Celestial Earth: From Mazdean Iran to Shī'ite Iran* (trans. Nancy Pearson; Bollingen Series 91:2; Princeton, NJ: Princeton University Press, 1977), 120–23; Bausani, *Religion in Iran*, 199–200.

510. The same epithet is used in Shahrastānī, *Kitāb al-milal wa'l-niḥal* (ed. Badrān), 1:628.10.

511. Compare Shahrastānī, *Kitāb al-milal wa'l-niḥal* (ed. Badrān), 1:626.9–628.9.

Ibn al-Murtaḍā, *K. al-munya* (ed. Taqīzādeh-Šīrāzī):[512]

... and (the Realm of Light) will not cease conducting its search until there remains only a small congealed portion (of Light) which is unable to be searched out. At that time the angel who is responsible for the earth will lift up, and the angel who is responsible for heaven will stop (supporting it), and that which is uppermost will collapse[513] onto that which is lowest. A fire will flare up in this lower region and will not cease burning until some of the portions of Light which are in the World of Darkness which are bound among the portions of Darkness have been set free.

They disagree over how long the burning lasts. It is said to be (by one tradition) 1,468 years, but it is also said to be (by another) 1,460 years.

When Darkness perceives the redemption of the Light, she will strive to fight back. But some of the hosts who surround her will restrain her, and in fright she will retreat into a tomb previously made ready for her. Then it (i.e., Light) will close the opening of this tomb with a rock, and it will be delivered from the corruption effected by Darkness.

Here they again disagree. Some of them maintain that when Light is redeemed from Darkness, it will construct a barrier between the two of them composed of Light and Darkness so that it (Darkness) may not return and molest it (Light). But some of them maintain that absolutely no amount of Light will remain (bound) within it.[514]

6. Some Concluding Observations

Close scrutiny of the various Islamicate testimonies about the teachings and practices of the Manichaeans underscores a perception of their overwhelming dependence upon what appears to be a limited, closely circumscribed amount of information that was repeatedly copied and sometimes editorially manipulated by successive generations of scholars and heresiographers. As has been most recently emphasized by François de Blois,[515] much of the Arabic language information about Mani and his religious system ultimately derives from the descriptive reports that were authored about non-Muslim religions by the mid-ninth century Muʿtazilī theologian Abū ʿĪsā al-Warrāq. Despite some later accusations which attribute this author's impressive knowledge about dualist religious speculations to his own affiliation with— or at least intellectual sympathy with—one of these

512. Taqīzādeh-Šīrāzī, *Mānī va dīn-e-ū*, 301 (§74); a variant text in Kessler, *Mani*, 348–49.

513. Read with the emendation suggested by Taqīzādeh-Šīrāzī, and cf. ʿAbd al-Jabbār above.

514. See also Kessler, *Mani*, 353–54.

515. François de Blois, "New Light on the Sources of the Manichaean Chapter in the *Fihrist*," in *Il Manicheismo, nuove prospettive della richerca: Dipartimento di Studi Asiatici Università degli Studi di Napoli "L'Orientale," Napoli, 2–8 Settembre 2001* (ed. Aloïs van Tongerloo and Luigi Cirillo; Turnhout: Brepols, 2005), 37–45.

schools of thought, it remains highly unlikely that he was actually guilty of these charges. This slur, which was perhaps the product of a scholastic rivalry or jealousy, is arguably nothing more than a sensationalist rumor floating a plausible explanation for why an intellectually talented member of the Muslim learned class would be *au courant* with such arcane topics.[516]

Yet if Muslim tradents were so dependent upon this literary testimonia for their expositions of the Manichaean system, it then seems legitimate to ask whether Manichaeism remained a viable and distinctive religious entity within the Islamicate cultural sphere after the time of Abū 'Īsā al-Warrāq, whose *floruit* is usually set in the middle of the ninth century. As we will see in the next chapter, individuals who were accused of *zandaqa* or Manichaeism became subject to brutal state-sponsored persecution during the initial decades of 'Abbāsid rule. This new policy of violent repression finds few parallels within the Islamicate realm in the preceding Umayyad period. It perhaps should be connected with the central government's military responses to a sequential series of so-called 'Irano-gnostic' or 'neo-Mazdakite' rebellions taking place in the northern and eastern fringes of the empire over approximately the first century of 'Abbāsid hegemony. These revolutionary movements were religiously tinged, combining messages of social reform and regime change with intriguing amalgams of prophetological and eschatological lore which infused Abrahamic scripturally based teachings with traditions and practices deriving from Zoroastrianism and other dualist sources, including Manichaeism.[517]

Reaction to the new climate of suspicion and suppression took a limited variety of forms. Some acquiesced to the charges leveled against them and dutifully accepted martyrdom at the hands of the state. Presumably a number of falsely accused individuals also fell afoul of this same fate, despite their best efforts to clear their names. Others acknowledged their guilt and formally repented of their 'error,' reportedly escaping execution by this tactic.[518] It remains however impossible to determine the number of such 'apostates' who were permitted to survive, or how many after their reprieve remained committed to their reintegration within the dominant religion. Physical flight from persecution was undoubtedly the most successful means of preserving life, scriptures, and institutional integrity. As we shall soon see, it was at the eastern frontiers of the empire and points beyond that Manichaeism survived and continued to function as a

516. Abū 'Īsā al-Warrāq was also the teacher of the notorious heretic Ibn al-Rāwandī, an association which did nothing to refute his alleged affiliation with *zandaqa* or to rehabilitate his reputation. See Stroumsa and Stroumsa, "Aspects of Anti-Manichaean Polemics," 53; also the testimony of al-Māturīdī above.

517. The most comprehensive study of these movements remains that of Gholam Hossein Sadighi, *Les mouvements religieux iraniens au IIe et au IIIe siècle de l'hégire* (Paris: Les Presses Modernes, 1938). An important recent study is Patricia Crone, "Zoroastrian Communism," *Comparative Studies of Society and History* 36 (1994): 447–62.

518. See the descriptions of the persecution of Manichaeans carried out by the caliph al-Mahdī which are excerpted in the following chapter.

recognizable religious entity after the ninth century. Whatever shadowy existence it may have maintained among the intelligentsia in the central provinces of the empire would remain understandably covert and largely indistinguishable from its cloaking Islamic veils.

— 5 —

'Historical' Testimonia about Manichaeism and Manichaeans

This chapter assembles and catalogs a number of testimonia which bear witness to the contestable vitality of Manichaeism as a religious identity in the Islamicate world. These comprise reports about the fate of its formal institutions in its Mesopotamian homeland and beyond, notices regarding official actions taken by governmental officials against suspected and self-confessed adherents, anecdotes featuring alleged (and actual) Manichaean agents and sympathizers, and accounts relating to the emergence of social fissures within the Manichaean community. Also included in this chapter is a series of reports discussing the infamous sixth-century Zoroastrian agitator Mazdak, an intriguing figure whom a number of ancient tradents and several modern scholars consider (probably erroneously) to be a 'neo-Manichaean' schismatic.

1. Post-Mani Historical Developments

Chronicon ad annum Christi 1234 (ed. Chabot):[1]

Aurelius (Aurelian?) ruled over Rome ten years. During his time Paul of Samosata[2] created a schism in the true faith, and so a synod met in Antioch and expelled him from the Church. Domnus replaced him as the seventeenth bishop.[3] The leader of the synod was Gregory Thaumaturgus[4] who had studied during his youth with Origen. At that same synod they anathematized Mānī the wicked.

1. J.-B. Chabot, ed., *Anonymi auctoris Chronicon ad annum Christi 1234 pertinens* (CSCO 81–82; 2 vols.; Paris: Reipublicae, 1916–20), 1:136.28–137.5.
2. Bishop at Antioch, 260–272 CE. See Henry Chadwick, *The Early Church* (Baltimore: Penguin Books, 1967), 114–15; Ian Gillman and Hans-Joachim Klimkeit, *Christians in Asia before 1500* (Ann Arbor: The University of Michigan Press, 1999), 37–38.
3. The proceedings are described in great deal in Eusebius, *Historia ecclesiastica* 7.27.1–30.19.
4. Literally 'Gregory the miracle-worker' (ܥܒܕ ܬܕܡܪܬܐ). Regarding this figure, see especially Raymond Van Dam, "Hagiography and History: The Life of Gregory Thaumaturgus," *Classical Antiquity* 1 (1982): 272–308.

Jāḥiẓ, *Kitāb al-ḥayawān* (ed. Taqīzādeh-Šīrāzī):[5]

One time Ibrāhīm b. al-Sindī[6] said: 'I wish the *zanādiqa* were not so eager to pay high prices for choice white paper and for the best shiny glossy black ink and for the accomplishments of calligraphy and the interests of the calligrapher. For I have never seen paper like the paper of their books or calligraphy like the calligraphy that is in them.[7] And while I am very fond of great wealth and together with my love for wealth hate to suffer (its) loss, I myself would liberally spend a large amount of money for books to prove (my) veneration of knowledge. Veneration of knowledge furnishes evidence for the nobility of one's soul and for (its) security against intoxicating impulses.'

I said to Ibrāhīm: 'Actually the *zanādiqa* expenditure on the production of (their) books is like the Christians' expenditure on (their) churches. Now if the books of the *zanādiqa* were books of legal opinions or of philosophy or of logic or customs or exposition and demonstration; or if their books were books which gave people knowledge about the different types of crafts or ways of earning a living and engaging in business; or books which were useful and practical; or something which would give people access to intelligent discourse and belles-lettres—even if these works do not increase wealth or avoid error—it would be possible to think they were among those who venerate information and who desire its exposition. But instead they contain within them religious doctrine and the exaltation of the ways of (their) faith! Their expenditure therefore is like the expenditure of the Zoroastrians on their fire temples or the expenditure of the Christians on golden crosses or the expenditure of the Indians on the shrine custodians for Buddha.'[8]

---

5. S. H. Taqīzādeh and A. A. Šīrāzī, *Mānī va dīn-e-ū* (Teheran: Ānjuman-e Irānshināsī, AH 1335/1956), 84–85 (§4). See also Konrad Kessler, *Mani: Forschungen über die manichäische Religion* (Berlin: Georg Reimer, 1889), 366–67; Alfred von Kremer, *Culturgeschichtliche Streifzüge auf dem Gebiete des Islams* (Leipzig: F. A. Brockhaus, 1873), 71.

6. An influential friend of Jāḥiẓ. See, e.g., the anecdote recounted in Charles Pellat, *The Life and Works of Jāḥiẓ: Translations of Selected Texts* (trans. D. M. Hawke; Berkeley: University of California Press, 1969), 168–70; also idem, "Ibrāhīm b. al-Sindī b. Sh̲āhak," *EI*[2] 3:990.

7. Note also Samuel N. C. Lieu, *Manichaeism in the Later Roman Empire and Medieval China* (2nd ed.; WUNT 63; Tübingen: J. C. B. Mohr, 1992), 176.

8. For more renditions, see Kessler, *Mani*, 366; von Kremer, *Streifzüge*, 36–37; Carl Schmidt and H. J. Polotsky, *Ein Mani-Fund in Ägypten: Originalschriften des Mani und seiner Schüler* (Berlin: Verlag der Akademie der Wissenschaften, 1933), 43; Thomas W. Arnold, "The Origins," in *A Survey of Persian Art From Prehistoric Times to the Present* (ed. Arthur Upham Pope and Phyllis Ackerman; 15 vols.; Oxford: Oxford University Press, 1964–65), 5:1817–1818; Geo Widengren, *Mani and Manichaeism* (trans. Charles Kessler; New York: Holt, Rinehart and Winston, 1965), 111; Jâhiz, *Le cadi et la mouche: Anthologie du Livre des Animaux* (ed. Lakhdar Souami; Paris: Sindbad, 1988), 140–41; Charles Pellat, "Le témoignage d'al-Jāḥiẓ sur les Manichéens," in *Essays in Honor of Bernard Lewis: The Islamic World, From Classical to Modern Times* (ed. C. E. Bosworth, et al.; Princeton, NJ: Darwin Press, 1989), 274–75.

Jāḥiẓ, *Kitāb al-radd ʻalā al-naṣārā* (ed. Taqīzādeh-Šīrāzī):[9]

Moreover, if it were not for Christian theologians as well as their physicians and their astrologers, not a thing from the writings (*kutub*) of the Manichaeans, Dayṣāniyya, Marcionites, or the Falāniyya (?) would have reached our own wealthy, clever, demented, and sociable circles. They would know nothing more than the Book of God Most Exalted and the *sunna* of His Prophet (may God bless and protect him!), and those writings would have remained concealed among those groups, passing into the possession of their heirs.[10]

Abū Yaʻqūb al-Sijistānī, *Ithbāt al-nubū'āt* (ed. Tāmir):[11]

The general populace of the land of China and Māčīn[12] follow the doctrine of Mānī. They employ his religious precepts (*sharīʻa*) and study his books, and they seek the favor of God Most Exalted through the religion (*dīn*) which he established among them.[13]

Ibn al-Nadīm, *Fihrist* (ed. Flügel):[14]

A section from a history of the Manichaeans, their migration through countries, and reports about their leaders:

Apart from the Sumaniyya (i.e., the Buddhists),[15] the first of the religions to enter the region which is beyond the river[16] (i.e., Transoxania) were the Manichaeans. The reason for this was that after the Persian king[17] had put Mānī to

9. Taqīzādeh-Šīrāzī, *Mānī va dīn-e-ū*, 99–100 (§8).

10. For other renderings, see Joshua Finkel, "A Risāla of al-Jāḥiẓ," *JAOS* 47 (1927): 331; *Sobriety and Mirth: A Selection of the Shorter Writings of al-Jāhiz* (trans. Jim Colville; London: Kegan Paul, 2002), 78.

11. Abū Yaʻqūb al-Sijistānī, *Kitāb ithbāt al-nubū'āt* (ed. ʻĀrif Tāmir; Beirut: al-Maṭbaʻah al-Kāthūlīkīyah, 1966), 83.2–3.

12. Emending the printed text's meaningless 'Mānīn.' For the cogency of Māčīn (also Mājīn) in this context, see especially C. E. Bosworth, "al-Ṣīn," *EI*[2] 9:616–17.

13. See also W[ladimir]. Ivanow, *Ibn al-Qaddah (The Alleged Founder of Ismailism)* (2nd rev. ed.; Bombay: Ismaili Society, 1957), 78; S. M. Stern, "Abū Ḥātim al-Rāzī on Persian Religion," in idem, *Studies in Early Ismāʻīlism* (Jerusalem: The Magnes Press, 1983), 35.

14. Gustav Flügel, *Mani: Seine Lehre und seine Schriften* (Leipzig, 1862; repr., Osnabrück: Biblio Verlag, 1969), 76.7–77.14; Ibn al-Nadīm, *Kitāb al-Fihrist* (ed. Riḍa Tajaddud; [Tehran: Maktabat al-Assadī, 1971]), 400–401; Taqīzādeh-Šīrāzī, *Mānī va dīn-e-ū*, 162–63 (§27).

15. See the sources cited by Flügel, *Mani*, 385-86; also Daniel Gimaret, "Bouddha et les bouddhistes dans la tradition musulmane," *Journal asiatique* 257 (1969): 273-316; Guy Monnot, "Sumaniyya," *EI*[2] 9:869–70.

16. The river which is meant is the Oxus in central Asia. See W. Barthold and C. E. Bosworth, "Mā Warā' al-Nahr," *EI*[2] 5:852–59.

17. Literally 'Kisrā' (= Khusrau or Khusrō), a proper name which like 'Caesar' in the West becomes a generic title for the Persian king.

death, suspended his corpse,[18] and prohibited the citizens of his realm from engaging in disputes about religion, he began killing the followers of Mānī in every place where he could find them. Therefore they did not cease fleeing from him until they had crossed the river at Balkh[19] and entered the kingdom of the *khān*, and they remained with him. In their language *khān* is the name with which they designate a ruler of the Turkish peoples.

So the Manichaeans lived in Transoxania until Persian authority dissipated and Arab sovereignty strengthened. Then they returned to this country, particularly at the time of the disturbances in Persia[20] and during the time of the Umayyad rulers. Khālid b. ʻAbd Allāh al-Qasrī protected them,[21] but the leadership did not convene in these locales except for in Bābil (i.e., Babylon).[22] Afterwards the leader would depart (Babylon) to (take refuge in) any region where he felt safe.

The last time when they were visible was during the reign of al-Muqtadir (908–932 CE), when they kept close to Khurāsān. Out of fear for their lives, those of them who were left concealed their affairs and roamed about in this region. (Eventually) around five hundred of their members gathered together in Samarkand.[23] When their business became public, the governor of Khurāsān sought[24] to put them to death. Then the king of China—I think it was (actually) the lord of the Toghuzghuz[25]—sent a message to him saying: 'In my country there are many more Muslims than there are people of my religion in your country,' and

18. Literally 'crucified him.'

19. I.e., the river Oxus, also referred to as the Āmū Daryā or Jayḥūn (= biblical Gihon [Gen 2:13]).

20. I.e., as the Persian Empire was breaking up due to the Muslim invasions.

21. Governor of ʻĪrāq (724–737 CE) during most of the caliphate of Hishām (724–743 CE). Sources accuse Khālid of showing favoritism to Zoroastrians and Christians; see Flügel, *Mani*, 321–22; Israel Friedlaender, "The Heterodoxies of the Shiites in the Presentation of Ibn Ḥazm," *JAOS* 29 (1908): 86–87; G. R. Hawting, "Khālid b. ʻAbd Allāh al-Ḳasrī," *EI*² 4:925–27; Said Amir Arjomand, "ʻAbd Allah Ibn al-Muqaffaʻ and the ʻAbbasid Revolution," *Iranian Studies* 27 (1994): 13–14. Ibn al-Nadīm also includes him in his list of officials who were suspected of harboring Manichaean sympathies (see below). Regarding the veracity of this charge, see especially Melhem Chokr, *Zandaqa et zindiqs en Islam au second siècle de l'hégire* (Damas: Institut français de Damas, 1993), 69–71.

22. Presumably Madā'in/Ktesiphon is the urban locale meant. See Josef van Ess, *Theologie und Gesellschaft im 2. und 3. Jahrhundert Hidschra: Eine Geschichte des religiösen Denkens im frühen Islam* (6 vols.; Berlin and New York: Walter de Gruyter, 1991–97), 1:419.

23. For a continuing presence of Manichaeans in Samarkand, see Bīrūnī below. Note also the remarks of Ulrich Rudolph, *Al-Māturīdī und die sunnitische Theologie in Samarkand* (Leiden: E. J. Brill, 1997), 183–84, 188–89, 193–97.

24. Read with Flügel's Ms. V.

25. I.e., the Uighur kingdom in central Asia which adopted Manichaeism as its state religion in 762 CE. See François de Blois, *Burzōy's Voyage to India and the Origin of the Book of Kalīlah wa Dimnah* (London: Royal Asiatic Society, 1990), 28 n.2; P. B. Golden, "To<u>gh</u>uz<u>gh</u>uz," *EI*² 10:555–57.

he swore to him that if he should kill a single one of them, he would kill the whole community (of Muslims) who were with him. (He also promised) he would demolish the mosques and leave among the remaining lands lookouts against the Muslims in order to (identify and) kill them. So the governor of Khurāsān refrained from harming them, and he accepted the *jizya* from them.

Now they (i.e., Manichaeans) have become few in Muslim areas. During the time of Mu'izz al-Dawlah,[26] I knew about three hundred of them in the 'City of Peace' (i.e., Baghdad), but now[27] there are not five of them present among us (in the capital). Those people whom they term *'ajārā*[28] live in the rural districts of Samarkand, Sogdia, and especially Nawīkath.[29]

Ibn al-Nadīm, *Fihrist* (ed. Tajaddud):[30]

A discussion about the script of Sogdia:

A trustworthy source said: 'I came to the land of Sogdia, and it is the region which is beyond the river.[31] Sogdia is called Upper Iran, and the Turks dwell there. Its main city is named Qara-<kent> (?).'[32] He also said: 'Its people are dualists and Christians, and they term dualists *aḥārkaf* in their language.'[33]

***Kitāb Ḥudūd al-'ālam* (ed. Taqīzādeh-Šīrāzī):**[34]

And in it (i.e., the city of Samarkand) is the monastery of the Manichaeans, and

---

26. The first Būyid ruler in Baghdad. He reigned from 945 to 967.

27. 987–88 CE.

28. See the analogous 'local' reference to *aḥārkaf* in the following testimony and the observations of François de Blois, "Glossary of Technical Terms and Uncommon Expressions in Arabic (and in Muslim New Persian) Texts Relating to Manichaeism," in *Dictionary of Manichaean Texts, Vol. II: Texts from Iraq and Iran (Texts in Syriac, Arabic, Persian and Zoroastrian Middle Persian)* (ed. François de Blois and Nicholas Sims-Williams; Turnhout: Brepols, 2006), 26–27. Note also Antonino Forte, "Deux études sur le manichéisme chinois," *T'oung Pao* 59 (1973): 231–32.

29. On this locale, see especially the remarks of de Blois, "Glossary," 82–83. For other translations of this passage, see Flügel, *Mani*, 105–106; Edward G. Browne, *A Literary History of Persia* (4 vols.; London and Cambridge, 1902–24; repr., Cambridge: The University Press, 1964), 1:163–64; Georges Vajda, "Les zindîqs en pays d'Islam au debut de la période abbaside," *RSO* 17 (1937–38): 178–79; Bayard Dodge, *The Fihrist of al-Nadīm: A Tenth-Century Survey of Muslim Culture* (2 vols.; New York: Columbia University Press, 1970), 2:801–803.

30. Ibn al-Nadīm, *K. al-Fihrist* (ed. Tajaddud), 20.

31. I.e., Transoxania, or the region beyond the Oxus river. See the immediately preceding testimony.

32. Tajaddud's text follows Flügel's which has قرنكث. Turkic for 'strong town'? Perhaps a corruption of Samarkand or Bukhārā? See de Blois, "Glossary," 82–83.

33. See also Dodge, *Fihrist*, 1:33.

34. Taqīzādeh-Šīrāzī, *Mānī va dīn-e-ū*, 481 (§172).

they are called *nighūshāk* (i.e., Hearers).[35]

Bīrūnī, *Āthār al-bāqiya 'an-il-qurūn al-khāliya* (ed. Sachau):[36]

There are still remnants of those who are obedient to it[37] (and) who belong to it dispersed among a number of lands. They are almost never found assembled together in a single locality in Muslim countries, except for the sect which is in Samarkand[38] that is known as 'the Ṣābians.'[39] As for outside the Muslim world, most of the Turks in the east, the people of China and Tibet, and some of those who live in India belong to his religion and his doctrine.[40]

Sam'ānī, *Kitāb al-ānsāb* (ed. Taqīzādeh-Šīrāzī):[41]

People who were his (i.e., Mani's) followers remained in areas of China and among the Turks and regions of 'Irāq and areas of Kirmān until the time of Hārūn al-Rashīd (786-809 CE). He placed his book known as the *Zand* on trial and condemned it to be burnt, and <he confiscated>[42] a *qalansūwa*-relic[43] that was in the possession

35. New Persian نغوشاك is equivalent to Middle Persian *nywš'g* 'Manichaean Hearer, Auditor.' Note Bertold Spuler, *Iran in früh-islamischer Zeit: Politik, Kultur, Verwaltung und öffentliches Leben zwischen der arabischen und der seldschukischen Eroberung, 633 bis 1055* (Wiesbaden: Franz Steiner Verlag, 1952), 207–208; Mary Boyce, *A Word-List of Manichaean Middle Persian and Parthian* (Acta Iranica 9a; Leiden: Brill, 1977), 65; also W. Barthold and C. E. Bosworth, "Mā Warā' al-Nahr," *EI²* 5:853; François C. de Blois, "The 'Sabians' (Ṣābi'ūn) in Pre-Islamic Arabia," *Acta Orientalia (Copenhagen)* 56 (1995): 52–53. For other translations of this passage, see V. Minorsky, *Hudūd al-'Ālam = 'The Regions of the World': A Persian Geography, 372 A.H.–982 A.D.* (London: Luzac, 1937), 113; Lieu, *Manichaeism²*, 224 n.29.

36. C. E. Sachau, ed., *Kitāb al-āthār al-bāqiya 'ani'l-qurūn al-khāliya: Chronologie orientalischer Völker von Albêrûnî* (Leipzig, 1878; repr., Leipzig: Otto Harrassowitz, 1923), 209.1–3; Taqīzādeh-Šīrāzī, *Mānī va dīn-e-ū*, 206 (§34).

37. I.e., to the Manichaean religion.

38. Note the testimony of Ibn al-Nadīm above about a large group of Manichaeans in Samarkand, as well as the notice about a Manichaean 'monastery' in the *Ḥudūd al-'ālam*. See also Rudolph, *Al-Māturīdī*, 189.

39. Manichaeans are sometimes compared to 'Ṣābians' in Muslim theological writings, but this is the only instance where a local Manichaean community is named 'Ṣābian.' This label, presumably self-applied, exploits the contested qur'ānic designation (2:62; 5:69; 22:17) for a licit scriptural religion. See also Christopher Buck, "The Identity of the Ṣābi'ūn: An Historical Quest," *The Muslim World* 74 (1984): 176–77.

40. For other translations, see C. Edward Sachau, *The Chronology of Ancient Nations: An English Version of the Arabic Text of the Athâr-ul-bâkiya of Albîrûnî* (London: William H. Allen and Co., 1879), 191; Gotthard Strohmaier, *In den Gärten der Wissenschaft: Ausgewählte Texte aus den Werken des muslimischen Universalgelehrten* (2nd ed.; Leipzig: Reclam-Verlag, 1991), 142.

41. Taqīzādeh-Šīrāzī, *Mānī va dīn-e-ū*, 246 (§46).

42. Read اخذ in place of اخد ?

43. Arabic *qalansūwa* refers to a kind of cone-shaped cap or hat. See Hugh Kennedy, *The*

of his (Mani's) adherents and ordered its burning. They were suppressed.

Ibn al-Jawzī, *Muntaẓam* (ed. Taqīzādeh-Šīrāzī):[44]

At the midpoint of Ramaḍān[45] he (the caliph Muqtadir) incinerated beside the 'Āmmah Gate (in Baghdad)[46] an image of Mānī[47] and four sacks of books which promoted *zanādiqa*. There dripped out from it (the fire) a quantity of gold and silver from what had adorned the volumes.[48]

Ibn al-Āthīr, *Lulāb fī tahdhīb al-ānsāb* (ed. Taqīzādeh-Šīrāzī):[49]

Factions of his followers remained in areas populated by the Turks and China and regions of 'Irāq and Kirmān until the time of Hārūn al-Rashīd. He burned his book, and there was a hat (*qalansūwa*) with it which was a relic from Mānī that he also put to the flame. He carried out many executions among them and stamped out their tradition.

2. Martyrological Traditions

a. Bahrām II (276–293 CE)

Sa'īd ibn al-Biṭrīq (Eutychius), *Naẓm al-jawhar*:[50]

And after him (i.e., Bahrām I) Bahrām b. Bahrām[51] ruled Persia for seventeen years. It was during his reign that a Persian who called himself Mānī appeared, and he promulgated the religion of Manichaeism. He claimed that he was a prophet. Bahrām b. Bahrām, who was king of Persia, seized him and cut him into two pieces. He also took into custody some of his sect and those who were propounding his doctrine: (it was) about one hundred people. He planted their heads upside down in the soil until they died. He said, 'I have made a garden and have planted

---

Court of the Caliphs: The Rise and Fall of Islam's Greatest Dynasty (London: Weidenfeld and Nicholson, 2004), 140.

44. Taqīzādeh-Šīrāzī, *Mānī va dīn-e-ū*, 207 (§50).

45. In the year AH 311, which was 923 CE.

46. The 'Public Gate,' regarding which see G. Le Strange, *Baghdad During the Abbasid Caliphate* (2nd ed.; Oxford: Clarendon Press, 1924), 255–59, 274–76.

47. An image of Mani was customarily employed during the celebration of the annual Bema-festival; see the testimony of Abu'l Faraj al-Iṣfahānī, *Kitāb al-aghānī*, 6:131–32 below for another example of a Mani image.

48. Schmidt-Polotsky, *Ein Mani-Fund*, 43 n.1; Thomas W. Arnold, *Painting in Islam: A Study of the Place of Pictorial Art in Muslim Culture* (Oxford, 1928; repr., New York: Dover Publications, 1965), 61; Spuler, *Iran in früh-islamischer Zeit*, 208 n.6. Their reference to 'fourteen' sacks should be corrected to 'four.' See also Chokr, *Zandaqa*, 56.

49. Taqīzādeh-Šīrāzī, *Mānī va dīn-e-ū*, 265 (§56).

50. Taqīzādeh-Šīrāzī, *Mānī va dīn-e-ū*, 123 (§19). Cf. also Flügel, *Mani*, 330.

51. I.e., Bahrām II, who indeed ruled for seventeen years after Bahrām I.

it with people instead of trees!'[52] Followers of his religion and proponents of his doctrine are called 'Manichaeans,' (a term) derived from the name of Mānī.[53]

***Chronicon Seertensis* (ed. Scher):**[54]

When this man (Bahrām II) became king over Persia in the year 590 of the era of Alexander (i.e., the Seleucid era),[55] he treated the people well and the army was pleased with him. At the beginning of his reign he proceeded to Ahwāz and conducted an inquiry into the Christian faith, just as his grandfather Sābūr had done. He was aware of some of its views, for according to what Mīlās al-Rāzī says[56] he had been brought up in Karkh Juddān[57] and had learned a certain amount of the Syriac language. He summoned a group of priests (lit. 'fathers'), questioned them, and they explained the doctrines to him. He said to them: 'I see that you glorify this unique entity whom you acknowledge and greatly exalt, but you are mistaken in your prohibition of the worship of the divine gods!'[58]

Later he changed his mind about it (i.e., Christianity). Finding that the Manichaeans declared themselves to be Christian and (that) they wore their garments in the same way and (that they) detested marriage and sexual procreation just as the *catholicos* and bishops (did), he wrongly concluded that the two faiths were in fact the same. He had decreed that the Manichaeans were to be killed and their churches demolished.[59] The Zoroastrians now attacked Christians without making any (doctrinal) distinctions. He executed his wife Qandīdā the Roman,[60]

52. The same tradition is found in the *Kitāb al-sinkisār* or Jacobite Synaxarion, although there it is integrated into the biographical trajectory popularized by the *Acta Archelai* calumnies. See Taqīzādeh-Šīrāzī, *Mānī va dīn-e-ū*, 454 (§159) and Chapter Two above.

53. See also Barthélemy d'Herbelot, *Bibliothèque orientale, ou Dictionaire universel* (Paris: Compagnie des Libraires, 1697), 549; Flügel, *Mani*, 330–31; A. V. Williams Jackson, *Researches in Manichaeism* (New York, 1932; repr., New York: AMS Press, 1965), 160.

54. Addai Scher, "Histoire Nestorienne inédite (Chronique de Séert)," *Patrologia Orientalis* 4 (1908): 237–38; reprinted in Taqīzādeh-Šīrāzī, *Mānī va dīn-e-ū*, 383-84 (§118).

55. 276/77 CE.

56. Miles of Rayy, bishop of Susa, who suffered martyrdom under Shāpūr II in 340 CE. See Sozomen, *Historia ecclesiastica* 2.14 and the sources cited by M.-L. Chaumont, *La christianisation de l'empire iranien: Des origines aux grandes persecutions du IVe siècle* (CSCO 499, Subsidia 80; Louvain: E. Peeters, 1988), 104 n.22.

57. The location of this city remains unclear. Chaumont (*La christianisation*, 105) proposes the reading 'Karkh Lēdān' or 'Karkā d-Lēdān,' a town near Susa.

58. Cf. Chaumont, *La christianisation*, 103–104.

59. This persecution is reflected in the largely fragmentary account preserved in Coptic *Homil.* 76.11–83.20. For an English rendering, see Iain Gardner and Samuel N. C. Lieu, eds., *Manichaean Texts From the Roman Empire* (Cambridge: Cambridge University Press, 2004), 102–108; also Nils Arne Pedersen, *Manichaean Homilies* (CFM Series Coptica 2; Turnhout: Brepols, 2006), 76–83.

60. Text reads Qandīrā, based on a faulty reading of the ambiguous Syriac character *d/r*. See especially Sebastian Brock, "A Martyr at the Sasanid Court under Vahrān II:

who was a Christian believer, and (also) killed the blessed Qārībā, son of Ḥananyā. The Zoroastrians inflicted pressure on the Christians. Pāpā[61] underwent terrible tortures and harsh calamities. The Christians lodged a complaint with Bahrām the king regarding what was happening to them, and he wanted to know the distinction between them and the Manichaeans. He asked them the reason for the abstention of the *catholicos* and bishops from marriage, and (why they refused) to raise up progeny in this world. He stated that if this (i.e., marriage and child-bearing) was impure and prohibited for them, they deserved execution for they strove for the destruction of this world; but if (this was) permitted (and) good (for them), then why did their leaders abstain from it and detest it?[62]

The Christians responded that the Manichaeans believe in two primal deities. (They also believe) that this earth is alive and possesses a spirit, (they believe) that souls relocate from one body to another, and they teach that marriage is impure. The Christians acknowledge a single deity who is the creator of everything (and) who is ancient and ceaseless (i.e., eternal). They teach that marriage is good, and they have stated this in their writings. However, their leaders abstain from it lest it divert them from what they were installed to supervise; namely, the direction of the (Christian) flock, the pursuit of prayer, and making intercession for the world and its people and the king and his kingdom. Moreover, the Manichaeans dress in Christian clothing so as to conceal themselves and their affairs.

The king was satisfied with how they spoke, and he decreed the suspension of their (persecution), and what was taking place against them came to an end and abated.[63]

b. Justinian (527–565 CE)

Zūqnīn Chronicle (ed. Chabot):[64]

(Lemma): At that time[65] Manichaeans were discovered in Constantinople, and they were (accordingly) immolated. (It transpired thusly): At that time numerous people were discovered who were caught up in the destructive error of the Manichaeans. They were assembling in private homes and performing the mysteries

Candida," *Analecta Bollandiana* 96 (1978): 167–81; Chaumont, *La christianisation*, 108–11; Christelle Jullien and Florence Jullien, "Aux frontières de l'Iranité: «*Nāṣrāyē*» et «*Krīstyonē*» des inscriptions du *mobad* Kirdīr: Enquête littéraire et historique," *Numen* 49 (2002): 294–95.

61. Patriarch of Seleucia, 247–326 CE.

62. Note Lieu, *Manichaeism*², 110.

63. See also Scher, "Histoire," 237–39; Chaumont, *La christianisation*, 105–106; and the brief discussion of Jullien and Jullien, "Aux frontières de l'Iranité," 285–86; 313–14.

64. J.-B. Chabot, ed., *Incerti auctoris Chronicon Pseudo-Dionysianum vulgo dictum* (CSCO 91, 104, scrip. syri 43, 53; 2 vols.; Paris: Reipublicae, 1927-33), 2:75.16–76.15. See also F. Nau, "Analyse de la seconde partie inedited de l'*Histoire Ecclésiastique* de Jean d'Asie, patriarche jacobite de Constantinople (d. 585)," *Revue de l'orient chrétien* 2 (1897): 455–93, esp. 478–79.

65. 540/41 CE.

of their filthy and erroneous doctrine. When they were arrested, the king[66] commanded that they come before him, for he hoped to be able to reprove them and turn them away from their destructive error. Then, when they entered, he argued with them about many (issues), and admonished (them) and showed them from the Scriptures that they were caught up in the error of 'paganism.'[67] Yet they remained unconvinced by him, but instead in a prideful tone (inspired) by Satan cried out fearlessly before him: 'We are prepared to be burned alive for the sake of the teaching of Mānī, and we (are prepared) to endure any sort of torment or affliction. We shall not change (our mind) about it.'

Then he (the king) gave command to fulfill their desire—that they be cast upon a boat[68] in the sea and set on fire and thereby be drowned in the sea—and to enter their wealth into the royal treasury, for prominent women, nobles, and patricians happened to be among them. Hence many Manichaeans perished on account of this sentence of burning with fire, and they could not be persuaded to defect from their error.[69]

c. al-Manṣūr (754–775 CE)

Ṭabarī, *Ta'rīkh al-rusul wa'l-mulūk* (ed. de Goeje):[70]

'Alī b. Muḥammad has reported on the authority of his father that Abū Ja'far (i.e., the caliph al-Manṣūr) directed Muḥammad b. Abu'l-'Abbās[71] to the *zanādiqa* and the shameless ones, and among them was Ḥammād 'Ajrad.[72] They remained with him in Baṣra, and their shamelessness became famous. He wished to do that only

---

66. The emperor Justinian.

67. A common charge against both Mani and resultant Manichaeism. Cf. the *Cologne Mani Codex* references which brand Mani's teachings and behavior as 'Greek,' a frequent synonym in Christian late antiquity for 'pagan' (as opposed to biblically sanctioned) doctrines. Note also Glenn W. Bowersock, *Hellenism in Late Antiquity* (Jerome Lectures 18; Ann Arbor: University of Michigan Press, 1990), 9–11.

68. Read ܒܡܥܕܘܒܢ? See *Chronicon Pseudo-Dionysianum* (ed. Chabot), 2:76 n.1; 82 n.4; 83.7.

69. Cf. Witold Witakowski, *Pseudo-Dionysius of Tel-Mahre Chronicle (known also as the Chronicle of Zuqnin) Part III* (Liverpool: Liverpool University Press, 1996), 70. This incident is briefly discussed by Richard Lim, *Public Disputation, Power, and Social Order in Late Antiquity* (Berkeley: University of California Press, 1995), 105. For general remarks on the persecution of Manichaeans by Justinian, see Samuel N. C. Lieu, *Manichaeism in Mesopotamia and the Roman East* (RGRW 118; Leiden: Brill, 1994), 112–17.

70. Ṭabarī, *Ta'rīkh ar-rusul wa-l-mulūk: Annales quos scripsit Abu Djafar Mohammed ibn Djarir at-Tabari* (15 vols.; ed. M. J. de Goeje; Leiden, 1879–1901; repr., Leiden: Brill, 1964–65), 3/1:422–23.

71. The nephew of al-Manṣūr and the son of his predecessor al-Saffāḥ (750–754 CE) who was serving as governor at Baṣra.

72. An infamous satirical poet who is frequently charged with Manichaean sympathies. Some traditions report that he was Muḥammad b. Abu'l-'Abbās's tutor. See Charles Pellat, "Ḥammād 'Adjrad," *EI*[2] 3:135–36; Chokr, *Zandaqa*, 265–72.

to make him odious to the people ....

(He continued on the authority of his father): (The caliph) al-Manṣūr lodged with my father for two years, and I came to know al-Khaṣīb the physician because of the many times he came to him there. Al-Khaṣīb pretended to be Christian, but he was an atheist *zindīq* who was unconcerned about the taking of life. Al-Manṣūr sent a messenger to him ordering him to plan the demise of Muḥammad b. Abu'l-'Abbās. He prepared a lethal poison (and) then waited for an illness to occur to Muḥammad. He came down with a fever, and al-Khaṣīb said to him: 'Will you take a drink of medicine?' He replied: 'Fix it for me,' so he prepared it for him, put that poison in it, gave it to him to drink, and he died from it.

The mother of Muḥammad b. Abu'l-'Abbās wrote to al-Manṣūr about it informing him that al-Khaṣīb had murdered her son. Al-Manṣūr wrote ordering that he be brought to him, and when he arrived, he scourged him with thirty light lashes of the whip and imprisoned him for a number of days. Then he gave him three hundred *dirhams* and freed him.[73]

d. al-Mahdī (775–785 CE)

Mas'ūdī, *Murūj al-dhahab* (ed. Barbier de Meynard-de Courteille):[74]

He (al-Mahdī) devoted himself to the extermination of the heretics and of those who had left the religion (of Islam), for they (heretics and apostates) were conspicuous during his time and openly publicized their doctrines under his caliphate.[75] The reason it (heresy) spread was due to the books of Mānī, Bardaiṣan, and Marcion which 'Abd Allāh Ibn al-Muqaffa'[76] and others translated from Persian and Pahlavi into Arabic and (then) expounded, and (also) due to books composed at that time by Ibn Abī al-'Awjā',[77] Ḥammad 'Ajrad, Yaḥyā b. Ziyād,[78] and Muṭī' b. Iyās[79] which endorsed the beliefs of the Manichaeans, the Dayṣānites, and the

73. See also Hugh Kennedy, *The History of al-Tabarī (Ta'rīkh al-rusul wa'l-mulūk), Volume XXIX: Al-Manṣūr and al-Mahdī* (Albany: State University of New York Press, 1990), 126–27.

74. Abū al-Ḥasan 'Alī b. al-Ḥusayn b. 'Alī al-Mas'ūdī, *Murūj al-dhahab wa-ma'ādin al-jawhar: Les prairies d'or* (9 vols.; ed. C. Barbier de Meynard and Pavel de Courteille; Paris: Imprimerie impériale, 1861-77), 8:292–93; Taqīzādeh-Šīrāzī, *Mānī va dīn-e-ū*, 132 (§21).

75. I.e., 775–785 CE. Compare the account of al-Mahdī's persecution of Manichaeans reported by Bar Hebraeus below.

76. With regard to this important figure, see below.

77. This personage, whom Vajda determined was the only eighth-century *zindīq* whose Manichaean affiliation was credible ("Les zindîqs," 221), is notorious for forging books and traditions which attack Islam and its Prophet and which lend support to dualist thought. See below.

78. For information on this figure, see Chokr, *Zandaqa*, 276–79.

79. A libertine poet who enjoyed favor among late Umayyad and early 'Abbāsid rulers. See G. E. von Grunebaum, "Three Arabic Poets of the Early Abbasid Age," *Orientalia*

Marcionites.[80] By this means the *zanādiqa* increased and promulgated their views among the populace. Al-Mahdī was the first (caliph) who commanded that disputants from the academy of theologians compose books to refute heretics such as those unbelievers we have already mentioned along with others. They (accordingly) formulated proofs against the deviants, eliminated the obscurities of the heretics, and clarified the truth for those who entertained doubts.[81]

Maqdisī, *Kitāb al-bad' wa'l-ta'rīkh* (ed. Huart):[82]

During his time *zandaqa* was rampant, and al-Mahdī executed some of them and successfully called on some of them to repent.[83]

Bar Hebraeus, *Chronicon syriacum* (ed. Bedjan):[84]

He (al-Mahdī) initiated a persecution against the Manichaeans. He destroyed the place named Padna Rabta,[85] (a place) completely full of Manichaeans, for many Arabs (Muslims?) had been ensnared by this heresy, and (now) they were put to death. Moreover, eight prominent members of the Gūmaye family (of Edessa) were ensnared in iniquity (Manichaeism?): after much torture, three died while in prison, and the (remaining) five were released.[86]

Ṭabarī, *Ta'rīkh* (ed. de Goeje):[87]

While there (in Aleppo), he sent 'Abd al-Jabbār the 'inspector' (*al-muḥtasib*)[88] to

---

17 (1948): 160-204, esp. 167–76.

80. The Arabic text of Mas'ūdī up to this point is provided in H. S. Nyberg, "Zum Kampf zwischen Islam und Manichäismus," *Orientalistische Literaturzeitung* 32 (1929): 432; correct his citation of volume 'VII' to 'VIII.'

81. See Guy Monnot, *Penseurs musulmans et religions iraniennes: 'Abd al-Jabbār et ses devanciers* (Paris: J. Vrin, 1974), 311-12; Roberto Giorgi, *Pour une histoire de la zandaka* (Firenze: La Nuova Italia Editrice, 1989), 131; David Marshall Lang, *The Wisdom of Balahvar: A Christian Legend of the Buddha* (London: George Allen and Unwin Ltd., 1957), 32; Dimitri Gutas, *Greek Thought, Arabic Culture: The Graeco-Arabic Translation Movement in Baghdad and Early 'Abbāsid Society* (London and New York: Routledge, 1998), 65.

82. Maqdisī, *Kitāb al-bad' wa'l-ta'rīkh* (6 vols.; ed. Cl. Huart; Paris: Leroux, 1899–1919), 6:98.6–7; see also Taqīzādeh-Šīrāzī, *Mānī va dīn-e-ū*, 146 (§25).

83. For another translation, see Cl. Huart, *Le livre de la création et de l'histoire de Motahhar ben Ṭâhir el-Maqdisî* (Paris: Ernest Leroux, 1919), 96.

84. Paul Bedjan, ed., *Gregorii Barhebraei Chronicon Syriacum* (Paris: Maisonneuve, 1890), 126.22–26.

85. A locale between Ḥarrān and Aleppo. See R. Payne Smith, *Thesaurus Syriacus* (2 vols.; Oxford: Clarendon, 1879–1901), 2:3039.

86. See J. B. Segal, *Edessa: 'The Blessed City'* (Oxford: Clarendon Press, 1970), 206; Chokr, *Zandaqa*, 63.

87. Ṭabarī, *Ta'rīkh* (ed. de Goeje), 3/1:499.

88. See Chokr, *Zandaqa*, 22–23.

arraign the *zanādiqa* who were in that district.[89] He did so and brought them to him when he was in Dābiq.[90] He executed a group of them and gibbeted them. Some of their books were brought, and they were chopped up with knives.[91]

Kitāb al-sinkisār; i.e., the Copto-Arabic Synaxarion (ed. Taqīzādeh-Šīrāzī):[92]

While he[93] was in Aleppo, he dispatched (an order) and assembled from those regions those who were *zanādiqa* (i.e., dualist heretics). Once they gathered, he killed them and chopped up their books with knives.[94]

Ṭabarī, *Ta'rīkh* (ed. de Goeje):[95]

In this (same year [AH 166/782 CE]) he arrested Dāwūd b. Rawḥ b. Ḥātim, Ismā'īl b. Sulaymān b. Mujālid, Muḥammad b. Abī Ayyūb al-Makkī, and Muḥammad b. Ṭayfūr for *zandaqa*. They admitted guilt, and al-Mahdī called on them to repent and then released them. He sent Dāwūd b. Rawḥ to his father, Rawḥ, who then was serving as governor of Baṣra. He treated him with benevolence, but he commanded him (i.e., his father) to supervise him.[96]

In this (same year) al-Waḍḍāḥ al-Sharawī arraigned 'Abdallāh who was the son of the vizier Abū 'Ubaydallāh, he being Mu'āwiyah b. 'Ubaydallāh al-Ash'arī of the people of Syria.[97] He was the one whom Ibn Shabābah undermined and who was charged with *zandaqa*. We have mentioned his case already and his execution.[98]

89. This incident is dated to the year AH 163/779 CE and is apparently the same incident that is reported in the preceding Bar Hebraeus notice and the following Synaxarion entry. See especially Chokr, *Zandaqa*, 62–63.

90. A locale in northern Syria lying upstream from Aleppo.

91. See also Kennedy, *History of al-Tabarī XXIX*, 214; J. L. Kraemer, "Heresy Versus the State in Medieval Islam," in *Studies in Judaica, Karaitica and Islamica Presented to Leon Nemoy on his Eightieth Birthday* (ed. Sheldon R. Brunswick; Ramat-Gan: Bar-Ilan University Press, 1982), 176–77.

92. Taqīzādeh-Šīrāzī, *Mānī va dīn-e-ū*, 455 (§159).

93. The caliph al-Mahdī.

94. See Vajda, "Les zindîqs," 183; Nabia Abbott, *Studies in Arabic Literary Papyri, III: Language and Literature* (OIP 77; Chicago, IL: The University of Chicago Press, 1972), 98 n.183. Abbott dates this event to 780 CE.

95. Ṭabarī, *Ta'rīkh* (ed. de Goeje), 3/1:517.

96. Kennedy points out that each of these defendants belonged to prominent families in the ruling class and that this might explain why the caliph treated them with such leniency. See also Chokr, *Zandaqa*, 74–75; Jonathan P. Berkey, *The Formation of Islam: Religion and Society in the Near East, 600–1800* (Cambridge: Cambridge University Press, 2003), 170.

97. According to Ma'sūdī, he was from Tiberias. See B. Carra de Vaux, *Maçoudi: Le livre de l'avertissement et de la revision* (Paris: L'Imprimerie Nationale, 1896), 441.

98. This episode was presented at length in Ṭabarī, *Ta'rīkh* (ed. de Goeje), 3/1:487–90, but there is no mention of the charge of *zandaqa* there. Instead the hapless defendant proves unable to recite from the Qur'ān when ordered to do so by the caliph.

Ibn al-Shiḥnah, *Rawḍ al-manāẓir fī akhbār al-awā'il wa'al-awākhir* (ed. Taqīzādeh-Šīrāzī):[99]

In the year AH 166 he (al-Mahdī) executed the poet Baššār b. Burd for (the crime of) *zandaqa*. He was blind from birth (and) had lived to be ninety years old.[100]

Ṭabarī, *Ta'rīkh* (ed. de Goeje):[101]

And in that year (AH 167) al-Mahdī was seriously committed to the search for heretics (*zanādiqa*), and the search for them encompassed even remote regions. He would execute them. He placed in charge as their superintendent[102] 'Umar al-Kalwādhanī. He arrested Yazīd b. al-Fayḍ, the secretary of al-Manṣūr. After he confessed what was reported (of him), he was imprisoned, but he managed to escape from prison and was no longer subject to his control.[103]

Jahshiyārī, *Kitāb al-wuzara' wa'l-kuttāb* (ed. Taqīzādeh-Šīrāzī):[104]

Al-Mahdī was seriously committed to the search for heretics (*zanādiqa*), and he appointed 'Umar al-Kalwādhānī to supervise the search for them. He took a group

---

See Vajda, "Les zindîqs," 187–89; Chokr, *Zandaqa*, 71–73; Moshe Gil, *A History of Palestine, 634–1099* (trans. Ethel Broido; Cambridge: Cambridge University Press, 1992), 289–90.

For another translation, see Kennedy, *History of al-Tabarī XXIX*, 234-35.

99. Taqīzādeh-Šīrāzī, *Mānī va dīn-e-ū*, 296 (§72).

100. Most scholars emend 'ninety' to 'seventy' on the basis of an orthographic confusion. Ibn al-Nadīm also includes Baššār b. Burd on his blacklist of intellectuals and poets who were alleged to sympathize with or practice *zandaqa*. Renowned for his satirical wit, he was frequently accused of endorsing heterodox beliefs and behaviors. See von Kremer, *Streifzüge*, 34–35; Reynold A. Nicholson, *A Literary History of the Arabs* (2nd ed.; Cambridge: The University Press, 1930), 373–74; Vajda, "Les zindîqs," 197–202; Charles Pellat, *Le milieu baṣrien et la formation de Ǧāḥiẓ* (Paris: Adrien-Maisonneuve, 1953), 176–78; Régis Blachère, "Bashshār b. Burd," *EI*[2] 1:1080–82; G. Schoeler, "Bashshār b. Burd, Abū'l-'Atāhiyah and Abū Nuwās," in *'Abbasid Belles-Lettres* (ed. Julia Ashtiany, et al.; The Cambridge History of Arabic Literature; Cambridge: Cambridge University Press, 1990), 276–86; Kennedy, *Court of the Caliphs*, 118-20.

101. Ṭabarī, *Ta'rīkh* (ed. de Goeje), 3/1:519–20; Taqīzādeh-Šīrāzī, *Mānī va dīn-e-ū*, 115 (§15).

102. Literally 'overseer of the heretics' (صاحب الزّنادقة), an inquisitional-type office dedicated to the exposure and punishment of 'heretics.' See Vajda, "Les zindîqs," 183; Geo Widengren, "Manichaeism and its Iranian Background," in *The Cambridge History of Iran, Volume 3(2): The Seleucid, Parthian and Sasanian Periods* (ed. Ehsan Yarshater; Cambridge: Cambridge University Press, 1983), 989.

103. See Vajda, "Les zindîqs," 186; Gholam Hossein Sadighi, *Les mouvements religieux iraniens au II*[e] *et au III*[e] *siècle de l'hégire* (Paris: Les Presses Modernes, 1938), 91; Kennedy, *History of al-Tabarī XXIX*, 237.

104. Taqīzādeh-Šīrāzī, *Mānī va dīn-e-ū*, 127 (§20). This tradition closely follows that of Ṭabarī, *Ta'rīkh* (ed. de Goeje), 3/1:519–20 above.

of them into custody, and arrested with them Yazīd b. al-Fayḍ, the secretary of al-Manṣūr. After he confessed he was a *zindīq*, he was imprisoned, but he managed to escape from prison and was no longer subject to his control.

Ṭabarī, *Ta'rīkh* (ed. de Goeje):[105]

In that year (AH 168) 'Umar al-Kalwādhanī, the 'overseer of the heretics,' died. Ḥamdawayh, who was Muḥammad b. 'Īsā from the people of Maysān, was appointed to take his place. That same year al-Mahdī put to death the *zanādiqa* who were in Baghdād.[106]

***Kitāb al-sinkisār*; i.e., the Copto-Arabic Synaxarion (ed. Taqīzādeh-Šīrāzī):**[107]

In it (i.e., that same year) 'Umar al-Kalwādhānī, the 'overseer of the heretics,' died. In his place he (al-Mahdī) appointed Muḥammad b. 'Īsa b. Ḥamdawayh,[108] and he executed many persons from among the *zanādiqa*.

Ṭabarī, *Ta'rīkh* (ed. de Goeje):[109]

An account which stems from 'Alī b. Muḥammad (b. Sulaymān b. 'Abdallāh) al-Hāshimī. He said: 'A son of Dāwūd b. 'Alī[110] was brought before al-Mahdī (and charged) as a *zindīq*, and Ya'qūb b. al-Faḍl b. 'Abd al-Raḥmān b. 'Abbās b. Rabī'a b. al-Ḥārith b. 'Abd al-Muṭṭalib[111] was brought (and charged) as a *zindīq*: (they were questioned) in two different trials. He (the caliph) spoke the same words to each of them after they confessed their *zandaqa* to him. As for Ya'qūb b. al-Faḍl, he said to him: "I confess it privately between the two of us. However, I will not divulge this to the people, even were you to cut me up with scissors." He (the caliph) said to him: "Woe to you! Even if the heavens have been unveiled to you and the matter is as you say, you should actually side with Muḥammad! If there was no Muḥammad (peace be upon him!), who would you be? Would you not be just one man from the general population? By God, if it were not for the fact that I took upon myself a sacred vow when God assigned me this office (i.e., the caliphate) that I would never execute a Hāshimite,[112] I would not have put you on trial: I would have put you to death!" Then he turned to Mūsā al-Hādī and said: "O Mūsā, I expressly entreat you that if you administer this office after me that you should not argue with these two for a single moment!" The son of Dāwūd b. 'Alī died in

105. Ṭabarī, *Ta'rīkh* (ed. de Goeje), 3/1:522; Taqīzādeh-Šīrāzī, *Mānī va dīn-e-ū*, 115 (§15).

106. See also Kennedy, *History of al-Tabarī XXIX*, 240–41.

107. Taqīzādeh-Šīrāzī, *Mānī va dīn-e-ū*, 455 (§159).

108. See Vajda, "Les zindîqs," 183.

109. Ṭabarī, *Ta'rīkh* (ed. de Goeje), 3/1:549–51; Taqīzādeh-Šīrāzī, *Mānī va dīn-e-ū*, 115–17 (§15).

110. Dāwūd b. 'Alī was the uncle of Abu'l-'Abbās al-Saffāḥ, the first 'Abbāsid caliph (750–754 CE).

111. He had served as secretary to the second 'Abbāsid caliph al-Manṣūr (754–775 CE).

112. The term can refer to both the 'Abbāsid house itself and the family of the Prophet.

confinement before the death of al-Mahdī. As for Ya'qūb, he remained (alive in prison) until al-Mahdī died.

Then Mūsā came from Jurjān (to assume the caliphate as al-Hādī).[113] At the moment he entered (the city), he remembered the directive of al-Mahdī, and so he sent someone to Ya'qūb who laid a pillow over him. Some men then sat down on top of it until he was dead. He afterwards forgot about him during his inauguration and the confirmation of his caliphal status. This took place on a very hot day.[114] (The corpse of) Ya'qūb remained in place until a portion of that night had passed, and then it was reported to Mūsā: "O Commander of the Faithful! Ya'qūb has begun to swell up and smell." He said: "Send him to his brother Isḥāq b. al-Faḍl and tell him that Ya'qūb died in prison." He was put in a small boat and was brought to Isḥāq. He examined (the body), and when he realized that washing (it) was not possible, he immediately buried him in his garden. When morning came, he sent a message to the Hāshimites informing them about the death of Ya'qūb and summoning them to his funeral. He instructed that a piece of wood be fashioned in the shape of a man. It was then wrapped in cotton bands and it was dressed in funerary shrouds. He then loaded it on the bier, and no one of those who were in attendance suspected that it was a substituted thing. Ya'qūb did have progeny who were his offspring: 'Abd al-Raḥmān, al-Faḍl, Arwā, and Fāṭima. As for Fāṭima, she was discovered to be pregnant by him (i.e., her father Ya'qūb), and she herself admitted this.'[115]

'Alī b. Muḥammad said: 'My father reported that Fāṭima and the wife of Ya'qūb b. al-Faḍl, the latter of whom was not a Hāshimite and who was called Khadīja, were brought before al-Hādī or previously before al-Mahdī. They both confessed to *zandaqa*, and Fāṭima admitted that she was pregnant by her father. He sent them to Rayṭa bt. Abī al-'Abbās.[116] She noticed that they both wore cosmetics and had tinged their hair/nails, and she censured them. She had many things to say against the daughter in particular. She (Fāṭima) said: "He forced me (to submit to him)." She (Rayṭa) replied: "Why then the paint, the eye-shadow, and the gaiety, if you were forced (to submit to sexual abuse)?" She cursed both of them.'

He continued: 'I was informed that they were both filled with terror and died of fright, being struck on their heads with a thing called the *ru'būb*: they were frightened by it and died. Arwā however remained, and al-Faḍl b. Ismā'īl b. al-Faḍl, the son of her uncle and a man who was unobjectionable with regard to religion, wed her.[117]

---

113. See Kennedy, *Court of the Caliphs*, 57–60.

114. His accession took place during the month of August in 785 CE.

115. The persecution of Manichaeans by al-Mahdī and his successors is briefly discussed by Berkey, *Formation of Islam*, 170–71.

116. Wife of al-Mahdī and the daughter of the first 'Abbāsid caliph al-Saffāḥ.

117. See also C. E. Bosworth, *The History of al-Ṭabarī, Volume XXX: The 'Abbāsid Caliphate in Equilibrium* (Albany: State University of New York Press, 1989), 10–14.

e. al-Hādī (785–786 CE)

Kitāb al-sinkisār; i.e., the Copto-Arabic Synaxarion (ed. Taqīzādeh-Šīrāzī):[118]

During it (i.e., that year [AH 169]) al-<Hādī>[119] vigorously prosecuted heretics (*zanādiqa*) and executed a group of them, among whom was 'Alī b. Yaqṭīn. Moreover he executed Ya'qūb b. al- Faḍl b. 'Abd al-Raḥmān b. 'Abbās b. Rabī'ah b. al-Ḥārith b. 'Abd al-Muṭṭalib. The reason why he was executed was that he had been brought before al-Mahdī and had confessed he was a *zindīq*. He said: 'If what you say is true, are you worthy to be counted among the relatives of Muḥammad? Were it not for Muḥammad, who would you be? Now, by God, had I not placed upon myself (an oath) not to kill a Hāshimite, I would certainly kill you.' Then he addressed al-Hādī: 'I adjure you that if you should exercise this emirate that you will put him to death!' So he imprisoned him. And after al-Mahdī died, al-Hādī had him executed. Similarly he also charged him with the execution of a son of Dāwūd b. 'Alī b. 'Abdallāh b. 'Abbās: he was a *zindīq*, but he died while in prison before (the death of) al-Mahdī. After Ya'qūb had been executed, his children were brought before al-Hādī, and his daughter Fāṭima confessed that she had been impregnated by her father. She was so terrified that she died from fright.

Ṭabarī, *Ta'rīkh* (ed. de Goeje):[120]

During this year (AH 169/785 CE), Mūsā (i.e., the caliph al-Hādī) vigorously searched for *zanādiqa* and put to death a large number of them. Among those whom he executed was a native of al-Nahrawān, Yazdān b. Bādhān,[121] the secretary of Yaqṭīn (b. Mūsā) and of his son 'Alī b. Yaqṭīn. It was said about him that he made the pilgrimage (to Mecca). He observed the people circumambulating (the Ka'ba) and exclaimed: 'They look like cattle trampling down a threshing floor!' Al-'Alā' b. al-Ḥaddād al-A'mā said to him (i.e., to al-Hādī):

> 'O one whom God has made superintendent over creation,
> and heir of the Ka'ba and the (Prophet's) pulpit!
>
> What do you think about an unbeliever
> who likens the Ka'ba to a threshing floor?
>
> And who deems the people when they run
> to be (like) asses trampling wheat and rye?'

Mūsā had him executed and then suspended him. A piece of wood from the scaffolding collapsed upon a man who was making pilgrimage, killing him and also his ass. He also executed the Hāshimite Ya'qūb b. al-Faḍl.[122]

---

118. Taqīzādeh-Šīrāzī, *Mānī va dīn-e-ū*, 455 (§159).
119. Correct the text's reading of al-Mahdī accordingly.
120. Ṭabarī, *Ta'rīkh* (ed. de Goeje), 3/1:548; Taqīzādeh-Šīrāzī, *Mānī va dīn-e-ū*, 115 (§15).
121. Also known as Izadayādār. See Maqdisī below and the discussion of Chokr, *Zandaqa*, 83–84.
122. Regarding this incident, see Sadighi, *Mouvements*, 92–93. For another translation, see

Maqdisī, *K. al-bad' wa'l-ta'rīkh* (ed. Huart):[123]

(The caliph) al-Hādī pursued the *zanādiqa* and ferociously exterminated them. Among those whom he put to death was Izadayādār, the secretary of Yaqṭīn b. Mūsa. He once observed the people who were hurriedly circumambulating (the Ka'ba) and exclaimed: 'They look like cattle trampling down a threshing floor!' A poet has said about him:

> 'What do you think about an unbeliever
> who likens the Ka'ba to a threshing floor?'
>
> Another has said:
>
> 'Mānī has been dead for ages,
> but Izadayādār has now appeared.
>
> Abū Khālid (i.e., Izadayādār) makes pilgrimage to the Sanctuary,
> fearing death or destitution (should he refuse to do so).
>
> But by God, Abū Khālid wishes
> that the House of God might be set afire!
>
> An unbeliever, yet according to his religion
> one may not kill serpents or sparrows in his home.
>
> He will not harm the mouse in its hole;
> for he says: "A divine spirit is within the mouse!"'

Al-Hādī had him executed and then suspended him. A piece of wood from the scaffolding collapsed upon a man who was making pilgrimage, killing him and also his ass.[124]

Ṭabarī, *Ta'rīkh* (ed. de Goeje):[125]

Muḥammad b. 'Aṭā' b. Muqaddam al-Wāsiṭī has mentioned that his father informed him that al-Mahdī once said to Mūsā,[126] this being after a *zindīq* had been brought before him and called on to repent, but he refused to repent, so he beheaded him and had him suspended: 'O my son, if this authority is granted to you, rid yourself of this group'—he meant the followers of Mānī—'for they are a sect who summon people to what appears to be right, such as avoidance of excess, renunciation of the material world, and preparation for the hereafter. Then they are trained to avoid meat, to handle (only) pure water, and to refrain from killing vermin, shunning and abstaining from sin. They then are led from this to the worship of two beings, one of them being Light and the other Dark-

---

Bosworth, *History of al-Tabarī XXX*, 10.

123. Maqdisī, *K. al-bad' wa'l-ta'rīkh* (ed. Huart), 6:100.7–101.5; Taqīzādeh-Šīrāzī, *Mānī va dīn-e-ū*, 146–47 (§25).

124. This episode is paralleled in the account of Ṭabarī above. For another translation, see Huart, *Le livre de la création* (1919), 98–99.

125. Ṭabarī, *Ta'rīkh* (ed. de Goeje), 3/1:588; Taqīzādeh-Šīrāzī, *Mānī va dīn-e-ū*, 117 (§15). See also Ibn al-Āthīr, *Kāmil fī al-ta'rīkh* 6:72 (*apud* Taqīzādeh-Šīrāzī, *Mānī va dīn-e-ū*, 264).

126. The future caliph al-Hādī (785-86 CE).

ness. Then after this, marriage with sisters and daughters, performing ablutions with urine, and stealing children off the streets are deemed permissible in order to deliver them from the straying path of Darkness to the rightly guided way of Light. Erect scaffolds for them, draw the sword against them, and by this action bring yourself closer to God, the One Who has no associate! For I had a dream where I saw your ancestor al-'Abbās arming me with two swords and ordering me to kill the followers of the dualists.'[127]

He related that Mūsā said after ten months (of his reign) had passed: 'Indeed, by God, if I live, I shall completely kill off this sect to the point that I will not leave them a single eye to blink!' It is reported that he gave orders for a thousand tree trunks (for gibbeting) to be prepared for him. He gave this directive in a certain month, but he died two months later.[128]

f. Hārūn al-Rashīd (786–809 CE)

Jāḥiẓ, *Risāla fī dhamm akhlāq al-kuttāb* (ed. Taqīzādeh-Šīrāzī):[129]

Then Yūnus b. Abī Farwa served as their secretary.[130] He was a Manichaean. He tried to hide himself in Kūfa, but he was kept fettered in irons until he perished.[131]

Ṭabarī, *Ta'rīkh* (ed. de Goeje):[132]

In that year (AH 170/786 CE), he (Hārūn al-Rashīd) granted amnesty to fugitives or to those who had gone into hiding, except for a group of the *zanādiqa* which included Yūnus b. Abī Farwa[133] and Yazīd b. al-Fayḍ.[134]

---

127. Regarding this description see Chokr, *Zandaqa*, 46.

128. For other translations, see Bosworth, *History of al-Tabarī XXX*, 69–70; Vajda, "Les zindîqs," 190.

129. Taqīzādeh-Šīrāzī, *Mānī va dīn-e-ū*, 100 (§9). Some think the attribution of this treatise to Jāḥiẓ is spurious. For references to this discussion, see Louise Marlow, *Hierarchy and Egalitarianism in Islamic Thought* (Cambridge: Cambridge University Press, 1997), 105 n.50.

130. I.e., he served for 'Īsā b. Mūsa, governor of Ahwāz and later Kūfa, and a nephew of the first two caliphs of the 'Abbāsid regime.

131. See also Vajda, "Les zindîqs," 213–14; Chokr, *Zandaqa*, 295–96; *Nine Essays of al-Jahiz* (trans. William M. Hutchins; New York: Peter Lang, 1989), 62.

132. Ṭabarī, *Ta'rīkh* (ed. de Goeje), 3/1:604; Taqīzādeh-Šīrāzī, *Mānī va dīn-e-ū*, 117 (§15).

133. He served as secretary for 'Īsā b. Mūsa, a nephew of the caliph al-Manṣūr and a potential rival to al-Mahdī for succession to rule. Note especially the discussion of Jacob Lassner, *The Shaping of 'Abbāsid Rule* (Princeton, NJ: Princeton University Press, 1980), 29, 50–57. Similarly Yazīd b. al-Fayḍ had been a secretary in the court of the same caliph. See Vajda, "Les zindîqs," 213–14; Chokr, *Zandaqa*, 295–96; van Ess, *Theologie und Gesellschaft*, 1:447.

134. For other translations, see Bosworth, *History of al-Tabarī XXX*, 98; Sadighi, *Mouvements*, 93.

Abu'l Faraj al-Iṣfahānī, *Kitāb al-aghānī* (ed. Taqīzādeh-Šīrāzī):[135]

Aḥmad b. Ibrāhīm b. Ismā'īl the scribe has mentioned that the daughter of Muṭī' b. Iyās was brought before (Hārūn) al-Rashīd among the *zanādiqa*. She had studied their scripture[136] and freely acknowledged it. She said: 'My father taught me this religion, but I have renounced it.' He accepted her repentance and restored her to her family.[137]

Ṭabarī, *Ta'rīkh* (ed. de Goeje):[138]

In that year (AH 180/796 CE), the Muḥammira[139] revolted in Jurjān. 'Alī b. 'Īsā b. Māhān[140] wrote that the person who incited that (rebellion) against him was 'Amr b. Muḥammad al-'Amrakī and that he was a *zindīq*. (Hārūn) al-Rashīd ordered that he be executed, and he was put to death at Merv.[141]

Ṭabarī, *Ta'rīkh* (ed. de Goeje):[142]

Once Mankah[143] was passing by the Khuld palace when he encountered a man of the Manichaean[144] sect. He had unrolled his coat and placed upon it many medicines. He was standing, praising a medication which was an ointment which he had with him, and said during his description: 'This is a medicine for incessant fever, intermittent fever, quartern, and tertian fever. It is good for pain in the back and the knees, hemorrhoids, and intestinal gas. It works for aching joints and pain in the eyes. It relieves abdominal pain, headache, and migraine. It is good for (difficulties in) passing urine, partial paralysis, and tremors.' He did not omit any physical disease without mentioning that medicine as its cure.

Mankah said to his interpreter: 'What does this one say?' The interpreter translated for him what he had heard. Then Mankah smiled and said: 'The ruler of the Arabs is certainly foolish! For if matters are as this one says, why would he bring me from my country, separate me from my family, and go to great trouble in maintaining me when this one was available, standing in plain view before him?

135. Taqīzādeh-Šīrāzī, *Mānī va dīn-e-ū*, 140 (§24).

136. Literally 'their *kitāb*'; i.e., 'their book' or 'their scripture.'

137. See Grunebaum, "Three Arabic Poets," 173; Vajda, "Les zindîqs," 213; Chokr, *Zandaqa*, 274.

138. Ṭabarī, *Ta'rīkh* (ed. de Goeje), 3/2:645.

139. The 'red-clad ones.' See the report of Ibn al-Nadīm below.

140. The military governor of Khurāsān.

141. For another translation, see Bosworth, *History of al-Tabarī XXX*, 163. With regard to this particular disturbance, see Spuler, *Iran in früh-islamischer Zeit*, 207; Elton L. Daniel, *The Political and Social History of Khurasan under Abbasid Rule 747–820* (Minneapolis and Chicago: Bibliotheca Islamica, 1979), 147; Chokr, *Zandaqa*, 84–85.

142. Ṭabarī, *Ta'rīkh* (ed. de Goeje), 3/2:747–48.

143. An Indian physician who came to Baghdad and translated Sanskrit medical works into Persian during the reign of Hārūn al-Rashīd. See Dodge, *Fihrist*, 2:710.

144. Emending the text in accordance with the critical apparatus supplied by the modern editors.

And if matters are not as this one says, why does he not put him to death? The *sharīʿa* (religious law) permits (the shedding of) his blood and the blood of those like him, for if he is executed, then many people will remain alive through the taking of that life. But if this fool is left alone, he will kill someone every day, and sometimes he will kill two, three, or four every day. This is a defect in governance and a weakness in the realm.'[145]

Samʿānī, *Kitāb al-ānsāb* (ed. Taqīzādeh-Šīrāzī):[146]

It is related that during the reign of [Hārūn] al-Rashīd there was a man who was a parasite who would go to extraordinary lengths in this (habit). He would borrow clothing and other items and was in the habit of insinuating himself among people for entertainments and social gatherings at grand houses. Now it happened that al-Rashīd had arrested the Manichaean *zanādiqa* in order to put them to death. They had in their possession a book called the *Zand* and the *qalansūwa* of Mānī. The freeloader thought they were on their way to a banquet and so he joined their group. He asked one of them if they had been invited to a social gathering. The man derisively answered: 'Yes!' When they arrived, they were seated before a leather drop-cloth and sword. They brought out the book which they had and the *qalansūwa* of Mānī and said to each one: 'Spit on it!' And if he refused to do so, he was killed. This continued until it was his own turn, whereupon he stood up, undid his trousers, and tried to urinate on it. He (the caliph) asked him about this, and so he recounted his story and his sycophantic habits. Al-Rashīd laughed, gave him some money, and released him, but he executed the Manichaeans.

g. al-Ma'mūn (813–833)

Jāḥiẓ, *Kitāb al-ḥayawān* (ed. Taqīzādeh-Šīrāzī):[147]

The Commander of the Faithful (al-Ma'mūn)[148] directed another question to the *zindīq* who bore the *kunya* Abū 'Alī. When he saw that Muḥammad b. al-Jahm was too long-winded, that al-'Utbī was incapable (of responding), and that al-Qasīm b. Sayyār was badly informed, al-Ma'mūn addressed him: 'I will ask you only about two matters. Tell me, can one who is an evildoer ever repent of his evildoing? Or can we never repent of anything which we have done?' He answered: 'No, many of those who have done evil have repented of their evildoing.' He responded: 'Tell me, is repentance for evildoing a bad or good thing?' He answered: 'A good thing.' He pressed: 'And the one who has repented, was he the one who did the evil, or was it another?' He answered: 'The one who repented was the one who did the

145. See also Bosworth, *History of al-Tabarī* XXX, 313–14.

146. Taqīzādeh-Šīrāzī, *Mānī va dīn-e-ū*, 246–47 (§46).

147. Taqīzādeh-Šīrāzī, *Mānī va dīn-e-ū*, 89–90 (§4).

148. There is a tradition (apocryphal?) which attributes the authorship of a 'book' (*kitāb*) refuting the Manichaeans to the caliph al-Ma'mūn. See Guy Monnot, "Les écrits musulmans sur les religions non-bibliques," in idem, *Islam et religions* (Paris: Éditions Maisonneuve et Larose, 1986), 52.

evil.' He said: 'Then it is apparent to me that the originator of what is good is the same as the originator of what is bad. It refutes your teaching that the one who views a threatening sight is different from the one who views a merciful sight.'

He retorted: 'Then I will maintain that the one who did evil is different from the one who repented!' He responded: 'Then this one who repented of evildoing—was it done by him, or was it a thing done by another?' But his question silenced him. He did not renounce (his error) or return (to the true faith); when he died, God gave him to the fire of Jahannam.[149]

Maʿsūdī, *Murūj al-dhahab* (ed. Barbier de Meynard-de Courteille):[150]

A report from Thumāma b. Ashras, who says: 'Information came to al-Ma'mūn about ten residents of Baṣra who were *zanādiqa* professing the teaching of Mānī and who spoke of Light and Darkness. After they had each been identified by name to him, he issued orders for them to be brought before him. While they were being rounded up, a freeloader noticed them and he thought, "They are surely being assembled for a banquet!" Unaware of their (true) circumstances, he inserted himself among them and proceeded with them until those in charge brought them to the boat. The freeloader thought, "Undoubtedly it is a pleasure cruise!" So he boarded the boat with them. It was not long before chains were produced and the whole group was fettered, the freeloader along with them. Then the freeloader thought, "My concern to freeload has resulted in chains!" Then he approached the sheikhs (among the prisoners) and asked, "I beg your pardon, but who are you?" They replied, "Rather, who are you? Are you indeed one of our brethren?" He answered, "By God, I do not know who you are, but as for me I am, by God, a freeloading man. I went out today from my house and came across you. I noticed (your) noble appearance, dignified demeanor, and obvious prosperity, and I thought '(some) distinguished elders, mature men, and youths must be assembling for a banquet.' So I inserted myself among you and imitated some of you as if I was one of your group. Then you came to this boat, and I saw that it was provided with these carpets and spreads, and I saw the filled dining tables and the bags and the baskets, and I thought 'a pleasure cruise, and they are departing for some palace or garden. Ah, what a blissful day!' And I was deliriously happy until these officers came among you and shackled you and me along with you. After I was fettered, I lost my mind. Inform me what it is going on!"'

But they laughed at him: they smiled and were amused and cheered by him. Then they said: "You are now counted among the total and you have been chained with irons. As for us, we are Manichaeans who have been defamed before al-Ma'mūn, and we are now being brought before him. He will question us about our affairs and interrogate us about our doctrine, and he will exhort us to repent and renounce it by subjecting us to different kinds of trials. Among these include his showing us a

149. For other translations, see Pellat, "Le témoignage," 272; Monnot, *Penseurs*, 293; Giorgi, *Pour une histoire*, 130; van Ess, *Theologie und Gesellschaft*, 6:116–17.

150. Masʿūdī, *Murūj* (ed. Barbier de Meynard-de Courteille), 7:12–16; also Taqīzādeh-Šīrāzī, *Mānī va dīn-e-ū*, 131–32 (§21).

picture of Mānī and ordering us to spit on it and thereby clear ourselves of suspicion. He will also order us to sacrifice an aquatic bird or a pheasant. Whoever complies with these saves himself, and whoever disobeys is put to death. When you are summoned and put on trial, let them know about yourself and your belief(s) so that the evidence for your testimony wins you favor. But you claim that you are a freeloader, and freeloaders have knowledge of a number of undertakings and stories: shorten our trip to the city of Baghdād with some tale or fable!"

When they reached Baghdād and were brought before al-Ma'mūn, he began summoning them by their names, one after the other, and interrogating each one about his doctrine. He informed each one about Islam, and then tested him: he called upon him to disavow Mānī and, showing him his picture, ordered that he should spit upon it and renounce him, and so on. However, they refused and he ordered them put to the sword. Finally—after the ten were no more and the number of the group had been fully extirpated—he came to the freeloader. Then al-Ma'mūn said to the officers: "Who is this?" They replied: "By God, we do not know, except that we found him with the rest of the group and so we brought him." Then al-Ma'mūn said to him: "What is your story?" He said: "O Commander of the Faithful! May I divorce my wife if I understood one thing of what they said! I am only a freeloader!" And he recounted to him his story, from beginning to end. Then al-Ma'mūn laughed, and then he showed him the picture (of Mani), but he cursed it and disavowed it and said: "Give it to me and I will shit upon it! By God, I do not know who Mānī is! Is he a Jew? A Muslim?" Then al-Ma'mūn said: "He was one given to excessive freeloading, but it proved hazardous to his health!""[151]

3. The Manichaean 'Blood-Libel'[152]

***Chronicon Anonymum* (ed. Guidi):**[153]

Again, in the region of Bih-Quwadh[154] some Manichaeans were caught in a town by the name of *Šṭrw* (Shaṭrū?). They say that they (Manichaeans) quarantine a man at the beginning of the year within an underground chamber. They feed him

151. See also Widengren, *Mani and Manichaeism*, 130-32. Note Sadighi, *Mouvements*, 95; Spuler, *Iran in früh-islamischer Zeit*, 208 n.6; Gotthard Strohmaier, "Al-Bīrūnī (973–1048) über Mani und Manichäer," in *Studia Manichaica: IV. Internationaler Kongress zum Manichäismus, Berlin, 14.–18. Juli 1997* (ed. Ronald E. Emmerick, Werner Sundermann, and Peter Zieme; Berlin: Akademie-Verlag, 2000), 591–92.

152. For a detailed discussion of this motif and the following texts, see John C. Reeves, "A Manichaean 'Blood-Libel'?" *Aram* 16 (2004): 217–32; note also Amir Harrak, "Anti-Manichaean Propaganda in Syriac Literature," *Journal of Eastern Christian Studies* 56 (2004): 49–67.

153. Ignatius Guidi, ed., *Chronica Minora I* (CSCO 1; Paris, 1903 ; repr., Louvain: Imprimerie Orientaliste, 1960), 33.14–34.2.

154. Presumably this is the district meant: it connotes the region between the ruins of ancient Babylon and the southern marshlands. See G. Le Strange, *The Lands of the Eastern Caliphate: Mesopotamia, Persia, and Central Asia from the Moslem Conquest to the Time of Timur* (Cambridge: University Press, 1905), 81; Michael G. Morony, *Iraq After the Muslim Conquest* (Princeton, NJ: Princeton University Press, 1984), 147–51.

anything he wants for an entire year, and then they slaughter him (as) a sacrifice to the demons, and use his head for divination and magical spells during the whole of that year. Every year they slaughter such a one.[155]

Moreover they bring (to him) maidens who have known no man, and they all have intercourse with him. Any child who is engendered from one of these (unions) they immediately boil until its flesh and bones become as (soft as) oil. Next they pound it in a mortar and mix it with flour and make little cakes from it. They feed each of their adherents one of these cakes (so that) he might never renounce Mānī.

All of them (in this instance) were caught by divine providence when a certain student whom they sought to quarantine managed to escape from them. They were hung along with some whores who were sequestered among them and who engaged in their misconduct. They were in all about seventy individuals.[156]

***Zūqnīn Chronicle* (ed. Chabot):**[157]

(Lemma): At that time[158] the religion of the Manichaeans in Ḥarrān, a city of Mesopotamia, became an object of scorn. (It transpired thusly): They happened to have a monastery to the east of Ḥarrān, removed about one mile from the city.[159] They would celebrate in that monastery once every year a great and horrible festival, and they would make sacrifice in it (the monastery). Therein that wicked (group's) bishop dwelt, that great festival transpired, and divinatory practices (occurred).

When their festival was drawing near, they had a custom of kidnapping a man and sequestering him from year to year. At (the time of) the festival they would sacrifice him, sever his head, and place a coin in his mouth. They would put it (the head) in a niche,[160] worship it, and practice divination by means of it.[161]

Now as the day of their impious festival approached, they wanted to bring a man whom they could prepare for quarantine so that he might serve as their sacrifice for the festival (the year) after the one which was approaching. The leaders of the

155. Parallels to this gruesome ritual are found in Muslim and Jewish accounts about the religious practices of the 'pagan' inhabitants of Ḥarrān. See Reeves, "Manichaean 'Blood-Libel'," 223–30.

156. See also Th[eodor]. Nöldeke, "Die von Guidi herausgegebene syrische Chronik," *Sitzungsberichte der kaiserlichen Akademie der Wissenschaften, phil.-hist. Klasse* (Wien, 1893), 9:36–38; Reeves, "Manichaean 'Blood-Libel'," 218–19; Morony, *Iraq After the Muslim Conquest*, 409; Samuel N. C. Lieu, *Manichaeism in Central Asia and China* (NHMS 45; Leiden: Brill, 1998), 170.

157. *Chronicon Pseudo-Dionysianum* (ed. Chabot), 2:224.1–226.3. See also J.-B. Chabot, ed., *Chronique de Denys de Tell-Maḥré: Quatrième partie* (Paris: Librairie Émile Bouillon, 1895), 80.1–82.2 (text).

158. The year previously mentioned was 1076 SE, corresponding to 764–65 CE.

159. Note the Ṣābian sanctuary named 'Dayr Kādī' mentioned by Ibn al-Nadīm, *Fihrist* (see Dodge, *Fihrist*, 2:757 n.54; 764; 767).

160. Options like 'window, shelf, recess, niche' are offered by Karl (*sic*) Brockelmann, *Lexicon Syriacum* (2nd ed.; Halle, 1928; repr., Tübingen: Max Niemeyer Verlag, 1982), 320.

161. Compare the testimony about the Ṣābian 'head' in Ibn al-Nadīm, *Fihrist* (Dodge, *Fihrist*, 2:753–54).

Manichaeans wrote a letter and went to the market-place in Ḥarrān. When a man was found whom they wanted, they took hold of him and said to him: 'Whatever wage you want (you will) receive: go and convey this letter from such-and-such a monastery to the head of the monastery; i.e., the (head) of (the Manichaean) monastery.' Due to the cleverness of the diabolical plan, he was unaware that it (the letter) was about the murder of the unfortunate fellow (i.e., his own). He made haste and departed, like a lamb to the slaughter. When he speedily arrived at that monastery, he approached the gate and asked those who were present before him for the head of their monastery and requested that they summon him. They quickly went in and informed him, and when the head of the monastery heard, he quickly came out and welcomed that man with honor and great rejoicing. He said to him, 'Come, enter (the compound) and relax for a short time: eat some food, and then you may take away an answer for your letter and depart in peace.'

When they brought the man in, they passed from one room into another, and a second, and a third, more than six or seven (in all), until they reached the man who had been previously quarantined since last year and who was appointed to serve as sacrifice for the approaching festival. He (the leader) instructed him, 'Sit here next to this man.' And after he sat down, that man (the imminent victim) said to him, 'You poor guy! How unfortunate for you!' Then that (other man) responded, 'Why so?' That (first) one continued, 'I acted the same (as you), and when I came here I found another man who was seated (here). During their festival they sacrificed him, and his head is now in that niche, before which they light a candle. They worship it and perform divination by means of it. Now they are preparing to kill me at this festival, and then you will sit here in my place until the next festival, when you yourself will become the sacrifice. However, if you want to escape from here, listen to me and prepare yourself. Watch for when they are ready to kill me (and) stand by my side. When my head falls upon the ground, snatch it up quickly while scattering my blood and directing (it) toward the door. (Even) if they cry out to you, or if they plead with you, or if they promise you numerous gifts, do not set it down; and if they want to seize you, shake some of the blood at them and they will flee from you.'

The man silently received (this advice) and then did and performed (it) with a noble passion just like he had said to him without omitting anything. When they killed him, he grabbed his head and ran toward the door. They for their part were pleading and shouting for him to put (it) down, but that (man) was not willing (to do so) for any (of their) gifts or promises, nor did he lose his nerve out of fear of them. They were unable to get close to him.

With swift feet he took it (the head) and came before 'Abbas,[162] the *'amīr* of Jazīra[163] at that time. When 'Abbas learned what had happened, he dispatched (police), arrested, and imprisoned all of them—men, women, and children.

162. The brother of the caliph al-Manṣūr (754–775 CE).

163. Syriac ܓܙܝܪܬܐ is Arabic الجزيرة, the district of upper Mesopotamia in which Ḥarrān was located. See Le Strange, *Lands of the Eastern Caliphate*, 86–114.

After subjecting them to various types of torture, he impounded everything which they owned, and (thereby) acquired from them more than four or five hundred thousand *minas*.[164]

Abu'l Faraj al-Iṣfahānī, *Kitāb al-aghānī* (ed. Taqīzādeh-Šīrāzī):[165]

It was related to me by Aḥmad b. al-'Abbās al-'Askarī what al-Ḥasan b. 'Ulayl al-'Anazī—Muḥammad b. Yazīd al-Muhallabī—Muḥammad b. 'Abdallāh Ibn Abī 'Uyayna reported about Ḥammād 'Ajrad when Baššār (b. Burd) recited a saying about him (Ḥammād 'Ajrad):

> O Nabataean (?), one 'head' is (already) heavy for me;
>
> Carrying two 'heads' is an even weightier matter!
>
> Charge someone other than me with the worship of two (lords),
>
> And I will occupy myself with the One!
>
> (Ḥammād replied): By God, I do not care for this saying, for he truly irritates me with his ignorance of *zandaqa*. People who believe that the *zanādiqa* worship a head are mistaken. He must think that fools do not know it, since this saying is spoken by the vulgar—there is no truth to it. Moreover, he, by God, knows *zandaqa* better than Mānī himself knew it![166]

4. Individual Manichaeans and Alleged Manichaeans

Abu'l Faraj al-Iṣfahānī, *Kitāb al-aghānī* (ed. Taqīzādeh-Šīrāzī):[167]

> [Ibn Munādhir[168] wrote]: O Ibn Ziyād! O Abū Ja'far![169]
>
> You affect a religion that is different from the one you conceal.
>
> On the outside, sounding like a *zindīq*;
>
> Yet inwardly (you remain) a virtuous Muslim youth.
>
> But you are not a *zindīq*!
>
> You just want to be regarded as clever![170]

---

164. See *Chronique* (ed. Chabot), 68-70; Reeves, "Manichaean 'Blood-Libel'," 219–20.
165. Taqīzādeh-Šīrāzī, *Mānī va dīn-e-ū*, 142 (§24).
166. See Vajda, "Les zindîqs," 205; Johann Fück, "The Rôle of Manicheism under the Early Abbasids," in idem, *Arabische Kultur und Islam im Mittelalter: Ausgewählte Schriften* (Weimar: H. Böhlaus, 1981), 262; Chokr, *Zandaqa*, 270; Reeves, "Manichaean 'Blood-Libel'," 217–18.
167. Taqīzādeh-Šīrāzī, *Mānī va dīn-e-ū*, 143 (§24); see also von Kremer, *Streifzüge*, 73.
168. The satirical poet Muḥammad Ibn Munādhir (d. 813). See Pellat, *Le milieu baṣrien*, 169; also Vajda, "Les zindîqs," 215; Chokr, *Zandaqa*, 292–94.
169. Apparently addressed to the brother of Yaḥyā b. Ziyād.
170. See von Kremer, *Streifzüge*, 42; Pellat, *Le milieu baṣrien*, 258; Chokr, *Zandaqa*, 279. This verse bears witness to how a reputation for *zandaqa* was thought to advance one's literary or intellectual bona fides.

Ibn al-Nadīm, *Fihrist* (ed. Flügel):[171]

The names and account of the leaders of the Manichaeans during the dynasty of the 'Abbāsids, and prior to them:

There was Ja'd b. Dirham[172] who was so tied to Marwān b. Muḥammad that he (the latter) was called 'Marwān the Ja'dite.'[173] He was a tutor for Marwān and his son and introduced him to *zandaqa*. Hishām b. 'Abd al-Malik executed Ja'd during his caliphate[174] after he had been jailed for a long time by Khālid b. 'Abd Allāh al-Qasrī. It is said that the relatives of Ja'd filed a report with Hishām wherein they complained about their impotence and the lengthy imprisonment of Ja'd. Hishām responded: 'Is he still alive?' He then wrote to Khālid about putting him to death. Following the order of Hishām, Khālid executed him on the Day of the Victims (i.e., the tenth day of the month Dhu'l-Ḥijjah or 'Īd al-Aḍḥā), after he announced from the pulpit that he was appointing him a substitute for the slaughtered animal.[175] Even he—I mean Khālid—was charged with *zandaqa*, for his mother was Christian.[176] 'Marwān the Ja'dite' was (also) a *zindīq*.

Among their leaders; i.e., *mutakallimūn* who were apparently Muslim but were concealing (their) *zandaqa*:

Ibn Ṭālūt; Abū Shākir; Ibn Akhī Abī Shākir; Ibn al-A'dā al-Ḥarīzī; Nu'mān; Ibn Abī al-'Awjā'; Ṣāliḥ b. 'Abd al-Quddūs.[177] These wrote books in support of the dualists and the teachings of their followers, and they refuted the numerous books which the (orthodox) *mutakallimūn* wrote about such things.[178]

---

171. Flügel, *Mani*, 77.15–79.7; Ibn al-Nadīm, *K. al-Fihrist* (ed. Tajaddud), 401; Taqīzādeh-Šīrāzī, *Mānī va dīn-e-ū*, 163-64 (§27).

172. A controversial thinker who reportedly denied the uncreated status of the Qur'ān and who disparaged the prophetic credentials of Abraham and Moses. See Vajda, "Les zindîqs," 180-81 n.1; Sadighi, *Mouvements*, 87–88; Francesco Gabrieli, "La «zandaqa» au Ier siècle abbasside," in *L'élaboration de l'Islam: Colloque de Strasbourg, 12-13-14 juin 1959* (Paris: Presses Universitaires de France, 1961), 29–30; W. Montgomery Watt, *The Formative Period of Islamic Thought* (Edinburgh: Edinburgh University Press, 1973), 242–43; Kraemer, "Heresy," 171–72; Chokr, *Zandaqa*, 187–89; van Ess, *Theologie und Gesellschaft*, 2:449–58; idem, *The Flowering of Muslim Theology* (trans. Jane Marie Todd; Cambridge, MA: Harvard University Press, 2006), 72–73.

173. Marwān II (745-750 CE), who became the last Umayyad caliph. Regarding this derogatory nickname, see Chokr, *Zandaqa*, 188–89.

174. Caliph from 724–743 CE.

175. Since Khālid was removed from his post in 737, the year of Ja'd's execution could not have been 742 as claimed by Louis Massignon, "Zindīḳ," *EI*[1] 8:1228; Watt, *Formative Period*, 242; Kraemer, "Heresy," 172; Morony, *Iraq After the Muslim Conquest*, 408.

176. Pellat endorses this accusation. See his *Le milieu baṣrien*, 219.

177. With regard to this figure, see Ignaz Goldziher, "Ṣâliḥ b. 'Abd-al-Ḳuddûs und das Zindîḳthum während der Regierung des Chalifen al-Mahdî," in *Transactions of the Ninth International Congress of Orientalists* (2 vols.; ed. E. Delmar Morgan; London: The Committee of the Congress, 1893), 2:104–29; Fück, "Rôle of Manicheism," 261–62.

178. See the important testimony of Jāḥiẓ below.

Among the poets:

Baššār b. Burd; Isḥāq b. Khalaf; Ibn Sayāba;[179] Salm al-Khāsir;[180] ʿAlī b. al-Khalīl; ʿAlī b. Thābit.

Some who have lately become notorious:

Abū ʿĪsā al-Warrāq; Abū'l-ʿAbbās al-Nāshī; al-Jayhānī Muḥammad b. Aḥmad.[181]

Account of some rulers and leaders who were charged with *zandaqa:*

It has been said that—with the exception of Muḥammad b. Khālid b. Barmak—the Barmakid family were *zanādiqa.*[182] It has been said that Faḍl and his brother Ḥasan were as well. Muḥammad b. [Abū] ʿUbayd Allāh, the secretary for al-Madhī, was a *zindīq*, and after he admitted this, al-Mahdī executed him.[183] I have read in a manuscript by one of the members of the sect that al-Ma'mūn was one of them, but he is not telling the truth about this. It is also said that Muḥammad b. ʿAbd al-Malik al-Zayyāt[184] was a *zindīq.*[185]

Ibn al-Nadīm, *Fihrist* (ed. Flügel):[186]

Some of the leaders of the sect during the ʿAbbāsid dynasty:

Abū Yaḥyā al-Ra'īs;[187] Abū ʿAlī Saʿīd;[188] Abū ʿAlī Rajā';[189] Yazdānbakht. He was the

179. I.e., Ibrāhīm b. Sayāba. See Vajda, "Les zindîqs," 215; Chokr, *Zandaqa*, 297-98.

180. See Chokr, *Zandaqa*, 298.

181. On the value of this list, see the remarks of Massignon, "Zindīḳ," *EI*[1] 8:1228-29.

182. A frequent slur directed with little foundation toward this family. See, e.g., the verse of Aṣmaʿī cited by Ibn Qutayba, *Kitāb al-maʿārif* (2nd ed.; ed. Tharwat ʿUkkāsha; Cairo: Dār al-Maʿārif, 1969), 382.10-12, where the poet represents the Barmakids responding to recited verses from the Qur'ān with the 'sayings (*'aḥādith*) of Mazdak.' Muḥammad b. Khālid was the only member of this family whom the caliph Harun al-Rashid spared during their precipitous fall from power in 803. For further information, see especially D. Sourdel, "Barāmika," *EI*[2] 1:1033-36; also Chokr, *Zandaqa*, 85; Kennedy, *Court of the Caliphs*, 71-79.

183. See especially the lengthy discussions of Vajda, "Les zindîqs," 187-89; Chokr, *Zandaqa*, 71-74. Note also Gil, *History of Palestine*, 289-90.

184. With regard to this figure, see Gutas, *Greek Thought*, 130-31.

185. For other translations, see Flügel, *Mani*, 106-107; Vajda, "Les zindîqs," 179-82; Dodge, *Fihrist*, 2:803-804.

186. Flügel, *Mani*, 79.8-80.2; Ibn al-Nadīm, *K. al-Fihrist* (ed. Tajaddud), 401-402; Taqīzādeh-Šīrāzī, *Mānī va dīn-e-ū*, 164 (§27).

187. Sadighi (*Mouvements*, 87 n.1) suggests that this otherwise unknown figure is to be identified with Abū Hilāl al-Dayḥūrī, the Manichaean leader who according to Ibn al-Nadīm (see below) emigrated from Africa (Egypt?) to Baghdad to replace Miqlāṣ as head of the Manichaean community.

188. This same figure is mentioned by Shahrastānī as one who imparted certain eschatological teachings pertaining to the length of time that Light and Darkness would persist in their mingled state. Therein he is dated to the year AH 271, which correlates with 884/5 CE. Since the anecdote about al-Ma'mūn and Yazdānbakht belongs to an earlier time, Ibn al-Nadīm's list of leaders is not arranged in a chronological sequence.

189. Perhaps the same figure as the Abū Saʿīd Raḥā mentioned by Ibn al-Nadīm below?

one whom al-Ma'mūn[190] brought from Rayy (for a disputation) after guaranteeing his safety. When the *mutakallimūn* had vanquished him, al-Ma'mūn said to him: 'Become a Muslim, O Yazdānbakht! Had I not granted you an assurance of safety, you and I would have a situation to resolve.'

Then Yazdānbakht said to him: 'O Commander of the Faithful! Your advice is heard and your words are received, but you are not one who compels people to abandon their religion.'[191] Al-Ma'mūn replied: 'It is as you say!' Then he lodged him in the Muḥarrim district and appointed him protection, fearing there might be disturbances on account of him. He was an eloquent speaker.[192]

'Abd al-Jabbār, *Mughnī* (ed. Ḥusayn):[193]

Al-Ḥasan b. Mūsā [al-Nawbakhtī] makes mention in his book of different dualist groups; e.g., the adherents of Mānī, whom are sometimes called 'Manichaeans' (*Manāniyya*). He also makes mention of the Mazdakites, the Dayṣānites, the Marcionites, and the Māhāniyya,[194] as well as the Zoroastrians. Aḥmad b. al-Ḥasan al-Misma'ī mentions another group whom he calls the Miqlāṣiyya.[195] Both of them say that among the leaders of the dualists were 'Abd al-Karīm Ibn Abī al-'Awjā', Nu'mān the Dualist,[196] Abū Shākir the Dayṣānite, Ibn Ṭālūt, Ibn Akhī Abū Shākir, 'Abd Allāh Ibn al-Muqaffa', Baššār the blind poet, Ghassān al-Ruhāwī, and Ḥammād 'Ajrad. He (al-Misma'ī?) has related where each one of them differs with his associate with regard to some of the details of the teachings,[197] but they are consistent in (their) dualism.[198]

---

190. Reigned as caliph 813-833 CE.
191. Cf. Q 2:256.
192. For other translations, see also Flügel, *Mani*, 108; Dodge, *Fihrist*, 2:805; Vajda, "Les zindîqs," 182; Berkey, *Formation of Islam*, 170–71.
193. 'Abd al-Jabbār b. Aḥmad al-Hamadhānī, *Al-Mughnī fī abwāb al-tawḥīd wa'l-'adl* (vols.; ed. Ṭāhā Ḥusayn, et al.; Cairo: Al-Shirkah al-'Arabīyah lil-Tibā'ah wa'l-Nashr, 1958–66), 5:9.12–10.1.
194. Mentioned by various authors as a Marcionite or Mazdakite sect. See especially the citation from Nashwān al-Ḥimyarī quoted by Monnot, *Penseurs*, 168 n.4; also Wilferd Madelung, "Abū 'Īsā al-Warrāq über die Bardesaniten, Marcioniten und Kantäer," in *Studien zur Geschichte und Kultur des Vorderen Orients: Festschrift für Bertold Spuler* (ed. Hans R. Roemer and Albrecht Noth; Leiden: Brill, 1981), 220–21.
195. A schismatic movement within Manichaeism. See Ibn al-Nadīm below.
196. I.e., Nu'mān b. al-Mundhir. He is sometimes referred to as a 'Manichaean'; see Chokr, *Zandaqa*, 214.
197. See the following entry.
198. For other translations, see Georges Vajda, "Le témoignage d'al-Māturidī sur la doctrine des Manichéens, des Dayṣānites et des Marcionites: Note annexe,"*Arabica* 13 (1966): 114–15; Monnot, *Penseurs*, 151–52.

ʿAbd al-Jabbār, *Mughnī* (ed. Ḥusayn):[199]

Al-Mismaʿī relates of Ibn Abī al-ʿAwjāʾ that he professed dualist teachings and that he was especially associated with propounding that each one of the Two Principles was divided into five senses, and that the sense which perceived colors was not the same as the sense which perceived tastes, nor was the one which perceived tastes the same as the one which perceived odors.

He said that Ibn al-Muqaffaʿ was especially associated with propounding that the Light only manages the Darkness and allowed itself to enter within it only for the purpose of self-restitution. He dismissed the repulsive tales which the Manichaeans recount about the conflict between the Two Principles. He (however) acknowledged (their) actions and their insubstantiality, and he maintained that action was natural for the Entities: the action associated with Light was always good, whereas the action associated with Darkness was always evil.[200]

He said that Nuʿmān the Dualist—he was the one whom al-Mahdī executed—distinguished himself by denying the movements upon which dualism is formed. He maintained that material substances could be divided until you reached a component that could not be divided (i.e., an atom), and that (such) a component of a substance had length, size, and depth (viz., was tri-dimensional) whether it is a constituent part of Light or a constituent part of Darkness.

Baššār (b. Burd) the blind (poet) distinguished himself by stating that most people lacked knowledge and did not avoid engaging in what was naturally disgusting, such as killing, violence, robbery, and immorality. He disapproved of the notion, which the dualists embrace, that the substance of Light could be simultaneously a deity and something controlled by a deity, a master and something bound by a master, a king and a slave. He also contested whether one portion of a substance could supplicate another portion or humble itself before it.

He reports that Abū Shākir was a proponent of the doctrine of Ibn Dayṣān (i.e., Bardaiṣan) and affirmed (the notion of random) movement. He maintained that it was an attribute of motion, neither being identical nor different from it; he denied that it could be either a thing or nothing, for he said the qualities of otherness and existence can only be predicated of substances, and movement is not a corporeal thing.

It was from him that Hishām b. al-Ḥakam[201] took this teaching about movements.

---

199. ʿAbd al-Jabbār, *Mughnī* (ed. Ḥusayn), 5:20.2–21.9.

200. Note the important remarks of de Blois, *Burzōy's Voyage*, 29.

201. An important early Shiʿite theologian who frequently interacted with dualist thinkers, particularly Abū Shākir the Dayṣānite. See Abu'l-Ḥusayn b. ʿUthmān al-Khayyāṭ, *Kitāb al-intiṣār: Le livre du triomphe et de la réfutation d'Ibn al-Rawandi l'hérétique* (trans. Albert N. Nader; Beyrouth: Éditions les Lettres Orientales, 1957), 37; Israel Friedlaender, "The Heterodoxies of the Shiites in the Presentation of Ibn Ḥazm," *JAOS* 28 (1907): 52–53, 63, 74–75; 29 (1908): 65–68; Ivanow, *Ibn al-Qaddah*, 80–86; Henry Corbin, "From the Gnosis of Antiquity to Ismaili Gnosis," in idem, *Cyclical Time and Ismaili Gnosis* (London: Kegan Paul International, 1983), 166–67; W[ilferd]. Madelung, "Hishām b. al-Ḥakam," *EI*[2] 3:496–98; Heinz Halm, *Shiʿism* (trans. Janet Watson and Marian Hill; 2nd ed.; New York: Columbia University Press, 2004), 39–40.

He relates about Ghassān al-Ruhāwī that he professed the doctrine of the Manichaeans. He maintained that movements are fine bodies which protract motion, and are substantially permanent without fading away.

He reports that Ibn Ṭālūt propounds the teaching of Ibn Abī al-'Awjā' regarding the senses. He maintains that each one of those Two Principles has a sixth sense in addition to the five senses which distinguishes between sensible perceptions and separates them from each other. Its substance differs from that of the Two Principles: it has a fine nature which is invisible, and only its results provide evidence for it. For if there did not exist something like this, one would be unable to distinguish between color and taste. But since one can distinguish (them), it proves there is a sixth sense.[202]

Abu'l Faraj al-Iṣfahānī, *Kitāb al-aghānī* (ed. Taqīzādeh-Šīrāzī):[203]

'Alā' b. al-Bandār said: Al-Walīd[204] was a *zindīq*. There was a man from Kalb who was advocating the doctrine of dualism. I visited al-Walīd one day and that Kalbī was with him, and between them there was a basket whose top was fastened with what appeared to me to be green silk. He (i.e., the caliph) said, 'Come closer, O 'Alā',' and so I approached and he lifted up the silk. Inside the basket was a human image. Because mercury and ammonia had been applied to its eyelid, it would blink as if it were moving. He said, 'O 'Alā', this is Mānī! God sent no prophet prior to him, nor has He sent a prophet after him!' I replied, 'O Commander of the Faithful! Fear God and do not allow this charlatan to mislead you from your faith!' The Kalbī said to him, 'O Commander of the Faithful! Did I not warn you that 'Alā' could not tolerate this tradition?'[205]

---

202. For other translations, see Vajda, "Le témoignage d'al-Māturidī: Note annexe," 127–28; Monnot, *Penseurs*, 172–74.

203. Taqīzādeh-Šīrāzī, *Mānī va dīn-e-ū*, 138 (§24).

204. The delinquent caliph Walīd II (743–744 CE). This Umayyad prince was often rumored to have Manichaean sympathies. Note Theophanes, *Chronographia* (ed. de Boor), 1:416.18–24: Οὐαλὶδ δὲ Πέτρον τὸν ἁγιώτατον μητροπολίτην Δαμασκοῦ γλωττοτομηθῆναι ἐκέλευσε ὡς ἀναφανδὸν ἐλέγχοντα τήν τῶν 'Αράβων *καὶ Μανιχαίων* δυσσέβειαν 'Walid commanded that Peter, who was the holy metropolitan of Damascus, have his tongue cut out because he openly convicted the Arabs *and the Manichaeans* of impiety,' a curious passage referenced by Ilse Rochow, "Zum Fortleben des Manichäismus im byzantinischen Reich nach Justinian I," *Byzantinoslavica* 40 (1979): 20. Compare too the *ḥadīth* found in al-Azdī that brands Walīd 'the *zindīq* of Quraysh and the Arabs,' cited by Suliman Bashear, *Arabs and Others in Early Islam* (Princeton, NJ: Darwin Press, 1997), 102. For more on Walīd II and his peculiarities, see Abbott, *Studies in Arabic Literary Papyri, III*, 90–103. The text of Theophanes is cited from *Theophanis Chronographia* (2 vols.; ed. Carolus de Boor; Lipsiae: B. G. Teubneri, 1883–85).

205. See also Chokr, *Zandaqa*, 254; Toufic Fahd, "Ṣābi'a," *EI*[2] 8:676; Reeves, "A Manichaean 'Blood-Libel'," 230–32.

Abū Nuwās *apud* Jāḥiẓ, *Kitāb al-ḥayawān* (ed. Taqīzādeh-Šīrāzī):[206]

(From a satirical set of verses directed against Abān al-Lāḥiqī):[207]
He (i.e., Abān) said: 'How can you bear witness[208] without having seen?
I could never bear witness unless my own eyes see (it)!'[209]
Then I said: 'Praised be the Lord!'
But he said: 'Praised be Mānī!'[210]
And I said: 'Jesus was a Messenger (*rasūl*)!'
But he responded: '(Yes), from Satan!'
I said: 'Moses was a faithful mouthpiece for the Benefactor!'
But he said: 'Does your Lord then have an eyeball and a tongue?!'[211]

Abu'l Faraj al-Iṣfahānī, *Kitāb al-aghānī* (ed. Taqīzādeh-Šīrāzī):[212]

Abū Nūwās[213] said: I had thought that Ḥammād 'Ajrad was accused of *zandaqa* only on account of the shamelessness of his poetry until (the time) when I was imprisoned in a jail with *zanādiqa*. Then (I learned) that Ḥammād 'Ajrad was an *imām* among their *imāms*, and that he had composed poetry which combined verse couplets (which) they would recite in their prayers![214]

206. Taqīzādeh-Šīrāzī, *Mānī va dīn-e-ū*, 93 (§4).

207. A Baṣran poet (d. ca. 815/16 CE) who enjoyed the patronage of the Barmakids and who prepared metrical versions of *Kalīla wa-Dimna* and *Kitāb Bilawhar wa-Yūdāsaf*, works of Indian origin which were adapted by Manichaeans. See Vajda, "Les zindîqs," 207-10; Pellat, *Le milieu baṣrien*, 179; Lang, *Wisdom of Balahvar*, 34; S. M. Stern, "Abān b. 'Abd al-Ḥamīd al-Lāḥiḳī," *EI*[2] 1:2; Chokr, *Zandaqa*, 298–301.

208. I.e., pronounce the *shahāda* bearing witness that only God is God and that Muḥammad is His Prophet.

209. For this typically Manichaean epistemological stance, see Sarah Stroumsa and Gedaliahu G. Stroumsa, "Aspects of Anti-Manichaean Polemics in Late Antiquity and under Early Islam," *Harvard Theological Review* 81 (1988): 46; van Ess, *Flowering of Muslim Theology*, 84–89.

210. Sarah Stroumsa, *Freethinkers of Medieval Islam: Ibn al-Rāwandī, Abū Bakr al-Rāzī, and Their Impact on Islamic Thought* (Leiden: Brill, 1999), 137.

211. An allusion to human creation after the likeness of God; cf. Gen 1:26–27. Augustine similarly depicts Manichaean critics carping about whether God had a nose, teeth, beard, or internal organs; note his *De Gen. contra Manichaeos* 1.17.27 and the remarks of Elizabeth A. Clark, *Reading Renunciation: Asceticism and Scripture in Early Christianity* (Princeton, NJ: Princeton University Press, 1999), 80.
See also Pellat, *Le milieu baṣrien*, 220–21; Chokr, *Zandaqa*, 245–46; H. T. Norris, "*Shu'ūbiyyah* in Arabic Literature," in *'Abbasid Belles-Lettres* (ed. Ashtiany, et al.), 42.

212. Taqīzādeh-Šīrāzī, *Mānī va dīn-e-ū*, 141 (§24).

213. For this infamous libertine poet, see the profile sketched by Nicholson, *Literary History*[2], 292–96.

214. See also Martin Schreiner, "Beiträge zur Geschichte der theologischen Bewegungen im Islâm," *ZDMG* 52 (1898): 475; Vajda, "Les zindîqs," 205; Gabrieli, "La «zandaqa»,"

Bīrūnī, *Risālah lil-Bīrūnī fī fihrist kutub Muḥammad ibn Zakarīyyā al-Rāzī* (ed. Sachau):[215]

... I am recording for you some of the books of Abū Bakr (i.e., Muḥammad b. Zakariyyā' al-Rāzī): those to which I can testify, or those (mentioned) within them whose names I stumbled upon when he referred to them and cited them. Did I not have such esteem for you, I would never have acted to provide it on account of (the risk) of earning the hatred of his opponents, for they may think that I belong to his school of thought and am one of those who make no difference between where he arrives during his exertion for what is right and to what he is favorably disposed and for which he is immoderately zealous. (Abū Bakr al-Rāzī was such a one) so that he became disgraced by his audacity. He was not content with harshness on the subject of religions: he neglected, shunned, and paid them no attention, aside from occupying himself with maligning them with wicked utterances and satanic deeds, until he was prompted to call attention to the books of Mānī and his followers as a stratagem against religions, including Islam.[216]

Ibn Abī Uṣaybi'a, '*Uyūn* (ed. Taqīzādeh-Šīrāzī):[217]

[Re: Abū Bakr Muḥammad b. Zakariyyā' al-Rāzī, *Refutation of Sīsan the dualist*]:[218] A book which alternates (statements) between he (i.e., al-Rāzī) and Sīsan the Manichaean.[219] He points out the issues wherein he errs and the weakness of his system in seven essays.[220]

26; Chokr, *Zandaqa*, 48, 271; Reeves, "A Manichaean 'Blood-Libel'," 217.

215. *Āthār* (ed. Sachau), XXXVIII-XXXIX; Taqīzādeh-Šīrāzī, *Mānī va dīn-e-ū*, 208-209 (§36).

216. For other translations, see D. M. Dunlop, *Arab Civilization to A.D. 1500* (New York: Praeger, 1971), 238; also Julius Ruska, "Al-Birūni als Quelle für das Leben und die Schriften al-Rāzi's," *Isis* 5 (1923): 29–30; Strohmaier, "Al-Bīrūnī über Mani und Manichäer," 594; cf. idem, *In den Gärten*[2], 146.

217. Taqīzādeh-Šīrāzī, *Mānī va dīn-e-ū*, 268–69 (§58).

218. This work appears as #140 (Ruska: #141) in Bīrūnī, *Risālah fī fihrist kutub Muḥammad b. Zakariyyā' al-Rāzī*. See Taqīzādeh-Šīrāzī, *Mānī va dīn-e-ū*, 210 (§36); Ruska, "Al-Biruni als Quelle," 46. It is also mentioned in Ibn al-Nadīm's *Fihrist*; note Stroumsa, *Freethinkers*, 101 n.97.

219. Mani's first successor as leader of the Manichaean religion. Greek sources (e.g., the so-called 'short' abjuration-formula) give his name as Σισίννιος, which Arabic sources shorten to Sīs or Sīsan. See Ibn al-Nadīm, *Fihrist* (Flügel, *Mani*, 66.9–11) translated herein; Flügel, *Mani*, 316–17. The text of the 'short' Greek abjuration is available in Alfred Adam, ed., *Texte zum Manichäismus* (2nd ed.; Berlin: Walter de Gruyter, 1969), 93–97, where the reference to Sisinnios is 94.35–36. His name should perhaps be restored in Coptic *Homil.* 50.24 (cf. 82.5–6, 20); also in M 5569 verso line 42. See F. C. Andreas and W. B. Henning, "Mitteliranische Manichaica aus Chinesisch-Turkestan III," *SPAW* (1934): 862.

220. See also Strohmaier, "Al-Bīrūnī über Mani und Manichäer," 596 n.33.

a. Traditions about 'Abd al-Karīm Ibn Abu'l-'Awjā'[221]

Jāḥiẓ, *Kitāb ḥujaj al-nubuwwa* (ed. Taqīzādeh-Šīrāzī):[222]

That which obstructed them (i.e., the Meccan opponents of the Prophet) is the same thing that obstructed Ibn Abī al-'Awjā', Isḥāq b. Ṭālūt, al-Nu'mān b. al-Mundhir, and other pieces of garbage like them. They substituted shame for honor, disbelief for belief, misery for fortune, and doubt for certainty. Yet doubt is characteristic of *zandaqa*, for they manufacture traditions, propagate stories, spread them throughout the cities, and defame the Qur'ān. They question its obscurity, validity, and universality, and they forge writings against its followers.[223]

Ṭabarī, *Ta'rīkh* (ed. de Goeje):[224]

It is said that 'Abd al-Karīm b. Abī al-'Awjā', the maternal uncle of Ma'n b. Zā'idah, was brought before Muḥammad b. Sulaymān when he was governor of Kūfa. He commanded that he be jailed. On the authority of Qutham b. Ja'far, al-Ḥusayn b. Ayyūb, and others, Abū Zayd says that many interceded for him in the 'City of Peace' (i.e., Baghdad) and pleaded with Abū Ja'far (i.e., the caliph al-Manṣūr). Since those who spoke about him were unreliable, he commanded Muḥammad in writing to refrain (from further action) regarding him until he (the caliph) had reached a decision about him.

Ibn Abī al-'Awjā' spoke to Abū al-Jabbār, who was devoted to Abū Ja'far and Muḥammad and later their sons after them, and said to him: 'If the *'amīr* delayed my case for three days, he would acquire one hundred thousand (*dirhams*) and you yourself would get so-and-so much.' Abū al-Jabbār informed Muḥammad and he said: 'You have reminded me about him! By God, I had forgotten about him. When I leave Friday prayers, remind me (again) about him.'

When he left (Friday prayers), he reminded him. Then he summoned Ibn Abī al-'Awjā' and gave orders for him to be beheaded. When he ascertained that he was going to be executed, he declared: 'Now by God, if you kill me, (know that) I have invented four thousand *ḥadīth*s in which I prohibit what is permitted and permit what is prohibited. By God, I have already made you break fast when you should be fasting, and fast when you should be breaking your fast!' Then he was beheaded.

Then the messenger from Abū Ja'far arrived with his letter to Muḥammad: 'Take care that you not make anything happen with regard to the case of Ibn Abī al-'Awjā'! If you have already acted, I will do such and such to you,' threatening him with punishment. Muḥammad said to the messenger: 'This is the head of Ibn Abī al-'Awjā', and that is his torso gibbeted by the garbage dump. Report to the

---

221. Perhaps the most notorious Manichaean of the early 'Abbāsid period. See Vajda, "Les zindîqs," 193–96; Fück, "Rôle of Manicheism," 260–61; van Ess, *Theologie und Gesellschaft*, 1:439–41; Chokr, *Zandaqa*, 109–11; 211-17.

222. Taqīzādeh-Šīrāzī, *Mānī va dīn-e-ū*, 97–98 (§6).

223. For another translation, see *Sobriety and Mirth* (trans. Colville), 130.

224. Ṭabarī, *Ta'rīkh* (ed. de Goeje), 3/1:375–77.

Commander of the Faithful what I have told you.'

When the messenger conveyed his reply to Abū Ja'far, he was furious with him. He ordered a letter to be written removing him (from office), and he said: 'By God, I should kill him in retaliation for executing him!' Later he sent for 'Īsā b. 'Alī and when he came to him he said: 'This is your doing! You suggested that this boy receive appointment (as governor) so I appointed him, a stupid boy with no knowledge of what he is bringing about! He had the audacity to kill a man without obtaining my opinion about him or waiting for my orders! I have just written about removing him (from office), and God help me if I do not do such and such to him,' threatening him with punishment.

'Īsā remained silent until his anger remitted (and) then he responded: 'O Commander of the Faithful, Muḥammad put this man to death only for *zandaqa*.[225] If his execution was justified, then the credit goes to you, but if it was wrong the responsibility is Muḥammad's. By God, O Commander of the Faithful, if you remove him for this lapse in what he did, he will depart (office) with commendation and renown, and the reports (about his dismissal) among the people will blame you.' He therefore commanded that the letters be shredded and that he continue in his job.[226]

Ibn Bābawayh, *Kitāb al-Tawḥīd* (ed. Ḥusaynī al-Ṭihrānī):[227]

Later during the following year he (Ja'far al-Ṣādiq[228]) met him (Ibn Abu'l-'Awjā') at the holy place (i.e., Mecca). One of his followers reported to him: 'Ibn Abu'l-'Awjā' has become a Muslim!' The sage (may the blessing of God be upon him!) replied: 'He is far too blind for this (to be true); he is no Muslim.' When he caught sight of the sage, he said: 'My leader and my master!' Then the sage said to him: 'What has brought you to this place?' He answered: 'Bodily habit, national custom, and a wish to see the foolishness practiced by people here who are shaving and casting stones!' The sage replied: 'O 'Abd al-Karīm, your insolence and your delusion are unsurpassed!' He was about to answer, but he said to him: 'There are no arguments during the Pilgrimage!'[229] He shook off his garment (*ridā'*) from his touch and said: 'If the matter were to be as you say—and it is certainly not as you say—then both we and you will be delivered. But if the matter is as we say—and it certainly is as we say—then we will be delivered and you will perish!' Then 'Abd al-Karīm turned to those who were with him and said: 'I feel a fever[230] in my heart; take me away!' They took him away and he died.[231] May God

225. This is the sole mention of the alleged crime in Ṭabarī's narrative.

226. See also Kennedy, *History of al-Tabarī XXIX*, 72–73.

227. Ibn Bābawayh, *[Kitāb] al-Tawḥīd* (ed. Abī Ja'far Muḥammad b. 'Alī Hāshim al-Ḥusaynī al-Ṭihrānī; Teheran: Maktabat al-Ṣudūq, 1967), 298.9–17.

228. The sixth Imām (d. 765 CE) and putative founder of Shi'ite law. Regarding his importance, see Berkey, *Formation of Islam*, 131–32; also Marshall G. S. Hodgson, "How Did the Early Shī'a Become Sectarian?" *JAOS* 75 (1955): 1–13.

229. For this and other precepts, see A. J. Wensinck and J. Jomier, "Iḥrām," *EI*² 3:1052–53.

230. Read with the critical apparatus حرارة in place of حزازة.

231. According to most of our sources, Ibn Abu'l-'Awjā' was executed seven years after

show him mercy![232]

Baghdādī, *al-Farq bayn al-firaq* (ed. Taqīzādeh-Šīrāzī):[233]

'Abd al-Karīm Ibn Abu'l-'Awjā', an uncle of Ma'n b. Zā'ida,[234] was one of them.[235] He combined within himself four sorts of errors. The first was that he privately observed the Manichaean religion, one of the dualist groups. Secondly, he accepted the doctrine of *tanāsukh* (i.e., metempsychosis).[236] Third, he sympathized with the Rāfiḍites[237] with regard to the imamate. Fourthly, he accepted the doctrine of the Qadarites[238] on matters of justice and injustice. He forged numerous *ḥadīths* with *isnāds* which have misled those who have no knowledge how to invalidate or confirm (such traditions). Those traditions which he forged are entirely erroneous regarding the ascription of human characteristics to God (*tashbīh*) and the denial of such attributes (*ta'ṭīl*), and in some of them he changes the stipulations of canonical law (*sharī'a*).[239]

He was the one who corrupted the Rāfiḍites: the fast of Ramaḍān (is synchronized) with the new moon, and he dissuaded them from regarding the new moon with a calculation which he devised for them. He attributed this calculation to Ja'far al-Ṣādiq!

An account of this deceiver was presented before Abu Ja'far Muḥammad b. Sulaymān, al-Manṣūr's governor over Kūfa, and he commanded that he be executed.[240] 'Abd al-Karīm said: 'By killing me you accomplish nothing! I have already fabricated four thousand *ḥadīths* in which I permit what is prohibited and prohibit

the death of Ja'far al-Ṣādiq. This is thus an apocryphal tale.

232. See also Monnot, *Penseurs*, 313–14.

233. Taqīzādeh-Šīrāzī, *Mānī va dīn-e-ū*, 190–91 (§32).

234. A general and governor during the late Umayyad and early 'Abbāsid periods. See Chokr, *Zandaqa*, 76; Arjomand, "'Abd Allah Ibn al-Muqaffa'," 35.

235. I.e., a Manichaean.

236. See Chapters 3 and 4 above.

237. An early term of abuse ('rejectors, deserters') for those Shi'ites who execrated Abū Bakr, 'Umar, and 'Uthmān for usurping the rightful succession of 'Alī to the caliphate. See Friedlaender, "Heterodoxies," *JAOS* 29 (1908): 137–57; W. Montgomery Watt, "The Rāfiḍites: A Preliminary Study," *Oriens* 16 (1963): 110–21; Etan Kohlberg, "al-Rāfiḍa or al-Rawāfiḍ," *EI*² 8:386–89; Halm, *Shi'ism*², 39–40; Patricia Crone, *God's Rule: Government and Islam* (New York: Columbia University Press, 2004), 73–75.

238. I.e., the proponents of free will. See Josef van Ess, "Ḳadariyya," *EI*² 4:368–72. For discussion of the political implications of this issue, see Majid Fakhry, *A History of Islamic Philosophy* (3d ed.; New York: Columbia University Press, 2004), 44–57.

239. Examples of such forgeries as reported by Ibn Qutayba are briefly described by Johann Fück, "Spuren des Zindīqtums in der islamischen Tradition," in idem, *Arabische Kultur und Islam im Mittelalter: Ausgewählte Schriften* (Weimar: H. Böhlaus, 1981), 267-71; note also Chokr, *Zandaqa*, 133–40. According to Yāqūt, he (also?) authored a book which was intended to subvert the Qur'ān and cast doubts on its alleged inimitability. See Sadighi, *Mouvements*, 98.

240. See Sadighi, *Mouvements*, 90.

what is permitted. I made the Rāfiḍites eat and drink on one of their fast days and made them fast on a day which was one during which they could eat and drink!'[241]

Bīrūnī, *Āthār al-bāqiya 'an-il-qurūn al-khāliya* (ed. Sachau):[242]

I have read some reports that Abū Ja'far Muḥammad b. Sulaymān, the governor of Kūfa during the administration of al-Manṣūr, arrested 'Abd al-Karīm Ibn Abī al-'Awjā', who was the uncle of Ma'n b. Zā'ida. He was one of the Manichaeans. However, he had many intercessors in 'the City of Peace' (i.e., Baghdad), and these persistently petitioned al-Manṣūr in order that he might write to Muḥammad to refrain (from further action) regarding him. Meanwhile 'Abd al-Karīm was expecting the arrival of the letter which would pertain to him. He said to 'Abū'l-Jabbār when he was alone with him: 'Should the prince (*'amīr*) delay my case for three days, he will have one hundred thousand dirhems!'

'Abū'l-Jabbār informed Muḥammad of this, and he said: 'You have reminded me about him, and I had already forgotten him. When I have returned from Friday prayers, remind me again about him.' When he returned, he reminded him of his words. He then sent for him and issued the command that he be beheaded. When he was certain that he was going to be executed, he said: 'By God, since you are truly going to kill me, (I should confess that) I have invented four thousand *ḥadīth*s (wherein) I forbid that which is permitted, and permit that which is proscribed. Already I have made you eat and drink on a fast day, and I have made you fast when you could be eating and drinking!' Then he was beheaded, and it was after it (i.e., his execution) that the letter pertaining to him arrived.[243]

b. Traditions about 'Abd Allāh Ibn al-Muqaffa'[244]

Qāsim b. Ibrāhīm, *K. al-radd 'alā al-zindīq al-la'īn Ibn al-Muqaffa'* (ed. Taqīzādeh-Šīrāzī):[245]

Then after Mānī the father of confusion and corruption came a wicked succes-

241. For another translation, see Abū Manṣūr 'Abd al-Qāhir b. Ṭāhir al-Baghdādī, *Moslem Schisms and Sects (Al-Fark Bain al-Firak) Part II* (ed. Abraham S. Halkin; Tel Aviv, 1935; repr., Philadelphia: Porcupine Press, 1978), 94–95. Note also Sadighi, *Mouvements*, 100–101.

242. *Āthār* (ed. Sachau), 67.17–68.3; Taqīzādeh-Šīrāzī, *Mānī va dīn-e-ū*, 202 (§34).

243. For another translation, see Sachau, *Chronology*, 80.

244. Regarding this tragic figure, see Sadighi, *Mouvements*, 96-100; Dominique Sourdel, "La biographie d'Ibn al-Muqaffa' d'après les sources anciennes," *Arabica* 1 (1954): 307–23; Francesco Gabrieli, "Ibn al-Muḳaffa'," *EI*² 3:883–85; Patricia Crone and Michael Cook, *Hagarism: The Making of the Islamic World* (Cambridge: Cambridge University Press, 1977), 102; Fück, "Rôle of Manicheism," 263–64; J. D. Latham, "Ibn al-Muqaffa' and Early 'Abbasid Prose," in *'Abbasid Belles-Lettres* (ed. Ashtiany, et al.), 48–77; idem, "Ebn al-Moqaffa'," *EncIr* 8:39–43; Arjomand, "'Abd Allah Ibn al-Muqaffa'," 9–36; van Ess, *Theologie und Gesellschaft*, 2:22–36, 5:104–108; Chokr, *Zandaqa*, 189–209.

245. Taqīzādeh-Šīrāzī, *Mānī va dīn-e-ū*, 81 (§3); Michelangelo Guidi, *La lotta tra l'Islam e il Manicheismo: Un libro di Ibn al-Muqaffa' contro il Corano confutato da al-Qāsim b. Ibrāhīm* (Roma: R. Accademia Nazionale dei Lincei, 1927), 8.4–11 (text).

sor appointed by Iblīs to succeed Mānī (in spreading his) delusions—one whose name was Ibn al-Muqaffaʿ, may he be forever cursed by God! He inherited Mānī's blasphemous legacy. He received his inheritance from Mānī his father, tied the nooses of his errors around his neck, and tightened the loops of his perditions around his throat. He raised up the error of his source, and uttered slanderous lies against God and against His messengers. He composed an incomprehensible book[246] in which he acquitted himself of all lies and untruths. He spoke about the faults of the messengers[247] and he invented lies about the 'Lord of the worlds.'[248]

Qāsim b. Ibrāhīm, *K. al-radd ʿalā al-zindīq al-laʿīn Ibn al-Muqaffaʿ* (ed. Guidi):[249]

The first thing that he began his book with was ... 'In the Name of Light the Merciful and Beneficent! ....' Then he says: 'Most Exalted is Light, the Mighty King! ....' Next he says: 'the One Who disclosed His greatness, wisdom, and luminescence to His friends ....' Then he says: 'the One Whose might compels His enemies—those who are ignorant of Him and blind to Him—to extol Him ....' Then he says: 'May Light be praised and sanctified!'[250]

Bīrūnī, *Taḥqīq mā lil-Hind* (ed. Sachau):[251]

I would love to have the ability to translate the book (entitled) *Pañcatantra*.[252] It is known among us as the *Book of Kalīla and Dimna*.[253] It has been widely reproduced in Persian, Indian, and then Arabic; and the Persian (was given) according to the version of persons who might be suspected of having altered its passages, such

---

246. Note John Wansbrough, *Quranic Studies: Sources and Methods of Scriptural Interpretation* (Oxford: Oxford University Press, 1977), 160.

247. I.e., the Muslim prophets.

248. A frequent qur'ānic epithet for God; see Q 1:2; 2:131; 5:28; 6:45; etc. Regarding its unique character, see Charles Cutler Torrey, *The Jewish Foundation of Islam* (New York: Jewish Institute of Religion Press, 1933), 52; note also the remarks and references in Arthur Jeffery, *The Foreign Vocabulary of the Quran* (Baroda, 1938; repr., Lahore: Al-Biruni, 1977), 208–209.

249. Guidi, *La lotta tra l'Islam*, 8.21–22, 9.8, 9.18, 10.14–15, 11.7 (text).

250. See also Schreiner, "Beiträge," 473–75; Nyberg, "Zum Kampf," 435; van Ess, *Theologie und Gesellschaft*, 5:104.

251. Edward Sachau, ed., *Kitāb fī taḥqīq mā l'il-Hind: Alberuni's India: An Account of the Religion, Philosophy, Literature, Chronology, Astronomy, Customs, Laws and Astrology of India about A.D. 1030* (London: Trübner, 1887), 76.7–10; also available in Taqīzādeh-Šīrāzī, *Mānī va dīn-e-ū*, 213 (§37).

252. The *Pañcatantra*, or 'Book of Five Topics,' a popular Indian collection of animal fables. See *The Panchatantra* (trans. Arthur W. Ryder; Chicago, IL: University of Chicago Press, 1925); *Pañcatantra: The Book of India's Folk Wisdom* (trans. Patrick Olivelle; Oxford: Oxford University Press, 1997).

253. With regard to the extraordinary popularity and influence of this anthology of animal fables, see Carl Brockelmann, "Kalīla wa-Dimna," *EI*² 4:503–506; Robert Irwin, "The Arabic Beast Fable," *Journal of the Warburg and Courtauld Institutes* 55 (1992): 36–50.

as 'Abd Allāh Ibn al-Muqaffa' in his expansion of its chapter about Burzōy.[254] He meant to engender doubts among those who were weak in the tenets of the faith and to break them away in the interests of summoning them to the teachings of the Manichaeans. And if he is to be suspected of making additions to it, it is hardly doubtful that he acted similarly when he translated.[255]

Bīrūnī, *Taḥqīq mā lil-Hind* (ed. Sachau):[256]

Another calamity occurred on account of the *zanādiqa*: (they are) the followers of Mānī like Ibn al-Muqaffa', 'Abd al-Karīm Ibn Abī al-'Awjā', and others like them. They sowed doubt among those who were weak-natured about the One Primal deity because of (His dispensing of) justice and injustice, and they inclined them to dualism. Moreover they extolled the biography of Mānī[257] until they (the weak-natured) were caught in his snare.[258] He was a man who exhibited no limits in the ignorance of his base teachings (and) sayings about the form of the world, as is evident from his misrepresentations, and he promulgated these in an eloquent fashion.[259] Joined to some of the preceding Jewish deceptions, it resulted in certain opinions being ascribed to Islam—God of course being far removed from anything like it![260]

Ibn Khallikān, *Wafayāt al-A'yān* (ed. Taqīzādeh-Šīrāzī):[261]

In spite of his excellence, Ibn al-Muqaffa' was suspected of *zandaqa*. Jāḥiẓ has said that Ibn al-Muqaffa', Muṭī' b. Iyās, and Yaḥyā b. Ziyād were (all) suspect with regard to their religions. (Someone remarked: 'And how did Jāḥiẓ forget about himself?'). The caliph al-Mahdī b. al-Manṣūr used to say: 'I have yet to find a book of *zandaqa* whose origin could not be traced back to Ibn al-Muqaffa'.[262]

---

254. Burzōy, physician to the Sasanian emperor Khusrau Anōshirvān (531–579 CE), and the supposed translator of *Kalīla wa-Dimna* from Sanskrit to Pahlavi, from which translations into Syriac and Arabic were subsequently made. For further information, see de Blois, *Burzōy's Voyage*; Chokr, *Zandaqa*, 197–202.

255. For other translations, see Sachau, *Alberuni's India*, 1:159; de Blois, *Burzōy's Voyage*, 26–27.

256. *Kitāb fī taḥqīq mā l'il-Hind* (ed. Sachau), 132.7–12; also available in Taqīzādeh-Šīrāzī, *Mānī va dīn-e-ū*, 214 (§37).

257. Arabic *sīrat Mānī*. This would seem to suggest that a hagiographic *vita* of Mani circulated in Arabic in competition with the similarly hagiographic *Sīra* of Muḥammad. Note Werner Sundermann, "Studien zur kirchengeschichtlichen Literatur der iranischen Manichäer I," *Altorientalische Forschungen* 13 (1986): 91.

258. See also de Blois, *Burzōy's Voyage*, 30.

259. Alternatively: 'he promulgated these in multiple languages.'

260. For other translations, see Sachau, *Alberuni's India*, 1:264; Strohmaier, *In den Gärten*[2], 184.

261. Taqīzādeh-Šīrāzī, *Mānī va dīn-e-ū*, 270 (§59).

262. See also *Ibn Khallikan's Biographical Dictionary* (4 vols.; trans. B[aro]n MacGuckin de Slane; Paris: Oriental Translation Fund of Great Britain and Ireland, 1842-71), 1:431–32; Browne, *Literary History*, 1:207–208 n.1.

5. Manichaean Sectarianism

Jāḥiẓ, *Kitāb al-tarbīʿ wa'l-tadwīr* (ed. Pellat):[263]

Are not all religious communities supporters of states and rulers except for the *zanādiqa*? Have not all past leaders put them to death? Are you not amazed that we continue to see the Miqlāṣiyya,[264] the Dīnāwariyya,[265] and the Toghuzghuziyya?[266]

Ibn al-Nadīm, *Fihrist* (ed. Flügel):[267]

Controversy among the Manichaeans with regard to the *Imāmate* after Mānī:

The Manichaeans say: Before Mānī completed his ascension to the Light-Paradises, he appointed Sīs to serve as *imām* after him, and he (i.e., Sīs) directed the pure religion of God[268] until he died.[269] (After him), the *imāms* transmitted the religion from one to the next with no disagreement among them until there appeared among them a dissident group known as the Dināwariyya.[270] They criti-

---

263. Charles Pellat, *Le Kitāb at-tarbīʿ wa-t-tadwīr de Ǧāḥiẓ* (Damas: Institut français de Damas, 1955), 77 (§138); also Taqīzādeh-Šīrāzī, *Mānī va dīn-e-ū*, 98 (§7).

264. All extant copies read this name as المصدقية (al-Muṣaddiqiyya?). Pellat suggests emending to either Mazdakiyya (he adopts this choice) or to Miqlāṣiyya. I have followed Sundermann and de Blois in opting for the second choice, thus endorsing Jāḥiẓ's awareness of at least three regional factions of Manichaean communities. See Werner Sundermann, "Dīnāvarīya," *EncIr* 7:419; also François de Blois, "*Naṣrānī* (Ναζωραῖος) and *ḥanīf* (ἐθνικός): Studies on the Religious Vocabulary of Christianity and of Islam," *BSOAS* 65 (2002): 7 n.32.

265. See the following entry from Ibn al-Nadīm.

266. Three distinct Manichaean communities differentiated by language and region, associated with Mesopotamia, central Asia, and the Uighur empire respectively. For other translations, see Maurice Adad, "Le *Kitāb al-Tarbīʿ wa-l-Tadwīr* d'al-Ǧāḥiẓ: Traduction française, III," *Arabica* 14 (1967): 186; *Sobriety and Mirth* (trans. Colville), 292.

267. Flügel, *Mani*, 66.8–69.5; Ibn al-Nadīm, *K. al-Fihrist* (ed. Tajaddud), 397–98; Taqīzādeh-Šīrāzī, *Mānī va dīn-e-ū*, 158–59 (§27).

268. Following the suggestion of Vajda ("Les zindîqs," 175 n.2) to read this phrase as a reflex of authentic Manichaean vocabulary as evidenced in Middle Iranian texts.

269. According to Kessler (*Mani*, 241), the language employed by this statement is not that of a hostile or even dispassionate observer, and he makes the plausible suggestion that it may stem from an early 'manichäischen Apostelgeschichte.'

270. I.e., the 'devout ones.' Although they did not emerge until the late sixth or early seventh century, the sect appears to have traced itself back to the initial missionary labors of Mār Ammō in Khurāsān. See M 2 I *apud* F. C. Andreas and W. B. Henning, "Mitteliranische Manichaica aus Chinesisch-Turkestan II," *SPAW* (1932): 304–305; also Mary Boyce, *A Reader in Manichaean Middle Persian and Parthian* (Acta Iranica 9; Leiden: Brill, 1975), 41; Lieu, *Manichaeism*^{2}, 220; Hans-Joachim Klimkeit, *Gnosis on the Silk Road: Gnostic Texts from Central Asia* (San Francisco: HarperCollins, 1993), 218 n.27. See also M 5815 *apud* Andreas-Henning, "Mitteliranische Manichaica ... III," 854–57, esp. 854 n.1; also Boyce, *Reader*, 50–52; Werner Sundermann, "Dīnāvarīya," *EncIr*

cized their *imām* and refused to obey him. The *imāmate* could not continue anywhere but in Bābil, and it was not permitted for the *imām* to be in any other place. This group spoke against that doctrine and they did not stop their opposition to it along with some other controversial things which are not worth mentioning here until Mihr was entrusted with the supreme leadership. This took place during the rule of al-Walīd b. 'Abd al-Malik while Khālid b. 'Abd Allāh al-Qasrī was governor in 'Irāq.[271]

A man named Zādhormuz joined them and remained with them for a time, but then he withdrew from them. He was a man who had extensive possessions, but he relinquished them to travel the path of *ṣiddīqūt*.[272] Later he claimed that he witnessed things which he found disreputable, and so he sought to join the Dināwariyya who lived on the other side of the river at Balkh. He came to Madā'in, (a place) where he had a friend who was very wealthy and who was serving as secretary to Ḥajjāj b. Yūsuf. He described his concerns to him and the reasons for his abandoning everything and heading for Khurāsān to join the Dināwariyya. Then the secretary said to him: 'Let me be your Khurāsān! I will build a church for you and I will furnish you with whatever you require for it.'[273]

So he stayed there with him, and he (i.e., the secretary) built a church for him. Zādhormuz then wrote a letter to the Dināwariyya wherein he invited them (to send) a leader whom he could install in it. They wrote back to him that it was not permitted for the leader to be anywhere other than at the center of imperial power in Bābil.[274] He sought someone who would be right for this (position), but there was no one apart from himself; accordingly, he decided (to assume leadership). When he was growing weak, which means that death was near, they[275] requested for him to appoint them a leader. He said: 'Here is Miqlāṣ: you already know his dignity. I approve of him and am confident in his leadership of you.' Therefore when Zādhormuz passed away, they unanimously advanced Miqlāṣ (to be their leader).

Then the Manichaeans split into two factions—the Mihriyya and al-Miqlāṣiyya:[276]

7:418–19.

271. An impossible synchronism, since Walīd b. 'Abd al-Malik was caliph from 705 to 714 CE and Khālid did not become governor of 'Irāq for at least another decade. See Sadighi, *Mouvements*, 85–86. According to another part of the *Fihrist* (see above), this happened during the reign of Hishām.

272. A valuable survival of the authentic Manichaean term for the lifestyle adopted by the 'elect.'

273. For an attempt to identify this helpful official, see Sadighi, *Mouvements*, 86 n.3.

274. They respond in this way because it is *after* their reconciliation with the Mesopotamian community headed by Mihr; see above.

275. Presumably his immediate associates and disciples.

276. For evidence of tension between the central Asian Dināwariyya-community and these two sects, see W. B. Henning, "Neue Materialen zur Geschichte des Manichäis-

Miqlāṣ opposed the (larger) community with regard to certain things about the religion, among which was the issue of *wiṣālāt*.[277] (This controversy continued) until Abū Hilāl al-Dayḥūrī arrived from Africa and assumed the leadership of the Manichaeans.[278] That happened during the reign of Abū Ja'far al-Manṣūr.[279] He made an appeal to the followers of Miqlāṣ to renounce what Miqlāṣ had prescribed for them with regard to *wiṣālāt*, and they consented to this.[280]

About that same time a man known as Buzurmihr appeared among the followers of Miqlāṣ. He assembled a group of them and innovated some other things. Their situation did not change until Abū Sa'īd Raḥā assumed the office of leader, and he brought them back to the opinion of the followers of Mihr with regard to the issue of *wiṣālāt*, and this position on *wiṣālāt* has not changed for the religion.

Things remained in this state until there appeared among them during the caliphate of al-Ma'mūn (813–833 CE) a man who I think was Yazdānbakht. He offered arguments against certain things and exercised cunning with them, and a small group of them favored him.

Why there is rancor between the followers of Miqlāṣ and the Mihriyya:

They claim that Khālid al-Qasrī[281] gave Mihr a she-mule to ride upon,[282] provided him with a silver signet ring, and presented him with embroidered garments.

During the reigns of al-Ma'mūn and al-Mu'taṣim, the leader of the Miqlāṣiyya was Abū 'Alī Sa'īd. Succeeding to the leadership after him was his secretary, Naṣr b. Hurmuzd al-Samarqandī. They declared permissible for the members of the sect and those who were joining it certain things which were prohibited by the

mus," *ZDMG* 90 (1936): 14–18; Werner Sundermann, "Iranian Manichaean Turfan Texts Concerning the Turfan Region," in *Turfan and Tun-Huang, The Texts: Encounter of Civilizations on the Silk Route* (ed. Alfredo Cadonna; Firenze: Leo S. Olschki Editore, 1992), 75–76; David Scott, "Manichaeism in Bactria: Political Patterns and East-West Paradigms," *Journal of Asian History* 41 (2007): 120–21; 124.

277. The meaning of this term has been a longstanding crux. See especially Vajda, "Les zindîqs," 177 n.2; van Ess, *Theologie und Gesellschaft*, 1:420 n.13; de Blois, "Glossary," 87.

278. Does this importation of a leader from 'Africa' (= Egypt?) connote that Manichaeism continued to survive there in the mid-eighth century? See, e.g., the remarks of D. W. Johnson, "Coptic Reactions to Gnosticism and Manichaeism," *Le Muséon* 100 (1987): 208–209; note also the broader range of evidence surveyed by Rochow, "Zum Fortleben des Manichäismus," 13–21. The suggested re-dating of the *Cologne Mani Codex* would seem to point in this direction as well. Van Ess equates this text's 'Africa' with Cyrenaica; see his *Theologie und Gesellschaft*, 1:418 n.3.

279. I.e., the 'Abbāsid caliph al-Manṣūr (754–775 CE).

280. See Sadighi, *Mouvements*, 86–87; Lieu, *Manichaeism in Mesopotamia*, 104–105.

281. The governor of 'Irāq who was mentioned in connection with Mihr above.

282. Within the Fatimid realm, a Jewish aspirant to the Palestinian gaonate was reportedly guilty of a similar affectation, 'evidently modeling himself after the Muslim *'ulamā'*, for whom riding on donkeys was both a privilege and a symbol of social status.' Cited from Marina Rustow, *Heresy and the Politics of Community: The Jews of the Fatimid Caliphate* (Ithaca, NY: Cornell University Press, 2008), 310.

religion. They socialized with the rulers and dined with them. Abū al-Ḥasan al-Dimashqī was also one of their leaders.[283]

'Abd al-Jabbār, *Mughnī* (ed. Ḥusayn):[284]

An account of the doctrine of the Miqlāṣiyya.[285] Al-Misma'ī relates that they follow the teaching of the Manichaeans, but they diverge from them when they say it is certain that a residue from the substance of Light will remain in the Mixture (that) Light will not be able to purify. For when its stay in the Mixture is a lengthy one, it is transformed and becomes Darkness. This is the power with which Darkness binds it when it (i.e., Light) is being strained from the Mixture.

Al-Ḥasan b. Mūsā [al-Nawbakhtī]—in reliance upon Ḥasan b. 'Alī who was also known as Abū Sa'īd al-Ḥuṣrī[286]—relates a number of their disagreements about space and air, about accidental qualities, about logical proof and refutation, about absolution and retaliation, about medical treatments, and about the installation of the *imām* and leader.[287] He says that they disagree about all these things.

He reports such disagreements by Abī al-'Awjā', al-Nu'mān, Ibn Akhī Abī Shākir, and Ibn Ṭālūt. Dualism is not peculiar in having these (divergent) teachings; we will mention their doctrines at the place where we discuss it.[288]

283. For other translations, see Flügel, *Mani*, 97–99; Vajda, "Les zindîqs," 175–78; Dodge, *Fihrist*, 2:791–94.

284. 'Abd al-Jabbār, *Mughnī* (ed. Ḥusayn), 5:18.12–19.5.

285. See the more detailed account in Ibn al-Nadīm above.

286. For what little is known about this figure, see Monnot, *Penseurs*, 61–63; Gabriel Said Reynolds, *A Muslim Theologian in the Sectarian Milieu: 'Abd al-Jabbār and the Critique of Christian Origins* (Leiden: Brill, 2004), 143 n.22.

287. Meaning the titular head of the Manichaean church.

288. This final sentence is especially difficult; see the remarks of Vajda, "Le témoignage d'al-Māturidī: Note annexe," 125 n.2; Monnot, *Penseurs*, 170 n.3. For other translations of this passage, see Vajda, "Le témoignage d'al-Māturidī: Note annexe," 125; Monnot, *Penseurs*, 169–70.

6. Mazdak as Manichaean?[289]

Pseudo-Joshua the Stylite, *Chronicle* (ed. Chabot):[290]

But when he[291] heard his (i.e., Kavād's) boastful words and learned about his wicked ways—he had authorized the institution of a foul Magian heresy which was known as that of the *Zaradushtaqan*:[292] this taught that women should be held in common and that any man might have intercourse with whomever he wished .... Even the nobles of his kingdom loathed him because he would allow their wives to commit adultery.[293]

Ya'qūbī, *Ta'rīkh* (ed. Houtsma):[294]

[Kisrā Anūshirwān] executed Mazdak, the one who directed the people to share equally with regard to wealth and females, and he executed Zarādusht b. Khurrakān because he effected an innovation in Zoroastrianism,[295] and he put

---

289. Mazdak and his movement are represented as a Manichaean aberration by Arthur Christensen, *Le règne du roi Kawādh et le communisme mazdakite* (Copenhagen: A. F. Høst, 1925), 107ff., whose arguments are repeated in his *L'Iran sous les Sassanides* (2nd ed.; Copenhagen: Ejnar Munksgaard, 1944), 316–62. According to Alessandro Bausani (*Religion in Iran: From Zoroaster to Baha'ullah* [New York: Bibliotheca Persica Press, 2000], 96), Mazdakism is 'directly derived from Manichaeism.' In actuality the Mazdakites should be viewed as a Zoroastrian reform movement which overlapped in significant ways with Manichaean ideology and in the post-Mazdak period with wider Jewish and Muslim 'messianic' currents. On the common confusion between Manichaeans and Mazdakites in our sources, see Jackson, *Researches*, 161; Lieu, *Manichaeism in Mesopotamia*, 116–17; 130–31. For a number of insightful remarks regarding the Mazdakites and their possible relationships with a number of Syro-Mesopotamian religious currents, see Erik Peterson, "Urchristentum und Mandäismus," *ZNW* 27 (1928): 76–84; also important is Marijan Molé, "Le problème des sectes zoroastriennes dans les livres pehlevis," *Oriens* 13 (1960–61): 1–28.

290. *Chronicon Pseudo-Dionysianum* (ed. Chabot), 1:249.3–7; 250.11–13. See also William Wright, *The Chronicle of Joshua the Stylite: Composed in Syriac A.D. 507* (Cambridge: University Press, 1882), 16.19–22; 18.5–6 (text).

291. The Byzantine emperor Anastasius (491–518 CE).

292. With regard to the form of this name, see especially Theodor Nöldeke, *Geschichte der Perser und Araber zur Zeit der Sasaniden* (Leiden, 1879; repr., Leiden: Brill, 1973), 457 nn.1–2.

293. See also Wright, *Chronicle of Joshua the Stylite*, 13-14; Otakar Klíma, *Mazdak: Geschichte einer sozialen Bewegung im sassanidischen Persien* (Praha: Československé Akademie Věd, 1957), 172 n.4; Patricia Crone, "Zoroastrian Communism," *Comparative Studies in Society and History* 36 (1994): 448.

294. M. T. Houtsma, ed., *Ibn Wadih qui dicitur al-Ja'qubi historiae* ... (2 vols.; Leiden: Brill, 1883), 1:185–86.

295. Rightly recognized as the 'innovator' of the Mazdakite 'heresy,' but erroneously situated in the early sixth century. According to the Syriac martyrology tied to Karkā de-Bēth Selōk (see Paul Bedjan, ed., *Acta martyrum et sanctorum syriace* [7 vols.; Paris, 1890-97; repr., Hildesheim: Georg Olms, 1968], 2:507-35), Zarādusht was a contem-

their followers to death.[296]

Ṭabarī, *Ta'rīkh* (ed. de Goeje):[297]

Then after Qubādh had reigned for ten years, the chief *mōbadh* and the aristocrats collectively agreed on removing Qubādh from rule. Therefore they removed him and imprisoned him. This was because he became a follower of a man named Mazdak and his adherents. They said: 'God has put sustenance on the earth for (His) servants to divide out among themselves equally, but people harm each other for it.' They claimed that they would take from the rich for the poor, and would give to those who had little from those who had a lot. Those who had a surplus of wealth, women, and material goods had no more right to them than anyone else. The lower echelons took advantage of this and seized the opportunity. They flocked to Mazdak and his party and sided with them. The people were afflicted by them: their power grew so strong that they would force their way into a man's house and take possession of his residence, his women, and his wealth, he being powerless to prevent them. They won over Qubādh to these pretenses, but they also threatened to remove him (from the throne). It did not take long before a man did not know his own child, nor did a child know who his father was, nor did a man control anything which was at his disposal.

They led Qubādh into a place which no one could come except them, and they installed his brother who was named Jāmāsb in his place. They informed Qubādh: 'You have sinned by what you have previously done, and the only thing that can purify you from it is to share your women.' They urged him to hand himself over to them so they could sacrifice him and make him an offering for the fire.[298]

When Zarmihr b. Sūkhrā[299] perceived this, he at the risk of his own life came forth (and was) joined by some from the nobles. He killed a large number of the Mazdakites, restored Qubādh to sovereignty, and expelled his brother Jāmāsb.

porary of Mani (ibid., 2:517.1–3). See Patricia Crone, "Kavād's Heresy and Mazdak's Revolt," *Iran* 29 (1991): 24; idem, "Zoroastrian Communism," 448.

296. See also Klíma, *Mazdak*, 172 n.5.

297. Ṭabarī, *Ta'rīkh* (ed. de Goeje), 1/2:885–87.

298. This is a confused account. It was not the Mazdakites who deposed Qubādh, but rather it was disaffected members of the ruling classes and the Zoroastrian clergy who effected this change in resistance to Qubādh's Mazdakite sympathies. Note also Averil Cameron, "Agathias on the Sassanians," *Dumbarton Oaks Papers* 23 (1969–70): 156.

299. A prominent aristocrat, leader of the Kārin family which was one of the traditional seven 'noble houses,' and perhaps the most powerful figure in Iranian politics during the last two decades of the fifth century. Information about his intrigues is provided by Christensen, *L'Iran sous les Sassanides*², 294–97; 336. With regard to the 'noble houses' (*vuzurgān*) and their place in Sasanian politics, see Zeev Rubin, "Nobility, Monarchy and Legitimation Under the Later Sasanians," in *The Byzantine and Early Islamic Near East, VI: Elites Old and New in the Byzantine and Early Islamic Near East* (Papers of the Sixth Workshop on Late Antiquity and Early Islam; ed. John Haldon and Lawrence I. Conrad; Princeton, N J: Darwin Press, 2004), 235–73, esp. 240–48.

After this, the Mazdakites never ceased provoking Qubādh against Zarmihr to the point that Qubādh eventually executed him. Qubādh had always been one of the best of their kings until Mazdak caused him to bear the message attributed to him. Afterwards the border regions fell into disorder and the ports of entry deteriorated.[300]

Someone educated in the history of the Persians has said that it was the Persian aristocrats who imprisoned Qubādh when he became a follower of Mazdak and joined him due to what he announced to him about his program and (it was they) who made his brother Jāmāsb b. Fīrūz king in place of him.[301]

Ṭabarī, *Ta'rīkh* (ed. de Goeje):[302]

When Kisrā had consolidated his rule, he abolished a sect which had been innovated within Zoroastrianism by a hypocritical person from the inhabitants of Fasā who was called Zarādhusht b. Khurrakān.[303] The people followed him in his innovation, and his power grew due to it. Among those who were propagandizing the people for him was a man from Madhariyā[304] called Mazdaq b. Bāmdādh. Some of what he prescribed for the people, extolled to them, and incited them about involved the sharing of their possessions and their families. He stated that this was a facet of the devout life that was pleasing to God, and that He would reward its observance with a most excellent recompense ....

In this way he incited the lower against the upper classes. Various kinds of sordid folk mingled with the noblest families. The way was open for robbers to extort, for scoundrels to commit outrages, and for adulterers to gratify their desires and have sexual intercourse with noble women to whom they would never have been able to aspire. Such severe distress encompassed the people that they had never experienced anything like it.

Then Kisrā prohibited the people from engaging in behavior associated with any of the innovations of Zarādusht b. Khurrakān and Mazdaq b. Bāmdādh. He

---

300. Compare the quotation from Ḥamza al-Iṣfahānī cited by Christensen, *L'Iran sous les Sassanides*², 345.

301. For other translations, see C. E. Bosworth, *The History of al-Tabarī (Ta'rīkh al-rusul wa'l-mulūk), Volume V: The Sāsānids, the Byzantines, the Lakhmids, and Yemen* (Albany: State University of New York Press, 1999), 132–35; Nöldeke, *Geschichte*, 140–44.

302. Ṭabarī, *Ta'rīkh* (ed. de Goeje), 1/2:893–94; see also Taqīzādeh-Šīrāzī, *Mānī va dīn-e-ū*, 114–15 (§15). For the Arabic text of the first sentence, see Molé, "Problème," 19.

303. Another translation of this sentence is in Giorgi, *Pour une histoire*, 142. Undoubtedly this is the same Zarādusht mentioned in the *Chronicle* of Pseudo-Joshua the Stylite and by Ya'qūbī above. According to the third book of the *Dēnkard*, a certain Zarādusht of Fasā asserted that women and property should be freely shared; for the text, see Mansour Shaki, "The Social Doctrine of Mazdak in the Light of Middle Persian Evidence," *Archív Orientální* 46 (1978): 290–92. For further discussion, see especially Ehsan Yarshater, "Mazdakism," in *The Cambridge History of Iran, Volume 3(2)*, 995–96; Crone, "Kavād's Heresy," 24.

304. Regarding this place, see Christensen, *L'Iran sous les Sassanides*², 340.

abolished their heresy and he executed many people who continued to follow it, but the people did not desist from their prohibited actions due to him. Also (he put to death) a group of Manichaeans,[305] and he stabilized for the Zoroastrians the religion which they had always practiced.[306]

Ṭabarī, *Ta'rīkh* (ed. de Goeje):[307]

Then he (Kisrā Anūshirwān) commanded that the leaders of the Mazdakites were to be beheaded and that their property was to be divided among the poor. He executed a large group of those who had confiscated people's possessions, and he restored these possessions to their original owners. He ordered that every child regarding whom there was a dispute about their parentage, and if their father was unknown, would be assigned to the family where they presently were, and that such children would be awarded a share of the property of the man to whom they were now assigned as long as the man was agreeable. As for every woman who had been seized against her will, the one who seized her would be under obligation to her and compelled to pay the bride price to her to the satisfaction of her family. Then the woman could choose whether to stay with him or to marry someone else, but if she had an original husband, she was to be restored to him. He also ordered that every one who had damaged the property of a person or who had maltreated an individual should make a full restitution: then that wrongdoer should undergo punishment in accordance with his crime.[308]

Mas'ūdī, *Tanbīh* (ed. de Goeje):[309]

Eighteenth: Qubād b. Fīrūz ruled for forty-three years. It was during his reign that Mazdak the *mōbad* interpreted the book of Zarādušt (i.e., Zoroaster) known as the Avesta: he maintained with regard to its surface meaning that an esoteric sense lies beneath its surface meaning. He was the first of those considered to be an interpreter and esoterist, for he refrained from (using) the surface meaning (to in-

305. It is unusual to see Manichaeans distinguished from Mazdakites in these reports of imperial repression. See also Jackson, *Researches*, 161; Sadighi, *Mouvements*, 83.

306. For other translations, see Bosworth, *History of al-Tabarī V*, 148-49; Nöldeke, *Geschichte*, 153–55.

307. Ṭabarī, *Ta'rīkh* (ed. de Goeje), 1/2:897.

308. See also Bosworth, *History of al-Tabarī V*, 155–56; Josef Wiesehöfer, *Ancient Persia from 550 BC to 650 AD* (trans. Azizeh Azodi; London and New York: I. B. Tauris, 2001), 173. Compare Nöldeke, *Geschichte*, 163. According to the latter scholar, this report of Kisrā's reforms (as opposed to the immediately preceding entry) stems from Ibn al-Muqaffa' (160 n.2).

309. Mas'ūdī, *Kitâb at-Tanbîh wa'l-Ischrâf* (2nd ed.; Bibliotheca Geographorum Arabicorum 8; ed. M. J. de Goeje; Leiden: Brill, 1967), 101.9–13; Molé, "Problème," 20.

terpret) the religious law of Zarādušt.[310] The Mazdakites are connected to him.[311]

Mas'ūdī, *Tanbīh* (ed. de Goeje):[312]

He (Anūshirwān) executed Mazdak and his followers. We have already talked about the difference between the teachings of Mazdak and how he practiced interpretation and what Mānī taught about it; and the difference between Mānī and the dualist sect founders who came before him such as Ibn Dayṣān (i.e., Bardaiṣan), Marcion, and the rest of them: how they all believed in two agents, one of them being good, praiseworthy, and desirable, whereas the other is evil, blameworthy, and dreadful; and the difference between all of these and what the Bāṭiniyya, the masters of interpretation at this present time, believe as is expressed in the book entitled *The Treasures of Religion and the Secret of the Worlds*.'[313]

Maqdisī, *K. al-bad' wa'l-ta'rīkh* (ed. Huart):[314]

This is the story of Qubādh and Mazdak. They say Qubādh b. Fīrūz was an amiable man: he was easily swung back and forth. He hated bloodshed and the ordering of punishment. Opinions multiplied during his time, and all sorts of religious factions and doctrines were embraced. Mazdak popped up; he was a man who welcomed depravity. He was active among the people. He said that God (may He be esteemed and honored!) had given possessions on earth to humanity to be shared among them equally so that no single person would be superior to another, but people acted badly and struggled with each other, and everyone took exclusive possession of whatever they wanted. What was needed was to take the excess that was possessed by the wealthy and return it to the poor so that they might become equals in rank. The lower classes sided with this and imposed his teaching upon themselves. They would burst in on men and forcibly take possession of their households, their property, their wives, and their slaves. Their power grew and the misery which they caused became so great that the ruler could not oppose them or resist them. Whoever refused them anything was killed.

After that they attacked Qubādh, removed him from office, jailed him, and made his brother Jāmāsb king.[315] The people's livelihoods were ruined, their genealogies became confused, and children did not know the identities of their

310. This 'deviant' hermeneutical activity connects Mazdak with dualist currents associated with Mani, who was likewise accused of engaging in an esoterist reading of Zoroastrian scriptures. Cf. Mas'ūdī, *Murūj* (ed. Barbier de Meynard-de Courteille), 2:167–68; Maqdisī, *Kitāb al-bad' wa'l-ta'rīkh* (ed. Huart), 3:157–58.

311. For other translations, see Carra de Vaux, *Le livre de l'avertissement*, 145; Yarshater, "Mazdakism," 997; Giorgi, *Pour une histoire*, 141–42.

312. Mas'ūdī, *Tanbīh* (ed. de Goeje), 101.13–20; Taqīzādeh-Šīrāzī, *Mānī va dīn-e-ū*, 134 (§22).

313. See also Carra de Vaux, *Le livre de l'avertissement*, 145.

314. Maqdisī, *K. al-bad' wa'l-ta'rīkh* (ed. Huart), 3:167.7–168.4.

315. See Christensen, *L'Iran sous les Sassanides*², 349–51.

fathers, and the weak could put up no resistance to the strong.[316]

Maqdisī, *K. al-bad' wa'l-ta'rīkh* (ed. Huart):[317]

Then Kisrā Anūshirwān b. Qubādh became king. He ruled for forty-seven years and seven months. He executed eighty thousand Mazdakites during the course of a single day, and brought the people back together into (orthodox) religion.[318]

Maqdisī, *K. al-bad' wa'l-ta'rīkh* (ed. Huart):[319]

A report about the teaching of the Khurramiyya:[320] they have factions and (different) categories, but they agree about the doctrine of 'return' (*raj'a*),[321] and they speak of a change of names and substitution of bodies. They assert that all the prophets, in spite of the difference(s) in their legislation and their religions, originate from a single spirit and that revelation has never ceased. Everyone who professes a religion is following the right course, if only they are hoping for recompense and are fearful of punishment, and they cannot be deemed to be incorrect or to be a promoter of something offensive (to God) as long as they do not intend to undermine their religion or disgrace their teaching. They diligently shun bloodshed, except for when they raise the banner of revolt. They venerate Abū Muslim and execrate Abū Ja'far (i.e., the caliph al-Manṣūr) for murdering him, and they recite many prayers for Mahdī b. Fīrūz, the one who is the son of Fāṭima, the daughter of Abū Muslim.[322] They have learned men (*imāms*) whom they consult for judicial decisions, and prophets who circulate among them whom they call *firīshtakān* (angels). They do not deem a thing blessed equal to that which they have blessed with wine and fruit beverages. The basic principle

316. For another translation, see Huart, *Le livre de la création* (1903), 170–71.

317. Maqdisī, *K. al-bad' wa'l-ta'rīkh* (ed. Huart), 3:168.12–14.

318. For another translation, see Huart, *Le livre de la création* (1903), 172.

319. Maqdisī, *K. al-bad' wa'l-ta'rīkh* (ed. Huart), 4:30–31.

320. A blanket term which encompasses a variety of neo-Mazdakite and extremist sects: 'No movement, however, is defined by our sources with greater vagueness,' so B. S. Amoretti, "Sects and Heresies," in *The Cambridge History of Iran, Volume 4: The Period from the Arab Invasion to the Saljuqs* (ed. R. N. Frye; Cambridge: Cambridge University Press, 1975), 503. See G. Flügel, "Bâbek, seine Abstammung und erstes Auftreten," *ZDMG* 23 (1869): 531–42; Sadighi, *Mouvements*, 187–228; Spuler, *Iran in früh-islamischer Zeit*, 200-206; and especially Wilferd Madelung, "Khurramiyya," *EI*[2] 5:63–65; idem, "Mazdakism and the Khurramiyya," in idem, *Religious Trends in Early Islamic Iran* (Albany, NY: Bibliotheca Persica, 1988), 1–12.

321. I.e., a return to this plane of existence after death by a prophet or other holy personage. See Israel Friedlaender, "Jewish-Arabic Studies," *Jewish Quarterly Review* n.s. 2 (1912): 481–507, and the careful remarks of Sadighi, *Mouvements*, 205–207.

322. An example of the 'messianic' aura with which some groups invested Abū Muslim after his murder. See the brief discussion above toward the end of Chapter Two, the reference to a kindred group in the testimony of Shahrastānī below, and Daniel, *Political and Social History of Khurasan*, 126–33; Mohamed Rekaya, "Le *Ḫurram-dīn* et les mouvements *Ḫurramites* sous les 'Abbāsides," *Studia Islamica* 60 (1984): 21–36.

of their religion is the doctrine of Light and Darkness.

Those whom I have observed from among them in their locales—Māsabadhān and Mihrajān-qadhaq[323]—I have found to be particularly attentive to cleanliness and purification, and to approaching people with courtesy and good deeds. I discovered among them some who professed free access to women, provided they (i.e., the women) were willing, and also the freedom to indulge in everything which one finds pleasurable and to satisfy one's yearnings as long as they do not cause harm to someone.[324]

Ibn al-Nadīm, *Fihrist* (ed. Tajaddud):[325]

Doctrines of the Khurramiyya and the Mazdakites:

Muḥammad b. Isḥāq (al-Nadīm) says the Khurramiyya comprise two sorts. The initial Khurramiyya were named the Muḥammira,[326] and they were dispersed throughout the mountainous regions of Azerbaijan and Armenia, the district of Daylam, Hamadān, and Dīnawar, and (also) between Iṣfahān and the region of al-Ahwāz. These were Zoroastrian originally, but later innovated their (own) teaching. They were among those known as the *Luqaṭa*.[327] Their leader, the 'older' Mazdak,[328] directed them to indulge in pleasures and to occupy themselves with fulfilling lusts, (consuming) foods and drinks, sharing and mingling together, and avoiding being independent of each other. They shared wives and families: no single one of them was prevented from (enjoying) the wife of another, and he (the husband) did not forbid her (from engaging in such relationships). With this being the case, they believe in good deeds, in avoiding killing, and in (avoiding) causing pain to living beings. They have a doctrine of hospitality which no other peoples have: when they entertain a person, they do not deny him anything he seeks, no matter what it might be. The 'later' Mazdak was connected with this doctrine. He was the one who appeared during the days of Qubād b. Fīrūz. (Kisrā) Anūshirwān executed him and put his adherents to death. His story is notorious and well known. Since al-Balkhi[329] has thoroughly investigated the accounts

323. The northern part of the Zagros mountain range. See Guy Monnot, "L'écho musulman aux religions d'Iran," in idem, *Islam et religions*, 86.

324. See also D. S. Margoliouth, "Khurramīya," *EI*[1] 4:975; Sadighi, *Mouvements*, 201–202; Yarshater, "Mazdakism," 1008-1009; Crone, "Zoroastrian Communism," 450–51; Bausani, *Religion in Iran*, 128–29.

325. Ibn al-Nadīm, *K. al-Fihrist* (ed. Tajaddud), 405–406.

326. I.e., 'those clad in red,' or 'who bear red standards.' See Daniel, *Political and Social History of Khurasan*, 147.

327. See especially Klíma, *Mazdak*, 229 n.59. The Arabic text of this and the preceding sentence is available in Molé, "Problème," 19.

328. According to Crone, this locution probably encodes the Zarādusht mentioned by Pseudo-Joshua and Ṭabarī ("Kavād's Heresy," 24).

329. Dodge (*Fihrist*, 2:817 n.445) suggests this may the geographer Abū Zayd Aḥmad b. Sahl al-Balkhī, although this particular title does not seem to be attributed to him anywhere else. Madelung identifies him as Abu'l-Qāsim al-Balkhī ("Khurramiyya,"

about the Khurramiyya and their doctrines and their practices with regard to drinking, enjoyments, and religious observances in the book *Sources of Questions and Answers*, there is no necessity for us to speak more about it since someone else who preceded us (has covered it).[330]

Khwārazmī, *Kitāb mafātīḥ al-'ulūm* (ed. Taqīzādeh-Šīrāzī):[331]

The Manichaeans are 'the Mānī-ones' whose name can be traced to Mānī, and it is unknown whether they have created this designation as a name following the analogy of others. Similarly the name of the Ḥarranāniyya can be traced to Ḥarrān, and the 'Anāniyya can be traced to <'Anān>[332] the Jew. The *zanādiqa* are the Manichaeans, and the Mazdakites are (also) designated with this name. Mazdak was the one who appeared in the days of Qubādh. He was the chief *mōbadh* or chief magistrate (*qāḍī*) of the Zoroastrians, and he asserted that possessions and women should be shared. He produced a book which he called *Zand* and maintained that it contained the (true) interpretation of the Avesta, which is the scripture of Zoroastrianism. It (i.e., the Avesta) is what Zarādusht (i.e., Zoroaster) brought, the one whom they allege is their prophet. The followers of Mazdak were named after (the) *Zand* and were called *Zandī*. Later the word was arabicized so that an individual came to be called a *zindīq* and a group *zanādiqa*.[333]

'Abd al-Jabbār, *Mughnī* (ed. Ḥusayn):[334]

Account of the doctrine of the Mazdakites. [Abū 'Īsā] al-Warrāq relates that their doctrine is similar to that of most of the Manichaeans with regard to the Two Entities; however, they maintain that Light acts purposefully, whereas Darkness acts haphazardly.

The Zoroastrians report that Mazdak was one who pronounced that (all) property and women were permitted (to whosoever desired them). He maintained

---

*EI*² 5:63); so also Sadighi, *Mouvements*, 150–51.

330. For other translations, see Sadighi, *Mouvements*, 198–99; Klíma, *Mazdak*, 203; Dodge, *Fihrist*, 2:817–18.

331. Taqīzādeh-Šīrāzī, *Mānī va dīn-e-ū*, 180 (§28); Molé, "Problème," 20.

332. The correct spelling of this name is recorded in Ms. E of the textual apparatus.

333. For another translation, see Giorgi, *Pour une histoire*, 142. Essentially the same testimony can be found in the later tradents Qalqashandī (*apud* Taqīzādeh-Šīrāzī, *Mānī va dīn-e-ū*, 298 [§73]), Kemāl Pasha-Zāde (*apud* Taqīzādeh-Šīrāzī, *Mānī va dīn-e-ū*, 307, 311 [§77]), Khafājī (*apud* Taqīzādeh-Šīrāzī, *Mānī va dīn-e-ū*, 319[(§80]), Mullā Ṣāliḥ Māzandarānī (*apud* Taqīzādeh-Šīrāzī, *Mānī va dīn-e-ū*, 320 [§81]), Ibn Ḥajar al-'Asqalānī (*apud* Taqīzādeh-Šīrāzī, *Mānī va dīn-e-ū*, 341, 342 [§93]), Muṭarrizī (*apud* Taqīzādeh-Šīrāzī, *Mānī va dīn-e-ū*, 401 [§128]), Sa'd al-Dīn al-Taftāzānī (*apud* Taqīzādeh-Šīrāzī, *Mānī va dīn-e-ū*, 414 [§138]), and Jazā'irī (*apud* Taqīzādeh-Šīrāzī, *Mānī va dīn-e-ū*, 432 [§148]). See also Taqīzādeh-Šīrāzī, *Mānī va dīn-e-ū*, 329 (§83).

334. 'Abd al-Jabbār, *Mughnī* (ed. Ḥusayn), 5:16.1–11. According to Vajda ("Le témoignage d'al-Māturidī: Note annexe," 122), it is only an abridgment of what can be found in Shahrastānī below.

that he did this so that the people would stop disliking and harming each other since this happens on account of property and women. He is the one who summoned Qubād the king[335] to (embrace) his teaching, and he complied with him. But Kisrā Anūshirwān[336] opposed him, and he is the one who executed him and put to death those who honored him.

Mazdak used to believe that Light possessed cognition (and) sensory perception, and that Darkness was ignorant (and) blind; and that (their) Mixture occurred accidentally, not purposely.

His adherents maintain that he was a prophet, and that he permitted sexual intercourse and the killing of his opponents. He however enjoined the killing of living beings[337] in order to free them from Evil and Mixture with Darkness.[338]

Miskawayh, *Tajārib al-umam* (ed. Taqīzādeh-Šīrāzī):[339]

And there arose as ruler after Qubād his son Kisrā Anūshīrwān. He applied himself diligently to governance and took matters firmly in hand ... He executed a group of Manichaeans and re-established the former religion of Zoroastrianism, writing announcements about this to the governmental officials and military leaders (*ispahbadīn*).[340]

Tha'ālibī, *Ghurar akhbār mulūk al-Furs wa-siyarihim* (ed. Zotenberg):[341]

Mazdak b. Bāmdādh was a devil in human form. He presented a handsome image, (but) he had an ugly plan; (he displayed) a clean appearance, (but) had an inner foulness; (his) speech was pleasing (but his) deeds were contentious. He succeeded in gaining access to Kavād, deceived him with his verbal misrepresentations, and enchanted him with his florid talk.[342]

---

335. I.e., the Sasanian ruler Kavād (488–96; 498–531 CE).

336. His successor Khusrau Anōshirvān (531–79 CE).

337. Literally 'killing of souls, selves.' This is interpreted as an endorsement of suicide by Moshe Gil, "The Creed of Abū 'Āmir," *Israel Oriental Studies* 12 (1992): 46; also Bausani, *Religion in Iran*, 104. Yarshater reads the 'killing of souls' less literally as simply a recommendation for asceticism (idem, "Mazdakism," 1012). See however the convincing arguments of Crone ("Kavād's Revolt," 27) for connecting this curious statement with a dispensation to slay group adversaries during situations of social crisis or danger.

338. For another translation, see Monnot, *Penseurs*, 164–65.

339. Taqīzādeh-Šīrāzī, *Mānī va dīn-e-ū*, 181-82 (§29).

340. See Ṭabarī, *Ta'rīkh* (ed. de Goeje), 1/2:894 above. The final sentence is paralleled in Nuwayrī, *Nihāyat al-arab fī funūn al-adab*, 15:191; see Taqīzādeh-Šīrāzī, *Mānī va dīn-e-ū*, 276 (§63).

341. H. Zotenberg, *Histoire des rois des Perses: Texte arabe publié et traduit* (Paris: Imprimerie nationale, 1890), 596.

342. See also Rubin, "Nobility," 252–53.

Bīrūnī, *Āthār* (ed. Sachau):[343]

After these appeared a man named Mazhdak b. Hamadādān, an inhabitant of Nasā. He was the chief *mōbadh* or chief magistrate during the time of Qubādh b. Fīrūz. He propounded dualism, but he disagreed with Zarādusht in regard to much of his teaching.[344] He said that people should enjoy communal access to wealth and to wives, and innumerable people became his followers.

Qubādh relied upon him, but some of the Persians maintain that his adherence was necessary at the time given that his power was not secure against the large number of his (i.e., Mazdak's) followers. Some others maintain that this Mazhdak was very sagacious: when he discerned that Qubādh was enamored with a woman who was married to his cousin, he ingeniously invented this doctrine and then announced it, and Qubādh quickly accepted it.[345] He (Mazdak?) commanded him to refrain from the sacrifice of cattle before its appointed time had come to it. He said: 'You will not complete what you are doing unless you give me possession of the mother of Anūshirwān so that I might enjoy her.' Then he agreed with him in this, and he commanded that she be given[346] to him. Anūshirwān came to him and spoke to him about her. He abased himself before him and kissed his feet so that he might favor him with her release.

Then when Anūshirwān became king, the first thing that he did was to seize Mazdak and those who had prevailed over him among his followers, and he set them in hollowed out pits and buried them upside-down until they died in them, and they were forced to die at their bottoms. He compelled his remaining followers from among the nobles and respectable families to renounce his ideas, and he executed anyone who refused to do so. He would often say: 'I could never turn toward any daily task without experiencing in my nose the stench of the sock of Mazdak when I kissed his foot!' A small group of his followers remains. They are termed after him 'Mazdakites' (*Mazdakiyya*) and Khurramdīniyya.[347]

Shahrastānī, *Kitāb al-milal wa'l-niḥal* (ed. Badrān):[348]

The Mazdakites are the followers of Mazdak. Mazdak was the one who appeared

343. *Āthār* (ed. Sachau), 209.11-17; Johann Fück, "Sechs Ergänzungen zu Sachaus Ausgabe von al-Bīrūnīs Chronologie Orientalischer Völker," in *Documenta Islamica Inedita* (Berlin: Akademie-Verlag, 1952), 79.

344. See Molé, "Problème," 19–20.

345. See Crone, "Zoroastrian Communism," 452.

346. Here is where the text in Sachau's *Chronologie* breaks off. This lacuna can now be restored thanks to Fück, "Sechs Ergänzungen," 79.

347. See also Remke Kruk, "Sharaf az-Zamân Ṭâhir Marwazî (fl. ca. 1100 A.D.) on Zoroaster, Mânî, Mazdak, and Other Pseudo-Prophets," *Persica* 17 (2001): 58, 67.

348. Muḥammad b. Fatḥ Allāh Badrān, ed., *Kitāb al-milal wa'l-niḥal* (2 vols.; [Cairo]: Matba'at al-Azhar, [1951–55]), 1:631.2–637.6; note also William Cureton, ed., *Kitāb al-milal wa-l-niḥal: Book of Religious and Philosophical Sects, by Muhammad al-Shahrastáni* (London, 1846; repr., Leipzig: O. Harrassowitz, 1923), 192.19–194.2.

during the reign of Qubād, the father of Anūshirwān. He summoned Qubād to (embrace) his teaching, and he complied with him. But Anūshirwān observed his vileness and his deceitfulness, and he sought for him, found him, and executed him.

[Abū 'Īsā] al-Warrāq relates that the doctrine of the Mazdakites is similar to that of most of the Manichaeans with regard to the Two Entities and the Two Principles. However, Mazdak said that Light acts purposefully and voluntarily, whereas Darkness acts haphazardly and coincidentally. Light possesses cognition (and) sensory perception, and Darkness is ignorant (and) blind. Moreover, (their) Mixture occurred by chance and accidentally, not purposely and deliberately. Similarly (their) purification will also transpire randomly instead of intentionally.[349]

Mazdak prohibited people from engaging in controversy, stirring up hatred, and the shedding of blood. Because the bulk of these (offenses) were occasioned by (disputes over) women and possessions, he made (all) women lawful (to all men)[350] and granted as permissible the taking of possessions, and he made the people share those things the same way they shared water, fire, and pasture.

He also relates about him that he enjoined the killing of living beings in order to free them from Evil and Mixture with Darkness.[351] His teaching with regard to fundamental principles and substances was that they were three; namely, water, earth, and fire. After they had mixed together, there was generated the Ruler of Good and the Ruler of Evil: what was from their pure portions became the Ruler of Good, and what was from their turbid portions became the Ruler of Evil.

It is also recounted about him that his deity was seated on his throne in the supernal world after the fashion of the installation of Khusrō (i.e., the Sasanian emperor) in the lower world. Four powers were present before him: the power(s) of discernment, understanding, mindfulness, and happiness, as similarly before Khusrō there were four officials; namely, the chief magistrate, the high priest, the commander-in-chief, and the minstrel.[352]

These four regulate the universe through seven who (serve) before them:[353] Sālār, Bīshkār, Bālūn, Birāwan, Kāzrān, Dustūr, and Kūdhak.[354] These seven powers

349. Compare Shahrastānī on Manichaean cosmology in Chapter Four above. The text of the present paragraph is also available in Taqīzādeh-Šīrāzī, *Mānī va dīn-e-ū*, 244 (§45).

350. Note Crone, "Kavād's Heresy," 38 n.104.

351. See the note in the report from 'Abd al-Jabbār cited above. Compare also the less garbled version of this testimony from Abū 'Īsā al-Warrāq found in Ibn al-Malāḥimī: see Rukn al-Dīn Maḥmūd b. Muḥammad al-Malāḥimī al-Khuwārazmī, *Kitāb al-mu'tamad fī uṣūl al-dīn* (ed. Martin McDermott and Wilferd Madelung; London: Al-Hoda, 1991), 584.4–5.

352. The Persian names of these officials are transcribed in Arabic characters respectively as *mōbadh-mōbadhān*, *al-hirbad al-akbar*, *isbahbud*, and *rāmishgar*.

353. A variant textual reading terms them 'viziers.'

354. Manuscripts and printed editions supply a number of variant readings for these names. For a careful analysis of the most meaningful possibilities, see Mansour Shaki, "The Cosmogonical and Cosmological Teachings of Mazdak," in *Papers in Honour of Professor Mary Boyce* (Acta Iranica 24–25; 2 vols.; ed. Jacques Duchesne-Guillemin and Pierre Lecoq; Leiden: Brill, 1985), 2:535–36.

are surrounded by twelve spiritual beings: Khwānandeh, Dihandeh, Satānandeh, Burandeh, Khūranindeh, Dawindeh, Khīzindeh, Kishandeh, Zanindeh, Kunindeh, Ābindeh, Shawindeh, and Pāyindeh.[355] Every person in whom these powers are united—the four, the seven, and the twelve—achieves lordly rank in the lower world and advances beyond the obligation to perform religious commandments.

He said that Khusrō of the supernal world ruled using the letters whose aggregate constitutes the Greatest Name. One who can imagine a thing employing those letters has the greatest mystery disclosed to him, while the one who refuses (to do so) remains in the blindness of ignorance, oblivion, stupidity, and confusion before the four spiritual powers.

These are (their) sects: the Kūdhiyya, the Abū Muslimiyya, the Māhāniyya,[356] and the Sabīd-jāmakiyya.[357] The Kūdhiyya are in the regions of Ahwāz, Fārs, and Shahrazūr, whereas the others are in the regions of Sogdia, Samarkand, Shāsh, and Ilāq.[358]

Nashwān b. Sa'īd b. Nashwān al-Ḥimyarī, *al-Ḥūr al-'īn* (ed. Taqīzādeh-Šīrāzī):[359]

The Mazdakites—the followers of the Persian Mazdak—teach a doctrine similar to that of the Manichaeans, except that they engage in sexual intercourse and the shedding of blood.[360]

---

355. Thirteen names, however, are provided. Moreover, manuscripts and printed editions supply a number of variant readings for these designations. See Shaki, "Cosmogonical and Cosmological Teachings of Mazdak," 2:537–39.

356. This group is here classified as a Mazdakite sect, but other sources label them as Marcionite. See Madelung, "Abū 'Īsā al-Warrāq," 220–21.

357. Referring to the Mubayyiḍa or so-called 'white-clad ones' (Persian *sapīdjāmagān*) who were involved in several 'messianic' disturbances in Khurāsān and Transoxania during the 'Abbasīd period. See Madelung, "K͟hurramiyya," *EI*[2] 5:64; Sadighi, *Mouvements*, 170 n.3; Spuler, *Iran in früh-islamischer Zeit*, 198–99.

358. For other translations, see Bausani, *Religion in Iran*, 102-103; Yarshater, "Mazdakism," 1006–1007; Shaki, "Cosmogonical and Cosmological Teachings of Mazdak," 2:527–29; Gil, "Creed of Abū 'Āmir," 46–47. Important remarks on this passage can be found in Michelangelo Guidi, "Mazdak," *EI*[1] 5:430–33; Sadighi, *Mouvements*, 109–10; Heinz Halm, "Die Sieben und die Zwölf: Die ismā'īlitische Kosmogonie und das Mazdak-Fragment des Šahrastānī," in *XVIII. Deutscher Orientalistentag, vom 1. bis 5. Oktober 1972, in Lübeck: Vorträge* (ZDMG Supplement II; ed. Wolfgang Voight; Wiesbaden: Franz Steiner Verlag, 1974), 170–77; Shaki, "Cosmogonical and Cosmological Teachings of Mazdak," 2:527–43; Shaul Shaked, *Dualism in Transformation: Varieties of Religion in Sasanian Iran* (London: School of Oriental and African Studies, 1994), 124–31. Crone is undoubtedly correct in stating that 'Gnosticism was certainly a factor in Mazdak's thought' ("Zoroastrian Communism," 461).

359. Taqīzādeh-Šīrāzī, *Mānī va dīn-e-ū*, 248 (§47).

360. See Monnot, *Penseurs*, 168 n.4.

***Chronicon ad annum Christi 1234* (ed. Chabot):**[361]

Regarding the Manichaeans in Persia.[362] At that time the doctrine of the Manichaeans was prevalent in Persia. Kavad, the king of the Persians,[363] entrusted his son Kusrō[364] to the Manichaeans in order for him to learn how to read and write from them. That child vowed to the Manichaeans that when he (the child) became king, their religion would dominate. When the child and his mother came before Kavad the king, they requested, in accordance with what he (the child) had promised the Manichaeans, that he (Kavad) should recognize his son (as) king while he (Kavad) was still alive. After the king made an investigation, it was reported to him by Christians that Manichaeans had (so) advised his son.

He summoned the Manichaean bishop[365] and said to him, 'You have devised this plan to cultivate my favor because you love both me and my son. Now summon all of the Manichaeans—the adherents of your religion—who have planned the royal accession of my son!' And when the Manichaeans proudly revealed themselves, the king ordered them put to the sword, and there did not remain a single one (alive). Their churches were (then) given to the orthodox (Christians).[366]

7. A Concluding Postscript

A close study of Islamicate Manichaeism—its personalities, doctrinal stances and attitudes, writings, internal struggles, and purported interactions with a variety of governmental and religious authorities—is a pursuit that has languished during the past fifty years or so. The lack of progress in this area is especially noticeable in view of the rapid advances now occurring in the recovery and study of western expressions of Manichaeism, especially in its Coptic and Latin forms. There are nevertheless some resources which can be used in the preliminary

361. *Chronicon ad annum Christi 1234* (ed. Chabot), 1:193.24–194.11.

362. It is clear from the chronological placement of this report and its analogues in other sources that the 'Manichaeans' featured here are actually the Mazdakites. See John Malalas, *Ioannis Malalae Chronographia* (CSHB 14; ed. Ludwig Dindorf; Bonn: E. Weber, 1831), 444.5–18; Theophanes, *Chronographia* (ed. de Boor), 1:169–70; *The Chronicle of Theophanes Confessor* (trans. Cyril Mango and Roger Scott; Oxford: Clarendon Press, 1997), 259–60; Crone, "Kavād's Heresy," 30–34. Note also Michael Syrus, *Chronicle* (ed. Chabot), 2:190–91.

363. The Sasanian emperor who ruled 488–496; 499–531 CE.

364. I.e., Khusrau I Anōshirvān (531–579 CE), who was definitely not favorably disposed to the followers of Mazdak. Theophanes identifies him as the king's 'third son' born to him by 'his daughter Sambikē' whom he names Phthasouarsan (Φθασουαρσάν). See Mango-Scott, *Chronicle*, 261 n.7.

365. Identified by Malalas as Ἰνδαράζαρ and by Theophanes as Ἰνδαζάρος. Following the brilliant insight of Arthur Christensen (*L'Iran sous les Sassanides*², 358), Crone points out the symbolic import of this cognomen (Persian *andarzgar* 'leader') and suggests this figure 'may well have been Mazdak himself' ("Kavād's Heresy," 30). See also Guidi, "Mazdak," 431; Mango-Scott, *Chronicle*, 261 n.6.

366. See also Klíma, *Mazdak*, 254–55.

reconstruction of the historical vicissitudes of Manichaeism within the religious universe of the Islamicate cultural sphere. Unlike the 'heresiological' accounts which concentrate upon outlining the doctrinal and ritual oddities which distinguish Manichaeans from members of other religious communities—accounts which by their relative uniformity betray their scholastic character and an ultimate dependence upon a paucity of literary sources—the notices about the 'historical' fortunes of named Manichaean leaders, the religion's alleged adherents and regional proponents (or detractors), their suppression and attempted extirpation by the state, and their communal schisms and migrations derive from a wider variety of tradents and writings, a number of whom were well situated within their social order to offer authoritative information about the subject. While it remains true that later historians and chroniclers freely utilize the traditions provided by their literary predecessors, some of them augment their reports with singular data and observations that shed potentially valuable light on the viability of Manichaeism for their own times and places. In spite of the increasingly systematic oppression which they would face in every region and cultural context wherein they dispersed, small groups of Manichaeans and their sympathizers persistently survived, clandestinely perpetuating their teachings and behavioral attitudes in a variety of political environments that were openly hostile to their overt expression.

It is perhaps then understandable why scholars might target the emergence of certain chiliastic or prophetically tinged resistance movements like Mazdakism and the later 'Irano-gnostic' eruptions against 'Abbāsid hegemony as possible instances of a recrudescent Manichaeism, now repackaged in the service of an Abrahamically inspired messianism or of a Zoroastrian timetable for the appearance of a deliverer and the end of a world age. Analogous motifs and themes are also visible in several of the forms of Shīʿite extremism which arose in Iraq and Iran during the eighth and ninth centuries. The 'schools of Chaldean dualists' surveyed by Ibn al-Nadīm at the close of the tenth century offer still further instances where Manichaeism and kindred ideologies have been adapted and transformed within the Islamicate religious world.[367] Very little work has been done to date toward a careful synoptic evaluation of all these movements and 'schools,' but there would seem to be an intriguing quantity of evidence that points to the continuing relevance of identifiably Manichaean ideas and imagery for their emergence and growth.[368]

The modern reconstruction of the history of Islamicate Manichaeism will not be an easy task. Yet I venture to say it is a task that can be accomplished, given the richness and breadth of the evidence that is currently available to us. It is my hope that the present work may play some small part in prompting scholars to join this effort and to begin exploring the vitality of Manichaeism in the Islamicate world.

---

367. Ibn al-Nadīm, *K. al-Fihrist* (ed. Tajaddud), 383.

368. A task taken up in my forthcoming *Shades of Light and Darkness: Studies in Chaldean Dualism and Gnosis*.

Chronological Arrangement of Authorities[1]

All dates are CE

Chronicon Maroniticum — ca. 650?
Chronicon anonymum (ed. Guidi) — ca. 680?
Jacob of Edessa — d. 708
Zūqnīn Chronicle — 775
Theodore bar Konai — d. ca. 800
Theodore Abū Qurra — d. ca. 820-25
Škand-Gumānīk Vičār — ca. 850?
Qāsim b. Ibrāhīm — d. 860
Abu ʿĪsā al-Warrāq — d. ca. 864
Jāḥiẓ — d. 868/9
Yaʿqūbī — d. 897
Dīnawarī — d. ca. 902/3
Ibn al-Faqīh — *Kitāb al-buldān* completed 902/3
Nawbakhtī — d. 912 or 922
Ṭabarī — d. 923
Abu'l Faraj al-Iṣfahānī — d. after 923
Abū Bakr al-Rāzī — d. 925
Abū Ḥātim al-Rāzī — d. 933/4
Saʿīd b. al-Biṭrīq (Eutychius) — d. 940
Agapius of Manbij — d. after 941
Saʿadyā b. Yōsēf — d. 942
Jahshiyārī — d. 942/3
Māturīdī — d. 944
Iṣṭakhrī — fl. ca. 950
Qirqisānī — d. ca. 950
Masʿūdī — d. 956
Ḥamza al-Iṣfahānī — d. 961-971
Maqdisī — *Kitāb al-bad'* written ca. 966

1. Authorities consulted for determining these dates include *EJ*, *EI*², and *EncIr*; also, Julie Scott Meisani and Paul Starkey, eds., *Encyclopedia of Arabic Literature* (2 vols.; London and New York: Routledge, 1998); Alexander P. Kazhdan, et al., eds., *The Oxford Dictionary of Byzantium* (3 vols.; Oxford: Oxford University Press, 1991); Aziz S. Atiya, ed., *The Coptic Encyclopedia* (8 vols.; New York: Macmillan, 1991). Where discrepancies occur among these sources, the most recent entry has been followed.

Abū Ya'qūb al-Sijistānī — d. ca. 975?
Ibn al-Nadīm — *Fihrist* completed 987
Sāwīrūs b. al-Muqaffa' — d. 987?
Ibn Bābawayh — d. 991/2
Khwārazmī — d. 997
Kitāb Ḥudūd al-'ālam — end of tenth century
Chronicon Seertensis (*Chronicle of Siirt*) — before 1020
'Abd al-Jabbār — d. 1025
Miskawayh — d. 1030
Baghdādī — d. 1037
Ibn Sīnā — d. 1037
Tha'ālibī — d. 1038
Yūsuf al-Baṣīr — d. ca. 1040
Bīrūnī — d. ca. 1050
Ibn Ḥazm — d. 1064
Asadī — after 1066
Abu'l-Ma'ālī — *Bayān al-adyān* completed 1092
Marwazī — d. ca. 1120
Abraham bar Ḥiyya — d. ca. 1136
Judah Halevi — d. 1141
Ibn al-Malāḥimī — d. 1141
Judah b. Elijah Hadassi — *Eshkol ha-kofer* written 1148
Shahrastānī — *Milal* completed 1153
Sam'ānī — d. 1166
Nashwān b. Sa'īd b. Nashwān al-Ḥimyarī — d. 1178
Abraham Ibn Daud — d. ca. 1180
Suhrawardī — d. 1191
Michael Syrus — d. 1199
Ibn al-Jawzī — d. 1201
Shams-i Qays — fl. 1204-1230
Fakhr al-Dīn al-Rāzī — d. 1209
Ibn al-Āthīr — d. 1233
Ghaḍanfar — fl. ca. 1250 (?)
Shahrazūrī — fl. ca. 1250
Ibn Abī l-Hadīd — d. 1257/8
Ibn Abī Uṣaybi'a — d. 1270
Ibn Khallikān — d. 1282
Bar Hebraeus — d. 1286
Copto-Arabic *Synaxarion* — early fourteenth century?
Abu'l-Barakāt Ibn Kabar — d. 1324
Nuwayrī — d. 1332
Ibn al-Murtaḍā — d. 1437
R. Simeon b. Ṣemaḥ Duran — d. 1444
Ibn al-Shiḥnah — d. 1485

Isaac b. Moses Arama — d. 1494
Mīrkhwānd — d. 1498
Elijah Levita — d. 1549
Ḥājjī Khalīfah — d. 1657

'Abbāsid caliphs
All dates AH/CE

Manṣūr — 136–158/754–775
Mahdī — 158–169/775–785
Hādī — 169–170/785–786
Hārūn — 170–193/786–809
Amīn — 193–198/809–813
Ma'mūn — 198–218/813–833
Mu'taṣim — 218–227/833–842

Muqtadir — 295–320/908–932

Bibliography

Abbott, Nabia. *Studies in Arabic Literary Papyri, III: Language and Literature*. Oriental Institute Publications 77. Chicago, IL: The University of Chicago Press, 1972.

ʿAbd al-Jabbār b. Aḥmad al-Hamadhānī. *Al-Mughnī fī abwāb al-tawḥīd wa'l-ʿadl*. 14 vols. Edited by Ṭāhā Ḥusayn, et al. Cairo: Al-Shirkah al-ʿArabīyah lil-Tibā'ah wa'l-Nashr, 1958–66.

———. *Tathbīt dālā'il al-nubūwwah*. 2 vols. Edited by ʿAbd al-Karīm ʿUthmān. Beirut: Dār al-Arabiyah, 1966–67.

Adad, Maurice. "Le *Kitāb al-Tarbīʿ wa-l-Tadwīr* d'al-Ğāḥiẓ: Traduction française, II." *Arabica* 14 (1967): 32–59.

———. "Le *Kitāb al-Tarbīʿ wa-l-Tadwīr* d'al-Ğāḥiẓ: Traduction française, III." *Arabica* 14 (1967): 167–90.

Adam, Alfred, ed. *Texte zum Manichäismus*. 2nd ed. Berlin: W. de Gruyter, 1969.

Ahrens, Karl. *Muhammad als Religionsstifter*. Leipzig: F. A. Brockhaus, 1935.

Aitken, Ellen Bradshaw. "The Cologne Mani Codex." In *Religions of Late Antiquity in Practice*, edited by Richard Valantasis, 161–76. Princeton, NJ: Princeton University Press, 2000.

Alfaric, Prosper. *Les écritures manichéennes*. 2 vols. Paris: E. Nourry, 1918–19.

———. "La vie chrétienne du Bouddha." *Journal asiatique* 10, 11th ser. (1917): 269–88.

Altmann, Alexander. "'The Ladder of Ascension.'" In *Studies in Mysticism and Religion presented to Gershom G. Scholem on his Seventieth Birthday by Pupils, Colleagues and Friends*, 1–32. Jerusalem: Magnes Press, 1967.

———. *Saadya Gaon: The Book of Doctrines and Beliefs: Abridged Edition*. Oxford: East and West Library, 1946.

Amoretti, B. S. "Sects and Heresies." In *The Cambridge History of Iran, Volume 4: The Period from the Arab Invasion to the Saljuqs*, edited by R. N. Frye, 481–519. Cambridge: Cambridge University Press, 1975.

Andrae, Tor. *Mohammed: The Man and His Faith*. Translated by Theophil Menzel. New York: Harper and Brothers, 1960.

Andreas, F. C. and W. B. Henning. "Mitteliranische Manichaica aus Chinesisch-Turkestan I." *Sitzungsberichte der preussischen Akademie der Wissenschaften* (1932): 175–222.

———. "Mitteliranische Manichaica aus Chinesisch-Turkestan II." *Sitzungsberichte der preussischen Akademie der Wissenschaften* (1933): 292–363.

———. "Mitteliranische Manichaica aus Chinesisch-Turkestan III." *Sitzungsberichte der preussischen Akademie der Wissenschaften* (1934): 846–912.

Arama, Isaac b. Moses. *Sefer ʿAqedat Yiṣḥaq*. 5 vols. Pressburg: Verlag von Victor Kittseer, 1849.

Arberry, A. J. *Razi's Traditional Psychology*. Damascus: Islamic Book Service, n.d.

Arjomand, Said Amir. "ʿAbd Allah Ibn al-Muqaffaʿ and the ʿAbbasid Revolution." *Iranian Studies* 27 (1994): 9–36.

Arnold, Thomas W. "The Origins." In *A Survey of Persian Art From Prehistoric Times to the*

Present, vol. 5. Edited by Arthur Upham Pope and Phyllis Ackerman, 1809–19. London and New York: Oxford University Press, 1964–65.

———. *Painting in Islam: A Study of the Place of Pictorial Art in Muslim Culture*. Oxford, 1928. Repr., New York: Dover Publications, 1965.

Arnold-Döben, Victoria. *Die Bildersprache des Manichäismus*. Köln: E. J. Brill, 1978.

Asmussen, Jes P. *Manichaean Literature: Representative Texts Chiefly from Middle Persian and Parthian Writings*. Delmar, N.Y.: Scholars' Facsimiles and Reprints, 1975.

Asmussen, Jes P. and Alexander Böhlig. *Die Gnosis III: Der Manichäismus*. Zürich: Artemis, 1980.

Ataç, Mehmet-Ali. "Manichaeism and Ancient Mesopotamian 'Gnosticism.'" *Journal of Ancient Near Eastern Religions* 5 (2005): 1–39.

Atiya, Aziz S., ed. *The Coptic Encyclopedia*. 8 vols. New York: Macmillan, 1991.

Babayan, Kathryn. *Mystics, Monarchs, and Messiahs: Cultural Landscapes of Early Modern Iran*. Cambridge, Mass.: Harvard University Press, 2002.

Badrān, Muḥammad b. Fatḥ Allāh, ed. *Kitāb al-milal wa'l-niḥal l'il-Shahrastānī*. 2 vols. [Cairo]: Matba'at al-Azhar, [1951–55].

Baghdādī, Abū Manṣūr 'Abd al-Qāhir b. Tāhir al-. *Moslem Schisms and Sects: Being the History of the Various Philosophic Systems Developed in Islam*. Translated by Kate Chambers Seelye. Columbia University Oriental Studies 15. New York, 1920. Repr., New York: AMS Press, 1966.

———. *Moslem Schisms and Sects (Al-Fark Bain al-Firak) Part II*. Edited by Abraham S. Halkin. Tel Aviv, 1935. Repr., Philadelphia: Porcupine Press, 1978.

Bailey, H. W. "Note on the Religious Sects Mentioned by Kartīr (Kardēr)." In *The Cambridge History of Iran, Volume 3(2): The Seleucid, Parthian and Sasanian Periods*, edited by Ehsan Yarshater, 907–908. Cambridge: Cambridge University Press, 1983.

———. *Zoroastrian Problems in the Ninth-Century Books*. Oxford: Clarendon Press, 1971.

Barnstone, Willis and Marvin Meyer, eds. *The Gnostic Bible*. Boston: Shambhala, 2003.

Baron, Salo W. "The Historical Outlook of Maimonides." *Proceedings of the American Academy for Jewish Research* 6 (1934–35): 5–113.

———. *A Social and Religious History of the Jews*. 2nd ed. 18 vols. Philadelphia and New York: Jewish Publication Society and Columbia University Press, 1952–83.

Barthold, W. and C. E. Bosworth. "Mā Warā' al-Nahr." In *Encyclopaedia of Islam*, vol. 5, 852–59. New ed. Leiden: Brill, 1954–2002.

Bashear, Suliman. *Arabs and Others in Early Islam*. Princeton, NJ: Darwin Press, 1997.

Bauer, Walter. *A Greek-English Lexicon of the New Testament and Other Early Christian Literature*. 2nd ed. Revised and translated by William F. Arndt and F. Wilbur Gingrich. Chicago, IL: University of Chicago Press, 1979.

Bausani, Alessandro. *Religion in Iran: From Zoroaster to Baha'ullah*. Translated by J. M. Marchesi. New York: Bibliotheca Persica Press, 2000.

Beck, Edmund, ed. *Des Heiligen Ephraem des Syrers Hymnen contra Haereses*. Corpus scriptorum christianorum orientalium 169. Louvain: Imprimerie orientaliste L. Durbecq, 1957.

Bedjan, Paul, ed. *Acta martyrum et sanctorum syriace*. 7 vols. Paris, 1890–97. Repr., Hildesheim: Georg Olms, 1968.

———. *Gregorii Barhebraei Chronicon Syriacum*. Paris: Maisonneuve, 1890.

BeDuhn, Jason David. *The Manichaean Body: In Discipline and Ritual*. Baltimore, MD: The Johns Hopkins University Press, 2000.

BeDuhn, Jason and Paul Mirecki, eds. *Frontiers of Faith: The Christian Encounter with Manichaeism in the Acts of Archelaus*. Nag Hammadi and Manichaean Studies 61. Leiden: Brill, 2007.

Bennett, Byard. "*Iuxta unum latus erat terra tenebrarum*: The Division of Primordial Space in Anti-Manichaean Writers' Descriptions of the Manichaean Cosmogony." In *The Light and the Darkness: Studies in Manichaeism and its World*, edited by Paul Mirecki and Jason BeDuhn, 68–78. Nag Hammadi and Manichaean Studies 50. Leiden: Brill, 2001.

Ben-Shammai, Haggai. *The Doctrines of Religious Thought of Abū Yūsuf Yaʿqūb al-Qirqisānī and Yefet ben ʿElī*. 2 vols. Ph.D. dissertation, Hebrew University, Jerusalem, 1977.

———. "Jewish Thought in Iraq in the 10th Century." In *Judaeo-Arabic Studies: Proceedings of the Founding Conference of the Society for Judaeo-Arabic Studies*, edited by Norman Golb, 15–32. Amsterdam: Harwood Academic Publishers, 1997.

Benveniste, E[mile]. "Le témoignage de Théodore bar Kōnay sur le zoroastrisme." *Le Monde Oriental* 26 (1932): 170–215.

Berkey, Jonathan P. *The Formation of Islam: Religion and Society in the Near East, 600–1800*. Cambridge: Cambridge University Press, 2003.

Betz, H. D. "Paul in the Mani Biography (Codex Manichaicus Coloniensis)." In *Codex Manichaicus Coloniensis: Atti del Simposio Internazionale (Rende-Amantea 3-7 settembre 1984)*, edited by Luigi Cirillo and Amneris Roselli, 215–34. Cosenza: Marra Editore, 1986.

Bevan, A. A. "Manichaeism." In *Encyclopaedia of Religion and Ethics*, edited by James Hastings, vol. 8, 394–402. 13 vols. New York: C. Scribner's Sons, 1908-1927.

Bickerman, E. J. *Chronology of the Ancient World*. 2nd ed. Ithaca, NY: Cornell University Press, 1980.

Bin Gorion, Micha Joseph. *Mimekor Yisrael: Classic Jewish Folktales*. 3 vols. Edited by Emanuel Bin Gorion. Bloomington: Indiana University Press, 1976.

Bīrūnī, Abu'l-Rayḥān Muḥammad b. Aḥmad al-. *Kitāb al-āthār al-bāqiya ʿani'l-qurūn al-khāliya: Chronologie orientalischer Völker von Albêrûnî*. Edited by C. E. Sachau. Leipzig, 1878. Repr., Leipzig: Otto Harrassowitz, 1923.

———. *Kitāb fī taḥqīq mā l'il-Hind: Alberuni's India: An Account of the Religion, Philosophy, Literature, Chronology, Astronomy, Customs, Laws and Astrology of India about A.D. 1030*. Edited by Edward Sachau. London: Trübner, 1887.

Blachère, Régis. "Bashshār b. Burd." *Encyclopaedia of Islam*, vol. 1, 1080–82. New ed. Leiden: Brill, 1954–2002.

Blochet, Edgar. *Le messianisme dans l'hétérodoxie musulmane*. Paris: Librairie Orientale et Américaine, 1903.

Blois, François de. *Burzōy's Voyage to India and the Origin of the Book of Kalīlah wa Dimnah*. London: Royal Asiatic Society, 1990.

———. "Elchasai – Manes – Muḥammad: Manichäismus und Islam in religionshistorischem Vergleich." *Der Islam* 81 (2004): 31–48.

———. "Glossary of Technical Terms and Uncommon Expressions in Arabic (and in Muslim New Persian) Texts Relating to Manichaeism." In *Dictionary of Manichaean Texts, Vol. II: Texts from Iraq and Iran (Texts in Syriac, Arabic, Persian and Zoroastrian Middle Persian)*, edited by François de Blois and Nicholas Sims-Williams, 21–120. Turnhout: Brepols, 2006.

———. "The Manichaean Daily Prayers." In *Studia Manichaica: IV. Internationaler Kongress zum Manichäismus, Berlin, 14.–18. Juli 1997*, edited by Ronald E. Emmerick, Werner Sundermann, and Peter Zieme, 49–54. Berlin: Akademie-Verlag, 2000.

———. "*Naṣrānī* (Ναζωραῖος) and *ḥanīf* (ἐθνικός): Studies on the Religious Vocabulary of Christianity and of Islam." *Bulletin of the School of Oriental and African Studies* 65 (2002): 1–30.

———. "New Light on the Sources of the Manichaean Chapter in the *Fihrist*." In *Il Manicheismo, nuove prospettive della richerca: Dipartimento di Studi Asiatici Università degli Studi di Napoli "L'Orientale," Napoli, 2-8 Settembre 2001*, edited by Aloïs van Tongerloo and Luigi Cirillo, 37–45. Turnhout: Brepols, 2005.

———. "[Review of *Atti del terzo congresso internazionale di studi "Manicheismo e Oriente Cristiano Antico"*]." *Journal of the Royal Asiatic Society* series 3,9,3 (1999): 441–42.

———. "The 'Sabians' (Ṣābi'ūn) in Pre-Islamic Arabia." *Acta Orientalia (Copenhagen)* 56 (1995): 39–61.

———. "Zindīḳ." *Encyclopaedia of Islam*, vol. 11, 510–13. New ed. Leiden: Brill, 1954–2002.

Blois, François de and Nicholas Sims-Williams, eds. *Dictionary of Manichaean Texts Vol. II: Texts from Iraq and Iran*. CFM Subsidia. Turnhout: Brepols, 2006.

Blumberg, Harry. "Theories of Evil in Medieval Jewish Philosophy." *Hebrew Union College Annual* 43 (1972): 149–68.

Bornkamm, Günther. *Mythos und Legende in den apokryphen Thomas-Akten: Beiträge zur Geschichte der Gnosis und zur Vorgeschichte des Manichäismus*. Forschungen zur Religion und Literatur des Alten und Neuen Testaments 31. Göttingen: Vandenhoeck and Ruprecht, 1933.

Bosworth, C. E. *The History of al-Tabarī (Ta'rīkh al-rusul wa'l-mulūk), Volume V: The Sāsānids, the Byzantines, the Lakhmids, and Yemen*. Albany: State University of New York Press, 1999.

———. *The History of al-Ṭabarī, Volume XXX: The 'Abbāsid Caliphate in Equilibrium*. Albany: State University of New York Press, 1989.

———. "Mānī b. Fāttik." In *Encyclopaedia of Islam*, vol. 6, 421. New ed. Leiden: Brill, 1954–2002.

———. "al-Ṣīn." In *Encyclopaedia of Islam*, vol. 9, 616–22. New ed. Leiden: Brill, 1954–2002.

Bousset, Wilhelm. *Hauptprobleme der Gnosis*. Göttingen, 1907. Repr., Göttingen: Vandenhoeck and Ruprecht, 1973.

———. "Manichäisches in den Thomasakten." *Zeitschrift für die neutestamentliche Wissenschaft und die Kunde der älteren Kirche* 18 (1917–18): 1–39.

Bowersock, Glenn W. *Hellenism in Late Antiquity*. Jerome Lectures 18. Ann Arbor: University of Michigan Press, 1990.

Boyce, Mary. *A Catalogue of the Iranian Manuscripts in Manichaean Script in the German Turfan Collection*. Berlin: Akademie-Verlag, 1960.

———. *A Reader in Manichaean Middle Persian and Parthian*. Acta Iranica 9. Leiden: Brill, 1975.

———. *A Word-List of Manichaean Middle Persian and Parthian*. Acta Iranica 9a; Leiden: Brill, 1977.

Brière, Maurice. "Les Homiliae Cathedrales de Sévère d'Antioche, traduction syriaque de Jacques d'Édesse CXX à CXXV." *Patrologia Orientalis* 29 (1960): 124–89.

Brinkmann, Augustus, ed. *Alexandri Lycopolitani contra Manichaei opinions disputatio*. Lipsiae: B. G. Teubner, 1895.

Brock, Sebastian. "A Martyr at the Sasanid Court under Vahrān II: Candida." *Analecta Bollandiana* 96 (1978): 167–81.

Brockelmann, Carl. "Kalīla wa-Dimna." In *Encyclopaedia of Islam*, vol. 4, 503–506. New ed. Leiden: Brill, 1954–2002.

———. *Lexicon Syriacum*. 2nd ed. Halle, 1928. Repr., Tübingen: Max Niemeyer Verlag, 1982.

Brooks, E.-W., ed. *Chronica Minora II*. Corpus scriptorum christianorum orientalium 3. Louvain: Secrétariat du CorpusSCO, 1904.

———. *Eliae metropolitae Nisibeni Opus chronologicum*. Corpus scriptorum christianorum orientalium 62–63a. 2 vols. in 4. Paris: Reipublicae, 1909–10.

———, ed. *John of Ephesus, Lives of the Eastern Saints, I*. Patrologia Orientalis 17.1. Paris: Firmin-Didot, 1923.

Browder, Michael H. "Al-Bîrûnî's Manichaean Sources." In *Manichaean Studies: Proceedings of the First International Conference on Manichaeism, August 5–9, 1987*, edited by Peter Bryder, 19–28. Lund: Plus Ultra, 1988.

Brown, Peter. *The Making of Late Antiquity*. Cambridge, MA: Harvard University Press, 1978.

Browne, Edward G. *A Literary History of Persia*. 4 vols. London and Cambridge, 1902–24. Repr., Cambridge: The University Press, 1964.

Buck, Christopher. "The Identity of the Ṣābi'ūn: An Historical Quest." *The Muslim World* 74 (1984): 172–86.

Budge, E. A. Wallis, ed. *The Book of Governors: The Historia Monastica of Thomas Bishop of Margâ A.D. 840*. 2 vols. London: Kegan Paul, Trench, Trübner, 1893.

Burkitt, F. C. *The Religion of the Manichees*. Cambridge: The University Press, 1925.

Butler, Alfred J. *The Arab Conquest of Egypt and the Last Thirty Years of the Roman Dominion*. Oxford: Clarendon Press, 1902.

Cameron, Averil. "Agathias on the Sassanians." *Dumbarton Oaks Papers* 23 (1969–70): 67–183.

———. "How to Read Heresiology." *Journal of Medieval and Early Modern Studies* 33 (2003): 471–92.

Cameron, Ron and Arthur J. Dewey. *The Cologne Mani Codex (P. Colon. inv. nr. 4780): "Concerning the Origin of his Body"*. Society of Biblical Literature Texts and Translations 15. Missoula, Mont.: Scholars Press, 1979.

Carra de Vaux, B. *Maçoudi: Le livre de l'avertissement et de la revision*. Paris: L'Imprimerie Nationale, 1896.

Casanova, Paul. *Mohammed et la fin du monde: Étude critique sur l'Islam primitive*. 2 vols. Paris: Librairie Paul Geuthner, 1911–24.

Cassel, David, ed. *Sefer ha-Kuzari: Das Buch Kuzari des Jehuda ha-Levi, nach dem hebräischen Texte des Jehuda Ibn-Tibbon*. Leipzig: A. M. Colditz, 1853.

Chabot, J.-B, ed. *Anonymi auctoris Chronicon ad annum Christi 1234 pertinens*. Corpus scriptorum christianorum orientalium 81-82. 2 vols. Paris: Reipublicae, 1916–20.

———, ed. *Chronique de Denys de Tell-Maḥré: Quatrième partie*. Paris: Librairie Émile Bouillon, 1895.

———. *Chronique de Michel le Syrien, patriarche jacobite d'Antioche, 1166–1199*. 4 vols. Repr., Bruxelles: Culture et Civilisation, 1963.

———. *Incerti auctoris Chronicon Pseudo-Dionysianum vulgo dictum*. Corpus scriptorum christianorum orientalium 91, 104. 2 vols. Paris: Reipublicae, 1927–33.

———. *Synodicon orientale ou Recueil de synods nestoriens*. Paris: Imprimerie nationale, 1902.

Chadwick, Henry. *The Early Church*. Baltimore, MD: Penguin Books, 1967.

Chaumont, M.-L. *La christianisation de l'empire iranien: Des origines aux grandes persécutions du IVe siècle*. Corpus scriptorum christianorum orientalium 499. Louvain: E. Peeters, 1988.

Chiesa, Bruno. "A New Fragment of al-Qirqisānī's *Kitāb al-Riyāḍ*." *Jewish Quarterly Review* 78 (1987–88): 175–85.

Chokr, Melhem. *Zandaqa et zindiqs en Islam au second siècle de l'hégire*. Damas: Institut français de Damas, 1993.

Christensen, Arthur. *L'Iran sous les Sassanides*. 2nd ed. Copenhagen: Ejnar Munksgaard, 1944.

———. *Le règne du roi Kawādh et le communisme mazdakite*. Copenhagen: A. F. Høst, 1925.

Church, F. Forrester and Gedaliahu G. Stroumsa. "Mani's Disciple Thomas and the Psalms of Thomas," *Vigiliae Christianae* 34 (1980): 47–55.

Chwolsohn, D[aniel]. *Die Ssabier und der Ssabismus*. 2 vols. St. Petersburg: Kaiserlichen Akademie der Wissenschaften, 1856.

Cirillo, Luigi, ed. *Codex Manichaicus Coloniensis: Atti del Secondo Simposio Internazionale (Cosenza 27–28 maggio 1988)*. Cosenza: Marra Editore, 1990.

Cirillo, Luigi and Amneris Roselli, eds. *Codex Manichaicus Coloniensis: Atti del Simposio Internazionale (Rende-Amantea 3–7 settembre 1984)*. Cosenza: Marra Editore, 1986.

Clackson, Sarah, et al., eds. *Dictionary of Manichaean Texts Vol. I: Texts from the Roman Empire*. CFM Subsidia II. Turnhout: Brepols, 1998.

Clark, Elizabeth A. *Reading Renunciation: Asceticism and Scripture in Early Christianity*. Princeton, NJ: Princeton University Press, 1999.

Cohen, Gerson D. *A Critical Edition with a Translation and Notes of the Book of Tradition (Sefer ha-Qabbalah) by Abraham ibn Daud*. Philadelphia, PA: The Jewish Publication Society of America, 1967.

Colpe, Carsten. "Anpassung des Manichäismus an den Islam (Abū ʿĪsā al-Warrāq)." *Zeitschrift der deutschen morgenländischen Gesellschaft* 109 (1959): 82–91.

———. "Bar Hebräus über die Manichäer." In *Pietas: Festschrift für Bernhard Kötting*, edited by Ernst Dassmann and K. Suso Frank, 237–42. Münster [Westfalen]: Aschendorffsche Verlagsbuchhandlung, 1980.

———. *Die religionsgeschichtliche Schule: Darstellung und Kritik ihres Bildes vom gnostischen Erlösermythus*. Forschungen zur Religion und Literatur des Alten und Neuen Testaments 78, Neue Folge 60. Göttingen: Vandenhoeck and Ruprecht, 1961.

Contini, Riccardo. "Hypothèses sur l'araméen manichéen." *Annali di Ca' Foscari: Rivista della Facoltà di lingue e letterature straniere di Ca' Foscari dell'Università di Venezia* 34 (1995): 65–107.

Corbin, Henry. "From the Gnosis of Antiquity to Ismaili Gnosis." In *Cyclical Time and Ismaili Gnosis*, 151–93. London: Kegan Paul International, 1983.

———. *Œuvres philosophiques et mystiques de Shihabaddin Yahya Sohrawardi I (Opera metaphysica et mystica II)*. Bibliothèque iranienne 2. Teheran/Paris: Institut franco-iranien/Adrien-Maisonneuve, 1952.

———. *Spiritual Body and Celestial Earth: From Mazdean Iran to Shīʿite Iran*. Translated by Nancy Pearson. Bollingen Series 91:2. Princeton, NJ: Princeton University Press, 1977.

———. *Trilogie ismaelienne: Textes édités avec traduction française et commentaries*. Bibliothèque iranienne 9. Teheran: Departement d'iranologie de l'Institut franco-iranien, 1961.

Crone, Patricia. *God's Rule: Government and Islam*. New York: Columbia University Press, 2004.

———. "Kavād's Heresy and Mazdak's Revolt." *Iran* 29 (1991): 21–42.

———. "Zoroastrian Communism." *Comparative Studies in Society and History* 36 (1994): 447–62.

Crone, Patricia and Michael Cook. *Hagarism: The Making of the Islamic World*. Cambridge: Cambridge University Press, 1977.

Crum, W. E. *A Coptic Dictionary*. Oxford: Clarendon Press, 1939.

———. "Eusebius and Coptic Church Histories." *Proceedings of the Society of Biblical Archaeology* 24 (1902): 68–84.

———. "A 'Manichaean' Fragment from Egypt." *Journal of the Royal Asiatic Society* (1919): 207–208.

Cumont, Franz and M.-A. Kugener. *Recherches sur le manichéisme*. Bruxelles: H. Lamertin, 1908–12.

Cureton, William, ed. *Kitāb al-milal wa al-niḥal: Book of Religious and Philosophical Sects by Muhammad al-Shahrastáni*. London, 1846. Repr., Leipzig: Otto Harrassowitz, 1923.

Daftary, Farhad. *The Ismāʿīlīs: Their History and Doctrines*. 2nd ed. Cambridge: Cambridge University Press, 2007.

Daiber, Hans. "Nestorians of Ninth Century Iraq as a Source of Greek, Syriac and Arabic: A Survey of Some Unexploited Sources." *Aram* 3 (1991): 45–52.

Daniel, Elton L. *The Political and Social History of Khurasan under Abbasid Rule, 747–820*. Minneapolis and Chicago: Bibliotheca Islamica, 1979.

Daryaee, Touraj. "Apocalypse Now: Zoroastrian Reflections on the Early Islamic Centuries," *Medieval Encounters* 4 (1998): 188–202.

Davidson, Israel. *Saadia's Polemic Against Ḥiwi al-Balkhi: A Fragment Edited from a Genizah MS*. New York: The Jewish Theological Seminary of America, 1915.

Delitzsch, Franz. *Etz Ḥayyim: Ahron ben Elia's aus Nikomedien des Karäers System der Religionsphilosophie*. Leipzig: Verlag von Johann Ambrosius Barth, 1841.

Dick, Ignace, ed. *Théodore Abuqurra: Traité de l'existence du Créateur et de la vraie religion*. Patrimoine arabe chrétien 3. Rome: Pontificio Istituto Orientale, 1982.

Dignas, Beate and Engelbert Winter. *Rome and Persia in Late Antiquity: Neighbours and Rivals*. Cambridge: Cambridge University Press, 2007.

Dīnawarī, Abū Ḥanīfah Aḥmad b. Dāwūd al-. *Kitāb al-akhbār al-ṭiwāl*. Edited by Vladimir Guirgass. Leiden: Brill, 1888.

Dodge, Bayard. *The Fihrist of al-Nadīm: A Tenth-Century Survey of Muslim Culture*. 2 vols. New York: Columbia University Press, 1970.

Dörfler, S. "Ahron ben Elia über die Manichäer." *Le Muséon* 38 (1925): 57–65.

Dozy, R. *Supplément aux dictionnaires arabes*. 2 vols. Leiden: E. J. Brill, 1881.

Drijvers, H. J. W. "Addai und Mani: Christentum und Manichäismus im dritten Jahrhundert in Syrien." In *IIIe Symposium Syriacum, 1980: Les contacts du monde syriaque avec les autres cultures, Goslar 7-11 septembre 1980*, edited by René Lavenant, 171–85. OrChrAn 221. Rome: Pontificium Institutum Studiorium Orientalium, 1983.

———. *Bardaiṣan of Edessa*. Assen: Van Gorcum, 1966.

———. "Early Syriac Christianity: Some Recent Publications." *Vigiliae Christianae* 50 (1996): 159–77.

———. "Jews and Christians at Edessa." *Journal of Jewish Studies* 36 (1985): 88–102.

Drower, E. S. *The Canonical Prayerbook of the Mandaeans*. Leiden: Brill, 1959.

———. *The Haran Gawaita and The Baptism of Hibil-Ziwa*. Città del Vaticano: Biblioteca Apostolica Vaticana, 1953.

———. "Mandaean Polemic." *Bulletin of the School of Oriental and African Studies* 25 (1962): 438–48.

Drower, E. S. and R. Macuch. *A Mandaic Dictionary*. Oxford: Clarendon Press, 1963.

Duchesne-Guillemin, Jacques. "Zoroastrian Religion." In *The Cambridge History of Iran, Volume 3(2): The Seleucid, Parthian and Sasanian Periods*, edited by Ehsan Yarshater,

866–908. Cambridge: Cambridge University Press, 1983.

Dunlop, D. M. *Arab Civilization to A.D. 1500*. New York: Praeger, 1971.

Duran, R. Simeon b. Ṣemaḥ. *Sefer Magen Avot*. Livorno: Abraham Isaac Qastillo, 1784/5.

Durkin-Meisterernst, Desmond. *Dictionary of Manichaean Texts Vol. III, Part 1: Dictionary of Manichaean Middle Persian and Parthian*. CFM Subsidia. Turnhout: Brepols, 2004.

———. "Erfand Mani die manichäische Schrift?" In *Studia Manichaica: IV. Internationaler Kongress zum Manichäismus, Berlin, 14.-18. Juli 1997*, edited by Ronald E. Emmerick, Werner Sundermann, and Peter Zieme, 161–78. Berlin: Akademie-Verlag, 2000.

Duval, Rubens. *La littérature syriaque*. 3rd ed. Paris: Librairie Victor Lecoffre, 1907.

Eisenberg, Isaac, ed. *Qiṣaṣ al-anbiyā': Vita Prophetarum auctore Muḥammed ben 'Abdallah al-Kisa'i*. 2 vols. Leiden: Brill, 1922–23.

Elman, Yaakov. "Middle Persian Culture and Babylonian Sages: Accommodation and Resistance in the Shaping of Rabbinic Legal Tradition." In *The Cambridge Companion to the Talmud and Rabbinic Literature*, edited by Charlotte Elisheva Fonrobert and Martin S. Jaffee, 165–97. Cambridge: Cambridge University Press, 2007.

Emmerick, Ronald E. "Buddhism among Iranian Peoples I: In Pre-Islamic Times." *Encyclopaedia Iranica*, edited by Ehsan Yarshater, vol. 2, 492–96. London and New York: Bibliotheca Persica, 1982- .

Epstein, J. N. "Gloses babylo-araméennes." *Revue des études juives* 73 (1921): 27–58; 74 (1922): 40–72.

Erder, Yoram. "The Origin of the Name Idrīs in the Qur'ān: A Study of the Influence of Qumran Literature on Early Islam." *Journal of Near Eastern Studies* 49 (1990): 339–50.

Ess, Josef van. *The Flowering of Muslim Theology*. Translated by Jane Marie Todd. Cambridge, MA: Harvard University Press, 2006.

———. "Ḳadariyya." In *Encyclopaedia of Islam*, vol. 4, 368–72. New ed. Leiden: Brill, 1954–2002.

———. "al-Naẓẓām." In *Encyclopaedia of Islam*, vol. 7, 1057–58. New ed. Leiden: Brill, 1954-2002.

———. *Theologie und Gesellschaft im 2. und 3. Jahrhundert Hidschra: Eine Geschichte des religiösen Denkens im frühen Islam*. 6 vols. Berlin: Walter de Gruyter, 1991–97.

Eusebius. *The Ecclesiastical History*. Loeb Classical Library. 2 vols. Translated by Kirsopp Lake and J. E. L. Oulton. Repr., Cambridge, MA: Harvard University Press, 1994.

Evetts, B. "History of the Patriarchs of the Coptic Church of Alexandria." *Patrologia Orientalis* 1 (1907): 103–214; 383–518.

Fahd, Toufic. "Ṣābi'a." In *Encyclopaedia of Islam*, vol. 8, 675-78. Leiden: Brill, 1954–2002.

Fakhry, Majid. *A History of Islamic Philosophy*. 3rd ed.; New York: Columbia University Press, 2004.

Faxian. *The Travels of Fa-hsien (399–414 A.D.), or Record of the Buddhistic Kingdoms*. Translated by H. A. Giles. Cambridge, 1923. Repr., Westport, Conn.: Greenwood Press, 1981.

Fiey, J.-M. "Īšō'dnāḥ et la Chronique de Séert." *Parole de l'Orient* 6-7 (1975–76): 447–59.

Finkel, Joshua. "A Risāla of al-Jāḥiẓ." *Journal of the American Oriental Society* 47 (1927): 311–34.

Flügel, G[ustav]. "Bâbek, seine Abstammung und erstes Auftreten." *Zeitschrift der deutschen morgenländischen Gesellschaft* 23 (1869): 531–42.

———. *Mani: Seine Lehre und seine Schriften*. Leipzig, 1862. Repr., Osnabrück: Biblio Verlag, 1969.

———. "Ueber Muhammad bin Isḥâq's Fihrist al-'ulûm." *Zeitschrift der deutschen morgenländischen Gesellschaft* 13 (1859): 559–650.

Foltz, Richard C. *Religions of the Silk Road: Overland Trade and Cultural Exchange from Antiquity to the Fifteenth Century*. New York: St. Martin's Press, 1999.

Forte, Antonino. "Deux études sur le manichéisme chinois." *T'oung Pao* 59 (1973): 220–53.

Fowden, Garth. *Empire to Commonwealth: Consequences of Monotheism in Late Antiquity*. Princeton, NJ: Princeton University Press, 1993.

Frank, Daniel. *The Religious Philosophy of the Karaite Aaron ben Elijah: The Problem of Divine Justice*. Ph.D. diss., Harvard University, 1991.

Frankfurter, David. "Apocalypses Real and Alleged in the Mani Codex." *Numen* 44 (1997): 60–73.

———. "The Legacy of Jewish Apocalypses in Early Christianity: Regional Trajectories." Pp. 129-200 in *The Jewish Apocalyptic Heritage in Early Christianity*. Compendia rerum iudaicarum ad Novum Testamentum III.4. Edited by James C. VanderKam and William Adler. Minneapolis, MN: Fortress, 1996.

Franzmann, Majella. "The Syriac-Coptic Bilinguals from Ismant el-Kharab (Roman Kellis): Translation Process and Manichaean Missionary Practice." In *Il Manicheismo, nuove prospettive della richerca: Dipartimento di Studi Asiatici Università degli Studi di Napoli "L'Orientale," Napoli, 2-8 Settembre 2001*, edited by Aloïs van Tongerloo and Luigi Cirillo, 115–22. Turnhout: Brepols, 2005.

Friedlaender, Israel. "The Heterodoxies of the Shiites in the Presentation of Ibn Ḥazm." *Journal of the American Oriental Society* 28 (1907): 1–80; 29 (1908): 1–183.

———. "Jewish-Arabic Studies," *Jewish Quarterly Review* n.s. 1 (1910): 183–215; n.s. 2 (1912): 481–516; n.s. 3 (1912): 235–300.

Friedmann, Yohanan. *Tolerance and Coercion in Islam: Interfaith Relations in the Muslim Tradition*. Cambridge: Cambridge University Press, 2003.

Frye, Richard N. "The Political History of Iran under the Sasanians." In *The Cambridge History of Iran, Volume 3(1): The Seleucid, Parthian and Sasanian Periods*, edited by Ehsan Yarshater, 116–77. Cambridge: Cambridge University Press, 1983.

Fück, Johann. "The Rôle of Manicheism under the Early Abbasids." In *Arabische Kultur und Islam im Mittelalter: Ausgewählte Schriften*, 258–66. Weimar: H. Böhlaus, 1981.

———. "Sechs Ergänzungen zu Sachaus Ausgabe von al-Bīrūnīs „Chronologie Orientalischer Völker"." In *Documenta Islamica Inedita*, edited by Johann Fück, 69–98. Berlin: Akademie-Verlag, 1952.

———. "Spuren des Zindīqtums in der islamischen Tradition." In *Arabische Kultur und Islam im Mittelalter: Ausgewählte Schriften*, 267–71. Weimar: H. Böhlaus, 1981.

Funk, Wolf-Peter. "The Reconstruction of the Manichaean *Kephalaia*." In *Emerging From Darkness: Studies in the Recovery of Manichaean Sources*, edited by Paul Mirecki and Jason BeDuhn, 143–59. Nag Hammadi and Manichaean Studies 43. Leiden: Brill, 1997.

Gabrieli, Francesco. "Ibn al-Muḳaffaʿ." In *Encyclopaedia of Islam*, vol. 3, 883–85. New ed. Leiden: Brill, 1954–2002.

———. "La «zandaqa» au Ier siècle abbasside." In *L'élaboration de l'Islam: Colloque de Strasbourg, 12-13-14 juin 1959*, 23–38. Paris: Presses Universitaires de France, 1961.

Gardner, Iain, ed. *Kellis Literary Texts: Volume 1*. Dakhleh Oasis Project Monograph No. 4. Oxford: Oxbow Books, 1996.

———. *Kellis Literary Texts: Volume 2*. Dakhleh Oasis Project Monograph 15. Oxford: Oxbow Books, 2007.

———. "The Manichaean Community at Kellis: A Progress Report." In *Emerging from Darkness: Studies in the Recovery of Manichaean Sources*, edited by Paul Mirecki and Jason BeDuhn, 161–75. Nag Hammadi and Manichaean Studies 43. Leiden: Brill, 1997.

———. "A Manichaean Liturgical Codex Found at Kellis." *Orientalia* 62 (1993): 30–59.

Gardner, Iain and Samuel N. C. Lieu, eds. *Manichaean Texts From the Roman Empire*. Cambridge: Cambridge University Press, 2004.

Gardner, Iain and K. A. Worp. "Leaves from a Manichaean Codex." *Zeitschrift für Papyrologie und Epigraphik* 117 (1997): 139–55.

Gardner, I[ain]. M. F. and Samuel N. C. Lieu. "From Narmouthis (Medinet Madi) to Kellis (Ismant el-Kharab): Manichaean Documents from Roman Egypt." *Journal of Roman Studies* 86 (1996): 146–69.

Genequand, Charles. "Philosophical Schools as Viewed by Some Medieval Muslim Authors." In *Muslim Perceptions of Other Religions: A Historical Survey*, edited by Jacques Waardenburg, 195–201. Oxford: Oxford University Press, 1999.

Gignoux, Philippe. *Man and Cosmos in Ancient Iran*. Roma: Istituto italiano per l'Africa e l'Oriente, 2001.

Gil, Moshe. "The Creed of Abū 'Āmir." *Israel Oriental Studies* 12 (1992): 9–57.

———. *A History of Palestine, 634–1099*. Translated by Ethel Broido. Cambridge: Cambridge University Press, 1992.

Gillman, Ian and Hans-Joachim Klimkeit. *Christians in Asia before 1500*. Ann Arbor: The University of Michigan Press, 1999.

Gimaret, Daniel. "Bouddha et les bouddhistes dans la tradition musulmane." *Journal asiatique* 257 (1969): 273–316.

———. "Tanāsukh." In *Encyclopaedia of Islam*, vol. 10, 181–83. New ed. Leiden: Brill, 1954–2002.

Giorgi, Roberto. *Pour une histoire de la zandaḳa*. Firenze: La Nuova Italia Editrice, 1989.

Gobillot, Geneviève. *Le livre de la profondeur des choses*. Villeneuve d'Ascq: Presses Universitaires du Septentrion, 1996.

Gökyay, O. Ş. "Kātib Čelebi." In *Encyclopaedia of Islam*, vol. 4, 760–62. New ed. Leiden: Brill, 1954-2002.

Golden, P. B. "Toghuzghuz." In *Encyclopaedia of Islam*, vol. 10, 555–57. New ed. Leiden: Brill, 1954-2002.

Goldziher, I[gnaz]. "Bemerkungen zur neuhebräischen Poesie." *Jewish Quarterly Review* o.s. 14 (1902): 719–36.

———. *Introduction to Islamic Theology and Law*. Translated by Andras and Ruth Hamori. Princeton: Princeton University Press, 1981.

———. "[Review of Hirschfeld, *Das Buch al-Chazarî*]." *Zeitschrift der deutschen morgenländischen Gesellschaft* 41 (1887): 691–707.

———. "Ṣâliḥ b. 'Abd-al-Ḳuddûs und das Zindîḳthum während der Regierung des Chalifen al-Mahdî." In *Transactions of the Ninth International Congress of Orientalists*, edited by E. Delmar Morgan, vol. 2, 104–29. 2 vols. London: The Committee of the Congress, 1893.

Gottheil, Richard J. H. "References to Zoroaster in Syriac and Arabic Literature." In *Classical Studies in Honour of Henry Drisler*, 24–51. New York: Macmillan and Company, 1894.

Griffith, Sidney H. "Free Will in Christian Kalām: The Doctrine of Theodore Abū Qurrah." *Parole de l'Orient* 14 (1987): 79–107.

———. "The Thorn Among the Tares: Mani and Manichaeism in the Works of St. Ephraem the Syrian." *Studia Patristica* 35 (2001): 403–35.

Grunebaum, G. E. von. "Three Arabic Poets of the Early Abbasid Age." *Orientalia* 17 (1948): 160–204.

Guidi, Ignatius, ed. *Chronica Minora I*. Corpus scriptorum christianorum orientalium 1. Paris, 1903. Repr., Louvain: Imprimerie Orientaliste, 1960.

Guidi, Michelangelo. *La lotta tra l'Islam e il Manicheismo: Un libro di Ibn al-Muqaffa' contro il Corano confutato da al-Qāsim b. Ibrāhīm*. Roma: R. Accademia Nazionale dei Lincei, 1927.

———. "Mazdak." In *Encyclopaedia of Islam*, vol. 5, 430–33. First edition. 9 vols. Leiden: E. J. Brill, 1913-38.

Guidi, Michelangelo and Michael G. Morony. "Mōbadh." In *Encyclopaedia of Islam*, vol. 7, 213–16. New ed. Leiden: Brill, 1954–2002.

Guillaume, Alfred. *The Life of Muhammad: A Translation of Isḥāq's Sīrat Rasūl Allāh*. Oxford, 1955. Repr., Karachi: Oxford University Press, 1967.

Gulácsi, Zsuzsanna. "Mani's 'Picture-Box'? A Study of a Chagatai Textual Reference and its Supposed Pictorial Analogy from the British Library (Or. 8212–1691)." In *Il Manicheismo: Nuove prospettive della richerca: Dipartimento di studi asiatici Università degli studi di Napoli "L'Orientale" Napoli, 2-8 settembre 2001*, edited by Aloïs van Tongerloo and Luigi Cirillo, 149–66. Manichaean Studies 5. Turnhout: Brepols, 2005.

Gutas, Dimitri. *Greek Thought, Arabic Culture: The Graeco-Arabic Translation Movement in Baghdad and Early 'Abbāsid Society*. London : Routledge, 1998.

Guttmann, J[acob]. *Die Religionsphilosophie des Saadia dargestellt und erläutert*. Göttingen: Vandenhoeck and Ruprecht, 1882.

———. "Ueber Abraham bar Chijja's ‚Buch der Enthüllung'." *Monatsschrift für Geschichte und Wissenschaft des Judentums* 47 (1903): 446–68; 545–69.

Guttmann, Julius. "The Sources of Hiwi al-Balkhi." In *Alexander Marx Jubilee Volume: On the Occasion of his Seventieth Birthday*, 95–102. 2 vols. New York: The Jewish Theological Seminary, 1950. (Hebrew).

Haase, Felix. *Altchristliche Kirchengeschichte nach orientalischen Quellen*. Leipzig: Verlag Otto Harrassowitz, 1925.

Hämeen-Anttila, Jaakko. "Arabian Prophecy." In *Prophecy in its Ancient Near Eastern Context: Mesopotamian, Biblical, and Arabian Perspectives*, edited by Martti Nissinen, 115–46. Atlanta: Society of Biblical Literature, 2000.

Halkin, Abraham S., ed. *Moses Maimonides' Epistle to Yemen: The Arabic Original and the Three Hebrew Versions*. New York: American Academy for Jewish Research, 1952.

Hallier, Ludwig. *Untersuchungen über die Edessenische Chronik*. Texte und Untersuchungen 9.1. Leipzig: J. C. Hinrichs, 1892.

Halm, Heinz. *Shi'ism*. Translated by Janet Watson and Marian Hill. 2nd ed. New York: Columbia University Press, 2004.

———. "Die Sieben und die Zwölf: Die ismā'īlitische Kosmogonie und das Mazdak-Fragment des Šahrastānī." In *XVIII. Deutscher Orientalistentag, vom 1. bis 5. Oktober 1972, in Lübeck: Vorträge*, edited by Wolfgang Voight, 170–77. ZDMG Supplement II. Wiesbaden: Franz Steiner Verlag, 1974.

Haloun, G. and W. B. Henning. "The Compendium of the Doctrines and Styles of the Teaching of Mani, the Buddha of Light." *Asia Major* 3 (1953): 184–212.

Haq, Syed Nomanul. *Names, Natures and Things: The Alchemist Jābir ibn Ḥayyān and his* Kitāb al-Aḥjār *(Book of Stones)*. Dordrecht: Kluwer Academic Publishers, 1994.

Harnack, Adolf. *Der Ketzer-Katalog des Bischofs Maruta von Maipherkat*. Texte und Untersuchungen zur Geschichte der altchristlichen Literatur, neue Folge 4.1b. Leipzig: J. C. Hinrichs, 1899.

Harrak, Amir. *The Acts of Mār Mārī the Apostle*. Atlanta: Society of Biblical Literature, 2005.
———. "Anti-Manichaean Propaganda in Syriac Literature." *Journal of Eastern Christian Studies* 56 (2004): 49–67.
Harris, J. Rendel. *The Gospel of the Twelve Apostles Together With the Apocalypses of Each One of Them*. Cambridge: The University Press, 1900.
Hartman, Sven S. "Les identifications de Gayōmart à l'époque islamique." In *Syncretism*, edited by Sven S. Hartman, 263–94. Stockholm: Almqvist and Wiksell, 1969.
Haug, Martin. *Essays on the Sacred Language, Writings, and Religion of the Parsis*. 3rd ed. Edited by E. W. West. London: Kegan Paul, Trench, Trübner, 1884.
Hawting, G. R. "Khālid b. 'Abd Allāh al-Ḳasrī." In *Encyclopaedia of Islam*, vol. 4, 925–27. New ed. Leiden: Brill, 1954–2002.
Hegemonius. *Acta Archelai*. Die griechische christliche Schriftsteller der ersten [drei] Jahrhunderte 16. Edited by Charles Henry Beeson. Leipzig: J. C. Hinrichs, 1906.
———. *Acta Archelai: The Acts of Archelaus*. Translated by Mark Vermes. Turnhout: Brepols, 2001.
Helm, Rudolf, ed. *Eusebius Werke VII Band: Die Chronik des Hieronymus*. 3rd ed. Berlin: Akademie-Verlag, 1984.
Henning, W. B. "The Book of the Giants." *Bulletin of the School of Oriental and African Studies* 11 (1943–46): 52–74.
———. "Ein manichäisches Bet- und Beichtbuch." *Abhandlungen der königlichen preussischen Akademie der Wissenschaften (Berlin)* 10. Berlin, 1936.
———. "Ein manichäisches Henochbuch." *Sitzungsberichte der preussischen Akademie der Wissenschaften* (1934): 27–35.
———. "Mani's Last Journey." *Bulletin of the School of Oriental and African Studies* 10 (1939–42): 941–53.
———. "Neue Materialen zur Geschichte des Manichäismus." *Zeitschrift der deutschen morgenländischen Gesellschaft* 90 (1936): 1–18.
———. "[Review of Jackson, *Researches in Manichaeism*]." *Orientalistische Literaturzeitung* 37 (1934): 749–56.
———. "A Sogdian Fragment of the Manichaean Cosmogony." *Bulletin of the School of Oriental and African Studies* 12 (1947–48): 306–18.
———. "Sogdian Tales." *Bulletin of the School of Oriental and African Studies* 11 [1943–46]: 465–87.
———. "Zwei Fehler in der arabisch-manichäischen Überlieferung." *Orientalia* 5 (1936): 84–87.
Henrichs, Albert and Ludwig Koenen. "Ein griechischer Mani-Codex." *Zeitschrift für Papyrologie und Epigraphik* 5 (1970): 97–217.
Herbelot, Barthélemy d'. *Bibliothèque orientale, ou Dictionaire universel*. Paris: Compagnie des Libraires, 1697.
Hespel, Robert and René Draguet. *Théodore bar Koni, Livre des scolies (recension de Séert): II. Mimrè VI-XI*. Corpus scriptorum christianorum orientalium 432, scrip. syri t. 188. Louvain: E. Peeters, 1982.
Hirschfeld, Hartwig, ed. *Das Buch al-Chazarî des Abû-l-Ḥasan Jehuda Hallewi*. Leipzig: Otto Schulze, 1887.
———. *Qirqisāni Studies*. Jews' College Publication 6. London: Oxford University Press, 1918.
Hodgson, Marshall G. S. "How Did the Early Shî'a Become Sectarian?" *Journal of the American Oriental Society* 75 (1955): 1–13.

———. *The Venture of Islam: Conscience and History in a World Civilization*. 3 vols. Chicago, IL: University of Chicago Press, 1974.

Hoffmann, Georg. *Auszüge aus syrischen Akten persischer Märtyrer*. Leipzig, 1880. Repr., Nendeln, Liechtenstein: Kraus Reprint Ltd., 1966.

Hope, C. A. "The Archaeological Context of the Discovery of Leaves from a Manichaean Codex." *Zeitschrift für Papyrologie und Epigraphik* 117 (1997): 156–61.

Houtsma, M. Th. "Bih'afrid." *Wiener Zeitschrift für die Kunde des Morgenlandes* 3 (1889): 30–37.

———, ed. *Ibn Wadih qui dicitur al-Ja'qubi historiae* .... 2 vols. Leiden: Brill, 1883.

Howard, George. *The Teaching of Addai*. Chico, CA: Scholars Press, 1981.

Hoyland, Robert G. *Arabia and the Arabs: From the Bronze Age to the Coming of Islam*. London: Routledge, 2001.

Hughes, Thomas Patrick. *A Dictionary of Islam*. London, 1885. Repr., Chicago, IL: Kazi Publications, 1994.

Hutter, Manfred. "Mani und das persische Christentum." In *Manichaica Selecta: Studies Presented to Professor Julien Ries on the Occasion of his Seventieth Birthday*, edited by Alois van Tongerloo and Søren Giversen, 125–35. Louvain: International Association of Manichaean Studies, 1991.

———. "Manichaeism in Iran in the Fourth Century." In *Studia Manichaica: IV. Internationaler Kongress zum Manichäismus, Berlin, 14.–18. Juli 1997*, edited by Ronald E. Emmerick, Werner Sundermann, and Peter Zieme, 308–17. Berlin: Akademie-Verlag, 2000.

———. *Manis kosmogonische Šābuhragān-Texte: Edition, Kommentar und literaturgeschichtliche Einordung der manichäisch-mittelpersischen Handschriften M 98/99 I und M 7980–7984*. Wiesbaden: Otto Harrassowitz, 1992.

Ibn al-Malāḥimī. *Kitāb al-mu'tamad fī uṣūl al-dīn*. Edited by Martin McDermott and Wilferd Madelung. London: Al-Hoda, 1991.

Ibn al-Nadīm. *Kitāb al-Fihrist*. Edited by Riḍa Tajaddud. Teheran: Maktabat al-Assadī, 1971.

Ibn Bābawayh. *[Kitāb] al-Tawḥīd*. Edited by Abī Ja'far Muḥammad b. 'Alī Hāshim al-Ḥusaynī al-Ṭihrānī. Teheran: Maktabat al-Ṣudūq, 1967.

Ibn Qutayba. *Kitāb al-ma'ārif*. 2d ed. Edited by Tharwat 'Ukkāsha. Cairo: Dār al-Ma'ārif, 1969.

Irwin, Robert. "The Arabic Beast Fable." *Journal of the Warburg and Courtauld Institutes* 55 (1992): 36–50.

———. *Islamic Art in Context: Art, Architecture, and the Literary World*. New York: Harry N. Abrams, 1997.

Ivanow, W[ladimir]. *Ibn al-Qaddah (The Alleged Founder of Ismailism)*. 2nd rev. ed. Bombay: Ismaili Society, 1957.

Jackson, A. V. Williams. *Researches in Manichaeism*. New York, 1932. Repr., New York: AMS Press, 1965.

———. "A Sketch of the Manichaean Doctrine Concerning the Future Life." *Journal of the American Oriental Society* 50 (1930): 177–98.

———. *Zoroaster: The Prophet of Ancient Iran*. New York, 1899. Repr., New York: AMS Press, 1965.

Jāḥiẓ. *Le cadi et la mouche: Anthologie du Livre des Animaux*. Edited by Lakhdar Souami. Paris: Sindbad, 1988.

———. *Nine Essays of al-Jahiz*. Translated by William M. Hutchins. New York: Peter Lang, 1989.

———. *Sobriety and Mirth: A Selection of the Shorter Writings of al-Jāhiz*. Translated by Jim Colville. London: Kegan Paul, 2002.

Jambet, Christian. *The Act of Being: The Philosophy of Revelation in Mullā Sadrā*. Translated by Jeff Fort. New York: Zone Books, 2006.

Jeffery, Arthur. *The Foreign Vocabulary of the Quran*. Baroda, 1938. Repr., Lahore: Al-Biruni, 1977.

John Malalas. *Ioannis Malalae Chronographia*. Corpus scriptorum historiae byzantinae 14. Edited by Ludwig Dindorf. Bonnae: E. Weberi, 1831.

Johnson, D. W. "Coptic Reactions to Gnosticism and Manichaeism." *Le Muséon* 100 (1987): 199–209.

Jones, F. Stanley. "The Astrological Trajectory in Ancient Syriac-Speaking Christianity." In *Atti del terzo congresso internazionale di studi "Manicheismo e Oriente Cristiano Antico": Arcavacata di Rende-Amantea 31 agosto–5 settembre 1993*, edited by Luigi Cirillo and Alois van Tongerloo, 183–200. Manichaean Studies 3. Turnhout: Brepols, 1997.

Judah ben Elijah Hadassi. *Sefer Eshkol ha-kofer*. Eupatoria, 1836. Repr., [Farnborough]: Gregg, 1971.

Judah ha-Levi. *Kitāb al-radd wa-'l-dalīl fī 'l-dīn al-dhalīl (al-Kitāb al-Khazarī)*. Edited by David H. Baneth. Jerusalem: The Magnes Press, 1977.

Jullien, Christelle and Florence Jullien. "Les *Actes de Mār Mārī*: Une figure apocryphe au service de l'unité communautaire." *Apocrypha* 10 (1999): 177–94.

———. *Apôtres des confins: Processus missionnaires chrétiens dans l'empire iranien*. Res Orientales 15. Bures-sur-Yvette: Groupe pour l'Étude de la Civilisation du Moyen-Orient, 2002.

———. "Aux frontières de l'Iranité: «*Nāṣrāyē*» et «*Krīstyonē*» des inscriptions du *mobad* Kirdīr: Enquête littéraire et historique." *Numen* 49 (2002): 282–335.

Kaestli, Jean-Daniel. "L'utilisation des actes apocryphes des apôtres dans le manichéisme." In *Gnosis and Gnosticism: Papers read at the Seventh International Conference on Patristic Studies (Oxford, September 8th-13th 1975)*, edited by Martin Krause, 107–16. Nag Hammadi Studies 8. Leiden: Brill, 1977.

Kazhdan, Alexander P., ed. *The Oxford Dictionary of Byzantium*. 3 vols. Oxford: Oxford University Press, 1991.

Kennedy, Hugh. *The Court of the Caliphs: The Rise and Fall of Islam's Greatest Dynasty*. London: Weidenfeld and Nicholson, 2004.

———. *The History of al-Tabarī (Ta'rīkh al-rusul wa'l-mulūk), Volume XXIX: Al-Manṣūr and al-Mahdī*. Albany: State University of New York Press, 1990.

Kessler, Konrad. *Mani: Forschungen über die manichäische Religion*. Berlin: Georg Reimer, 1889.

Khayyāṭ, Abu'l-Ḥusayn b. 'Uthmān al-. *Kitāb al-intiṣār: Le livre du triomphe et de la réfutation d'Ibn al-Rawandi l'hérétique*. Translated by Albert N. Nader. Beyrouth: Éditions les Lettres Orientales, 1957.

Kister, M. J. "The Struggle Against Musaylima and the Conquest of Yamāma." *Jerusalem Studies in Arabic and Islam* 27 (2002): 1–56.

Klein, Wassilios. "The Epic *Buddhacarita* by Aśvaghoṣa and its Significance for the 'Life of Mani.'" In *Il Manicheismo: Nuove prospettive della richerca: Dipartimento di studi asiatici Università degli studi di Napoli "L'Orientale" Napoli, 2-8 settembre 2001*, edited by Aloïs van Tongerloo and Luigi Cirillo, 223–32. Manichaean Studies 5. Turnhout: Brepols, 2005.

———. "War Mani Priester der Perserkirche?" In *Atti del terzo congresso internazionale di studi "Manicheismo e Oriente Cristiano Antico": Arcavacata di Rende-Amantea 31 agosto–5 settembre 1993*, edited by Luigi Cirillo and Alois van Tongerloo, 201–16. Manichaean Studies 3. Turnhout: Brepols, 1997.

Klijn, A. F. J. *Seth in Jewish, Christian and Gnostic Literature*. Novum Testamentum Supplements 46. Leiden: Brill, 1977.

Klijn, A. F. J. and G. J. Reinink. *Patristic Evidence for Jewish-Christian Sects*. Novum Testamentum Supplements 36. Leiden: Brill, 1973.

Klíma, Otakar. *Mazdak: Geschichte einer sozialen Bewegung im sassanidischen Persien*. Praha: Nakladatelství Československé Akademie Věd, 1957.

Klimkeit, Hans-Joachim. *Gnosis on the Silk Road: Gnostic Texts from Central Asia*. San Francisco, CA: Harper Collins, 1993.

———. *Hymnen und Gebete der Religion des Lichts: Iranische und türkische liturgische Texte der Manichäer Zentralasiens*. Opladen: Westdeutscher Verlag, 1989.

Koenen, Ludwig. "Manichaean Apocalypticism at the Crossroads of Iranian, Egyptian, Jewish and Christian Thought." In *Codex Manichaicus Coloniensis: Atti del Simposio Internazionale (Rende-Amantea 3–7 settembre 1984)*, edited by Luigi Cirillo and Amneris Roselli, 285–332. Cosenza: Marra Editore, 1986.

Koenen, Ludwig and Cornelia Römer. *Der Kölner Mani-Kodex. Über das Werden seines Leben: Kritische Edition*. Papyrologica Coloniensia 14. Opladen: Westdeutscher Verlag, 1988.

Kohlberg, Etan. "al-Rāfiḍa or al-Rawāfiḍ." In *Encyclopaedia of Islam*, vol. 8, 386–89. New ed. Leiden: Brill, 1954-2002.

Kotter, Bonifatius, ed. *Die Schriften des Johannes von Damaskos, IV: Liber de haeresibus; Opera polemica*. Berlin: Walter de Gruyter, 1981.

Kraeling, Carl H. *Anthropos and Son of Man: A Study in the Religious Syncretism of the Hellenistic Orient*. New York: Columbia University Press, 1927.

Kraemer, J[oel]. L. "Heresy Versus the State in Medieval Islam." Pp. 167-80 in *Studies in Judaica, Karaitica and Islamica Presented to Leon Nemoy on his Eightieth Birthday*. Edited by Sheldon R. Brunswick. Ramat-Gan: Bar-Ilan University Press, 1982.

———. *Humanism in the Renaissance of Islam: The Cultural Revival during the Buyid Age*. 2d rev. ed. Leiden: Brill, 1992.

———. "al-Nawbakhtī, al-Ḥasan b. Mūsā." Page 1044 in vol. 7 of the *Encyclopaedia of Islam*. New ed. Leiden: Brill, 1954–2002.

Kraus, Paul. *Alchemie, Ketzerei, Apokryphen im frühen Islam: Gesammelte Aufsätze*. Edited by Rémi Brague. Hildesheim: Georg Olms Verlag, 1994.

———. "Beiträge zur islamischen Ketzergeschichte: Das *Kitâb az-Zumurrud̲* des Ibn-ar-Râwandî." *Rivista degli Studi Orientali* 14 (1933–34): 93–129; 335–79.

Kremer, Alfred von. *Culturgeschichtliche Streifzüge auf dem Gebiete des Islams*. Leipzig: F. A. Brockhaus, 1873.

Kruisheer, Dirk. "Reconstructing Jacob of Edessa's *Scholia*." In *The Book of Genesis in Jewish and Oriental Christian Interpretation: A Collection of Essays*, edited by Judith Frishman and Lucas Van Rompay, 187–96. Louvain: Peeters, 1997.

Kruk, Remke. "Sharaf az-Zamân Ṭâhir Marwazî (fl. ca. 1100 A.D.) on Zoroaster, Mânî, Mazdak, and Other Pseudo-Prophets." *Persica* 17 (2001): 51–68.

Labourt, J[érôme]. *Le christianisme dans l'empire perse sous la dynastie sassanide (224–632)*. Paris: Librairie Victor Lecoffre, 1904.

Lamoreaux, John C., trans. *Theodore Abū Qurrah*. Library of the Christian East 1. Provo: Brigham Young University Press, 2005.

Lampe, G. W. H. *A Patristic Greek Lexicon*. Oxford: Clarendon Press, 1961.

Landauer, S., ed. *Kitâb al-Amânât wa'l-I'tiqâdât von Sa'adja b. Jûsuf al-Fajjûmî*. Leiden: Brill, 1880.

Lang, David Marshall. *The Wisdom of Balahvar: A Christian Legend of the Buddha*. London: George Allen and Unwin, 1957.

Lassner, Jacob. "Abū Muslim al-Khurāsānī: The Emergence of a Secret Agent from Kurāsān, Irāq, or Was It Iṣfahān?" *Journal of the American Oriental Society* 104 (1984): 165–75.

———. *Islamic Revolution and Historical Memory: An Inquiry into the Art of 'Abbāsid Apologetics*. American Oriental Series 66. New Haven, CT: American Oriental Society, 1986.

———. *The Shaping of 'Abbāsid Rule*. Princeton, NJ: Princeton University Press, 1980.

Latham, J. D. "Ebn al-Moqaffa'." *Encyclopaedia Iranica*, edited by Ehsan Yarshater, vol. 8, 39–43. London and New York: Bibliotheca Persica, 1982– .

———. "Ibn al-Muqaffa' and Early 'Abbasid Prose." In *'Abbasid Belles-Lettres*. The Cambridge History of Arabic Literature, edited by Julia Ashtiany, et al., 48–77. Cambridge: Cambridge University Press, 1990.

Le Strange, G. *Baghdad During the Abbasid Caliphate*. 2nd ed. Oxford: Clarendon Press, 1924.

———. *The Lands of the Eastern Caliphate: Mesopotamia, Persia, and Central Asia from the Moslem Conquest to the Time of Timur*. Cambridge: University Press, 1905.

Levita, Elijah. *Sefer ha-Tishbi: le-Eliyahu ha-Tishbi shoroshav ke-minyan Tishbi*. Isny: [Paul Fagius], 1540/41.

Lidzbarski, Mark, ed. *Ginzā: Der Schatz oder das grosse Buch der Mandäer*. Göttingen: Vandenhoeck and Ruprecht, 1925.

———. *Das Johannesbuch der Mandäer*. 2 vols. Giessen: Alfred Töpelmann, 1905–15.

———. "Warum schrieb Mānī aramäisch?" *Orientalistische Literaturzeitung* 30 (1927): 913–17.

Lieu, Samuel N. C. "Fact and Fiction in the *Acta Archelai*." In *Manichaean Studies: Proceedings of the First International Conference on Manichaeism, August 5-9, 1987*, edited by Peter Bryder, 69–88. Lund: Plus Ultra, 1988.

———. *Manichaeism in Central Asia and China*. Nag Hammadi and Manichaean Studies 45. Leiden: Brill, 1998.

———. *Manichaeism in Mesopotamia and the Roman East*. Religions in the Graeco-Roman World 118. Leiden: Brill, 1994.

———. *Manichaeism in the Later Roman Empire and Medieval China*. 2nd ed. Wissenschaftliche Untersuchungen zum Neuen Testament 63. Tübingen: J. C. B. Mohr, 1992.

———. "[Review of Reeves, *Jewish Lore in Manichaean Cosmogony*]," *Journal of Semitic Studies* 40 (1995): 161–63.

Lim, Richard. *Public Disputation, Power, and Social Order in Late Antiquity*. Berkeley: University of California Press, 1995.

Lippert, Julius. *Ibn al-Qifti's Tar'īḫ al-Ḥukamā'*. Leipzig: Dieterich'sche Verlagsbuchhandlung, 1903.

Lupieri, Edmondo. *The Mandaeans: The Last Gnostics*. Translated by Charles Hindley. Grand Rapids, MI: William B. Eerdmans, 2002.

MacKenzie, D. N. "I, Mani ...." In *Gnosisforschung und Religionsgeschichte: Festschrift für Kurt Rudolph zum 65. Geburtstag*, edited by Holger Preissler and Hubert Seiwert, 183–98. Marburg: Diagonal-Verlag, 1994.

———. "Mani's *Šābuhragān*." *Bulletin of the School of Oriental and African Studies* 42 (1979): 500–534; 43 (1980): 288–310.

Madelung, Wilferd. "Abū 'Īsā al-Warrāq über die Bardesaniten, Marcioniten und Kantäer." In *Studien zur Geschichte und Kultur des Vorderen Orients: Festschrift für Bertold Spuler zum siebzigsten Geburtstag*, edited by Hans R. Roemer and Albrecht Noth, 210–24. Leiden: Brill, 1981.

———. "Hishām b. al-Ḥakam." In *Encyclopaedia of Islam*, vol. 3, 496–98. New ed. Leiden: Brill, 1954–2002.

———. "Khurramiyya." In *Encyclopaedia of Islam*, vol. 5, 63–65. New ed. Leiden: Brill, 1954–2002.

———. "Mazdakism and the Khurramiyya." In *Religious Trends in Early Islamic Iran*, 1–12. Albany, NY: Bibliotheca Persica, 1988.

Maqdisī. *Kitāb al-bad' wa'l-ta'rīkh: Le livre de la création et de l'histoire de Motahhar ben Ṭâhir el-Maqdisî*. 6 vols. Edited by Cl[ément]. Huart. Paris: Leroux, 1899–1919.

Margoliouth, D. S. "'The Devil's Delusion' of Ibn al-Jauzi." *Islamic Culture* 9 (1935): 1–21.

———. "Khurramīya." In *Encyclopaedia of Islam*, vol. 4, 974–75. First edition. 9 vols. Leiden: E. J. Brill, 1913–38.

———. "Notes on Syriac Papyrus Fragments from Oxyrhynchus." *Journal of Egyptian Archaeology* 2 (1915): 214–16.

Marlow, Louise. *Hierarchy and Egalitarianism in Islamic Thought*. Cambridge: Cambridge University Press, 1997.

Marquet, Yves. "Sabéens et Iḫwān al-Ṣafā'." *Studia Islamica* 24 (1966): 35–80; 25 (1966): 77–109.

Martin, Richard C. "Inimitability." In *Encyclopaedia of the Qur'ān*, edited by Jane Dammen McAuliffe, vol. 2, 526–36. 6 vols. Leiden, 2001–2006.

Massignon, Louis. *Essay on the Origins of the Technical Language of Islamic Mysticism*. Translated by Benjamin Clark. Notre Dame, IN: University of Notre Dame Press, 1997.

———. *The Passion of al-Ḥallāj: Mystic and Martyr of Islam*. 4 vols. Translated by Herbert Mason. Princeton, NJ: Princeton University Press, 1982.

———. "Zindīḳ." In *Encyclopaedia of Islam*, vol. 8, 1228–29. First edition. 9 vols. Leiden: E. J. Brill, 1913–38.

Mas'ūdī, Abū al-Ḥasan 'Alī b. al-Ḥusayn b. 'Alī al-. *Kitâb at-Tanbîh wa'l-Ischrâf*. 2nd ed. Bibliotheca Geographorum Arabicorum 8. Edited by M. J. de Goeje. Repr., Leiden: Brill, 1967.

———. *Murūj al-dhahab wa-ma'ādin al-jawhar: Les prairies d'or*. 9 vols. Edited by C. Barbier de Meynard and Pavet de Courteille. Paris: Imprimerie impériale, 1861–77.

Masuzawa, Tomoko. *The Invention of World Religions, Or, How European Universalism was Preserved in the Language of Pluralism*. Chicago, IL: University of Chicago Press, 2005.

Māturīdī, Abū Manṣūr Muḥammad b. Muḥammad b. Maḥmūd al-. *Kitāb al-tawḥīd*. Edited by Fathalla Kholeif. Beyrouth: Dar el-Machreq Éditeurs, 1970.

Meisani, Julie Scott and Paul Starkey, eds. *Encyclopedia of Arabic Literature*. 2 vols. London: Routledge, 1998.

Menasce, Pierre Jean de. *Une apologétique mazdéenne du IXe siècle: Škand-Gumānīk Vičār*. Fribourg: Librairie de l'Université, 1945.

Meyer, Marvin, ed. *The Nag Hammadi Scriptures: The International Edition*. New York: HarperOne, 2007.

Mikkelsen, Gunner B. *Dictionary of Manichaean Texts Vol. III, Part 4: Dictionary of Manichaean Texts in Chinese*. CFM Subsidia. Turnhout: Brepols, 2006.

Milik, J. T. *The Books of Enoch: Aramaic Fragments of Qumrân Cave 4*. Oxford: Clarendon Press, 1976.

———. "Problèmes de la littérature hénochique à la lumière des fragments araméennes de Qumran." *Harvard Theological Review* 64 (1971): 333–78.

———. "Turfân et Qumran: Livre des Géants juif et manichéen." In *Tradition und Glaube: Das frühe Christentum in seiner Umwelt,* edited by Gert Jeremias, Heinz-Wolfgang Kuhn, and Hartmut Stegemann, 117–27. Göttingen: Vandenhoeck and Ruprecht, 1971.

Minorsky, V[ladimir], trans. *Calligraphers and Painters: A Treatise by Qāḍī Aḥmad, son of Mīr-Munshī (circa A.H. 1015/A.D. 1606).* Freer Gallery of Art Occasional Papers vol. 3, no. 2. Washington, DC: Smithsonian Institution, 1959.

———. *Hudūd al-ʿĀlam = 'The Regions of the World': A Persian Geography, 372 A.H.–982 A.D.* London: Luzac, 1937.

Minorsky, Vladimir and C. E. Bosworth. "Rām-Hurmuz." In *Encyclopaedia of Islam,* vol. 8, 416–17. New ed. Leiden: Brill, 1954–2002.

Mitchell, C. W., ed. *S. Ephraim's Prose Refutations of Mani, Marcion, and Bardaisan.* 2 vols. London: Williams and Norgate, 1912–21.

Mizuno, Kōgen. *Buddhist Sutras: Origin, Development, Transmission.* Tokyo: Kōsei, 1982.

Molé, Marijan. "Le problème des sectes zoroastriennes dans les livres pehlevis." *Oriens* 13 (1960–61): 1–28.

Monnot, Guy. "Abū Qurra et la pluralité des religions." *Revue de l'histoire des religions* 208 (1991): 49–71.

———. "L'écho musulman aux religions d'Iran." In *Islam et religions,* 83–96. Paris: Éditions Maisonneuve et Larose, 1986.

———. "Les écrits musulmans sur les religions non-bibliques." In *Islam et religions,* 39–82. Paris: Éditions Maisonneuve et Larose, 1986.

———. "Māturīdī et le manichéisme." In *Islam et religions,* 129-56. Paris: Éditions Maisonneuve et Larose, 1986.

———. *Penseurs musulmans et religions iraniennes: ʿAbd al-Jabbār et ses devanciers.* Paris: J. Vrin, 1974.

———. "Sumaniyya." In *Encyclopaedia of Islam,* vol. 9, 869–70. New ed. Leiden: Brill, 1954–2002.

———. "Th̲anawiyya." In *Encyclopaedia of Islam,* vol. 10, 439–41. New ed. Leiden: Brill, 1954–2002.

Montgomery, James A. *Aramaic Incantation Texts from Nippur.* Philadelphia, PA: The University Museum, 1913.

Morony, Michael G. *Iraq After the Muslim Conquest.* Princeton, NJ: Princeton University Press, 1984.

Moscati, Sabatino. "Abū Muslim." In *Encyclopaedia of Islam,* vol. 1, 141. New ed. Leiden: Brill, 1954–2002.

Mottahedeh, Roy. *The Mantle of the Prophet: Religion and Politics in Iran.* New ed. Oxford: Oneworld Publications, 2000.

Müller, F. W. K. "Eine Hermas-Stelle in manichäischer Version." *Sitzungsberichte der königlich preussischen Akademie der Wissenschaften* (1905): 1077–83.

Natan b. Yeḥiel. *ʿArukh ha-shalem.* 9 vols. Edited by Alexander Kohut. Repr., New York: Pardes, 1955.

Nattier, Jan. "Church Language and Vernacular Language in Central Asian Buddhism." *Numen* 37 (1990): 195–219.

Nau, F. "Analyse de la seconde partie inedited de l'*Histoire Ecclésiastique* de Jean d'Asie, patriarche jacobite de Constantinople (d. 585)." *Revue de l'orient chrétien* 2 (1897): 455–93.

———. "Bardesanes: Liber legum regionum." In *Patrologia Syriaca*, edited by R. Graffin, vol. 2, 492–658. 3 vols. Paris: Firmin-Didot, 1894–1926.

Nautin, Pierre. "L'auteur de la «Chronique de Séert»: Išōʿdenaḥ de Baṣra." *Revue de l'histoire des religions* 186 (1974): 113–26.

Nemoy, Leon. *Karaite Anthology: Excerpts from the Early Literature*. Yale Judaica Series 7. New Haven, CT: Yale University Press, 1952.

Neubauer, Adolf, ed. *Mediaeval Jewish Chronicles and Chronological Notes: Edited from Printed Books and Manuscripts*. 2 vols. Oxford, 1887–95. Repr., Amsterdam: Philo Press, 1970.

Nicholson, Reynold A. *A Literary History of the Arabs*. 2nd ed. Cambridge: The University Press, 1930.

Nöldeke, Theodor. *Geschichte der Perser und Araber zur Zeit der Sasaniden aus der arabischen Chronik des Tabari*. Leiden, 1879. Repr., Leiden: Brill, 1973.

———. "Die Namen der aramäischen Nation und Sprache." *Zeitschrift der deutschen morgenländischen Gesellschaft* 25 (1871): 113–31.

———. "[Review of Pognon, *Inscriptions*]." *Wiener Zeitschrift für die Kunde des Morgenlandes* 12 (1898): 353–61.

———. "Die von Guidi herausgegebene syrische Chronik." In *Sitzungsberichte der kaiserlichen Akademie der Wissenschaften, phil.-hist. Klasse*, Abhandlung 9, 1–48. Wien, 1893.

Norris, H. T. "*Shuʿūbiyyah* in Arabic Literature." In *ʿAbbasid Belles-Lettres*, edited by Julia Ashtiany, et al., 31–47. The Cambridge History of Arabic Literature. Cambridge: Cambridge University Press, 1990.

Nyberg, H. S. "Zum Kampf zwischen Islam und Manichäismus." *Orientalistische Literaturzeitung* 32 (1929): 425–41.

Ogden, C. J. "The 1468 Years of the World-Conflagration in Manichaeism." In *Dr. Modi Memorial Volume: Papers on Indo-Iranian and Other Subjects*, 102–105. Bombay: Fort Printing Press, 1930.

Olivelle, Patrick, trans. *Pañcatantra: The Book of India's Folk Wisdom*. Oxford: Oxford University Press, 1997.

Palmer, Andrew. *The Seventh Century in the West-Syrian Chronicles*. Liverpool: Liverpool University Press, 1993.

Parker, Grant. *The Making of Roman India*. Cambridge: Cambridge University Press, 2008.

Payne Smith, R. *Thesaurus Syriacus*. 2 vols. Oxford: Clarendon, 1879–1901.

Pearson, Birger A. "Jewish Sources in Gnostic Literature." In *Jewish Writings of the Second Temple Period*, edited by Michael E. Stone, 443–81. Compendia rerum iudaicarum ad Novum Testamentum 2.2. Assen/Philadelphia: Van Gorcum/Fortress, 1984.

Pedersen, Nils Arne. "A Manichaean Historical Text." *Zeitschrift für Papyrologie und Epigraphik* 119 (1997): 193–201.

———. *Manichaean Homilies*. CFM Series Coptica 2. Turnhout: Brepols, 2006.

Pellat, Charles. "Ḥammād ʿAdjrad." In *Encyclopaedia of Islam*, vol. 3, 135–36. New ed. Leiden: Brill, 1954–2002.

———. "Ibrāhīm b. al-Sindī b. Shāhak." In *Encyclopaedia of Islam*, vol. 3, 390. New ed. Leiden: Brill, 1954–2002.

———. *Le Kitāb at-tarbīʿ wa-t-tadwīr de Ğāḥiẓ*. Damas: Institut français de Damas, 1955.

———. *The Life and Works of Jāḥiẓ*. Translated by D. M. Hawke. Berkeley: University of California Press, 1969.

———. *Le milieu baṣrien et la formation de Ğāḥiẓ*. Paris: Adrien-Maisonneuve, 1953.

———. *Les prairies d'or*. 5 vols. Paris: Société asiatique, 1962–97.

———. "Le témoignage d'al-Jāḥiẓ sur les Manichéens." In *Essays in Honor of Bernard Lewis: The Islamic World, From Classical to Modern Times*, edited by C. E. Bosworth, et al., 269–79 Princeton, NJ: Darwin Press, 1989.
Pessagno, J. Meric. "The Reconstruction of the Thought of Muḥammad Ibn Shabīb." *Journal of the American Oriental Society* 104 (1984): 445–53.
Petermann, H. *Thesaurus s. Liber Magnus vulgo "Liber Adami" appellatus opus Mandaeorum summi ponderis*. 2 vols. Lipsiae: P. O. Weigel, 1867.
Peterson, Erik. "Urchristentum und Mandäismus." *Zeitschrift für die neutestamentliche Wissenschaft und die Kunde der älteren Kirche* 27 (1928): 55–98.
Pines, Shlomo. *The Collected Works of Shlomo Pines, Volume V: Studies in the History of Jewish Thought*, edited by Warren Zev Harvey and Moshe Idel. Jerusalem: Magnes Press, 1997.
———. "Jewish Philosophy." In *The Encyclopedia of Philosophy*, edited by Paul Edwards, vol. 4, 261–77. 8 vols. New York: Macmillan, 1967.
———. "Studies in Christianity and in Judaeo-Christianity Based on Arabic Sources." *Jerusalem Studies in Arabic and Islam* 6 (1985): 107–61.
———. "Two Passages Concerning Mani." In *The Jewish Christians of the Early Centuries of Christianity According to a New Source*, 66–69. Proceedings of the Israel Academy of Sciences and Humanities 2.13. Jerusalem: The Israel Academy of Sciences and Humanities, 1966.
Pococke, Edward, ed. *Historia compendiosa Dynastiarum authore Gregorio Abul-Pharagio ....* 2 vols. Oxoniae: Excudebat H. Hall ... impensis Ric. Davis, 1663.
Pognon, Henri. "Extraits du «Livre des Scholies» de Théodore bar Khouni." In *Inscriptions mandaïtes des coupes de Khouabir*, 105–58. Paris, 1898. Repr., Amsterdam: Philo Press, 1979.
———. *Inscriptions mandaïtes des coupes de Khouabir*. Paris, 1898. Repr., Amsterdam: Philo Press, 1979.
Poirier, Paul-Hubert. "Les *Actes de Thomas* et le manichéisme." *Apocrypha* 9 (1998): 263–90.
Polotsky, Hans Jakob, ed. *Manichäische Homilien*. Stuttgart: W. Kohlhammer, 1934.
———. "Manichäismus." In *Paulys Realencyclopädie der classischen Altertumswissenschaft*. Neue Bearbeitung, edited by Georg Wissowa, Supplementband 6, 240–71. München: A. Druckenmüller, 1980.
Poznanski, Adolf and Julius Guttmann, ed. *Sefer Megillat ha-Megalle von Abraham bar Chija*. Berlin: H. Itzkowski, 1924.
Prémare, Alfred Louis de. "«Comme il est écrit»: L'histoire d'un texte." *Studia Islamica* 70 (1989): 27–56.
———. "Les textes musulmans dans leur environment." *Arabica* 47 (2000): 391–408.
Puech, Henri-Charles. "Dates manichéennes dans les chroniques syriaques." In *Mélanges syriens offerts à Monsieur René Dussaud*, vol. 2, 593–607. 2 vols. Paris: Librairie Orientaliste Paul Geuthner, 1939.
———. "Gnostic Gospels and Related Documents." In *New Testament Apocrypha*, by Edgar Hennecke, vol. 1, 231–362. 2 vols. Edited by Wilhelm Schneemelcher. Philadelphia, PA: The Westminster Press, 1963–65.
———. "Liturgie et pratiques rituelles dans le manichéisme (Collège de France, 1952–1972)." In *Sur le manichéisme et autres essais*, 235–394. Paris: Flammarion, 1979.
———. *Le manichéisme: Son fondateur - sa doctrine*. Paris: Civilisations du Sud, 1949.
Qirqisānī. *Kitāb al-anwār wa'l-maqārib*. 5 vols. Edited by Leon Nemoy. New York: Alexander Kohut Memorial Foundation, 1939–43.

Rabin, Chaim. *Qumran Studies*. London: Oxford University Press, 1957.

Rāzī, Abū Ḥātim Aḥmad b. Ḥamdān al-. *A'lām al-nubuwwah (The Peaks of Prophecy)*. Edited by Salah al-Sawy. Teheran: Imperial Iranian Academy of Philosophy, 1977.

———. *Kitâb al-Iṣlâḥ*. Wisdom of Persia 42. Edited by Hasan Mīnūchehr. Teheran: Institute of Islamic Studies, 1998.

Reeves, John C. "The 'Elchasaite' Sanhedrin of the Cologne Mani Codex in Light of Second Temple Jewish Sectarian Sources." *Journal of Jewish Studies* 42 (1991): 68–91.

———. "An Enochic Citation in *Barnabas* 4:3 and the *Oracles of Hystaspes*." In *Pursuing the Text: Studies in Honor of Ben Zion Wacholder on the Occasion of his Seventieth Birthday*, edited by John C. Reeves and John Kampen, 260–77. Journal for the Study of the Old Testament Supplement Series 184. Sheffield: Sheffield Academic Press, 1994.

———. *Heralds of That Good Realm: Syro-Mesopotamian Gnosis and Jewish Traditions*. Nag Hammadi and Manichaean Studies 41. Leiden: Brill, 1996.

———. *Jewish Lore in Manichaean Cosmogony: Studies in the Book of Giants Traditions*. Cincinnati, OH: Hebrew Union College Press, 1992.

———. "Jewish Pseudepigrapha in Manichaean Literature: The Influence of the Enochic Library." In *Tracing the Threads: Studies in the Vitality of Jewish Pseudepigrapha*, edited by John C. Reeves, 173–203. Society of Biblical Literature Early Judaism and Its Literature 6. Atlanta: Scholars Press, 1994.

———. "A Manichaean 'Blood-Libel'?" *Aram* 16 (2004): 217–32.

———. "Manichaean Citations from the *Prose Refutations* of Ephrem." In *Emerging from Darkness: Studies in the Recovery of Manichaean Sources*, edited by Paul Mirecki and Jason BeDuhn, 217–88. Nag Hammadi and Manichaean Studies 43. Leiden: Brill, 1997.

———. "Manichaica Aramaica: Adam, Seth, and Magical Praxis." *Journal of the American Oriental Society* 119 (1999): 432–39.

———. "Reconsidering the 'Prophecy of Zardūšt.'" In *A Multiform Heritage: Studies on Early Judaism and Early Christianity in Honor of Robert A. Kraft*, edited by Benjamin G. Wright, 167–82. Atlanta, GA: Scholars Press, 1999.

———. *Shades of Light and Darkness: Studies in Chaldean Dualism and Gnosis*. In preparation.

Rehm, Bernhard and Georg Strecker, eds. *Die Pseudoklementinen, [Bd.] I: Homilien*. Die griechische christliche Schriftsteller der ersten [drei] Jahrhunderte. 3rd ed. Berlin: Akademie Verlag, 1992.

———. *Die Pseudoklementinen, [Bd.] II: Rekognitionen in Rufins Übersetzung*. Die griechische christliche Schriftsteller der ersten [drei] Jahrhunderte. 2nd ed. Berlin: Akademie Verlag, 1994.

Reitzenstein, Richard. *Hellenistic Mystery-Religions: Their Basic Ideas and Significance*. Translated by John E. Steely. Pittsburgh, PA: Pickwick Press, 1978.

———. *Das iranische Erlösungsmysterium: Religionsgeschichtliche Untersuchungen*. Bonn a. Rh.: A. Marcus and E. Weber's Verlag, 1921.

Reitzenstein, R[ichard]. and H. H. Schaeder. *Studien zum antiken Synkretismus aus Iran und Griechenland*. Leipzig: B. G. Teubner, 1926.

Rekaya, Mohamed. "Le *Ḫurram-dīn* et les mouvements *Ḫurramites* sous les 'Abbāsides," *Studia Islamica* 60 (1984): 5–57.

Reynolds, Gabriel Said. *A Muslim Theologian in the Sectarian Milieu: 'Abd al-Jabbār and the Critique of Christian Origins*. Leiden: Brill, 2004.

Richter, Siegfried G. *Die Herakleides-Psalmen*. CFM Series Coptica 1; Liber Psalmorum, Pars II, Fasc. 2. Turnhout: Brepols, 1998.

Ries, Julien. *Les études manichéennes: Des controverses de la Réforme aux découvertes du XXe siècle*. Louvain-la-Neuve: Centre d'histoire des religions, 1988.

Robinson, Chase F. *Islamic Historiography*. Cambridge: Cambridge University Press, 2003.

Rochow, Ilse. "Zum Fortleben des Manichäismus im byzantinischen Reich nach Justinian I." *Byzantinoslavica* 40 (1979): 13–21.

Rompay, Lucas Van. "Bardaisan and Mani in Philoxenus of Mabbog's *Mēmrē Against Habib*." In *Syriac Polemics: Studies in Honour of Gerrit Jan Reinink,* edited by Wout Jac. Van Bekkum, Jan Willem Drijvers, and Alex C. Klugkist, 77–90. Orientalia Lovaniensia Analecta 170. Leuven: Peeters, 2007.

Rosenblatt, Samuel. *Saadia Gaon: The Book of Beliefs and Opinions*. Yale Judaica Series 1. New Haven, CT: Yale University Press, 1948.

Rosenthal, Franz. *Aḥmad b. aṭ-Ṭayyib as-Saraḫsî*. New Haven, CT: American Oriental Society, 1943.

———. *Die aramaistische Forschung seit Th. Nöldeke's Veröffentlichungen*. Leiden, 1939. Repr., Leiden: Brill, 1964.

———. "Some Pythagorean Documents Transmitted in Arabic." *Orientalia* 10 (1941): 104–15; 383–95.

Rubin, Uri. *The Eye of the Beholder: The Life of Muḥammad as Viewed by the Early Muslims*. Princeton, NJ: The Darwin Press, 1995.

Rubin, Zeev. "Nobility, Monarchy and Legitimation Under the Later Sasanians." In *The Byzantine and Early Islamic Near East, VI: Elites Old and New in the Byzantine and Early Islamic Near East,* edited by John Haldon and Lawrence I. Conrad, 235–73. Papers of the Sixth Workshop on Late Antiquity and Early Islam. Princeton, N J: Darwin Press, 2004.

Rudolph, Kurt. *Gnosis: The Nature and History of Gnosticism*. Translated by Robert McLachlan Wilson. San Francisco: Harper and Row, 1983.

———. *Die Mandäer*. 2 vols. Göttingen: Vandenhoeck and Ruprecht, 1960–61.

Rudolph, Ulrich. *Al-Māturīdī und die sunnitische Theologie in Samarkand*. Leiden: E. J. Brill, 1997.

Ruska, Julius. "Al-Birūni als Quelle für das Leben und die Schriften al-Rāzi's." *Isis* 5 (1923): 26–50.

Russell, James R. "Alphabets." In *Late Antiquity: A Guide to the Postclassical World,* edited by G. W. Bowersock, Peter Brown, and Oleg Grabar, 288–90. Cambridge, MA: Harvard University Press, 1999.

———. "Kartīr and Mānī: A Shamanistic Model of Their Conflict." In *Iranica Varia: Papers in Honor of Professor Ehsan Yarshater,* 180–93. Leiden: Brill, 1990.

Rustow, Marina. *Heresy and the Politics of Community: The Jews of the Fatimid Caliphate*. Ithaca, NY: Cornell University Press, 2008.

Ryder, Arthur W., trans. *The Panchatantra*. Chicago, IL: University of Chicago Press, 1925.

Sachau, Edward. *Alberuni's India: An Account of the Religion, Philosophy, Literature, Geography, Chronology, Astronomy, Customs, Laws and Astrology of India about A.D. 1030*. 2 vols. London: K. Paul, Trench, Trübner, 1888.

———. *The Chronology of Ancient Nations: An English Version of the Arabic Text of the Athâr-ul-bâkiya of Albîrûnî*. London: William H. Allen, 1879.

Sadighi, Gholam Hossein. *Les mouvements religieux iraniens au IIe et au IIIe siècle de l'hégire*. Paris: Les Presses Modernes, 1938.

Sako, Louis R. M. "Les sources de la Chronique de Séert." *Parole de l'Orient* 14 (1987): 155–66.

Salemann, Carl. "Ein Bruchstük (*sic*!) manichäischen Schrifttums im Asiatischen Museum." *Mémoires de l'Academié Impériale des Sciences de Saint-Pétersbourg*, 8ème série, VI.6 (1904): 2–7.

Salmond, S. D. F. "Archelaus: The Acts of the Disputation with the Heresiarch Manes." In *The Ante-Nicene Fathers: Translations of the Writings of the Fathers down to A.D. 325*, edited by Alexander Roberts and James Donaldson, vol. 6, 175–236. Repr., Grand Rapids, MI: Wm. B. Eerdmans, 1978.

Samir, Khalil Samir, ed. *Teodoro Abū Qurra: La libertà*. Patrimonio culturale arabo cristiano 6. Translated by Paola Pizzi. Turin: Silvio Zamorani, 2001.

Sarton, George. "[Review of Siggel, *Katalog*, vol. 1]." *Journal of Near Eastern Studies* 10 (1951): 284–85.

Schaeder, H. H. *Iranische Beiträge I*. Halle, 1930. Repr., Darmstadt: Wissenschaftliche Buchgesellschaft, 1972.

———. "Die Kantäer." *Die Welt des Orients* 1(1947–52): 288–98.

———. "Rezension von Carl Schmidt und H. J. Polotsky, *Ein Mani-Fund in Ägypten*." *Gnomon* 9 (1933): 337–62.

Schefer, Ch[arles]. *Chrestomathie persane à l'usage des élèves de l'École spéciale des langues orientales vivantes*. 2 vols. Paris: Ernest Leroux, 1883–85.

Scheftelowitz, I. *Die Entstehung der manichäischen Religion und des Erlösungsmysteriums*. Giessen: A. Töpelmann, 1922.

Scher, Addai. "Histoire Nestorienne inédite (Chronique de Séert)." *Patrologia Orientalis* 4 (1908): 215–313.

Schimmel, Annemarie. *Mystical Dimensions of Islam*. Chapel Hill: University of North Carolina Press, 1975.

Schipper, Hendrik Gerhard and Johannes van Oort. *St. Leo the Great, Sermons and Letters Against the Manichaeans: Selected Fragments*. CFM Series Latina 1. Turnhout: Brepols, 2000.

Schmidt, Carl and H. J. Polotsky. *Ein Mani-Fund in Ägypten: Originalschriften des Mani und seiner Schüler*. Berlin: Verlag der Akademie der Wissenschaften, 1933.

Schoeler, G. "Bashshār b. Burd, Abū'l-ʿAtāhiyah and Abū Nuwās." In *ʿAbbasid Belles-Lettres*, edited by Julia Ashtiany, et al., 275–99. The Cambridge History of Arabic Literature. Cambridge: Cambridge University Press, 1990.

Scholem, Gershom. *On the Mystical Shape of the Godhead: Basic Concepts in the Kabbalah*. Translated by Joachim Neugroschel. New York: Schocken, 1991.

Schreiner, Martin. "Beiträge zur Geschichte der theologischen Bewegungen im Islâm." *Zeitschrift der deutschen morgenländischen Gesellschaft* 52 (1898): 463–563; 53 (1899): 51–88.

Schwartz, Martin. "Qumran, Turfan, Arabic Magic, and Noah's Name." In *Charmes et sortilèges, magie et magiciens*, edited by Rika Gyselen, 231–38. Res Orientales 14. Bures-sur-Yvette: Groupe pour l'Étude de la Civilisation du Moyen-Orient, 2002.

Scopello, Madeleine. "Hégémonius, les *Acta Archelai* et l'histoire de la controverse antimanichéenne." In *Studia Manichaica: IV. Internationaler Kongress zum Manichäismus, Berlin, 14.–18. Juli 1997*, edited by Ronald E. Emmerick, Werner Sundermann, and Peter Zieme, 528–45. Berlin: Akademie-Verlag, 2000.

———. "Vérités et contre-vérités: La vie de Mani selon les *Acta Archelai*." *Apocrypha* 6 (1995): 203–34.

Scott, David A. "Christian Responses to Buddhism in Pre-Medieval Times." *Numen* 32 (1985): 88–100.

———. "Manichaean Responses to Zoroastrianism (Politico-Religious Controversies in Iran, Past to Present: 3)." *Religious Studies* 25 (1989): 435–57.

———. "Manichaean Views of Buddhism." *History of Religions* 25 (1985): 99–115.

———. "Manichaeism in Bactria: Political Patterns and East-West Paradigms." *Journal of Asian History* 41 (2007): 107–30.

Segal, Alan F. *Two Powers in Heaven: Early Rabbinic Reports about Christianity and Gnosticism*. Leiden, 1977. Repr., Leiden: Brill, 2002.

Segal, J. B. *Edessa: 'The Blessed City'*. Oxford: Clarendon Press, 1970.

Seybold, Chr. Fred., ed. *Severus ben el Moqaffa' Historia patriarcharum alexandrinorum*. Corpus scriptorum christianorum orientalium, script. arabici 8–9. 2 vols. Paris: Carolus Poussielgue, 1904–10.

Sezgin, Fuat. *Geschichte des arabischen Schriftums*. 9 vols. Leiden: Brill, 1967–1995.

Sfameni Gasparro, Giulia. "Addas-Adimantus unus ex discipulis Manichaei: For the History of Manichaeism in the West." In *Studia Manichaica: IV. Internationaler Kongress zum Manichäismus, Berlin, 14.–18. Juli 1997*, edited by Ronald E. Emmerick, Werner Sundermann, and Peter Zieme, 546–59. Berlin: Akademie-Verlag, 2000.

Shahrastānī. *Kitāb al-milal wa'l-niḥal*. 2 vols. Edited by M. S. Kaylānī. Beirut: Dār al-Ma'rifah, n.d.

Shaked, Shaul. *Dualism in Transformation: Varieties of Religion in Sasanian Iran*. London: School of Oriental and African Studies, 1994.

———. "Esoteric Trends in Zoroastrianism." *Proceedings of the Israel Academy of Sciences and Humanities* 3 (1969): 175–221.

———. "First Man, First King: Notes on Semitic-Iranian Syncretism and Iranian Mythological Transformations." In *Gilgul: Essays on Transformation, Revolution and Permanence in the History of Religions*, edited by S[haul] Shaked, D[avid] Shulman, and G[uy] G. Stroumsa, 238–56. Leiden: E. J. Brill, 1987.

———. "Manichaean Incantation Bowls in Syriac." *Jerusalem Studies in Arabic and Islam* 24 (2000): 58–92.

———. "Some Islamic Reports Concerning Zoroastrianism." *Jerusalem Studies in Arabic and Islam* 17 (1994): 43–84.

Shaki, Mansour. "The Cosmogonical and Cosmological Teachings of Mazdak." In *Papers in Honour of Professor Mary Boyce*, edited by Jacques Duchesne-Guillemin and Pierre Lecoq, vol. 2, 527–43. Acta Iranica 24–25. 2 vols. Leiden: E. J. Brill, 1985.

———. "Gayōmart." Pp. 345-47 in vol. 10 of the *Encyclopaedia Iranica*. Edited by Ehsan Yarshater. London and New York: Bibliotheca Persica, 1982– .

———. "The Social Doctrine of Mazdak in the Light of Middle Persian Evidence." *Archív Orientální* 46 (1978): 289–306.

Shams-i Qays. *al-Mu'jam fī ma'āyīr ash'ār al-'ajam*. Edited by Muḥammad Qazvīnī. Revised by Muḥammad Taqī Mudarris Raḍavī. Teheran: Dānishgāh-i Tihrān, 1959.

Shapira, Dan D. Y. "Manichaeans (Marmanaiia), Zoroastrians (Iazuqaiia), Jews, Christians and Other Heretics: A Study in the Redaction of Mandaic Texts." *Le Muséon* 117 (2004): 243–80.

Sharon, Moshe. "People of the Book." In *Encyclopaedia of the Qur'ān*, edited by Jane Dammen McAuliffe, vol. 4, 36–43. 6 vols. Leiden, 2001–2006.

Siggel, Alfred. *Arabisch-deutsches Wörterbuch der Stoffe aus den drei Naturreichen, die in arabischen alchemistischen Handschriften vorkommen*. Deutsche Akademie der Wissenschaften zu Berlin, Institut für Orientforschung Veröffentlichung Nr. 1. Berlin: Akademie-Verlag, 1950.

———. *Katalog der arabischen alchemistischen Handschriften Deutschlands*. 3 vols. Berlin: Akademie-Verlag, 1949–56.

Sijistānī, Abū Ya'qūb al-. *Kitāb ithbāt al-nubū'āt*. Edited by 'Ārif Tāmir. Beirut: al-Maṭba'ah al-Kāthūlīkīyah, 1966.

Simon, Róbert. "Mānī and Muḥammad." *Jerusalem Studies in Arabic and Islam* 21 (1997): 118–41.

Simon-Shoshan, Moshe. "The Tasks of the Translators: The Rabbis, the Septuagint, and the Cultural Politics of Translation." *Prooftexts* 27 (2007): 1–39.

Sims-Williams, Nicholas. "*Aurentēs*." In *Studia Manichaica: IV. Internationaler Kongress zum Manichäismus, Berlin, 14.–18. Juli 1997*, edited by Ronald E. Emmerick, Werner Sundermann, and Peter Zieme, 560–63. Berlin: Akademie-Verlag, 2000.

———. "The Manichaean Commandments: A Survey of the Sources." In *Papers in Honour of Professor Mary Boyce*, edited by Jacques Duchesne-Guillemin and Pierre Lecoq, vol. 2, 573–82. Acta Iranica 24–25. 2 vols. Leiden: Brill, 1985.

Skjærvø, Prods Oktor. "Aramaic Scripts for Iranian Languages." In *The World's Writing Systems*, edited by Peter T. Daniels and William Bright, 515–35. Oxford: Oxford University Press, 1996.

———. "Iranian Elements in Manicheism, A Comparative Contrastive Approach: Irano-Manichaica I." In *Au carrefour des religions: Mélanges offerts à Philippe Gignoux*, edited by Rika Gyselen, 263–84. Res Orientales 7. Bures-sur-Yvette: Group pour l'étude de la civilisation du Moyen-Orient, 1995.

———. "Iranian Epic and the Manichean *Book of Giants*: Irano-Manichaica III." *Acta Orientalia Academiae Scientiarum Hungaricae* 48 (1995): 187–223.

———. "Venus and the Buddha, or How Many Steps to Nirvana? Some Buddhist Elements in Manichaean Literature." In *Iranian and Indo-European Studies: Memorial Volume of Otakar Klíma*, edited by Petr Vavroušek, 239–54. Prague: Enigma Corporation, 1994.

Slane, William MacGuckin, Baron de, trans. *Ibn Khallikan's Biographical Dictionary*. 4 vols. Paris: Oriental Translation Fund of Great Britain and Ireland, 1842–71.

Smith, Jonathan Z. "A Matter of Class: Taxonomies of Religion." *Harvard Theological Review* 89 (1996): 387–403.

———. *Relating Religion: Essays in the Study of Religion*. Chicago, IL: University of Chicago Press, 2004.

Sokoloff, Michael. *A Dictionary of Jewish Babylonian Aramaic of the Talmudic and Geonic Periods*. Ramat-Gan: Bar Ilan University Press, 2002.

Sourdel, D[ominique]. "Barāmika." In *Encyclopaedia of Islam*, vol. 1, 1033–36. New ed. Leiden: Brill, 1954–2002.

———. "La biographie d'Ibn al-Muqaffa' d'après les sources anciennes." *Arabica* 1 (1954): 307–23.

Spuler, Bertold. *Iran in früh-islamischer Zeit: Politik, Kultur, Verwaltung und öffentliches Leben zwischen der arabischen und der seldschukischen Eroberung, 633 bis 1055*. Wiesbaden: Franz Steiner Verlag, 1952.

Steinschneider, Moritz. *Polemische und apologetische Literatur in arabischer Sprache zwischen Muslimen, Christen und Juden, nebst Anhängen verwandten Inhalts*. Leipzig, 1877. Repr., Hildesheim: Georg Olms, 1966.

Stern, S. M. "Abān b. 'Abd al-Ḥamīd al-Lāḥiḳī." In *Encyclopaedia of Islam*, vol. 1, 2. New ed. Leiden: Brill, 1954–2002.

———. "Abū Ḥātim al-Rāzī on Persian Religion." In *Studies in Early Ismā'īlism*, 30–46. Jerusalem: The Magnes Press, 1983.

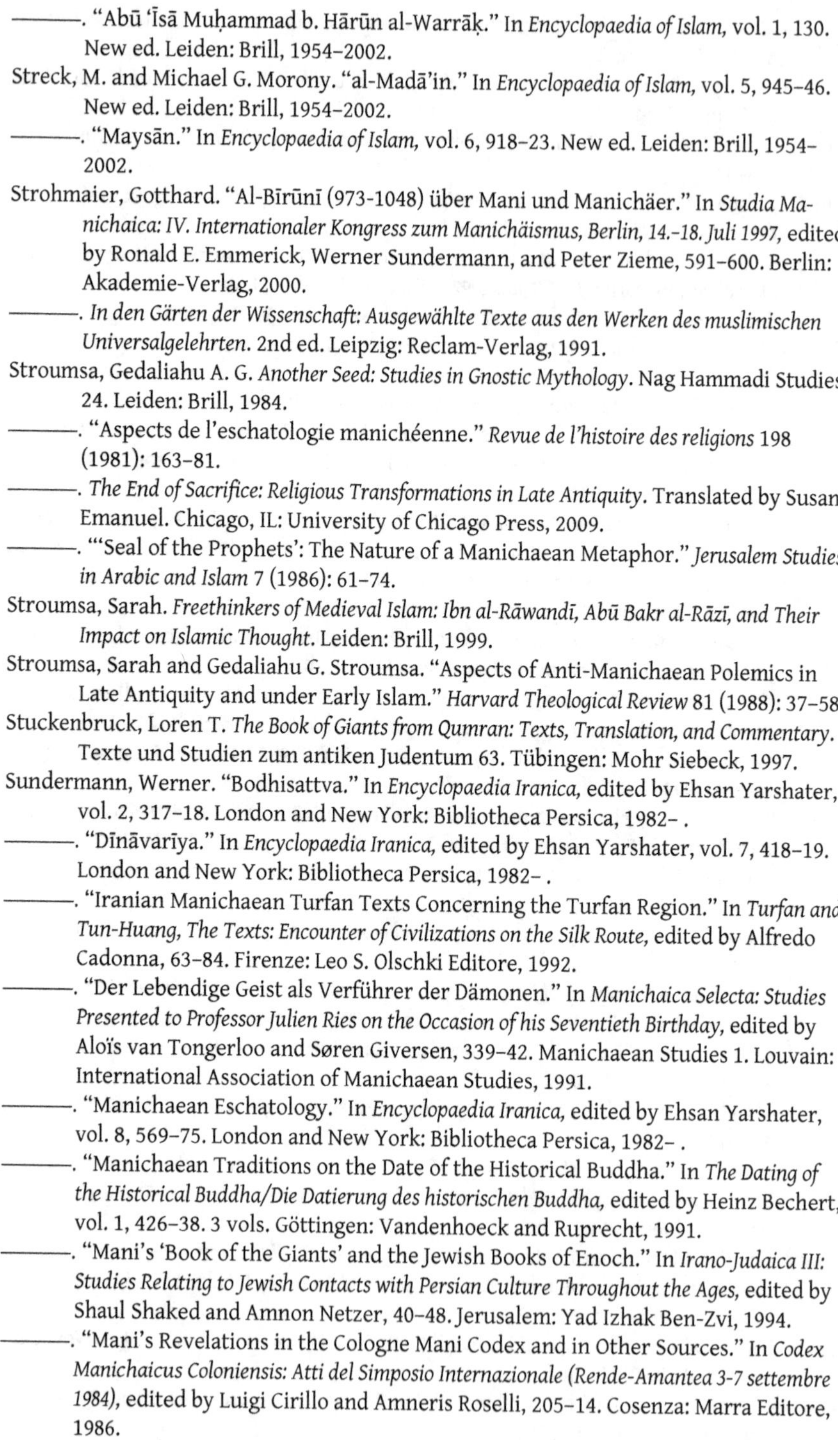

———. "Abū ʿĪsā Muḥammad b. Hārūn al-Warrāḳ." In *Encyclopaedia of Islam*, vol. 1, 130. New ed. Leiden: Brill, 1954–2002.

Streck, M. and Michael G. Morony. "al-Madāʾin." In *Encyclopaedia of Islam*, vol. 5, 945–46. New ed. Leiden: Brill, 1954–2002.

———. "Maysān." In *Encyclopaedia of Islam*, vol. 6, 918–23. New ed. Leiden: Brill, 1954–2002.

Strohmaier, Gotthard. "Al-Bīrūnī (973-1048) über Mani und Manichäer." In *Studia Manichaica: IV. Internationaler Kongress zum Manichäismus, Berlin, 14.-18. Juli 1997*, edited by Ronald E. Emmerick, Werner Sundermann, and Peter Zieme, 591–600. Berlin: Akademie-Verlag, 2000.

———. *In den Gärten der Wissenschaft: Ausgewählte Texte aus den Werken des muslimischen Universalgelehrten*. 2nd ed. Leipzig: Reclam-Verlag, 1991.

Stroumsa, Gedaliahu A. G. *Another Seed: Studies in Gnostic Mythology*. Nag Hammadi Studies 24. Leiden: Brill, 1984.

———. "Aspects de l'eschatologie manichéenne." *Revue de l'histoire des religions* 198 (1981): 163–81.

———. *The End of Sacrifice: Religious Transformations in Late Antiquity*. Translated by Susan Emanuel. Chicago, IL: University of Chicago Press, 2009.

———. "'Seal of the Prophets': The Nature of a Manichaean Metaphor." *Jerusalem Studies in Arabic and Islam* 7 (1986): 61–74.

Stroumsa, Sarah. *Freethinkers of Medieval Islam: Ibn al-Rāwandī, Abū Bakr al-Rāzī, and Their Impact on Islamic Thought*. Leiden: Brill, 1999.

Stroumsa, Sarah and Gedaliahu G. Stroumsa. "Aspects of Anti-Manichaean Polemics in Late Antiquity and under Early Islam." *Harvard Theological Review* 81 (1988): 37–58.

Stuckenbruck, Loren T. *The Book of Giants from Qumran: Texts, Translation, and Commentary*. Texte und Studien zum antiken Judentum 63. Tübingen: Mohr Siebeck, 1997.

Sundermann, Werner. "Bodhisattva." In *Encyclopaedia Iranica*, edited by Ehsan Yarshater, vol. 2, 317–18. London and New York: Bibliotheca Persica, 1982– .

———. "Dīnāvarīya." In *Encyclopaedia Iranica*, edited by Ehsan Yarshater, vol. 7, 418–19. London and New York: Bibliotheca Persica, 1982– .

———. "Iranian Manichaean Turfan Texts Concerning the Turfan Region." In *Turfan and Tun-Huang, The Texts: Encounter of Civilizations on the Silk Route*, edited by Alfredo Cadonna, 63–84. Firenze: Leo S. Olschki Editore, 1992.

———. "Der Lebendige Geist als Verführer der Dämonen." In *Manichaica Selecta: Studies Presented to Professor Julien Ries on the Occasion of his Seventieth Birthday*, edited by Aloïs van Tongerloo and Søren Giversen, 339–42. Manichaean Studies 1. Louvain: International Association of Manichaean Studies, 1991.

———. "Manichaean Eschatology." In *Encyclopaedia Iranica*, edited by Ehsan Yarshater, vol. 8, 569–75. London and New York: Bibliotheca Persica, 1982– .

———. "Manichaean Traditions on the Date of the Historical Buddha." In *The Dating of the Historical Buddha/Die Datierung des historischen Buddha*, edited by Heinz Bechert, vol. 1, 426–38. 3 vols. Göttingen: Vandenhoeck and Ruprecht, 1991.

———. "Mani's 'Book of the Giants' and the Jewish Books of Enoch." In *Irano-Judaica III: Studies Relating to Jewish Contacts with Persian Culture Throughout the Ages*, edited by Shaul Shaked and Amnon Netzer, 40–48. Jerusalem: Yad Izhak Ben-Zvi, 1994.

———. "Mani's Revelations in the Cologne Mani Codex and in Other Sources." In *Codex Manichaicus Coloniensis: Atti del Simposio Internazionale (Rende-Amantea 3-7 settembre 1984)*, edited by Luigi Cirillo and Amneris Roselli, 205–14. Cosenza: Marra Editore, 1986.

———. *Mitteliranische manichäische Texte kirchengeschichtlichen Inhalts*. Berliner Turfantexte 11. Berlin: Akademie-Verlag, 1981.

———. *Mittelpersische und parthische kosmogonische und Parabeltexte der Manichäer*. Berliner Turfantexte 4. Berlin: Akademie-Verlag, 1973.

———. "Parthisch 'bšwdg'n 'die Täufer.'" *Acta Antiqua Academiae Scientiarum Hungaricae* 25 (1977): 237–42.

———. "Der Paraklet in der ostmanichäischen Überlieferung." In *Manichaean Studies: Proceedings of the First International Conference on Manichaeism, August 5–9, 1987*, edited by Peter Bryder, 201–12. Lund: Plus Ultra, 1988.

———. "Studien zur kirchengeschichtlichen Literatur der iranischen Manichäer I." *Altorientalische Forschungen* 13 (1986): 40–92.

———. "Studien zur kirchengeschichtlichen Literatur der iranischen Manichäer II." *Altorientalische Forschungen* 13 (1986): 239–317.

———. "Was the *Ārdhang* Mani's Picture-Book?" In *Il Manicheismo, nuove prospettive della richerca: Dipartimento di Studi Asiatici Università degli Studi di Napoli "L'Orientale," Napoli, 2–8 Settembre 2001*, edited by Aloïs van Tongerloo and Luigi Cirillo, 373–84. Manichaean Studies 5. Turnhout: Brepols, 2005.

———. "Ein weiteres Fragment aus Manis Gigantenbuch." In *Orientalia J. Duchesne-Guillemin emerito oblate*, 491–505. Leiden: Brill, 1984.

———. "Zoroastrian Motifs in Non-Zoroastrian Traditions." *Journal of the Royal Asiatic Society* series 3, 18, 2 (2008): 155–65.

Ṭabarī, Abū Ja'far Muḥammad b. Jarīr al-. *Ta'rīkh ar-rusul wa-l-mulūk: Annales quos scripsit Abu Djafar Mohammed ibn Djarir at-Tabari*. 15 vols. Edited by M. J. de Goeje. Leiden, 1879–1901. Repr., Leiden: Brill, 1964-65.

Tailleu, Dieter. "Glossary to the Zoroastrian Middle Persian Polemics Against Manichaeism." In *Dictionary of Manichaean Texts, Vol. II: Texts from Iraq and Iran (Texts in Syriac, Arabic, Persian and Zoroastrian Middle Persian)*, edited by François de Blois and Nicholas Sims-Williams, 121–45. Turnhout: Brepols, 2006.

Taqizadeh, S. H. "A New Contribution to the Materials Concerning the Life of Zoroaster." *Bulletin of the School of Oriental Studies* 8 (1935–37): 947–54.

Taqīzādeh, S. H. and A. A. Šīrāzī. *Mānī va dīn-e-ū*. Teheran: Ānjuman-e Irānshināsī, 1335 AH/1956.

Taqizadeh, S. H. and W. B. Henning. "The Dates of Mani's Life." *Asia Major* 6 (1957): 106–21.

Tardieu, Michel. "Principes de l'exégèse manichéenne du Nouveau Testament." In *Les règles de l'interpretation*, edited by Michel Tardieu, 123–46. Paris: Éditions du Cerf, 1987.

———. *Manichaeism*. Translated by M. B. DeBevoise. Urbana: University of Illinois Press, 2008.

———. *Le manichéisme*. Paris: Presses Universitaires de France, 1981; 2nd ed.; Paris: Presses Universitaires de France, 1997.

Theodore bar Konai. *Liber Scholiorum*. Edited by Addai Scher. 2 vols. Corpus scriptorum christianorum orientalium, scrip. syri series II, t. 65–66. Paris: Carolus Poussielgue, 1910–12.

Theophanes. *The Chronicle of Theophanes Confessor*. Translated by Cyril Mango and Roger Scott. Oxford: Clarendon Press, 1997.

———. *Theophanis Chronographia*. 2 vols. Edited by Carolus de Boor. Lipsiae: B. G. Teubneri, 1883–85.

Thomas, David. "Abū 'Īsā al-Warrāq and the History of Religions." *Journal of Semitic Studies* 41 (1996): 275–90.

———, ed. *Early Muslim Polemic Against Christianity: Abū 'Īsā al-Warrāq's "Against the Incarnation"*. Cambridge: Cambridge University Press, 2002.

Tongerloo, Aloïs van. "The Buddha's First Encounter in a Manichaean Old Turkic Text." In *Il Manicheismo: Nuove prospettive della richerca: Dipartimento di studi asiatici Università degli studi di Napoli "L'Orientale" Napoli, 2-8 settembre 2001*, edited by Aloïs van Tongerloo and Luigi Cirillo, 385–96. Manichaean Studies 5. Turnhout: Brepols, 2005.

———. "The Father of Greatness." In *Gnosisforschung und Religionsgeschichte: Festschrift für Kurt Rudolph zum 65. Geburtstag*, edited by Holger Preissler and Hubert Seiwert, 329–42. Marburg: diagonal-Verlag, 1994.

Torrey, Charles Cutler. *The Jewish Foundation of Islam*. New York: Jewish Institute of Religion Press, 1933.

Touati, Charles, trans. *Le Kuzari: Apologie de la religion méprisée*. Louvain: Peeters, 1994.

Tubach, Jürgen. "Mani, der bibliophile Religionsstifter." In *Studia Manichaica: IV. Internationaler Kongress zum Manichäismus, Berlin, 14.–18. Juli 1997*, edited by Ronald E. Emmerick, Werner Sundermann, and Peter Zieme, 622–38. Berlin: Akademie-Verlag, 2000.

Tucker, William L. *Mahdis and Millenarians: Shī'ite Extremists in Early Muslim Iraq*. Cambridge: Cambridge University Press, 2008.

Vacca, V. "Sadjāḥ." In *Encyclopaedia of Islam*, vol. 8, 738–39. New ed. Leiden: Brill, 1954–2002.

Vajda, Georges. "La démonstration de l'unité divine d'après Yūsuf al-Baṣīr." In *Studies in Mysticism and Religion presented to Gershom G. Scholem on his Seventieth Birthday*, 288–306. Jerusalem: Magnes Press, 1967.

———. "Du prologue de Qirqisānī à son commentaire sur la Genèse." In *In Memoriam Paul Kahle*, edited by Matthew Black and Georg Fohrer, 222–31. Beihefte zur Zeitschrift für die alttestamentliche Wissenschaft 103. Berlin: A. Töpelmann, 1968.

———. *Al-Kitāb al-Muḥtawī de Yūsuf al-Baṣīr: Texte, traduction et commentaire*. Edited by David R. Blumenthal. Leiden: Brill, 1985.

———. "Note annexe: L'aperçu sur les sectes dualistes dans *al-Muġnī fī abwāb al-tawḥīd wa-l-'adl* du cadi 'Abd al-Ğabbār." *Arabica* 13 (1966): 113–28.

———. "Le témoignage d'al-Māturidī sur la doctrine des manichéens, des dayṣānites et des marcionites." *Arabica* 13 (1966): 1–38.

———. "Les zindîqs en pays d'Islam au début de la période abbaside." *Rivista degli studi orientali* 17 (1937–38): 173–229.

Van Dam, Raymond. "Hagiography and History: The Life of Gregory Thaumaturgus." *Classical Antiquity* 1 (1982): 272–308.

Vasiliev, Alexandre. "*Kitāb al-Unvān*: Histoire universelle écrite par Agapius (Mahboub) de Menbidj." *Patrologia Orientalis* 7 (1911): 458–591.

Ventura, M[oise]. *La philosophie de Saadia Gaon*. Paris: J. Vrin, 1934.

Vielhauer, Philip. "Jewish-Christian Gospels." In *New Testament Apocrypha*, by Edgar Hennecke, vol. 1, 117–65. 2 vols. Edited by Wilhelm Schneemelcher. Philadelphia, PA: The Westminster Press, 1963–65.

Vööbus, Arthur, ed. *The Canons Ascribed to Mārūtā of Maipherqaṭ and Related Sources*. Corpus scriptorum christianorum orientalium 439–440, scrip. syri t. 191–192. 2 vols. Louvain: Peeters, 1982.

Walker, Joel Thomas. *The Legend of Mar Qardagh: Narrative and Christian Heroism in Late Antique Iraq*. Berkeley: University of California Press, 2006.

Walker, Paul E. *The Wellsprings of Wisdom: A Study of Abū Ya'qūb al-Sijistānī's Kitāb al-Yanābī'*. Salt Lake City: University of Utah Press, 1994.

Wansbrough, John. *Quranic Studies: Sources and Methods of Scriptural Interpretation*. Oxford: Oxford University Press, 1977.

Wasserstein, Abraham and David J. Wasserstein. *The Legend of the Septuagint: From Classical Antiquity to Today*. Cambridge: Cambridge University Press, 2006.

Wasserstrom, Steven M. *Between Muslim and Jew: The Problem of Symbiosis Under Early Islam*. Princeton, NJ: Princeton University Press, 1995.

Watt, W. Montgomery. "al-Aswad b. Ka'b al-'Ansī." In *Encyclopaedia of Islam*, vol. 1, 728. New ed. Leiden: Brill, 1954–2002.

———. *The Formative Period of Islamic Thought*. Edinburgh: Edinburgh University Press, 1973.

———. *Muhammad at Medina*. Oxford: Clarendon Press, 1956.

———. "Musaylima." In *Encyclopaedia of Islam*, vol. 7, 664–65. New ed. Leiden: Brill, 1954–2002.

———. "The Rāfiḍites: A Preliminary Study." *Oriens* 16 (1963): 110-21.

Wensinck, A. J. and J. Jomier. "Iḥrām." In *Encyclopaedia of Islam*, vol. 3, 1052–53. New ed. Leiden: Brill, 1954–2002.

West, E. W. *Pahlavi Texts: Part III*. Sacred Books of the East 24. Oxford, 1855. Repr., Delhi: Motilal Banarsidass, 1970.

Widengren, Geo. *Mani and Manichaeism*. Translated by Charles Kessler. New York: Holt, Rinehart and Winston, 1965.

———. "Manichaeism and its Iranian Background." In *The Cambridge History of Iran, Volume 3(2): The Seleucid, Parthian and Sasanian Periods*, edited by Ehsan Yarshater, 965–90. Cambridge: Cambridge University Press, 1983.

———, ed. *Der Manichäismus*. Wege der Forschung 168. Darmstadt: Wissenschaftliche Buchgesellschaft, 1977.

———. *Muhammad, The Apostle of God, and His Ascension*. Uppsala: A.-B. Lundequistska Bokhandeln, 1955.

Wiesehöfer, Josef. *Ancient Persia: From 550 BC to 650 AD*. Translated by Azizeh Azodi. London: I. B. Tauris, 1996.

Wilkens, Jens. "Neue Fragmente aus Manis Gigantenbuch." *Zeitschrift der deutschen morgenländischen Gesellschaft* 150 (2000): 133–76.

Wisnovsky, R. "Yaḥyā al-Naḥwī." In *Encyclopaedia of Islam*, vol. 11, 251–53. New ed. Leiden: Brill, 1954–2002.

Witakowski, Witold. *Pseudo-Dionysius of Tel-Mahre Chronicle (known also as the Chronicle of Zuqnin) Part III*. Liverpool: Liverpool University Press, 1996.

———. "Sources of Pseudo-Dionysius of Tel-Mahre for the Christian Epoch of the First Part of His *Chronicle*." In *After Bardaisan: Studies on Continuity and Change in Syriac Christianity in Honour of Professor Han J. W. Drijvers*, edited by G. J. Reinink and A. C. Klugkist, 329–66. Orientalia Lovaniensia Analecta 89. Leuven: Peeters, 1999.

Wright, William. *The Chronicle of Joshua the Stylite: Composed in Syriac A.D. 507*. Cambridge: University Press, 1882.

Wurst, Gregor. *Die Bema-Psalmen*. CFM Series Coptica 1; Liber Psalmorum, Pars II, Fasc. 1. Turnhout: Brepols, 1996.

Yarshater, Ehsan. "Iranian National History." In *The Cambridge History of Iran, 3(1): The Seleucid, Parthian and Sasanian Periods*, edited by Ehsan Yarshater, 359–480. Cambridge: Cambridge University Press, 1983.

———. "Mazdakism." In *The Cambridge History of Iran, Volume 3(2): The Seleucid, Parthian and Sasanian Periods*, edited by Ehsan Yarshater, 991–1024. Cambridge: Cambridge University Press, 1983.

Yu-Kung, Kao. "Source Materials on the Fang La Rebellion." *Harvard Journal of Asiatic Studies* 26 (1966): 211–40.

Yūsofī, Ğ. Ḥ. "Abu Moslem Ḵorāsānī." In *Encyclopaedia Iranica*, edited by Ehsan Yarshater, vol. 1, 341–44. London and New York: Bibliotheca Persica, 1982– .

Zaehner, R. C. *The Teachings of the Magi: A Compendium of Zoroastrian Beliefs*. Repr., New York: Oxford University Press, 1976.

Zarrīnkūb, 'Abd al-Ḥusain. "The Arab Conquest of Iran and its Aftermath." In *The Cambridge History of Iran, Volume 4: The Period from the Arab Invasion to the Saljuqs*, edited by R. N. Frye, 1–56. Cambridge: Cambridge University Press, 1975.

Zotenberg, H[ermann]. *Histoire des rois des Perses: Texte arabe publié et traduit*. Paris: Imprimerie nationale, 1890.

Indices

Index of Citations of Primary Sources

1. Hebrew Bible

2. New Testament

3. Qur'ān

4. Jewish and Christian Apocrypha and Pseudepigrapha

5. Rabbinic literature

6. Christian writers

7. Muslim writers

8. Manichaica

9. Manuscripts

10. Miscellaneous writings

Index of Ancient and Medieval Authors, Tradents, and Personages

Index of Scriptural and Parascriptural Characters

Index of Manichaeans and of Individuals Suspected or Accused of *Zandaqa*

Index of Modern Authors

www.ingramcontent.com/pod-product-compliance
Lightning Source LLC
Chambersburg PA
CBHW071359300426
44114CB00016B/2122

* 9 7 8 1 7 8 1 7 9 0 3 8 0 *